THE STEPHEN BECHTEL FUND

IMPRINT IN ECOLOGY AND THE ENVIRONMENT

The Stephen Bechtel Fund has

established this imprint to promote

understanding and conservation of

our natural environment.

The publisher gratefully acknowledges the generous contribution to this book provided by the Stephen Bechtel Fund.

MERCURY IN THE ENVIRONMENT

Mercury in the Environment

PATTERN AND PROCESS

Edited by

MICHAEL S. BANK

UNIVERSITY OF CALIFORNIA PRESS
Berkeley   Los Angeles   London

APR 2 5 2014

University of California Press, one of the most distinguished university presses in the United States, enriches lives around the world by advancing scholarship in the humanities, social sciences, and natural sciences. Its activities are supported by the UC Press Foundation and by philanthropic contributions from individuals and institutions. For more information, visit www.ucpress.edu.

University of California Press
Berkeley and Los Angeles, California

University of California Press, Ltd.
London, England

Library of Congress Cataloging-in-Publication Data

Mercury in the environment : pattern and process / edited by Michael S. Bank. — 1st ed.
 p. cm.
 Includes bibliographical references and index.
 ISBN 978-0-520-27163-0 (hardback)
 1. Mercury—Environmental aspects.   2. Mercury—Bioaccumulation.   3. Mercury—Toxicology.   4. Mercury—Health aspects.   I. Bank, Michael S.
 TD196.M38M466 2012
 363.738′4—dc23   2011052057

19 18 17 16 15 14 13 12
10 9 8 7 6 5 4 3 2 1

The paper used in this publication meets the minimum requirements of ANSI/NISO Z39.48-1992 (R 1997) (*Permanence of Paper*).

Cover image: Miao settlements near Tianhe Pool Scenic Area, Guizhou Province, China, June 2009. Photo by Michael S. Bank.

CONTENTS

CONTRIBUTORS

ARIA AMIRBAHMAN, University of Maine, Orono
aria@umit.maine.edu

MICHAEL S. BANK, Harvard Medical School,
Boston, Massachusetts
michael_bank@hms.harvard.edu

NILADRI BASU, University of Michigan, Ann Arbor
niladri@umich.edu

FRANK J. BLACK, University of California, Santa Cruz
fblack@westminstercollege.edu

KEVIN BISHOP, Swedish University of Agricultural Science,
Uppsala, Sweden
kevin.bishop@slu.se

WILLIAM E. BROOKS, United States Geological Survey,
Reston, Virginia
wbrooks@usgs.gov

JOANNA BURGER, Rutgers University, Piscataway, New Jersey
burger@biology.rutgers.edu

CELIA Y. CHEN, Dartmouth College,
Hanover, New Hampshire
celia.y.chen@dartmouth.edu

CHRISTOPHER H. CONAWAY, University of California,
Santa Cruz
kitconaway@hotmail.com

JOHN DELLINGER, Concordia University, Mequon, Wisconsin
john.dellinger@cuw.edu

MATTHEW DELLINGER, University of Wisconsin, Milwaukee
delling2@uwm.edu

CHARLES T. DRISCOLL, Syracuse University, New York
ctdrisco@syr.edu

DAVID C. EVERS, Biodiversity Research Institute,
Gorham, Maine
david.evers@briloon.org

A. RUSSELL FLEGAL, University of California, Santa Cruz
flegal@ucsc.edu

IVAN J. FERNANDEZ, University of Maine, Orono
ivanjf@maine.edu

SARAH GEROULD, United States Geological Survey,
Reston, Virginia
sgerould@usgs.gov

GARY A. GILL, Pacific Northwest National Laboratory,
Sequim, Washington
gary.gill@pnl.gov

SIMONE CHARLES, Georgia Southern University, Statesboro
scharles@georgiasouthern.edu

MICHAEL GOCHFELD, Robert Wood Johnson Medical School,
Piscataway, New Jersey
gochfeld@eohsi.rutgers.edu

GARY H. HEINZ, United States Geological Survey,
Beltsville, Maryland
gheinz@usgs.gov

HOLGER HINTELMANN, Trent University,
Peterborough, Ontario
hhintelmann@trentu.ca

MILENA HORVAT, Jozef Stefan Institute, Ljubljana, Slovenia
milena.horvat@ijs.si

DANIEL JAFFE, University of Washington, Bothell
djaffe@u.washington.edu

NEIL C. KAMMAN, Vermont Department of Environmental
Conservation, Waterbury
neil.kamman@state.vt.us

BRENDA K. LASORSA, Pacific Northwest National Laboratory,
Sequim, Washington
brenda.lasorsa@pnl.gov

ROBERT P. MASON, University of Connecticut, Groton
robert.mason@uconn.edu

WENDY MCKELVEY, New York City Department of Health and
Mental Hygiene, New York
wmckelve@health.nyc.gov

JEROME NRIAGU, University of Michigan, Ann Arbor
jnriagu@umich.edu

EMILY OKEN, Harvard Medical School and Harvard
Pilgrim Health Care Institute, Boston, Massachusetts
emily_oken@hphc.org

MARK B. SANDHEINRICH, University of Wisconsin, La Crosse
sandhein.mark@uwlax.edu

ANTON M. SCHEUHAMMER, Environmental Canada,
Ottawa, Ontario
tony.scheuhammer@ec.gc.ca

NOELLE ECKLEY SELIN, Massachusetts Institute of
Technology, Cambridge
selin@mit.edu

JAMES B. SHANLEY, United States Geological Survey,
Montpelier, Vermont
jshanley@usgs.gov

C. MARK SMITH, Massachusetts Department of Environmental
Protection, Boston
c.mark.smith@state.ma.us

PHIL SWARTZENDRUBER, Puget Sound Clean Air Agency,
Seattle, Washington
phils@pscleanair.org

JENNIFER S. YAUCK, University of Wisconsin, Milwaukee
jsy_ireland@hotmail.com

FOREWORD

SARAH GEROULD

I was a teenager when *Life* magazine published W. Eugene Smith's famous pictures of Tomoko Uemura, her body ravaged by deformities from Minamata disease. I remember poring over the pictures while sitting on our living room couch, wondering how such a thing could have happened and about how mercury could have caused these devastating deformities. In 1972, the science of mercury in the environment was in its infancy. Although the neurologic symptoms of Minamata disease were recognized well enough for specialists to identify mercury as the causative agent, the understanding of mercury's environmental impacts and global dispersal would require several decades of research.

The science of mercury has advanced considerably since those pictures were published. The global dispersion and speciation of mercury are now well recognized. The potential for methylmercury to cause neurologic deficits in segments of the world's population that rely on a diet of piscivorous fish has been established (Mergler et al., 2007). Although the understanding of mercury's implications for human health has advanced far enough to permit the development of criteria and consumption advisory levels for the protection of humans (United States Environmental Protection Agency, 2001, 2007a), field studies of effects in fish and fish-eating wildlife species continue to unveil new understanding of its impacts on these species. Scientists now recognize that mercury enters the environment through many sources, not just through point sources such as chloralkali plants and mining. Treatment technologies for removing mercury from air and water have advanced (United States Environmental Protection Agency 2007b). Monitoring has given us a wealth of data on concentrations in many environmental media. Our understanding of the environmental factors that control mercury speciation have made significant advances (Munthe et al., 2007), although many important questions remain, such as the complexities of the relationship between mercury loading and the resulting concentrations in fish and the biogeochemical controls on the mercury methylation process (Munthe et al., 2007). Finally, the science of mercury sources and cycling is now mature enough to allow society to recognize and anticipate the effects of things such as fire and fluctuating reservoir levels (Grigal, 2002) as cofactors in controlling mercury cycling in the environment.

Scientific understanding is not the only thing that has changed since W. Eugene Smith's pictures were published. Regulatory agencies have recognized and reduced emissions from incinerators and other mercury sources in the United States (Lindberg et al., 2007). Though many sources of mercury have been regulated in recent years (United Nations Environment Programme, 2002), several new issues are now upon us. For example, the need for energy conservation leads our society to use more compact fluorescent light bulbs, all of which contain mercury; and as U.S. sources are controlled, emissions from Asia, driven by increases in coal combustion and economic development, have sent more mercury into the air (Wong et al., 2006). Clouds of dust containing mercury are blown across the Atlantic and Pacific oceans and deposited onto distant landmasses (Garrison et al., 2003). Increases in atmospheric deposition of mercury in dust into parts of the arctic and subarctic environments (Pacyna and Keeler, 1995) are paralleled by increases in concentrations of mercury in wildlife (Braune, 2007).

As the dynamics of global mercury sources and cycling continue to evolve, and science grows in its ability to document and explain mercury dynamics and effects, it is important to establish benchmarks of those changes and the progress toward understanding them. Michael Bank's book provides a welcome update to the state of the art on mercury pollution. The contributors to the book are a strong list of experts who describe the latest findings relative to the fate and effects of mercury in the environment.

The book summarizes mercury cycling and transport and dynamics in terrestrial, aquatic, and atmospheric environments and exposure and effects in humans and wildlife. It includes information on historical uses and production of mercury. The book's final section synthesizes issues affected by mercury or by which mercury is affected, such as climate change and landscape change. The book will be a reliable source of information for environmental managers, health professionals, scientists, and the educated public. It shows how far we've come in understanding this important issue since W. Eugene Smith published his pictures of Tomoko Uemura.

References

Braune, B. "Temporal trends of organochlorines and mercury in seabird eggs from the Canadian Arctic." 1975–2003. *Environmental Pollution* 148 (2007): 599–613.

Garrison, V.H., E.A. Shinn, W.T. Foreman, D.W. Griffin, C.W. Holmes, C.A. Kellogg, M.S. Majewski, L.L. Richardson, K.B. Ritchie, and G.W. Smith. "African and Asian dust from desert soils to coral reefs." *Bioscience* 53 (2003): 469–480.

Grigal, D.F. "Inputs and outputs of mercury from terrestrial watersheds: A review." *Environmental Reviews* 10 (2002): 1–39.

Lindberg, S.,R. Bullock, R. Ebinghaus, D. Engstrom, X. Feng, W. Fitzgerald, N. Pirrone, E. Prestbo, and C. Seigneur. "A synthesis of progress and uncertainties in attributing the sources of mercury in deposition." *Ambio* 36 (2007): 19–32.

Mergler, D., H.A. Anderson, L.H.M. Chan, K.R. Mahaffey, M. Murray, M. Sakamoto, and A.H. Stern. "Methylmercury exposure and health effects in humans: A worldwide concern." *Ambio* 36 (2007): 3–11.

Munthe, J., R.A. Bodaly, B.A. Branfireun, C.T. Driscoll, C.C. Gilmour, R. Harris, M. Horvat, M. Lucotte, and O. Malm. "Recovery of mercury-contaminated fisheries." *Ambio* 36 (2007): 33–44.

Pacyna, J.M., and G.J. Keeler. "Sources of mercury in the Arctic." *Water, Air, & Soil Pollution* 80 (1995): 621–632.

United Nations Environment Programme. "Chapter 7: current production and use of mercury." in *Global Mercury Assessment*. pp. 117–134. Geneva, Switzerland: UNEP Chemicals, 2002. http://new.unep.org/gc/gc22/Document/UNEP-GC22-INF3.pdf (accessed February 5, 2008).

United States Environmental Protection Agency. "Methylmercury criteria document." (EPA-823-R-01-001) January 2001, http://www.epa.gov/waterscience/criteria/methylmercury/document.html (accessed February 5, 2008).

United States Environmental Protection Agency. National Listing of Fish Advisories. Technical Fact Sheet: 2005/06 National Listing. Fact Sheet, EPA-823-F-07-003, July 2007a. http://www.epa.gov/waterscience/fish/advisories/2006/tech.html (accessed February 5, 2008).

United States Environmental Protection Agency. Office of Solid Waste and Emergency Response. Treatment Technologies for Mercury in Soil, Waste, and Water. EPA-542-R-07-003. August 2007b http://www.epa.gov/tio/download/remed/542r07003.pdf (accessed February 5, 2008).

Wong, C.S., N.S. Duzgoren-Aydin, A. Aydin, and M.H. Wong. "Sources and trends of environmental mercury emissions in Asia." *Science of the Total Environment* 368 (2006): 649–662.

INTRODUCTION

Mercury on the Rise

MICHAEL S. BANK

Mercury science is a rapidly growing interdisciplinary field and touches on nearly all academic and scientific disciplines, including biogeochemistry, economics, sociology, public health, decision sciences, physics, global change, and mathematics. Only recently have scientists really begun to establish more holistic approaches to studying mercury pollution, including investigations that have furthered the integration of a multitiered approach, especially by using chemistry, biology, and human health sciences.

The study of mercury pollution has contributed a variety of domestic and international policies related to the management of this ubiquitous contaminant. The target audience for this book is graduate and undergraduate students, natural resource managers, and technical scientists. The book focuses on integrating the diverse sciences involved in the process of mercury cycling in the environment from the atmosphere, through terrestrial and aquatic food webs, and in human populations to help the reader develop a more holistic perspective on this important environmental pollution topic.

The original idea for the book was developed at a conference in 2004, after an associate of the University of California Press who had viewed my oral presentation suggested that I consider writing a book on mercury pollution. After some investigating, I soon realized that although there were strong volumes on mercury pollution, none of them had a solid focus on aspects related to human dimensions and new topics such as advances in mercury isotope chemistry, and that current public health summaries were not readily available in the literature. This book largely stems from my desire to impart knowledge from worldwide experts on their areas of expertise and to disseminate the most current scientific information available about mercury.

The book has four parts: (I) mercury cycling in the environment: an introduction; (II) methods for research, monitoring, and analysis; (III) mercury in terrestrial and aquatic environments; and part (IV) toxicology, humans, policy, and risk analysis.

Part I, "Mercury Cycling in the Environment: An Introduction," serves as a basic introduction to the book. Chapter 1 focuses on sources, fate, and transport of mercury in the environment as a global problem and provides the reader with the critical background information on mercury pollution. Chapter 2 discusses historical and industrial uses of mercury in the environment, with a focus on ancient civilizations. The use of mercury by ancient civilizations has not received much attention, and this chapter describes mercury as a utility of human societies.

Part II, "Methods for Research, Monitoring, and Analysis," is dedicated to summarizing and highlighting recent advances in the study methods used in mercury investigations. Recent advances in the analytical methods used to measure mercury in the environment are discussed in Chapter 3. Because these methods are advancing rather quickly in the field, this chapter will be an important source for students, chemists, and laboratory scientists. Chapter 4 focuses specifically on mercury isotope fractionation and the use and application of mercury isotopes in source apportionment research and in determining biogeochemical pathways of mercury in the environment. Chapter 5 is devoted to the atmospheric chemistry and modeling of mercury. This sole atmospheric deposition chapter discusses, in detail, the reactions, behavior, and chemical properties of mercury in the earth's atmosphere and the role of scale and uncertainty assessments and their collective applications to monitoring, research, and policy. The chapter concludes by summarizing future challenges for mercury atmospheric deposition research. Chapter 6 focuses on indicators of environmental changes in mercury contamination in different ecosystem compartments and discusses the need for a national mercury monitoring network. This chapter discusses measurement approaches from the atmosphere to different wildlife indicator species that inhabit freshwater, terrestrial, and coastal ecosystems. The indicators identified in this chapter involve measurements made at several spatial and temporal scales and were selected to provide the best information to policymakers and other stakeholders and with regard to identifying the reasons and rates of change in mercury concentrations.

Part III, "Mercury in Terrestrial and Aquatic Environments," includes four chapters that focus on mercury in soils, forested watersheds, freshwater ecosystems, and marine environments. Chapter 7 summarizes the current knowledge about mercury in soils, which is critical to our understanding of the accumulation and loss of mercury in the environment and outlines the relationships between kinetics, climate, vegetation, disturbances, soil chemistry, and mercury speciation. Chapter 8 goes beyond soils and discusses mercury in forested watersheds. In this chapter, the authors review and synthesize information about mercury in terrestrial landscapes and describe how total mercury and methylmercury move through forested catchments. The authors also discuss, in detail, the role and effects of disturbance (forest harvesting, urbanization, etc.) on total mercury and methylmercury fluxes and their sensitivity to changes in mercury emission rates, land-use practices, and climate. Chapter 9 deals with mercury in freshwater ecosystems. In this chapter, the authors describe biotic and abiotic mechanisms that govern mercury methylation, bioaccumulation, and trophic transfer in a wide array of aquatic food webs and ecosystems, including natural lakes and ponds, reservoirs, wetlands, and rivers. The authors provide examples of mercury cycling and bioaccumulation by examining case studies from the Everglades, Adirondack mountain lakes, man-made reservoirs, large lakes such as Lake Michigan, and the Nyanza Superfund site on the Sudbury River in Massachusetts. Chapter 10 is a comprehensive summary of mercury in the marine environment, with regard to human and environmental health concerns. In this chapter the authors discuss the source of mercury in marine ecosystems, methylation of mercury, and bioaccumulation and biomagnification in marine food webs.

Part IV, "Toxicology, Risk Analysis, Humans, and Policy," includes five chapters that discuss and summarize the recent advances in each of these important disciplines. Chapter 11 focuses on the ecotoxicology of mercury, primarily as methylmercury, in wildlife such as fish, amphibians, birds, and mammals. Chapters 12 through 15 are dedicated to risk assessment, public health, and environmental justice. These chapters report on a variety of topics, including risk assessment models, human exposure routes of the different mercury species, and fish consumption patterns related to socioeconomic dynamics. Chapter 16 integrates many scientific aspects discussed throughout the book and summarizes mercury policy initiatives in the context of both environmental and human health.

The field of mercury science is tremendous in scope and scale and I hope this book serves as a preliminary, introductory step for students, researchers and scientists to develop a further interest and understanding of mercury pollution and cycling in the environment.

ACKNOWLEDGMENTS

Although I am the sole editor of this volume, I could not have edited it without support from a variety of sources. I received support during the course of editing this book from Harvard University, the Massachusetts Department of Environmental Protection, the National Science Foundation, the National Oceanic and Atmospheric Administration, the United States Department of Agriculture, Harvard School of Public Health (HSPH), the United States Geological Survey, HSPH-National Institute of Environmental Health Sciences Center for Environmental Health (NIEHS grant number ES000002), the New York Department of Environmental Conservation, the International Union for Conservation of Nature-Amphibian Specialist Program, and the Akira Yamaguchi Endowment at Harvard School of Public Health.

In addition to all the contributors, I am grateful to Anh-Thu Vo, Jeff Crocker, Colin Davies, Philippe Grandjean, Jennifer Wachtl, Art Lage, and John Spengler for their support, guidance, and encouragement throughout various stages of the project. I am grateful to all of the individual chapter reviewers, and I thank the two anonymous reviewers for their comments on the entire volume manuscript. I am grateful to Harvard Medical School and HSPH, Department of Environmental Health and their exceptional administrative staff, especially Renee Costa, Joan Arnold, Tracy Mark, Rose West, and Linda Fox. I thank Blake Edgar, Hannah Love, Lynn Meinhardt, Kate Marshall, and Kate Hoffman at the University of California Press in Berkeley, for their patience and guidance throughout all phases of the book's development. I am also grateful to project manager Michael Bohrer-Clancy of Macmillan Publishing Solutions.

PART ONE

MERCURY CYCLING IN THE ENVIRONMENT

CHAPTER 1

Sources and Transport

A Global Issue

PHIL SWARTZENDRUBER and DANIEL JAFFE

Chemical Forms of Mercury in Water and Air

The Roman deity, Mercury, was the god of trade, commerce, thievery, and messengers. His reputation as a cunning and swift messenger led to the modern adjective, *mercurial*, meaning labile, volatile, and erratic. Many contemporary scientists who study mercury would emphatically agree that its behavior in the environment and in the laboratory often seems erratic and mysterious. Indeed, it was only relatively recently that we became aware of the global nature of mercury contamination, partly because of the difficulty in detecting it at the extremely low concentrations that are typical in air and water. Thus, we encounter an apparent paradox fitting of Mercury's reputation; why are there toxic levels of mercury in fish in remote regions throughout the globe despite water and air concentrations that are very low? The answer is a complex process of emission, transport, deposition, and accumulation up through the food chain. All of the major steps in this process have been clearly identified, although a number of the specific mechanisms remain poorly understood. In this chapter we will give an overview of the chemical forms present in the air and water, their sources, and how they are transported.

The chemical symbol for mercury, Hg, is derived from the Latin name, *hydragyrum*, which means silver water. Elemental mercury is found in the Earth's crust in only a limited number of regions in the world. Mercury is more abundant in mineral form, with cinnabar (HgS) being the most prevalent. Several of the less abundant minerals include calomel, Livingstonite, and Tiemannite. Mercury is predominantly found in deposits formed by hydrothermal systems, which are most common at convergent tectonic margins. It also tends to be enriched in some base-metal ores and present with other chalcophilic (having a sulfur affinity) elements (Kesler, 1994). The elemental form of mercury (Hg^0) has had a great number of uses historically, including barometers, thermometers, electrical switches, fluorescent light bulbs, and ballast for submarines. Elemental mercury has a unique combination of properties that seem to make it ideal for these applications. Hg^0 is the only abundant metal that is liquid at room temperature. It has a melting

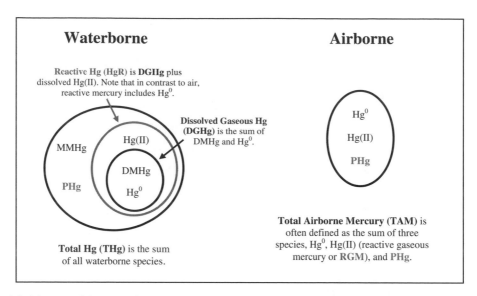

FIGURE 1.1 A simplified diagram of the major chemical forms of mercury found in water and air. See the section on "Chemical Forms of Mercury in Water and Air" for a description of the forms. DGHg = dissolved gaseous mercury; DMHg = dimethylmercury; HgR = reactive mercury; MMHg = monomethylmercury; PHg = particulate-bound mercury; RGM = reactive gaseous mercury; TAM = total airborne mercury; THg = total mercury.

point of –39°C and a boiling temperature of 357°C. It also has a rather high vapor pressure despite having a density 13 times greater than water and slightly greater than lead. This anomalous behavior is caused by weak inter-atomic bonding, which is due to the nucleus having a tight hold on its valence electrons. Hg^0 is also relatively insoluble in water (49 μg/L or 4.4 ppt at 20°C which is 4 to 6 orders of magnitude smaller than the solubility of the predominant Hg compounds) and will readily avoid liquids. So, it is often described as preferring to be in the gas phase. Mercury can also be found in two ionic forms, oxidation states +1 and +2, which are more prevalent in water than in the atmosphere (Schroeder and Munthe, 1998).

A number of the mercury compounds that occur in the environment have not been directly identified. Rather, several different fractions of mercury have been defined based on how they are collected (e.g., on a filter) and how elemental mercury can be released from them (e.g., heating the filter to 800°C). These distinctions, called "operationally defined fractions," are then used in place of specific compounds. The properties of the different fractions (e.g., solubility, volatility, etc.) are used in modeling the fate of mercury. As instrumentation and techniques have developed, the definitions of the fractions have evolved, and, not surprisingly, there is still some controversy as to the names and definitions of some of the fractions. A simplified chart of the forms of mercury that occur in water and air is shown in Figure 1.1. The major operationally defined fractions are indicated with color.

One of the challenges of studying the cycling of mercury is that because it is an element, it is never destroyed, but it can be recycled through the environment. In specific terms, mercury that is deposited to soils, lakes, wetlands, or oceans may later be re-released to the atmosphere. So,

soil and ocean reservoirs, and therefore soil and ocean emissions, include a component that is natural, plus a portion resulting from human activities at a prior time.

Research has shown that most natural samples exhibit measurable mass-dependent isotope fractionation and some exhibit mass-independent fractionation. Although this subfield of mercury research is in its infancy, it shows promise in providing new insights into the sources and history of ambient mercury (Bergquist and Blum, 2007).

CHEMICAL SPECIES OF MERCURY

Hg^0 is elemental mercury. Hg^0 has an anomalously high vapor pressure (Brown et al., 2008) for a heavy metal. It is slightly water-soluble (~50 μg/L at 20°C) (Clever et al., 1985) and has a high Henry's law coefficient (729 at 20°C) (Schroeder and Munthe, 1998). In the natural environment, it can exist in the gaseous or liquid state. Gaseous element mercury (GEM), is the dominant form in the atmosphere. Most natural waters are nearly saturated, or are supersaturated with respect to atmospheric Hg^0 (Fitzgerald et al., 2007).

$Hg(II)$ or divalent mercury. Inorganic and organic divalent mercury compounds exist in gaseous, dissolved, and solid states. Their toxicity, solubility, vapor pressure, and reactivity vary greatly. $Hg(II)$ is much more prevalent in waters than in the atmosphere. Methylated mercury compounds (below) are of particular interest because of their role in the biologic cycling of Hg and accordingly make up >95% of the mercury in fish (Chen et al., 2008).

DMHg is dimethylmercury, $(CH_3)_2Hg$. DMHg is significantly more toxic than Hg^0 on a milligrams per kilogram of body weight ingestion basis (due to more efficient absorption in the gut). It is believed to be present in the atmosphere in only negligible concentrations, but it is thought to be ubiquitous in the deeper ocean (Mason et al., 1998).

MMHg is monomethylmercury, CH_3Hg+. MMHg is significantly more toxic than Hg^0 on a milligrams per kilogram of body weight ingestion basis (due to more efficient absorption in the gut) and readily bio-accumulates up the food chain (National Research Council, 2000). MMHg has not been reliably detected in the open oceans apart from the Equatorial Pacific Ocean (Fitzgerald et al., 2007).

OPERATIONALLY DEFINED FORMS OF MERCURY

DGHg is dissolved gaseous Hg. It is a fraction of mercury measured in water that is defined by its ability to be volatilized only by purging with a clean, inert gas. It includes **DMHg** (Fitzgerald et al., 2007).

HgR is reactive Hg dissolved in water. It is defined based on its ability to be volatilized after reduction with $SnCl_2$, and purging with a clean, inert gas (Fitzgerald et al., 2007).

Hg(II) has also been used as an operationally defined fraction of dissolved Hg. It is determined by subtracting mercury that is readily volatilized **(DGHg)** from reactive Hg **(HgR)** (Mason et al., 1998). It has been used as a measure of bio-available mercury, but is known to not be universally appropriate (Fitzgerald et al., 2007).

Hg-Col is colloidal mercury. It is mercury associated with colloidal matter that can be trapped on an ultrafine membrane after filtration of larger particulate matter. Colloidal mercury is generally considered to be larger than 1000 Da (molecular weight) but smaller than 0.1–0.5 µm (Guentzel et al., 1996).

RGM or reactive gaseous mercury, refers to Hg that can be captured on a KCl surface (Landis et al., 2002). RGM is believed to consist primarily of gaseous Hg(II) compounds. It is regarded as the fraction of airborne Hg that is readily deposited to the surface via wet or dry deposition. The exact chemical form of RGM is not known, but likely candidates include HgO (Hall, 1995), $HgCl_2$ (Landis et al., 2002), and $HgBr_2$ (Holmes et al., 2009). In many reports, RGM and gaseous Hg(II) are used interchangeably, but it is important to recognize that RGM is an operation definition whereas Hg(II) is a chemical definition.

PHg, or particulate-bound mercury, refers to mercury that is extracted from particles, either airborne or waterborne. The observed PHg concentration can be dependent on the size of particles that are collected; for example, most airborne PHg measurements include only particles <2.5 µm (aerodynamic diameter), so mercury on larger particles would be excluded from the reported concentration.

The amount of mercury extracted from the particles can be dependent on the technique used. Waterborne particulate mercury is generally determined by filtration, addition of BrCl, reduction with $SnCl_2$, and purging with a clean, inert gas. Measuring airborne PHg also requires capturing particles on a filter. The filters can be analyzed in the aqueous phase using the previously described technique. Or, the mercury on particles can be thermally reduced/desorbed, and quantified as GEM (Landis et al., 2002).

The Changing Global Cycle of Mercury

Sediments and Ice Cores as Archives of Geochemical Cycles

Lake sediment cores and glacial ice cores have been used as historical records of preindustrial and anthropogenic deposition. Trace metal and hydrocarbon concentrations in cores have been shown to accurately reflect the impact of industrialization on air concentrations and increased deposition of pollutants to the earth (e.g., Wong et al., 1984) and oceans (Véron et al., 1987). Mercury has also been studied in ice cores and lake sediments, and similar increases in deposition are seen across a wide range of geologic and hydrologic environments (e.g., Swain et al., 1992; Schuster et al., 2002). These records are powerful evidence of the recent anthropogenic influence on the global Hg cycle.

The Preindustrial Cycle

A diagram of the simplified global mercury cycle is shown in Figure 1.2 (after Mason and Sheu, 2002). Preindustrial values are shown in parentheses below the modern values. The glacial and sediment records have shown that in the millennium before industrialization, mercury and other metals had a relatively steady deposition flux, with an occasional perturbation due to volcanic activity (e.g., Schuster et al., 2002). This implies that the net flux of mercury coming into the atmosphere approximately equaled the net flux deposited to the land and oceans. There is substantial evasion from the ocean and land, but it is nearly balanced by deposition. There is also local recycling of mercury over the ocean surface (not shown) that makes no contribution to the net evasion or deposition (Strode et al., 2007). Rivers also make a small contribution to the open ocean (~1% of ocean reservoir), but this is omitted from the figure for the sake of simplicity. In the preindustrial cycle, the annual flux into and out of the atmosphere (~2–4000 tons/yr) is similar to the total airborne burden, suggesting a lifetime for atmospheric Hg of approximately 1 year (Mason and Sheu, 2002; Selin et al., 2008). In the oceans, the total burden is more than a factor of

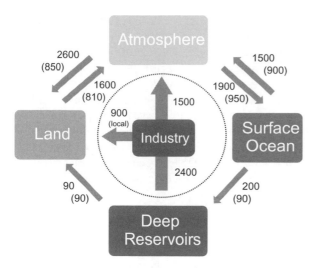

FIGURE 1.2 A simplified global geochemical mercury cycle. All values are tons per year. Preindustrial values are given in parentheses below the modern values. The inner, dashed circle indicates the perturbation of industrial activities that significantly increased the extraction of mercury from deep reservoirs. This results in significantly greater local deposition and also increased input to the global atmospheric pool, which increases global deposition. Upward arrows from the land and ocean are net evasion and downward arrows are wet and dry deposition. (*Source:* Adapted from Mason and Sheu, 2002.)

100 greater than the annual flux, indicating a much longer lifetime for Hg. Therefore, for any given change in the global cycle (e.g., anthropogenic emissions), we can expect that the atmosphere will respond much more rapidly than the ocean. Further, since the mixing and circulation of the atmosphere occurs much more rapidly than that of the ocean, we can expect that changes in the atmospheric burden will be seen much more rapidly throughout the globe than changes in the ocean. The net lifetime of mercury against long-term burial (i.e. lifetime in the atmosphere, surface ocean, and land surface system) is on the order of 1000 years (Selin et al., 2008).

Evidence of Recent Changes in Deposition of Mercury

Significant advances in mercury detection and sampling have occurred in the past 20 years. These advances have allowed for reliable determination of current and historical levels of Hg deposited in sediments and ice cores. Despite some initial contradictory reports, there is now a good consistency between studies of deposition from a large number of locations in North America, South America, New Zealand, and Europe. These studies show a compelling pattern of increasing deposition to lake sediments and glacial ice (Swain et al., 1992; Fitzgerald et al., 1998; Lamborg et al., 2002; Landers et al., 2008) and a generally consistent pattern in peat cores (Biester et al., 2002, 2007).

As an example, Figure 1.3 shows lake sediment profiles of Hg enrichment from four lakes in the Western United States. Here, enrichment is the Hg enhancement, relative to another element that is assumed to be purely lithospheric in origin, titanium. These data are from a study of Hg and persistent organic pollutants from eight National Parks in the western United States and Alaska that receive only atmospheric input (Landers et al., 2008). Enrichment is relative to titanium concentrations in the sediment cores and is defined by:

$$\text{Percent Sediment Enrichment} = \frac{(M_x/Ti_x) - (M_b/Ti_b)}{(M_b/Ti_b)} \times 100$$

where

Hg_x = mercury concentration (ng/g) at interval depth x

Ti_x = titanium concentration (ng/g) at interval depth x

Hg_b = mercury concentration (ng/g) at interval closest to year 1870

Ti_b = titanium concentration (ng/g) at interval closest to year 1870

These lake sediments show a clear enhancement in mercury deposition from the preindustrial era to the present, consistent with other studies (e.g., Swain et al., 1992; Schuster et al., 2002). Increases in the deposition rate, averaging about threefold, are widely observed, although there are significant variations between sites. Individual lakes and cores can vary because of local geography, geology, and local emissions. These factors are not well understood and limit our overall understanding of the Hg cycle. For example, once deposited, Hg can be sequestered by organic carbon. Thus, a change in organic carbon in the air or lake can change the fraction of Hg that is permanently captured. Nonetheless, the increased atmospheric deposition to the catchment, from both regional and global sources, is required to explain the enhancements in Hg deposition in the lake sediment cores. (Swain et al., 1992; Fitzgerald et al., 1998; Schuster et al., 2002; Landers et al., 2008).

Observations of wet and dry deposition and large-scale modeling of the global Hg cycle indicate that input from the atmosphere is the primary cause of the increased accumulation in the sediments. There is, nonetheless, still significant uncertainty in some of the mechanisms involved (e.g., Calvert and Lindberg 2005; Lin et al., 2006; Lindberg et al., 2007). The fraction of the mercury deposition that can be attributed to local (or regional) sources versus the global background is an area of continued research. A number of modeling studies have apportioned local and regional deposition to various sources, including anthropogenic (local and global), natural, and recycled. For example, in the United States, Seigneur et al., (2004) estimate that 30% of total deposition is from North American anthropogenic sources, 40% is due to anthropogenic sources outside North America, and 33% is from natural sources. Selin et al., (2008)

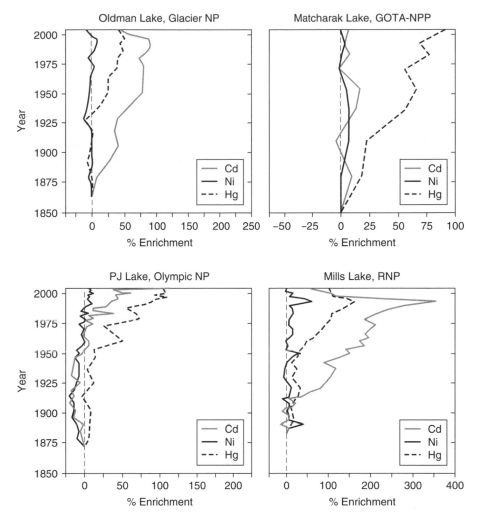

FIGURE 1.3 Four examples of the enrichment in Hg deposition found in lake cores in the Western United States. Oldman Lake is in Glacier National Park, Montana; Matcharak Lake is in Gates of the Arctic National Park and Preserve, Alaska; PJ Lake is in Olympic National Park, Washington; and Mills Lake is in Rocky National Park, Colorado. (*Source:* Landers et al., 2008).

found that 68% of the deposition is anthropogenic, with 31% coming from outside North America. As primary anthropogenic sources emit some mercury in forms that can be deposited locally (RGM and PHg) (Pacyna and Pacyna, 2002), the issue of source attribution encompasses multiple spatial scales (Seigneur et al., 2004; Selin et al., 2007).

The Modern Mercury Cycle

The modern, industrial cycle of mercury differs from the preindustrial cycle (Figure 1.2) because of the extraction and mobilization of Hg from deep reservoirs. (Deep reservoirs are defined as reservoirs that are physically below the surface ocean and land surface which contain a large mass of mercury relative to the mass that cycles through the land, air, and water, on an annual basis). Anthropogenic activities have greatly increased the mobilization of Hg (e.g., coal combustion and mining) from deep reservoirs. This

enhanced Hg extraction is thought to have increased the total atmospheric burden of Hg by about a factor of 3, which has resulted in a nearly threefold increase in deposition to the land and ocean. But, it should be noted that the observational record of Hg in the atmosphere is relatively short, so no clear pattern of change has been found (Ebinghaus et al., 2009). Increased concentrations in the surface ocean and land surface have accordingly increased emissions back to the atmosphere. Thus, the total amount of mercury cycling through the land surface, surface oceans, and atmosphere, has increased significantly (Selin et al., 2008; Sunderland et al., 2009). The burden of total mercury in the deep oceans has also increased, but by a much smaller factor. The smaller increase in deep ocean concentrations is largely a result of the much greater reservoir of Hg and slower mixing and turnover times. This produces a lag in uptake on the order of decades to centuries in the surface waters and deep ocean, respectively (Sunderland and Mason, 2007).

Sources of Mercury in Water

Atmospheric Wet and Dry Deposition

The largest and most important source of mercury in water is wet and dry deposition from the atmosphere. This includes both a natural and anthropogenic component. Globally, about 1% of the total oceanic burden is deposited and emitted each year (Mason and Sheu, 2002; Sunderland and Mason, 2007). Most of the mercury deposited to oceans in precipitation is either bound to particles or is dissolved in an ionic state, Hg(II). Over the oceans, the overwhelming portion that is dry deposited is RGM, which has been produced near the water surface from photochemically driven oxidation by halogens (Laurier et al., 2003; Sprovieri et al., 2003; Laurier and Mason, 2007; Holmes et al., 2009). A portion (~10%) of the RGM that is deposited to the ocean is reduced to elemental mercury in the surface waters, either directly by sunlight, or through biologic activity (Fitzgerald et al., 2007; Strode et al., 2007). This tends to make the surface waters supersaturated with respect to dissolved elemental mercury (Schroeder and Munthe, 1998). Therefore, (gaseous) elemental mercury is generally evading from the ocean surface. Lakes and wetlands are more variable in their interaction with GEM. Some studies have reported supersaturations in surface waters with net evasion (Poissant et al., 2000, 2004), and others have observed slow net deposition or near equilibrium with the air (Zhang and Lindberg, 2000) or diurnal cycles (Marsik et al., 2005).

Mercury that is bound to particles and bound to soluble organic complexes can also be incorporated into the hydrologic cycle as a part of runoff after rain or flooding events and through the movement of subsurface pore water. Subsurface geothermal and hydrothermal vents are also sources of mercury in the ocean, although the magnitude of these inputs is believed to be negligible as compared with the total oceanic burden. Subsurface vents may, nonetheless, be important in enhancing the concentrations in ambient waters and sediments near the vent site (Stoffers et al., 1999; King et al., 2006; Lamborg et al., 2006). Some mercury is also thought to enter (or perhaps reenter) the hydrologic cycle from diagenetic reactions, which are physical, chemical, or biologic changes that occur as sediment (settled particulate matter that contains mercury) is deposited, compressed, and transformed to rock.

Industrial Point Sources

Industrial waste is an important source of Hg to some watersheds. The most prominent example of anthropogenic input of mercury to aquatic system occurred in Minimata, Japan, in the early 1950s. Throughout this period, the Chisso Corporation dumped more than 20 tons of mercury that had been used as a catalyst in the production of acetaldehyde, into Minamata Bay. The mercury contaminated the sediments, water, and ecosystem and ultimately the fish, which were a staple of the local diet. In the following years, more than 100 people died and more than 1000 were permanently disabled from the resulting methylmercury poisoning, which consequently bears the name, Minimata Disease (Clarkson, 1997).

It is also important to note that, by definition, the increased deposition (of RGM and particulate-bound Hg) to oceans and lakes throughout the globe as compared with preindustrial times is ultimately attributable to anthropogenic activities. Though the input occurs after transport through the atmosphere, it is nonetheless of anthropogenic origin.

Mining Runoff

An additional important source of mercury to aquatic systems is runoff or leaching resulting from mining activities. Large-scale mercury mines often produce large quantities of tailings or leave mining passages open after operations cease (e.g., Sulfur Bank Mercury Mine, California [Engle et al., 2007]; Almadén, Spain [Gray et al., 2004]; Idrija, Slovenia [Hines et al., 2006]). Early gold and silver mining also produced large quantities of Hg-enriched tailings because Hg was added to crushed ore in order to amalgamate and extract the gold and silver (e.g., Bonzongo et al., 1996). The wastes, along with the open mine passages, allow rain and groundwater to leach and mobilize mercury. Even smaller-scale mining activities, in particular artisanal mining practiced in China, Indonesia, South America, and Africa (reviewed by Veiga et al., 2006) produce significant amounts of waste matter that is enriched in mercury. This is often dumped into streams or lakes, or otherwise allowed to leach in an uncontrolled manner.

Methylated Species

Perhaps the most crucial process in the global cycling of mercury, at least from the standpoint of toxicity, is the concentration and accumulation of MMHg or DMHg up the food chain (called "bio-accumulation"). Most of the DMHg and MMHg that is bio-accumulated is produced in situ in natural waters or near the sediment–water interface. The production of MMHg and DMHg from dissolved Hg(II) (methylation) occurs primarily in sulfate-reducing bacteria in anoxic environments and has been hypothesized to be a cellular detoxification mechanism. A limited number of other methylation mechanisms have been proposed, but bacteria appear to be the largest producers in lakes and wetlands (Rudd, 1995; Fitzgerald et al., 2007).

Little DMHg and MMHg is found in the surface waters of the open ocean. Higher concentrations of DMHg can be found below the mixed layer of the open ocean and peripheral seas, while MMHg has been unambiguously detected only in coastal zones, peripheral seas, and the Equatorial Pacific Ocean (Fitzgerald et al., 2007).

Natural Processes That Emit Mercury into the Air

A number of natural processes emit mercury to the atmosphere. The origins of the mercury emitted from these processes may be purely natural, or they may be a mix of natural and anthropogenic (reemissions) (Gustin et al., 2008). Volcanoes, geothermal vents, and naturally enriched soils release mercury that originated in deep reservoirs, so can be considered purely natural emissions. Land, emissions, forest fires, and ocean emissions are mixed sources because a significant fraction of their Hg burden was previously deposited, which includes some anthropogenic mercury (Selin et al., 2008).

Quantifying natural sources of mercury in the air is difficult because of the large range of source types, natural variability, concomitance with anthropogenic mercury, and the global scale of the problem. Nonetheless, it is critical to quantify these sources, as without an understanding of natural sources it is difficult to understand the scale of anthropogenic influence. Ideally, we would like to quantify preindustrial mercury emissions as a reference point for present-day emissions. Since we obviously cannot go back in time and make direct observations, the estimation of preindustrial emissions must be done indirectly through models and sediment records.

Based on a small number of measurements, estimated mercury releases from volcanoes are 100–800 tons/yr (Varekamp and Buseck, 1986; Nriagu and Becker 2003; Pyle and Mather 2003). The only known estimate of global geothermal emissions (60 tons/year) is from Varekamp and Buseck (1986) based on average Hg content in hot springs and a global estimate of convective heat flux.

The emission of Hg from naturally enriched soils and exposed mineral deposits has been studied on small scales. A very limited number of global estimates have been made by scaling up the local emissions, but these are highly uncertain (Gustin et al., 2008). An early estimate of 500 tons/yr for global mercury emissions from soils was made by Lindqvist, et al. (1991). The flux of mercury from soil is a complicated function of soil concentration, light, moisture, temperature, and other factors (e.g. Gustin, et al., 1999; Ericksen, et al., 2006; Xin, et al., 2007). In one study, rainfall was found to increase the flux of mercury from desert soils by approximately an order of magnitude (Lindberg, et al., 1999), thus showing the complexity of quantifying soil flux. Based on recent observations and an understanding of soil mercury concentrations in geologically enriched regions across the United States, Ericksen et al., (2006) estimated a release of 100 tons/yr from soils in the contiguous United States. Several models of the global mercury cycle have used a global land flux of 500 tons/yr (Seigneur, et al., 2004; Selin et al., 2007).

Oceanic emissions are believed to be the largest component of all natural emissions. Mason and Sheu (2002) estimated that oceanic emissions of mercury are 2600 tons/yr; however, a significant fraction of this is "recycled: back into surface waters locally through photochemical processing. They estimated that the net flux out of the marine boundary layer is only about 1500 tons/yr. Using a three-dimensional global model that was constrained to observed mercury concentrations in the ocean, Strode et al. (2007) calculated a significantly larger net flux of 2800 tons/yr. A large fraction of this, however, was considered to be reemission of previously deposited mercury.

For forest fires, most of the mercury released probably came from recent deposition to the soil and vegetation, and so is partly reemission of previous anthropogenic and natural emissions (see the section on "Mercury Emissions: Summary, Uncertainty, and Validation," below). Weiss-Penzias et al. (2007) estimated global emissions of mercury from forest fires of 670 ± 330 tons/yr based on observations of the Hg:CO ratio in 10 biomass burning plumes. Wiedinmeyer and Friedli (2007) used a similar approach to estimate U.S. emissions of mercury from wildfires, and arrived at 44 tons/ yr with an uncertainty of 50%. In summary, natural emissions of Hg are an important component of the global cycle, but there are large uncertainties with regard to our estimates of these emissions.

Anthropogenic Sources of Mercury in the Air

Emissions inventories of anthropogenic sources of mercury have been compiled for most developed countries. These are based on direct stack tests to determine the amount of mercury being emitted for a particular facility. The emission per unit of production is termed an "emission factor." The emission factor from one facility is often used to estimate the emissions from another facility that has not had a direct stack test. This, of course, assumes that both factories operate similarly, with identical fuel and emission controls. While the emissions for large facilities can be relatively well known, emissions from smaller facilities are often excluded from emission inventories, and this can result in a significant error in the total emissions. The most important example is Chinese emissions from coal combustion and metals smelting. Because of less centralized consumption of coal (Wong et al., 2006) and a lack of data regarding activity levels and emissions factors from smaller operations and remote regions (Wu et al., 2006), there is considerable uncertainty (±44%) about the total estimate (Streets et al., 2005).

Based on emissions inventories, anthropogenic sources are believed to emit approximately 2200–3400 tons/yr of mercury to the atmosphere. While there are many different source types, the largest sources, in order of importance, are coal combustion, gold production, nonferrous metal smelting, cement production, caustic soda manufacturing, and waste incineration (Pacyna et al., 2006; Selin et al., 2008). Coal combustion is the largest source globally, and is responsible for about 1400 tons/yr, which is nearly two thirds of the global anthropogenic total (Pacyna et al., 2006). In most first-world countries, coal combustion is carried out almost entirely in the industrial and power generation sectors, whereas in developing countries, notably China, a significant fraction of coal combustion also occurs in the residential sector (Wu et al., 2006).

Emissions from coal combustion can vary substantially from facility to facility. The mercury emission factor from coal combustion depends mainly on two factors:

1. Concentration of mercury in the coal
2. The degree of emission controls

The concentration of mercury in coal can vary by more than two orders of magnitude, from 0.01 to 1.5 g of Hg/ton of coal (Pacyna et al., 2006). In addition, there are also large variations in control technologies. For example, the simplest particulate control technology, a cyclone, has almost no ability to capture mercury. A more complicated technique that is widely used, electrostatic precipitators (ESP), can remove approximately 30% of mercury in the stack emissions. Flue-gas desulfurization with an ESP can remove up to 74% of the mercury (Streets et al., 2005; Wu et al., 2006, Pacyna et al., 2006). Thus, emission factors (e.g., kilograms of Hg emitted per ton of coal consumed) vary greatly from plant to plant and country to country. Coal combustion can produce Hg as GEM, RGM, or PHg.

Gold production is the second largest source of mercury globally. These emissions are primarily the result of large-scale mining activities of gold-rich ores (which are almost always enriched in mercury) and small-scale, artisanal mining, which extracts gold by amalgamating it with mercury. Since gold and mercury are often colocated in the same deposit, these regions generally have naturally high emissions of mercury in the form of GEM (Engle et al., 2001; Coolbaugh et al., 2002). Mining activities, including digging, pulverizing, and roasting the ore, will significantly increase the mercury emissions. While the use of mercury to amalgamate and concentrate gold is now illegal in most parts of the world, this method is still used, especially in remote, third-world locations. Emissions from the disturbed deposits and wastes can continue for years, and thus current emissions are a result of both current and past practices. Some historically contaminated mining sites can accumulate substantial water and soil mercury concentrations and result in significant atmospheric emissions, for example, the Carson River Superfund site in Nevada (Gustin et al., 1996; Leonard et al., 1998). In Venezuela, Garcia-Sanchez et al. (2006) studied several sites polluted from past mining activities. In some gold processing shops, they found GEM concentrations of 50 to >100 μg/m³, which is more than 20,000 times greater than background concentrations.

Lacerda (1997) published a summary of Hg emissions from past and current gold mining. In this estimate, 460 tons/yr are released to the environment globally, an d65% of this is released to the atmosphere. Of the total atmospheric emissions, nearly 60% is released in South America. Lacerda's (1997) estimate of atmospheric emissions of Hg in South America by gold mining (179 tons/yr) is nearly twice the total Hg emissions from all sources in South America estimated by Pacyna et al. (2006). But, it should be noted that the Pacyna et al. (2006) inventory does not quantify Hg emissions from South American gold mining, nor does it attempt to quantify Hg emissions from illegal gold mining activities. In addition, the Pacyna study used an Hg emission factor of 0.5 g of Hg emitted/g of gold produced, whereas Lacerda used a factor of 1.5. Thus, while emissions of Hg from gold mining are clearly a substantial source for the global atmosphere, there is significant uncertainty in the actual values.

In developed countries, emissions of mercury have decreased in the past two decades, partly because of some direct emission controls, but mostly as a side benefit to controls on other pollutants (US EPA, 1997; Pacyna et al., 2006). Emissions in Europe have decreased nearly 50%, partly because of controls on other pollutants, but also because of political and economic changes that led to plant closures and reductions in coal use.

China is the world's largest emitter of mercury, with emissions of ~700 tons/yr (Pacyna et al., 2006; Wu et al., 2006). This is approximately one third of the global anthropogenic total. The next five top-emitting countries, in order, are South Africa, India, Japan, Australia, and the United States. Chinese emissions are rapidly increasing because of strong growth in the economic output and the increasing utilization of coal (e.g., Kim and Kim, 2000; Tan et al., 2000; Wu et al., 2006). It should also be noted that Chinese Hg emissions are expected to continue to increase for some time because of China's large coal reserves (Zhang et al., 2002) that have moderate to high Hg content (Zheng et al., 2007). Coal combustion and metal smelting are the two largest sources in China, although the larger of these is still somewhat uncertain. Metal smelting is the largest source of mercury in China in the Wu et al. (2006) and Streets et al. (2005) inventories, whereas coal combustion is the largest source in the Pacyna et al. (2006) inventory. While coal consumption is increasing rapidly in China, there is also greater utilization of ESPs for particulate removal, which can partially offset this increase (Wu et al., 2006). According to Wu et al. (2006), Chinese mercury emissions increased by 2.9% per year from 1995 to 2003.

For the United States, the anthropogenic emissions were recently quantified as part of the Clean Air Mercury Rule (CAMR), for the years 1990, 1996, and 1999. The mercury emissions were found to have decreased from 245 metric tons in 1990 to 124 tons in 1999. The drop was largely due to controls on medical and municipal incineration, as well as controls on other pollutants, such as SO₂ and aerosols, which had a side benefit of also reducing mercury. As of 1999, the largest single category for mercury emissions in the United States is coal combustion, which is responsible for 43% of total U.S. emissions. (see http://www.epa.gov/camr/charts.htm).

The CAMR was finalized in March 2005 to reduce emissions of mercury from coal power plants. This rule (along with the Clean Air Interstate Rule), would reduce mercury emissions from coal power plants in the United States from 48 tons/yr to 15 tons/yr by the year 2018. However, the rule proposes to use a "cap and trade" method, whereby not all power plants need to reduce their emissions uniformly. Under a cap-and-trade system, one plant can reduce their emissions more than is required and sell the resulting "credits" to a plant that did not reduce their emissions as much, or at all. This could result in "hotspots," where mercury deposition remains high and unaffected by the national emission reductions (e.g., Evers et al., 2007). The situation is further complicated by several lawsuits regarding the way the United States Environmental Protection Agency (EPA) regulated mercury via the CAMR. Prior to 2005, mercury was listed as a Hazardous Air Pollutant (HAP) in section 112 of the U.S. Clean Air Act (see http://www.epa.gov/oar/caa/caa112.txt). This would require the "maximum achievable" control of a listed pollutant on a plant-by-plant basis and would be inconsistent with a cap-and-trade approach. As part of its March 2005 decision, mercury was de-listed as a hazardous air pollutant and the CAMR regulations were put into place by the EPA. As a result of this action by the EPA, the CAMR rules were challenged in court by a broad coalition of states, Native American groups, and an array of health and environmental organizations. On February 8, 2008, the U.S. Court of Appeals for the District of Columbia overturned the EPA's CAMR. Thus, at the time of this writing (mid-2009), the final form for any rules on mercury emissions from coal power plants in the United States are in question.

Chemical Speciation

While most natural mercury sources emit Hg^0 (GEM), this is not the case for anthropogenic emissions, which consist of a mix of particle-bound mercury (PHg), Hg(II) compounds (or RGM), and Hg^0. The relative proportions of these is specific to each facility and source type. The chemical speciation is important for the simple reason that the different forms have vastly different lifetimes and thus vastly different impacts on the local environment. Hg^0 has a long enough lifetime in the atmosphere (about 1 year) that it mixes throughout the globe before reentering the terrestrial cycle, whereas PHg and RGM are removed from the atmosphere in a matter of hours to days and are thus much more important for local and regional bioaccumulation. In short, GEM is largely a global problem, whereas PHg and RGM are of regional concern. A further complication is that in some industries, stack tests are often only required to measure total mercury, without regard to the chemical form. For understanding and modeling the deposition and environmental influence, the chemical form can easily be more important than the total amount being emitted.

Mercury emissions that result from low-temperature volatilization (e.g., evaporation of mercury from concentrated mining waste) are emitted nearly 100% as GEM. Sources that involve high-temperature combustion (e.g., coal combustion or metal smelting) are more likely to contain some mercury in other forms. Depending on the coal type and combustion conditions, RGM and PHg could be as much as 46% of the mercury emissions (Seigneur et al., 2001). Globally, anthropogenic mercury emissions are believed to be 53% GEM, 37% RGM, and 10% PHg (Pacyna et al., 2006). For the United States, emissions are reported as 50% GEM, 46% RGM, and 4% PHg. For China, the Hg emissions are reported to be 57% GEM, 33% RGM, and 10% PHg. As mentioned previously, RGM and PHg will primarily deposit locally, so the large emissions in China have a significant contribution to deposition within Asia (Jaffe and Strode, 2008). Unfortunately, the values given above have significant uncertainty, and thus limit our ability to model the relative importance of global versus regional sources at any particular location.

Reemission of Previously Deposited Mercury

Evidence for reemission of previously deposited mercury has been shown in a number of studies. For example, Landis and Keeler (2002) estimated the evasion of mercury from Lake Michigan to be 38% of the annual wet and dry deposition flux. A study using mercury isotopes in a Canadian lake showed conclusively that recently deposited mercury could be reemitted to the atmosphere (Southworth, et al., 2007). Nearly all reemissions of mercury are in the form of Hg^0, regardless of how the mercury entered the system.

With respect to reemission, the key question is how much of the emissions from any one source is natural and how much is due to anthropogenic activities that may have taken place months to years ago? This question is important in that it directs us to identify the natural component of the global mercury cycle against which human-caused changes can be understood (e.g., the anthropogenic contribution to Hg in fish). However, quantifying the total fraction of current emissions that is natural versus anthropogenic is a challenging task. Probably the ice-core records and the lake-sediment cores, which document historic deposition trends, are the best evidence for large-scale changes in global mercury cycling (see the section on "The Changing Global Cycle of Mercury," above).

Mercury Emissions: Summary, Uncertainty, and Validation

Current estimates are that emissions of mercury are 6000–11,000 tons/yr, with the sources divided approximately equally between natural, direct anthropogenic, and reemissions from past activities. Table 1.1 gives a summary of the direct anthropogenic emissions from several

TABLE I.I
Direct Anthropogenic Emissions of Mercury (tons/yr)

Source	China	Asia	United States	Global	Global
Coal combustion	257	879	54[a]	NR	1422
Gold mining	45	47	6[b]	300	248
Nonferrous smelting	320	88	NR	NR	149
Cement production	35	90	NR	NR	140
Total all sources	696	1180	126	NR	2190
Year	2003	2000	1998/1999	NR	2000
Reference	Wu et al., 2006	Pacyna et al., 2006	Seigneur et al., 2001	Lacerda, 1997	Pacyna et al., 2006

NR = not reported.

a. Includes all fossil fuel stationary sources, but the total is dominated by facilities burning coal.

b. All mining sources.

sources Note that an estimate by Selin et al, (2008) has a much higher emission total for anthropogenic sources (3400 tons/yr).

Emission inventories should be considered as a "work in progress." By this we mean that source tests often omit both large and small facilities, emissions are constantly changing, factories are omitted, new information is uncovered, and chemical processes and fuels change. This is not meant as a criticism of emission inventories, only as a realistic assessment of their limitations and uncertainties. Emission inventories need validation against atmospheric observations to examine consistency.

Observations downstream of a major source region can give quantitative information on the emission. For example Jaffe et al. (2005) used observations on the island of Okinawa to quantify the emissions and outflow of mercury from Asia. They found that a much larger source of Hg was required to reconcile the atmospheric observations with the existing emission inventory. Combining observations with a transport model can improve the estimate of emissions. Two studies that examined the same Okinawa data along with data from the Mt. Bachelor Observatory in central Oregon and using the GEOS-CHEM model (Selin et al., 2007; Strode et al., 2008) also confirmed a much larger Asian source of Hg than had been previously assumed. Strode et al. (2008) compared the Hg:CO ratio in GEOS-Chem to observations at Okinawa and at Mt. Bachelor in central Oregon, and found that an Asian source of 1260–1470 tons/yr of Hg^0 was consistent with the observations. Models can also be run in "inverse" mode, whereby the emission inventories are derived directly from the best fit with observations. Using this approach with aircraft observations from the western Pacific, Pan et al. (2007) also found that Hg^0 emissions were significantly greater from China than the current emission inventory, consistent with the earlier studies mentioned above. These studies are fairly convincing that the total outflow of mercury from Asia is significantly larger than that reported by the anthropogenic inventory alone. This is due to a combination of underestimates in the industrial sources, combined with land emissions, both natural and reemissions.

In the most complete examination of anthropogenic emissions, Selin et al. (2008) suggested that all categories of Hg emissions were significantly larger than previously assumed, with anthropogenic emissions of 3400 tons/yr, natural emissions of 3200 tons/yr, and reemissions of 4100 tons/yr. However, as stated previously, all of these estimates have significant uncertainty.

From Release to Global Transport

The transport and deposition of mercury from the atmosphere is a crucial pathway for contamination in remote ecosystems. Hydrologic transport also plays a role in redistributing mercury, but because of the slower movement and mixing of the oceans, this plays only a small role in the enhancements of mercury in remote ecosystems. On continents, the transport of mercury in surface and subsurface waters is primarily important in redistributing high mercury levels near contaminated sites.

Aqueous Transport

RIVERINE

Rivers play an important role in the local transport of mercury from contaminated sites, but have a less significant role in the global cycle. Mason et al. (2002) and Sunderland and Mason (2007) estimate that about 1–2% of the total sources to the ocean come from inputs from rivers, with dissolved and particle-bound Hg being the largest fractions. Sunderland and Mason (2007) note that a large fraction of the particulate mercury carried by rivers is deposited in estuarine regions and oceanic shelves and does not reach the open ocean. Also, because wetlands can be strong producers of MMHg, the outflow from wetlands can be significant sources to downstream water bodies (St. Louis et al., 1996). One study of fate and transport in a boreal wetland found that over the course of several months, significant fractions of a newly deposited isotope (^{202}Hg) were converted to MMHg and were transported below the water table and toward a neighboring lake via groundwater (Branfireun et al., 2005).

Ocean Settling and Transport

The world's oceans play an important role in transporting and redistributing heat throughout the globe, but they do not play as prominent a role for mercury. This is primarily due to the much shorter intrahemispheric mixing time of the atmosphere (~10–20 days [Jacob, 1999]) as compared to the oceans (10s to 1000s of years [Sunderland and Mason, 2007]). Also, the short lifetime of Hg in the surface oceans against reemission (~0.6 year [Selin et al., 2008]) means that the surface ocean and atmosphere are in steady state on an annual time scale. Thus, the atmosphere will act to damp local perturbations from the surface ocean. Noteworthy oceanic transport processes include up/downwelling, interhemispheric transport, particle settling, and transport of MMHg from coastal sediments.

Mason et al. (1994) estimated that upwelling of thermocline waters in the equatorial Pacific is similar to the net atmospheric input to the surface, and in some places it may be greater. This, along with observations of elevated mercury in subsurface waters (Mason and Fitzgerald, 1993; Mason and Sullivan, 1999; Horvat et al., 2003) suggests that mercury-enriched water masses may sink from the surface and be transported as a record of historical deposition. Nonetheless, because of the relatively slow exchange rate of the world's oceans, the fluxes in and out of intermediate and deep reservoirs are a very small fraction of their overall burden.

Oceanic transport also likely contributes to interhemispheric transport. The lifetime of mercury in deep ocean compartments is much longer, 10s to 1000s of years (Sunderland and Mason, 2007) than surface reservoirs and would allow for interhemispheric transport. The impact of this mercury on atmospheric concentrations and deposition to land, however, would depend on the deep waters reaching the surface. The settling of particulate mercury, from the surface to deep waters and the ocean floor, is an important component in the oceanic cycle, particularly in the North Atlantic. In the surface waters, carbon-rich biomass or waste matter produced by phytoplankton or zooplankton sequesters mercury and falls to the intermediate and deep ocean. It is believed that about 50% of the sinking mercury is buried on the ocean floor and is lost to deep reservoirs (Sunderland and Mason, 2007).

The transport of MMHg from coastal sediments is also an important form of oceanic transport. Fitzgerald et al. (2007) estimate that coastal benthic MMHg production rates and diffusional efflux are sufficient that they are likely a major source to nearby ecosystems and potentially the open ocean.

Atmospheric Transport

DISPERSION OF POINT AND AREA SOURCE PLUMES

The majority of direct anthropogenic mercury emissions are from point sources such as coal-fired power plants, municipal waste incinerators, metal refineries, and chlor-alkali plants. The dispersion of these types of plumes has been widely studied, and a range of tools exist to describe the fate of chemicals in those plumes (e.g., Mossio et al., 2001). GEM emitted from these sources is largely unreactive and has been suggested to be useful tracer of sources (Friedli et al., 2004; Jaffe et al., 2005). RGM and PHg have much different fates. RGM is rapidly deposited to particles and surfaces, and can be sequestered by cloud and rain drops (Schroeder and Munthe, 1998). Particulate mercury can also settle out of the atmosphere or become incorporated into rain and cloud drops. Depending on the ambient conditions and the chemistry of the emitted plume, some of the RGM may be reduced to GEM (Lohman et al., 2006). Thus, if an airmass remains in contact with the surface, a large fraction of the RGM and PHg will be lost to the surface within hours to days of emission.

Continental Export and Long-Range Transport

Large, polluted airmasses can be exported from their source region, and then transported and dispersed over thousands of kilometers in the jet stream through their interaction with a midlatitude cyclone. Because the lifetime of GEM in the atmosphere is about 1 year (Selin et al., 2007), in some cases plumes have been observed for 7–10 days or more after emission (Jaffe et al., 2005; Slemr et al., 2006; Ebinghaus et al., 2007; Weiss-Penzias et al., 2007; Swartzendruber et al., 2008). In these studies, the mercury source region was identified through a combination of trajectory and synoptic analysis, and the calculation of enhancement ratios of copollutants. The enhancement ratios reflect the emission ratio (under certain assumptions) and, because of a significant difference in emission ratios between the major emitters (Jaffe et al., 2005; Weiss-Penzias et al., 2007), can suggest a source type. The suggested source type and backward air-parcel trajectories can then be compared with emissions maps. This approach has been successful in identifying intercontinental transport of Hg from sources in East Asia, Europe, and Africa. Modeling studies have confirmed the long-range transport of Hg seen in observations (e.g., Selin et al., 2007; Jaffe and Strode, 2008; Strode et al., 2008).

Global Transport

Once polluted airmasses are lofted into the jet stream, they can circle the northern hemisphere in as little as 7–10 days and will

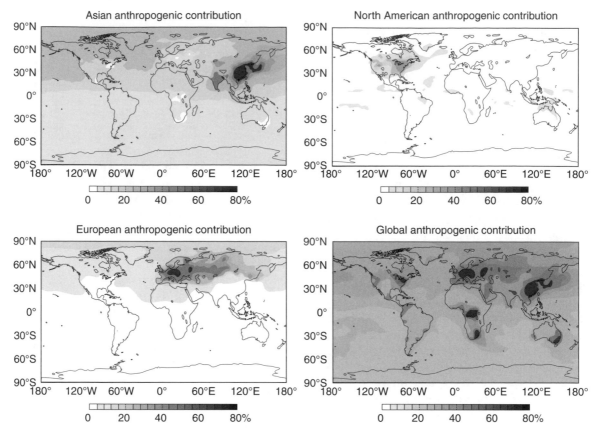

FIGURE 1.4   GEOS-Chem global chemical transport model estimates of annual average fraction of deposition that is due to anthropogenic emissions from Asia, North America, Europe, and all anthropogenic sources for 2004. Note that this is simply the direct deposition that does not include mercury that has been previously deposited to, and reemitted from the ocean and land. (Figures and modeling work provided by S. Strode.)

generally be dispersed in the midlatitude "pollution belt" in 1–2 weeks (Jacob, 1999). During transport, the airmasses tends to be stretched into long filaments and begin mixing into to the global background. Although the pollution and plumes can be swiftly transported over long distances at higher altitudes, their impact on the surface obviously depends upon them descending to the surface, which can be a slow process.

There is also transport and exchange of Hg between the hemispheres, although this is considerably slower, and requires on the order of 1 year for exchange to occur. The slower interhemispheric exchange along with the greater anthropogenic emissions in the northern hemisphere creates a very useful property, an interhemispheric gradient, which is a powerful constraint on the sources and global lifetime of Hg. The interhemispheric gradient provides clear evidence for increasing anthropogenic emissions, especially in the northern hemisphere (e.g., Slemr and Langer, 1992; Lamborg et al., 2002, Strode et al., 2007).

Industrial emissions of RGM and PHg are relatively short-lived and deposit to surfaces within a day or two of being emitted. In contrast, most GEM will be exported from the source region and continue to mix into the hemispheric background. Thus, the chemical form of Hg emissions are key to understanding the impacts. In their modeling study, Seigneur et al. (2004) show that North American industrial sources contribute between 25 and 32% to total deposition within the contiguous United States, but that there is considerable spatial variability in this value (9–81%). This is due to the significant emissions of RGM and PHg in the Eastern United States, which makes a significant contribution to deposition regionally.

On the other hand, GEM will be intercontinentally transported in 7–10 days, and within 1–2 months it will be distributed throughout the hemisphere. Slowly, GEM is oxidized to RGM, which is more readily removed by wet and dry deposits. While the GEM oxidation mechanism remains uncertain (Lindberg et al., 2007), its impact is felt in a variety of environments (Swartzendruber et al., 2006; Steffen et al., 2008; Weiss-Penzias et al., 2009). This is a key process that makes Hg a global pollutant. Figure 1.4 shows the percent deposition that can be attributed to emissions from the major industrial regions: Asia, United States, Europe, and the sum of all anthropogenic sources. Note that this includes only the deposition due to recent anthropogenic sources and does not include anthropogenic mercury that has been previously deposited and reemitted. Each source region contributes to global Hg deposition in proportion to its total emissions (see Table 1.1).

What is clear from Figure 1.4 is that Hg is a global pollutant that knows no boundaries. To substantially reduce deposition and bioaccumulation of Hg in any part of the world will require reductions in the global emissions.

Summary

Mercury is a global pollutant. It is emitted to the atmosphere in both reactive and more inert forms so that individual sources can impact ecosystems near and far. Once deposited Hg has a complex biogeochemistry. It can be converted to methyl mercury and bioaccumulate in ecosystems. Because of the global transport of Hg, emissions in one region significantly impact other regions of the globe.

References

Bergquist, B.A., and Blum, J.D. 2007. Mass-dependent and -independent fractionation of Hg isotopes by photoreduction in aquatic systems. *Science* 318: 417–420.

Biester, H., R. Bindler, A. Martinez-Cortizas, and D.R. Engstrom. 2007. Modeling the past atmospheric deposition of mercury using natural archives. *Environmental Science and Technology* 41(14): 4851–4860.

Biester, H., R. Kilian, C. Hertel, C. Woda, A. Mangini, and H.F. Scholer. 2002. Elevated mercury concentrations in peat bogs of South Patagonia, Chile—an anthropogenic signal. *Earth and Planetary Science Letters* 201: 609–620.

Bonzongo, J.C., K.J. Heim, J.J. Warwick, W.B. Lyons. 1996. Mercury levels in surface waters of the Carson River-Lahontan reservoir system, Nevada: influence of historic mining activities. *Environmental Pollution* 92(2): 193–201.

Branfireun, B.A., D.P. Krabbenhoft, H. Hintelmann, R.J. Hunt, J.P. Hurley, and J.W.M. Rudd. 2005. Speciation and transport of newly deposited mercury in a boreal forest wetland: A stable mercury isotope approach. *Water Resources Research* 41: W06016, doi:10.1029/2004WR003219.

Brown, A.S., R.J.C. Brown, W.T. Corns, and P.B. Stockwell. 2008. Establishing SI traceability for measurements of mercury vapour, *Analyst* 133: 946–953. DOI: 10.1039/b803724h.

Calvert, J.G., and S.E. Lindberg. 2005. Mechanisms of mercury removal by O_3 and OH in the atmosphere. *Atmospheric Environment* 39(18): 3355–3367.

Chen, C., A. Amirbahman, N. Fisher, G. Harding, C. Lamborg, D. Nacci, and D. Taylor. 2008. Methylmercury in Marine Ecosystems: Spatial Patterns and Processes of Production, Bioaccumulation, and Biomagnification. *EcoHealth* doi: 10.1007/s10393-008-0201-1.

Clarkson, T.W. 1997. The toxicology of mercury. *Critical Reviews in Clinical Laboratory Sciences* 34: 369–403.

Clever, H.L., S.A. Johnson, and M.E. Derrick. 1985. The solubility of mercury and some sparingly soluble mercury salts in water and aqueous electrolyte solutions. *Journal of Physical and Chemical Reference Data* 14: 631.

Coolbaugh, M.F., M.S. Gustin, and J.J. Rytuba. 2002. Annual emissions of mercury to the atmosphere from natural sources in Nevada and California. *Environmental Geology* 42(4): 338–349.

Ebinghaus, R., C. Banic, S. Beauchamp, D. Jaffe, H.H. Kock, N. Pirrone, L. Poissant, F. Sprovieri, and P.S. Weiss-Penzias. 2009. Spatial coverage and temporal trends of land-based atmospheric mercury measurements in the Northern and Southern Hemispheres. In: N. Pirrone, and R. Mason (Eds.). *Mercury fate and transport in the global atmosphere emissions, measurements and models.* Springer, New York.

Ebinghaus, R., F. Slemr, C.A.M. Brenninkmeijer, P. van Velthoven, A. Zahn, M. Hermann, D.A. O'Sullivan, and D.E. Oram. 2007. Emissions of gaseous mercury from biomass burning in South America in 2005 observed during CARIBIC flights. *Geophysical Research Letters* 34: L08813. doi:10.1029/2006GL028866.

Ebinghaus, R., H.H. Kock, C. Temme, J.W. Einax, A.G. Lowe, A. Richter, J.P. Burrows, and W.H. Schroeder. 2002. Antarctic springtime depletion of atmospheric mercury. *Environmental Science and Technology* 36: 1238–1244.

Engle, M.A., F. Goff, D.G. Jewett, G.J. Reller, and J.B. Bauman. 2007. Application of environmental groundwater tracers at the Sulphur Bank Mercury Mine, California, USA. *Hydrogeology Journal* 1431–2174, doi:10.1007/s10040-007-0240-7.

Engle, M.A., M.S. Gustin, and H. Zhang. 2001. Quantifying natural source mercury emissions from the Ivanhoe Mining District, north-central Nevada. *Atmospheric Environment* 35(11): 3987–3997.

Ericksen, J.A., M.S. Gustin, and M. Xin. 2006. Air-soil exchange of mercury from background soils in the United States. *Science of the Total Environment* 366: 851–863.

Evers, D.C., Y.J. Han, C.T. Driscoll, N.C. Kamman, M.W. Goodale, K.F. Lambert, T.M. Holsen, C.Y. Chen, T.A. Clair, and T. Butler. 2007. Biological mercury hotspots in the northeastern United States and Southeastern Canada. *BioScience* 57(1): 29–43.

Fernandez, P., R.M. Vilanova, C. Martinez, P.G. Appleby, and J.O. Grimalt. 2000. The historical record of atmospheric pyrolitic pollution over Europe registered in the sedimentary PAH from remote mountain lakes. *Environmental Science and Technology* 34: 1906–1913.

Fitzgerald, W.F., D.R. Engstrom, R.P. Mason, and E.A. Nater. 1998. The case for atmospheric mercury contamination in remote areas, *Environmental Science and Technology* 32 (1): 1–7.

Fitzgerald, W.F., C.H. Lamborg, and C.R. Hammerschmidt. 2007. Marine biogeochemical cycling of mercury. *Chemical Reviews* 107: 641–662.

Friedli, H.R., L.F. Radke, R. Prescott, P. Li, J.-H. Woo, and G.R. Carmichael. 2004. Mercury in the atmosphere around Japan, Korea, and China as observed during the 2001 ACE-Asia field campaign: Measurements, distributions, sources, and implications. *Journal of Geophysical Research* 109:D19S25.doi:10.1029/2003JD004244.

Garcia-Sanchez, A., F. Contreras, M. Adams, and F. Santos. 2006. *Airborne total gaseous mercury and exposure in a Venezuelan mining area. International Journal of Environmental Health Research* 16(5): 361–373. http://www.informaworld .com/smpp/462289770-42942271/title~content=t713425582 ~db=all~tab=issueslist~branches=16 - v16.

Gray, J.E., M.E. Hines, P.L. Higueras, I. Adatto, and B.K. Lasorsa. 2004. Mercury speciation and microbial transformations in mine wastes, stream sediments, and surface waters at the Almadén Mining District, Spain. *Environmental Science and Technology* 38: 4285–4292.

Guentzel, J.L., R.T. Powell, W.M. Landing, and R.P. Mason. 1996. Mercury associated with colloidal material in an estuarine and an open ocean environment. *Marine Chemistry* 55: 177–188.

Gustin, M.S., S. Lindberg, F. Marsik, A. Casimir, R. Ebinghaus, G. Edwards, C. Hubble-Fitzgerald, R. Kemp, H. Kock, T. Leonard, J. London, M. Majewski, C. Montecinos, J. Owens, M. Pilote, L. Poissant, P. Rasmussen, F. Schaedlich, D. Schneeberger, W. Schroeder, J. Sommar, R. Turner, A. Vette, D. Wallschlaeger, Z. Xiao, and H. Zhang. 1999. Nevada STORMS project: Measurement of mercury emissions from naturally enriched surfaces. *Journal of Geophysical Research* 104: 21831–21844.

Gustin, M.S., G.E. Taylor, T.L. Leonard, and T.E. Keislar. 1996. Atmospheric mercury concentrations associated with geologically and anthropogenically enriched sites in central western Nevada. *Environmental Science and Technology* 30(8): 2572–2579.

Gustin, M.S., S.E. Lindberg, and P.J. Weisberg. 2008. An update on the natural sources and sinks of atmospheric mercury. *Applied Geochemistry* 23: 482–493.

Hall, B. 1995. The gas-phase oxidation of elemental mercury by ozone, *Water Air Soil Pollution*, 80, 301–315.

Hines, M.E., J. Faganeli, I. Adatto, and M. Horvat. 2006. Microbial mercury transformations in marine, estuarine and freshwater sediments downstream of the Idrija Mercury Mine, Slovenia. *Applied Geochemistry* 21: 1940–1954.

Holmes, C.D., D.J. Jacob, R.P. Mason, and D.A. Jaffe. 2009. Sources and deposition of reactive gaseous mercury in the marine atmosphere. *Atmospheric Environment* 43: 2278–2285.

Horvat, M., J. Kotnik, M. Logar, V. Fajon, T. Zvonaric, and N. Pirrone. 2003. Speciation of mercury in surface and deep-sea waters in the Mediterranean Sea. *Atmospheric Environment* 37: S93–S108.

Jacob, D.J. 1999. *Introduction to atmospheric chemistry.* Princeton, NJ: Princeton University Press.

Jaffe, D., and Strode, S. 2008. Sources, fate and transport of atmospheric mercury from Asia. *Environmental Chemistry* 5: 121. doi:10.1071/EN08010.

Jaffe, D.A., E. Prestbo, P. Swartzendruber, P. Weiss-Penzias, S. Kato, A. Takami, S. Hatakeyama, and Y. Kajii. 2005. Export of Atmospheric Mercury from Asia. *Atmospheric Environment* 39: 3029–3038. doi:10.1016/j.atmosenv.2005.01.30.

Johansson, K. 1989. Metals in sediment of lakes in Northern Sweden. *Water, Air and Soil Pollution* 47: 441–455.

Kesler, S.E. 1994. *Mineral resources, economics, and the environment.* New York: Macmillan College Publishing.

Kim, K.H., and M.Y. Kim. 2000. The effects of anthropogenic sources on temporal distribution characteristics of total gaseous mercury in Korea. *Atmospheric Environment* 34: 3337–3347.

King, S.A., S. Behnke, K. Slack, D.P. Krabbenhoft, D.K. Nordstrom, M.D. Burr, and R.G. Striegl. 2006. Mercury in water and biomass of microbial communities in hot springs of Yellowstone National Park, USA. *Applied Geochemistry* 21: 1868–1879.

Lacerda, L.D. 1997. Global mercury emissions from gold and silver mining. *Water, Air and Soil Pollution* 97(3–4): 209–221.

Lamborg, C.H., K.L. Von Damm, W.F. Fitzgerald, C.R. Hammerschmidt, and R. Zierenberg. 2006. Mercury and monomethylmercury in fluids from Sea Cliff submarine hydrothermal field, Gorda Ridge. *Geophysical Research Letters* 33: L17606. doi:10.1029/2006GL026321.

Lamborg, C.H., W.F. Fitzgerald, A.W.H. Damman, J.M. Benoit, P.H. Balcom, and D.R. Engstrom. 2002. Modern and historic atmospheric mercury fluxes in both hemispheres: Global and regional mercury cycling implications. *Global Biogeochemical Cycles* 16(4): 1104. doi:10.1029/2001GB001847.

Landers, D.H., et al. 2008. *The fate, transport, and ecological impacts of airborne contaminants in western national parks.* Final report of the NPS WACAP study. EPA/600/R-07/138, January 2008.

Landis, M.S., and G.J. Keeler. 2002. Atmospheric mercury deposition to Lake Michigan during the Lake Michigan Mass Balance Study. *Environmental Science and Technology* 36: 4518–4524.

Landis, M.S., R.K. Stevens, F. Schaedlich, and E.M. Prestbo. 2002. Development and characterization of an annular denuder methodology for the measurement of divalent inorganic reactive mercury in the ambient air. *Environmental Science and Technology* 36: 3000–3009.

Laurier, F., and R.P. Mason. 2007. Mercury concentration and speciation in the coastal and open ocean boundary layer. *Journal of Geophysical Research* 112: D06302. doi:10.1029/2006JD007320.

Laurier, F.J.G., R.P. Mason, L. Whalin, and S. Kato. 2003. Reactive gaseous mercury formation in the North Pacific Ocean's marine boundary layer: A potential role of halogen chemistry. *Journal of Geophysical Research* 108(D17): 4529. doi:10.1029/2003JD003625.

Leonard, T.L., G.E. Taylor, M.S. Gustin, and G.C. Fernandez. 1998. Mercury and plants in contaminated soils: 1. uptake partitioning and emission to the atmosphere. *Environmental Toxicology and Chemistry* 17(10): 2063–2071.

Lin, C.-J., P. Pongprueksa, S.E. Lindberg, S.O. Pehkonen, D. Byun, and C. Jang. 2006. Scientific uncertainties in atmospheric mercury models I: Model science evaluation. *Atmospheric Environment* 40: 2911–2928.

Lindberg, S., R. Bullock, R. Ebinghaus, D. Engstrom, X. Feng, W. Fitzgerald, N. Pirrone, E. Prestbo, and C. Seigneur. 2007. A synthesis of progress and uncertainties in attributing the sources of mercury in deposition. *Ambio* 36(1): 19–33.

Lindberg, S.E., H. Zhang, M. Gustin, A. Vette, F. Marsik, J. Owens, A. Casimir, R. Ebinghaus, G. Edwards, C. Fitzgerald, J. Kemp, H.H. Kock, J. London, M. Majewski, L. Poissant, M. Pilote, P. Rasmussen, F. Schaedlich, D. Schneeberger, J. Sommar, R. Turner, D. Wallschläger, and Z. Xiao. 1999. Increases in mercury emissions from desert soils in response to rainfall and irrigation. *Journal of Geophysical Research* 104(17): 21879–21888.

Lindqvist, O., K. Johansson, M. Aastrup, A. Andersson, L. Bringmark, G. Hovsenius, L. Hakanson, A. Iverfeldt, M. Meili, and B. Timm. 1991. Mercury in the Swedish environment – Recent research on causes, consequences and corrective methods. *Water, Air and Soil Pollution* 55: xi–261. doi: 10.1007/BF00542429.

Lohman, K., C. Seigneur, E. Edgerton, and J. Jansen. 2006. Modeling mercury in power plant plumes. *Environmental Science an Technology* 40(12): 3848–3854.

Lucotte, M., A. Mucci, C. Hillaire-Marcel, P. Pichet, and A. Grondin. 1995. Anthropogenic mercury enrichment in remote lakes of Northern Quebec (Canada). *Water, Air and Soil Pollution* 80: 467–476.

Marsik, F., G.J. Keeler, S.E. Lindberg, and H. Zhang. 2005. Air-surface exchange of gaseous mercury over a mixed sawgrass-cattail stand within the Florida Everglades. *Environmental Science and Technology* 39: 4739–4746.

Mason, R.P., and G.R. Sheu. 2002. Role of the ocean in the global mercury cycle. *Global Biogeochemical Cycles* 16(4): 1093. doi: 10.1029/2001GB001440.

Mason, R.P., and K.A. Sullivan. 1999. The distribution and speciation of mercury in the *South and equatorial Atlantic. Deep Sea Research Part II*, 46: 937–956.

Mason, R.P., K.R. Rolfhus, and W.F. Fitzgerald. 1998. Mercury in the North Atlantic. *Marine Chemistry* 61: 37–53.

Mason, R.P., W.F. Fitzgerald, and F.M.M. Morel. 1994. The biogeochemical cycling of elemental mercury – anthropogenic influences. *Geochemica et Cosmochimica Acta* 58: 3191–3198.

Mason, R.P., and W.F. Fitzgerald. 1993. The distribution and biogeochemical cycling of mercury in the equatorial Pacific Ocean. *Deep Sea Research* 40: 1897–1924.

Mossio, P., A.W. Gnyp, and P.F. Henshaw. 2001. A fluctuating plume dispersion model for the prediction of odour-impact frequencies from continuous stationary source. *Atmospheric Environment* 35(16): 2955–2962.

National Research Council. 2000. *Toxicological effects of methylmercury.* Washington DC: National Academies Press.

Nriagu, J., and C. Becker. 2003. Volcanic emissions of mercury to the atmosphere: global and regional inventories. *Science of the Total Environment* 304: 3–12.

Pacyna, E.G., J.M. Pacyna, F. Steenhuisen, and S. Wilson. 2006. Global anthropogenic mercury emission inventory for 2000. *Atmospheric Environment* 40: 4048–4063.

Pacyna, E.G., and J.M. Pacyna. 2002. Global emission of mercury from anthropogenic sources in 1995. *Water, Air and Soil Pollution* 137: 149–165.

Pan, L., T. Chai, G.R. Carmichael, Y. Tang, D. Streets, J.-H. Woo, H.R. Friedli, and L.F. Radke. 2007. Top-down estimate of mercury emissions in China using four-dimensional variational data assimilation. *Atmospheric Environment* 41: 2804–2819.

Poissant, L., A. Amyot, M. Pilote, and D.R.S. Lean. 2000. Mercury water-air exchange over the Upper St. Lawrence River and Lake Ontario. *Environmental Science and Technology* 34: 3069–3078.

Poissant, L., M. Pilote, X. Xu, H. Zhang, and C. Beauvais. 2004. Atmospheric mercury speciation and deposition in the Bay St. Francois wetlands. *Journal of Geophysical Research* 109: D11301. doi:10.1029/2003JD004364.

Pyle, D.M., and T.A. Mather. 2003. The importance of volcanic emissions for the global atmospheric mercury cycle. *Atmospheric Environment* 37: 5115–5124.

Rudd, J.W.M. 1995. Sources of methylmercury to aquatic ecosystems: a review. *Water, Air and Soil Pollution* 80: 697–713.

Schroeder, W.H., and J. Munthe. 1998. Atmospheric mercury—An overview. *Atmospheric Environment* 32(5): 809–822.

Schroeder, W.H., K. Anlauf, L.A. Barrie, J.Y. Lu, A. Steffen, D.R. Schneeberger, and T, Berg. 1998. Arctic springtime depletion of mercury. *Nature* 394: 331–332.

Schuster, P.F., D.P. Krabbenhoft, D.L. Naftz, L.D. Cecil, M.L. Olson, J.F. Dewild, D.D. Susong, J.R. Green, and M.L. Abbott. 2002. Atmospheric mercury deposition during the last 270 years: A glacial ice core record of natural and anthropogenic sources. *Environmental Science and Technology* 36: 2303–2310.

Seigneur, C., P. Karamchandani, K. Lohman, and K. Vijayaraghavan. 2001. Multiscale modeling of the atmospheric fate and the transport of mercury. *Journal of Geophysical Research* 106(D21): 27795–27809.

Seigneur, C., K. Vijayaraghavan, K. Lohman, P. Karamchandani, and C. Scott. 2004. Global source attribution for mercury deposition in the United States. *Environmental Science and Technology* 38: 555–569.

Selin, N.E., D.J. Jacob, R.J. Park, R.M. Yantosca, S. Strode, L. Jaeglé, and D. Jaffe. 2007. Chemical cycling and deposition of atmospheric mercury: global constraints from observations, *Journal of Geophysical Research*, 112, D02308, doi:10.1029/2006JD007450.

Selin, N.E., D.J. Jacob, R.M. Yantosca, S. Strode, L. Jaeglé, and E.M. Sunderland. 2008. Global 3-D land-ocean-atmosphere model for mercury: Present-day versus preindustrial cycles and anthropogenic enrichment factors for deposition. *Global Biogeochemical Cycles* 22: GB2011. doi:10.1029/2007GB003040.

Slemr, F., R. Ebinghaus, P.G. Simmonds, and S.G. Jennings. 2006. European emissions of mercury derived from long-term observations at Mace Head, on the western Irish coast. *Atmospheric Environment* 40: 6966–6974.

Slemr, F., and F. Langer. 1992. Increase in global atmospheric concentrations of mercury inferred from measurements over the Atlantic Ocean. *Nature* 355: 434–437.

Southworth, G., S. Lindberg, and H. Hintelmann. 2007. Evasion of added isotopic mercury from a northern temperate lake. *Environmental Toxicology and Chemistry* 26(1): 53–60.

Sprovieri, F., N. Pirrone, and J. Sommar. 2003. Mercury speciation in the marine boundary layer along a 6000 km cruise path around the Mediterranean Sea. *Atmospheric Environment* 37(suppl. 1): S63–S71.

St. Louis, V.L., J.W.M. Rudd, C.A. Kelly, K.G. Beaty, R.J. Flett, and N.T. Roulet. 1996. Production and loss of methylmercury and loss of total mercury from boreal forest catchments containing different types of wetlands. *Environmental Science and Technology* 30: 2719.

Steffen, A., T. Douglas, M. Amyot, P. Ariya, K. Aspmo, T. Berg, J. Bottenheim, S. Brooks, F. Cobbett, A. Dastoor, A. Dommergue, R. Ebinghaus, C. Ferrari, K. Gardfeldt, M.E. Goodsite, D. Lean, A.J. Poulain, C. Scherz, H. Skov, J. Sommar, and C. Temme. 2008. A synthesis of atmospheric mercury depletion event chemistry in the atmosphere and snow. *Atmospheric Chemistry and Physics* 8(6): 1445–1482.

Stoffers, P., M. Hannington, I. Wright, P. Herzig, C. de Ronde and Shipboard Scientific Party. 1999. Elemental mercury at submarine hydrothermal vents in the Bay of Plenty, Taupo volcanic zone, New Zealand, *Geology* 1999;27;931–934, doi:10.1130/0091-7613(1999)027<0931:EMASHV>2.3.CO;2

Streets, D.G., J.M. Hao, Y. Wu, J.K., Jiang, M. Chan, H.Z. Tian, and X.B. Feng. 2005. Anthropogenic mercury emissions in China. *Atmospheric Environment* 39: 7789–7806.

Strode, S.A., L. Jaegle, N.E. Selin, D.J. Jacob, R.J. Park, R.M. Yantosca, R.P. Mason, and F. Slemr. 2007. Air-sea exchange in the global mercury cycle. *Global Biogeochemica Cycles* 21: GB1017. doi:10.1029/2006GB002766.

Strode, S., L. Jaeglé, D. Jaffe, P. Swartzendruber, N. Selin, C. Holmes, and R. Yantosca. 2008. Trans-Pacific transport of mercury. *Journal of Geophysical Research* doi:10.1029/2007JD009428.

Sunderland, E.M., and R.P. Mason. 2007. Human impacts on open ocean mercury concentration. *Global Biogeochemical Cycles* 21: GB4022. doi:10.1029/2006GB002876.

Sunderland, E.M., D.P. Krabbenhoft, J.W. Moreau, S.A. Strode, and W.M. Landing. 2009. Mercury sources, distribution and bioavailability in the North Pacific Ocean: Insights from data and models. *Global Biogeochemical Cycles* 23: GB2010. doi:10.1020/2008GB003425.

Swain, E.B., D.R. Engstron, M.E. Brigham, T.A. Henning, and P.L. Brezonik. 1992. Increasing rates of atmospheric mercury deposition in mid-continental North America. 1992. *Science* 257: 784–787.

Swartzendruber, P.C., D.A. Jaffe, E.M. Prestbo, P. Weiss-Penzias, N.E. Selin, R. Park, D.J. Jacob, S. Strode, and L. Jaegle. 2006. Observations of reactive gaseous mercury in the free troposphere at the Mount Bachelor Observatory. *Journal of Geophysical Research* 111: D24301. doi:10.1029/2006JD007415.

Swartzendruber, P.C., D. Chand, D.A. Jaffe, J. Smith, D. Reidmiller, L. Gratz, J. Keeler, S. Strode, L. Jaegle, and R. Talbot. 2008. Vertical distribution of mercury, CO, ozone, and aerosol scattering coefficient in the Pacific Northwest during the spring 2006 INTEX-B campaign. *Journal of Geophysical Research.* 2008, 113, D10305, doi: 10.1029/2007JD009579.

Tan, H., J.L. He, L. Liang, S. Lazoff, J. Sommar, Z.F. Zeo, and O. Lindqvist. 2000. Atmospheric mercury deposition in Giuzhou, China. *Science of the Total Environment* 259 (1–3): 223–230.

US EPA. 1997. Mercury Study Report to Congress, EPA-452-R-97-004.

Varekamp, J.C., and Buseck, P.R. 1986. Global mercury flux from volcanic and geothermal sources. *Applied Geochemistry* 1: 65–73.

Veiga, M.M., P.A. Maxson, and L.D. Hylander. 2006. Origin and consumption of mercury in small-scale gold mining. *Journal of Cleaner Production* 14(3–4): 436–447.

Véron, A., C.E. Lambert, A. Isley, P. Linet, and F. Grousset. 1987. Evidence of recent lead pollution in deep North-East Atlantic sediments. *Nature* 326: 278–281.

Weiss-Penzias, P., M.S. Gustin, and S.N. Lyman. 2009. Observations of speciated atmospheric mercury at three sites in Nevada: evidence for a free tropospheric source of reactive gaseous mercury. *Journal of Geophysical Research* 114: D14302. doi:10.1029/2008JD011607.

Weiss-Penzias, P., D.A. Jaffe, P.C. Swartzendruber, W. Hafner, D. Chand, and E.M. Prestbo. 2007. Quantifying Asian and biomass burning sources of mercury using the Hg/CO ratio in pollution plumes observed at the Mount Bachelor observatory. *Atmospheric Environment* 41(21): 4366–4379.

Wiedinmeyer, C., and H. Friedli. 2007. Mercury emission from fires: an initial inventory for the United States. *Environmental Science and Technology* 41(23): 8092–8098.

Wong, H.K.T., J.O. Nriagu, and R.D. Coker. 1984. Atmospheric deposition of metals into lakes in the Algonquin Provincial Park, Ontario. *Chemical Geology* 44: 187–201.

Wong, C.S.C., N.S. Duzgoren-Aydin, A. Aydin, and M.H. Wong. 2006. Sources and trends of environmental mercury emissions in Asia. *Science of the Total Environment* 368: 649–662.

Wu, Y., S. Wang, D.G. Streets, J. Hao, M. Chan, and J. Jiang. 2006. Trends in anthropogenic mercury emissions in China from 1995 to 2003. *Environmental Science and Technology* 40(17): 5312–5318.

Xin, M., M. Gustin, and D. Johnson. 2007. Laboratory investigation of the potential for reemission of atmospherically derived Hg from soils. *Environmental Science and Technology* 41(14): 4946–4951.

Zhang, H., and S.E. Lindberg. 2000. Air/water exchange of mercury in the Everglades I: the behavior of dissolved gaseous mercury in the Everglades Nutrient Removal Project. *Science of the Total Environment* 259: 123–133.

Zhang, M.Q., Y.C. Zhu, and R.W. Deng. 2002. Evaluation of mercury emissions to the atmosphere from coal combustion, China. *Ambio* 31(6): 482–484.

Zheng, L., G. Liu, and C.-L. Chou. 2007. The distribution, occurrence and environmental effect of mercury in Chinese coals. *Science of the Total Environment* 384: 374–383.

Industrial Use of Mercury in the Ancient World

WILLIAM E. BROOKS

THE OLD WORLD AND ASIA

THE NEW WORLD

CONCLUSION

Mercury and cinnabar, the common ore of mercury, were known and used by ancient people in Africa, Asia, Central America, Europe, Mexico, and South America. Archaeologists have shown that cinnabar was mined and mercury was produced more than 8000 years ago in Turkey. Cinnabar was a multiuse pigment in many parts of the ancient world, and mercury was used for gilding or placer gold amalgamation. Mercury was the earliest known treatment for syphilis, and its use is described in the Canon of Medicine by the Persian physician Ibn Sina (Avicenna) in 1025 CE.

Even though cinnabar and mercury are found worldwide, the most well-known occurrences include those in Almaden, Spain; California; Huancavelica, Peru; Idrija, Slovenia; the Sizma district, Turkey; and the Yangtze region, China. The mineral name "cinnabar" may have been derived from Sinop, also called Cinab, a Black Sea port that was an export center for cinnabar and mercury (also called "ruddle") produced in ancient Turkey (Barnes and Bailey, 1972). An undated Chinese saying "where there is cinnabar above, yellow gold will be found below" (Herz and Garrison, 1998) suggests that the Chinese understood the geometry of mineral deposits and that the presence of cinnabar might be used to locate some types of gold occurrences.

Far more is known about mercury in the 1500s and later. For example, Agricola (1556) details mercury use and retorting techniques and discusses the health effects of breathing the fumes released during mercury retorting in Europe in the 1500s. In the 1600s, mercury from the Santa Barbara Mine, Huancavelica, Peru was essential to Spanish Colonial silver processing at Potosí, Bolivia, and

soon replaced mercury brought across the Atlantic from the centuries-old Almaden Mine in Spain (Putman, 1972). The slaves and indigenous workers at Huancavelica were exposed to cinnabar powder from mining, mercury fumes from mining and retorting, dust that contained silica and arsenic compounds, cold, high altitude, carbon monoxide, cave-ins, and poor ventilation; therefore, Huancavelica came to be known as the "mina de la muerte" [mine of death] (Brown, 2001).

In Europe in the 1800s, mercury was widely used for gilding domes and interiors of cathedrals, domes of government buildings, and religious figures and also for mirror backing. Mercuric nitrate was widely used for making hats, and the term "mad hatter" was associated with those who were affected by the fumes released during the process. The term "vermeil" was also used in the 19th century; it referred to a sterling silver product, for example, a wine cooler, with all surfaces coated with a minimum of 10 karat gold that was of a minimum thickness of 2.5 µm; however, this process was banned because the artisans became blind as a result of exposure to mercury. Tableware made by this metallurgical process is kept on display in the Vermeil Room in the White House, Washington, DC. Along with polished copper, brass, silver, and obsidian, the reflective qualities and movement of native mercury made it intriguing as a scrying, or fortune-telling, mirror. Mercury has also been used as a mirror to reflect light for transmitted light microscopes.

Powdered cinnabar, or vermillion, was widely used as an artist's pigment in Europe from the 1300s until the 1900s (Windhaven Guild, 2004) and is still available from art suppliers (Iconofile, 2010). Mercury compounds were used to inhibit mold in some household paints; however, because of its toxicity, mercury is no longer used for this application.

Worldwide, artisanal gold mining is the leading industrial use of mercury, for example, in Colombia (Delgado, 2010), Brazil (Fialka, 2006), and Peru (Brooks et al., 2007). Mercury is also widely used as an electrolyte to produce chlorine and caustic soda from brine and is also used for some batteries, children's light-up toys and shoes, compact and traditional fluorescent lamps, dental amalgam, switches, and thermostats. Fever thermometers and some medical measuring devices still use mercury; however, the use of digital substitutes is increasing. The mercury used in these products can be recycled, thereby, eliminating releases that may potentially affect human health (Brooks and Matos, 2005). Some skin-lightening creams and beauty soaps may also contain mercury (al-Saleh and al-Doush, 1997). Information on global mercury production, use, and releases since 1500 CE is provided by Hylander and Meili (2003, 2005). Statistics on annual world mercury production, domestic import sources and export destinations, and prices are compiled in Brooks (2007).

Since 1927, mercury has been measured and priced by the flask, a unique commercial unit that was introduced at Almaden, Spain (Meyers, 1951). The flask itself is made of welded steel, has a screw cap, and is about the size of a 2-L container. When filled, the flask weighs 34.5 kg, and 29 flasks of mercury are contained in a metric ton.

The Old World and Asia

Archaeological evidence indicates that mercury and cinnabar were known and widely used for industrial applications before 1500 CE. In southwestern Turkey, in the Sizma district, cinnabar was mined as early as 6300 BCE from what may be the oldest known underground mine, a mercury mine. A ^{14}C date of 6280 BCE on cinnabar-painted skulls that were excavated in the area suggests that the cinnabar may have been sourced from occurrences in the Sizma district. Near Ladik, also in the Sizma district, the 3 m^2 hearth of a mercury retort, carved into marble, was found. Cinnabar would have been used for pigments or cosmetics and the mercury would have been used for gilding or amalgamation with alluvial gold found in the streams in the region. Thus, it is very likely that cinnabar mining and mercury production first originated in Turkey more than 8000 years ago (Barnes and Bailey, 1972; Yildiz and Bailey, 1978).

Mercury was known in Spain before the Christian Era, and the Moorish name of the mine "Almaden" and the metal "azogue" (mainly in Latin America) are still in use today. Near Valencia, Spain, well-preserved human bones covered with powdered cinnabar were found in a tomb that dates to 5000 BCE (Maravelaki-Kalaitzaki and Kallithrakas-Kontos, 2003). Was the powdered cinnabar used because of the life symbolism suggested by its blood-red color? Or, perhaps, powdered cinnabar, now known to be toxic (Sax, 1984), was selectively used because of its toxicity and preservative qualities. These properties were also understood in ancient India, where cinnabar was used

as a preservative to keep fine silks intact (Srinivasan and Ranganathan, 2004).

Mercury was found in a ceremonial cup in an Egyptian tomb that dates to 1600–1500 BCE (D'Itri and D'Itri, 1977). Was the mercury placed in the tomb because it was silvery, liquid, reflective, and needed in the afterlife? Or was mercury intentionally used because its fumes, which volatize at ambient temperatures, were known to be toxic and therefore, inhibited biologic activity and decay?

A kilogram of mercury, which may have been used for amalgamation or gilding, was found near the Greek trading site of al Mina, on the Syrian coast, which dates to 500 BCE (Ramage and Craddock, 2000). Theophrastus (372–287 BCE) was the first to describe refining and condensation of mercury from cinnabar (Healy, 1978). He wrote the earliest work on minerals and mining, "Peri Lithon" [On Stones], and described the mining and processing of cinnabar in Iberia and Colchis. However, the "Iberia" of Theophrastus' time was north of Turkey, the current republic of Georgia, and not Spain. Colchis was to the south. Later, the cinnabar workshops were transferred to Rome because cinnabar had been discovered in Spain (Caley and Richards, 1956).

Native mercury was associated with cinnabar occurrences in Asia Minor at Ephesus, Turkey, and in Europe at Almaden, Spain. Pliny the Elder (23–79 CE) described native mercury droplets associated with silver and lead mines in Greece (Healy, 1978). Pliny the Younger (61–113 CE) described a method of recycling and purifying used mercury by squeezing it through leather (D'Itri and D'Itri, 1977). At about the same time, mercury was used to recycle gold from worn-out golden embroideries by first ashing the material and then treating the dampened ashes with mercury (Ramage and Craddock, 2000).

In ancient China, cinnabar was also used for pigments and the tomb of Emperor Ch'i-Huang-Ti, who died in 210 BCE, contained a large relief map of China in which the oceans and rivers were represented by mercury (Schuette, 1931). The Chinese also believed that mercury or cinnabar medications could prolong life, perhaps because of their preservative qualities; however, several emperors died from mercury poisoning in their attempts to attain immortality (Leicester, 1961). Over 4000 years ago women in China drank mercury as a contraceptive (Simon, 2004).

Mercury and gold were used as a part of the finishing process on ceremonial swords in 12th century Japan. A paste of mercury and gold was applied to decorate the protective collar (habaki) between the blade of the sword and the user's hand. The amalgam paste was then heated to drive off the mercury. This process gilded the habaki with a decorative gold accent (Kapp et al., 1987).

Whether or not mercury was used for amalgamation and recovery of alluvial gold in the ancient world is controversial. For example, Davies (1935), considered it unlikely that mercury was used to recover gold, and scanning electron microscope analyses of gold artifacts from Sardis did not detect mercury (Ramage and Craddock, 2000). However, by

77 CE, Rome imported 4–5 metric tons of mercury annually from the mines in Spain, which was used for gold amalgamation (D'Itri and D'Itri, 1977).

As early as 600 BCE, cinnabar was used by the Greeks as a pigment to color statues (Healy, 1978). Powdered cinnabar was used to paint Roman villas and also as a cosmetic. Researchers found that cinnabar was one of the mineral pigments used on the frescoes that were later buried by ash from volcanic eruptions at Pompeii (Lorenzi, 2004). Roman criminals and slaves were sent to work at firesetting (an ancient mining practice in which wood was burned at the face of the ore zone and water was poured on the face, causing the rock to crack and spall) in the Spanish mercury mines (D'Itri, and D'Itri, 1977); they subsequently died from inhaling the toxic mercury fumes released by the process.

In the Middle East, according to the 11th century scientist Abu Rayhan al-Biruni, author of texts on mineralogy, gems, and metals, gold was processed from the ore by crushing, then the ore was washed and mercury was added. Gold was also recovered from the Sind River by leaving mercury in small pits dug in the bedrock in the stream. The gold-bearing sediment would wash over the puddles of mercury and the gold would amalgamate with the mercury. In both examples, the gold-bearing amalgam was then recovered and squeezed through leather to separate the gold from the mercury and recover some of the mercury. Then, as a final step, the amalgam was burned in order to volatilize the mercury and purify the gold (al-Hassan and Hill, 1986).

The amalgamation process for small-scale mining of quartz veins was introduced to West Africa in the 12th century and the amalgam was similarly burned to recover the gold (Blanchard, 2006).

The New World

There are mercury occurrences in Guerrero, Queretaro, San Luis Potosí, and Zacatecas, Mexico. However, in the late 1500s, mercury from Peru was brought to Mexico for silver processing. Spain prohibited the exploitation of mercury in Mexico from 1680 to 1811; therefore, records of mercury mining in Mexico were inconsistent (Consejo de Recursos Minerales, 1992; Acosta y Asociados, 2001).

Underground mining of cinnabar dates to the 1000 BCE in Queretaro, and it was used for rituals and celebrations (Langenscheidt, 1986; Consejo de Recursos Minerales, 1992). Archaeological evidence indicates that cinnabar was also mined at Guadalcázar, in central San Luis Potosí (Wittich, 1922; Zaragoza, 1993). In south-central Mexico, cinnabar was used as a pigment by the Olmec to decorate figures during the Pre-Classic (1200 to 400 BCE) (Martín del Campo, 2005).

At the Temple of Inscriptions, Palenque, Mexico, the sarcophagus of the Maya king Pacal, who died in 683 CE, was painted with cinnabar as a toxic warning to looters. The body of Pacal and the body of a woman, perhaps related to Pacal, in a nearby tomb and known as the "Red Queen" were covered in powdered cinnabar (Hawkes and Hammond, 1997; Miller, 2001). Cinnabar was one of several pigments used to decorate incense burners used for funeral rituals at Palenque (Vazquez and Velazquez, 1996). A photograph available on the Internet shows the cinnabar-covered remains of a Mayan woman at Copan, Honduras (250–900 CE) (Garrett, 2007).

In Central America, mercury occurrences are known in Guatemala, Honduras, and El Salvador, but the only occurrences for which production has been reported are in Honduras (Roberts and Irving, 1957). Of these, only the La Cañada Mine, Departamento Tegucigalpa, Honduras, was worked during the Spanish Colonial period. The cinnabar occurrences in Central America were known and exploited from early prehistory as sources of the intense red pigment that was used for painting ceramics and other artifacts (Karen Bruhns, Ph.D., professor, San Francisco State University, written communication, October 9, 2007).

In the mud in Lake Amatitlan, Guatemala, marine archaeologists found two containers with mercury that date to the Early Classic Period (300–600 CE) (Mata Amado, 2002). Jade and shell fragments were found floating on a tiny, approximately 130-g pool of mercury in a closed container in a Mayan tomb that dates to 900–1000 CE in Belize (Pendergast, 1982).

There are a number of gold, silver, or lead–zinc occurrences in Central America and South America that, geologically, may have had minor mercury or cinnabar in the upper parts of the mineral deposits. For example, bedrock occurrences of cinnabar were exploited in the 1900s and later, in the 1950s, at Witlage Creek in eastern Suriname (Capps et al., 2004).

Approximately 20 mercury occurrences are known in Peru (Petersen, 1970); however, the occurrences in Huancavelica are the most well-known (Yates et al., 1951; McKee et al., 1986) and the most likely source of mercury and cinnabar used in ancient Peru. There are also cinnabar occurrences near Azoguines and Cuenca, Ecuador, which are not as well known as those at Huancavelica, that were also exploited (Truhan et al., 2005).

Archaeological studies (e.g., Petersen, 1970; West, 1994) indicate that ancient Peruvians exploited placer gold; however, the use of mercury for amalgamation and recovery of the gold is rarely discussed or is considered to have been a European technological import. However, the volume of gold artifacts provided by Atahualpa, the Inca king, for his release from the Spanish in 1532 is hard evidence of the volume of gold in Peru as well as the advanced small-scale mining technology used by the ancient Andeans. Larco Hoyle (2001) indicates that mercury was used by the Moche (100 BCE–750 CE), in northern Peru, to amalgamate placer gold. The mercury was cleaned and recycled by squeezing the gold-bearing amalgam through a scrap of leather, and the recovered mercury was reused. This process is similar to the method described by al-Biruni (al-Hassan and Hill,

1986) for mercury recovery. Posnansky (in Petersen, 1970) describes a site near Machu Picchu where amalgamation was used, before the arrival of the Europeans, to recover gold from crushed quartz vein material. Kaufmann Doig (1978) also describes the use of mercury for gilding precontact copper artifacts with gold.

The Inca (1300–1533 CE), as did the Romans, recognized the health hazards of mercury and that exposure to mercury and cinnabar during mining and retorting would cause the ancient miners "to shake and lose their senses"; therefore, the use of mercury by the Inca declined (Garcilaso de la Vega, in Larco Hoyle, 2001). As in the Old World, whether or not the ancient Andean metallurgists retorted cinnabar for mercury is controversial; however, retorts have been found near the mercury mines at Huancavelica (Kendall Brown, Ph.D., professor, Brigham Young University, written communication, May 9, 2003). Mercury was recovered from drainages and, according to Petersen (1970), from retorting cinnabar near Huancavelica. And, only 15 km from Huancavelica is Atalla, an archaeological site interpreted as an ancient cinnabar pigment production center (Burger and Matos, 2002). Isotopic data on mercury in lake sediments, combined with ^{14}C geochronology, indicate that mercury mining at Huancavelica began around 1400 BCE. and that mercury production peaked at approximately 500 BCE and at 1450 CE, corresponding to the heights of Chavin and Inka rule, respectively, in the region (Cooke et al., 2009).

In describing the early history of the amalgamation process, Craddock (2000) indicated that if mercury had been used, then trace amounts of mercury would be present in the chemical analyses of the gold foils. The implication is that the quantity of mercury used in the amalgamation process would have been reduced by firing the gold, which would have volatilized most, but not all, of the mercury.

Therefore, using SEM-EDX (scanning electron microscope combined with energy dispersive x-ray spectroscopy), Ramage and Craddock (2000) analyzed gold samples from Sardis and found mainly gold and silver. They concluded that since mercury was not detected, no mercury had been used to amalgamate the gold.

However, using induced coupled plasma (ICP) analysis, 8 ppm mercury was found in gold after the gold–mercury amalgam (>300,000 ppm mercury) was burned (refogado), to volatilize the mercury, in the modern gold shops in Madre de Dios, Perú. From 12.3 to 13.9 ppm mercury was found in worked gold artifacts from Huaca la Ventana, a Middle Sicán (900–1200 CE) site at Lambayeque, Perú, and low levels of mercury were found in precontact worked gold samples from Colombia and Ecuador. Similarly low levels of mercury in the ICP analyses of modern refogado gold and precontact worked gold are consistent with a comparable, ancient small-scale mining technology that would have used mercury to amalgamate the fine-grained placer and vein gold, and then, as now, burning the amalgam to volatilize the mercury, beautify, and recover the gold for craft production (Brooks et al., 2009).

Powdered cinnabar was used to decorate gold masks during the Formative Period in Peru (1000–400 BCE) (De Lavalle, 1992; Shimada and Griffin, 2005); as a mural pigment (Muelle and Wells, 1939; Bonavia, 1985; Brooks et al., 2006); for painting warriors' bodies and as a cosmetic for the elite Inca women (Brown, 2001); and for funeral preparations (Maravelaki-Kalaitzaki and Kallithrakas-Kontos, 2003; John Verano, Ph.D., anthropologist, Dumbarton Oaks, Washington, DC, oral communication, December 12, 2005). Wooden funerary figures painted with cinnabar were recovered from Huaca Tacaynamo and Huaca El Dragón, both of which are Chimu (800–1450 CE) ceremonial sites in northern Peru (Jackson, 2004). Mollusk shells, some with cinnabar found in the interior of the shell, suggests that the shells were used as ancient palettes (Petersen, 1970).

A variety of "reds" were readily available in ancient Peru. Sources for "red" included plant-derived achiote, Spondylus (a mollusk), insect-derived cochineal, feathers, plant pigments, and mineral-derived cinnabar, goethite, hematite, and jasper. However, ancient Peruvians selectively used powdered cinnabar for funeral preparations (Shimada and Griffin, 2005; John Verano, Ph.D., anthropologist, Dumbarton Oaks, Washington, DC, oral communication, January 25, 2006). Therefore, in ancient Peru and elsewhere in the New World, as in the Old World, the question persists as to whether or not cinnabar was used because of its blood-red life symbolism or because of its toxicity and preservative qualities.

In 1566, the mercury mines of Huancavelica were rediscovered by the Spaniards. In 1571, mercury once again became an important industrial metal in mining when Pedro Fernandez de Velasco used mercury for silver amalgamation at Porco and Potosí, Bolivia (Arana, 1901). Until that time, mercury had been transported from Spain for use in the New World, and Spanish shipwrecks, which still contain mercury, are known in Samaná Bay, Dominican Republic, and Cartagena Bay, Colombia (Petersen, 1979). In the late 1500s, mercury from Huancavelica was also used in the "patio process" for silver processing in Chile, Bolivia, and Mexico. Salt, mercury, and vitriol (mixed copper and iron sulfates) were mixed with crushed silver ore that contained argentite (Ag_2S), cerargyrite (AgCl), or pyragyrite (Ag_3SbS_3), also known as the "dry ores," in a large open area, or patio, and at Potosí, Bolivia, the cold climate required that the patios be heated from below to speed silver production, which also increased mercury losses (Craddock, 1995). Mercury's role was well established in mineral processing in Spanish Colonial Peru and adding mercury, "el azogado," was an essential step in silver recovery (Del Busto Duthurburu, 1996).

Conclusion

Since ancient times, mercury has been used for a variety of industrial applications and one of those, its use for artisanal gold mining continues today in many parts of the world. The selective use of powdered cinnabar as a preservative in ancient funeral rituals to stop biologic decomposition can only be inferred; however, now, the toxicity of cinnabar is well established. Age-old awareness of the toxicity of mercury fumes and cinnabar powder by the Romans, the Maya, and the Inca has largely been overridden by mercury's widespread usefulness in modern industrial applications.

References

Acosta y Asociados. 2001. *Inventory of sites in Mexico with elevated concentrations of mercury, Acosta y Asociados Project CEC-01, Agua Prieta, Sonora, Mexico.* http://www.chem.unep.ch/mercury/2001-gov-sub/sub79govatt2.pdf (accessed October 10, 2007).

Agricola, G. 1556. *De Re Metallica: London.* Translated by H.C. Hoover and L.H. Hoover and reprinted in 2005 from the 1912 edition, New York: Kessinger.

al-Hassan, A.Y., D.R. Hill. 1986. *Islamic technology, an illustrated history.* Cambridge: Cambridge University Press, p. 247.

al-Saleh, I., and I. al-Doush. 1997. Mercury content in skin lightening creams and potential health hazards to the health of Saudi women. *Journal of Toxicology and Environmental Health* 51(1): 123–145.

Arana, P.P. 1901. *Las minas de azogue del Peru* [Mercury mines of Peru]. Lima: Imprenta El Lucero, p. 6.

Barnes, J.W., and E.H. Bailey. 1972. Turkey's major mercury mine today and how it was mined 8000 years ago. *World Mining* 25(4): 49–55.

Blanchard, I. 2006. African gold and European markets, c.1300-c.1800. Presented at the International Institute of Economic Studies, Volume and Commercial Relations between Europe and the Islamic World, University of Edinburgh-CEU-Budapest, 1-5 May. http://www.ianblanchard.com (accessed August 27, 2008).

Bonavia, D. 1985. *Mural painting in ancient Peru.* Bloomington: Indiana University Press, p. 179.

Brooks, W.E. 2007. Mercury, chapters in *U.S. Geological Survey Minerals Yearbook.* http://minerals.usgs.gov (accessed December 15, 2008).

Brooks, W.E., and G.R. Matos. 2005. Mercury recycling in the United States in 2000, *U.S. Geological Survey Circular 1196-U.* http://minerals.usgs.gov (accessed August 27, 2007).

Brooks, W.E., V. Piminchumo, H. Suarez, J.C. Jackson, and J.P. McGeehin. 2006. Mineral pigments from Huaca Tacaynamo, northern Peru. *Geological Society of America Abstracts with Programs* 38(7): 233.

Brooks, W.E., E. Sandoval, M. Yepez, and H. Howard. 2007. Peru mercury inventory. *U.S. Geological Survey Open-File Report 2007-1252.* http://pubs.usgs.gov/of/2007/1252 (accessed October 15, 2007).

Brooks, W.E., G. Schworbel, and L.E. Castillo. 2009. Mercury and small-scale gold mining in ancient Peru. *Geological Society of America Abstracts with Programs* 41(7): 435.

Brown, K.W. 2001. Workers' health and colonial mercury mining at Huancavelica, Peru. *The Americas, The Academy of American Franciscan History*, 57(4): 467–496.

Burger, R., and R. Matos. 2002. Atalla, a center on the periphery of the Chavin horizon. *Latin American Antiquity* 13(2): 10–25.

Caley, E.R., and J.F.C. Richards, eds. 1956. *Theophrastus, On stones, introduction, Greek text, English translation, and commentary*, p. 57. http://onlinebooks.library.upenn.edu (accessed October 22, 2007).

Capps, R.C., W.W. Malfait, and D.J. LaPoint. 2004. Bedrock sources of placer gold-mercury at the Witlage Creek prospect, eastern Surinam. *Geological Society of America Abstracts with Programs* 36(2): 43.

Consejo de Recursos Minerales. 1992. *Geological mining monograph of the State of Queretaro, Mexico.* Consejo de Recursos Minerales, Secretaria de Energía, Minas E Industria Paraestatal, Mexico, M-4e, pp. 27, 140.

Cooke, C.A., P.H. Balcom, H. Biestar, and A.P. Wolfe. 2009. *Over three millennia of mercury pollution in the Peruvian Andes:* Proceedings of the National Academy of Sciences. http://www.pnas.org/cgi/doi/10.1073/pnas.0900517106 (accessed September 10, 2010).

Craddock, P.T. 1995. *Early metal mining and production.* Washington, DC: Smithsonian Institution Press, p. 216.

Craddock, P.T. 2000. Early history of the amalgamation process, appendix 3. In: A. Ramage, and P.T. Craddock (Eds.). *King Croesus' gold*, London: British Museum Press, pp. 103–107, 233.

Davies, O.R. 1935. *Roman mines in Europe.* London: Oxford Press, p. 45.

De Lavalle, J.A. 1992. *Oro del antiguo Peru* [Gold of ancient Peru]. Lima, Peru: Banco de Credito del Peru en la Cultura, p. 39.

Del Busto Duthurburu, J.A. 1996. *La plateria en el Peru* [Silvercraft in Peru]. Colección Enrico Poli, Banco Sur del Peru, Lima: Cuzzi y Cia, S.A., p. 98.

Delgado, D. 2010. *Colombia's gold boom laced with mercury.* http://www.mineweb.co.za (accessed July 14, 2010).

D'Itri, P.A., and F.M. D'Itri. 1977. *Mercury contamination, a human tragedy.* New York: Wiley, pp. 6, 7.

Fialka, J.J. 2006. How mercury rules designed for safety end up polluting. *Wall Street Journal*, April 20, p. A1.

Garrett, K. 2007. Cinnabar-covered remains of a Maya woman. http://www.art.com (accessed September 12, 2007).

Hawkes, N., and N. Hammond. 1997. Scientists seek DNA clues to Mayan Queen. http://home.netcom.com/~the-iaa/number38.html (accessed October 15, 2007).

Healy, J.F. 1978. *Mining and metallurgy in the Greek and Roman world.* London: Thames and Hudson, pp. 190, 191.

Herz, N., and E.G. Garrison. 1998. *Geological methods for archaeology.* New York: Oxford University Press, p. 241.

Hylander, L.D., and M. Meili. 2003. 500 years of mercury production, global annual inventory by region until 2000 and associated emissions. *The Science of the Total Environment* 30(1): 13–27.

Hylander, L.D., and M. Meili. 2005. The rise and fall of mercury, converting a resource to refuse after 500 years of mining and pollution. *The Science of the Total Environment* 32(2): 24–41.

Iconofile, 2010. *Natural mineral pigments, cinnabar.* http://www.iconofile.com (accessed July 12, 2010).

Jackson, M.A. 2004. The Chimu sculptures of Huacas Tacaynamo and El Dragón, Moche Valley, Peru. *Latin American Antiquity* 15(3): 298–322.

Kapp, L., H. Kapp, and A. Yoshira. 1987. *The craft of the Japanese sword.* Tokyo: Kodansha International.

Kaufmann Doig, F. 1978. *Manual de arqueologia Peruana* [Manual of Peruvian archaeology]. Lima, Peru: Ediciones Peisa, p. 747.

Langenscheidt, A. 1986. El cinabrio y el azogue en el Mexico antiguo [Cinnabar and mercury in ancient Mexico]. *Revista Minero-Americana*, Mexico City, 17(1): 24–29.

Larco Hoyle, R. 2001. *Los Mochicas, tomo II* [The Moche, volume II]. Lima: Museo Arqueologico Rafael Larco Herrera, pp. 128, 135.

Leicester, H.M. 1961. *The historical background of chemistry.* New York: Wiley, p. 12.

Lorenzi, R. 2004. *Pompeii artists painted the town red.* http://www.abc.net.au (accessed January 15, 2007).

Maravelaki-Kalaitzaki, N., and N. Kallithrakas-Kontos. 2003. *Cinnabar find in Cretan Hellenistic tombs, preservative or cosmetic purposes.* Presented at the 4th Symposium on Archaeometry, Hellenic Society for Archaeometry, Athens, Greece, May 28–31, 2003. http://www.archaeometry.gr/eae/HSA.htm (accessed August 27, 2006).

Martín del Campo, E. 2005. *Mesoamerican art.* http://members.aol.com/emdelcamp/edgar2.htm (accessed October 10, 2007).

Mata Amado, G. 2002. Exploraciónes subacuaticas en los Lagos de Guatemala [Underwater archaeology in the lakes of Guatemala]. In: J. La Porte (Ed.). *XV Simposio de Investigaciónes Arqueológicas en Guatemala.* Teguchigalpa: Museo Nacional de Arqueologia y Ethologia, p. 45.

McKee, E.H., D.C. Noble, and C. Vidal. 1986. Timing of volcanic and hydrothermal activity, Huancavelica mercury district, Peru. *Economic Geology* 81(2): 489–492.

Meyers, D.K. 1951. History of the mercury flask. *Journal of Chemical Education* 28: 127.

Miller, M.E. 2001. The art of Mesoamerica, from Olmec to Aztec. http://mayaruins.com/palenque/al_223.html (accessed October 15, 2007).

Muelle, J.C., and R. Wells. 1939. Las pinturas del templo de Pachacamac [Paints used at Pachacamac]. Lima, Peru, *Revista del Museo Nacional*, 8(2): 27.

Pendergast, D.M. 1982. Ancient Maya mercury. *Science* 217(6): 533–535.

Petersen, G. 1970. *Mining and metallurgy in ancient Peru* [translation by Brooks, W.E., 2010, of Minería y Metalurgia en el Antiguo Perú, Arqueologicas 12, Publicaciones del Instituto de Investigaciones Antropologícas, Museo Nacional de Antropología y Arqueología, Pueblo Libre, Lima, Perú]: *Geological Society of America Special Paper 467.* pp. 4, 29, 45, 55; Fig. 7.

Petersen, M. 1979. December. Graveyard of the quicksilver galleons. *National Geographic* 156(6): 850–876.

Putman, J.J. 1972. Quicksilver and slow death. *National Geographic*, October, 142(4): 507–527.

Ramage, A., and P.T. Craddock. 2000. *King Croesus' gold.* London: British Museum Press, p. 233.

Roberts, R.J., and E.M. Irving. 1957. Mineral deposits of Central America. *U.S. Geological Survey Bulletin* 1034: 169.

Sax, N.I. 1984. *Dangerous properties of industrial minerals.* New York: Van Nostrand, p. 1756.

Schuette, C.N. 1931. Quicksilver. *U.S. Bureau of Mines Bulletin* 335: 3.

Shimada, I., and J.A. Griffin. 2005. Precious metal objects of the Middle Sican. *Scientific American* 15(1): 80–89.

Simon, S. 2004. There's the rhythm method. *The Washington Post*, December 31, p. C8.

Srinivasan, S., and S.M. Ranganathan. 2004. *Metallurgical heritage of India.* http://metalrg.iisc.ernet.in/~wootz/heritage/Heritage.htm (accessed September 26, 2007).

Truhan, D.L., J.H. Burton, and K.O. Bruhns. 2005. El cinabrio en el mundo Andino: *Revista de Antropología 18*, La Casa de La Cultura Ecuatoriana Benjamin Carrion, Cuenca, Ecuador, p. 201.

Vazquez, J., and R. Velazquez. 1996. Analisis quimico de materiales encontrados en excavacion, dos casos: Porta-incensarios tipo Palenque y cinabrio usado en practicas funerarias: La Octava Mesa Redonda de Palenque, 6-12 de Junio de http://mesoweb.com/pari/publications/RT10/08_Analisis.html (accessed July 21, 2008).

West, R.C. 1994. Aboriginal metallurgy and metalworking in Spanish America, in Craig, A.K. and West, R.C., eds., In Quest of Mineral Wealth, Aboriginal and Colonial Mining and Metallurgy in Spanish America. Department of Geography and Anthropology, Louisiana State University, Baton Rouge, *Geoscience and Man* 33: 5–20.

Windhaven Guild. 2004. *Natural pigment watercolors.* http://www.baronyofwindhaven.org (accessed February 10, 2007).

Wittich, E.F. 1922. La geología de la región minera de Guadalcázar [Geology of the Gualdacazar mining district]. *Memorias de la Sociedad Científica Antonio Alzate*, Mexico City, 40: 145–178.

Yates, R.G., D.F. Kent, and J.F. Concha. 1951. Geology of the Huancavelica quicksilver district. *U.S. Geological Survey Bulletin* 975-A.

Yildiz, M., and E.H. Bailey. 1978. Mercury deposits in Turkey. *U.S. Geological Survey Bulletin* 1456, p. 80.

Zaragoza, D.M. 1993. Guadalcázar, San Luis Potosí, una zona minera prehispánica [Guadalcazar, San Luis Potosi, a prehispanic mining district]. Abstract presented at *III Reunión de Historiadores de la Minería Latinoamericana*, Taxco, Mexico, November 22–26, 1993.

PART TWO

METHODS FOR RESEARCH, MONITORING, AND ANALYSIS

CHAPTER 3

Analytical Methods for Measuring Mercury in Water, Sediment, and Biota

BRENDA K. LASORSA, GARY A. GILL, and MILENA HORVAT

Mercury (Hg) exists in a large number of physical and chemical forms with a wide range of properties. Conversion between these different forms provides the basis for mercury's complex distribution pattern in local and global cycles and for its biologic enrichment and effects. Since the 1960s, the growing awareness of environmental mercury pollution has stimulated the development of more accurate, precise and efficient methods of quantifying mercury and its compounds in a wide variety of matrices. During recent years new analytical techniques have become available that have contributed significantly to the understanding of mercury chemistry in natural systems. In particular, these include ultrasensitive and specific analytical equipment and contamination-free methods. These improvements allow for the determination of total mercury as well as major species of mercury to be made in water, sediments and soils, and biota. Analytical methods are selected depending on the nature of the sample, the concentration levels of mercury, and what species or fraction is to be quantified. The terms "speciation" and "fractionation" in analytical chemistry were addressed by the International Union for Pure and Applied Chemistry (IUPAC) that published guidelines (Templeton et al., 2000) or recommendations for the definition of speciation analysis: "Speciation analysis is the analytical activity of identifying and/or measuring the

TABLE 3.1
Typical Ranges of Environmental Mercury Concentrations

Matrix	Total Hg	MMHg
Freshwater (rivers)	0.3–100 ng/L	0.01–2 ng/L
Freshwater (lakes)	0.2–50 ng/L	0.01–5 ng/L
Seawater	0.2–5 ng/L	0.01–0.5 ng/L
Rain	1–20 ng/L	0.01–0.5 ng/L
Snow	1–150 ng/L	0.01–1 ng/L
Lake sediment	10–1000 ng/g	0.01–100 ng/g
Marine sediment	5–2000 ng/g	0.05–100 ng/g
Soils	5–500 ng/g	0.05–20 ng/g
Terrestrial mammals	0.01–0.2 μg/g (wet)	0.005–0.15 μg/g (wet)
Freshwater fish	0.01–2 μg/g (wet)	0.005–2 μg/g (wet)
Marine fish	0.01–13 μg/g (wet)	0.01–12 μg/g (wet)
Marine mammals	0.03–35 μg/g (wet)	0.02–35 μg/g (wet)
Algae	0.01–0.2 μg/g	0.001–0.1 μg/g
Blood	0.2–50 μg/L	0.2–50 μg/L
Human hair	0.1–10 μg/g	0.1–10 μg/g

SOURCE: Pirrone and Mahaffey, 2005; personal experience of the authors.

quantities of one or more individual chemical species in a sample. The chemical species are specific forms of an element defined as to isotopic composition, electronic or oxidation state, and/or complex or molecular structure. The speciation of an element is the distribution of an element amongst defined chemical species in a system. In case that it is not possible to determine the concentration of the different individual chemical species that sum up the total concentration of an element in a given matrix, meaning it is impossible to determine the speciation, it is a useful practice to do fractionation instead. Fractionation is the process of classification of an analyte or a group of analytes from a certain sample according to physical (e.g. size, solubility) or chemical (e.g. bonding, reactivity) properties."

Typical concentrations of Hg and monomethylmercury (MMHg) found in a variety of environmental matrices are given in Table 3.1. This table is by no means exhaustive, but it does illustrate the wide range of concentrations that must be quantified in a great variety of matrices of varying complexity in order to understand Hg cycling in the environment and its effects on human and ecosystem health (Figure 3.1). The selection of an analytical technique that is rigorous enough to overcome any matrix issues yet sensitive enough to produce meaningful data in the range of typical concentrations is critical to the success of environmental Hg research.

Physical and Chemical Properties of Mercury Species

Metallic Mercury

Elemental mercury (Hg^0), referred to as Hg vapor when present in the atmosphere, or as metallic Hg in liquid form, is of considerable toxicologic as well as of environmental importance because it has a relatively high vapor pressure (14 mg m^{-1} at 20°C, 31 mg m^{-3} at 30°C) and appreciable water solubility (~60 μg L^{-1} at room temperature). Because it is highly lipophilic, elemental Hg dissolves readily in fatty compartments. Of equal significance is the fact that the vapor exists in a monatomic state.

Inorganic Ions of Mercury

Many salts of divalent mercury, Hg(II), are readily soluble in water, such as mercury sublimate ($HgCl_2$, 62 g L^{-1} at 20°C), and, thereby, highly toxic. In contrast, the water solubility of cinnabar (HgS) is extremely low (~10 ng L^{-1}), and, correspondingly, HgS is much less toxic than $HgCl_2$ (Simon and Wuhl-Couturier, 2002). The extremely high affinity of the free mercury ion, Hg^{2+}, for sulfhydryl groups of amino acids such as cysteine and methionine in enzymes explains its high toxicity. However, its affinity to SeH-groups is even greater, which may explain the

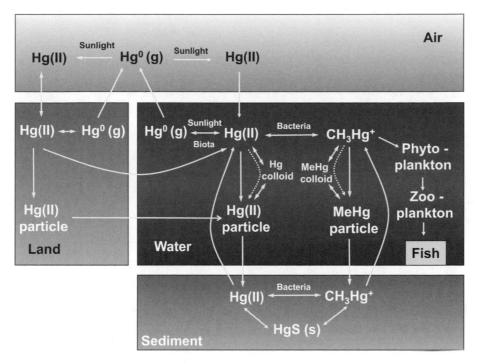

FIGURE 3.1   A biogeochemical cycle of mercury in the environment, illustrating the common forms of mercury often quantified.

protective role of selenium from Hg intoxication (Yaneda and Suzuki, 1997). Monovalent Hg, Hg (I), is found only in dimeric salts such as Hg_2Cl_2 (calomel), which is sparingly soluble in water and therefore correspondingly much less toxic than $HgCl_2$ (sublimate).

Organo-Mercury Compounds

Organo-Hg compounds consist of diverse chemical structures in which divalent Hg forms one covalent bond (R-Hg-X) or two covalent bonds (R-Hg-R) with carbon. In environmental samples, organo-Hg compounds are, for the most part, limited to the alkylmercurials monomethylmercury, mono-ethylmercury and, more rarely, dimethylmercury, as well as alkoxymercury compounds, and arylmercurials (phenylmercury). Organo-Hg cations (R-Hg$^+$) form salts with inorganic and organic acids (e.g., chlorides and acetates), and react readily with biologically important ligands, notably sulfhydryl groups. Organo-mercurials also pass easily across biologic membranes, since the halides (e.g., CH_3HgCl) and dialkylmercury are lipid-soluble. The major difference among these various organo-Hg compounds is that the stability of carbon-mercury bonds in vivo varies considerably. Thus, alkylmercury compounds are much more resistant to biodegradation than either arylmercury or alkoxymercury compounds. The term "methylmercury" is used throughout this text to represent monomethylmercury (MMHg) compounds. In many cases, the complete identity of these compounds is not known except for the MMHg cation, CH_3Hg^+, which is associated either with a simple anion, like chloride, or a large charged molecule (e.g., a protein)

(Horvat, 2005). Monomethylmercury compounds are of the greatest concern, as these highly toxic compounds are formed by microorganisms in sediments and bio-accumulated and biomagnified in aquatic food chains, thus resulting in exposures of fish-eating populations, often at levels exceeding what is regarded as safe. MMHg is also bio-accumulated and biomagnified in terrestrial food chains. Although it is less researched and not typically an issue for human consumption, this is still a major concern for wildlife health.

Determination of Total Mercury and Inorganic Mercury Species

There are numerous analytical techniques available for the analysis of total Hg and the inorganic Hg species in environmental samples. A brief summary of the methods available for analysis of Hg species in environmental samples is given in Table 3.2. Traditional analytical methods for Hg detection are largely based upon room temperature, gas phase (often referred to as cold vapor), and atomic absorption techniques, but inductively coupled plasma mass spectrometry (ICP-MS) can also be used for parts-per-million to higher parts-per-billion level measurements in solids. More recently, cold-vapor atomic fluorescence techniques have been developed that allow determination at parts-per-trillion and subparts-per-trillion concentration levels. The most appropriate specific method is dictated by the detection limit required to produce meaningful data, as well as the sample size, sample matrix and potential interferences specific to the method.

TABLE 3.2

Selected Methods for the Analysis of Mercury

Analyte	Matrix	Detector	Reference or EPA method	Typical MDL
Total Hg	Water	CVAAS	EPA Method 245.1	5–10 ng/L
Total Hg	Water	CVAFS	EPA Method 245.7	0.5–5 ng/L
Total Hg	Water	CVAFS	EPA Method 1631	0.1–0.3 ng/L
Total Hg	Water	ICP-MS	EPA Method 200.8	10 ng/L
Total Hg	Water	ICP-AES	EPA Method 200.7	200 ng/L
Elemental Hg	Water	CVAFS	EPA Method 1631 mod[a]	0.1–0.3 ng/L
Reactive Hg	Water	CVAFS	EPA Method 1631 mod[b]	0.1–0.3 ng/L
MMHg	Water	CVAFS	EPA Method 1630 (draft)	0.01–0.05 ng/L
Total Hg	Sediment	CVAAS	EPA Method 245.5	5–10 ng/g
Total Hg	Sediment	CVAAS	EPA Method 7471	10–50 ng/g
Total Hg	Sediment	DTDAAS	EPA Method 7473	5–10 ng/g
Total Hg	Sediment	CVAFS	EPA Method 1631 appendix	0.5–1 ng/g
MMHg	Sediment	CVAFS	EPA Method 1630 mod[c]	0.01–0.05 ng/g
MMHg	Sediment	GC-ICP-MS	Bjorn et al. (2007)[c]	0.01–0.05 ng/g
Total Hg	Tissue	CV AAS	EPA Method 245.6	5–10 ng/g
Total Hg	Tissue	DTDAAS	EPA Method 7473	5–10 ng/g
Total Hg	Tissue	CVAFS	EPA Method 1631 appendix	0.5–1 ng/g
Total Hg	Blood	ICP-MS	Palmer et al. (2006)	0.17 µg/L
Total Hg	Blood	FI-AAS	Palmer et al. (2006)	0.6 µg/L
MMHg	Tissue	CVAFS	EPA Method 1630 mod[d]	0.5–2 ng/g

AAS = atomic absorption spectrometry; CVAAS = cold-vapor atomic absorption spectrometry;
CVAFS = cold-vapor atomic fluorescence spectrometry; FI = Flow Injection; GC = gas chromatography;
ICP-AES = inductively coupled plasma atomic emission spectrometry; ICP-MS = inductively coupled
plasma mass spectrometry; MDL = Method Detection Limit; DTD = Direct Thermal Decomposition.
a. Without oxidation or reduction.
b. Without oxidation.
c. Using extraction or distillation to isolate MMHg.
d. Using KOH/methanol digestion to release MMHg (Bloom 1989)

Another factor that must be weighted in choosing a suitable analytical method is the recognition that mercury can exist in a wide variety of chemical forms that may or may not be liberated for analysis by the procedures adopted. Illustrated in Figure 3.2 are the various fractions or pools of inorganic Hg(II) that can exist in natural water systems. The common aqueous species of inorganic Hg(II) in oxygenated freshwater are $Hg(OH)_2^0$, and $HgCl_2^0$. In seawater, the dominant inorganic forms are the chloride species ($HgCl_4^{-2}$, $HgCl_3^{-1}$, etc). In suboxic to anoxic waters, polysulfide species can dominant (e.g., HgS^0) if sulfide concentration levels exceed Hg concentration levels. Hg(II) also strongly interacts with colloids and suspended particles in aqueous systems to form colloidal or particulate-bound Hg forms. Mercury also forms numerous stable complexes with well-defined organic ligands (e.g., ethylenediaminetetraacetic acid [EDTA]) and with dissolved organic matter (DOM) to form organic mercury compounds. Biologic transformations can convert Hg(II) to gaseous elemental Hg and methylated Hg forms (see Figure 3.1). In tissues, mercury can be present in both inorganic and organo-Hg forms, with higher trophic level species usually containing predominantly MMHg. In sediments, mercury tends to adsorb preferentially to carbon-based particles.

To perform a meaningful total Hg analysis, it is essential to perform a suitable preparation step to release the Hg from whatever matrix or complexes in which it may reside.

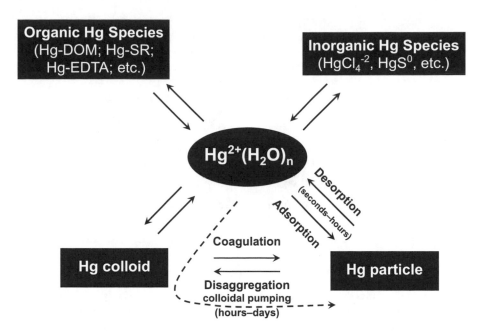

FIGURE 3.2 Competition for the partitioning of the free mercury ion into various pools or fractions in natural waters.

This removes any matrix interferences with the analysis that result in a biased determination and allows the detection method to quantify the mercury.

Finally, because Hg is ubiquitous in the environment and is used in so many chemical manufacturing processes, finding suitably clean reagents for sample preparation or digestion steps can be difficult. For low-level aqueous mercury measurements, it is essential, therefore, that all reagents used be rigorously checked for Hg contamination prior to use and that all laboratory ware that comes in contact with the sample be of appropriate materials and be rigorously cleaned to maintain contamination at suitably low levels (Gill and Fitzgerald, 1985, 1987; Bloom, 1994; Parker and Bloom, 2005).

Total Mercury and Inorganic Mercury Species in Water

Recent improvements in analytical methods have demonstrated that much of the historical data for total Hg in environmental water samples collected prior to the early 1990s was biased, either high because of contamination during sampling and analysis or low because of improper sample collection containers or improper preservation techniques (Fitzgerald, 1999). Problems arising in the analysis of total Hg in natural water samples are not connected with the final measurement, but rather with difficulties associated with contamination-free sampling and losses due to volatilization and adsorption during storage. There have been remarkable improvements in sampling and analytical techniques that have resulted in a dramatic increase in the reliability of data for Hg in

aqueous samples over the past 15 years (Gill and Fitzgerald, 1985, 1987; Bloom, 1995; Fitzgerald, 1999; Parker and Bloom, 2005).

As noted previously, the total Hg in a water sample can be composed of several distinct forms or pools, including "dissolved" Hg (usually operationally defined as that mercury passing through a 0.45-µm filter), Hg associated with particulate and colloidal matter, volatile elemental Hg^0, and labile (or reactive) Hg(II). All these forms can all be quantified as long as the samples are collected and preserved properly for the species to be determined.

SAMPLING AND STORAGE

Collection and handling of aqueous samples for low-level determination of Hg must address several factors, including whether or not the sample is representative, possible interconversion processes, contamination, and preservation and storage of the matrix before analysis. The measurement (sampling and analysis) protocol must be carefully designed if speciation of Hg forms in the aqueous samples is intended. The stability of Hg in solution is affected by many factors, including: (a) the concentration of Hg and its compounds, (b) the type of water sample, (c) the type of containers used, (d) the cleaning and pretreatment of the containers, and (e) the preservative added. Table 3.3 lists recommended sample-collection containers, hold times, and preservation methods for the most common environmental samples collected for inorganic or total Hg analysis.

The best materials for sample storage and sample processing are Pyrex and silica (quartz) glass or Teflon

TABLE 3.3
Recommended Containers and Preservation Methods for Inorganic and Total Mercury Measurements

Analyte	Matrix	Preservative	Container	Hold time
Total Hg	Water	0.5% HCl	Teflon or glass	90 days[a]
Total Hg	Water	0.5% HCl	Teflon or glass	180 days[b]
Elemental Hg	Water	NA	Teflon or glass	0 days[b]
Reactive Hg	Water	$4 \pm 2°C$	Teflon or glass	2–3 days[b]
Total Hg	Sediment	Frozen/freeze-dried	Teflon, glass or plastic	1 year[a]
Total Hg	Tissue	Frozen/freeze-dried	Teflon, glass or plastic	1 year[a]

NA = not applicable.

a. According to EPA Method 1631.

b. According to Parker and Bloom 2005.

Polytetrafluoroethylene (PTFE) or fluorinated ethylene propylene (FEP). Significant contamination can occur with plastics such as polyethylene and polypropylene, and therefore these are not recommended for aqueous samples. Plastic containers cannot be as rigorously cleaned as glass or Teflon and are highly permeable to vapor-phase Hg^0, allowing Hg to readily freely diffuse into (or out of) samples depending on the concentration gradient between the sample and surrounding air (Gill and Fitzgerald, 1987). Rigorous cleaning procedures must be used for all laboratory ware and other equipment that comes into contact with samples. There are several cleaning procedures that are suitable for laboratory ware and sampling equipment: (1) aqua regia treatment followed by soaking in dilute (~5–10%) nitric acid for a week; (2) soaking in a hot oxidizing mixture of $KMnO_4$ and $K_2S_2O_8$, followed by NH_4OCl rinsing and soaking for a week in 5M HNO_3; (3) soaking in a 1:1 mixture of concentrated chromic and nitric acids for a few days; and (4) soaking in a BrCl solution (mixture of HCl and $KBrO_3$).

Teflon ware is usually cleaned in hot concentrated HNO_3 for 48 hours, followed by numerous rinses with a high-purity (low Hg content) laboratory water supply (e.g., 18 MΩ deionized water or double distilled water) and dried on a class-100 clean air bench. Items are then generally placed in a sealed plastic bag to avoid dust contamination and stored in an environment known to be low in atmospheric mercury content. Some authors recommend storage of laboratory ware in dilute HNO_3 or HCl acids until use. For collection of samples to be analyzed for both total Hg and MMHg analyses, the bottles must be prepared with extreme caution to ensure that the containers do have residual HNO_3 from the cleaning process. Soaking of laboratory ware, particularly Teflon, in hot (70°C) 1% HCl removes any traces of oxidizing compounds that may subsequently destroy MMHg in solution.

Water samples are often collected by grab sampling upstream of sources of contamination. Collection of surface waters is usually performed by hand, using arm-length plastic gloves. Samples are taken upwind of a rubber raft or a fiberglass boat. When it is not possible to collect a grab sample, acid-cleaned, contamination-free sampling devices (e.g., Teflon or Go-Flo samplers) are commonly used for the collection of water samples. Alternatively, the water can be pumped through acid-cleaned Teflon tubing using a peristaltic pump. Precipitation samples can be collected by automatic samplers, with in-line filtration if desired (Landing et al., 1998).

Water samples should be collected in acid-cleaned glass or Teflon bottles. If the samples are to be analyzed for dissolved Hg, the sample must either be filtered using a peristaltic pump with precleaned in-line filters during sample collection or within 48 hours of collection once samples are returned, on ice, to the laboratory. Samples for total or dissolved Hg should be preserved as soon as possible after collection (generally within 48 hours) with high-purity, low-mercury-content HCl (typically 0.5%) or HNO_3 (typically 0.2%). Water samples for the analysis of total mercury only may also be preserved by direct addition of the oxidizing agent 0.2N BrCl (typically 0.5%) as described in Environmental Protection Agency (EPA) Method 1631 (EPA, 2002). If MMHg is also to be analyzed along with total Hg on the same sample, only HCl preservation should be used, as HNO_3 can destroy MMHg. Water samples for the determination of elemental Hg should not be preserved with acid and the Hg^0 isolated from the solution immediately upon collection to avoid loss from solution. Samples for the analysis of reactive Hg cannot be preserved and must be stored cold and processed as soon as possible after collection (Parker and Bloom, 2005). Ideally, samples for reactive mercury are reduced and purged to gold amalgamation traps in the field immediately after collection.

Containers and other sampling equipment that come into contact with water samples should be made of borosilicate glass, Teflon, or silica glass and rigorously cleaned with strong acid prior to use. These materials have been found to be free from Hg contamination and therefore suitable for work at low, ambient levels. However, Teflon shows the best performance regarding both contamination and loss-free storage of aqueous samples. Sampling devices (such as Go-Flo water-sampling bottles) should be Teflon-coated if possible and the surface in contact with the sample acid should be cleaned with dilute acid (e.g., 1N HCl for 8 hours or more).

Approximately 250 mL of water is typically needed for a total Hg analysis. Personnel handling sample containers should do so with gloved hands (clean, nonpowdered latex or vinyl gloves), and samples should be double bagged in clean plastic bags for shipping as outlined in EPA Method 1669, *Sampling Ambient Water for Trace Metals at EPA Water Quality Criteria Levels* (EPA, 1996).

Determination of Total Mercury in Natural Waters

Analytical techniques suitable for total Hg determination in natural waters at the picogram level are either based on cold-vapor atomic absorption spectrometry (CVAAS), cold-vapor atomic fluorescence spectrometry (CVAFS), ICP-MS, inductively coupled plasma atomic emission spectrometry (ICP-AES), or atomic absorption spectrometry (AAS). Of these, CVAAS is the most widespread method, although CVAFS is rapidly replacing CVAAS because of its superior detection limits.

Mercury detection by CVAAS is based on the gas phase absorption of 254 nm radiation by elemental Hg atoms in an inert gas stream. Mercuric ions in the digested sample are reduced to Hg^0 with $SnCl_2$ or a similar reductant and then are purged out of the sample and directly into a gas cell, where absorption is determined. The absorption signal (peak height or area) is proportional to the concentration of Hg in the gas cell. The mass of Hg in a sample is quantified using a standard curve, which is a function of the volume of sample purged. This method has been promulgated as EPA Method 245.1, *Determination of Mercury in Water by Cold Vapor Atomic Absorption Spectrometry* (in EPA, 1994). However, the achievable detection limits for CVAAS methods are not low enough to be useful for most ambient water samples.

In recent years, CVAFS techniques have become increasingly important, since the instrumental detection limit is often less than 1 pg, which is an order of magnitude better than ICP-MS, ICP-AES, or CVAAS. Since the development of a simple, very sensitive (~0.3 pg) and inexpensive CVAFS detector (Bloom and Fitzgerald, 1988; Kvietkus et al., 1983) many research groups have used this instrumental approach for Hg measurements of low-level air and natural water samples (Bloom and Fitzgerald, 1988; Gill and Bruland, 1990; Liang and Bloom 1993; Mason and Fitzgerald, 1993; Cai, 2000;

Logar et al., 2004). This method has been promulgated as EPA Method 1631 (EPA, 2002).

Sample decomposition of all organo-, organic-, and particulate Hg species in a water sample is necessary if total Hg is to be measured. This is generally achieved using the oxidizing agent BrCl in an HCl solution (Bloom and Crecelius, 1983) or techniques based on UV oxidation in HCl solution (Ahmed et al., 1987; May et al., 1987). The use of other wet chemical oxidative mixtures is limited because of relatively high reagent blanks. In the case of humic-rich water samples, a combination of BrCl and UV oxidation is very effective and results in complete recovery.

After the decomposition step, mercury is usually isolated from the aqueous sample matrix for gas-phase detection by reducing the Hg in a sparging vessel and purging it from solution with an inert, Hg-free, gas flow. The most common reducing agent used is $SnCl_2$, but $NaBH_4$ may also be used (Iverfeldt, 1988; Heraldsson et al., 1989; Gill and Bruland, 1990). The evolved Hg^0 is then swept from the purging cell either onto an amalgamation media or directly into the detector. Preconcentration of the Hg^0 in the gas stream onto a gold trap by amalgamation is applied in nearly all analytical procedures used for the most sensitive measurement of Hg in natural waters (Bloom and Crecelius, 1983; Gill and Fitzgerald, 1987). Like the CVAAS methods, the fluorescence signal is proportional to the mass of Hg collected, which is quantified using a standard curve.

Most of the trace-level analytical methods for water samples, such as EPA Method 1631, were written for ambient environmental water samples. The sample-preparation techniques described in these methods may not be rigorous or adequate for all types of water samples. For waters with complex matrices, such as highly organic industrial wastes and sewage influent, it is important to modify the techniques to ensure that the digestion of the sample is complete. Verification of digestion can be determined by performing matrix spikes on the most complex matrices to be analyzed. Interferences in the method can result with unusual samples. For example, high concentrations of iron can result in the formation of iron chloride during the oxidation step that will precipitate and scavenge Hg out of the sample. Method modifications often used to overcome matrix interferences include sample dilution, the addition of extra oxidizer, and heating the sample (e.g., ~50°C for several hours) (Lytle et al., 2007).

For the analysis of elemental and reactive Hg in water, CVAFS is recommended, as it is the only method with a sufficiently low detection limit to accurately quantify the relatively low concentration of these forms of Hg in water samples. For the analysis of elemental Hg, no oxidation or reduction step is performed; the elemental Hg is simply purged directly from the sample, preconcentrated onto an amalgamation media (generally gold) and then quantified using CVAFS. Similarly, for the analysis of reactive Hg, no oxidation step is performed; the sample is reduced with a reducing agent and purged onto the amalgamation media and then eluted into the detector. It is important to note that reactive mercury is operationally defined as readily reducible mercury, and in a nonoxidized sample, the Hg that is reducible is greatly impacted by the method and duration of reduction. There is some evidence to suggest that a neutral pH reduction (or certainly something less acidic than standard $SnCl2$) provides a better measure of "methylatable" mercury (Bloom, 1994).

Total Mercury in Solid Matrices

In sediments and soils, Hg is frequently associated with humic matter. In contaminated sites (particularly mining areas), it is mostly present as cinnabar (HgS). Because the Hg can be adsorbed to carbon or strongly bonded within sediment grains, it is essential that the samples be properly digested to release all of the Hg present in the samples. In biologic samples, Hg concentrations can range widely, from less than 0.5 ng/g (0.5 ppb) to over 100 µg/g (100 ppm) and be present in both inorganic and organo-Hg forms. At low trophic levels in a food chain, the percentage of mercury as inorganic mercury is much higher than at high trophic levels, where the dominant form of mercury is usually MMHg (Bloom 1992; Boudou and Ribeyre, 1997; Morel et al., 1998; Wiener et al., 2003). The wide variety of biologic samples, from invertebrates and feathers to blood and muscle tissue, requires that the sample-preparation techniques be tailored to the sample type. Frequently, tissue samples such as algae or single invertebrates have very small masses combined with low Hg concentrations, in which case it is essential to use analytical methods that are sensitive enough to detect the Hg.

SAMPLING AND STORAGE

Sediment samples should be collected in acid-cleaned glass, plastic, or Teflon containers. Samples should be stored frozen until analysis or freeze-dried to increase sample holding time. For biologic samples, the sample-collection and storage methods must be modified to suit the tissue type. Dry samples such as feathers and hair (or fur) can be sealed in plastic bags and stored at room temperature in a clean laboratory environment. It may be necessary to gently wash hair or feather samples with high-purity deionized water and/or acetone to remove any dirt on the surface of the samples. Muscle or organ tissue should be collected in precleaned glass, polypropylene, or polyethylene containers and frozen or freeze-dried until digestion. Total Hg in freeze-dried biologic samples, such as biologic certified reference materials (CRMs), are stable for years. Any required dissection or homogenization should be done with Teflon, titanium, or Teflon-coated stainless steel utensils.

Blood samples require special care. Ideally, they should be collected without the addition of any preservative or coagulant. If preservatives or coagulants must be used, it is important to verify low Hg concentrations in the preservative prior to use because some preservatives contain an Hg compound or may be contaminated with Hg impurities. If organic species are also to be determined in a blood sample it is important to note that preservatives and/or anticoagulants are likely to break up the original Hg species. Most anticoagulants are either polyanions (e.g., heparin) or metal chelators (e.g., EDTA, citrate) and therefore have a high affinity for metal species. After blood has been sampled without an anticoagulant, it will clot spontaneously and separate into serum and packed cells. For determination of total Hg, it is therefore advisable to collect only about 200 µL of blood and to digest the entire sample, thus avoiding any chance of bias if the sample coagulates or separates.

Solid-phase samples must be digested to liberate Hg into aqueous solution for analysis for all analytical methods, except those based on direct thermal decomposition, A common digestion media for sediments is strong mixed acids such as aqua regia. A review of the older literature shows that the strong oxidant potassium permanganate was often used in the digestion process to promote complete digestion. It is essential to carefully assess the reagents for Hg content prior to use. Potassium permanganate in particular is notorious for Hg contamination, which can be inconsistent even within the same container of dry reagent. When methods using digestion reagents like permanganate were first described, the instrument detection limits for Hg were such that this contamination was not always evident. In the past 20 years, instrument detection limits have improved to the point at which reagent or method blanks are now usually the limiting factor in setting the sensitivity of the analytical method for Hg. This improvement in instrumental sensitivity has resulted in high-biased data for low concentration samples. Note that other digestion techniques, such as those written for the digestion of tissue and sediment samples for the National Oceanic and Atmospheric Administration (NOAA) Status and Trends Program (NOAA, 1997) work well with these analytical techniques and do not use potassium permanganate.

Determination of Total Mercury in Solid-Phase Materials

COLD-VAPOR ATOMIC ABSORPTION SPECTROMETRY METHODS

The most commonly used standard methods for total Hg in tissue and sediment (and high concentration wastewaters) uses a CVAAS technique similar to those described above for water samples. An aliquot of the digested sample is diluted in water, reduced with stannous chloride or other reducing agent, and the evolving elemental Hg is passed through an adsorption cell and quantified against standards of known concentration. The typical detection limit for these methods is ~10 ng/g (ppb) as Hg for both tissues and sediments. When first described, CVAAS systems for tissues and sediments were manual, but today there are several commercially available automated CVAAS analytical systems. The EPA has promulgated several CVAAS methods for determination of total Hg in solid environmental matrices, including EPA 245.5 *Determination of Mercury in Sediment by Cold Vapor Atomic Absorption Spectrometry* (in EPA 1994), EPA 245.6 *Determination of Mercury in Tissue by Cold Vapor Atomic Absorption Spectrometry* (in EPA, 1994), EPA 7470 *Mercury in Liquid Waste—Manual Cold Vapor Technique* (EPA, 1993), and EPA 7471 *Mercury in Solid or Semisolid Waste (Manual Cold-Vapor Technique)* (EPA, 2007). The CVAFS technique described previously for aqueous samples can also be used for solid phases if very high sensitivity is required. A small aliquot of a strong acid digest of the solid is spiked into a purging system in a manner identical to that used for the preparation of a standard curve.

THERMAL DECOMPOSITION

A relatively new analytical method for the determination of total Hg in solids uses direct thermal decomposition, preconcentration by amalgamation onto gold and detection by CVAAS (Hall and Pelchat, 1997; Cizdziel, et al., 2002; Lowery et al., 2007). The method uses complete combustion of solid samples in an oxygen carrier gas to release Hg vapor instead of the chemical reduction step used in most liquid-based analyzers. The combustion process does not require the conversion of Hg to mercuric ions, so lengthy sample pretreatments are unnecessary. Sample analysis is rapid, and automated systems are commercially available. Because chemical reduction is not used, there is no need for sample digestion. This method has been promulgated as EPA Method 7473 (EPA, 1998a). This method can also be applied to liquid samples such as industrial wastes, but is not sensitive enough for ambient environmental water samples.

INDUCTIVELY COUPLED PLASMA ATOMIC EMISSION SPECTROMETRY

ICP-MS has been increasingly used in Hg research studies and has been demonstrated to be a very powerful tool (Hintelmann and Ogrinc, 2003). Although standard-configuration ICP-MS is not sufficiently sensitive for the analysis of many solid matrix environmental samples, specialized sample introduction systems that introduce Hg in the form of gaseous species into a dry plasma greatly reduced the occurrence of memory effects, which was one of the major problems for the effective use of ICP-MS initially. ICP-MS can achieve absolute detection limits of less than 100 pg of Hg. Moreover, the capability of ICP-MS to take advantage of special isotope-dilution methods makes this technique suitable for very precise and accurate measurements. In addition, multiple stable tracer experiments to study the fate of Hg species in the environment and biologic systems are available for the investigation of multiple transformation processes simultaneously (Demuth and Heumann, 2001; Stoichev et al., 2004; Tseng et al., 2000).

Researchers have been using multiple collectors (MC-ICP-MS) tuned to specific Hg isotopes to determine variation in Hg isotopic ratios that may be used to determine the origin of Hg in the environment (Hintelmann and Lu, 2003; Foucher and Hintelmann, 2006; Blum and Bergquist, 2007).

X-RAY SPECTROSCOPY

X-ray fluorescence (XRF) is convenient because the sample preparation is minimal, analysis is quick and nondestructive and it is indifferent to the chemical or physical state of the analyte. However, it is less sensitive than AAS and neutron activation analysis (NAA). Typical detection limits of x-ray techniques are in the ppm range. The sensitivity can be improved by preseparation and preconcentration of Hg (D'Silva and Fassel, 1972; Bennun and Gomez, 1997). In vivo determination of Hg was investigated and applied (O'Meara et al., 2000). Synchrotron radiation XRF has successfully been applied to biologic monitoring using hair. Its advantage is in studying Hg dynamics in a small sample (Shimijo et al., 1997). X-ray absorption spectroscopy (XAS), in particular extended x-ray absorption fine structure (EXAFS) spectroscopy has been applied for Hg speciation in Hg-bearing mine wastes (Kim et al., 2004).

ELECTROCHEMICAL METHODS

An electrochemical method using chronopotentiometric stripping analysis on gold film electrodes for the determination of total mercury in fish and shrimp was described by Augelli et al. (2007). They achieved a detection limit of 5 ng/g, which is comparable to methods based on CVAA.

Other Total Mercury Analytical Methods

NEUTRON ACTIVATION ANALYSIS

NAA can be performed as nondestructive instrumental NAA (Dams et al., 1970; Das and van der Sloot, 1976) or radiochemical NAA (Kosta and Byrne, 1969; Byrne and Kosta, 1974). k_0 standardization instrumental NAA (k_0-INAA) is now available and can be used on a routine basis (Jaćimović and Horvat, 2004). Good agreement of the results obtained by k_0-INAA with other methods was observed in environmental samples such as soil, sediments, and sewage sludge with elevated Hg values (>1 mg/kg), while at lower concentrations agreement is good in the absence of major interferences in k_0-INAA. In biologic samples (plants, algae, and tissues) the agreement is satisfactory at concentrations higher than 0.05 mg/kg. The sensitivity of k_0-INAA largely depends on the presence of other elements that interfere with the gamma line of ^{203}Hg. k_0-INAA may suffer from spectral interferences and, when plastic irradiation vials are used, from volatilization losses. Therefore, the use of standard reference materials of known chemical composition close to those of the samples should be used for validation purposes. Sample contamination issues are not as big a concern because sample preparation and handling steps are minimal before the irradiation of the sample. NAA has often been used as a reference method against which other methods were checked and compared (Jaćimović and Horvat, 2004). A major limitation in the widespread adoption of activation techniques for Hg analysis is that the technique requires very expensive facilities and well-trained personnel. NAA procedures also tend to be lengthy and they cannot be adapted for use in the field.

ELECTROCHEMICAL METHODS

The use of electrochemical methods for total mercury analysis of environmental waters is limited, primarily because of its lack of sensitivity. Detection limits are typically in the low nanomolar range. Another limitation is that many of the electrochemical approaches used for other trace-element determinations use mercury-based electrodes (e.g., hanging drop mercury electrodes or thin film Hg electrodes). Electrochemical methods developed for mercury analysis of water typically use noble metal electrodes (Turyan and Mandler, 1994; Wu et al., 1997; Falter et al., 1999; Bonfil et al., 2000; Giacominoa et al., 2008). One important advantage of electrochemical methods is that, for example, using anodic stripping voltammetry (ASV), it is possible to separate Hg(I) and Hg(II) in aqueous solutions. However, the sensitivity is poor as compared with other techniques for determination of total Hg (Sipos et al., 1980; Švarc-Gajić et al., 2009).

PHOTO-ACOUSTIC SPECTROSCOPY

Mercury is first preconcentrated on a gold trap and after thermal release it is quantified by measuring the sound produced from fluorescent quenching when the sample vapor is irradiated with a modulated Hg vapor lamp. The detection limit is 0.05 ng. The method has been successfully used for detection of ultratrace levels of Hg in air and snow (de Mora et al., 2005; Patterson, 1984).

ATOMIC EMISSION SPECTROMETRY

Several types of plasma sources, including direct current, inductively coupled, and microwave-induced gas (helium and argon) plasmas have been used for the determination of Hg (Fukushi et al., 1993). These methods are very sensitive, but as compared with AAS and atomic fluorescence spectrometry (AFS) they are too complex and expensive for routine work.

Determination of Organo-Mercury Species

There are no promulgated standard methods for the analysis of organo-Hg compounds in environmental samples. Most of the methods come from published papers detailing methods developed for a specific analyte and matrix.

In recent years, however, significant improvements of analytical methods in terms of specificity and sensitivity have been achieved. This has allowed the determination of Hg speciation in many environmental compartments.

Occurrence of Organo-Mercury Species in Natural Waters

Concentrations of organo-Hg compounds (predominantly MMHg) in water samples are generally very low (at the nanogram per liter level or below), so that accurate analysis requires great care in sample handling and analysis. The theoretical approach via stability calculations can be of great help in making rough estimates of the predominant Hg species under various conditions. Mercury compounds occurring in natural waters (see Figure 3.1) are most often defined by their ability to be reduced to elemental Hg. In lake waters, MMHg species account for 1–30% of total Hg. Most of the MMHg is probably associated with DOM. Thiol groups (-RSH) have been shown, however, to have a higher capability to bind MMHg in comparison with ligands containing oxygen and nitrogen donor atoms and the inorganic ions (CN^-, Cl^-, OH^-). Monomethylmercury compounds in surface runoff waters, soil pore waters, and groundwaters are similar to the species in lake waters and are generally quite strongly associated with DOM (see section on "Determination of Organo-Hg Compounds in Aqueous Media"). Dimethylmercury has rarely been reported in surface waters except in the deep ocean (Mason and Fitzgerald, 1993; Cossa et al., 1994; Vandal et al., 1998; Horvat et al., 2003) and during some seasons in the slurry of salt marshes (Weber et al., 1998). Monomethylmercury concentrations in seawater are generally lower than in lake waters. The presence of organo-Hg species, including dimethylmercury, was also detected in geothermal gases and waters (Hirner et al., 1998).

Sampling and Storage

The same techniques described previously for collection of inorganic Hg samples are also applicable to organo-Hg samples. Samples may be collected in precleaned glass or Teflon, but it is essential that all residual oxidative acid used in the cleaning process be leached from the walls of Teflon bottles prior to use for collection of samples. This can be accomplished by filling the bottles with dilute (0.5%) HCl and warming overnight. For the analysis of organo-mercurials, preservation with oxidative reagents (as advised for total Hg analysis) should be avoided, since organo-mercurials are converted into inorganic Hg. Stabilization by HNO_3 results in a decrease in MMHg, while Hg(II) remains stable in the presence of HNO_3 (Leermakers et al., 1990; Parker and Bloom, 2004). Hydrochloric acid is the most appropriate acid for storing aqueous MMHg solutions (Ahmed et al., 1987). Sulfuric acid is usually used for preservation of MMHg solutions in seawater (Leermakers et al.,

TABLE 3.4
Recommended Containers and Preservation Methods for Organo-Mercury

Analyte	Matrix	Preservative	Container	Hold time
MMHg	Freshwater	0.5% HCl/dark	Teflon or glass	180 days[a]
MMHg	Seawater	0.5% H_2SO_4/dark	Teflon or glass	180 days[a]
MMHg	Sediment	Frozen	Glass or plastic	Undetermined
MMHg	Tissue	$4 \pm 2°C$[b], frozen[c]/freeze-dried	Glass or plastic	Undetermined
MMHg	Blood	$4 \pm 2°C$[b]/frozen[c]	Glass or plastic	Undetermined

a. EPA Method 1630.
b. Not recommended for long-term storage.
c. Samples should never be thawed and refrozen.

1990; Parker and Bloom, 2005). Some authors claim that for MMHg determinations, storage of unpreserved samples at low temperatures (or even deep-frozen) is better than adding acid (Bloom, 1989; Horvat et al., 2003). Horvat and Byrne (1992) noted that long periods of deep-freeze storage do not affect the methylmercury concentration in fish muscle, but losses of up to 30% were observed in shellfish. Freeze-drying is therefore recommended as the best method for long-term preservation of tissue samples. Table 3.4 lists recommended sample-collection containers, hold times, and preservation methods for the most common environmental samples collected for organo-Hg analysis.

Determination of Organo-Mercury Compounds in Aqueous Media

A large number of articles describing methods for the determination of MMHg compounds in biologic and sediment samples have been published. Far fewer analytical methods have been described for the reliable determination of organo-Hg species in water samples at ambient concentration levels. In many studies, Hg compounds in aquatic environments are "speciated" according to their ability to reduce the various forms of Hg present to the elemental state. Because dimethylmercury and Hg^0 are highly volatile, they must be isolated immediately after sampling to avoid gas-phase exchanges. The most common isolation approach used with volatile species is direct aeration and adsorption on a suitable adsorbent (e.g., Carbotrap or Tenax), coupled with noble metal amalgamation for Hg^0 (Horvat et al., 2003). Alternatively, volatile species can be directly isolated by cryogenic trapping, separation on a gas chromatography (GC) column and detected by one or more suitable Hg detectors, most recently by ICP-MS (Hintelmann and Ogrinc, 2003; Monperrus et al., 2004; Stoichev et al., 2004). It is important that samples not be acidified prior to such separations to avoid conversion of dimethylmercury and Hg^0 into MMHg and Hg(II), respectively.

A common method used for the determination of organo-Hg species (usually focusing on MMHg) involves a derivatization step using an ethylating or other similar reagent in which the organo-Hg species present are converted to volatile analogs for isolation from solution by gas-phase stripping. A critical part of this procedure is the preparation of samples prior to derivatization. Often, a pre-separation and preconcentration step is necessary for this isolation method to be effective, regardless of which detection system is used to quantify the organo-Hg compounds. Monomethylmercury compounds must be removed from bound sites to facilitate the ethylation reaction. Interfering compounds (such as sulfides) must also be removed. Two basic approaches have been described to prepare the sample prior to the derivatization step. The first method is based on extraction of MMHg compounds into methylene chloride and then back-extraction into water by solvent evaporation (Bloom, 1989). The second is based on water vapor distillation (see, e.g., De Wild et al., 2002). Distillation has advantages, since it quantitatively releases MMHg from sulfur and organic-rich water samples (Horvat et al., 1993).

ORGANO-MERCURY DETERMINATIONS USING A DISTILLATION STEP

Analytical methods for the determination of organo-Hg species based on a distillation step are perhaps the most widely used approaches for the determination of MMHg (Bloom, 1989; Horvat et al., 1993; Bloom and von der Geest, 1995; Olsen et al., 1997; De Wild et al., 2002). The method is based on the distillation of a water sample to isolate MMHg (as a chloride formed by acidification with hydrochloric acid) (Figure 3.3).

Following isolation by distillation, the sample is ethylated with sodium tetraethylborate, $3NaB(C_2H_5)_4$. During the derivatization step using $3NaB(C_2H_5)_4$, both inorganic Hg and organo-Hg species in the sample become ethylated:

$$[CH_3Hg^+] + [Hg^{2+}] + 3NaB(C_2H_5)_4 \rightarrow [CH_3HgC_2H_5] + [Hg(C_2H_5)_2] + 3Na^+ + 3B(C_2H_5)_3$$

Ethylated Hg species are volatile and therefore can be purged from solution at room temperature using a sparging vessel; the volatile species are collected on adsorbent

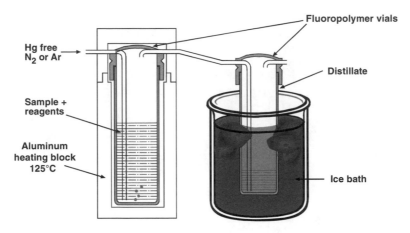

FIGURE 3.3 Schematic diagram of the distillation system used to separate monomethylmercury from complex matrices prior to the derivatization step. (*Source:* EPA. 1998b.)

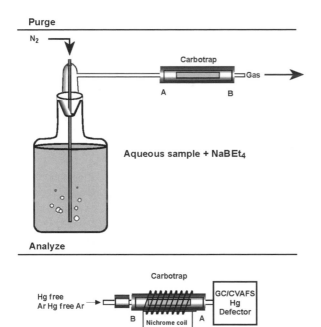

FIGURE 3.4 Schematic diagram of the purging system to strip derivatized mercury species from solution onto an absorbent material. NaBEt$_4$ = sodium tetraethylborate. (*Source:* EPA. 1998b.)

materials such as Carbotrap or Tenax at room temperature (Figure 3.4).

Subsequent separation of the various Hg species is then conducted by heating the adsorbed Hg species off of the collection column and into a GC column. After thermal release, individual Hg compounds are separated by cryogenic or isothermal GC. As the species are eluted they are thermally decomposed (pyrolyzed) at high temperature (>750°C) and are quantified as Hg^0 using a CVAFS detector that achieves very low detection limits (<10 pg, equating to about 0.02 ng/L at typical sample volumes) (Figure 3.5). A CVAAS detector can also be used, but its detection limit is much higher, equating to about 0.3 ng/L at typical sample volumes (Rapsomanikis and Craig, 1991).

This method has been published by the EPA as Method 1630 (EPA, 1998b) and has frequently been adopted in laboratories involved in studies of the biogeochemical cycle of Hg. EPA Method 1630 remains in draft status and has not yet been fully promulgated by EPA.

ORGANO-MERCURY DETERMINATIONS USING AN EXTRACTION STEP

In a typical extraction method, MMHg halide (Br$^-$, Cl$^-$ or I$^-$) is extracted into an organic solvent (benzene or toluene) after acidification. This is followed by derivatization to a water-soluble adduct of methylmercury–cysteine, which is extracted into the aqueous phase. After acidification, CH$_3$HgX (X is a halide ion) is back-extracted into a small amount of organic solvent. An aliquot is then injected onto a gas–liquid chromatography (GLC) column and detected by electron capture detection (ECD) or any other suitably sensitive detector (such as a plasma emission detector). Packed or capillary columns can be used as described later for MMHg determination in other environmental samples.

Craig (1986) has reviewed the many modifications to this extraction procedure. For example, the MMHg compound may be transferred into organic solvent as dithizonates followed by clean-up steps and detection by GC-ECD (Akagi and Nishimura, 1991). Inorganic and organic Hg species can be preconcentrated on dithiocarbamate or sulfhydryl cotton-fiber adsorbent that is then extracted as described above (Lee and Mowrer, 1989; Jones et al., 1995). However, in some water samples, artifact formation of MMHg was observed during solid-phase extraction of water samples (Celo et al., 2004). The common drawbacks of most of these extraction procedures are the large sample requirements, low extraction yields, and nonspecific separation of dimethylmercury, if present.

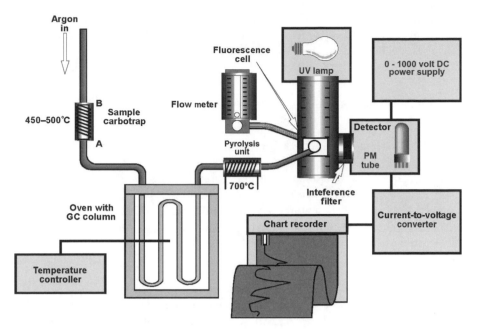

FIGURE 3.5.   Schematic diagram of the CVAFS detector interfaced with the isothermal GC and pyrolytic decomposition column. (*Source*: EPA. 1998b.)

There are also methods for determination of "total" organo-Hg compounds. Inorganic and organic Hg are preconcentrated on a dithiocarbamate resin and are subsequently eluted with thiourea. Separation of organic and inorganic Hg is achieved by differential reduction and detection by CVAAS (Minagawa et al., 1979). Inorganic and organic Hg can also be separated using anion exchange resins. Organic Hg is then decomposed (by UV irradiation) and measured by CVAAS. However, it has been shown that the concentration levels obtained by this method do not necessarily correspond to MMHg (owing to the lack of specificity of the protocol). The method has been improved by the introduction of more specific separations of organic and inorganic Hg species by water vapor distillation (Padberg and Stoeppler, 1991).

In recent years, ICP-MS is being used more and more frequently as a detector for inorganic and organo-Hg determinations. Propylation has been shown to be an even more suitable derivatization procedure, being free from interferences caused by halide ions (Demuth and Heumann, 2001). Hydration was also proven to be a useful derivatization method, in particular when coupled with preconcentration by cryotrapping (Tseng et al., 1998; Monperrus et al., 2004; Stoichev et al., 2004).

HYPHENATED TECHNIQUES

Within the past decade, a number of methods have been described that interface a gas or liquid chromatographic separation technique to a sensitive detector such as CVAFS or ICP-MS. These methods have the potential advantage of allowing for the simultaneous determination of both inorganic Hg and a variety of organo-Hg species. Because

the chromatographic separation techniques use such small sample volumes, a preconcentration step is required to bring the analytes to a detection range suitable for natural waters. Cairns et al. (2008) describe a high-performance liquid chromatography (HPLC)-ICP-MS technique using online microcolumn preconcentration for speciation of mercury in seawater. The method achieved a detection limit of 0.07 ng/L for inorganic mercury and 0.02 ng/L for MMHg. Other examples of hyphenated methods include ion chromatography (IC)-ICP-MS as described by Chen, K.-J. et al. (2009) and a HPLC-ICP-MS technique described by dos Santos et al. (2009). However, these methods had detection limits of 30 ng/L (MMHg) and 100 ng/L (inorganic Hg) and 5.2 ng/L (MMHg) and 4.6 ng/L (inorganic Hg), respectively. These latter methods do not have sufficient sensitivity to detect natural levels of mercury in water and illustrate the necessity to use an appropriate preconcentration technique in order to detect natural levels of inorganic mercury and MMHg in water samples.

Determination of the Chemical and Phase Speciation of Mercury in Natural Waters

The interaction of Hg with organic matter in natural waters is important in controlling the solubility, mobility, and bioavailability of Hg (Ravichandran et al., 1998, 1999). The recognition that Hg can strongly interact with dissolved organic matter and aquatic colloids to form both solution and colloidal phases has spawned an interest in developing methods to determine the chemical and phase speciation of Hg in natural waters and in assessing the significance of Hg–DOM interactions. Many of the methods that have been described in recent years are based on the pioneering work for determining the interaction of trace elements with dissolved organic matter (van den Berg, 1984; Moffett and Zika, 1987; Sigleo and Means, 1990; Rue and Bruland, 1995; Wen et al., 1996; Miller and Bruland, 1997; Wells et al., 1998).

Methods to Assess Divalent Mercury–Organic Matter Interactions

Several approaches to determine the interaction of inorganic Hg(II) with dissolved organic matter in natural waters based on competitive ligand equilibrium (CLE) approaches have been described. The technique is based on an equilibrium competition between the natural ligands present in the solution and an added ligand that has well-characterized formation constants for free ionic Hg^{2+}.

The technique allows for the determination of the strength of binding between the natural ligand(s) present and Hg^{2+} (i.e., determination of a conditional stability constant) and also provides a measure of the abundance of the Hg binding ligand concentration (L). Although this information is highly useful for equilibrium modeling and bioavailability predictions, it does not provide direct information on the composition of the binding ligand(s).

Methods for determining the interaction of inorganic Hg(II) species with DOM in natural waters and wastewaters using the CLE approach have been described by Hsu and Sedlak (2003), Han and Gill (2005), and Black et al. (2007). Details about these analytical approaches and results for determining the binding of inorganic Hg(II) with natural organic matter are given in Table 3.5.

TABLE 3.5

Selected Summary of Analytical Approaches and Results for Determining the Binding of Inorganic Divalent Mercury with Natural Organic Matter in Natural Waters

Matrix	Method	Log K^{cond} (HgL')	[L']^a	Reference
Fresh and saline water	Osteryoung square wave anodic stripping voltammetry using a gold disk electrode	9.7–10.8	1.4–4.5 nM	Wu et al. (1997)
Freshwater	Dual CLE using thiosalicylic acid and diethyldithiocarbamate with isolation and separation of Hg-competing ligand complexes by SPE on C18	29.9–33.5	0.022–11 nM	Black et al. (2007)
Coastal and estuarine water	CLE using thiosalicylic acid and chloride with solvent extraction using toluene to isolate the natural ligand Hg complex from the competing ligand–Hg complex	26.5–29.0 (TSA) 23.1–24.4 (Cl)	0.013–0.10 nM (using TSA); 0.5–9.6 nM (using Cl)	Han and Gill (2005)
Lake, river, and sea water	Isolation of an operationally defined "reducible mercury" fraction using stannous chloride or sodium borohydride wet chemical reduction combined with ligand titrations	21–24	<1–60 nM	Lamborg et al. (2003)
Wastewater	CLE using glutathione and with isolation and separation of Hg-competing ligand complexes by SPE on C18	>30	0.09–0.54 nM	Hsu and Sedlak (2003)
Hydrophobic DOM isolates	Equilibrium dialysis and ligand exchange using EDTA	22.5–23.5^b	5 nmol/mg DOM	Haitzer et al. (2003)
DOM isolates from the Florida Everglades	CLE–SPE method involving the titration of solutions containing DOM and Hg with glutathione	25–31 (units = M^{-1})		Gaspar et al. (2007)

CLE = competitive ligand exchange; SPE = solid-phase extraction; TSA = thiosalicylic acid.

a. [L'] represents the concentration of natural ligand not bound to Hg.

b. log K^{cond} for the formation of Hg–DOM, units of L kg^{-1}.

Isolation steps included solvent–solvent and solid-phase extraction. The other major approach to study Hg(II)–DOM interactions involves studies of DOM fractions isolated from a bulk DOM or OM pool. The isolation process tends to favor separation of DOM into hydrophilic and hydrophobic fractions that are then assessed for their ability to bind with Hg(II) by a variety of approaches. Haitzer et al. (2003) separated hydrophobic organic acid fractions from surface water using AMBERLITE™ XAD™-8 resin and then used equilibrium dialysis to determine distribution coefficients for Hg–DOM interactions. Gaspar et al. (2007) used several XAD resin techniques to isolate DOM of varying hydrophobicities and then applied a modified version of the CLE-SPE method of Hsu and Sedlak (2003) to determine equilibrium reactions between free ionic Hg^{2+} and the DOM isolates. Lamborg et al. (2003) developed an Hg speciation technique based on the operational "reactive Hg" assay. The authors describe the method as a technique for determining the labile fraction of Hg, which they assume represents only complexes of Hg that have stability constants that are too low to protect the Hg(II) from wet chemical reduction.

Electrochemical techniques have also been described to determine the concentration and speciation of Hg in aqueous systems, but the sensitivity of these methods is currently limited and hence cannot be used to determine binding constants or concentrations at levels that other techniques currently can achieve (Turyan and Mandler, 1994; Wu et al., 1997).

Phase-Speciation Methods

Natural waters contain a variety of colloidal particles, including organic biopolymers and inorganic nanoparticles that readily interact with many trace elements to remove them from the solution phase (Honeyman and Santschi, 1988; Buffle and Leppard, 1995; Santaschi et al., 2002). One of the most common techniques to isolate colloids and colloidally bound metals from aqueous solutions is cross-flow ultrafiltration (Buffle et al., 1992; Buesseler et al., 1996; Guo and Santschi, 2007). Cross-flow ultrafiltration techniques have been described to determine the phase speciation of Hg and MMHg in both marine and freshwater systems (Stordal et al., 1996; Babiarz et al., 2000; Guentzel et al., 1996; Choe and Gill, 2001). Table 3.6 is a brief summary illustrating the importance of colloidal Hg and MMHg. Determinations of colloidal Hg using ultrafiltration techniques involve significant attention to operational characteristics, including concentration factors and careful calibration of the membrane for size fractionation (Babiarz et al., 2000; Choe and Gill, 2001). To date, most ultrafiltration studies have observed significant levels of colloidal Hg and MMHg in estuarine, marine, and freshwater systems.

TABLE 3.6
Colloidal Mercury and Methylmercury Levels Observed in Natural Water Systems

System	Filter-passing[a] mean and/or (range) (pM)	Colloidal Hg[b] mean and/or (range) (pM)	Truly dissolved[c] mean and/or (range) (pM)	% of filter-passing phase that is colloidal	Reference
Total Hg					
Freshwaters	20.5	12	9.5	59	Babiarz et al. (2001)
Estuarine	3.3 (0.32–8.2)	(0.29–4.4)	(0.9–2.9)	57 ± 20	Stordal et al. (1996)
San Francisco Bay	(1.8–7.8)			38 ± 18 (fall) 57 ± 10 (spring)	Choe and Gill (2003)
MMHg					
Freshwaters	1.1	0.60	0.50	54	Babiarz et al. (2001)
Galveston Bay	(0.025–0.105)	(0–0.07)	(0.015–0.06)	52–60	Choe and Gill (2001)
San Francisco Bay				34 ± 11 (fall) 56 ± 15 (spring)	Choe and Gill (2003)

a. Filter-passing Hg is defined as Hg that is observed in a water sample that has been filtered with a 0.4- or 0.45-μm filter.

b. Colloidal Hg is defined as Hg in the filter-passing fraction that has been retained by ultrafiltration. The minimal size fraction isolated varies with investigation, but is typically between 1 and 10 kDa.

c. The truly dissolved fraction is defined as Hg observed in the natural water sample that has passed through the ultrafiltration system. Plus–minus values are means ±SD.

Organo-Mercury Species in Other Environmental Matrices

Sampling and Storage

SEDIMENTS AND SOILS

Monomethylmercury generally does not occur in sediments at a level of more than about 2% of the total Hg present. There appears to be an approximate equilibrium level between MMHg production and destruction. Methylation–demethylation reactions are assumed to be widespread in the environment, and each ecosystem attains its own steady state with respect to the individual species of Hg. Dimethylmercury is considered to be unstable in sediments, but is assumed to be stabilized by a conjunction of factors, such as high sulfide levels, salinity, anoxic conditions, and constant inputs of methane into the media (Weber et al., 1998).

Sediment and soil samples should be collected and stored with caution because the percentage of MMHg in these samples is very low (e.g., <2% of total Hg) and improper handling and storage may lead to inaccurate results. Changes in in situ pH, reduction–oxidation potential and moisture content as a result of sampling can lead to conversion of Hg species (methylation, demethylation, or reduction) and may significantly influence the stability of MMHg in sediments. This is particularly true in the case of sediments taken from zones where bottom waters are oxygen-depleted (Horvat et al., 2004). Samples collected from such environments are best analyzed fresh or, if long-term storage is unavoidable, samples should be kept in the dark in an inert atmosphere and deep frozen.

BIOLOGIC SAMPLES

In upper-trophic-level piscivorous fish, the percentage of MMHg to total Hg in fish muscle varies from 80 to 100%, but in other organs its concentration is smaller (typical values in liver and kidney are ≤20%). In lower-trophic-level fish and other aquatic organisms, the percentage of MMHg is much more variable. Relatively high Hg and MMHg concentrations have been reported for fish-eating marine birds. Birds feeding on wild vegetation generally have much lower levels of Hg. There have been many studies performed on terrestrial ecosystems (particularly in Canada, Sweden, and the United States). Mercury also passes from vegetation into the food chains of fauna (Gnamuš et al., 2000).

Most biologic samples are preferably analyzed fresh or after lyophilization. Deep-freezing of fresh samples, especially with long storage, should be avoided, since it has been observed that in some organisms MMHg may decompose with repeated freezing and unfreezing (particularly in bivalves) (Horvat and Byrne, 1992). Monomethylmercury and total Hg in freeze-dried biologic samples, such as biologic CRMs, are stable for years. CRMs are, however, sterilized either by autoclaving or by gamma irradiation. This important step prevents bacteriologic activity, which may otherwise lead to methylation and demethylation processes. In general, very little is known about the effects of sterilization on the stability of MMHg compounds. More studies are needed to investigate the stability of organo-Hg compounds in biologic samples, particularly under various sample preparation and long-term storage conditions. Significant external contamination of biologic samples with MMHg is unlikely to occur; however, precautions are necessary to avoid contamination by inorganic Hg.

Blood and hair samples are often analyzed in order to estimate exposure of humans to Hg and its compounds. Blood and hair should be collected as described above. After blood has been sampled without an anticoagulant, it will clot spontaneously and separate into serum and packed cells. The process takes 15 to 30 minutes at room temperature. The samples should then be centrifuged within 1 hour. This separation should be done as soon as possible to avoid hemolysis of blood. Hemolyzed samples cannot be considered for speciation analysis. The distribution of the different trace element species between serum and cells may vary by several orders of magnitude. Serum and packed cells may be deep-frozen only once, as repeatedly frozen and thawed samples have shown a remarkable decrease in MMHg concentrations. There is also some evidence that MMHg may be destroyed during lyophilization of blood samples (Horvat and Byrne, 1992; LaFleur, 1973).

Analysis of human hair offers several advantages over analysis of blood samples, such as ease of sampling and sample storage. The concentration of MMHg in hair is approximately 250 times higher than in blood, and analysis of different longitudinal sections of hair can give information on the history of the exposure to MMHg ingested through food. Adhering dust and grease should be removed by washing with a solvent such as hexane, alcohol, acetone, water, diethylether, or detergents. The International Atomic Energy Agency (IAEA) and the World Health Organization (WHO) recommend the use of only water and acetone (UNEP/WHO/IAEA 1987). Long-term storage of human hair samples has shown that MMHg is stable for a period of a few years if stored dry and in the dark at room temperature (Horvat, 2005).

Determination of Organo-Mercury in Solid Matrices

Environmental samples can have complex matrices, necessitating that several steps be used to release the organic Hg from the sample prior to analysis: (1) liberation of MMHg from its matrix, (2) extraction/cleanup/preconcentration, (3) separation of Hg species of interest, and (4) quantification. These steps can vary widely from one matrix to another, depending on the potential interferences present in the sample and how tightly bound the organic Hg is within the sample matrix.

LIBERATION OF MONOMETHYLMERCURY FROM SOLID MATRICES

Most methods are based on the method originally developed by Westöö (1966), which involves the extraction of organo-Hg chloride from acidified homogeneous samples into benzene (however, the use of toluene is strongly recommended, for health and safety reasons). Organo-Hg compounds are then back-extracted into an aqueous cysteine solution. The aqueous solution is then acidified and organo-Hg compounds are reextracted with benzene or toluene. This double partitioning facilitates the removal of many interferences such as benzene-soluble thiols. Finally, MMHg is analyzed by GC with ECD.

More recently, several modifications have been made to the Westöö protocol for the separation and identification of organo-Hg in biologic and other samples. In tissue matrices, such as homogenized fish muscle tissue, a simple digestion using 25% KOH in methanol (Bloom, 1989) will completely dissolve the sample, which can then be derivatized and analyzed as described previously for aqueous samples. In more complex matrices, such as plant matter and soil/sediment samples, more rigorous cleanup and extraction techniques are required. For example, in the initial step the addition of Cu(II) ions enhances the removal of Hg bound to sulfur. The method has also been modified in terms of the quantity of chemicals used. A semi-micro scale method developed by Uthe et al. (1972) has been widely applied. However, inorganic Hg cannot be determined using this procedure unless a reagent is added to form, for example, alkyl- and aryl-derivatives, which can then be extracted and determined by GLC (Zarnegar and Mushak, 1974).

In general, solvent-extraction procedures are time consuming, corrections for the recovery of the procedure vary from sample to sample, and with some sample types (e.g., those rich in lipids) phases are difficult to separate because of the presence of persistent emulsions, particularly during the separation of the aqueous cysteine phase. To overcome these problems, MMHg can be adsorbed on cysteine paper (instead of into cysteine solution) during the cleanup stage (Horvat et al., 1988). Using additional preseparations prior to extraction, such as volatilization of MMHg in a microdiffusion cell (Zelenko and Kosta, 1973) and distillation (Horvat et al., 1988, 1994) may also facilitate the separation of phases during extraction. Because various extraction and cleanup procedures are used to extract organo-Hg from its matrix, it is essential to quantify recovery, especially when speciation is performed on insoluble samples such as sediments and soils.

It is also important to note that some extraction protocols may lead to artifact MMHg production, especially in procedures in which MMHg is isolated at higher temperatures (Falter, 1999). A study by Bloom et al. (1997) investigated artifact formation of MMHg and proposed an extraction technique using cold acidic bromide and extraction into methylene chloride that appears to avoid this problem.

This extraction method is frequently used in conjunction with EPA Method 1630 (EPA, 1998b) for the determination of MMHg in sediment and soil samples. Regardless of which extraction technique is used, results should be checked regularly by the use of appropriate CRMs, if available, or by comparison of the results from different laboratories and/or the use of different analytical approaches.

The use of ICP-MS with isotope dilution analysis (IDA) can help overcome problems associated with incomplete recovery of organo-Hg species, particularly in biologic samples. If equilibration of the isotopically modified spike and the sample MMHg is achieved, the spike material acts as an ideal internal standard. So far, such a protocol has been successfully applied to numerous environmental and biologic samples (Falter, 1999; Hintelmann, 1999; Snell et al., 2000; Clough et al., 2003).

EXTRACTION/CLEANUP/PRECONCENTRATION

DERIVATIZATION METHODS

Most methods use the formation of a volatile organo-Hg derivative (through ethylation, propylation, butylation, hydration, and iodination) in order to separate the organo-Hg from the bulk of the sample by simple purge and trap techniques. The same ethylation method as described above for water samples has also been applied to biologic and sediment samples (Bloom, 1989). An aliquot of the digested or extracted sample is subjected to ethylation by sodium tetraethylborate, which transforms MMHg into methylethylmercury. At the same time Hg(II) is transformed into diethylmercury. The two species can be quantified simultaneously (Liang et al., 1994) if diethylmercury is not naturally present in the sample. If diethylmercury is present in the sample, a different derivatization technique, such as propylation, must be used.

Volatile ethylated Hg compounds, as well as elemental Hg and dimethylmercury, are removed from solution by aeration and are then trapped on an adsorbent (Carbotrap or Tenax). Mercury compounds are separated on a GC column, and pyrolyzed to elemental Hg^0 at high temperatures (>750°C) for subsequent Hg determination by CVAFS, CVAAS, or ICP-MS. As mentioned previously, very low detection limits may be achieved using CVAFS and ICP-MS (6 pg/L for water and 1 pg/g for biota and sediment samples). Instead of sodium tetraethyl borate, sodium borohydride may also be used to form volatile Hg hydride, which is then quantified by GC in line with a Fourier transform infrared spectrophotometer (Fillipelli et al., 1992). CH_3I formed in a headspace vial may also be introduced onto a GC column and detected by microwave-induced plasma atomic emission spectrometry (MIP-AES) or AFS detectors. Propylation and hydration have also been applied with great success as described above (Demuth and Heuman, 2001; Logar et al., 2004).

DIFFERENTIAL REDUCTION

Magos (1971) reported a method in which the inorganic Hg in an alkaline-digested sample is selectively reduced by stannous chloride, while organo-Hg compounds are reduced to elemental Hg by a combination of stannous chloride and cadmium chloride. The released elemental Hg can be measured by CVAAS. The method has been successfully applied to biologic samples in toxicologic, epidemiologic, and clinical studies. May et al. (1987) developed a method using CVAAS for the detection of organo-Hg compounds after preseparation of organo-Hg by anion exchange. Other researchers have used volatilization and trapping on cysteine paper (Zelenko and Kosta, 1973) or water vapor distillation (Horvat et al., 1993). Organo-Hg compounds must be destroyed by either UV irradiation or acid digestion prior to detection by CVAAS. In most biologic samples, the organo-Hg concentrations usually correspond to MMHg. In some environmental samples, such as sediment, soil, and water samples, the concentrations of organic Hg (particularly if separated by anion exchange) have been found to be much higher than those of MMHg compounds. This is probably due to presence of some other organic mercury compounds that have not, as yet, been identified.

SEPARATION OF MERCURY SPECIES OF INTEREST

In addition to choosing proper extraction techniques, it is essential to choose proper chromatographic conditions for the separation of the organo-Hg species. Apart from the above-mentioned problems associated with the extraction of organo-mercurials, problems also exist in the chromatography of organo-mercurial halides. Many investigators have recommended that columns packed with 5% DEGS-PS on 100-120 mesh Supelco support be used. Some other polar stationary phases have also been used (e.g. PEGS, Carbowax 20M, Durapak, Carbowax 400, PDEAS and HIEFF-2AP). In order to prevent ion-exchange and adsorption processes on the column (which cause undesirable effects such as tailing, changing of the retention time, and decrease of peak areas/heights) passivation of the packing material is needed with Hg(II) chloride in benzene (O'Reilly, 1982). Although the more inert nature of capillary columns would be expected to minimize such effects, improved chromatographic performance over packed columns cannot be readily achieved. Some workers still prefer to use packed columns because the analytical protocols using capillary columns require additional research to optimize performance. The following capillary columns have so far been reported to give good results: OV-17 WCOT, Beijing Chemical Industry Works; Superox 20M FSOT, and OV 275. Several workers have chosen to derivatize Hg species to their corresponding nonpolar, alkylated analogues such as butyl derivatives, which can then be separated on nonpolar packed or capillary columns (Bulska et al., 1992).

As described above for aqueous samples, hyphenated techniques have also been developed for the determination of Hg species in solid phases. Shade (2008) describes a technique for the determination of inorganic Hg and MMHg in biotic samples using Hg–thiourea complex ion chromatography with CVAFS detection. Mercury species were extracted using an acidic leaching solution containing thiourea. The cationic Hg–thiourea complexes are separated by ion chromatography, followed by sequential oxidation of the methylmercury ion (CH_3Hg^+) to inorganic Hg(II), and stannous chloride reduction of Hg(II) to Hg^0 to permit detection by CVAFS. The method achieved detection limits of ~0.5 ng/g for both MMHg and inorganic Hg(II) using sample masses as low as 100 mg. Hight and Chen (2006) describe an HPLC-ICP-MS technique using L-cysteine extraction for the determination of MMHg and total Hg in seafood. They achieved a detection limit of 7 ng/g for MMHg and 5 ng/g for inorganic Hg using a 0.5-g sample. Chang et al. (2007) describe an HPLC-ICP-MS technique for the determination of Hg (and lead) speciation in fish samples using 2-mercaptoethanol and L-cysteine microwave-assisted extraction. They achieved a detection limit of 10 ng/g for both inorganic Hg and MMHg. Even though these latter methods do not have the sensitivity of the Shade method, they are nonetheless adequate for measuring Hg species in biologic samples. Other hyphenated methods have been described by Santoyo et al. (2009), Margetínová et al (2008), and Chen, J. et al. (2009), but the sensitivity of these methods may not be adequate for some biologic samples from lower trophic levels, where Hg concentration levels are low.

QUANTIFICATION

Various detectors can be used in combination with chromatography for the determination of Hg species. The ECD is a very sensitive detector with an absolute detection limit of approximately a few picograms. It does not, however, measure Hg directly, but responds to the halide ion attached to the CH_3Hg^+ ion. The identification of small MMHg peaks can sometimes be subject to positive systematic error owing to co-eluting contaminants. The use of an ICP-AES detector, a mass spectrometric detector, CVAAS, CVAFS, or ICP-MS can avoid such problems, since Hg is measured directly. Miniaturized automated speciation analyzers have been developed for the determination of organo-Hg compounds, based on microwave induced plasma emission detector (Slaets and Adams, 2000).

Other Methods

Gage (1961) presented the first practical method for differentiating between organic and inorganic Hg. It was a colorimetric method in which organo-Hg compounds were extracted into an organic solvent and determined spectrophotometrically to be dithizone complexes. The method suffers from low sensitivity. Simple extraction procedures have also been successfully used followed by AAS. HPLC has proven of use with reductive amperometric electrochemical detection, UV detection, inductively coupled plasma emission spectrometric detection, or AAS detection. NAA has been used for MMHg determinations in fish, blood, and hair samples after suitable preseparation procedures. Graphite furnace AAS has also been used for the final determination of MMHg in toluene extracts to which dithizone was added. An anodic stripping voltammetry technique has been developed for determination of MMHg. However, the method has never been used for environmental samples. Methylmercury has also been extracted into dichloromethane (CH_2Cl_2). This was then evaporated down to 0.1 mL and subjected to GC with an atmospheric pressure active nitrogen detector (Horvat, 1996). An enzymatic method for specific detection of organo-mercurials in bacterial cultures has been developed. It is based on the specific conversion of MMHg (no other methyl-metallo groups are enzymatically converted) to methane by organo-mercurial lyase. Ethyl and phenylmercury can also be detected (Baldi and Fillipelli, 1991).

Other Organo-Mercurials

Among other organo-Hg species currently of interest, ethylmercury (EtHg) is a compound that requires further attention because it is still used in thiomerosal for preservations of vaccines. It is important to analyze EtHg in vaccines, in wastewater from waste treatment plants in industries using EtHg, as well biologic samples in order to understand EtHg uptake, distribution, excretion, and effects. In principle, methods developed for MMHg can also be used for EtHg, except in protocols using derivatization by ethylation. In such cases propylation is recommended (Logar et al., 2004).

Only a few investigations concerning the determination of other organo-mercurials used in agriculture and for other purposes have been reported (Horvat and Schroeder, 1995). Methoxyethylmercury and ethoxyethylmercury have been examined by thin-layer chromatography (TLC) and GLC. It would appear that the only method that can separate and measure many of the compounds simultaneously is HPLC with UV detection (Hempel et al., 1992; Hintelmann and Wilken, 1993). It offers several advantages. The separation of the compounds is performed at ambient temperatures; hence, thermal decomposition does not occur. It offers the possibility to separate less volatile or nonvolatile species such as mersalyl acid or the aromatic organo-mercurials, that usually present a problem for GLC. It is, however, very important to isolate these compounds from environmental samples quantitatively. Methylmercury and ethylmercury can easily be isolated from soils by extraction from acidified samples. Several extraction agents have been tested in order to release organo-mercurials from soils. Methylmercury and phenylmercury can be extracted by potassium iodide–ascorbic acid and oxalic acid with

satisfactory yields, whereas ethylmercury is only partly extracted. No suitable extraction techniques have been found for methoxyethylmercury and ethoxyethylmercury in soils (due to decomposition of these compounds under acidic conditions) (Horvat, 2005).

Fractionation of Mercury in Soils and Sediments

Frequently, for the purpose of risk assessment, it is important to understand the relative availability of the forms of Hg present in a soil or sediment sample. The biogeochemical and especially the ecotoxicologic significance of Hg input is determined by its specific binding form and coupled reactivity rather than by its concentration in the solid material. Consequently, these are the parameters that have to be determined in order to assess the potential for Hg transformation processes (such as methylation, reduction, and demethylation) and to improve data for environmental risk assessment. EPA Method 3200 (EPA, 2005)—*Mercury species fractionation and quantification by microwave-assisted extraction, selective solvent extraction and/or solid phase extraction*—uses sequential extraction and separation procedures to differentiate mercury species that are present in soils and sediments into four distinct fractions: extractable organic mercury, extractable inorganic mercury, semimobile mercury, and nonmobile mercury. Hg pyrolysis followed by AAS detection was developed to distinguish among cinnabar-bound Hg, metallic Hg, and matrix-bound Hg (Biester et al., 1999; Bloom et al., 2003). Alternative approaches used for Hg fractionation are based on sequential extractions and leaching to provide information on the solubility and reactivity of Hg. A sequential extraction method developed by Bloom et al. (2003) consists of six steps that extract increasing recalcitrant forms of Hg, including water-soluble, "human stomach acid"—soluble, organo-chelated, elemental Hg, mercuric sulfide, and residual fraction. An additional step was incorporated into this scheme in order to provide information on the volatilization potential of Hg present in soil (Kocman et al., 2004). An alternative approach to Hg speciation in soils has been described by Cattani et al. (2008) based on HPLC-ICP-MS quantification of a diffusive gradient in thin-film fractionation. The technique is designed to quantify inorganic Hg and organo-Hg (e.g., methyl, ethyl, and phenyl Hg) species. Issaro et al. (2009) reviewed the extractants used to speciate mercury in soils and sediments. They found a lack of consensus between the existing methods and argued for a standard protocol and appropriate standard reference materials.

Use of Mercury Isotopic and Radiochemical Tracers

In order to understand the fate and transformation of Hg in the environment, it is necessary to assess the potential for Hg transformation rates under various environmental conditions and matrices. Analytical protocols using enriched stable and radioactive isotopes of Hg in combination with the ICP-MS are increasingly used (Monperrus et al., 2004). Multiple stable tracer experiments allow studies of the fate of Hg species in the environment and in biologic systems. This concept allows the investigation of multiple transformation processes simultaneously (Demuth and Heumann, 2001; Hintelmann and Ogrinc, 2003; Monperrus et al., 2004). The use of radioisotopes to trace different transport and transformation processes is also widespread; in the case of Hg, the most frequently used radiotracer is ^{203}Hg ($t_{1/2}$ = 46 days) (Guimaraes et al., 1995; Stordal et al., 1996; Gilmour et al., 1998; Mauro et al., 2002). However, when adequate facilities are available ^{197}Hg ($t_{1/2}$ = 64.14 hours) can also be used successfully, as it was demonstrated in Hg methylation–demethylation studies in soils and sediments (Guevara et al., 2004). Demethylation has been studied by the use of $^{14}CH_3Hg^+$, where the $^{14}CH_4$ produced indicates reductive demethylation, and $^{14}CO_2$ oxidative pathways of detoxification mechanisms (Hines et al., 2000; Oremland et al., 1991). A review of improvements on this topic is presented by Bjorn et al. (2007).

Calibration and Quality Control

It is essential that any analytical method used be carefully calibrated using standards available from various certifying agencies such as the National Institute of Standards and Technology (NIST) or manufacturers such as High Purity Standards. Because most commercially available standards must be diluted to be in the working range for most environmental Hg samples, it is recommended that two or more dilutions be used for calibration, as described in EPA Method 1631 (EPA, 2002), so that any loss of titer in one of the standards will be obvious when the two standards are plotted together. In addition, the calibration should be verified using a CRM from NIST, the National Research Council of Canada (NRCC), the IAEA, or another trusted certifying agency. CRMs are available for total Hg and MMHg for many sample types. It is best to match the CRM matrix as closely as possible to the samples being analyzed.

The difficulty of preventing losses of low-level Hg from aqueous solutions is well known, so care must be taken that standards prepared for instrument calibration are stable. Losses during storage are due to adsorption on container walls and volatilization losses due to reduction of inorganic Hg to elemental Hg. Numerous papers have been written describing various treatments of samples to prevent losses of inorganic Hg during storage (Coyn and Callins, 1972; Carr and Wilkniss, 1973; Lo and Wai, 1975). Strong acids and oxidants (such as HNO_3, HCl, or BrCl) can be added as preservatives. Losses are very much dependent on the container materials used; the best materials are quartz, Pyrex glass, and Teflon. Polyethylene or polypropylene containers are not recommended for storage of standards. Any working standard solution with a concentration less than 10 ng/mL should be prepared in Teflon and monitored frequently for titer.

Methods using dual amalgamation can also be calibrated using the Hg saturated air calibration method (Fitzgerald and Gill, 1979; Dumarey et al., 1985). Elemental Hg is placed in a closed glass container, and the temperature is kept at a constant value. The temperature dependence of the saturated Hg vapor concentration is calculated from the ideal gas law. An appropriate volume of Hg vapor is taken by gas-tight syringe and injected into the gas train through the chromatographic septum on the sampling gold trap. This approach has the advantage of preventing problems associated with the stability of aqueous Hg solutions and is ideal for calibration of methods for determining total Hg in air. However, when total Hg is measured by the reduction–aeration method, calibration of the analytical instrument with aqueous standards is preferable because it acts as a control for the reduction amalgamation conditions and represents less danger for possible contamination in the case of damage of the calibration vessel (Horvat, 2005).

There are very few commercially available standards for organo-Hg compounds. Most must be made in the laboratory from pure liquid or powder compounds. Care must be taken to ensure that the compounds are prepared in solvents and containers that will keep them stable as long as possible. There have been quite a few studies performed concerning the stability of organo-mercurials in standard solutions (Lansens et al., 1990; Meuleman et al., 1993). A decrease of MMHg in aqueous solutions can be caused by adsorption onto the container walls. Losses of MMHg chloride due to volatilization is unlikely to occur [K_d (gas–liquid distribution coefficient: C_{gas}/C_{H2O}) is 1.07×10^{-5} at 20°C]. The stability is strongly dependent on the concentration, the container materials, and the storage temperature. Stock MMHg standard solutions made up in organic solvents and stored in Pyrex glass bottles are very stable and can last for years. Working dilutions of the stock standards can be made in a solution of 0.2% hydrochloric acid and 0.5% acetic acid that, if stored in Teflon at 4±2°C, will last at least a year. Aqueous MMHg solutions are somewhat less stable. An aqueous solution with a concentration of 10 µg/L, stored in Pyrex at low temperature (e.g., in a refrigerator) is stable for approximately one month. If Teflon containers are used, the solution is stable for several months if stored in the dark at room temperature. A new CRM for calibration of Me^{202}Hg was produced by the European Institute for Reference Materials and Measurements (Snell et al., 2004) for calibration and quality control using ICP-MS detection and isotope-dilution analysis.

Volatile organo-Hg compounds (in particular dimethlymercury) can also be prepared in the gas phase. This is important for the optimization of methods for organo-Hg speciation in air and dimethylmercury in water. An aliquot of vapor is removed from a temperature-stabilized vessel using a gas-tight syringe. The concentration can be calculated from data on the partial pressure of the individual compound and the gas–law equation (Dumarey et al., 1985).

Because there are very few certified calibration standards for organo-Hg compounds, it is essential to test the titer of the standards frequently by cross-calibrating with multiple standards, exchanging standards with other laboratories, and analyzing frequent standard reference materials (there are several tissue and sediment Standard Reference Materials from IAEA and National Research Council Canada certified for MMHg).

It is recommended that the quality-control samples be analyzed with each batch of 20 or fewer samples to verify the validity of the data. Field blanks, method blanks and bottle blanks, blank spikes, matrix spikes/spike duplicates, analytical duplicates, and CRM (when available) are all recommended. All of the standard EPA methods stipulate recovery and precision data quality objectives.

Summary and Conclusions

A comparison of typical analytical sensitivities given in Table 3.2, with typical ranges of concentrations of Hg and MMHg in biological samples and sediments given in Table 3.1, indicate that current analytical methods for the determination of Hg and MMHg in most cases are sensitive enough to achieve a reliable quantification of most solid matrices as long as sufficient mass is available for analysis.

Determination of aqueous Hg and Hg species is a different story. Manufacturers who make CVAFS analytical instruments for aqueous Hg determinations report that instrumental sensitivities of 0.02 to 0.03 ng/L (0.1 to 0.15 pM) can be achieved using small sample volumes (< 50 mL). Assuming that instrument sensitivity is the limiting factor controlling Hg detection, then this level of sensitivity should be sufficient for most freshwater systems, but it is just barely sufficient for open ocean seawater determinations. Total Hg concentrations in open ocean seawater around 0.2 ng/L (1 pM) are often observed, with a few reports of even lower concentrations, in the 0.02-0.04 ng/L (0.1-0.2 pM) range (Laurier et al., 2004; Kotnik et al., 2007; Sunderland et al, 2009). More typically, aqueous total Hg analytical sensitivity will be limited by control of the method blank, which mandates that extremely strict contamination control measures be implemented in order to achieve the sensitivity necessary to study total Hg at ambient levels, and especially so in open ocean seawater.

Aqueous MMHg measurements in seawater are even more challenging given current sensitivity levels. Typical sample volumes used for a MMHg analyses of an aqueous sample is 100-200 mL, which result in detection limits between 0.01 and 0.03 ng/L (50 and 150 fM). This level of sensitivity is sufficient for most freshwater (e.g. Hurley et al., 1995; Dennis et al., 2005; Brigham et al., 2009; Scudder et al., 2009) and estuarine and coastal marine systems (Choe and Gill, 2003; Hammerschmidt and Fitzgerald, 2006; Han et al., 2007), but appear to be insufficient for some oceanic areas where concentrations have been reported to fall below 0.010 ng/L (50 fM) (Mason and Fitzgerald, 1990, 1993; Mason et al., 1998; Cossa et al., 2009; Kotnik et al; 2007).

A common approach to improve analytical sensitivity with mercury determinations is simply to preconcentrate a larger volume of sample prior to analysis. However, this approach will likely also result in sacrifice of sample throughput and use of currently available instrumentation and automation approaches. Without continued improvements in new methodology and enhanced analytical sensitivity for Hg and especially MMHg measurements of aqueous samples, our ability to study biogeochemical processes in some natural waters and particularly open ocean areas will be limited.

Acknowledgments

We would like to acknowledge Dr. Eric Crecelius and Mr. Nicolas Bloom for their pioneering research and analytical methods development that opened the door to understanding speciation, transport, and fate of mercury in the environment.

References

Ahmed, R., K. May, and M. Stoppler. 1987. Ultratrace analysis of mercury and methylmercury in rainwater using cold vapour absorption spectrometry. *Fresenius Zeitschrift Analytische Chemie* 326: 510–516.

Akagi, H., and H. Nishimura. 1991. Speciation of mercury in the environment. In T. Suzuki, I. Nobumassa, and T. W. Clarkson eds. *Advances in mercury toxicology.* New York: Plenum.

Augelli, M. A., R. A. A. Munoz, E. M. Richter, M. I. Cantagallo and L. Angnes. 2007. Analytical procedure for total mercury determination in fishes and shrimps by chronopotentiometric stripping analysis at gold film electrodes after microwave digestion. *Food Chemistry*, 101: 579–584.

Babiarz, C. L., S. R. Hoffman, M. M. Shafer, J. P. Hurley, A. W Andren, and D. E. Armstrong. 2000. A critical evaluation of tangential-flow ultrafiltration for trace metal studies in freshwater systems: 2. Total mercury and methylmercury. *Environmental Science and Technology* 34: 3428–3434.

Babiarz, C. L., J. P. Hurley, S. R. Hoffman, A. A. Andren, H. H. Shater, and D. E. Armstrong. 2001. Partitioning of Total Mercury and methylmercury to the Colloidal Phase in Freshwaters. *Environmental Science and Technology,* vol. 35, pp. 4773–4782.

Baldi, F., and M. Fillipelli. 1991. New method for detecting methylmercury by its enzymatic conversion to methane. *Environmental Science and Technology* 25: 302–305.

Bennun, L., J. Gomez. 1997. Determination of mercury by total reflection x-ray fluorescence using amlgamation with gold. *Spectochim. Acta B.,* 52, 1195–1200.

Biester, H., M. Gosar, and G. Müller. 1999. Mercury speciation in tailings of the Idrija mercury mine. *Journal of Geochemical Exploration* 65: 195–204.

Bjorn, E., T. Larsson, L. Lambertsson, U. Skyllberg, and W. Frech. 2007. Recent advances in mercury speciation analysis with focus on spectrometric methods and enriched stable isotope applications. *Ambio* 36(6): 443–451.

Black, F.J., K.W. Bruland, and A.R. Flegal. 2007. Competing ligand exchange-solid phase extraction method for the determination of the complexation of dissolved inorganic mercury (II) in natural waters. *Analytica Chimica Acta* 598: 318–333.

Bloom, N.S. 1989. Determination of picogram levels of methylmercury by aqueous phase ethylation, followed by cryogenic gas chromatography with cold vapour atomic fluorescence detection. *Canadian Journal of Fisheries and Aquatic Science* 46: 1131–1140.

Bloom, N.S. 1992. On the chemical form of mercury in edible fish and marine invertebrate tissue. *Canadian Journal of Fisheries and Aquatic Sciences* 49: 1010–1017.

Bloom, N.S. 1994. Influence of analytical conditions on the observed "reactive mercury" concentrations in natural freshwaters. In: Watras, C., and Huchabee, J. (Eds.). *Mercury pollution: Integration and synthesis*. Boca Raton, FL: Lewis, pp. 541–552.

Bloom, N.S. 1995. Mercury as a case study of ultra-clean sample handling and storage in aquatic trace metal research. *Environmental Laboratory* 3–4: 20–25.

Bloom, N.S., and E.A. Crecelius. 1983. Determination of mercury in sea water at sub-nanogram per liter levels. *Marine Chemistry* 14: 49–59.

Bloom, N.S. and E.J. von der Geest. 1995. Matrix modification to improve recovery of CH$_3$Hg from clear waters using the acid/chloride distillation procedure. *Water, Air, & Soil Pollution* 80: 1319.

Bloom, N.S., and W.F. Fitzgerald. 1988. Determination of volatile mercury species at the picogram level by low-temperature gas chromatography with cold vapour atomic fluorescence detection. *Analytica Chimica Acta* 208: 151–161.

Bloom, N., J. Colman, and L. Barber. 1997. Artifact formation of methylmercury during aqueous distillation and alternative techniques for the extraction of methylmercury from environmental samples. *Fresenius Journal of Analytical Chemistry* 358: 371–377.

Bloom, N.S., E. Preus, J. Katon, and M. Hiltner. 2003. Selective extractions to assess the biogeochemically relevant fractionation of inorganic mercury in sediments and soils. *Analytica Chimica Acta* 79: 33–248.

Blum, J.D., and B.A. Bergquist. 2007. Reporting of variations in the natural isotopic composition of mercury. *Analytical and Bioanalytical Chemistry* 388: 353–359.

Bonfil, Y., M. Brand and E. Kirowa-Eisner. 2000. Trace determination of mercury by anodic stripping voltammetry at the rotating gold electrode. *Analytica Chimica Acta*, 424 (1): 65–76.

Boudou, A., and F. Ribeyre. 1997. Mercury in the food web: accumulation and transfer mechanisms, in metal ions in biological systems, Vol. 34, Mercury and Its Effects on Environment and Biology, Sigel, A. and Sigel, H., Eds., Marcel Dekker, *New York*, 1997, 289–319.

Brigham, M.E., D.A. Wentz, G.R. Aiken, and D.P. Krabbenhoft. 2009. Mercury cycling in stream ecosystems; 1. Water column chemistry and transport. *Environmental Science & Technology*, 43: 2720–2725.

Buesseler, K.O., J. Bauer, R. Chen, T. Eglinton, O. Gustafsson, W. Landing, K. Mopper, S.B. Moran, P.H. Santschi, R. Vernon-Clark, and R.M. Wells. 1996. An intercomparison of cross-flow filtration techniques used for sampling marine colloids: overview and organic carbon results. *Marine Chemistry* 55: 1–32.

Buffle, J., and G.G. Leppard. 1995. Characterization of aquatic colloids and macromolecules. *Environmental Science and Technology* 29: 2169–2175.

Buffle, L., D. Perret, and M. Newmann. 1992. The use of filtration and ultrafiltration for size fractionation of aquatic particles, colloids and macromolecules. In J. Buffle and H.P. van Leeuwen eds. *Environmental particles*, Col., vol. 1. Boca Raton, FL: Lewis, pp. 171–230.

Bulska, E., H. Emteborg, D.C. Baxter, and W. Frech. 1992. Speciation of mercury in human whole blood by capillary gas chromatography with a microwave-induced plasma emission detector system following complexometric extraction and butylation. *Analyst* 117: 657–665.

Byrne, A.R., and L. Kosta. 1974. Simultaneous neutron activation determination of selenium and mercury in biological samples by volatilization. *Talanta* 211: 1083.

Cai, Y. 2000. Speciation and analysis of mercury, arsenic, and selenium by atomic fuorescence spectrometry. *Trends in Analytical Chemistry* 19 (1): 62–66.

Cairns, W.R.L., M. Ranaldo, R. Hennebelle, C. Turetta, G. Capodaglio, C.F. Ferrari, Aur´elien Dommergue, P. Cescon and C. Barbante. 2008. Speciation analysis of mercury in seawater from the lagoon of Venice by on-line pre-concentration HPLC–ICP-MS. *Analytica Chimica Acta* 622: 62–69.

Carr, R.A., and P.E. Wilkniss. 1973. Mercury: Short-term storage of natural waters. *Environmental Science and Technology* 7(1): 62–63.

Cattani, I., S. Spalla, G.M. Beone, A.A.M. Del Re, R. Boccelli and M. Trevisan. 2008. Characterization of mercury species in soils by HPLC–ICP-MS and measurement of fraction removed by diffusive gradient in thin films. *Talanta* 74: 1520–1526.

Celo, V., R.V. Ananth, S.L. Scott, and D.R.S Lean. 2004. Methylmercury artifact formation during solid-phase extraction of water samples using sulfhydryl cotton fiber adsorbent. *Analytica Chimica Acta* 516: 171–177.

Chang, L.-F., S.-J. Jiang and A.C. Sahayam. 2007. Speciation analysis of mercury and lead in fish samples using liquid chromatography–inductively coupled plasma mass spectrometry. *Journal of Chromatography A* 1176: 143–148.

Chen, J., H. Chen, X. Jin and H. Chen. 2009. Determination of ultra-trace amount methyl-, phenyl- and inorganic mercury in environmental and biological samples by liquid chromatography with inductively coupled plasma mass spectrometry after cloud point extraction preconcentration. *Talanta* 77: 1381–1387.

Chen, K.-J, I-H. Hsu and Y.-C. Sun. 2009. Determination of trace mercury species by high performance liquid chromatography–inductively coupled plasma mass spectrometry after cloud point extraction. *Journal of Chromatography A* 1216: 8933–8938.

Choe K.-Y., and G.A. Gill. 2001. Isolation of colloidal monomethyl mercury in natural waters using cross-flow ultrafiltration techniques. *Marine Chemistry* 76: 305–318.

Choe, K.-Y. and G.A. Gill. 2003. Distributions of particulate, colloidal and dissolved mercury in the San Francisco Bay estuary: 2. Monomethyl mercury. *Limnology and Oceanography* 48(4): 1547–1556.

Choe K.-Y., G.A. Gill, and R. Lehman. 2003. Distribution of particulate, colloidal, and dissolved mercury in San Francisco Bay estuary. 1. Total mercury. *Limnology and Oceanography* 48(4): 1535–1546.

Cizdziel, J.V., T.A. Hinners and E.M. Heithmar. 2002. Determination of total mercury in fish tissues using combustion atomic absorption spectrometry with gold amalgamation. *Water, Air, and Soil Pollution* 135: 355–370.

Clough, R., S. Belt, E.H. Evans, B. Fairman, and T. Catterick. 2003. Investigation of equilibration and uncertainty contributions for the determination of inorganic mercury and methylmercury by isotope dilution inductively coupled plasma mass spectrometry. *Analytica Chimica Acta* 500: 155–170.

Cossa, D., B. Averty, and N. Pirrone. 2009. The origin of methylmercury in open Mediterranean waters. *Limnology and Oceanography* 54: 837–844.

Cossa, D., J.-M. Martin, and J. Sanguine. 1994. Dimethylmercury formation in the Alboran Sea. *Marine Pollution Bulletin* 28: 381–384.

Coyn, R.V., and J. Collins. 1972. Loss of mercury from water during storage. *Analytical Chemistry* 44:1093–1096.

Craig, P.J. 1986. Organometallic compounds in the environment—principles and reactions. London: Longman.

Dams, R., J.A. Robbins, K.A. Rahn, and J.W. Winchester. 1970. Nondestructive neutron activation analysis of air pollution particulates. *Analytical Chemistry* 42(8): 861–867.

Das, H.A., and H.A. van der Sloot. 1976. Sampling problems and the determination of mercury in surface water, seawater, and air. *NBS Special Publication No. 422*, Washington, DC: US Government Printing Office.

de Mora, S.J., J.E. Patterson, and D.M. Bibby. 1995. Baseline atmospheric mercury studies at Ross Island, Antarctica. *Antarctic Science* 7: 323–326.

Demuth, N., and K.G. Heuman. 2001. Validation of methylmercury determinations in aquatic systems by alkyl derivatization methods for GC analysis using ICP-IDMS. *Analytical Chemistry* 73: 4020–4027.

Dennis, I.F., T.A. Clair, C.T. Driscoll, N. Kamman, A. Chalmers, J. Shanley, S.A. Norton, and S. Kahl. 2005. Distribution patterns of mercury in lakes and rivers of northeastern north america. *Ecotoxicology* 14: 113–123.

De Wild, J.F., M.L. Olson, and S.D. Olund. 2002. Determination of methyl mercury by aqueous phase ethylation, followed by gas chromatographic separation with cold vapor atomic fluorescence detection. *U.S. Geological Survey Open-File Report* 01–445, 14p.

dos Santos, J.S., M. de la Guárdia, A. Pastor and M.L.P. dos Santos. 2009. Determination of organic and inorganic mercury species in water and sediment samples by HPLC on-line coupled with ICP-MS. *Talanta* 80: 207–211.

D'Silva, A.P., and V.A. Fassel, 1972. Ultratrace level detection of mercury by an x-ray excited optical fluorescence technique, *Analytical Chemistry* 44: 2115–2116.

Dumarey, R., E. Temmerman, R. Dams, and J. Hoste. 1985. The accuracy of the vapour-injection calibration method for the determination of mercury by amalgamation/cold vapour atomic absorption spectrometry. *Analytica Chimica Acta* 170: 337–340.

EPA. 1993. *Test methods for evaluating solid waste, physical/chemical methods*. EPA SW-846. Cincinnati: USEPA Office of Research and Development Environmental Monitoring Systems Laboratory.

EPA. 1994. *Methods for the determination of metals in environmental samples*. EPA-600/R-94/111. Cincinnati: USEPA Office of Research and Development Environmental Monitoring Systems Laboratory.

EPA. 1996. *Method 1669: Sampling ambient water for trace metals at EPA water quality criteria levels*. EPA-821/R-96/011. Washington, DC: U.S. Environmental Protection Agency Office of Water.

EPA. 1998a. *Method 7473: Mercury in solids and solutions by thermal decomposition amalgamation and atomic absorption spectrophotometry*. EPA SW-846 Cincinnati: USEPA Office of Research and Development Environmental Monitoring Systems Laboratory.

EPA. 1998b. *Method 1630: Methyl mercury in water by distillation, aqueous ethylation, purge and trap, and CVAFS*. EPA-821/R-02/019. Washington, DC: U.S. Environmental Protection Agency Office of Water.

EPA. 2002. *Method 1631 revision e: mercury in water by oxidation, purge and trap, and cold vapor atomic fluorescence spectrometry*. EPA-821/R-02/019. Washington, DC: U.S. Environmental Protection Agency Office of Water.

EPA. 2005. EPA Method 3200-Mercury Species Fractionation and Quantification by Microwave Assisted Extraction, Selective Solvent Extraction and/or Solid Phase Extraction in SW–846: Test Methods for Evaluating Solid Waste, Physical/Chemical Methods.

EPA. 2007. *Method 7471b: Mercury in solid or semisolid waste (manual cold-vapor technique)*. EPA SW-846. Cincinnati: USEPA Office of Research and Development Environmental Monitoring Systems Laboratory.

Falter, R. 1999. Experimental study on the unintentional abiotic methylation of inorganic mercury during analysis: part 1: Localisation of the compounds effecting the abiotic mercury methylation. *Chemosphere* 39(7): 1051–1073.

Fillipelli, M., F. Baldi, F.E. Brinckman, and G.J. Olson. 1992. Methylmercury determination as volatile methylmercury hydride by purge and trap gas chromatography in line with Fourier Transform Infrared Spectroscopy. *Environmental Science and Technology* 25: 1457–1462.

Fitzgerald, W.F. 1999. Clean hands, dirty hands: Clair Patterson and the aquatic biogeochemistry of mercury. In Clean hands: Clair Patterson's crusade against environmental lead contamination. Cliff I. Davison, ed. Commack, NY: Nova Scientific Publishers, Inc., pp. 119–137.

Fitzgerald, W.F., C.H. Lamborg, and C.R. Hammerschmidt. 2007. Marine biogeochemical cycling of mercury. *Chemical Reviews,* 107: 641–662.

Fitzgerald, W.F. and G.A. Gill. 1979. Subnanogram determination of mercury by two-stage gold amalgamation and gas phase detection applied to atmospheric analysis. *Analytical Chemistry* 51: 1714–1720.

Foucher, D., and H. Hintelmann. 2006. High-precision measurement of mercury isotope ratios in sediments using cold-vapor generation multi-collector inductively coupled plasma mass spectrometry. *Analytical and Bioanalytical Chemistry* 384: 1470–1478.

Fukushi K., N.S. Willie, and R.E. Sturgeon. 1993. Subnanogram determination of inorganic and organic mercury by helium-microwave induced plasma-atomic emission spectrometry. *Analytical Letters* 26(2): 325–340.

Gage, J.C. 1961. The trace determination of phenyl- and methylmercury salts in biological material. *Analyst* 86: 457–459.

Gaspar, J.D., G.R. Aiken, and J.N. Ryan. 2007. A critical review of three methods used for the measurement of mercury (Hg^{2+})-dissolved organic matter stability constants. *Applied Geochemistry* 22: 1583–1597.

Giacominoa, A., O. Abollino, M. Malandrinoa and E. Mentasti. 2008. Parameters affecting the determination of mercury by anodic stripping voltammetry using a gold electrode. *Talanta* 75 (1): 266–273.

Gill, G.A. and W.F. Fitzgerald. 1987. Picomolar mercury measurements in sea water and other materials using stannous chloride reduction and two-stage gold amalgamation with gas phase detection. *Marine Chemistry* 20: 227–243.

Gill, G.A. and K.W. Bruland. 1990. Mercury in surface freshwater systems in California and other areas. *Environmental Science and Technology* 24: 1392–1400.

Gnamuš, A., A.R. Byrne, and M. Horvat. 2000. Mercury in the soil-plant-deer-predator food chain of a temperate forest in Slovenia. *Environmental Science and Technology* 34: 3337–3345.

Guentzel, J.L., R.T. Powell, W.M. Landing, and R.P. Mason. 1996. Mercury associated with colloidal material in an estuarine and an open-ocean environment. *Marine Chemistry* 55: 177–188.

Guevara, S., V. Jereb, M. Arribere, S. Perez Catan, and M. Horvat. 2004. The production and use of 197Hg radiotracer to study mercury transformation processes in environmental matrices. *Materials and Geoenvironment* 51: 1928–1931.

Guimaraes, J.R.D., O. Malm, and W.C. Pfeiffer. 1995. A simplified radiochemical technique for measurement of mercury methylation rates in aquatic systems near goldmining areas, Amazon, Brazil. *Science of the Total Environment* 175: 151–162.

Guo, L., and P.H. Santschi. 2007. *Ultrafiltration technique and its applications to sampling and characterization of aquatic colloids*. In K. Wilkinson and J. Lead, eds. *Environmental colloids and particles*. IUPAC Series on Analytical and Physical Chemistry of Environmental Systems. New York: Wiley, pp. 159–221.

Haitzer, M., G.R. Aiken, and J.N. Ryan. 2003. Binding of mercury (II) to aquatic humic substances: influence of pH and source of humic substances. *Environmental Science and Technology* 37: 2436–2441.

Hall, G.E.M. and P. Pelchat. 1997. Evaluation of a direct solid sampling atomic absorption spectrometer for the trace determination of mercury in geological samples. *Analyst* 122: 921–924.

Hammerschmidt, C.R., and W.F. Fitzgerald. 2006. Bioaccumulation and trophic transfer of methylmercury in Long Island Sound. *Archives of Environmental Contamination & Toxicology* 51: 416–424.

Han, S., and G.A. Gill. 2005. Determination of mercury complexation in coastal and estuarine waters using competitive ligand exchange methods. *Environmental Science and Technology* 39: 6607–6615.

Han, S., R.D. Lehman, K.-Y. Choe, and G.A. Gill. 2007. Chemical and physical speciation of mercury in Offatts Bayou: a seasonally anoxic bayou in Galveston Bay. *Limnology and Oceanography* 52: 1380–1392.

Hempel, M., H. Hintelman, and R.-D. Wilken. 1992. Determination of organic mercury species in soils by high-performance liquid chromatography with ultraviolet detection. *Analyst* 117: 669–674.

Heraldsson, C., S. Westerlund, and P. Öhman. 1989. Determination of mercury in natural samples in the sub-nanogram level using inductively coupled plasma/mass spectrometry after reduction to elemental mercury. *Analytica Chimica Acta* 221: 77–84.

Hight, S.C. and J. Cheng. 2006. Determination of methylmercury and estimation of total mercury in seafood using high performance liquid chromatography (HPLC) and inductively coupled plasma-mass spectrometry (ICP-MS): method development and validation. *Analytica Chimica Acta* 567: 160–172.

Hines, M.E., M. Horvat, J. Faganeli, J.C.J Bonzongo, T. Barkay, E.B. Major, K.J. Scott, E.A. Bailey, J.J. Warwick, and W.B. Lyons. 2000. Mercury biogeochemistry in the Idrija River, Slovenia, from above the mine into the Gulf of Trieste. *Environmental Research* 83: 129–139.

Hintelmann, H. 1999. Comparison of different extraction techniques used for methylmercury analysis with respect to accidental formation of methylmercury during sample preparation. *Chemosphere* 39: 1093–1105.

Hintelmann, H., and S.Y. Lu. 2003. High precision isotope ratio measurements of mercury isotopes in cinnabar ores using multi-collector inductively coupled plasma mass spectrometry. *Analyst* 128: 635–639.

Hintelmann, H., and N. Ogrinc. 2003. Determination of stable mercury isotopes by ICP-MS and their application in environmental studies. In *Biogeochemistry of environmentally important trace elements*, ACS Symposium Series 835, Y. Cai, O.C. Braids eds. *The American Chemical Society*, Washington, DC, pp. 321–338.

Hintelmann, H., and R.-D. Wilken. 1993. The analysis of organic mercury compounds using liquid chromatography with on-line atomic fluorescence spectrometric detection. *Applied Organometallic Chemistry* 7: 173–180.

Hirner, A.V., J. Feldmann, E. Krupp, R. Grumping, R. Guguel and W.R. Cullen. 1998. Metal(loid)organic compounds and geothermal gases and waters. *Organic Geochemistry* 29(5–7): 1765–1778.

Honeyman, B.D. and P.H. Santschi. 1988. Metals in aquatic systems. *Environmental Science and Technology* 22 (8): 862–871.

Horvat, M. 1996. Mercury analysis and speciation in environmental samples. In Global and Regional Mercury Cycles: Sources, Fluxes and Mass Balances. Proceedings of the NATO Advanced Research Workshop on Regional and

Global Mercury Cycles: Sources, Fluxes and Mass Balances, Novosibirsk, Russia, July 10–14, 1995. NATO Science Partnership Sub-Series: 2:, Vol. 21. Baeyens, W.; Ebinghaus, Ralf; Vasiliev, Oleg eds., Dordrecht, The Netherlands: Kluwer Academic Publishers, 588 pages.

Horvat, M. 2005. *Determination of mercury and its compounds in water, sediment, soil, and biological samples.* In Dynamics of mercury pollution on regional and global scales: exposures around the world. N. Pirrone, K. Mahaffey eds. New York: Springer Science + Business Media.

Horvat, M., and A.R. Byrne. 1992. Preliminary study of the effects of some physical parameters on the stability of methylmercury in biological samples. *Analyst* 117: 665–668.

Horvat, M., and W.H. Schroeder. 1995. Mercury (a) determination of organomercurials. In *Encyclopedia of analytical science.* London: Harcourt Brace.

Horvat, M., L. Liang, and N.S. Bloom. 1993. Comparison of distillation with other current isolation methods for the determination of methylmercury compounds in low level environmental samples Part I. Sediments. *Analytica Chimica Acta* 281: 135–152.

Horvat, M., J. Kotnik, M. Logar, V. Fajon, T. Zvonaric, and N. Pirrone. 2003. Speciation of mercury in surface and deep sea waters in the Mediterranean sea. *Atmospheric Environment* 37: 93–108.

Horvat, M., M. Logar, N. Ogrinc, V. Fajon, S. Lojen, H. Akagi, T. Ando, T. Tomiyasu, and A. Matsuyama. 2004. The effect of sampling and sample pretreatment on MeHg concentration in coastal marine sediments. *Materials and Geoenvironment* 51: 1939–1943.

Horvat, M., V. Mandic, L. Liang, N.S. Bloom, S. Padberg, Y.-H. Lee, H. Hintelmann, and J. Benoit. 1994. Certification of methylmercury compounds concentration in marine sediment reference material, IAEA-356. *Applied Organometallic Chemistry* 8: 533–540.

Horvat, M., K. May, M. Stoeppler, and A.R Byrne. 1988. Comparative studies of methylmercury determination in biological and environmental samples. *Applied Organometallic Chemistry* 2: 515–524.

Hsu, H., and D.L. Sedlak. 2003. Strong Hg(II) complexation in municipal wastewater effluent and surface waters. *Environmental Science and Technology* 37: 2743–2749.

Hurley, J.P., Benoit, J.M., Shafer, M.M., Andren, A.W., Sullivan, J.R., Hammond, R., and Webb, D.A. 1995. Influences of watershed characteristics on mercury levels in Wisconsin rivers. *Environmental Science and Technology* 29 (7): 1867–1875.

Issaro, N., C. Abi-Ghanem and A. Bermond. 2009. Fractionation studies of mercury in soils and sediments: a review of the chemical reagents used for mercury extraction. *Analytica Chimica Acta* 631: 1–12.

Iverfeldt, Å. 1988. Mercury in the Norwegian fjord Framvaren. *Marine Chemistry* 23: 441–445.

Jaćimović, R., and M. Horvat. 2004. Determination of total mercury in environmental and biological samples using k0-INAA, RNAA and CVAAS/AFS techniques: advantages and disadvantages. *Journal of Radioanalytical and Nuclear Chemistry* 259: 385–390.

Jones, R., M.F. Jacobson, R. Jaffe, A.C. West-Thomas, and A. Alli. 1995. Method development and sample processing of water, soil, and tissue for the analyses of total and organic mercury by CV AFS. *Water, Air, and Soil Pollution* 80(1–4): 1285–1294.

Kim, C.S., J.J., Rytuba, and G.E. Brown, Jr. 2004. EXAFS study of mercury(II) sorption to Fe- and Al-(hydr)oxides: I. Effects of pH. *J. Journal of Colloid and Interface Science* 27, 1–15.

Kocman, D., M. Horvat, and J. Kotnik. 2004. Mercury fractionation in contaminated soils of the Idrija mercury mine region. *Journal of Environmental Monitoring* 8: 696–703.

Kosta, L., and A.R. Byrne. 1969. Activation analyses for mercury in biological samples at nanogram levels. *Talanta* 16: 1297.

Kotnik, J., M. Horvat, E. Tessier, N. Ogrinc, M. Monperrus, D. Amouroux, V. Fajon, D. Gibičar, S. Žižek, F. Sprovieri and N. Pirrone. 2007. Mercury speciation in surface and deep waters of the Mediterranean Sea. *Marine Chemistry* 107: 13–30.

Kvietkus, K., J. Sakalys, and K. Sopauskas. 1983. The application of the atomic fluorescence method for determining mercury concentrations by a photon counter. *Atmospheric Physics* 8: 127–135.

LaFleur, P.D. 1973. Retention of mercury when freeze-drying biological materials. *Analytical Chemistry* 45: 1534–1536.

Lamborg, C.H., C.-M. Tseng, W.F. Fitzgerald, P.H. Balcom, and C.R. Hammerschmidt. 2003. Determination of the mercury complexation characteristics of dissolved organic matter in natural waters with "reducible Hg" titrations. *Environmental Science and Technology* 37: 3316–3322.

Lamborg, C.H., O. Yiğiterhan, W.F. Fitzgerald, P.H. Balcom, C.R. Hammerschmidt and J. Murray. 2008. Vertical distribution of mercury species at two sites in the Western Black Sea. *Marine Chemistry* 111: 77–89.

Landing, W.M., J.L. Guentzel, J.J. Perry, Jr., G.A. Gill, and C.D. Pollman. 1998. Methods for measuring mercury and other trace species in rainfall and aerosols in Florida. *Atmospheric Environment* 32: 909–918.

Lansens, P., C. Meuleman, and W. Baeyens. 1990. Long-term stability of methylmercury standard solutions in distilled, deionized water. *Analytica Chimica Acta* 229: 281–285.

Laurier, F.J.G., R.P. Mason, G.A. Gill, and L. Whalin. 2004. Mercury distributions in the North Pacific Ocean – 20 years of observations. *Marine Chemistry* 90: 3–19.

Lee, Y.H., and J. Mowrer. 1989. Determination of methylmercury in natural waters at sub-nanogram per liter level by capillary gas chromatography after adsorbent preconcentration. *Analytica Chimica Acta* 221: 259–264.

Leermakers, M., P. Lansens and W. Baeyens. 1990. Storage and stability of inorganic and methylmercury solutions. *Fresenius' Journal of Analytical Chemistry.* 336 (8): 655–662.

Liang L. and N.S. Bloom. 1993. Determination of total mercury by single-stage gold amalgamation with cold vapour atomic spectrometric detection. *Journal of Analytical Atomic Spectrometry* 8: 591–594.

Liang, L., N. Bloom, and M. Horvat. 1994. Simultaneous determination of mercury speciation in biological materials by GC/CVAFS after ethylation and room temperature precollection. *Clinical Chemistry* 40: 602–607.

Lo, J., and C. Wai. 1975. Mercury loss from water during storage: Mechanisms and preservation. *Analytical Chemistry* 47: 1869–1871.

Logar, M., M. Horvat, N. Horvat, M. Benedik, A. Marn-Pirnat, R. Ponikvar, and J. Osredkar. 2004. Determination of ethyl mercury and methylmercury in blood samples. *Materials and Geoenvironment* 51: 1976–1978.

Lowery, T. A., R. S. Winters and E. S. Garrett. 2007. Comparison of total mercury determinations of fish fillet homogenates by thermal decomposition, amalgamation, and atomic absorption spectrophotometry versus cold vapor atomic absorption spectrophotometry. *Journal of Aquatic Food Product Technology* 16 (2): 5–15.

Lytle, Charles, J. Dahl, E. Farkas, and J. Wilson. 2007. *Analysis of mercury in wastewater by microwave digestion followed by ICP-MS: Comparison to EPA Methods at 40 CFR 136.3.* Alexandria, VA: Water Environment Federation.

Magos, L. 1971. Selective atomic-absorption determination of inorganic mercury and methylmercury in undigested biological samples. *Analyst* 96: 847–852.

Margetínová, J., P. Houserová-Pelcová and V. Kubán. 2008. Speciation analysis of mercury in sediments, zoobenthos and river water samples by high-performance liquid chromatography hyphenated to atomic fluorescence spectrometry following preconcentration by solid phase extraction. *Analytical Chimica Acta* 615: 115–123.

Mason, R. P., and W. F. Fitzgerald. 1990. Alkylmercury species in the equatorial Pacific. *Nature* 347: 457–459.

Mason, R. P., and W. F. Fitzgerald. 1993. The distribution and cycling of mercury in the equatorial Pacific Ocean. *Deep Sea Res.*, Part I, 40(9): 1897–1924.

Mason, R. P., K. Rolfhus, and W. F. Fitzgerald. 1998. Mercury in the North Atlantic. *Marine Chemistry* 61: 37–53.

Mauro, J. B. N., Guimaraes, J. R. D., Hintelman, H., Watras, C. J., Haack, E. A., Coelho, and S. A.-Souza. 2002. Mercury methylation in mycrophytes, periphyton, and water—comparative studies with stable and radio-mercury additions. *Analytical and Bioanalytical Chemistry* 374, 983–989.

May, K., M. Stoeppler, and K. Reisinger. 1987. Studies in the ratio total mercury/methylmercury in the aquatic food chain. *Toxicological and Environmental Chemistry* 13: 153–159.

Meuleman, C., C. C. Laino, P. Lansens, and W. Baeyens. 1993. A study of the behaviour of methylmercury compounds in aqueous solutions, and of gas/liquid distribution coefficients, using had space analysis. *Water Research* 1431–1446.

Miller, L. A., and K. W. Bruland. 1997. Competitive equilibration techniques for determining transition metal speciation in natural waters: Evaluation using model data. *Analytica Chimica Acta* 343: 161–181.

Miller, L. A., and K. W. Bruland. 1994. Determination of copper speciation in marine waters by competitive ligand equilibration/liquid–liquid extraction: an evaluation of the technique. *Analytica Chimica Acta* 284: 573–586.

Minagawa, K., Y. Takizawa, and I. Kifune. 1979. Determination of very low levels of inorganic and organic mercury in natural waters by CV AAS after preconcentration on a chelating resin. *Analytica Chimica Acta* 115: 103–110.

Moffett, J. W., and R. G. Zika. 1987. Solvent extraction of copper acetylacetonate in studies of copper(II) speciation in seawater. *Marine Chemistry* 21: 301–313.

Monperrus, M., E. Krupp, D. Amouroux, O. F. X. Donard, and R. C. Rodríguez Martín-Doimeadios. 2004. Potential and limits of speciated isotope-dilution analysis for metrology and assessing environmental reactivity. *Trends in Analytical Chemistry* 23: 261–272.

NOAA. 1997. Technical Memorandum NOS ORCA 130: Sampling and Analytical Methods of the National Status and Trends Program Mussel Watch Project: 1993–1996 Update. G.G. Lauenstein and A.Y. Cantillo, Eds.

Olson, M. L., L. B., Cleckner, S. A., King, J. P., Hurley, and D. P., Krabbenhoft. 1997. Resolution of matrix effects on analysis of total and methyl mercury in aqueous samples from the Florida Everglades: *Fresenius Journal of Analytical Chemistry* 358: 392–396.

O'Reilly, J. E. 1982. Gas chromatographic determination of methyl and ethyl mercury: "passivation" of the chromatographic column. *Journal of Chromatography* 238: 433.

Oremland, R. S., C. W. Culbertons, and M. R. Winfrey. 1991. Methylmercury decomposition in sediments and bacterial cultures. Involvement of methanogens and sulfate reducers in oxidative demethylation. *Applied Environmental Microbiolology* 57: 130–137.

Padberg, S., and M. Stoeppler. 1991. *Studies of transport and turnover of mercury and methylmercury.* In Metal Compounds in Environment and Life (Interrelation between Chemistry and Biology); 4: 329–340.

Palmer, C. D., M. E. Lewis, C. M. Geraghty, F. Barbosa, and P. Parsons. 2006. Determination of lead, cadmium and mercury in blood for assessment of environmental exposure: a comparison between inductively coupled plasma-mass spectrometry and atomic absorption spectrometry. *Spectrochimica Acta Part B* 61: 980–990.

Parker, J. L., and N. S. Bloom. 2004. Preservation and storage techniques for low-level aqueous mercury speciation. *Science of the Total Environment* 337: 253–263.

Parker, J. L., and N. S. Bloom. 2005. Preservation and storage techniques for low-level aqueous mercury speciation. *Science of the Total Environment* 337: 253–263.

Patterson, J. E. 1984. A differential photoacoustic mercury detector. *Analytica Chimica Acta* 164: 119–126.

Pirrone, N., and K. Mahaffey eds. 2005. *Dynamics of mercury pollution on regional and global scales: exposures around the world.* New York: Springer Science + Business Media.

Rapsomanikis, S., and P. J. Craig. 1991. Speciation of mercury and methylmercury compounds in aqueous samples by chromatography—AAS after ethylation with sodium tetraethylborate. *Analytica Chimica Acta* 248: 563–567.

Ravichandran, M., G. R. Aiken, M. M. Reddy, and J. Ryan. 1998. Enhanced dissolution of cinnabar (mercuric sulfide) by dissolved organic matter isolated from the Florida Everglades. *Environmental Science and Technology* 32: 3305–3311.

Ravichandran, M., G. R. Aiken, J. N. Ryan, and M. M. Reddy. 1999. Inhibition of precipitation and aggregation of metacinnabar (mercuric sulfide) by dissolved organic matter isolated from the Florida Everglades. *Environmental Science and Technology* 33: 1418–1423.

Rue, E. L., and K. W. Bruland. 1995. Complexation of iron(III) by natural organic ligands in the Central North Pacific as determined by a new competitive ligand equilibration/ adsorptive cathodic stripping voltammetric method. *Marine Chemistry* 50(1–4): 117–138.

Santoyo, M. M., J. A. L. Figueroa, and K. Wrobel. 2009. Analytical speciation of mercury in fish tissues by reversed phase liquid chromatography–inductively coupled plasma mass spectrometry with Bi^{3+} as internal standard. *Talanta* 79: 706–711.

Santschi, P. H., K. A. Roberts, and L. Guo. 2002. The organic nature of colloidal actinides transported in surface water environments. *Environmental Science and Technology* 36: 3711–3719.

Scudder, B. C., L. C. Chasar, D. A. Wentz, N. J. Bauch, M. E. Brigham, P. W. Moran and D. P. Krabbenhoft. 2009. Mercury in fish, bed sediment, and water from streams across the United States, 1998–2005: U.S. Geological Survey Scientific Investigations Report 2009–5109, p. 74.

Shade, C. W. 2008. Automated simultaneous analysis of and mercuric Hg in biotic samples by Hg-thiourea complex liquid chromatography following acidic thiourea leaching. *Environmental Science and Technology* 42, 6604–6610.

Shimojo, N., S. Homma-Takeda, K., Ohuchi, M., Shinyashiki, GF, Sun, and Y. Kumagai. 1997. Mercury dynamics in hair of rats exposed to methylmercury by synchrotron radiation x-ray fluorescence imaging. *Life Science* 60, 2129–2137.

Sigleo, A. C., and J. C. Means. 1990. Organic and inorganic components in estuarine colloids: implications for sorption and transport of pollutants. *Reviews of Environmental Contamination and Toxicology* 112: 123–147.

Simon, M. and G. Wuhl-Couturier. 2002. *Mercury.* In F. Bohnet ed. *Ullmann's encyclopedia of industrial chemistry,* 6th completely revised edition. Weinheim, Germany: Wiley-VCH.

Sipos, L., H. W. Nurnberg, P. Valenta, and M. Branica. 1980. The reliable determination of mercury tracers in sea water by subtractive differential pulse voltammetry at the twin gold electrodes. *Analytica Chimica Acta* 115: 25–42.

Slaets, S., and F. C. Adams. 2000. Determination of organomercury compounds with a miniaturised automated speciation analyzer. *Analytica Chimica Acta* 414: 141–149.

Snell, J. P., E. Bjorn, and W. Frech. 2000. Investigation of errors introduced by the species distribution of mercury in organic solutions on total mercury determination by electro vaporization-inductively coupled plasma mass spectrometry. *Journal of Analytical Atomic Spectrometry* 15: 397–402.

Snell, J. P., C. R. Quetel, L. Lambertsson, and J. Qvarnstrom. 2004. A new 202 Hg isotopically enriched methylmercury spike material with SI-traceable reference values for isotope dilution measurements in biological and environmental samples. *Materials and Geoenvironment* 51: 2026–2029.

Stoichev, T., R. C. Rodriguez Martin-Doimeadios, E. Tessier, D. Amouroux, and Q. F. X. Donard. 2004. Improvement of analytical performance of mercury speciation by on-line derivatization, cryofocussing and atomic fluorescence. *Talanta* 62: 433–438.

Stordal, M. C., G. A Gill, L.-S. Wen, and P. H. Santschi. 1996. Mercury phase speciation in the surface waters of three Texas estuaries: importance of colloidal forms. *Limnology and Oceanography* 41(1): 52–61.

Stordal, M. C., P. H. Santschi, and G. A. Gill. 1996. Colloidal pumping: evidence for the coagulation using colloids tagged with 203-Hg. *Environmental Science and Technology* 30: 3335–3340.

Sunderland, E. M., D. P. Krabbenhoft, J. M. Moreau, S. A. Strode, and W. M. Landing. 2009. Mercury sources, distribution, and bioavailability in the North Pacific Ocean: insights from data and models. *Global Biogeochemical Cycles* 23, GB2010, doi:10.1029/2008GB003425.

Švarc-Gajić, J., Z. Stojanović, Z. Suturović, N. Marjanović and S. Kravić. 2009. Direct mercury determination in natural waters by chronopotentiometric stripping analysis in macroelectrode process vessel. *Desalination* 249: 253–259.

Templeton, D. M., F. Ariese, R. Cornelis, L.-G. Danielsson, H. Muntau, H. P. van Leeuwen, and R. Lobinski. 2000. IUPAC Guidelines for Terms Related to Speciation of Trace Elements. *Pure and Applied Chemistry* 72/8: 1453–1470.

Tseng, C. M., A. de Diego, H. Pinaly, D. Amoroux and O. F. X Donard. 2000. Field cryofocussing hydride generation applied to the simultaneous multi-elemental determination of alkyl-metal(loid) species in natural waters using ICP-MS detection. *Journal of Environmental Monitoring* 2: 603–612.

Turyan, I., and D. Mandler. 1994. Electrochemical determination of ultralow levels ($<10^{-12}$ M) of mercury by anodic stripping voltammetry using a chemically modified electrode. *Electroanalysis* 6:838–843.

UNEP/WHO/IAEA. 1987. The determination of methylmercury, total mercury and total selenium in human hair. In: *Reference methods for marine pollution studies,* no. 46. Geneva, Switzerland: United Nations Environment Programme.

Uthe, J. F., J. Solomon, and B. Grift. 1972. A rapid semi-micro method for the determination of methylmercury in fish tissue. *Journal of the Association of Official Analytical Chemists* 55: 583–594.

Vandal, G. M., R. P. Mason, D. McKnight, and W. Fitzgerald. 1998. Mercury speciation and distribution in a polar desert lake (Lake Hoare, Antarctica) and two glacial meltwater streams. *Science of the Total Environment* 213: 229–237.

van den Berg, C. M. G. 1984. Determination of the complexing capacity and conditional stability constants of complexes of copper(II) with natural organic ligands in seawater by cathodic stripping voltammetry of copper-catechol complex ions. *Marine Chemistry* 15: 1–18.

Weber, J., R. Evans, S. H. Jones, and M. E. Hines. 1998. Conversion of mercury(II) into mercury(0), monomethylmercury cation, and dimethylmercury in saltmarsh sediment slurries. *Chemosphere* 6: 1669–1687.

Wells, M. L., P. B. Kozelka, and K. W. Bruland. 1998. The complexation of "dissolved" Cu, Zn, Cd and Pb by solute and colloidal organic matter in Narragansett Bay, RI. *Marine Chemistry* 62: 203–217.

Wen L.-S., M. C. Stordal, D. Tang, G. A. Gill, and P. H. Santschi. 1996. An ultraclean cross-flow ultrafiltration technique for the study of trace metal phase speciation in seawater. *Marine Chemistry* 55: 129–152.

Westöö, G. 1966. Determination of methylmercury compounds in foodstuffs I. Methylmercury compounds in fish, identification and determination. *Acta Chemica Scandinavica* 20: 2131–2137.

Wiener, J. G., D. P. Krabbenhoft, G. H. Heinz, and A. M. Scheuhammer. 2003. Ecotoxicology of mercury. In Hoffman, D. J., Rattner, B. A., Burton Jr., G. A., Cairns Jr. eds. Handbook of Ecotoxicology. Boca Raton, FL: Lewis Publishers, pp. 409–463.

Wu, Q., S. C. Apte, G. E. Batley, and K. C. Bowles. 1997. Determination of the mercury complexing capacity of natural waters by anodic stripping voltammetry. *Analytica Chimica Acta* 350: 129–134.

Yaneda, S., and K. T. Suzuki. 1997. Equimolar Hg-Se complex binds to selenoprotein. *Biochemical and Biophysical Research Communications* 231: 7–11.

Zarnegar, P., and P. Mushak. 1974. Quantitative measurements of inorganic mercury and organomercurials in water and biological media by gas liquid chromatography. *Analytica Chimica Acta* 69: 389–407.

Zelenko, V., and L. Kosta. 1973. A new method for the isolation of methylmercury from biological tissues and its determination at the parts-per-million level by gas chromatography. *Talanta* 20: 115–123.

CHAPTER 4

Use of Stable Isotopes in Mercury Research

HOLGER HINTELMANN

Mercury, with an average atomic weight of 200.59 ± 0.02, has seven stable isotopes and numerous radioactive isotopes. The representative abundance percentages (De Laeter et al., 2003) of the individual isotopes are ^{196}Hg (0.15 ± 0.01), ^{198}Hg (9.97 ± 0.20), ^{199}Hg (16.87 ± 0.22), ^{200}Hg (23.10 ± 0.19), ^{201}Hg (13.18 ± 0.09), ^{202}Hg (29.86 ± 0.26), and ^{204}Hg (6.87 ± 0.15). The provided uncertainties are rather large, presumably caused either by measurement uncertainties or as a result of actual variations in natural isotope abundance. All radiogenic Hg isotopes, including ^{197}Hg ($t_{1/2} = 64.14$ hours) and ^{203}Hg ($t_{1/2} = 46.612$ days) (Korea Atomic Energy Research Institute, 2000), do not occur naturally, and are not subject of this chapter.

A Brief History of Mercury Isotope Ratio Measurements

The measurement of isotope fractionation was originally established for studying biogeochemical pathways of light elements (H, C, N, O, and S). More recently, this concept was extended to almost the entire periodic table and applied to many fields, including geology and environmental, planetary, and earth sciences. Mercury is one of the heaviest stable elements and has an intriguing isotope system. Its chemical–physical properties, a relatively large mass range ($m/z = 196–204$), high elemental volatility, multiple redox states, and the ability to form covalent bonds provide many opportunities to fractionate isotopes. Unlike lead, there is no radiogenic source of Hg, and any isotopic variation would clearly be the result of fractionation processes. Early investigations deliberately generated rather large Hg isotope fractionations in laboratory experiments (Brönsted and von Hevesy, 1920). However, analytical limitations hampered progress in observing naturally occurring smaller deviations (Nier, 1950). First reports regarding natural variations were obtained by gas-source isotope ratio mass spectrometry (Nier and Schlutter, 1986; Obolenskii and Doilnitsyn, 1976). They were later viewed with some skepticism (Koval et al., 1977; Nier and Schlutter, 1986) because the achievable analytical precision with this method was less than 20‰, and observed variations were typically within this range as well. Instrumental neutron activation analysis (INAA) provided results on Hg isotope ratio variations in extraterrestrial materials (Lauretta et al., 2001). However, INAA is applicable only to measure ^{196}Hg and ^{202}Hg, which complicated data confirmation. In fact, the values were later called into question by high-precision mass spectrometry (MS) measurements (De Laeter et al., 2003; Lauretta et al., 2001).

Measurement of Mercury Isotopes by Mass Spectrometry

Technological advances in MS technology have led to substantial improvements in the precision of Hg isotope ratio measurements. Inductively coupled plasma–time-of-flight–mass spectrometry (ICP-ToF-MS) offers simultaneous detection of multiple isotopes using a detector array. Reaction and collision cell techniques dramatically improved sensitivity and precision through the reduction of the ion energy spread, and magnetic-sector instruments generate flat-topped peaks, which are desirable for precise isotope ratio determinations. However, each of these technologies has also some inherent disadvantages for very precise isotope ratio determinations. While ICP-ToF-MS suffers from low sensitivity, the other technologies are restricted to having a single detector, which necessitates the measurement of multiple isotopes sequentially in time. Effects such as plasma noise or minute variations in sample uptake and transmission quickly compounded uncertainties. Ultimately, a multidetector arrangement following the MS separation of isotopes is required to obtain the necessary precision. Thermal ionization mass spectrometry (TIMS) is a technique widely applied to determine very precise isotope ratios. Unfortunately, the high ionization potential of mercury makes TIMS unsuitable for measuring this element.

Only mating multicollector MS with the inductively coupled plasma (ICP) ionization source greatly improved the precision of isotope ratio measurements for heavy elements in general and Hg in particular. A comparison of typical precisions obtained by the various MS techniques is presented in Table 4.1. To be consistent with the nomenclature in this chapter relative standard deviations (RSDs) are given in‰. Clearly, multicollector-ICP/MS (MC-ICP/MS) offers precision that is at least one order of magnitude better than the other instruments. This power is required, since natural variations are too small to be resolved by single collector instruments, and today, Hg isotope fractionation studies are conducted exclusively using MC-ICP/MS.

Sample Introduction

Similar to the quantitative determination of Hg in environmental samples, Hg isotope ratio measurements also require

TABLE 4.1

Typical Precision of Mercury Isotope Ratio Measurements Using Different ICP/MS Systems

Instrument	RSD (‰)
Magnetic-sector high resolution	1.7
Time of flight	0.8
Collision cell	2.8
Multicollector	0.020

unique solutions to address and overcome element-specific challenges in sample preparation and sample introduction. As with conventional ICP/MS analysis (Hintelmann and Ogrinc, 2003), introduction of the Hg analyte into the MC-ICP/MS requires careful consideration. First and foremost, the analytical strategy must take into account the minimum mass of Hg required for highly precise isotope ratio measurements. Based on the experience in my laboratory, it is desirable to have at least 10 ng of Hg available for the measurement. This is in stark contrast to the picogram or even femtogram detection limits achievable nowadays with the most sensitive equipment used for quantitative measurements. It should be stressed that the absolute sensitivity of the MC-ICP/MS is on a par with, if not better than, the most sensitive atomic fluorescence spectrometers (AFS) or single collector ICP/MS. However, sensitive ion-counting detectors typically found in single detector ICP/MS instruments, and now also available for MC-ICP/MS, are not suitable for ultraprecise isotope ratio measurements, and less sensitive, but more precise, Faraday detectors must be used instead. Second, the counting statistic theory predicts that the precision of isotope ratio measurements improves with increasing signal strength. Therefore, nanogram quantities of Hg must reach the ICP source to obtain a precision that is sufficient to distinguish natural isotope abundance variations.

Gold Trap Amalgamation and Preconcentration

Gold trap amalgamation is a convenient preconcentration method that is widely used for quantitative Hg determinations and relatively easy to interface with ICP/MS (Hintelmann and Ogrinc, 2003; Schauble, 2007). In principle, this technique offers several advantages: (a) When used in combination with a cold vapor generation system, there is theoretically no limit to the amount of sample and analyte mass that could be processed. Hence, in principle, even background air and aqueous samples with low Hg concentrations could be analyzed, but they would require reducing, purging, and trapping Hg from up to several liters of water or several cubic meters of air. (b) When used in combination with a sample combustion system (Biswas et al., 2008; Evans et al., 2001; Xie et al., 2005) the use of any chemical reagents required for wet digestions is avoided, reducing the risk of sample contamination. (c) For certain samples, such as Hg in air, it is probably the only realistic approach for sample collection and analysis. However, MC-ICP/MS instruments are optimized for acquiring steady and continuous signals, which vary only little in intensity for the duration of the measurement. The signal resulting from heating up a gold trap, on the other hand, is transient in nature—that is, the signal intensity changes continuously with time. Frequently, changes in Hg isotope ratios during peak evolution were observed during the measurement (Evans et al., 2001). In addition, it is not possible to determine the internal precision of the measurement for an individual sample. Evaluation of transient signals is further complicated by low signal intensities on both tails of the peak, which leads to large variations in ratios during the leading and trailing portions of the signal. Eventually, the authors decided to calculate intensity-weighted isotope ratios and achieved a precision of ±0.5‰ RSD (n = 4–6), which was deemed insufficient to detect isotope ratio variations among coal samples. Subsequent modifications aimed at extending and flattening the peak improved the precision and accuracy of the method and succeeded in improving the precision of the isotope ratio measurement to better than 0.1‰ (Xie et al., 2005).

Direct Injection of Gaseous Elemental Mercury

One technique collects Hg(0) vapor, which is thermodesorbed from gold, in the barrel of a gas-tight glass syringe for temporal storage (Sonke et al., 2008). The syringe is then connected to the nebulizer gas stream of the MC-ICP/MS. Using a syringe pump, the Hg(0) is slowly injected at a continuous rate, generating a steady Hg signal. Depending on the Hg concentration in the syringe, the rate of injection can be varied between 0.1 and 20 mL/min to optimize the Hg signal. This technique provided a precision of 0.24‰ (±2 SD) for δ^{202}Hg.

Continuous-Flow Cold-Vapor Generation

The need to generate a steady signal for data acquisition has established continuous-flow cold-vapor generation as the method of choice for sample introduction (Foucher and Hintelmann, 2006; Hintelmann and Lu, 2003; Klaue and Blum, 1999, 2000). Typically, the acidic sample is continuously mixed with a reducing solution using peristaltic pumps and Ar gas is introduced into a gas–liquid separator. The gaseous Hg(0) is stripped from solution and transported to the ICP. Usually, stannous chloride is used as the reductant, but also borohydride has been evaluated (Hintelmann and Lu, 2003).

Ideally, the Hg concentration in the sample solution is between 2 and 30 ng/mL. At sample uptake rates of approximately 1 mL/min, up to 10 minutes of data acquisition are required to introduce sufficient Hg for a precise measurement. The memory effects associated with Hg measurements are well documented (Hintelmann, 2003). Therefore, thorough rinsing of the cold-vapor system is

necessary before the next sample (or standard) can be analyzed. Washing out the entire system with a dilute solution of nitric acid (delivered through the sample line) for a few minutes or until the Hg signal drops to approximately 1% of the intensity of measured samples is normally required.

It should be noted that the most straightforward approach of directly nebulizing an acidic sample solution is not advisable. The sensitivity of such sample introduction is inferior, dropping the limit of detection (LOD) by at least a factor of 10–100. Even more disconcerting are the severe memory effects expected when introducing high concentrations of ionic Hg into conventional spray chambers. Nevertheless, a precision of ±0.08‰ is achievable, when introducing an acidic Hg solution by means of a tandem quartz spray chamber arrangement with a perfluoroalkoxy (PFA) nebulizer. As much as 250 ng/mL of Hg was required for the measurement, though (Malinovsky et al., 2008).

Gas Chromatography

The next frontier in Hg isotope ratio measurements is the determination of compound specific isotope ratios, specifically for methylmercury (MMHg). This requires either an offline isolation of MMHg from the sample or a chromatographic separation of Hg species, which is directly interfaced with the MC-ICP/MS. Offline separation techniques must recover 100% of the MMHg in the sample (to avoid fractionation during sample processing) and remove divalent mercury [Hg(II)] quantitatively at the same time. On the other hand, direct coupling of gas chromatography (GC) to ICP/MS is a standard technology used routinely for quantitative mercury speciation, and numerous suitable sample-processing schemes exist for measuring MMHg by GC-ICP/MS (this book, chapter 5). However, this technique again generates transient signals (chromatographic peaks), which are difficult to process for precise isotope ratio determinations. To make matters worse, isotope ratios change continuously while the peak eluted from a packed GC column (Dzurko et al., 2009). This apparent fractionation was not caused by fractionation of MMHg on the column, but instead relates to the amplifier–detector arrangement. By carefully optimizing the peak integration and isotope ratio calculation algorithm, the authors achieved a precision of 0.16‰ RSD (n = 8) for the ^{202}Hg:^{198}Hg ratio of MMHg and 0.18‰ RSD for the same ratio of inorganic Hg. Drifting isotope ratios during peak elution were also observed when using a capillary GC column interfaced to MC-ICP/MS (Krupp and Donard, 2005). The authors provided a thorough analysis of potential sources for this behavior, including drift in mass bias, chromatographic fractionation, drift in background signal, and influence of analyte concentration, but were unable to find a satisfactory explanation. The lower sample-loading capacity of the capillary GC technique allowed a maximum injection of only 500 pg of Hg per measurement, resulting in an isotope ratio precision of only ~0.5‰ RSD for MMHg standards (Epov et al., 2008).

Sample Preconcentration Strategies

Clearly, environmental samples with low Hg concentrations are still a challenge for measuring precise Hg isotope ratios. Preconcentration is required for many matrices, such as air and water, to obtain a sufficient mass of Hg and for samples of average concentration but little available sample mass, such as zooplankton or thin slices of sediment cores. Two major strategies have emerged to deal with this challenge. As mentioned earlier, combustion techniques will volatilize Hg from larger sample masses, which can subsequently be collected on gold traps or inline with acidic permanganate solution (Biswas et al., 2008; Xie et al., 2005). Similarly, Hg in large volumes of solutions can be reduced, purged from solution, and collected as above. Dissolved gaseous mercury can be purged from aqueous solutions into permanganate solution, which was acidified with sulfuric acid (Zheng et al., 2007). My colleagues and I have determined the Hg isotope ratio in arctic snow by collecting 4 L of snow, which subsequently melted in a clean room. Hg in solution was reduced by the addition of $SnCl_2$ and Hg(0) purged onto gold traps in the field station. The traps were conveniently transported back to the analytical laboratory, where Hg was thermodesorbed into an acidic permanganate solution, which was then measured by continuous-flow cold-vapor MC-ICP/MS.

Nomenclature of Mercury Isotope Fractionation

With mercury being a new and rapidly emerging field of isotope ratio determinations, there is a risk of confusion with regard to terminology. To complicate matters, different studies chose to express results using a bewildering array of nomenclatures, making it often very difficult to compare data among laboratories or to evaluate the accuracy and precision of each study. In addition, the measurement of extremely precise Hg isotope ratios is an exceptionally challenging exercise and requires strict adoption of quality-control measures. The following sections try to summarize the state of the field and to suggest a common, promising and useful nomenclature.

Mass Bias Correction

In principle, there are two alternatives to report Hg isotope ratio differences: in the form of absolute ratios or as the deviation from a common standard. Although the former is the traditional format used by analytical chemists, it is extremely difficult if not impossible to determine correct absolute ratios at the level of accuracy required for distinguishing natural variations. Hence, geochemists typically use a relative comparison using the delta notation $\delta^{xxx}Hg$ in‰. It should be stressed that every isotope ratio measurement by MC-ICP/MS is subject to instrumental mass bias and will therefore deliver inaccurate results. Hence, the initially measured ratios must

be mass bias–corrected, which is achieved by: (a) external correction by measuring the (accurately known) isotope ratio of another element, (b) internal correction by measuring two additional Hg isotopes, which were added in a known ratio to the sample of interest, or (c) bracketing the unknown sample with a standard of known isotope composition. For maximum accuracy, a combination of strategies a and c is most commonly used and highly advisable.

EXTERNAL MASS BIAS CORRECTION

This strategy works best if an element of similar atomic mass and chemical characteristics is available. Typically, thallium is chosen to correct for Hg isotope mass bias and a Tl reference material (Standard Reference Material issued by the National Institute of Standards and Technology, SRM NIST 997) is available with a certified $^{205/203}Tl$ ratio of 2.38714. The possibility of using $^{208/206}Pb$ from concurrently produced PbH_4 for mass bias correction of Hg ratios has also been explored (Hintelmann and Lu, 2003). The mass bias–corrected ratios for Hg obtained by using known Tl and Pb isotope ratios, however, led to significantly different results. The authors concluded that the hydride generation step itself is prone to fractionate PbH_4 and therefore is unsuitable for correcting measured Hg isotope ratios. Using Tl isotopes on the other hand is also potentially problematic, since Tl is chemically quite different from Hg. First, the ionization potential of Hg (10.437 eV) is much higher than that of Tl (6.108 eV), resulting in less efficient ionization of Hg in an argon plasma. Second, Hg is often introduced in gaseous from (either as Hg(0) after cold-vapor generation or in form of gaseous species from a GC column), while Tl species are not volatile. Typically, a dry aerosol of Tl is produced in a separate desolvation unit (e.g., Aridus [Sonke et al., 2008] or Apex [Foucher and Hintelmann, 2006]) and subsequently mixed with the Hg(0)-containing gas stream prior to reaching the plasma. Detailed measurements revealed that the mass bias factors for Hg and Tl are very similar, but not identical. Most mass bias corrections apply an exponential law assuming invariant mass bias factors. Hence, even those "corrected" Hg isotope ratios are not likely to be completely accurate, which may explain why measurements by different laboratories and even measurements conducted in the same laboratory, but under different instrumental conditions, lead to varying absolute ratios. This is probably inevitable and has resulted in the adoption of the delta notation to express Hg isotope variations among samples relative to each other rather than in absolute terms.

DOUBLE SPIKE (INTERNAL MASS BIAS CORRECTION)

This is often the most accurate, but also the most technically challenging, mass bias–correction strategy. It requires a total of four isotopes that must be available with the element of interest. Two are used for the calculation of the ratio of interest and two are added to the unknown sample in known proportions prior to the measurement (Albarède and Beard, 2003). While mercury has a total of seven isotopes, it appears that at least two (^{199}Hg and ^{201}Hg) are potentially subject to anomalous fractionation effects (see below), leaving five isotopes for the double-spike procedure. The performance of a double-spike method using ^{196}Hg and ^{204}Hg has been demonstrated for Hg isotope ratio measurements, achieving very similar precision as compared with the more widely used standard-sample bracketing technique with internal mass–bias correction (Mead and Johnson, 2010).

STANDARD-SAMPLE BRACKETING

This proven strategy was originally developed for the field of light isotope ratio measurements. Before and after measurement of the unknown sample, a standard of known isotopic composition is measured and the ratios are compared to compute a relative difference between the two. This comparison of isotope ratios generates a scale of deviations relative to the standard material, which is set to zero. In fact, exact knowledge of the standard's isotope ratio is not even required, as long as its isotope composition is identical in every measurement. The procedure implicitly requires the instrumental mass bias not to change during the measurement of the sample sequence, a requirement that is not necessarily fulfilled. In addition, for the procedure to work, exact matrix and concentration matching is mandatory, because the instrumental mass bias can be very sensitive to matrix and concentration changes.

For these reasons, it has been shown that a combination of external mass bias correction and standard bracketing delivers the most accurate and precise data. External correction compensates for any subtle drifts in mass bias during the measurement, while sample bracketing and comparison to a common standard avoids the challenges associated with calculating correct absolute isotope ratios.

Theory of Mercury Isotope Fractionation

Isotope fractionation is a proven tool for examining biogeochemical pathways of light element isotope systems (H, C, N, O, and S), in which fractionation is caused by classical isotope effects (CIEs). CIEs are based on differences in zero-point vibrational energies of isotopes (i.e., differences in bond strengths), which is a function of their mass differences (Bigeleisen and Mayer 1947; Urey 1947). Because of the small relative difference in mass of heavy isotope systems, scientists were initially skeptical that Hg isotope fractionation would be detectable at all. However, the dominant source of fractionation in heavy isotopes (mass $\geq$40) was suggested to be the nuclear volume effect (NVE, or nuclear field shift effect) (Bigeleisen, 1996; Schauble 2007). Schauble modeled the expected fractionation for Hg species in equilibrium with Hg(0) vapor and found the NVE to be much larger than CIE. The NVE

influences reactions, where s-electron occupations change between reactants and products. Smaller (lighter) isotopes are concentrated in reduced species. Hence, redox reactions involving changes in oxidation states of Hg(II) to Hg(0) ([Xe]4f^{14}5d^{10}6s^{0} $\rightarrow$ [Xe]4f^{14}5d^{10}6s^{2}) or vice versa show a strong NVE effect. Such redox conversions are extremely important reactions in the environmental Hg cycle, mobilizing Hg as Hg(0) and transporting it globally through the atmosphere. However, nuclear volume, and thus NVE fractionation, does not scale linearly with mass. Instead, odd isotopes (^{199}Hg and ^{201}Hg) are slightly smaller (appear to be lighter) than their mass suggests, leading to even–odd staggered isotope effects and creating mass independent fractionation (MIF). It is expressed in both kinetic and equilibrium fractionation. While Schauble was basing his calculations in part on a compilation of published nuclear radii (Angeli, 2004), another group of authors (Ghosh et al., 2008) used a different set of experimental data (Hahn et al., 1979) for their recalculation of nuclear radii and arrived at values that are close to those obtained by Schauble, with the notable exception of ^{204}Hg. According to Schauble, the nuclear radius of ^{204}Hg is slightly larger than its mass would predict, while the calculations by Ghosh et al., put ^{204}Hg in a linear relationship with the other even-numbered Hg isotopes. As a consequence, the latter data would predict no MIF of ^{204}Hg, which is consistent with the currently available experimental results for this isotope.

Another mechanism by which isotopes are fractionated independently of mass is the magnetic isotope effect (MIE) (Buchachenko, 2001; Buchachenko et al., 2004, 2006). MIE is usually induced after hemolytic cleavage of bonds, leading to pairs of radical triplets, which are spin-forbidden to recombine. However, fragments with magnetic nuclei (^{199}Hg, I = 1/2; ^{201}Hg, I = 3/2) undergo very fast triplet-singlet conversion. Radical pairs can now recombine in the singlet state to the starting reagents. This spin conversion is much slower in diamagnetic nuclei, typically leading to an enrichment of odd (paramagnetic) isotopes in starting reagents and of even (diamagnetic) nuclei in the products. MIE is a purely kinetic effect, not observed for equilibrium fractionation processes, and should be predominant in reactions with radical intermediates. Indeed, photodemethylation and photoreduction experiments have already shown to create large MIFs (Bergquist and Blum, 2007).

Delta Notation

To minimize the effects of instrumental fractionation, isotope ratios are commonly determined by standard–sample–standard bracketing (and internal mass bias correction for the most accurate data) and reported using the δ (‰) notation:

$$\delta\,^{xxx}Hg/^{yyy}Hg\ (\text{‰}) = [(^{xxx}Hg/^{yyy}Hg)_{sample}\ /$$
$$(^{xxx}Hg/^{yyy}Hg)_{standard} - 1] \times 1000$$

While looking deceptively simple, this equation has the potential of generating great confusion, particularly for systems having more than two isotopes. The first source for confusion is the choice of isotopes to be used for reporting variations. There are over 40 permutations of how Hg isotope ratios could be calculated. Some researchers prefer to express Hg isotope ratios relative to ^{202}Hg (Jackson et al., 2004; Ghosh et al., 2008), probably led by the idea that ratios containing ^{202}Hg (which is the most abundant Hg isotope) will provide the highest measurement precision. It is fortuitous that for many isotope systems this approach puts the lighter isotope (often being the most abundant isotope) into the denominator, which then provides additional intuitive information—that is, negative deviations will indicate an enrichment of the sample with light isotopes, while positive deviations are consistent with an enrichment of heavy isotopes. Unfortunately, the most abundant Hg isotope, ^{202}Hg, is also one of the heaviest of this isotope system. To save the intuitive information contained in delta values, it is therefore proposed to choose a light Hg isotope as the common denominator. When using this strategy, it makes sense to avoid the lightest Hg isotope, ^{196}Hg, because of its very low natural abundance (~0.15%) and use the next heavier isotope, ^{198}Hg, in the denominator for all calculations and comparisons. This notation was recently informally proposed and is now used by most research groups (Foucher and Hintelmann, 2006; Bergquist and Blum, 2007; Estrade et al., 2008; Sonke et al., 2008).

A second source for misunderstandings is the fact that the standard, to which all unknowns are compared, is currently not defined. A perennial challenge for nontraditional isotope systems is the absence of reference materials certified for isotope ratios. This information may be available, if the element in question is amenable to determination by TIMS, which has been used to establish absolute isotope ratios. This is not possible for Hg, though. However, as explained above, it is not strictly necessary to have a material with a known absolute Hg isotope ratio. There is currently a strong trend toward using a NIST mercury standard solution as the common Hg standard to which all other Hg ratios are compared. Initially, SRM NIST 1641d (1.590 mg/kg ± 0.018 mg/kg mercury in water, acidified to 2% nitric acid and stabilized with 1 mg/kg Au) was selected for reference, but this solution contains a high concentration of gold. Although this does not affect the measurement of Hg in the solution, concerns about potential matrix effects causing unpredictable mass bias have led to the recommendation of using SRM NIST 3133 (9.954 mg/g ± 0.053 mg/g mercury in water, acidified to 10% nitric acid) instead. In fact, SRM NIST 1641d is a derivative of SRM NIST 3133 and measurements have shown that the two solutions have identical Hg isotope ratios (Blum and Bergquist, 2007). For quality-control purposes, it would be further desirable to have a (common) secondary standard to ensure that the deviations measured on different occasions and among different laboratories are comparable. A solution of Almadén (Spain) cinnabar (UM-Almadén) was proposed for this purpose (Blum and Bergquist, 2007). The university of Michigan prepared a large batch of this material and generously offered

samples to interested laboratories free of charge. A value of δ^{202}Hg $= -0.54 \pm 0.08‰$ has been suggested for this solution, with no measurable mass independent deviations for odd isotopes. Ultimately, it would be attractive if one of the established reference material producers would take on the task certifying a set of materials with respect to their δ^{202}Hg, Δ^{199}Hg, and Δ^{201}Hg deviations. The recently discovered MIF of odd Hg isotopes may require an additional reference material with anomalous fractionation, which are most frequently observed in biologic tissues with large proportions of MMHg. I therefore propose a reference material such as NRC DORM-2 (National Research Council Canada Dogfish Muscle Reference Material) or ERM-CE 464 (European Reference Material CE-464, Tuna Fish) as an alternative widely available material. Measurements have demonstrated not only large MIFs in both materials but also large mass dependent fractionation (MDF) relative to SRM NIST 3133. Table 4.2 shows measured deviations for selected (certified) reference materials, which are potentially useful as a secondary Hg isotope ratio standard. In contrast to NIST 3133 or UM-Almadén, which are Hg solutions ready for measurement, a biologic tissue (or other solid) CRM would require additional sample preparation prior to the determination. Use of such material would therefore offer the opportunity to validate all sample manipulations required for the determination of real samples as well as the actual isotope ratio measurement.

For sample preparation and introduction schemes that are based on gaseous Hg(0), it would be advantageous to compare the measurement directly to a gaseous or metallic Hg standard (e.g. NIST 2555), which has been used in a gold trap introduction scheme (Xie et al., 2005). One potential problem is that Hg vapor drawn from the headspace over a drop of Hg is most likely already fractionated relative to the metallic bulk sample.

All the above considerations lead to following propose nomenclature for stating Hg isotope ratio deviations:

$$\delta^{xxx}\text{Hg (‰)} = [(^{xxx}\text{Hg}/^{198}\text{Hg})_{\text{sample}} / (^{xxx}\text{Hg}/^{198}\text{Hg})_{\text{NIST 3133}} - 1] \times 1000$$

δ^{202}Hg values are most commonly reported. Although δ^{204}Hg would take advantage of a larger mass difference, this isotope has potential analytical issues because of isobaric overlap with ^{204}Pb and much lower natural abundance than ^{202}Hg.

As explained in the previous section, the mercury isotope system exhibits anomalous behavior. The even-numbered isotopes (^{196}Hg, ^{198}Hg, ^{200}Hg, ^{202}Hg, and likely also ^{204}Hg) are subject only to MDF, which is well covered by the above notation. However, the odd Hg isotopes (^{199}Hg and ^{201}Hg) also display mass independent fractionation, necessitating additional nomenclature. Using the proposed δ^{202}Hg value to characterize mass dependent effects and, thus, predicting theoretical values of $\delta^{xxx}\text{Hg}_{\text{MDF}}$ one can calculate the deviations from MDF as follows:

$$\Delta^{xxx}\text{Hg} = \delta^{xxx}\text{Hg}_{\text{measured}} - \delta^{xxx}\text{Hg}_{\text{MDF}}$$

TABLE 4.2

Mercury Isotope Variations Relative to NIST SRM 3133 in a Variety of Biologic and Sediment Reference Materials

CRM	Matrix	δ^{202}Hg (‰)	Δ^{199}Hg (‰)	Δ^{201}Hg (‰)	Reference
NIST SRM-1641d	Solution	+0.03 ± 0.10	ND	ND	Blum and Bergquist, 2007
UM-Almadén	Solution	−0.54 ± 0.08	ND	ND	Blum and Bergquist, 2007
		−0.52 ± 0.07	ND	ND	Foucher et al., 2009
NRC DORM-2	Fish	+0.18	+1.07	+0.88	Bergquist and Blum, 2007
		+0.15 ± 0.06	+1.11 ± 0.01	+0.89 ± 0.06	This chapter
		+0.11 ± 0.08	+1.08 ± 0.03	+0.93 ± 0.05	Malinovsky et al., 2008
BCR CRM-464	Fish	+0.68 ± 0.06	+2.21 ± 0.04	+1.81 ± 0.04	This chapter
NRC DOLT-2	Biologic	+0.1	+0.71	+0.59	Bergquist and Blum, 2007
NRC DOLT-3	Biological	−1.26 ± 0.05	+0.57 ± 0.04	+0.65 ± 0.02	Malinovsky et al., 2008
NRC TORT-2	Biological	−0.18 ± 0.04	+0.70 ± 0.03	+0.59 ± 0.01	This chapter
IAEA-356	Sediment	−0.32 ± 0.04	ND	ND	Foucher et al., 2009
BCR CRM-580	Sediment	−0.46 ± 0.04	ND	ND	Foucher et al., 2009
NIST SRM-1944	Sediment	−0.54 ± 0.04	ND	ND	Foucher et al., 2009
NRC MESS-3	Sediment	−2.50 ± 0.28	ND	ND	Foucher et al., 2009
NRC PACS-2	Sediment	−0.28 ± 0.09	ND	ND	Malinovsky et al., 2008

ND = not detected.

or

$$\Delta^{xxx}\text{Hg} = \delta^{xxx}\text{Hg}_{measured} - \delta^{202}\text{Hg}_{measured} \times f,$$

where f is an isotope-pair specific scaling factor.

The most commonly used equations are to calculate:

$$\Delta^{199}\text{Hg} = \delta^{199}\text{Hg}_{measured} - \delta^{202}\text{Hg}_{measured} \times 0.25,$$
$$\Delta^{200}\text{Hg} = \delta^{200}\text{Hg}_{measured} - \delta^{202}\text{Hg}_{measured} \times 0.50,$$
$$\Delta^{201}\text{Hg} = \delta^{201}\text{Hg}_{measured} - \delta^{202}\text{Hg}_{measured} \times 0.75,$$
$$\Delta^{204}\text{Hg} = \delta^{204}\text{Hg}_{measured} - \delta^{202}\text{Hg}_{measured} \times 1.49.$$

Table 4.3 precisely summarizes scale factors (based on the δ^{202}Hg system) for MDF as well as MIF caused by NVE, derived by Schauble (2007) and by Ghosh et al. (2008). Although both authors calculated similar factors, subtle differences exist. Ghosh et al. predict no mass-independent fractionation for ^{204}Hg, which is consistent with current experimental results. Both authors develop scale factors for odd Hg isotopes leading to significant MIF, which is indeed often observed for biologic materials. The differences between odd isotope scale factors are small and cannot be

resolved experimentally with existing technology. While Schauble derives a purely mass-dependent behavior for ^{200}Hg, Ghosh et al.'s scale factor should cause some mass-independent fractionation for ^{200}Hg as well, which has not been observed so far, but may be too small to be detectable. It appears that additional nuclear radii determinations and calculations are required to resolve the remaining differences or, alternatively, very precise isotope ratio measurements must be conducted to decide which set of scale factors is most accurate.

The Hg isotope system offers now a unique opportunity to deconvolute mechanisms leading to MIF. It has not one but two magnetic isotopes, both subject to NVE and MIE. Plots of Δ^{199}Hg versus Δ^{201}Hg should reveal the relative contribution of both effects. MIF caused by NVE alone should show a slope between 0.366 (Schauble, 2007) and 0.457 (Ghosh et al., 2008). The challenge is to predict the MIF caused by MIE. Whereas the latter authors speculate that MIE fractionation will reflect the ratio of the magnetic moment of the two isotopes resulting in a ratio of Δ^{201}Hg/Δ^{199}Hg = 0.560225/0.5058852 = 1.11 (Korea Atomic Energy Research Institute, 2000), this assumption is so far not supported by any experimental or theoretical evidence.

TABLE 4.3
Scale Factors for Converting $^{202/198}$Hg Fractionation Factors for Other Isotope
Ratios with ^{198}Hg as the Denominating Isotope

	$^{196/198}$Hg	$^{199/198}$Hg	$^{200/198}$Hg	$^{201/198}$Hg	$^{202/198}$Hg	$^{204/198}$Hg	Reference
MD$_{equ}$	−0.515	0.254	0.505	0.754	1.000	1.486	Young et al., 2002
MD$_{kin}$		0.252	0.502	0.752	1.000	1.492	Young et al., 2002
NV	−0.466	0.107	0.497	0.700	1.000	1.654	Schauble, 2007
NV		0.080	0.471	0.674	1.000	1.499	Ghosh et al., 2008

NOTE: Provided are factors following equilibrium and kinetic mass-dependent fractionation laws (MD$_{equ}$ and MD$_{kin}$) and two solutions for nuclear volume (NV) fractionation, based on modeled and experimentally derived nuclear radii.

Precision of the Analytical Measurement

As for any other analytical measurement, it is important to report a measure of uncertainty for each determination to allow for the evaluation and comparison of data. The most important parameter is the reproducibility of the overall analytical method, including sampling, sample preparation, and measurement. For unknown samples, this can be assessed only by replicate analysis—that is, measurement of replicate sample preparations. This uncertainty is often referred to as the external reproducibility (or sometimes called "between-run precision") and characterizes the distribution of independent measurements around the population mean. The external reproducibility is expressed in multiples of the standard deviation of the sample (in analytical chemistry, commonly 1 SD) and requires the measurement of at least three individual sample preparations. However, often there is not sufficient sample material (or mass of Hg) available to allow replicate Hg isotope ratio analyses. In this situation, a conservative estimate of uncertainty should be provided. A related sample that is similar or close in matrix to the sample in question and that is available in sufficient quantity could be measured repeatedly to provide a measure of the combined uncertainty resulting from sample preparation and measurement. Preferably, this surrogate sample should be an actual environmental sample rather than a CRM to truly account for uncertainties associated with in-house sample homogenization.

Another useful performance indicator is the accuracy of the deviation measurement (accuracy, with which δ^{202}Hg can be determined). This can be evaluated by analyzing a reference sample (CRM or in-house standard), which has a different isotope composition than the bracketing standard. Measured δ^{202}Hg for this secondary standard should be consistent for each analytical session. The precision with which this deviation can be measured over an extended period of time should also be the limiting value when reporting the external reproducibility. Currently, the reported precision for such comparisons is slightly better than 0.10‰ (2 SD). Hence, applying today's technology and instruments, measured Hg isotope ratio deviations (δ^{202}Hg) between two samples must be >0.10‰ to be significant.

Often, researchers also report the internal precision of an isotope ratio measurement, usually expressed as two times the standard error (2 SE) of repeated isotope ratio measurements during a single analytical run. Although this value is an indication for the precision of the individual measurement, it does not take into account potential variability introduced during sample preparation or by inherent sample inhomogeneities, which is often considerable for matrices such as soils or sediments. At any rate, authors should clearly state the level of uncertainty of their measurement and how it was derived.

Mercury Isotope Data of Natural Samples

At time of this writing, there have been only a dozen or so published studies describing Hg isotope ratio variations in natural samples. Although only 10 years ago many scientists were skeptical that the Hg isotope system is subject to natural fractionation in the first place, some pioneering studies have now unequivocally shown that variations exist and that Hg exhibits rich and often unexpected fractionation patterns. Figure 4.1 illustrates the range of δ^{202}Hg that has been observed in nature so far; this is discussed in more detail in the following section. Although initial determinations concentrated on document variations in natural Hg isotope ratios, more recent investigations have started to focus on the (bio)geochemical processes causing the observed differences. Newer studies have confirmed that analytical methods have matured to a point at which routine measurements have now become possible. Note that all of the following δ values conform to the notation described in the previous section, report δ^{202}Hg, and were converted from the original literature where necessary and possible.

Sediments

Hg isotope ratios in a series of sediments obtained from many different locations have been determined (Foucher and Hintelmann, 2006). The δ^{202}Hg displayed a range of almost 5‰, ranging from −4.00 to +0.74‰. Large variations were observed near a gold mine in New Brunswick, Canada, where cyanide leaching mobilized large concentrations of

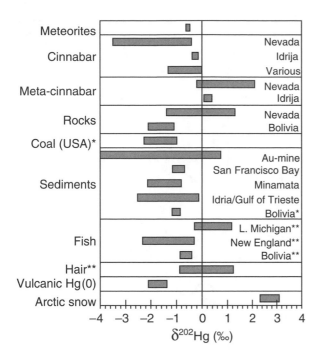

FIGURE 4.1   Reported ranges of Hg isotope composition for environmental samples, analyzed by MC-ICP/MS and expressed relative to NIST 3133 (vertical line at 0 ‰). Mass-independent fractionation has been reported for some terrestrial (*) and many biological (**) samples.

Hg as well. Depending on the location of the sample, measured Hg isotope ratios varied greatly between the source Hg at the mine (−0.15 to +0.05‰) and the background Hg in river sediments (−2.83 to −2.75‰) (Foucher and Hintelmann, 2004). Based on these data, a simple mixing model was developed to estimate the proportion of discharged Hg in the total Hg measured downstream of the mine (Foucher and Hintelmann, unpublished). δ^{202}Hg in Minamata Bay spans from −2.0 to −1.0‰, depending on the location in the bay. Samples collected in the Northern San Francisco Bay area showed little variation (−1.1 to −1.0‰). Another study determined Hg isotope variations in Arctic lake sediments (Jackson et al., 2004). The authors reported data for a dated sediment core from the anoxic zone of Romulus Lake, a small oligotrophic, saline and meromictic lake in the high arctic desert of Ellesmere Island, Nunavut, Canada, and found that deeper (older) sediments were enrichment with lighter isotopes. They hypothesize that the observed Hg isotope fractionation was caused by microbial activities linked to redox processes in the lake. However, they also do not rule out that the measured Hg isotope ratios may be indicative of different Hg sources in the lake.

Ores

Few data have been reported for Hg isotope ratios in Hg ores. One study (Hintelmann and Lu, 2003) compared cinnabar ores from many different locations and detected deviations between −1.3‰ and 0.00‰. Another study measured Hg isotope ratios in materials obtained from

two hydrothermal systems in Nevada (Smith et al., 2005). The authors measured deviations ranging from −3.5 to −0.4‰ for cinnabar and from −1.4 to +1.3‰ for meta-cinnabar, while the underlying rock showed values of −0.2 to +2.1‰. They explained the observed light isotope enrichment in cinnabar relative to meta-cinnabar and the underlying veins through a combined process of boiling hydrothermal fluid, surface oxidation, and kinetic effects during mineral precipitation. A similar fractionation between cinnabar and meta-cinnabar was observed in ores from an Hg mine in Idria, Slovenia (Foucher et al., 2009), where −0.26‰ for red and +0.23‰ for black cinnabar was measured. This relatively larger range of isotope deviation in related ores points to the importance of temperature causing boiling, evaporation, and precipitation of Hg phases in some deposits, while other deposits such as Almadén, Spain are low-temperature systems, in which boiling is not common. Those deposits are expected to show more uniform δ^{202}Hg.

Meteorites

Most Hg isotope ratio measurements of meteorites, mostly chondrites, were conducted with techniques other than MC-ICP/MS. Because of the associated larger uncertainty with these methods, many of the older data are now considered suspect. MC-ICP/MS measurements were conducted to determine the isotope composition in the Murchison and Allende carbonaceous chondrites (Lauretta et al., 2001). In contrast to earlier NAA studies, this newer study did not find anomalous deviations from terrestrial values. Instead, the bulk isotope composition did not deviate statistically from their reference standard (UM-Almadén), suggesting −0.54‰ for Allende and Murchinson Hg. In contrast to earlier NAA studies, no anomalous $\delta^{202/196}$Hg fractionation was found.

Coal

Since coal burning is one of the main ways that Hg is introduced into the atmosphere, the Hg isotope ratio signature of coal is of great interest for studies trying to track Hg from sources to receptor sites. However, one early investigation was unable to differentiate Hg isotope ratios in coal— Evans et al. (2001) found variations between −1.5‰ and 0‰ relative to NIST 1632b. Unfortunately, the precision of the isotope ratio determination for the reference material was less than 2‰ (RSD) at the time, which did not allow conclusive differentiation between coal samples. Nevertheless, considering that analytical techniques have matured greatly since then, it is worthwhile to revisit the question with optimized methods. More recent work indicated significant Hg isotope abundance differences in coal from various locations in the United States, China, and Kazakhstan, with δ^{202}Hg from −0.9 to −3.0‰ and Δ^{201}Hg from −0.1 to 0.4‰ (Biswas et al., 2008).

Water

Concentrations of Hg in (uncontaminated) aqueous sources are too low for directly measuring isotope ratios by MC-ICP/MS. However, Foucher and Hintelmann (2004) were able to determine fractionation of Hg isotopes in mine leachate, contaminated groundwater and rivers. Not surprisingly, the initial δ^{202}Hg in the receiving water body was identical to the source material at the mine. However, over a length of 3000 m, significant amounts of Hg evaporated from the river, resulting in a progressive enrichment of heavy isotopes in the water.

As a proof-of-concept study, my colleagues and I collected large quantities of polar snow. After melting it down under clean room conditions and preconcentrating the Hg in 4 L of sample onto gold traps in the field, the Hg isotope ratio was determined for the original snow sample. At total Hg concentrations of 5.2 to 9.9 ng/L (n = 3), initial δ^{202}Hg values between +2.32 and +3.10‰ were obtained for snow collected in early May 2007 at Ny Ålesund, Svalbard. Considering that background sediments typically have negative δ^{202}Hg values, the observation of such large positive deviations is remarkable. More recently, a new method using ion exchange resins has been developed to concentrate Hg from pristine water samples, facilitating the Hg isotope ratio measurement at nanograms per liter levels (Chen et al., 2010).

Air

Owing to the extremely low concentration of typically 1.5–2 ng/m^3 Hg in air, this matrix is as challenging for MC-ICP/MS measurements as water samples. The only study reporting Hg(0) in atmospheric samples (Sonke et al., 2008) collected Hg(0) emissions from the passively degassing volcano—Vulcano, Italy—and determined −1.74 ± 0.36‰ for this source.

Aquatic Food Web Samples

Similar to δ^{15}N, which is used in food web studies to identify trophic levels of specimen and δ^{13}C, which is used to identify food sources, one of the great potentials of applying Hg isotope ratios is to better understand Hg bioaccumulation. However, except for fish, which typically have high enough Hg concentrations and provide sufficient sample mass for a precise isotope ratio determination, most other aquatic biota are either low in Hg or are available only in small quantities (e.g., zooplankton, algae, and benthos) or both, which makes isotope ratio measurements challenging.

A comprehensive investigation measured Hg isotope ratios in food chains of Lake Ontario and two boreal lakes (Jackson et al., 2007). Hg isotope variations from the original literature have been converted to δ^{202}Hg values and are summarized in Figure 4.2. In general, δ^{202}Hg increased with increasing Hg concentration of the specimen. Depending on the lake, zooplankton showed between −2.60‰ and

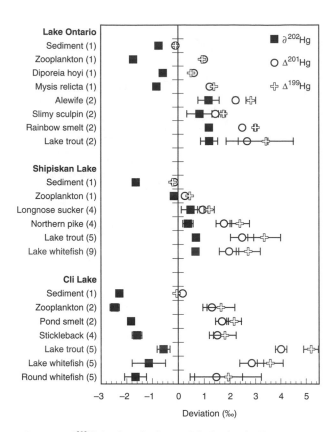

FIGURE 4.2 δ^{202}Hg in three freshwater lake food webs. Data were converted from Jackson et al. (2007), and deviations are expressed relative to a standard solution of Hg (but not relative to SRM NIST 3133, which was not measured in this study).

−0.16‰ and was always the most negative biologic sample. The top predator lake trout ranged from −0.57 to +1.43‰ and always displayed the most positive values. The wide variation in δ^{202}Hg among samples of the same fish species collected at different locations is intriguing. However, the database and number of analyzed samples is still very small. It is too early to decide whether the variations reflect differences in Hg sources, differences in habitat and MMHg accumulation, or differences in Hg cycling (e.g., photoreduction, methylation, and demethylation). Nevertheless, a clear trend was visible in all three ecosystems, with δ^{202}Hg increasing with increasing MMHg. However, it must be noted that all data so far report δ^{202}Hg for total Hg—that is, the composite value for δMe^{202}Hg and δ^{202}Hgi (Hgi = inorganic Hg). This means that in fish (> 95% MMHg) the composite δ^{202}Hg reflects δMe^{202}Hg. In lower-food-chain organisms such as zooplankton (up to 40% MMHg), δ^{202}Hg is a concentration-weighted average of δMe^{202}Hg and δ^{202}Hgi. At the other end of the spectrum, the measured δ^{202}Hg in sediments (<1% MMHg) represents δ^{202}Hgi. Bearing in mind the vast differences in the geochemistry and bioaccumulation behavior of MMHg and inorganic Hg, it is likely that individual samples may exhibit very different δMe^{202}Hg and δ^{202}Hgi values. Therefore, comparisons based on δ^{202}Hg must consider potential bias when using composite isotope ratio data. Jackson et al. (2007) also reported the extraction of MMHg from fish samples for subsequent compound-specific isotope ratio measurement. Unfortunately, their data are inclusive. Although δ^{202}Hg for lake trout was reported with +0.62 to +0.83‰ (Shipiskan Lake) and −0.74 to −0.57‰ (Cli Lake), the corresponding values for δMe^{202}Hg (−1.04 and −0.35‰ in Shipiskan and Cli Lake, respectively) and δ^{202}Hgi (−0.11 and −0.33‰) do not match up.

In Lake Michigan, δ^{202}Hg for burbot fish varied between −0.29 and + 1.2‰ and values for New England (mainly yellow perch and chain pickerel) ranged from −0.30 to –2.33‰ (Bergquist and Blum, 2007). While δ^{202}Hg varied greatly within and among locations and fish species, in general, a strong correlation between δ^{202}Hg and the Hg concentration in fish muscle was again observed. The authors speculated, therefore, that δ^{202}Hg values might indicate fish age and trophic status. The enrichment of ^{202}Hg in fish having higher Hg concentrations is noteworthy. A preferential elimination of lighter isotopes by fish leading to the observed fractionation in older and more contaminated fish was suggested. This idea may well be supported by a study by Van Walleghem et al. (2007), which showed that fish are able to eliminate MMHg, creating an opportunity for significant isotope fractionation.

The most striking result of both studies, however, is the observation of mass independent fractionation (MIF) in fish and food-web samples. Δ^{201}Hg between +0.59‰ and +4.21‰ and Δ^{199}Hg between +0.29 and +5.51‰ were observed (Bergquist and Blum, 2007). The more comprehensive food-web data in Figure 4.2 show frequently large Δ^{199}Hg—up to +5.19‰ in biota. It is striking that sediments in all three lakes were the only samples with undetectable MIF. Despite the large variation among different samples, the ratio of Δ^{199}Hg go Δ^{201}Hg is very consistent and was, on average, 1.28 for all fish samples in both studies. Interestingly, almost identical MIF was measured in the laboratory when subjecting MMHg in water to photodemethylation (Bergquist and Blum, 2007). The MMHg remaining in solution had a similar Δ^{199}Hg:Δ^{201}Hg ratio as that observed in fish in the wild. The authors interpreted this finding as an imprinting of the aqueous MMHg MIF onto the food web. This hypothesis would imply that the original MMHg MIF remains unperturbed regardless of potential (mass-dependent or mass-independent) fractionation during bioaccumulation. Jackson et al. (2007) observed an increase of Δ^{199}Hg with Hg concentration (and trophic level) in their food-web study (Figure 4.2), which would be in contrast with the theory that the MIF is unaffected by bioaccumulation. However, Δ^{199}Hg measured in lower-food-web organisms might be biased by Δ^{199}Hgi, which is likely different from ΔMe^{199}Hg measured in fish. In addition, the effects of biotic methylation and demethylation as well as bioaccumulation on Hg isotope fractionation are mostly unknown to date. Only a small fraction of MMHg in water is subject to photoreduction, while the majority of MMHg is produced in sediments or deep anoxic water. Considering the postulated strong magnetic isotope effect (MIE) in the interaction of MMHg with cysteine residues (Buchachenko, 2001), a (bio)accumulation process involving MMHg binding to cysteine in proteins may also introduce a significant MIF. It remains to be seen whether the similarity of the Δ^{199}Hg:Δ^{201}Hg ratio in photodemethylation reactions and fish tissue is directly related or merely a coincidence. The determination of ΔMe^{199}Hg and ΔMe^{201}Hg in water would greatly aid in answering this question. Unfortunately, MMHg in surface water is extremely low, making these measurements nearly impossible. Regardless, the combined use of MDF and MIF in food web studies offers a new powerful tool to unravel the complexities of Hg sources and accumulation in food webs.

Mercury Isotope Systematics and Processes Causing Mercury Isotope Fractionation

Clearly, to fully understand the observed Hg isotope ratio deviations in nature, a comprehensive theoretical framework describing the processes leading to Hg isotope fractionation is necessary. Many studies have investigated individual reactions and processes and reveal deeper insight into the Hg isotope system. Table 4.4 summarizes those investigations and the following section provides additional insight.

Reduction Processes

Owing to its rich redox chemistry, many mercury species are subject to photoreduction, microbial reduction, and chemical reduction processes. All three reduction pathways have in common that they supply Hg(0) to the pool of atmospheric Hg. Consequently, any fractionation during reduction processes has the potential to regulate or alter the Hg isotope signature of the atmosphere on a local, regional, and maybe even global scale.

PHOTOREDUCTION

Using a solar simulator, our laboratory systematically investigated photoreduction of ionic Hg in natural waters to identify, which environmental parameter affects Hg isotope fractionation (Zheng and Hintelmann, 2009). Filtered lake water from Harp Lake (Haliburton, Ontario, Canada) with a residual dissolved organic carbon (DOC) content of 12 mg/L was amended with 10 µg/L of Hg and irradiated under a solar simulator. Reduced Hg(0) was continuously purged from the reactor and trapped in acidic permanganate solution. Every 2 hours, subsamples were collected, for a total reaction time of 10 hours, after which 30% of the initial Hg was reduced and lost from the reactor. The Hg isotope composition was determined for the residual aqueous Hg, and for the first time also for the reduced Hg(0) product of the reaction. A mass balance confirmed that all the experimental Hg could be accounted for in either the remaining or the trapping solution. An exemplary plot is shown in

TABLE 4.4
Mercury Isotope Fractionation During Chemical Reactions and Phase Transfer Processes

Process	Maximum observed deviation in ‰			$^{202/198}\alpha$ Values	Reference
	$\Delta^{202}Hg$	$\Delta^{199}Hg$	$\Delta^{201}Hg$		
Microbial reduction					
Reactant	+6.16	NR[a]	NR	1.0013−1.0020	Kritee et al., 2007
Product	−2.56	NR	NR		
Photoreduction, reactant	+2.24	+2.15	+2.16	0.9994	Bergquist and Blum, 2007
Photoreduction					
Reactant	+0.46	+2.21	+1.77		Zheng and Hintelmann, 2009
Product	−1.20	−7.74	−6.27		
Dark reduction					
Reactant	+0.09	ND[b]	ND		
Product	−1.89	+0.20	+0.18		
Abiotic reduction, reactant	+5.58	NR	NR	1.0011	
Photodemethylation	+0.36	+1.67	+1.21	0.9983−0.9987	Bergquist and Blum, 2007
DGHg volatilization					
Reactant	+1.50	ND	ND	1.00044−1.00047	Zheng et al., 2007
Product	−0.75	ND	ND		
Evaporation					
Liquid to gas	+0.86	NR	NR	1.0062−1.0068	Estrade et al., 2008
Liquid to gas	+0.93	ND	ND		Sonke et al., 2008
Methylation	−1.40	NR	NR		Dzurko, 2006
Octanol/water partitioning					
Octanol	−2.43	ND	ND		Malinovsky et al., 2008
Water	+0.28	ND	ND		
Creatine kinase, reaction with MeHg	422	781	578		Buchachenko et al., 2004

NOTE: Deviations are expressed relative to the starting material of the reaction or transfer process.

DGHg = dissolved gaseous mercury; ND = not detected; NR = not reported.

[a.] Authors did not provide data to evaluate whether mass, independent fractionation exists.

[b.] Authors tested for, but did not observe, any mass, independent fractionation.

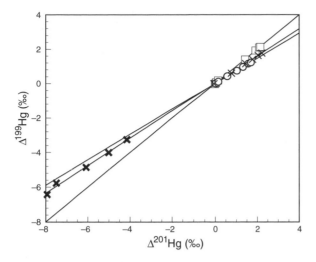

FIGURE 4.3 Δ^{199}Hg and Δ^{199}Hg for photochemical reduction of Hg(II) and MeHg. Positive data are for Hg remaining in solution and negative values represent reduced Hg(0). Open squares (MeHg) and open circles (Hg(II)) depict results obtained by. Thin and bold crosses summarize results obtained in the author's laboratory. The slopes are 1.36 for MeHg, 1.00 for Hg(II) and 1.26 for the Hg(II)/Hg(0) data.

Figure 4.3 revealing not only strong fractionation caused by the photoreduction, but also a significant MIF. After 10 hours of incubation, the remaining Hg was depleted with light isotopes, showing a δ^{202}Hg of +0.46‰, while the reduced Hg was enriched with light isotopes at −0.80‰. The even isotopes of Hg were preferentially reduced resulting in an even greater enrichment of ^{199}Hg and ^{201}Hg in solution. The corresponding Δ^{199}Hg and Δ^{201}Hg values were +1.77 and +2.22‰, respectively, for Hg remaining in solution, and −6.43 and −7.94‰ for the photoreduced Hg.

Other investigators (Bergquist and Blum, 2007) amended Hg in solution (100 µg/L) with Suwannee River Fulvic Acid (SRFA) (1 mg/L) and obtained reduction rates of >90% after exposing the sample to 6 hours of natural sunlight. Unfortunately, this study did not provide a mass balance, so it is unknown whether the loss was entirely due to reduction. Nevertheless, δ^{202}Hg values of 1.67‰ were obtained at the end of their incubation. This high value is probably explained by a small residual fraction of Hg, which leads to a large enrichment of heavy isotopes in Rayleigh-type systems. Δ^{199}Hg and Δ^{201}Hg were of similar magnitude, at +2.13 and 2.14‰, respectively, resulting in a ratio of approximately 1.0 between the two MIF processes in the latter study, while the former experiment using natural DOC sources gave a ratio of 1.26. Subsequent investigations observed that the nuclear volume effect contributes to odd isotope anomalies during abiotic reduction in the absence of light (Zheng and Hintelmann, 2010a) and identified a characteristic fractionation pattern for different pathways of Hg(II) reduction by low-molecular-weight organic substances (Zheng and Hintelmann, 2010b). Clearly, more work is required to fully understand the controlling forces behind MDF and MIF during photoreduction.

PHOTODEMETHYLATION

In similar experiments, solutions of MMHg (66–133 µg/L) were amended with SRFA (1–10 mg/L) and exposed to natural sunlight (Bergquist and Blum, 2007). Although the rate of photoreduction was slower (only 20% reduction after 6 hours of incubation), a larger Rayleigh fractionation as observed: $^{202/198}\alpha_{\text{product/reactant}}$ = 0.9983 to 0.9987 for MMHg versus 0.9994 for Hg(II). Again a significant MIF was detected.

MICROBIAL REDUCTION

Microbial reduction of Hg(II) is an alternative pathway of adding to the pool of Hg(0) available for atmospheric transport. By exposing bacteria capable of expressing the enzyme mercury reductase (MerA) to high concentrations of Hg (NIST SRM 3133), elemental Hg was volatilized and subsequently trapped in an acidic permanganate solution (Kritee et al., 2007). The isotopic composition of the growth medium as well as the volatilized Hg(0) product were measured. Regardless of the experimental conditions, the bacteria preferentially reduced the lighter Hg isotopes. In all cases, Hg underwent Rayleigh fractionation. The authors estimated $^{202}\alpha$ values ranging from 1.0013 to 1.0020. The overall observed fractionation will be the net effect of several steps, including diffusive transport of Hg(II) across the outer membrane, MerT- and MerP-mediated active transport of Hg(II) through periplasm and the inner membrane, and finally reduction by MerA. Nevertheless, the magnitude of fractionation was consistent and independent of temperature (22 to 37°C), reactor size and type of culture (pure and natural consortium). Although enzyme-catalyzed reactions normally lead to increased fractionation at lower temperatures, the authors speculate that slow transport through membranes compensates for the expected, but not observed, increased fractionation. The study did not report or observe any MIF.

CHEMICAL (ABIOTIC) REDUCTION

A fractionation factor for the abiotic reduction of Hg(II) by chemical reagents was determined by adding substoichiometric amounts of Sn(II) to Hg(II) in solution (Zheng and Hintelmann, 2010a). The instantaneously produced Hg vapor was purged from solution and trapped in acidic permanganate. Both, the Hg in the trapping and the remaining solution were measured for Hg isotope ratios. As was the case with the other reduction processes, lighter isotopes were preferentially reduced, resulting in δ^{202}Hg of 5.58‰ in the remaining solution when 99% of the initial Hg was reduced. The process followed a Rayleigh-type fractionation with $^{202}\alpha$ = 1.0011. Only MDF was observed during abiotic reduction.

Evaporation and Volatilization

A few studies have been conducted to compare the fractionation of Hg(0) between the gas phase in contact with the liquid metal and determined a $\Delta^{202/198}Hg_{vap/liq}$ fractionation of $-0.86 \pm 0.05\text{‰}$ (Estrade et al., 2008) and $-0.93 \pm 0.17\text{‰}$ (Sonke et al., 2008)—that is, the vapor phase in both studies was enriched with lighter isotopes relative to the liquid metal.

The evasion of reduced Hg in the form of gaseous mercury from surface waters, such as lakes and oceans is deemed to be a major pathway of delivering geogenic Hg to the pool of atmospheric Hg. The process itself is expected to be purely physical. After reducing Hg(II) in solution using stannous chloride, evaporation of the formed Hg(0) was followed over time (Zheng et al., 2007). The gaseous mercury was collected in acidic permanganate traps and Hg isotope ratios in the volatilized Hg(0) were compared to the ratio of Hg(0) isotopes remaining in solution. The pattern during volatilization followed a Rayleigh fractionation with an observed maximum $\delta^{202}Hg$ of -1.48‰. As expected for a purely physical process, volatilization enriched the light isotopes in the gas phase. The experiments fit perfectly to a Rayleigh system with $^{202}\alpha = 1.00044$ to 1.00047.

Methylation

Currently, it is unknown whether or to what degree the Hg isotope ratio signature is altered when Hg(II) is converted to MMHg. This is crucial information to link Hg sources, which are commonly dominated by inorganic Hg to Hg in biota, which is predominantly MMHg, at least in fish. A method was developed to determine compound-specific Hg isotope ratios (Dzurko et al., 2009). The authors applied a novel "reference standard addition" technique to determine the isotope fractionation during microbial methylation. An inorganic mercury standard was added to pure cultures of the sulfate-reducing bacteria (SRB) *Desulfovibrio sulfuricans* and *D. propionicus*, which were grown in four different media (Postgate's Media B and C for growth of SRB and a medium for fermentative growth of SRB, with and without addition of sulfate) and the produced MMHg was isolated from the culture by atmospheric pressure distillation. Prior to the subsequent analytical procedures, the same inorganic Hg standard that was used in the methylation assay was again added to the isolated MMHg. During the following online separation/determination of MMHg and inorganic Hg, it was possible to determine the Hg isotope ratio of the original Hg(II) starting material and the methylated product in a single run. The Hg isotope ratio deviations between the reactant and the product immediately revealed the fractionation during microbial methylation. Figure 4.4 illustrates the results obtained for *D. desulfuricans*. While the individual absolute isotope ratios fluctuate from day to day, the deviation between Hg(II) reactants and MMHg products is remarkably consistent, as expressed by the $\delta^{202}Hg$.

For the *D. proprionicus* strain, the $\delta^{202}Hg$ values are $-1.41\text{‰} \pm 0.41$, $-1.25\text{‰} \pm 0.16$, $-0.78\text{‰} \pm 0.20$, and -1.05‰ for

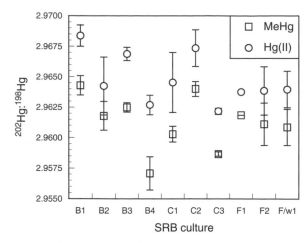

FIGURE 4.4 $\delta^{202}Hg$ for Hg methylation experiments with *D. desulfuricans* in various media. Circles indicate the isotope ratios of MeHg produced by the bacteria and squares represent the Hg(II) starting material. Error bars represent 2 SD of 3–6 replicate measures from a single culture assay.

SRB grown in media B, C, F, and F w/SO$_4$, respectively. For the *D. desulfuricans* strain, the corresponding $\delta^{202}Hg$ values are $-1.10\text{‰} \pm 0.53$, $-0.96\text{‰} \pm 0.09$, $-1.05\text{‰} \pm 0.30$, and -1.18‰ (Dzurko, 2006).

Judging by these preliminary data, it appears that microbial methylation imparts a fractionation between -0.8 and -1.4‰ relative to the Hg(II) starting material. The variation in isotope fractionation among different cultures with the same growth medium was too large to observe any effect of the growth medium on the degree of fractionation. On average, methylation by the *D. proprionicus* and *D. desulfuricans* strains caused a fractionation of $1.12 \pm 0.27\text{‰}$ and $1.07 \pm 0.1\text{‰}$, respectively. Data regarding MIF were inclusive. Because of the relatively large uncertainty of the chromatographic method, no significant MIF was detected.

Binding of Monomethylmercury to Proteins

ATP-synthesizing creatine kinase (CK) is a phosphorylating enzyme that is strongly inhibited in the presence of MMHg. By studying the effect as a function of the Hg isotope binding to the enzyme, it was found that magnetic Hg isotopes were much more efficient inhibitors than nonmagnetic nuclei (Buchachenko et al., 2004). The authors postulated that the reaction between CK and MMHg is spin selective—that is the active site of the enzyme generates ion-radical pairs with MeHgCl and cysteine residues as reaction partners, causing mass independent isotope fractionation. The data are reproduced in Table 4.5 and were used to calculate $\delta^{202}Hg$, $\Delta^{199}Hg$, and $\Delta^{201}Hg$. According to these results, the CK reaction would generate an unheard of mass independent isotope fractionation of several percent. Regrettably, the authors do not present quality-control data to assess the quality of their isotope abundance

TABLE 4.5
Fractionation of Methylmercury after Reaction
with Creatine Kinase (CK)

	Hg isotope composition (%)			
	^{199}Hg	^{200}Hg	^{201}Hg	^{202}Hg
Starting MeHg	17.0	23.1	13.2	26.6
CK-bound MeHg	34.0	7.4	28.2	10.3

	Fractionation (‰)
$\delta^{202/200}$Hg	209
$\delta^{202/198}$Hg = δ^{202}Hg[a]	422
$\delta^{202/199}$Hg	−806
$\delta^{202/201}$Hg	−819
$\delta^{199/198}$Hg = δ^{199}Hg[b]	888
$\delta^{201/198}$Hg = δ^{201}Hg[b]	895
Δ^{199}Hg	781
Δ^{201}Hg	578
Δ^{199}Hg/Δ^{201}Hg	1.35

SOURCE: Hg isotope composition data are from published data (Buchachenko et al., 2004), and deviations were obtained as indicated in footnotes.

a. δ^{202}Hg was obtained using scale factors from Table 4.3 according to δ^{202}Hg = δ^{202}Hg × 2.02.

b. To calculate the deviations relative to the ^{198}Hg ratio (in the absence of ^{198}Hg fractions or ratios), the delta notation was converted from δ^{xxx}Hg = [(^{xxx}Hg/^{198}Hg)$_{sample}$/(^{xxx}Hg/^{198}Hg)$_{NIST\ 3133}$ − 1] × 1000 into

(δ^{xxx}Hg/1000 + 1) × ^{xxx}Hg$_{std}$/^{xxx}Hg$_{sample}$ = ^{198}Hg$_{std}$/^{198}Hg$_{sample}$.
Since this is true for all Hg isotope pairs, one can set up the equation
(δ^{202}Hg/1000 + 1) × ^{202}Hg$_{std}$/^{202}Hg$_{sample}$ = (δ^{199}Hg/1000 + 1) × ^{199}Hg$_{std}$/^{199}Hg$_{sample}$
and solve for δ^{199}Hg to obtain this value:
δ^{199}Hg = (^{202}Hg$_{std}$/^{199}Hg$_{std}$)/(^{202}Hg$_{sample}$/^{199}Hg$_{sample}$) × δ^{202}Hg + [(^{202}Hg$_{std}$/^{199}Hg$_{std}$)/(^{202}Hg$_{sample}$/^{199}Hg$_{sample}$) − 1] × 1000
or
δ^{199}Hg = (^{202}Hg$_{std}$/^{199}Hg$_{std}$)/(^{202}Hg$_{sample}$/^{199}Hg$_{sample}$) × δ^{202}Hg − $\delta^{202/199}$Hg.
δ^{201}Hg was calculated in similar fashion.

measurements, which were conducted by gas isotope ratio mass spectrometry. In addition, the assumption that the CK-MMHg reaction produces intermediate ion-radical pairs is not supported in the literature. Hence, independent corroboration of this reaction and the corresponding isotope fractionation is urgently needed. If binding of MMHg to enzymes, proteins, and other cysteine residues would indeed strongly favor odd Hg isotopes as suggested, it would have profound consequences for Hg isotope fractionation during bioaccumulation considering that MMHg in fish is thought to be bound to cysteine residues (Harris et al., 2003). As well, it would constitute a unique example

of different isotopes of the same element exhibiting drastic differences in toxicity.

Source Tracking

A pioneering study illustrated the power of Hg isotope ratio measurements to trace sources of contamination (Foucher et al., 2009). The authors investigated the well-documented Hg mining region near Idrija, Slovenia, and measured sediments alongside the Idrijca River, the Soča/Isonzo River and in the Gulf of Trieste to determine the variation in Hg isotopic composition versus distance from the Hg mine. Samples collected from the rivers Idrijca and Soča/Isonzo and near the shore in the Gulf of Trieste had very uniform δ^{202}Hg values of −0.32 ± 0.15‰, which was not different from Hg ore at the Idrija Mine (−0.26 ± 0.12‰) suggesting that sediments throughout the watershed of the Soča/Isonzo River to the Gulf of Trieste are dominated by Hg exported from the mining area. In contrast, the regional background of the Adriatic Sea was determined to be −2.53 ± 0.46‰. Sediments from the southern part of the Gulf outside the river plume showed intermediate δ^{202}Hg, ranging from −1.19 to −2.00‰. Using a simple binary mixing model, the authors were able to demonstrate that all samples investigated in this study were a result of combinations of Hg originating from the Idrija Mine and from the Adriatic Sea. They estimated that the contribution of Hg from the mining area in surficial sediments of the Gulf of Trieste progressively decreases from 90% or more in the northern part to less than 45% in the south. These results are a promising first demonstration of tracking mercury sources in natural systems using mercury stable isotope ratios.

Future Directions

The field of mercury isotope geochemistry is rapidly emerging and the analytical protocols and methods are now well enough defined to measure Hg isotope ratios in many matrices. However, there are still many unresolved questions that will be answered only through a combination of careful, well-designed laboratory experiments and collection of field data. Hg is an important environmental pollutant that continues to be under close scrutiny. It is expected that Hg isotope analyses will contribute to our understanding of the Hg cycle and in the future may even be the critical tool to resolve the "holy grail" of Hg biogeochemistry—that is, the differentiation between geogenic and anthropogenic sources of Hg in the environment.

In particular, the following areas will likely receive increased attention in the future. Our database of well-constrained Hg isotope fractionation factors is still very limited and requires expansion to fully understand Hg isotope variations in nature. We also need to expand our database on natural Hg isotope variations. Additional work is needed to extend it to environmental compartments with low Hg concentrations or mass. In particular, we are lacking information on Hg isotope fractionation in water and the atmosphere, which is of crucial importance when it comes to regional or even global source tracking of Hg pollution. Since the instrumental technology seems to be used already to its maximum potential, future gains will be possible mainly by processing very large quantities of samples. To this end, we must optimize quantitative pre-concentrations methods.

The next frontier is likely the compound-specific measurement of Hg isotope ratios. Hg is a prime example for the need of species-specific information. The different Hg species exhibit vastly different chemical, physical, and toxicologic characteristics. It is therefore expected that isotope ratio measurements will follow previous analytical and environmental studies and use species-specific measurements to shed more light on the complex Hg biogeochemical cycle. And lastly, it should be noted that MIF is not only an academic curiosity, but instead offers enormous potential for tracking Hg through the ecosystem. Nevertheless, we are only at the beginning of establishing a theoretical framework for the Hg isotope system, which has the unique characteristic of multiple independent fractionation pathways.

References

Albarède, F., and B.L. Beard. 2003. Analytical methods for non-traditional isotopes. In: C.M. Johnson, B.L. Beard, and F. Albarède, eds. *Geochemistry of non-traditional stable isotopes,* Vol. 55. Washington, DC: Mineralogical Society of America, pp. 113–152.

Angeli, I. 2004. A consistent set of nuclear rms charge radii: properties of the radius surface R(N,Z). *Atomic Data and Nuclear Data Tables* 87: 185–206.

Bergquist, B.A., and J.D. Blum. 2007. Mass-dependent and -independent fractionation of Hg isotopes by photoreduction in aquatic systems. *Science* 318: 417–420.

Bigeleisen, J. 1996. Nuclear size and shape effects in chemical reactions. Isotope chemistry of the heavy elements. *Journal of the American Chemical Society* 118: 3676–3680.

Bigeleisen, J., and M.G. Mayer. 1947. Calculation of equilibrium constants for isotopic exchange reactions. *Journal of Chemical Physics* 15: 261–267.

Biswas, A., J.D. Blum, B.A. Bergquist, G.J. Keeler, and Z. Xie. 2008. Natural mercury isotope variation in coal deposits and organic soils. *Environmental Science & Technology* 42: 8303–8309.

Blum, J.D., and B.A. Bergquist. 2007. Reporting of variations in the natural isotopic composition of mercury. *Analytical and Bioanalytical Chemistry* 388: 353–359.

Brönsted, J.N., and G. von Hevesy. 1920. The separation of mercury isotopes. *Nature (London)* 106: 144–147.

Buchachenko, A.L. 2001. Magnetic isotope effect: nuclear spin control of chemical reactions. *Journal of Chemical Physics* 105: 9995–10011.

Buchachenko, A.L., V.L. Ivanov, V.A. Roznyatovsky, and Y.A. Ustynyuk. 2006. Magnetic isotope effect in the photolysis of organotin compounds. *Journal of Physical Chemistry* 110: 3857–3859.

Buchachenko, A.L., D.A. Kouznetsov, and A.V. Shishkov. 2004. Spin biochemistry: magnetic isotope effect in the reaction of creatine kinase with CH_3HgCl. *Journal of Physical Chemistry* 108: 707–710.

Chen, J., H. Hintelmann, and B. Dimock. 2010. Chromatographic pre-concentration of Hg from dilute aqueous solutions for isotopic measurement by MC-ICP-MS. *Journal of Analytical Atomic Spectrometry* 25: 1402–1409.

De Laeter, J.R., J.K. Böhlke, P. De Bièvre, H. Hidaka, H.S. Peiser, K.J.R. Rosman, and P.D.P. Taylor. 2003. Atomic weights of the elements: review 2000 (IUPAC Technical Report). *Pure and Applied Chemistry* 75: 683–800.

Dzurko, M. 2006. Fractionation of mercury isotopes during methylation by sulfate-reducing bacteria. Master's thesis, Trent University, Peterborough, ON, Canada.

Dzurko, M., D. Foucher, and H. Hintelmann. 2009. Determination of compound-specific Hg isotope ratios from transient signals using gas chromatography coupled to multicollector inductively couple plasma mass spectrometry (MC-ICP/MS). *Analytical and Bioanalytical Chemistry* 393: 345–355.

Epov, V.N., P. Rodriguez-Gonzalez, J. Sonke, E. Tessier, D. Amouroux, L.M. Bourgoin, and O.F.X. Donard. 2008. Simultaneous determination of species-specific isotopic composition of Hg by gas chromatography coupled to multicollector ICPMS. *Analytical Chemistry* 80: 3530–3538.

Estrade, N., J. Carignan, J. Sonke, and O.F.X. Donard. 2008. Mercury isotope fractionation during liquid-vapor evaporation experiments. *Geochimica et Cosmochimica Acta* 73: 2693–2711.

Evans, R.D., H. Hintelmann, and P.J. Dillon. 2001. Measurement of high precision isotope ratios for mercury from coals using transient signals. *Journal of Analytical Atomic Spectrometry* 16: 1064–1069.

Foucher, D., and H. Hintelmann. 2004. Determination of highly precise mercury isotope ratios by using the multi-collector inductively coupled plasma mass spectrometry. *Materials and Geoenvironment* 51: 1913–1916.

Foucher, D., and H. Hintelmann. 2006. High precision measurement of mercury isotope ratios in sediments using cold-vapor generation multi-collector inductively coupled plasma mass spectrometry. *Analytical and Bioanalytical Chemistry* 384: 1470–1478.

Foucher, D., N. Ogrinc, and H. Hintelmann. 2009. Tracing mercury contamination from the Idrija mining region (Slovenia) to the Gulf of Trieste using Hg isotope ratio measurements. *Environmental Science and Technology* 43: 33–39.

Ghosh, S., Y. Xu, M. Humayun, and L. Odom. 2008. Mass independent fractionation of mercury isotopes in the environment. *Geochemistry, Geophysics, Geosystems* 9: Q03004. doi:10.1029/2007GC001827.

Hahn, A.A., J.P. Miller, R.J. Powers, A. Zehnder, A.M. Rushton, R.E. Welsh, A.R. Kunselman, P. Robertson, and H.K. Walter. 1979. An experimental study of muonic x-ray transitions in mercury isotopes. *Nuclear Physics A* 314: 361–386.

Harris, H.H., I.J. Pickering, and G.N. George. 2003. The chemical form of mercury in fish. *Science* 301(5637): 1203.

Hintelmann, H. 2003. Trace element speciation: Mercury. In: Z. Mester and R. Sturgeon (Eds.). *Sample preparation for trace element analysis.* New York: Elsevier, pp. 1063–1080.

Hintelmann, H., and S. Lu. 2003. High precision isotope ratio measurements of mercury isotopes in cinnabar ores using multi-collector ICP/MS. *Analyst* 128: 635–639.

Hintelmann, H., and N. Ogrinc. 2003. Determination of stable mercury isotopes by ICP/MS and their application in environmental studies. In: Y. Cai and C.O. Braids, eds. *Biogeochemistry of environmentally important trace elements.* ACS Symposium Series Vol. 835. *American Chemical Society,* Washington: DC, pp. 321–338.

Jackson, T.A., D.C.G. Muir, and W.F. Vincent. 2004. Historical variations in the stable isotope composition of mercury in arctic lake sediments. *Environmental Science and Technology* 38: 2813–2821.

Jackson, T.A., D.M. Whittle, M.S. Evans, and D.C.G. Muir. 2007. Evidence for mass-independent and mass-dependent fractionation of the stable isotopes of mercury by natural processes in aquatic ecosystems. *Applied Geochemistry* 23: 547–571.

Klaue, B., and J.D. Blum. 1999. Trace analyses of arsenic in drinking water by inductively coupled plasma mass spectrometry: high resolution versus hydride generation. *Analytical Chemistry* 71: 1408–1414.

Klaue, B., and J.D. Blum. 2000. Mercury isotopic analyses by single- and multi-collector magnetic sector inductively coupled plasma mass spectrometry. *Journal of Conference Abstracts: Goldschmidt 2000* 5: 591.

Korea Atomic Energy Research Institute. 2000. Table of nuclides. http://atom.kaeri.re.kr (April 08, 2008).

Koval, N.A., V.V. Zakharchenko, O.R. Savin, V.I. Vinogradov, V.A. Shkurdoda, and V.I. Simonovskii. 1977. Problems of natural fractionation of mercury isotopes. *Doklady Akademii Nauk* 235: 936–938.

Kritee, K., J.D. Blum, M.W. Johnson, B.A. Bergquist, and T. Barkay. 2007. Mercury stable isotope fractionation during reduction of Hg(II) to Hg(0) by mercury resistant microorganisms. *Environmental Science and Technology* 41: 1889–1895.

Krupp, E.M., and O.F.X. Donard. 2005. Isotope ratios on transient signals with GC–MC–ICP-MS. *International Journal of Mass Spectrometry* 242: 233–242.

Lauretta, D.S., B. Klaue, J.D. Blum, and P.R. Buseck. 2001. Mercury abundances and isotopic composition in the Murchinson (CM) and Allende (CV) carbonaceous chondrites. *Geochimica et Cosmochimica Acta* 65: 2807–2818.

Malinovsky, D., R.E. Sturgeon, and L. Yang. 2008. Anion-exchange chromatographic separation of Hg for isotope ratio measurements by multicollector ICPMS. *Analytical Chemistry* 80: 2548–2555.

Mead, C., and T.M. Johnson. 2010. Hg stable isotope analysis by the double-spike method. *Analytical and Bioanalytical Chemistry* 388: 353–359, 397: 1529–1538.

Nier, A.O. 1950. A redetermination of the relative abundances of the isotopes of krypton, rubidium, xenon and mercury. *Physical Review A* 79: 450–454.

Nier, A.O., and D.J. Schlutter. 1986. Mass spectrometric study of the mercury isotopes in the Allende meteorite. *Proceedings of the 17th Lunar and Planetary Sciences Conference* E124–E128.

Obolenskii, A.A., and E.F. Doilnitsyn. 1976. Natural fractionation of mercury isotopes. *Doklady Akademii Nauk* 230: 701–704.

Schauble, E.A. 2007. Role of nuclear volume in driving equilibrium stable isotope fractionation of mercury, thallium, and other very heavy elements. *Geochimica et Cosmochimica Acta* 71: 2170–2189.

Smith, C.N., S.E. Kesler, B. Klaue, and J.D. Blum. 2005. Mercury isotope fractionation in fossil hydrothermal systems. *Geology* 33: 825–828.

Sonke, J.E., T. Zambardi, and J.-P. Toutain. 2008. Indirect gold trap–MC-ICP-MS coupling for Hg stable isotope analysis using a syringe injection interface. *Journal of Analytical Atomic Spectrometry* 23: 569–573.

Urey, H.C. 1947. The thermodynamic properties of isotopic substances. *Journal of the Chemical Society (London)* 562–581.

Van Walleghem, J.L.A., P.J. Blanchfield, and H. Hintelmann. 2007. Elimination of mercury by yellow perch in the wild. *Environmental Science and Technology* 41: 5895–5901.

Xie, Q., S. Lu, R.D. Evans, P. Dillon, and H. Hintelmann. 2005. High precision Hg Isotope analysis of environmental samples using gold trap-MC-ICP-MS. *Journal of Analytical Atomic Spectrometry* 20: 515–522.

Young, E.D., A. Galy, and H. Nagahara. 2002. Kinetic and equilibrium mass-dependent isotope fractionation laws in nature and their geochemical and cosmochemical consequence. *Geochimica et Cosmochimica Acta* 66: 1095–1104.

Zheng, W., and H. Hintelmann. 2009. Mercury isotope fractionation during photoreduction in natural water is controlled by its Hg/DOC ratio. *Geochimica et Cosmochimica Acta* 73: 6704–6715.

Zheng, W., and H. Hintelmann. 2010a. Nuclear field shift effect in isotope fractionation of mercury during abiotic reduction in the absence of light. *Journal of Physical Chemistry* 114: 4238–4245.

Zheng, W., and H. Hintelmann. 2010b. Isotope Fractionation of mercury during its photochemical reduction by low-molecular-weight organic compounds. *Journal of Physical Chemistry* 114: 4246–4253.

Zheng, W., D. Foucher, and H. Hintelmann. 2007. Mercury isotope fractionation during volatilization of Hg(0) from solution into the gas phase. *Journal of Analytical Atomic Spectrometry* 22: 1097–1104.

CHAPTER 5

Atmospheric Chemistry, Modeling, and Biogeochemistry of Mercury

NOELLE ECKLEY SELIN

GLOBAL BUDGET OF MERCURY

FORMS AND DISTRIBUTION OF MERCURY IN THE ATMOSPHERE

OXIDATION AND REDUCTION PROCESSES

DEPOSITION PROCESSES

ATMOSPHERIC MODELS AND APPLICATIONS

FUTURE CHALLENGES

Mercury in the environment is of increasing concern globally because it can travel long distances through the atmosphere. For example, atmospheric transport and deposition of mercury from lower latitudes to the Arctic environment poses environmental and human health risks, despite few sources within the Arctic. On a more local scale, atmospheric chemical reactions and meteorologic processes can determine whether mercury deposits near sources or circulates globally. Understanding the chemistry and transport of atmospheric mercury is thus vitally important for managing mercury pollution.

There remain several critical uncertainties surrounding the behavior of mercury in the atmosphere. The global biogeochemical budget of mercury is not well constrained, particularly the magnitude of fluxes from land and ocean surfaces. The chemical reactions that control the transformation of mercury between its forms in the atmosphere are uncertain. However, some improvements in measurement techniques and the development of models at scales from local to global have provided important new insights into atmospheric mercury.

This chapter addresses the atmospheric chemistry and transport of mercury. It begins with an overview of the global biogeochemical budget of mercury, with particular attention to fluxes into and out of the atmosphere. It then surveys the different forms of atmospheric mercury

and their distribution in the atmosphere. This includes the oxidation and reduction reactions that alter the form and properties of atmospheric mercury, and the wet and dry deposition processes that control its deposition to ecosystems. This is followed by a brief survey of atmospheric models that have been used in combination with measurements to further scientific understanding of atmospheric mercury. The chapter concludes by summarizing future challenges for atmospheric mercury research.

Global Budget of Mercury

Prior to the onset of human industrial activities, the amount of natural mercury cycling through the land–ocean–atmosphere system was roughly one third of present levels. This represents the natural background level of mercury in the environment, which human activities have augmented. The origin of this natural background is geologic activity, including erupting volcanoes and emissions from the so-called global mercuriferous belts, where land is enriched with mercury (Fitzgerald and Lamborg, 2005).

The natural cycle accounts for about a third of present-day mercury entering the atmosphere; however, direct anthropogenic emissions are roughly comparable in magnitude. Anthropogenic activities that release mercury to the atmosphere include coal burning, industrial processes, waste incineration, and mining and metallurgical activities (Pacyna et al., 2006). The total amount of anthropogenic emissions to the atmosphere has remained relatively stable over the past decade; however, decreases in North America and Europe have been offset by increasing emissions in rapidly developing regions such as Asia (Pacyna et al., 2006).

The remaining third of emissions to the atmosphere is a result of the legacy of anthropogenic activity that has released mercury since industrialization. Human activities have taken mercury from its long-term storage in geologic reservoirs and transferred it to the atmosphere. While the lifetime of mercury in the atmosphere is about a year, cycling between the atmosphere and the land and ocean surface effectively lengthens the amount of time mercury circulates in the environment (Selin et al., 2008). Mason and Sheu (2002) estimate that it will take about 10,000 years for mercury to return to long-term sedimentary storage. Until then, this historical mercury continues to be released again to the atmosphere from land and ocean surfaces. The magnitude of these fluxes and the processes controlling them are not well constrained, but measurements have shown that fluxes can depend on temperature (Kim et al., 1995; Lindberg et al., 1995), solar radiation (Carpi and Lindberg, 1998; Gustin et al., 2002), or soil moisture (Gustin and Stamenkovic, 2005). Isotopic field studies have also shown that mercury recently deposited to ecosystems is more available for emission (Graydon et al., 2006; Hintelmann et al., 2002).

Forms and Distribution of Mercury in the Atmosphere

In the atmosphere, mercury exists in three major forms. The majority of mercury in the atmosphere is in the form of gaseous, elemental mercury, which is termed Hg(0) (Mason and Sheu, 2002; Schroeder and Munthe, 1998). Typical concentrations of Hg(0) in the atmosphere are about 1.6 ng m^{-3} at the surface. Hg(0) has a Henry's law constant of 0.11 M atm^{-1} at 298 K (Lin and Pehkonen, 1999), which makes it less soluble than other forms of atmospheric Hg, and therefore more likely to be present in the gas phase in the atmosphere. Hg(0) has a lifetime of between 0.5 and 2 years in the global atmosphere, which means that it has the ability to transport globally. The two other forms of mercury are both shorter-lived. Divalent mercury [Hg(II)] is more soluble than Hg(0), which means that it is more likely to deposit to the surface through wet deposition and also dry deposition (which is enhanced for more soluble species). Because it deposits so readily, its lifetime in the atmosphere is shorter than that of Hg(0)—on the order of days to weeks. Typical concentrations of atmospheric Hg(II) vary between 1 and 100 pg m^{-3}. It is thought that most divalent mercury in the atmosphere is in the form of HgCl$_2$ (Lin et al., 2006). Mercury can also be associated with atmospheric particulate matter, termed Hg(P). Atmospheric concentrations of Hg(P) are of the same order of magnitude as Hg(II). Depending on particle size, it will also be deposited to the surface through wet and dry deposition on timescales of days to weeks. Mercury can also exist in organic forms in the atmosphere (e.g., methylmercury), though concentrations are more than an order of magnitude smaller than inorganic forms (Hammerschmidt et al., 2007).

Measurements of Hg(0) in the atmosphere are available at a number of land-based stations and from some ocean cruises and aircraft missions. Most land-based measurements are from the northern midlatitudes. Measurements from the Southern Hemisphere at Cape Point (Baker et al., 2002), from Antarctica (Ebinghaus et al., 2002) ,and from ocean cruises (Lamborg et al., 1999; Laurier et al., 2003; Temme et al., 2003) have generally reported lower concentrations than in the Northern Hemisphere, which indicates that most mercury sources are in the Northern Hemisphere. The interhemispheric gradient of Hg(0), in combination with the balance of sources between the Northern and Southern hemispheres, provides constraints on the atmospheric lifetime of Hg(0), as the interhemispheric exchange time for air is about a year (Jacob et al., 1987). The longer the atmospheric lifetime of mercury, the smaller the interhemispheric gradient is expected to be, since mercury would have an opportunity to mix between the hemispheres before it is removed from the atmosphere.

Seasonal variation of Hg(0) is consistent at most sites in the Northern Hemisphere (Kellerhals et al., 2003; Selin et al., 2007), with a maximum in winter and minimum in late summer. This behavior has been measured, for example, at a network of stations in Canada (CAMNet) (Kellerhals et al., 2003), and the seasonal variation is statistically significant for available sites in the northern midlatitudes (Selin et al., 2007). This suggests a photochemical sink of Hg(0), which is oxidation to Hg(II). However, the dominant atmospheric oxidant of Hg(0) is at present uncertain, as discussed below. Seasonal variation of Hg(0) in the Southern Hemisphere is more puzzling. Hg(0) measurements at Cape Point observatory in South Africa (Slemr et al., 2008) are maximum in summer and minimum in winter, opposite what would be expected from photochemical oxidation in this hemisphere. Slemr et al. suggest, based on the Cape Point data, that the seasonal behavior of mercury is driven by its sources rather than its sinks. Obrist (2007) reviewed the seasonal data from mercury measurements and suggested that the spring and summer declines in atmospheric mercury could be driven by the uptake of mercury by vegetation rather than its oxidation sink. This is a subject of continuing scientific investigation and discussion.

Measurements of Hg(II) and Hg(P) are fewer, though the number of measurements of these species are increasing. Hg(II) is measured in the atmosphere as reactive gaseous mercury (RGM) using an operationally defined method. Typically, Hg(II) measurements are made by collecting the species on KCl-coated denuders and reducing it to Hg(0) before measurement (Landis et al., 2002).

RGM has been shown to vary diurnally in the atmosphere, with a peak around midday and at a minimum at night. Jaffe et al. (2005) measured RGM at Okinawa, Japan, and found that levels peaked in the afternoon and were at a minimum at night. RGM at this site did not correlate with Hg(0), indicating that RGM results here from oxidation of Hg(0) and is not directly emitted from anthropogenic sources. It is thought that this reflects production of Hg(II) via oxidation of Hg(0). Laurier and Mason (2007) measured RGM at two sites in Maryland and on an Atlantic cruise and reported diurnal variation in RGM consistent with in situ photochemical production at background sites. At more urban sites in Baltimore, Maryland, they reported that local sources contributed to RGM concentrations. While these measurements of RGM suggest the influence of photochemical production, the major oxidation reactions producing RGM remain uncertain. The details and uncertainties surrounding mercury oxidation and reduction reactions are discussed further in the next section.

Some aircraft measurements of Hg(0) show relatively constant levels as altitude increases (Banic et al., 2003), while others show depletion of Hg(0) with increasing altitude (Friedli et al., 2004; Talbot et al., 2007). A number of measurements of RGM at altitudes above the surface (Landis et al., 2005; Sillman et al., 2007; Swartzendruber et al., 2006) have shown that RGM is higher there than at sea level. Swartzendruber et al. (2006) measured RGM at Mt. Bachelor, Oregon (2.7 km), and observed RGM enhancements up to 600 pg m^{-3} at night, associated with downslope flows of free tropospheric air. Sillman et al. (2007) reported aircraft measurements in the free troposphere (up to 4 km) between 10 and 250 pg m^{-3}, with concentrations increasing with higher altitudes. As total mercury is expected to be conserved, RGM increases with higher altitudes are consistent with aircraft measurements that show depletion of Hg(0) with increasing altitude, such as the measurements of Talbot et al. (2007) of near-total depletion of Hg(0) in the stratosphere. Single-particle measurements have measured mercury attached to particles around the tropopause (Murphy et al., 2006). Mercury is thought to adsorb to elemental carbon (soot) particles (Seigneur et al., 1998), but the dynamics of gas-particle exchange for mercury are not well understood. The influence of high-altitude mercury on the surface is uncertain, but this question has been explored with models as discussed below.

Oxidation and Reduction Processes

Hg(0) is converted to Hg(II) by oxidation in the atmosphere, which is thought to be a photochemically driven process. Based on laboratory data, it was previously thought that O$_3$ (Hall, 1995) and OH radicals (Pal and Ariya, 2004; Sommar et al., 2001) were the primary oxidants of mercury in the global atmosphere. However, more recent theoretical research has demonstrated that the reactions with O$_3$ and OH are unlikely to occur under atmospheric conditions (Calvert and Lindberg, 2005). At present, it is thought that Br could be the dominant global oxidant of mercury (Holmes et al., 2006; Seigneur and Lohman, 2008) and measurements have established kinetic parameters for its reaction with Hg(0) (Donohoue et al., 2006).

In polar regions, observations of Hg(0) and RGM have shown that these species exhibit unusual behavior in springtime. Shortly after Arctic sunrise, a series of so-called Atmospheric Mercury Depletion Events (AMDEs) have been observed to occur, in which Hg(0) levels show a very rapid decline, accompanied by concurrent increases in RGM. Hg(0) is depleted and recovers in a series of such events, which have been measured throughout the Arctic, sub-Arctic, and Antarctic coasts (Steffen et al., 2008). These depletion events are highly correlated with depletion events of tropospheric ozone in the Arctic (Simpson et al., 2007), which are caused by reactions involving halogen chemistry. It is thus thought that halogens, specifically Br, are responsible for AMDEs. At present, it is unknown how much of the depleted mercury remains in the ecosystem, and how much is revolatilized to the atmosphere, during AMDEs. Some measurements have indicated that much of the deposited mercury is revolatilized, but this remains a topic of active scientific interest. In particular, this is because mercury is of concern in Arctic ecosystems because of its accumulation in sensitive food chains (Arctic Monitoring and Assessment Programme [AMAP], 2002). Mercury deposition during the springtime period of productivity could thus contribute to these levels.

Reduction of Hg(II) to Hg(0) is an uncertain process in the atmosphere. Hg(II) is known to be reduced to Hg(0) in natural waters, and this process has been observed to occur in rainwater. It has been hypothesized that an aqueous reaction could reduce Hg(II) in the atmosphere, though its exact mechanism remains unknown. Hg(II) can also be reduced in power plant plumes (Vijayaraghavan et al., 2008). The extent to which reduction of Hg(II) occurs in the atmosphere is important both for the global budget (Lin et al., 2007) as well as for regional chemistry. As reduction produces the longer-lived Hg(0), it can lengthen the lifetime of mercury, and/or reduce regional deposition of anthropogenically emitted Hg(II). Thus, better constraints on the oxidation and reduction reactions of mercury are critical for policy.

Deposition Processes

Processes of wet and dry deposition bring mercury from the atmosphere to the surface. Measurements are available for wet deposition of mercury through the U.S. Mercury Deposition Network (MDN) (National Atmospheric Deposition Program, 2009), which was established in 1996. The MDN measures wet deposition of mercury in weekly precipitation samples at over 100 sites in the United States, Canada, and Mexico. This is the most extensive network of wet deposition monitoring data for mercury that is available, although some stations in Europe also measure mercury wet deposition as part of the Co-Operative Programme for Monitoring and Evaluation of the Long-Range Transmissions of Air Pollutants in Europe (EMEP, 2009). In the United States, wet deposition of mercury varies both regionally and seasonally. The highest measurements of wet deposition are in the southeastern United States, and an additional area of elevated deposition has been measured near Hg(II) sources in the Midwest (e.g., the Ohio River Valley region, which has a high concentration of coal power). Deposition can vary seasonally, and is generally highest in the summer months in the eastern United States.

Dry deposition could be more important than wet deposition to many ecosystems, though few measurements are available. Methods for mercury dry deposition are not well developed (Lyman et al., 2009), and thus the total global magnitude of dry deposition is unknown. Measurements of the deposition velocity of Hg(II) to forest canopies and wetlands are very high (Lindberg et al., 1998; Poissant et al., 2004), as expected for a species of high solubility. The importance of dry deposition of Hg(0) is unknown. Uptake of Hg(0) by vegetation is thought to occur at the leaf interior, controlled by gas exchange at the stomata (Lindberg et al., 1992). While measured deposition velocities for Hg(0) are much slower than those for Hg(II) (Lindberg et al., 1995; Poissant et al., 2004), the significantly higher concentrations of Hg(0) in the atmosphere mean that this could be an important atmospheric sink. However, as the Hg(0) land–atmosphere and ocean–atmosphere flux is bidirectional, measurements and models must take this into account in estimating the net flux. Because the total amount of deposition of mercury is roughly equal to its source to the atmosphere, the total amount of dry deposition in particular is a key constraint in the global biogeochemical budget of mercury.

Atmospheric Models and Applications

Atmospheric models can help to constrain uncertainties in the global mercury cycle, evaluate the importance of various chemical reactions, and assist in policy-making applications. A variety of atmospheric models have been applied to mercury at scales from regional to global (Bullock et al., 2008). In addition, modeling applications have been used to estimate the global biogeochemical budget of mercury.

Lamborg et al. (2002) used a simple, multibox model of mercury to estimate the present-day and preindustrial global biogeochemical budgets of mercury, constrained by the interhemispheric gradient and the enhancement of deposition since the preindustrial era. Mason and Sheu (2002), in contrast, scaled up from individual measurements to estimate preindustrial and present-day cycles. Sunderland and Mason (2007) used an ocean cycling model to assess preindustrial and present ocean fluxes, and Selin et al. (2008) constructed preindustrial and present-day cycles using a coupled three-dimensional land–ocean–atmosphere model. Estimates of global mercury fluxes vary, with the largest uncertainties in fluxes to and from the ocean and land (Selin, 2009).

Despite the uncertainties in modeling mercury, substantial insights can nevertheless be gained from their application in combination with measurements. Most mercury models show reasonable agreement with data on atmospheric Hg(0) and wet deposition (although, as suggested by Lin et al. [2006], it should be recognized that model uncertainties could be compensating for each other). For example, Shia et al. (1999) reported agreement with spatial and seasonal trends for the Chemical Transport Model for Mercury (CTM-Hg) model,

and Selin et al. (2007, 2008) showed that GEOS-Chem agreed with mean concentrations at land-based sites as well as spatial variations. A large number of models have also been compared with constraints from MDN measurements (Bullock et al., 2009; Seigneur et al., 2004; Selin and Jacob, 2008).

Lin et al. (2006, 2007) have used the CMAQ mercury model in an extensive evaluation of the sensitivity of the atmospheric behavior of mercury to different model assumptions about chemistry and deposition processes. They suggested that chemical speciation and kinetics introduce the greatest uncertainties in atmospheric mercury modeling. Bullock et al. (2008) conducted a model intercomparison of the regional mercury models CMAQ (Bullock and Brehme, 2002), Regional Modeling System for Aerosols and Deposition (REMSAD) (ICF, 2005), and the Trace Element Analysis Model (TEAM) (Pai et al., 1997). They found significant differences among the models, driven both by initial and boundary conditions and by model processes. In their study, initial and boundary conditions were supplied by three different global models, CTM-Hg (Shia et al., 1999; Seigneur et al., 2001), GEOS-Chem (Selin et al., 2007), and the Global/Regional Atmospheric Heavy Metals (GRAHM) Model (Dastoor and Larocque, 2004). For some mercury species, monthly average boundary conditions varied by over an order of magnitude, especially at higher altitudes. Bullock et al. (2009) compared wet deposition measurements to output from these models, and found that adjusting for errors in precipitation data improved the agreements between models and observations.

One application of mercury modeling that is of particular interest to policy makers involves diagnosing and attributing the sources of mercury in deposition. Seigneur et al. (2004) used CTM-Hg to calculate that on average 25–32% of deposition to the United States is from North American sources, but at some locations their contribution was as high as 81%. They also estimated that Asian sources contributed 5–36%. Cohen et al. (2004) used the Hybrid Single-Particle Lagrangian Integrated Trajectory (HYSPLIT) model to investigate the sources of mercury to the Great Lakes, and found that coal combustion was the largest contributor. Selin and Jacob (2008) estimated, using the GEOS-Chem model, that North American sources contributed 20% on average to U.S. deposition, exceeding 50% in the industrial Midwest and Northeast. They also estimated that high-altitude RGM contributed over 50% to U.S. deposition, in particular contributing to high levels of deposition in the U.S. Southeast in summertime from convective scavenging.

Future Challenges

Though concentrations of mercury in the atmosphere are low, it is atmospheric transport that makes mercury a global pollution concern. Understanding the pathways by which mercury travels long distances in the environment thus requires a better understanding of the reactions and processes that mercury undergoes in the atmosphere.

Despite increasing attention to mercury in the atmosphere, there remain several scientific uncertainties that limit our understanding of mercury chemistry, transport, and global biogeochemical cycling.

First, constraining the global budget of mercury, and in particular the interactions between land and ocean surfaces and the atmosphere, is a priority. From the atmospheric perspective, this will require improved measurements of land and ocean fluxes as well as dry deposition measurements, and comparison of these measurements with atmospheric models. Improved knowledge of land–atmosphere fluxes will also help to address the influence of historical mercury that continues to reside in these reservoirs, and its interactions with processes such as land-use and climatic changes.

Second, as Hg(II) is the predominant form depositing to ecosystems and Hg(0) represents the majority of emissions, understanding the oxidation and reduction reactions that control the speciation of mercury is necessary to better constrain where and when deposition is most likely to occur. Better understanding of where and under what conditions Hg(II) is formed can help to trace pollutants from source to receptor as well as identify gaps in measurements in potentially impacted ecosystems.

Finally, to support policy applications, better integration and analysis of the fate of atmospheric mercury across local, regional, and global scales is necessary. Deposition to ecosystems comprises mercury from anthropogenic sources nearby and faraway, in combination with historical mercury loadings as well as natural background. These source attributions vary spatially and temporally in ways that are only beginning to be understood. Effective controls on mercury pollution will thus likely require coordinated policy actions at a variety of scales (Selin and Selin, 2006).

References

Arctic Monitoring and Assessment Programme (AMAP). 2002. *Arctic Pollution*. Oslo, Norway: AMAP.

Baker, P. G. L., E. G. Brunke, F. Slemr, and A. M. Crouch. 2002. Atmospheric mercury measurements at Cape Point, South Africa. *Atmospheric Environment* 36 (14): 2459–2465.

Banic, C. M., S. T. Beauchamp, R. J. Tordon, W. H. Schroeder, A. Steffen, K. A. Anlauf, and H. K. T. Wong. 2003. Vertical distribution of gaseous elemental mercury in Canada. *Journal of Geophysical Research-Atmospheres* 108 (D9).

Bullock, O. R., and K. A. Brehme. 2002. Atmospheric mercury simulation using the CMAQ model: formulation description and analysis of wet deposition results. *Atmospheric Environment* 36: 2135–2146.

Bullock, O. R., Jr., D. Atkinson, T. Braverman, K. Civerolo, A. Dastoor, D. Davignon, J.-Y. Ku, K. Lohman, T. C. Myers, R. J. Park, C. Seigneur, N. E. Selin, G. Sistla, and K. Vijayaraghavan. 2008. The North American Mercury Model Intercomparison Study (NAMMIS): Study description and model-to-model comparisons. *Journal of Geophysical Research* 113 (D17310).

Bullock, O. R., Jr., D. Atkinson, T. Braverman, K. Civerolo, A. Dastoor, D. Davignon, J.-Y. Ku, K. Lohman, T. Myers, R. Park, C. Seigneur, N. E. Selin, G. Sistla, and K. Vijayaraghavan. 2009. An analysis of simulated wet deposition of mercury from the North American Mercury Model Intercomparison Study (NAMMIS). *Journal of Geophysical Research,* in press.

Calvert, J. G., and S. E. Lindberg. 2005. Mechanisms of mercury removal by O3 and OH in the atmosphere. *Atmospheric Environment* 39: 3355–3367.

Carpi, A., and S. E. Lindberg. 1998. Application of a Teflon (TM) dynamic flux chamber for quantifying soil mercury flux: Tests and results over background soil. *Atmospheric Environment* 32 (5): 873–882.

Cohen, M., R. Artz, R. Draxler, P. Miller, L. Poissant, D. Niemi, D. Ratté, M. Deslauriers, R. Duval, and R. Laurin. 2004. Modeling the atmospheric transport and deposition of mercury to the Great Lakes. *Environmental Research* 95 (3): 247–265.

Co-operative Programme for Monitoring and Evaluation of the Long-Range Transmissions of Air Pollutants in Europe (EMEP). 2009. Heavy Metals and POP Measurements, 2007. Kjeller, Norway: Norwegian Institute for Air Research. EMEP/CCC Report 3/2009.

Dastoor, A. P., and Y. Larocque. 2004. Global circulation of atmospheric mercury: a modelling study. *Atmospheric Environment* 38 (1): 147–161.

Donohoue, D. L., D. Bauer, B. Cossairt, and A. J. Hynes. 2006. Temperature and pressure dependent rate coefficients for the reaction of Hg with Br and the reaction of Br with Br: A pulsed laser photolysis-pulsed laser induced fluorescence study. *Journal of Physical Chemistry A* 110 (21): 6623–6632.

Ebinghaus, R., H. H. Kock, C. Temme, J. W. Einax, A. G. Lowe, A. Richter, J. P. Burrows, and W. H. Schroeder. 2002. Antarctic springtime depletion of atmospheric mercury. *Environmental Science and Technology* 36 (6): 1238–1244.

Fitzgerald, W. F., and C. H. Lamborg. 2005. Geochemistry of mercury in the environment. In: *Treatise on Geochemistry*, edited by B. S. Lollar. New York: Elsevier.

Friedli, H. R., L. F. Radke, R. Prescott, P. Li, J.-H. Woo, and G. R. Carmichael. 2004. Mercury in the atmosphere around Japan, Korea and China as observed during the 2001 ACE-Asia field campaign: Measurements, distributions, sources and implications. *Journal of Geophysical Research* 109 (D19S25): 1–13.

Graydon, J. A., V. L. St Louis, S. E. Lindberg, H. Hintelmann, and D. P. Krabbenhoft. 2006. Investigation of mercury exchange between forest canopy vegetation and the atmosphere using a new dynamic chamber. *Environmental Science and Technology* 40 (15): 4680–4688.

Gustin, M. S., H. Biester, and C. S. Kim. 2002. Investigation of the light-enhanced emission of mercury from naturally enriched substrates. *Atmospheric Environment* 36 (20): 3241–3254.

Gustin, M. S., and J. Stamenkovic. 2005. Effect of watering and soil moisture on mercury emissions from soils. *Biogeochemistry* 76 (2): 215–232.

Hall, B. 1995. The gas phase oxidation of elemental mercury by ozone. *Water, Air, and Soil Pollution* 80: 301–315.

Hammerschmidt, C. R., C. H. Lamborg, and W. F. Fitzgerald. 2007. Aqueous phase methylation as a potential source of methylmercury in wet deposition. *Atmospheric Environment* 41 (8): 1663–1668.

Hintelmann, H., R. Harris, A. Heyes, J. P. Hurley, C. A. Kelly, D. P. Krabbenhoft, S. Lindberg, J. W. M. Rudd, K. J. Scott, and V. L. St Louis. 2002. Reactivity and mobility of new and old mercury deposition in a Boreal forest ecosystem during the first year of the METAALICUS study. *Environmental Science and Technology* 36 (23): 5034–5040.

Holmes, C., X. Yang, and D. J. Jacob. 2006. Is atomic bromine a major global oxidant of atmospheric mercury? *Geophysical Research Letters* 33 (L20808). doi:10.1029/2006GL027176.

ICF. 2005. User's guide to the Regional Modeling System for Aerosols and Deposition (REMSAD). San Francisco, CA: ICF Consulting/SAI.

Jacob, D. J., M. J. Prather, S. C. Wofsy, and M. B. McElroy. 1987. Atmospheric distribution of 85 Kr simulated with a general circulation model. *Journal of Geophysical Research* 92: 6614–6626.

Jaffe, D., E. Prestbo, P. Swartzendruber, P. Weiss-Penzias, S. Kato, A. Takami, S. Hatakeyama, and Y. Kajii. 2005. Export of atmospheric mercury from Asia. *Atmospheric Environment* 39: 3029–3038.

Kellerhals, M., S. Beauchamp, W. Belzer, P. Blanchard, F. Froude, B. Harvey, K. McDonald, M. Pilote, L. Poissant, K. Puckett, B. Schroeder, A. Steffen, and R. Tordon. 2003. Temporal and spatial variability of total gaseous mercury in Canada: results from the Canadian Atmospheric Mercury Measurement Network (CAMNet). *Atmospheric Environment* 37 (7): 1003–1011.

Kim, K. H., S. E. Lindberg, and T. P. Meyers. 1995. Micrometeorological measurements of mercury-vapor fluxes over background forest soils in eastern Tennessee. *Atmospheric Environment* 29 (2): 267–282.

Lamborg, C. H., W. F. Fitzgerald, J. O'Donnell, and T. Torgersen. 2002. A non-steady-state compartmental model of global-scale mercury biogeochemistry with interhemispheric gradients. *Geochimica et Cosmochimica Acta* 66 (7): 1105–1118.

Lamborg, C. H., K. R. Rolfhus, W. F. Fitzgerald, and G. Kim. 1999. The atmospheric cycling and air-sea exchange of mercury species in the South and equatorial Atlantic Ocean. *Deep-Sea Research II* 46: 957–977.

Landis, M. S., M. M. Lynam, and R. K. Stevens. 2005. The monitoring and modelling of mercury species in support of local, regional and global modelling. In: *Dynamics of mercury pollution on regional and global scales*, edited by N. Pirrone and K. R. Mahaffey. Norwell, MA: Springer.

Landis, M. S., R. K. Stevens, F. Schaedlich, and E. M. Prestbo. 2002. Development and characterization of an annular denuder methodology for the measurement of divalent inorganic reactive gaseous mercury in ambient air. *Environmental Science and Technology* 36: 3000–3009.

Laurier, F., and R. P., Mason. 2007. Mercury concentration and speciation in the coastal and open ocean boundary layer. *Journal of Geophysical Research D Atmospheres* 112.

Laurier, F. J. G., R. P. Mason, and L. Whalin. 2003. Reactive gaseous mercury formation in the North Pacific Ocean's marine boundary layer: A potential role of halogen chemistry. *Journal of Geophysical Research* 108 (D17): 4529.

Lin, C.-J., and S. O. Pehkonen. 1999. The chemistry of atmospheric mercury: a review. *Atmospheric Environment* 33 (13): 2067–2079.

Lin, C.-J., P. Pongprueksa, O. R. Bullock, S. E. Lindberg, S. O. Pehkonen, C. Jang, T. Braverman, and T. C. Ho. 2007. Scientific uncertainties in atmospheric mercury models II: Sensitivity analysis in the CONUS domain. *Atmospheric Environment* 41 (31): 6544–6560.

Lin, C.-J., P. Pongprueksa, S. E. Lindberg, S. O. Pehkonen, D. Byun, and C. Jang. 2006. Scientific uncertainties in atmospheric mercury models I: Model science evaluation. *Atmospheric Environment* 40: 2911–2928.

Lindberg, S. E., P. J. Hanson, T. P. Meyers, and K.-H. Kim. 1998. Air/surface exchange of mercury vapor over forests—the need for a reassessment of continental biogenic emissions. *Atmospheric Environment* 32 (5): 895–908.

Lindberg, S. E., K. H. Kim, T. P. Meyers, and J. G. Owens. 1995. Micrometeorological gradient approach for quantifying air-surface exchange of mercury-vapor—tests over contaminated soils. *Environmental Science and Technology* 29 (1): 126–135.

Lindberg, S. E., T. P. Meyers, G. E. Taylor Jr., R. R. Turner, and W. H. Schroeder. 1992. Atmosphere-surface exchange of mercury in a forest: Results of modeling and gradient approaches. *Journal of Geophysical Research* 97 (D2): 2519–2528.

Lyman, S. N., M. S. Gustin, E. M. Prestbo, P. I. Kilner, E. Edgerton, and B. Hartsell. 2009. Testing and application of surrogate surfaces for understanding potential gaseous oxidized mercury dry deposition. *Environmental Science and Technology* 43 (16):6235–6241.

Mason, R. P., and G. R. Sheu. 2002. Role of the ocean in the global mercury cycle. *Global Biogeochemical Cycles* 16 (4): 1093.

Murphy, D. M., P. K. Hudson, D. S. Thomson, P. J. Sheridan, and J. C. Wilson. 2006. Observations of mercury-containing aerosols. *Environmental Science and Technology* 40 (7): 2357–2362.

National Atmospheric Deposition Program. 2009. Mercury Deposition Network (MDN): A NADP Network. Champaign, IL: NADP Program Office, Illinois State Water Survey.

Obrist, D. 2007. Atmospheric mercury pollution due to losses of terrestrial carbon pools? *Biogeochemistry* 85 (2): 119–123.

Pacyna, E.G., J.M. Pacyna, F. Steenhuisen, and S. Wilson. 2006. Global anthropogenic mercury emission inventory for 2000. *Atmospheric Environment* 40 (22): 4048–4063.

Pai, P., P. Karamchandni, and C. Seigneur. 1997. Simulation of the regional atmospheric transport and fate of mercury using a comprehensive Eulerian model. *Atmospheric Environment* 31: 2271–2732.

Pal, B., and P. A. Ariya. 2004. Studies of ozone initiated reactions of gaseous mercury: kinetics, product studies, and atmospheric implications. *Physical Chemistry Chemical Physics* 6 (3): 572–579.

Poissant, L., M. Pilote, P. Constant, C. Beauvais, H. H. Zhang, and X. H. Xu. 2004. Mercury gas exchanges over selected bare soil and flooded sites in the bay St. Francois wetlands (Quebec, Canada). *Atmospheric Environment* 38 (25): 4205–4214.

Schroeder, W. H., and J. Munthe. 1998. Atmospheric mercury—An overview. *Atmospheric Environment* 32 (5): 809–822.

Seigneur, C., and K. Lohman. 2008. Effect of bromine chemistry on the atmospheric mercury cycle. *Journal of Geophysical Research* 113: D22309.

Seigneur, C., H. Abeck, G. Chia, M. Reinhard, N. S. Bloom, E. Prestbo, and P. Saxena. 1998. Mercury adsorption to elemental carbon (soot) particles and atmospheric particulate matter. *Atmospheric Environment* 32 (14/15): 2649–2657.

Seigneur, C., P. Karamchandani, K. Lohman, and K. Vijayaraghavan. 2001. Multiscale modeling of the atmospheric fate and transport of mercury. *Journal of Geophysical Research* 106 (D21): 27,795–27,809.

Seigneur, C., K. Vijayaraghavan, K. Lohman, P. Karamchandani, and C. Scott. 2004. Global source attribution for mercury deposition in the United States. *Environmental Science and Technology* 38 (2): 555–569.

Selin, N. E. 2009. Global biogeochemical cycling of mercury: a review. *Annual Review of Environment and Resources* 34: 43–63.

Selin, N. E., and D. J. Jacob. 2008. Seasonal and spatial patterns of mercury wet deposition in the United States: constraints on the contribution from North American anthropogenic sources. *Atmospheric Environment* 42 (21): 5193–5204.

Selin, N. E., and H. Selin. 2006. Global politics of mercury pollution: the need for multi-scale governance. *Review of European Community and International Environmental Law* 15 (3): 258–269.

Selin, N. E., D. J. Jacob, R. J. Park, R. M. Yantosca, S. Strode, L. Jaegle, and D. A. Jaffe. 2007. Chemical cycling and deposition of atmospheric mercury: Global constraints from observations. *Journal of Geophysical Research* 112: D02308.

Selin, N. E., D. J. Jacob, R. M. Yantosca, S. Strode, L. Jaegle, and E. M. Sunderland. 2008. Global 3-D land-ocean-atmosphere model for mercury: present-day vs. pre-industrial cycles and anthropogenic enrichment factors for deposition. *Global Biogeochemical Cycles* 22 (22): GB2011.

Shia, R.-L., C. Seigneur, P. Pai, M. Ko, and N. D. Sze. 1999. Global simulation of atmospheric mercury concentrations and deposition fluxes. *Journal of Geophysical Research* 104 (D19): 23,747–23,760.

Sillman, S., F. J. Marsik, K. I. Al-Wali, G. J. Keeler, and M. S. Landis. 2007. Reactive mercury in the troposphere: model formation and results for Florida, the northeastern United States, and the Atlantic Ocean. *Journal of Geophysical Research* 112: D23305.

Simpson, W. R., R. von Glasow, K. Riedel, P. Anderson, P. Ariya, J. Bottenheim, J. Burrows, L. Carpenter, U. Frieß, M. E. Goodsite, D. Heard, M. Hutterli, H.-W. Jacobi, L. Kaleschke, J. Plane, U. Platt, A. Richter, H. Roscoe, R. Sander, P. Shepson, J. Sodeau, A. Steffen, T. Wagner, and E. Wolff. 2007. Halogens and their role in polar boundary-layer ozone depletion. *Atmospheric Chemistry and Physics* 7 (16): 4375–4418.

Slemr, F., E. G. Brunke, C. Labuschagne, and R. Ebinghaus. 2008. Total gaseous mercury concentrations at the Cape Point GAW station and their seasonality. *Geophysical Research Letters* 35: L11807.

Sommar, J., K. Gårdfeldt, D. Strömberg, and X. Feng. 2001. A kinetic study of the gas-phase reaction between the hydroxyl radical and atomic mercury. *Atmospheric Environment* 35: 3049–3054.

Steffen, A., T. Douglas, M. Amyot, P. Ariya, K. Aspmo, T. Berg, J. Bottenheim, S. Brooks, F. Cobbett, and A. Dastoor. 2008. A synthesis of atmospheric mercury depletion event chemistry in the atmosphere and snow. *Atmospheric Chemistry and Physics* 8 (6): 1445–1482.

Sunderland, E. M., and R. P. Mason. 2007. Human impacts on open ocean mercury concentrations. *Global Biogeochemical Cycles* 21 (4): GB4022.

Swartzendruber, P., D. A. Jaffe, E. M. Prestbo, J. E. Smith, P. Weiss-Penzias, N. E. Selin, D. J. Jacob, R. J. Park, S. Strode, and L. Jaegle. 2006. Observations of reactive gaseous mercury at the Mt. Bachelor Observatory. *Journal of Geophysical Research* 111 (D24301). doi:10.1029/2006JD007415.

Talbot, R., H. Mao, E. Scheuer, J. Dibb, and M. Avery. 2007. Total depletion of Hg in the upper troposphere-lower stratosphere. *Geophysical Research Letters* 34: L23804.

Temme, C., F. Slemr, R. Ebinghaus, and J. W. Einax. 2003. Distribution of mercury over the Atlantic Ocean in 1996 and 1999–2001. *Atmospheric Environment* 37 (14): 1889–1897.

Vijayaraghavan, K., P. Karamchandani, C. Seigneur, R. Balmori, and S.-H. Chen. 2008. Plume-in-grid modeling of atmospheric mercury. *Journal of Geophysical Research* 113: D24305.

CHAPTER 6

A Framework for a Mercury Monitoring and Assessment Program

Synthesis and Future Research

ROBERT P. MASON

POLICY AND MANAGEMENT REQUIREMENTS

MODELING REQUIREMENTS

A MERCURY MONITORING FRAMEWORK

THE NETWORK DESIGN

PROPOSED INDICATORS

CONCLUDING REMARKS

Mercury (Hg), especially in its more toxic and bio-accumulative form as methylmercury (MeHg), is an important environmental health concern (Clarkson, 1994; Wolfe et al., 1998; Wiener et al., 2003; Pirrone and Mahaffey, 2005; Mergler et al., 2007). Therefore, in recent years there has been a global effort to limit its input to the atmosphere, especially from anthropogenic sources. Many regulations limiting Hg emissions from specific sources in developing countries, and elsewhere, are already in place, mandated, or likely to happen in the future (USEPA, 1997, 2008; UNEP, 2009). As these regulations are implemented, there is a crucial need to document the impact of their changes on human and ecosystem health in order to assess the effectiveness of regulation and the need for further controls (Mason et al., 2005; Harris et al., 2007a; USEPA, 2008). There are advisories against the overconsumption of fish with elevated MeHg from many water bodies in the United States and other countries, because it is documented that elevated intake of MeHg can cause neurologic damage (Clarkson, 1994; Mahaffey, 1998). Mercury is emitted into the biosphere, either via emission to the atmosphere or to other regions (water or land), from both natural and anthropogenic sources and is effectively transported, primarily as inorganic Hg, from its source to remote locations where it is converted and bio-accumulated as MeHg into aquatic food chains (Mason and Sheu, 2002;

Morel et al., 1998). This transport, transformation, and bio-accumulation make the control and management of Hg a complex problem.

The importance of the atmosphere in the local, regional, and global redistribution of Hg is well known, and anthropogenic release of Hg into the atmosphere since industrialization has increased the global pool of Hg about threefold, on average, and to a higher extent in some locations, such as the eastern United States (Mason and Sheu, 2002; Lindberg et al., 2007; Selin et al., 2008; Pirrone and Mason, 2009). Evidence of long-term changes in the atmospheric Hg burden are recorded in a number of proxies, and the extent of change can be determined using a variety of methods, such as the analysis of lake sediments, ice cores, and peat deposits (Engstrom and Swain, 1997; Lamborg et al., 2002a; Barbante et al., 2004; Krabbenhoft et al., 2007). Such increases in the global atmospheric pool should also be reflected in the atmospheric Hg concentration, but this has been difficult to demonstrate given that the extent to which measurement is possible is still limited (Slemr et al., 2003; Lindberg et al., 2007) and the historical record of accurate measurement is relatively short (<20 years, typically) (Ebinghaus et al, 2009). Given the confounding effect of climate variability and other factors on atmospheric Hg concentration and distribution, it has been difficult to derive a multidecade regional or global trend based on the current situation, since data collection is spatially and temporally uncoordinated (Mason et al., 2005; Lindberg et al., 2007; Ebinghaus and Banic, 2009; Keeler et al., 2009).

In addition, increases in Hg emissions in some regions of the world are being offset by decreases in emissions in other regions (Pacyna et al., 2006; Selin et al., 2008; Pirrone et al., 2009, 2010), and given the relatively long atmospheric residence time of Hg (0.5–1 year) (Lamborg et al., 2002b), emissions in one region of the world can impact Hg deposition to other continents and to the ocean (Dastoor and Larocque, 2004; Jaffe et al., 2005; Selin et al., 2007; Dastoor and Davignon, 2009; Jaegle et al., 2009; Jung et al., 2009; Seigneur et al., 2009; Travnikov and Ilyin, 2009). Significant efforts, especially in developed countries and in the Northern Hemisphere, have been made to understand the atmospheric transport and fate of Hg, which is complicated by the fact that the transformation processes that convert Hg between its different oxidation states and forms in the atmosphere is dynamic and can markedly impact the rate at which Hg is removed from the atmosphere by wet and dry deposition (Schroeder and Munthe, 1998; Ariya et al., 2009; Hynes et al., 2009). Mercury can exist in two oxidation states in the atmosphere (elemental Hg [Hg^0] and ionic Hg [Hg^{II}]). Whereas Hg^0 is found entirely in the gas phase, Hg^{II} can be present as a variety of forms in the gas phase and can also be found within or attached to atmospheric particles. Thus, operationally, three phases have been defined in many studies: gaseous elemental Hg (Hg^0), reactive gaseous Hg (RGHg), and particulate Hg (PHg) (Schroeder and Munthe, 1998; Landis et al., 2002). Developments in the measurement and analytical techniques for Hg have led to a much improved understanding of the sources and cycling of Hg in the environment, but the exact impact of anthropogenic activities on the global Hg cycle is still unclear (Slemr et al., 2003; Laurier and Mason, 2007; Pirrone et al., 2009), as is the subsequent conversion and bioaccumulation of MeHg in aquatic food chains.

Understanding the fate of Hg in the environment, and the impact of human activity on the biosphere, requires improved knowledge of Hg fate, transport, and transformation, which must be derived from a series of coordinated scientific endeavors in terms of measurement and modeling, coupled with interpretation of the results within a policy framework (Mason et al., 2005; Harris et al., 2007a; Keeler et al., 2009). An improved understanding of Hg biogeochemical cycling is important if there is to be a focused and concerted effort to set national and international priorities and goals for Hg management and reduction and to develop and implement policies and strategies. The need to establish baseline concentrations and to document changes to allow assessment of the effectiveness of global Hg emission reductions, or other changes in emission distribution, is apparent. Modeling efforts also require sufficient data to test and validate the model parameters (Ryaboshapko et al., 2007a), and long-term datasets are needed for model testing (Ryaboshapko et al., 2007b). Finally, by comparing and contrasting model output and measurements it is possible to understand more clearly the exchange of Hg between reservoirs and the important reactions. Without this knowledge, the impact of changes in MeHg in fish in response to changes in atmospheric inputs cannot be properly assessed (Munthe et al., 2007; Wiener et al., 2003, 2007; Pirrone and Mason, 2009).

Current atmospheric Hg models have had some success in predicting the levels and trends in ambient Hg levels in the atmosphere (Ryaboshapko et al., 2002, 2007a, 2007b; Lindberg et al., 2007), and similarly, biogeochemical models of the ecosystem cycling of Hg and MeHg formation have been relatively successful in the estimation of changes and trends (Harris et al., 2007a). However, the linking of atmospheric and biogeochemical models for Hg is still in its infancy.

There is a critical need for a coordinated Hg monitoring network designed to track the changes that are occurring in a variety of ecosystem compartments over time and to sustain the development of Hg models that can be used to support policy decisions (Gbondo-Tugbawa and Driscoll, 1998; Hudson et al., 1994; Beals et al., 2002; Roue-Legall et al., 2005; Trudel and Rasmussen, 2006). A well-planned network is required to provide a consistent, standardized set of long-term data on the concentrations and forms of Hg in all compartments of the biosphere. The overarching benefit of such a coordinated monitoring network would be the universal availability of high-quality measurement data that can support various related activities (e.g., modeling and management and policy decisions) (Mason et al., 2005; Harris et al., 2007a). The data from the set of coordinated monitoring sites would support the evaluation and validation of models as research and management tools. Clearly, there is a need to monitor and assess progress on mandated Hg reductions of controllable anthropogenic inputs to the atmosphere, as well as the impact of changes in emissions due to natural variability and human-induced climate change. A reexamination of the current status of the measurement and monitoring of Hg in the global atmosphere is needed to promote the activities required to support a coordinated and consistent monitoring program.

In addition, there are many unanswered questions about the environmental benefits of Hg emission reductions in terms of spatial differences and timescales of response, and it is not clear what site-specific parameters affect these changes. Some intensive studies have been conducted (e.g., Evers and Clair, 2005), but the overall applicability of the results to different ecosystems, or at the continental scale, is uncertain. Overall, it does not appear that the present, mostly uncoordinated, data-collection networks are sufficient to describe spatial and temporal trends in environmental Hg contamination (Ebinghaus and Banic, 2009). Clearly, it is crucial for scientists and policy makers to develop a monitoring framework that can accurately evaluate the effectiveness of current and impending Hg regulation.

The notion of a national Hg monitoring network was first promoted by Dr. William Fitzgerald at an international Hg meeting in Whistler, Canada, in 1994 (Fitzgerald, 1995). More recently, development of a monitoring strategy outline for North America began when a group of 32 Hg scientists from academia, industry, government, and nonprofit organizations in the United States, Canada, and Europe convened during a workshop in Pensacola, Florida, in September 2003. The workshop's aim was to identify suitable Hg indicators and to propose a national (North American) monitoring and assessment network to measure and document the changes in atmospheric loading resulting from changes in Hg emissions in the United States and their impact on aquatic biota MeHg. A holistic, multimedia monitoring approach was designed, as this is needed to detect change across a diverse and complex system. Products of this workshop were a paper published in 2005 (Mason et al., 2005) and a more detailed book (Harris et al., 2007a), which expanded the ideas of the paper and put forward a detailed plan and approach for such a monitoring network.

Since the workshop and the publication of the book, there have been a series of meetings in the United States with federal officials from the United States Environmental Protection Agency (EPA) and other agencies and for U.S. congressional staff. This resulted in the introduction of two bills by Congress to support the formation and structure of a comprehensive national monitoring network. These bills have not been acted on, but activities are ongoing to continue to promote and develop the monitoring network. In this regard, EPA and other Federal agencies organized a workshop in Annapolis, Maryland, in May 2008 to further a comprehensive and integrated monitoring network (MercNet; http://nadp.sws.uiuc.edu/mercnet).

In addition to the efforts in North America, there are a number of international efforts to develop an integrated global monitoring network and regional initiatives in Asia and elsewhere. Such initiatives are focused on evaluating the current information and reassessing Hg emissions and cycling in the atmosphere and the importance of long-range transport (Pirrone and Mason 2009), as well as on coordinating monitoring efforts. The various activities have been coordinated through the United Nations Environmental Program Global Partnership for Mercury Air Transport and Fate Research (UNEP-MFTP) (Pirrone and Mason, 2009; UNEP, 2009) and the Hemispheric Transport of Air Pollutants (HTAP) Task Force (HTAP, 2010). An HTAP report on hemispheric transport of air pollutants, including mercury, is in its final stages of preparation (HTAP, 2010).

In addition, the notion of a global Hg network has been incorporated into the Global Earth Observation System of Systems (GEOSS) program as Sub-Task HE-09-02d. The sub-task initiates the development of:

> a global observation system for mercury by harmonizing standard operating procedures for monitoring mercury and its compounds in air, atmospheric deposition, water, soil, sediments, vegetation and biota. The sharing of data from this network, allowing access to comparable and long-term data from a wide array of locations, will help understand temporal and spatial patterns of mercury transport and deposition to, and evasion from, terrestrial and aquatic ecosystems. The data produced will support the validation of

regional and global atmospheric mercury models for use in evaluations of different policy options for reducing mercury pollution impacts on human health and ecosystems. Build upon the contributions of, among others, the UNEP Mercury Programme, the Hemispheric Transport of Air Pollutants Task Force (TF HTAP), and the European Monitoring and Evaluation Program (EMEP). Moreover, this sub-task will build upon the US MercNet initiative and international monitoring and modelling efforts undertaken by Italy, Japan and South Africa (Global Earth Observation System of Systems [GEOSS], 2009).

Policy and Management Requirements

A monitoring and assessment network must be developed with a clear understanding of the policy and management requirements, and with knowledge of the current situation in order to inform policy development, including answers to policy questions such as: (1) What further Hg reductions are needed to improve human and ecosystem health? (2) What sources should the agencies focus on first in terms of Hg control? and (3) What regulation will be the most cost-effective? Any network will be developed and initiated during a time (Schmeltz et al., 2011), when regulations are already being implemented; therefore the monitoring information that is being gathered may need to be modified to ensure its relevancy and its ability to assess the impact of Hg changes on human and ecosystem health. In addition, sufficient information must be available for all areas so that scientists and policymakers can accurately assess the environmental benefits and effectiveness of Hg control, as this is not the case at present.

Currently, much research is being conducted in an uncoordinated and nonstandard manner, and this is insufficient for determining spatial and temporal trends in environmental contamination. Also, there is insufficient information to establish the baseline concentrations in multiple ecosystem compartments that are needed to assess the effectiveness of future Hg emission reductions or other changes in emission distribution globally. Comprehensive Hg monitoring information is needed to assess progress on mandated Hg reductions of controllable anthropogenic inputs to the atmosphere, as well as the impact of changes in emissions due to natural variability and human-induced climate change.

Modeling Requirements

In designing the network, it is crucial to incorporate the needs of models/modelers (Keeler et al., 2009) and to understand the role of these models in a national Hg assessment and their limitations. The data collected must be sufficient to allow for the testing and validation of model parameters; this includes the need for long-term datasets (Ryaboshapko et al., 2007a; Bullock and Jaegle, 2009; Keeler et al., 2009) and for data collected simultaneously in a variety of ecosystem compartments over time (Harris et al., 2007a). Modeling is an integral part of a national Hg assessment because comparing and contrasting model output and monitored data enables improved understanding of the exchange of Hg between reservoirs and the important governing reactions. Global Hg models (Selin et al., 2007; Dastoor and Davignon, 2009; Jaegle et al., 2009; Jung et al., 2009; Seigneur et al., 2009; Travnikov and Ilyin, 2009) allowing assessment of the input and export from the monitoring domain are needed in support of regional modeling efforts (Bullock and Jaegle, 2009; Keeler et al., 2009). Without knowledge of the link between atmospheric Hg input and bioaccumulation, the impact of changes in MeHg in fish in response to changes in atmospheric inputs cannot be properly assessed. Current atmospheric Hg models have had some success in predicting the levels and trends in ambient Hg levels in the atmosphere (Ryaboshapko et al., , 2002, 2007a, 2007b; Lindberg et al., 2007), and similarly, biogeochemical models of ecosystem cycling of Hg and MeHg formation have been relatively successful in the estimation of changes and trends (Hudson et al., 1994; Gbondo-Tugbawa and Driscoll, 1998; Beals et al., 2002; Roue-Legall et al., 2005; Trudel and Rasmussen, 2006). However, the development of coupled atmospheric and biogeochemical models for Hg is just beginning, and a comprehensive research framework that integrates observations covering a wide range of temporal and spatial scales with modeling and process studies is needed to support such efforts.

Although a monitoring program is primarily a data-collection exercise, models are needed to extrapolate between monitoring sites, to interpret data, and to critically examine the causality of the response of the indicators to changes in atmospheric Hg deposition (Harris et al., 2007a, 2007b). The models could also be used to guide monitoring-site selection, although current efforts are relying more on building the monitoring program around existing sites and databases (Schmeltz et al., 2011). Aquatic ecosystem modeling will be used to test anticipated changes against the observed response and to ascertain the magnitude of the response due to changes in Hg deposition and allow for the exclusion or examination of the impact of confounding factors. For example, it is entirely possible that other factors, such as those impacting trophic status and an organism's growth rate, could cause a decrease in fish Hg concentrations even as atmospheric deposition does not change. Models can be used to predict the spatial and temporal patterns of atmospheric Hg concentrations and fluxes under various future scenarios (e.g., Selin et al., 2008). The models could determine the relative contributions of various sources of Hg over time, based on emission inventories and other estimates of point source and areal inputs, and estimate the likely Hg attenuation rate and recovery timeline under various environmental scenarios. Overall, models allow integration and synthesis, and the data required to run them are a necessary part of any monitoring plan.

Given the complexities in Hg cycling, currently no simulation models accurately predict the response of Hg concentrations (total or MeHg) in the various compartments of terrestrial and aquatic ecosystems to changes in Hg loading rates without modification of the model to a particular situation (Hudson et al., 1994; Gbondo-Tugbawa and Driscoll, 1998; Beals et al., 2002; Roue-Legall et al., 2005; Trudel and Rasmussen, 2006). Such models are needed in conjunction with field and laboratory studies to advance our understanding of Hg cycling. Simulation models have only been calibrated and tested against field data from several sites (e.g., Gbondo-Tugbawa and Driscoll, 1998; Beals et al., 2002); therefore, their accuracy is limited by data availability and by our understanding of the response of more diverse systems. Further model development requires the collection of specific field data for validation. Clearly, there is a critical need to develop models that can reasonably simulate Hg and MeHg cycling and concentrations based on site characteristics and external Hg loading.

A Mercury Monitoring Framework

As outlined and discussed in detail in the other chapters in this book, the link between Hg deposition and MeHg bio-accumulation in aquatic food chains is complex and involves many steps (Mason et al., 2005). Mercury in the atmosphere is removed by both wet and dry deposition to the biosphere. In surface waters, the dissolved Hg^{II} species can be reduced to Hg^0, and if waters become saturated with Hg^0, then it is returned to the atmosphere via evasion (Mason and Sheu, 2002). Reduction and reemission also occur in terrestrial ecosystems (St. Louis et al., 2001; Mason, 2009). For Hg deposited to the watershed, its route to the aquatic system is complex, and the timescale of this pathway is not well known (Grigal, 2003). Most of the total Hg input to watersheds remains sequestered and is not transported to the associated aquatic system. However, for some systems, this input is still significant as compared with direct deposition to the water surface. The bioavailability of Hg supplied from the watershed to methylating bacteria and the potential for reduction to Hg^0 are still not well understood (Sellers et al., 1995; St. Louis et al., 2001). In comparison, some research suggests that Hg added directly to the water surface is efficiently transformed into MeHg and bio-accumulated (Harris et al., 2007b). Sites of methylation are typically the upper reaches of saturated, but anoxic, zones, such as sediments and wetlands in both marine and freshwater ecosystems, as the microbial communities responsible for Hg methylation are primarily sulfate-reducing bacteria (Benoit et al., 2003). Many chemical, biologic, and physical factors—such as bacterial community structure, pH, redox, nutrients, and sulfate—influence MeHg production, and human impacts such as eutrophication and other terrestrial disturbances also affect the extent of Hg methylation. Because MeHg can be degraded (demethylated) to Hg^{II}, by both biotic and abiotic processes, there is rapid cycling between the Hg and MeHg pools, and measured concentrations represent short-term steady-state standing stocks (Benoit et al., 2003).

In designing a monitoring program, it is necessary that the program accurately measures and quantifies the sources of the changes being documented. Because of differences in the lifetime of the various Hg species in surface waters, and their different source profiles and their transformation in the atmosphere, the tracking and detecting of changes in atmospheric Hg deposition relative to reductions in emissions of Hg from anthropogenic sources can be complex (Morel et al., 1998; Ryaboshapko et al., 2007b). The atmospheric transformations are also influenced by the concentration and reactivity of atmospheric oxidants (Schroeder and Munthe, 1998; Hynes et al., 2009). Overall, the ability to detect the response to changes in anthropogenic Hg emissions in the continental United States, for example, will be confounded by changes in natural emissions, in the rate of reemission of previously deposited Hg (Mason, 2009), as well as by changes in Hg emissions in other countries (Bullock and Brehme, 2002, Ryaboshapko et al., 2002, 2007a). Thus, any framework for monitoring atmospheric wet and dry deposition needs to measure or estimate the contribution from all forms of Hg in the atmosphere.

The timescale of a particular ecosystem response to Hg emission reductions is not well known, and it will most likely involve an initial rapid change followed by a slower response, and these rates of change will be different for different ecosystems (Saltman et al., 2007). Therefore, the indicators used must respond on different timescales. Concentrations in upper-trophic-level organisms change relatively slowly (over years) because of growth dilution, as MeHg is only slowly depurated. Conversely, lower-trophic-level organisms, such as zooplankton, respond rapidly (within weeks) to changes in water-column MeHg concentration, and their concentration reflects a transient signal reflecting short-term variability of Hg dynamics and other factors rather than longer-term changes in Hg (Hudson et al., 1994; Harris et al., 2007a). Clearly, the careful choice of Hg monitoring indicators will help reduce these confounding factors due to short-term variability, but they must also be able to integrate the signal so that the direction of change can be determined. Therefore, short-term measurements will be needed to assess variability imparted by ancillary ecosystem changes; however, the monitoring program should be maintained for a sufficient time (at least 10 years) to assess longer-term trends

in atmospheric Hg input. Furthermore, a baseline of information in addition to Hg speciation and distribution is needed to allow for the detection of change. Given that change is already occurring (Pacyna et al., 2006; Pirrone et al., 2009, 2010), the monitoring program needs to be instituted as soon as possible to ensure that adequate background information is gathered. In this context, therefore, there is much to be gained by using existing sites where measurements are being made, as these will have the necessary and required background information, even if only some of the indicators and ancillary information are being measured.

As noted, factors other than changes in Hg deposition also impact Hg methylation and the bio-accumulation (Schmeltz et al., 2011) and fate of MeHg (Benoit et al., 2003), and ancillary data must be collected to properly assess the impact of these confounding variations to ensure that the interpretation of the indicators is scientifically robust and defensible. Confounding factors include land-use changes, global warming impacts, changes in food-web structure and species, existing point-source discharges, changes in climate and atmospheric chemistry and acidic deposition, in situ chemical and physical properties, and hydraulic retention time. Such changes impact all environments; therefore, a cross-section of systems with varying sensitivities to loading needs to be examined, as well as sampling locations that are impacted by local/regional atmospheric Hg emissions. Clearly, while the environmental settings (e.g., water-body type, geographic location) most responsive to short-term changes in atmospheric Hg deposition need to be examined, less responsive and "background" environments should also be monitored. Each ecosystem is unique, and the ability to discern trends in Hg concentrations in indicators will depend on a detailed and clear understanding of the factors that influence Hg biogeochemical cycling.

The Network Design

A regional network should preferably be continental in scale and should include a finite number of study sites that are intensively monitored for all the required variables and indicators (so-called intensive sites) as well as a broad range of colocated monitoring locations (called cluster sites) across different ecosystems, where a more limited number of measurements are made (Mason et al., 2005; Harris et al., 2007a). As it is not possible to provide details for all locations, the proposed network design for North America will be presented here as an example. Depending on the final approach and rationale for choosing sites, it appears that 10–20 intensive sites would provide (Schmeltz et al., 2011) sufficient spatial coverage for North America in terms of Hg deposition levels and ecosystem types. North America consists of four ecosystem domains (polar, desert,

TABLE 6.1
Proposed Indicators for Both the Intensive and the Cluster Sites within the Monitoring Program

Indicator	Location	Frequency	Indicator of
Atmospheric Hg speciation and flux	I	Continuous	Causality
Wet deposition Hg and Flux	C & I	Weekly & event	Causality
Throughfall and litterfall Hg speciation/flux	I	Weekly	Causality
Hg in snowpack	C & I	Annual	Both
Soil/sediment speciation (i.e., Hg, MeHg and %MeHg)	C & I	Annual & quarterly	Both
Soil solution speciation	I	Quarterly	Both
Forest floor survey	I	Every 10 yrs	Causality
Methylation/demethylation rates	I	Biannual	Both
Sediment Hg accumulation rate	C & I	Every 5–10 yrs	Both
Surface water Hg speciation/Hg^0 flux	C & I	Annual & quarterly	Both
Stream water and groundwater Hg speciation and flux	I	Weekly & quarterly	Causality
Algae/phytoplankton and zooplankton Hg speciation	I	Quarterly	Causality
Hg speciation in prey fish or estuarine invertebrates	C & I	Annual	Both
Total Hg in piscivorous fish	C & I	Annual	Trend
Total Hg in mammal/bird blood and fur/feather/egg	C & I	Annual	Both

SOURCE: Information summarized from Harris et al. (2007) and Mason et al. (2005).

C = cluster sites; I = intensive sites.

humid temperate, and humid tropical) and 14 divisions (Bailey, 2004), and in terms of Hg monitoring it appears that the terrestrial regions could be subdivided into 10 "ecoregions." In addition, estuarine and coastal sites should be included in the network (Evers et al., 2008a) because these are impacted by local and regional inputs from the atmosphere and the watershed. The number of estuarine and marine sites is dependent on the total number of intensive sites, but there should be at least 2–3 to cover spatial and regional differences and to account for sites directly impacted versus remote locations. On the east coast of North America, for example, it could be possible to choose an intensive site near the coast so that the cluster sites incorporate different water types, such as lakes, tidal river reaches, and the estuarine and coastal environment.

It is scientifically reasonable to have 10–20 cluster sites corralled around each intensive site, and these sites would be chosen based on their similar atmospheric loading within each ecoregion. At these sites, the primary indicators would be measured over a prolonged period of time (Table 6.1). It is envisioned that a set of cluster sites would have ecologic characteristics that are as similar as possible but would have differing site characteristics (Schmeltz et al., 2011) (e.g., pH, dissolved organic carbon (DOC), acid neutralizing capacity (ANC), and watershed:water body ratio). Cluster site selection criteria would be based on multiple factors, such as water-body type (lake, reservoir, river, or estuary/coastal)

and would represent remote and impacted sites, dry regions and saline waters, as well as a wide range of ecosystem types, and include exposure "hotspots" (Evers et al., 2007).

Intensive sites would be locations where intensive, multimedia, more continuous monitoring is conducted, and where the specific objective is both the careful monitoring of anticipated changes to Hg loading (trend analysis) and detailed documentation of the environmental response in terms of MeHg accumulation in biota (causal response). Emphasis would be placed on choosing sites where change is expected. To maximize existing monitoring, information, and resources, these sites should be established in conjunction with current deposition monitoring stations and/or ecosystem study sites. Clearly, sites from the National Atmospheric Deposition Program (NADP) Mercury Deposition Network (MDN), which currently measures only wet deposition, but which is being expanded to include atmospheric Hg speciation measurements (MDN, 2008), would be desirable as would be sites from other regional monitoring programs, which include Hg and related ancillary measurements, because of the longer-term records at these locations. Measurements would include detailed atmospheric, watershed, aquatic, and biota sampling. Priority should be also given to sites with other intensive ongoing monitoring programs (including sites, such as the Long Term Ecological Research [LTER] Network, which may not have existing Hg data) and would seek to develop ongoing collaborations with other efforts that meet multiple needs (e.g., global change, urban sprawl, and changing-land-use issues).

Therefore, based on the discussion above, the following criteria for site location (Schmeltz et al., 2011) can be listed in order of importance. The chosen sites should, most importantly, be those sites with (Harris et al., 2007a) existing longer-term Hg data (atmospheric and ecosystem data) and supporting information on site characteristics and ancillary measurements; if possible, sites that are expected to be sensitive to Hg inputs and to exhibit large changes in response to changes in Hg deposition should also be included. Sites should preferably reflect a particular ecosystem type (e.g., forest, lake, wetland, urban, of coastal) and/or ecoregions and should be chosen to span ecosystems with a range of characteristic response times to changes in deposition (e.g., rapid-perched seepage lakes and slow sites with substantial groundwater input) and should also include reference sites (i.e., those that are currently impacted only minimally by anthropogenic sources). In addition, preference should be given to sites with existing facilities and infrastructure to support the overall monitoring program. Given the importance of modeling, sites that are useful test beds for evaluation of atmospheric and watershed Hg models should be targeted, and these should include sites where a clearly defined response to changes in Hg emissions and deposition is anticipated (i.e., sites whose response will not be confounded by other disturbances and which are remote from point source inputs). Finally, some sites should be near point emission sources to evaluate the importance of and response to local deposition from elevated Hg inputs.

Although it is not clear to what extent anthropogenic inputs within the United States have impacted offshore open ocean waters (Sunderland and Mason, 2007; Selin et al., 2008), especially the Pacific Ocean, it is clear that human activity and local inputs have impacted many U.S. estuaries and the associated coastal zones, for example. Therefore, a monitoring program cannot ignore these saline waters (Evers et al., 2008a) and should not focus exclusively on freshwater environments. These environments are complex, given the potential impact of local point source inputs and the legacy of past inputs that are in estuarine sediments. However, with the proper choice of locations, and with the careful selection of the indicator species to be monitored, the impact of changes in Hg inputs can be ascertained. Indeed, the usefulness of using estuarine/coastal organisms in a monitoring program is exemplified by the National Oceanic and Atmospheric Administration (NOAA) Mussel Watch program (NCCOS, 2008), which has been tracking contaminants in the coastal zone for many years already, and total Hg is one of the analytes included in this program.

In ascertaining ecosystem response in the United States, the modeling efforts of NOAA, EPA, and others (Bullock and Brehme, 2002; Cohen et al., 2004; Seigneur et al., 2004; Selin et al., 2008; Bullock and Jaegle, 2009) can be used to evaluate the relative change across the continent. At present, these model outputs suggest that the largest decreases in atmospheric deposition, given current projected regulatory impact, would be in the eastern states, while there may be increases in the western states, reflecting overall changes in U.S. and global emissions (Dastoor and Davignon, 2009; Jaegle et al., 2009; Jung et al., 2009; Seigneur et al., 2009; Travnikov and Ilyin 2009). An initial evaluation of potential sites within the United States has found up to 40 candidate locations with approximately 50% in the Eastern United States (east of the Mississippi), ~25% in the Great Lakes/Midwest region and ~25% in the Western United States (Schmeltz et al., 2011). Clearly, this initial evaluation, based on existing Hg monitoring locations, does not cover all the requirements outlined above. Reference (i.e., low-impact) sites would likely include higher-elevation locations, islands, or forested, undeveloped regions in the Western United States. Finally, efforts such as the U.S. Hg sensitivity maps, developed by the United States Geological Survey (USGS) (Myers et al., 2007), can provide the information needed to target sensitive ecosystems and those that are likely to show the largest biogeochemical response to changes in Hg inputs. There is also an effort within the EPA to collate and provide maps showing the locations of ongoing and longer-term measurements of Hg and MeHg in water, sediments, and various biota (fish and wildlife) and these efforts at summarizing the existing information and databases will provide the necessary background and assist in site selection. Thus, substantial effort and progress is currently underway to identify potential monitoring sites, to coalesce the information from current efforts, and to move toward a consensus on the location of the intensive monitoring sites (Schmeltz et al., 2011).

Proposed Indicators

Choice of suitable measurements for the network is the key to the success of the overall program. Suitable indicators are those that are: (1) comparable across ecosystems or, for biota, have a large geographic distribution; (2) able to integrate variability in space and time; (3) relatively simple to interpret, and for biologic indicators, relevant in terms of human and ecologic health; (4) easy to sample, process, and quantify analytically; (5) already measured or part of an existing database, and ideally have historical data available; (6) able to show a response to Hg loading on a relatively short timescale without influence from confounding factors; (7) able to detect, or reflect, changes in MeHg production and bioaccumulation; and (8) theoretically and empirically sound. In addition, indicators should reflect changes in exposure to humans and wildlife (Harris et al., 2007). Such criteria allow the determination of the relative value of each metric within any study design, given a balance between financial resources and scientific rationale. Based on this rationale, the indicators that are most suitable for both the intensive and cluster sites are shown in Table 6.1.

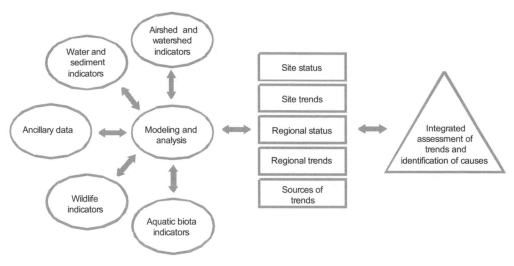

FIGURE 6.1 Diagram representing the factors that need to be integrated into the network design. (*Source:* Saltman et al., 2007. Used with permission.)

In the table, the indicators for a site type are listed as well as the proposed frequency of sampling. In addition, it is noted whether the indicator is useful for determining trends in Hg concentration/deposition over time only, indicative of causal relationships between changes in input and changes in MeHg production and accumulation, or indicative of both. The relationship between indicators for the various media, modeling, and integration is shown in Figure 6.1 (Saltman et al., 2007).

Measurements of Hg in wet deposition are relatively easily accomplished and are currently monitored at the national level through the MDN, which has around 100 active sites (MDN, 2008). This weekly collection program has limitations in coverage, and does not provide data suitable for some computer-model simulations. Even given these concerns, the recommendation is for a widely distributed weekly Hg wet deposition monitoring program at the cluster sites (Table 6.1). At intensive sites, event-based wet deposition collection is recommended (Driscoll et al., 2007). The intensive sites, ranging from background to urban environments, and including continental and coastal locations, should measure Hg atmospheric speciation. Atmospheric Hg^0 concentration is strongly reflective of the global atmospheric Hg pool and does not necessarily provide a sensitive local indicator of short-term regional change (Slemr et al., 2003). In contrast, the concentrations of RGHg and PHg show a higher regional variability and will likely show a response to changes in emissions, as these species have a relatively short residence time in the atmosphere, are easier to control at the emission source, and have a strong anthropogenic signal (Schroeder and Munthe, 1998; Hedgecock and Pirrone, 2001; Ryaboshapko et al., 2007a, 2007b). They are, however, relatively difficult to measure (Landis et al., 2002; Munthe et al., 2001; Sheu and Mason, 2001) and are formed in situ to some extent via atmospheric chemical reactions (Laurier and Mason, 2007). There is large uncertainty in the current estimates

of Hg dry deposition (Ryaboshapko et al., 2007a), and methods for the measurement of atmospheric Hg speciation and dry deposition will need to be standardized and rigorously calibrated for this program; some new approaches are being developed (Skov et al., 2006).

Atmospheric Hg speciation measurements at intensive sites would be coupled with estimates of deposition and ecosystem fluxes, including litterfall, throughfall, and event-based wet deposition, as well as measurements of other atmospheric compounds in both the atmosphere and in wet deposition (e.g., atmospheric ozone and NO_x, sulfate and major ions in precipitation) (Table 6.2) (Driscoll et al., 2007). Therefore, benefit would be obtained from choosing locations that are already making measurements. For example, in the United States, there are existing NADP networks, the MDN, the National Trends Network (NTN) and the Atmospheric Integrated Research Monitoring Network (AIRMON) and other atmospheric sampling programs (e.g., the Clean Air Status and Trends Network [CASTNET]). Such intensive site measurements would serve two primary purposes: (1) generate atmospheric data in support of regional and global-scale atmospheric modeling efforts; and (2) collect data for local-scale modeling of atmospheric deposition, and specifically dry deposition to complex surfaces, such as forests. Soil, groundwater, and surface water measurements would also be made (Table 6.1) to examine the role of air–surface exchange of Hg^0, and the fluxes of Hg and MeHg within the watershed, in impacting Hg transport to methylation sites, in conjunction with the other indicators discussed below.

Mercury export from watersheds is typically a small fraction of the yearly input from the atmosphere (Grigal, 2003) and is influenced to some extent by changes in Hg input, although the timescale of response is very slow (Harris et al., 2007a). Larger responses are possible over shorter timescales from other disturbances, such as changes in land use. Rainfall amount and other climatic variables also

TABLE 6.2
Proposed Ancillary Measurements Needed to Be Collected in Conjunction with the Mercury Measurements

Ancillary measurement	Location	Frequency	Indicator of
Atmospheric deposition of sulfate and nitrogen	I & C	Weekly or event	Causality
Rainfall	I & C	Weekly or event	Causality
Watershed area and land use; % wetlands	I & C	Once	Causality
Aquatic system morphology	I & C	Once	Causality
Water chemistry (pH, DOC, major ions, TSS, chlorophyll, ANC, DO, nutrients)	I & C	Quarterly	Both
Water physical metrics (temperature, degree of stratification, salinity)	I & C	Annually	Both
Organism characteristics (size, weight, sex, condition, food consumption, age)	I & C	With biodata feedback	Both

SOURCE: Saltman et al. (2007).

ANC = acid neutralizing capacity; C = cluster sites; DO = dissolved oxygen; DOC = dissolved organic carbon; I = intensive sites.

influence export, especially with respect to sporadic and extreme events. Export of MeHg is similarly influenced by a number of variables that have little relationship to short-term changes in atmospheric Hg input (Sellers et al., 1995). Thus, export fluxes are not good indicators for monitoring short-term changes in atmospheric deposition and its direct impact on MeHg levels in fish, but they must be examined at intensive sites to gain important information about long-term changes within the ecosystems. Given the complications associated with the interpretation of data on export from the terrestrial landscape, both intensive and cluster sites should include water bodies with little or no watershed.

Changes in atmospheric deposition are recorded by the Hg concentration gradient in sediments, peat bogs, and glacial ice (Porcella, 1996). Carefully selected cores are therefore appropriate trend indicators because they smooth short-term variations in Hg deposition and integrate spatial variability. There is a large body of experimental and observational evidence for their reliability, and well-established protocols for the collection, processing, and interpretation of these records (Benoit et al., 1994; Porcella, 1996), despite the extent of watershed input, and sediment mixing, and other potentially confounding factors. However, because of the rate of surface sediment mixing relative to sediment accumulation, sediment cores cannot provide resolution of changes at intervals shorter than about 5 years. Estimated accumulation rates could be matched with information from atmospheric deposition monitoring at colocated sites.

While the relationship between biota and sediment Hg and MeHg levels is difficult to construct (Mason, 2002), measurements of sediment MeHg provide an integrative measure of the impact of changes in Hg input and other factors on MeHg net production (Benoit et al., 2003). Thus, it is recommended that total Hg and MeHg be measured in

surficial sediments at all sites (Table 6.1). Because it has been shown for numerous ecosystems that there is a relationship between short-term methylation rate measured using assays and in situ MeHg concentration and %MeHg in sediments (Benoit et al., 2003), these difficult assays are not recommended for the cluster sites. There is a reasonable relationship across a variety of ecosystems between %MeHg and the relative methylation rate constant; therefore, it appears that %MeHg is a relatively good proxy for such measurements (Heyes et al., 2006) and sediment MeHg concentration and %MeHg are useful indicators of the rate of change in bulk MeHg concentration. The %MeHg in sediment signal will allow the determination of whether change is directly or indirectly related to changes in atmospheric Hg input.

Total Hg and MeHg measurements in water, or in the dissolved and particulate fractions, have been made in many ecosystems studied to date, and these indicators are recommended for all intensive sites (Table 6.1) even though it may be difficult to interpret the response of these measurements to changes in Hg input (Watras et al., 1994; Morel et al., 1998; Hrabik and Watras, 2002; Mason, 2002; Orihel et al., 2006). Water concentrations can be influenced by factors unrelated to Hg inputs, such as the variation in particulate matter, DOC, and particulate organic carbon (POC) concentrations, and these need to be measured (Table 6.2). However, in a number of locations, primarily those with a dominantly pelagic food web, studies have shown a reasonable correlation between MeHg in water and MeHg in fish, reflecting the changes occurring at the base of the pelagic food chain (Watras et al., 1998; Mason et al., 2000; Brumbaugh et al., 2001; Mason, 2002). As water concentrations vary seasonally and with depth within a particular water body, these measurements must be assessed with consideration of the anticipated spatial variability.

The best indicator of short-term MeHg change in the food chain is yearling fish for lakes and rivers (Table 6.1) (Wiener et al., 2007). Most yearling fish feed on invertebrates and have a relatively limited diet and thus provide a relatively consistent interannual indicator. Despite seasonal variation, it has been shown that there is a strong relationship between the MeHg concentration in yearling fish and piscivorous fish. However, it is recommended that yearling fish be sampled in the same season over time to reduce any interannual variability (Wiener et al., 2007). These smaller fish are easily sampled, and their sampling is less intrusive than sampling larger fish. The monitoring of piscivorous fish, especially those that are recreationally or commercially important, is also recommended, even though these organisms may take 3–5 years to respond to changes in MeHg bioavailability (Exponent, 2003). As fish MeHg concentration increases with age, there is a need to normalize fish concentration (Wiener et al., 2003, 2007). Ancillary information on fish length and weight, and feeding habits, is required to provide a statistically defensible size-normalized MeHg value (Table 6.2).

Other factors, such as nutrient input, watershed land-use change, fluctuating water levels in shallow ecosystems, overfishing, changes in food chain structure, and changing species competition, can also alter fish MeHg concentration (Morel et al., 1998; Mason et al., 2000; Exponent, 2003). Because MeHg is the dominant form in fish, measurement of total Hg is often an adequate metric. Of all indicators, there is substantial information already available on piscivorous-fish–muscle Hg concentrations across ecosystems, because of fish consumption advisory programs. There are large and growing databases, such as the EPA's National Fish Tissue Study, which involves a coordinated random sampling for Hg and other chemicals in fish (USEPA, 1996). Such studies increasingly record both Hg and the necessary ancillary information and are therefore useful benchmarks for assessing long-term changes in fish concentration. Overall, it is recommended that piscivorous fish be sampled on a schedule of every 3–5 years as part of the monitoring program at all sites (Table 6.1).

Sampling of phytoplankton, periphyton, or zooplankton is not recommended for the cluster sites (Table 6.1) (Wiener et al., 2007). Although zooplankton are an important trophic link (Watras et al., 1998), they respond too rapidly to change (days to months), and the population consists of a complex mix of organisms that varies both spatially and temporally within and across ecosystems (Back et al., 2003). In addition, MeHg concentrations vary seasonally and the fraction of the total Hg as MeHg varies between species. Some benthic invertebrates within freshwater systems, such as crayfish, are potential indicators as they live for multiple years, have a short home range, and are ubiquitous (Resh and McElvary, 1993). In estuarine and coastal environments, crustaceans and bivalves are candidate monitors, and have been successfully used (NCCOS, 2008). However, the Mussel Watch program has measured only total Hg, and for these organisms, %MeHg should also be determined. In addition, other factors, such as organic matter content, can obscure the relationship between sediment MeHg and MeHg in benthic invertebrates (Mason, 2002), so this can reduce the effectiveness of these organisms as monitors of change in MeHg concentration and as indicators of change in Hg deposition.

Wildlife indicators should be chosen based on the criteria outlined by Wolfe et al. (2007) as well as to describe pathways of MeHg bioaccumulation. Field sampling feasibility, species distribution, and existing data were some of the criteria used for indicator species selection. Nonlethal sampling techniques are now common for wildlife. Tissue types and their interpretation are relatively well understood for blood, eggs, and keratin materials such as fur, feathers, and scales (Evers et al., 2005; Wolfe et al., 2007). Blood is the favored matrix for understanding short-term dietary uptake, while keratinous materials are generally good indicators of longer-term dietary Hg uptake. Therefore, the sampling of one individual can provide both short- and long-term information on Hg uptake. Hg concentrations in the above tissue types are typically over 95% MeHg (Evers et al., 2005; Rimmer et al., 2005) and thus total Hg is a suitable and more affordable analysis.

Because the primary objective for this monitoring framework is to track an aquatic-based MeHg signal resulting from changes in atmospheric Hg input, indicators that have a strong aquatic link (including wetlands), have small home ranges, and are widely distributed are preferred. Spatiotemporal comparisons of wildlife MeHg concentrations require standardization of species, or at least of representative foraging guilds. Cross-taxa conversions can be used to help standardize comparisons. Geographically and temporally, there are multiple examples of species that are targeted because of well-known and well-accepted attributes, including conservation need and high public value. For example, significant research has been conducted on birds, including the common loon (*Gavia immer*), at broad geographical levels for Hg exposure (Evers et al., 1998, 2003) and for understanding pharmacokinetics (Kenow et al., 2007a, 2007b) and adverse effect levels in the field (Burgess and Meyer, 2008; Evers et al., 2008b). New evidence indicates that avian invertivores are generally at greater risk from current environmental Hg loads than previously modeled and therefore will likely be an important target taxa, because this finding and the logistical ease of sampling suitable sample sizes (Evers et al., 2005; Rimmer et al., 2005; Brasso and Cristol 2008; Tsao et al., 2009). Commonly investigated freshwater mammals are the northern river otter (*Lontra canadensis*) and the American mink (*Neovison vison*) (Yates et al., 2005). Although marine mammals are also often investigated for Hg (Law et al., 1996; Muir, 1999), the level of their inclusion in this Hg monitoring program is undetermined.

The value and need for measuring Hg in wildlife is related to the lack of definitive relationships that can be reliably predicted from either prey Hg levels or abiotic measurements. Although efforts are underway to better model these relationships through wildlife criterion values based on water Hg concentrations (Nichols et al., 1999) and other means, direct field measurements are still required to confidently track changes in environmental Hg loads. The challenge to choose the best indicator organism is even greater because more recent evidence indicates substantial differences in species' sensitivities to MeHg toxicity (Heinz et al., 2009) and uptake (Evers et al., 2005); however, the ability to interpret short- and long-term Hg body burdens with nonlethal sampling and to relate those concentrations to adverse effects at taxonomically relevant levels is promising. Therefore, the value of measuring spatiotemporal trends in Hg in wildlife is particularly strong for tracking changes as well as for species conservation purposes and determining the health of the overall ecosystem.

Concluding Remarks

The proposed monitoring strategy embraces the need for detailed sample collection and analysis at a relatively small number of locations to document the extent of change resulting from future proposed Hg emission reductions. In addition, it is necessary to collect samples on a subset of indicators (Tables 6.1 and 6.2) at a large number of sites that are widely distributed on a continental scale and that cover a wide variety of ecosystems. This monitoring framework will be integrated with the application of atmospheric and watershed Hg models. Monitoring sites should be clustered together within ecoregions to allow for the assessment of the importance of local environmental effects not directly related to Hg deposition changes. At the intensive sites a broad array of atmospheric, water, sediment, terrestrial, and biotic sampling would be done, while at the cluster sites, wet Hg deposition would be measured only in conjunction with seasonal sediment collections for total Hg and MeHg. Aquatic biota sampling would consist of yearling fish and, on a 3- to 5-year timescale, the sampling of piscivorous fish. Wildlife sampling would be conducted under a similar framework with yearly nondestructive sample collection combined with the 3- to 5-year sampling of larger predators. Overall, such a framework would answer the questions of both whether change is occurring in atmospheric Hg input and how this change is reflected in biota MeHg concentrations across a variety of aquatic ecosystems. In addition, this program would provide the information necessary to demonstrate the impact of reductions in Hg emissions from anthropogenic sources on fish and wildlife MeHg concentration.

This chapter has identified the most useful indicators for the examination of environmental changes in Hg contamination in different compartments of the environment, for the atmosphere to wildlife that live in freshwater, terrestrial, and coastal ecosystems. The indicators identified are wide-ranging and involve measurements made at several different scales of time and space but are judged to be those that will provide the best information to policymakers and other stakeholders on the degree to which environmental concentrations are changing with identification of the reasons for the changes occurring. The need for baseline data is crucial for the success of the program, as changes are already occurring in a number of sectors, and further emission reductions are expected from power plants and other sources. It is therefore critical that an assessment program be implemented soon, and there is urgency for the responsible federal and state agencies, and other interested partners, to continue to promote the process of designing and implementing an ecologic Hg monitoring program through legislative action.

To adequately assess ecologic changes in Hg concentrations, it will be necessary to make a long-term commitment to ecologic monitoring and modeling. It could take up to 20 years before the full scope of the impacts of the emission reductions are determined, depending on the types of systems being monitored, and especially for large water bodies, for those with relatively large watersheds, and for the coastal environment. For this reason, it is critical for federal agencies and others in cooperation to make a firm commitment to support the monitoring effort for many years into the future at both the regional and the global scale. Even given the fiscal realities of government that limit long-term planning, it is still possible for federal agencies, states, private-sector organizations, and others to provide long-term support for the proposed monitoring program. A monitoring program is a substantial undertaking that will require a sustained commitment and substantial resources and is likely too large and complex to be housed in any particular federal agency or academic institution. Indeed, for the United States, as outlined in the bills submitted to U.S. Congress, participation for a North American network would involve many organizations (USEPA, USGS, NOAA, US Fish and Wildlife Service, and US Park Service) with each agency being responsible for the monitoring that falls under their charge, and for these agencies to coordinate and involve academic and other institutions in the various activities. Such an approach for the United States is based on the model used in current monitoring programs such as the NADP, a consortium of more than 250 sponsors that depends on substantial funding support from at least a half-dozen different federal agencies and departments. Similarly, the bills propose the formation of a nonfederal oversight management committee that will provide guidance and which would be composed of scientists from a wide range of backgrounds and organizations. Currently, such a structure is the basic structure being considered, with federal agencies working with each other and with other interested organizations to develop a broad consortium to support and guide a monitoring and assessment program.

Acknowledgements

This publication was made possible by NIH Grant Number P42 ES007373 from the National Institute of Environmental Health Sciences. Its contents are solely the responsibility of the authors and do not necessarily represent the official views of NIH.

References

Ariya, P.A., K. Peterson, G. Snider, and M. Amyot. 2009. Mercury chemical transformation in the gas, aqueous and heterogeneous phases: state-of-the-art science and uncertainties. In: Pirrone, N., and R.P. Mason (Editors). *Mercury fate and transport in the global atmosphere.* Springer, Dordrecht, the Netherlands, pp. 459–501.

Back, R.C., P.R. Gorski, L.B. Cleckner, and J.P. Hurley. 2003. Mercury content and speciation in the plankton and benthos of Lake Superior. *The Science of The Total Environment* 304: 349–354.

Bailey, R.G. 2004. Description of ecoregions of the United States. http://www.fs.fed.us/land/ecosysmgmt/index.html (accessed September 23, 2009).

Barbante, C., M. Schwikowski, T. Doring, H.W. Gaggeler, U. Schotterer, L. Tobler, K. Van De Velde, C. Ferrari, G. Cozzi, A. Turetta, K. Rosman, M. Bolshov, G. Capodaglio, P. Cescon, and C. Boutron. 2004. Historical record of European emissions of heavy metals to the atmosphere since the 1650s from Alpine snow/ice cores drilled near Monte Rosa. *Environmental Science and Technology* 38(15): 4085–4090.

Beals, D.I., R.C. Harris, and C. Pollman. 2002. Predicting fish mercury concentrations in everglades marshes: handling uncertainty in the everglades mercury cycling model (E-MCM) with a Monte Carlo approach. *Abstracts of Papers of the American Chemical Society* 223: U542.

Benoit, J., W.F. Fitzgerald, and A.W.H. Damman. 1994. Historical atmospheric mercury deposition in the mid-continental United States as recorded in an ombrotrophic peat bog. In: Watras, C.J., and J.W. Huckabee (Editors). *Mercury as a global pollutant: towards integration and synthesis.* Lewis, Boca Raton, FL, pp. 187–202.

Benoit, J.M., C.C. Gilmour, A. Heyes, R.P. Mason, and C.L. Miller. 2003. Geochemical and biological controls over methylmercury production and degradation in aquatic ecosystems. In: Cai, Y., and O.C. Brouds (Editors). *Biogeochemistry of environmentally important trace elements.* ACS Symposium Series, Washington, DC, pp. 262–297.

Brasso, R.L., and D. A. Cristol. 2008. Effects of mercury exposure on the reproductive success of tree swallows (*Tachycineta bicolor*). *Ecotoxicology* 17: 133–141.

Brumbaugh, W.G., D.P. Krabbenhoft, D.R. Helsel, J.G. Wiener, and K.R. Echols. 2001. A national pilot study of mercury contamination of aquatic ecosystems along multiple gradients—bioaccumulation in fish. U.S. Geological Survey Report USGS/BRD/BSR—2001-0009.2001. Reston, VA: U.S. Geological Survey.

Bullock, O.R., and K.A. Brehme. 2002. Atmospheric mercury simulation using the CMAQ model: formulation description and analysis of wet deposition results. *Atmospheric Environment* 36(13): 2135–2146.

Bullock, O.R., and L. Jaegle. 2009. Importance of a global scale approach to using regional models in the assessment of source-receptor relationships for mercury. In: Pirrone, N., and R.P. Mason (Editors). *Mercury fate and transport in the global atmosphere.* Springer, Dordrecht, the Netherlands, pp. 503–517.

Burgess, N.M., and M.W. Meyer. 2008. Methylmercury exposure associated with reduced productivity in common loons. *Ecotoxicology* 17: 83–91.

Clarkson, T. 1994. The toxicology of mercury and its compounds. In: Watras, C.J., and J.W. Huckabee (Editors). *Mercury as a global pollutant: towards integration and synthesis.* Lewis, Boca Raton, FL, pp. 631–642.

Cohen, M., R. Artz, R. Draxler, P. Miller, L. Poissant, D. Niemi, D. Ratte, M. Deslauriers, R. Duval, R. Laurin, J. Slotnick, T. Nettesheim, and J. McDonald. 2004. Modeling the atmospheric transport and deposition of mercury to the Great Lakes. *Environmental Research* 95(3): 247–265.

Dastoor, A.P., and Y. Larocque. 2004. Global circulation of atmospheric mercury: a modelling study. *Atmospheric Environment* 38(1): 147–161.

Dastoor, A.P., and D. Davignon. 2009. Global mercury modeling at Environment Canada. In: Pirrone, N., and R.P. Mason (Editors). *Mercury fate and transport in the global atmosphere.* Springer, Dordrecht, the Netherlands, pp. 519–531.

Driscoll, C.T., M. Abbott, R. Bullock, J. Jansen, D. Leonard, S. Lindberg, J. Munthe, N. Pirrone, and M. Nilles. 2007. Airsheds and watersheds. In: Harris, R., D.P. Krabbenhoft, R.P. Mason, M.W. Murray, R. Reash and T. Saltman (Editors). *Ecosystem response to mercury contamination: indicators of change.* CRC Press, Boca Raton, FL, pp. 13–46.

Ebinghaus, R., C. Banic, S. Beauchamo, D. Jaffe, H.H. Kock, N. Pirrone, L. Poissant, F. Sprovieri, and P. S. Weiss-Penzias. 2009. Spatial coverage and temporal trends of land-based atmospheric mercury measurements in the Northern and Southern Hemispheres. In: Pirrone, N., and R. P. Mason (Editors). *Mercury fate and transport in the global atmosphere.* Dordrecht, the Netherlands, Springer, pp. 223–291.

Engstrom, D.R., and E.B. Swain. 1997. Recent declines in atmospheric mercury deposition in the upper Midwest. *Environmental Science and Technology* 31(4): 960–967.

Evers, D.C., and Clair, T.A., 2005. Mercury in northeastern North America: a synthesis of existing databases. *Ecotoxicology* 14(1–2): 7–14.

Evers, D. C., J. D. Kaplan, M. W. Meyer, P. S. Reaman, A. Major, N. Burgess, and W. E. Braselton. 1998. Bioavailability of environmental mercury measured in common loon feathers and blood across North America. *Environmental Toxicology and Chemistry* 17: 173–183.

Evers, D.C., K.M. Taylor, A. Major, R.J. Taylor, R.H. Poppenga, and A.M. Major. 2003. Common loon eggs as indicators of methylmercury availability in North America. *Ecotoxicology* (12): 69–81.

Evers, D.C., N. Burgess, L Champoux, B. Hoskins, A. Major, W. Goodale, R. Taylor, R. Poppenga, and T. Daigle. 2005. Patterns and interpretation of mercury exposure in freshwater avian communities in northeastern North America. *Ecotoxicology* 14: 193–222.

Evers, D.C. Y.J. Han, C.T. Driscoll, N.C. Kamman, M.W. Goodale, K.F. Lambert, T.M. Holsen, C.Y. Chen, T.A. Clair, and T. Butler. 2007. Biological mercury hotspots in the northeastern United States and southeastern Canada. *Bioscience* 57(1): 29–43.

Evers, D.C., L. Savoy, C.R. DeSorbo, D. Yates, W. Hanson, K.M. Taylor, L. Siegel, J.H. Cooley, M. Bank, A. Major, K. Munney, H.S. Vogel, N. Schoch, M. Pokras, W. Goodale, and J. Fair. 2008a. Adverse effects from environmental mercury loads on breeding common loons. *Ecotoxicology* 17: 69–81.

Evers, D.C., R.P. Mason, N.C. Kamman, C.Y. Chen, A.L. Bogomolni, D.L. Taylor, C.R. Hammerschmidt, S.H. Jones, N.M. Burgess, K. Munney, and K.C. Parsons. 2008b. An integrated mercury monitoring program for temperate estuarine and marine ecosystems on the North American Atlantic Coast. *EcoHealth* 5: 426–441.

Exponent. 2003. Fish contaminant monitoring program: Review and recommendations, Exponent Report.

Fitzgerald, W.F. 1995. Is mercury increasing in the atmosphere? the need for an atmospheric mercury network (AMNET). *Water, Air, and Soil Pollution* 80: 245–254.

Gbondo-Tugbawa, S., and Driscoll, C.T. 1998. Application of the regional mercury cycling model (RMCM) to predict the fate and remediation of mercury in Onondaga Lake, New York. *Water, Air, and Soil Pollution* 105: 417–426.

GEOSS (Global Earth Observation System of Systems). 2009. Website: http://earthobservations.org/documents/tasksheets/latest/HE-09-02d.pdf (accessed September 23, 2009).

Grigal, D.F. 2003. Mercury sequestration in forests and peatlands: a review. *Journal of Environmental Quality* 32(2): 393–405.

Harris R.C., D.P. Krabbenhoft, R.P. Mason, M.W. Murray, R. Reash, and T. Saltman (Editors). 2007a. *Ecosystem response to mercury contamination: indicators of change.* CRC Press, Boca Raton, FL.

Harris, R.C., J.W.M. Rudd, M. Amyot, C. Babiarz, K.G. Beaty, P.J. Blanchfield, R.A. Bodaly, B.A. Branfireun, C.C. Gilmour, J.A Graydon, A. Heyes, H. Hintelmann, J.P. Hurley, C.A. Kelly, D.P. Krabbenhoft, S.E. Lindberg, R.P. Mason, M.J. Paterson, C.L. Podemski, A. Robinson, K.A. Sandilands, G.R. Southworth, V.L. St. Louis, and M.T. Tate. 2007b. Whole-ecosystem study shows rapid fish-mercury response to changes in mercury deposition. *Proceedings of the National Academy of Sciences of the United States of America*, 104(42): 16586–16591.

Hedgecock, I.M., and N. Pirone. 2001. Mercury and photochemistry in the marine boundary layer-modelling studies suggest the in situ production of reactive gas phase mercury. *Atmospheric Environment* 35(17): 3055–3062.

Heinz, G.H., D.J. Hoffman, J.D. Klimstra, K.R. Stebbins, S.L. Kondrad, and C.A. Erwin. 2009. Species differences in the sensitivity of avian embryos to methylmercury. *Archives of Environmental Contamination and Toxicology* 56: 129–138.

Heyes, A., R.P. Mason, E.-H. Kim, and E. Sunderland. 2006. Mercury methylation in estuaries: insights from using measuring rates using stable mercury isotopes. *Marine Chemistry* 102(1–2): 134–147.

Hrabik, T.R., and C.J.W. Watras. 2002. Recent declines in mercury concentration in a freshwater fishery: Isolating the effects of deacidification and decreased atmospheric mercury deposition in Little Rock Lake. *Science of the Total Environment* 297: 229–237.

HTAP. 2010. Webpage http://www.htap.org (accessed November 11, 2010).

Hudson, R.J.M., S. Gherini, C.J.W. Watras, and D. Porcella. 1994. Modeling the biogeochemical cycling of mercury in lakes. In: Watras, C.J., and J.W. Huckabee (Editors). *Mercury as a global pollutant: towards integration and synthesis.* Lewis, Boca Raton, FL, pp. 473–526.

Hynes, A.J., D.L. Donohoue, M.E. Goodsite, and I. Hedgecock. 2009. Our current understanding of major chemical and physical processes affecting mercury dynamics in the atmosphere and at the air-water/terrestrial interfaces. In: Pirrone, N., and R.P. Mason (Editors). *Mercury fate and transport in the global atmosphere.* Springer, Dordrecht, the Netherlands, pp. 427–457.

Jaegle, L., S. Strode, N.E. Selin, and D.J. Jacob. 2009. The Geos-Chem model. In: Pirrone, N., and R.P. Mason (Editors). *Mercury fate and transport in the global atmosphere,* Springer, Dordrecht, the Netherlands, pp. 533–545.

Jaffe, D., E. Prestbo, P. Swartzendruber, P. Weiss-Penzias, S. Kato, A. Takami, S. Hatakeyama, and Y. Kajii. 2005. Export of atmospheric mercury from Asia. *Atmospheric Environment* 39(17): 3029–3038.

Jung, G., I.A. Hedgecock and N. Pirone. 2009. The ECHMERIT model. In: Pirrone, N., and R.P. Mason (Editors). *Mercury fate and transport in the global atmosphere.* Springer, Dordrecht, the Netherlands, pp. 547–569.

Keeler, G.J., N. Pirrone, R. Bullock, and S. Sillman. 2009. The need for a coordinated global mercury monitoring network for global and regional model validation. In: Pirrone, N., and R.P. Mason (Editors). *Mercury fate and transport in the global atmosphere.* Springer, Dordrecht, the Netherlands, pp. 391–425.

Kenow, K.P., M.W. Meyer, R.K. Hines, and W.H. Karasov. 2007a. Distribution and accumulation of mercury in tissues and organs of captive-reared common loon (*Gavia immer*) chicks. *Environmental Toxicology and Chemistry* 26: 1047–1055.

Kenow, K.P., K.A. Grasman, R.K. Hines, M.W. Meyer, A. Gendron-Fitzpatrick, M. Spalding, and B.R. Gray. 2007b. Effects of methylmercury exposure on the immune function of juvenile common loons. *Environmental Toxicology and Chemistry* 26: 1460–1469.

Krabbenhoft, D., D. Engstrom, C. Gilmour, R. Harris, J. Hurley, and R.P. Mason. 2007. Monitoring and evaluating trends in sediment and water indicators. In: Harris, R., D.P. Krabbenhoft, R.P. Mason, M.W. Murray, R. Reash, and T. Saltman (Editors). *Ecosystem response to mercury contamination: indicators of change.* CRC Press, Boca Raton, FL, pp. 47–86.

Lamborg, C.H., W.F. Fitzgerald, A.W.H. Damman, J.M. Benoit, P.H. Balcom, and D.R. Engstrom. 2002a. Modern and historic atmospheric mercury fluxes in both hemispheres: Global and regional mercury cycling implications. *Global Biogeochemical Cycles* 16(4). doi: 10.1029/2001GB001847.

Lamborg, C.H., W.F. Fitzgerald, J. O'Donnell, and T. Torgersen. 2002b. A non-steady-state compartment model of global-scale mercury biogeochemistry with interhemispheric atmospheric gradients. *Geochimica et Cosmochimica Acta* 66(7): 1105–1118.

Landis, M.S., R.K. Stevens, F. Schaedlich, and E.M. Prestbo. 2002. Development and characterization of an annular denuder methodology for the measurement of divalent inorganic reactive gaseous mercury in ambient air. *Environmental Science and Technology*, 36(13): 3000–3009.

Laurier, F., and R.P. Mason. 2007. Mercury concentration and speciation in the coastal and open ocean boundary layer. *Journal of Geophysical Research-Atmospheres* 112(D6): D06302. doi: 10.1029/2006JD007320.

Law, R.L. 1996. Metals in marine mammals. In: Beyer, W.N., G.H. Heinz, and A.W. Redmon-Norwood (Editors). *Environmental contaminants in wildlife: interpreting tissue concentrations.* Lewis, Boca Raton, FL, pp. 357–376.

Lindberg, S.R. Bullock, R. Ebinghaus, D. Engstrom, X.B. Feng, W.F. Fitzgerald, N. Pirrone, E. Prestbo, and C. Seigneur. 2007. A synthesis of progress and uncertainties in attributing the sources of mercury in deposition. *Ambio* 36(1): 19–32.

Mahaffey, K. 1998. Methylmercury exposure and neurotoxicity. *JAMA* 280: 737–738.

Mason, R.P. 2002. The bioaccumulation of mercury, methylmercury and other toxic trace metals into pelagic and benthic organisms. In: Newman, M.C., and Hale, R.C. (Editors). *Coastal and estuarine risk assessment.* CRC Press, Boca Raton, FL, pp. 127–149.

Mason, R.P. 2009. Mercury emissions from natural processes and their importance in the global mercury cycle. In: Pirrone, N., and R.P. Mason (Editors). *Mercury fate and transport in the global atmosphere*, Springer, Dordrecht, the Netherlands, pp. 193–221.

Mason, R.P., J.M. Laporte, and S. Andres. 2000. Factors controlling the bioaccumulation of mercury, methylmercury, arsenic, selenium, and cadmium by freshwater invertebrates and fish. *Archives of Environmental Contamination and Toxicology* 38(3): 283–297.

Mason, R.P., and G.R. Sheu. 2002. Role of the ocean in the global mercury cycle. *Global Biogeochemical Cycles* 16(4): 1093. doi: 10.1029/2001GB001440.

Mason, R.R., M.L. Abbott, R.A. Bodaly, O.R. Bullock, C.T. Driscoll, D. Evers, S.E. Lindberg, M. Murray, and E.B. Swain. 2005. Monitoring the response to changing mercury deposition. *Environmental Science and Technology* 39(1): 14A–22A.

MDN. 2008. The Mercury Deposition Network webpage. http://nadp.sws.uiuc.edu/mdn (accessed September 23, 2009).

Mergler, D., H. A. Anderson, L.H.N. Chan, K.R. Mahaffey, M. Murray, M. Sakamoto, and A.H. Stern. 2007. Methylmercury exposure and health effects in humans: A worldwide concern. *Ambio* 36(1): 3–11.

Morel, F.M.M., A. Kraepiel, and M. Amyot. 1998. The chemical cycle and bioaccumulation of mercury. *Annual Review of Ecology and Systematics* 29: 543–566.

Muir, D., B. Braune, B. DeMarch, R. Norstrom, R. Wagemann, L. Lockhart, B. Hargrave, D. Bright, R. Addison, J. Payne, and K. Reimer. 1999. Spatial and temporal trends and effects of contaminants in the Canadian Arctic marine ecosystem: A review. *Science of the Total Environment* 230: 83–144.

Munthe, J., I. Wangberg, N. Pirrone, A. Iverfeldt, R. Ferrara, R. Ebinghaus, X. Feng, K. Gardfeldt, G. Keeler, E. Lanzillotta, S.E. Lindberg, J. Lu, Y. Mamane, E. Prestbo, S. Smolke, W.H. Schroeder, J. Sommar, F. Sprovieri, R.K. Stevens, W. Stratton, G. Tuncel, and A. Urba. 2001. Intercomparison of methods for sampling and analysis of atmospheric mercury species. *Atmospheric Environment* 35(17): 3007–3017.

Munthe, J., R.A. Bodaly, B.A. Branfireun, C.T. Driscoll, C.C. Gilmour, R. Harris, M. Horvat, M. Lucotte, and O. Malm. 2007. Recovery of mercury-contaminated fisheries. *Ambio* 36(1): 33–44.

Myers, M.D., M. A. Ayers, J. S. Baron, P. R. Beauchemin, K. T. Gallagher, M. B. Goldhaber, D. R. Hutchinson, J. W. LaBaugh, R. G. Sayre, S. E. Schwarzbach, E. S. Schweig, J. Thormodsgard, C. van Riper III, and W. Wilde. 2007. USGS Goals for the Coming Decade. *Science* 318(5848): 200–201.

NCCOS. 2008. National Centers for Coastal Ocean Science Mussel Watch Webpage. http://coastalscience.noaa.gov (accessed March 15, 2011).

Nichols, J., S. Bradbury, and J. Swartout. 1999. Derivation of wildlife values for mercury. *Journal of Toxicology and Environmental Health Part B: Critical Reviews* 2:325–355.

Orihel, D.M., M.J. Paterson, C.C. Gilmour, R.A. Bodaly, P.J. Blanchfield, H. Hintelmann, R.C. Harris, and J.W.M. Rudd. 2006. Effect of loading rate on the fate of mercury in littoral mesocosms. *Environmental Science and Technology* 40(19): 5992–6000.

Pacyna, E.G., J.M. Pacyna, F. Steenhuisen, and S. Wilson. 2006. Global anthropogenic mercury emission inventory for 2000. *Atmospheric Environment* 40: 4048–4063.

Pirrone, N., and K.R. Mahaffey. 2005. Where we stand on mercury pollution and its health effects on regional and global scales. In: Pirrone, N., and K.R. Mahaffey (Editors). *Dynamics of mercury pollution on regional and global scales.* Springer, New York, pp. 1–24.

Pirrone, N., and R.P. Mason. 2009. *Mercury fate and transport in the global atmosphere.* Springer, Dordrecht, the Netherlands.

Pirrone, N., S. Cinnirella, X. Feng, R.B. Finkelman, H.R. Friedli, J. Leaner, R.P. Mason, A.B. Muhkerjee, G. Stracher, D.G. Streets, and K. Telmer. 2009. In: Pirrone, N., and R.P. Mason (Editors). *Mercury fate and transport in the global atmosphere.* Springer, Dordrecht, the Netherlands, pp. 3–49.

Pirrone, N.S., S. Cinnirella, X. Feng, R. B. Finkelman, H. R. Friedli, J. Leaner, R. Mason, A. B. Mukherjee, G. B. Stracher, D. G. Streets, and K. Telmer. 2010. Global mercury emissions to the atmosphere from anthropogenic and natural sources. *Atmospheric Chemistry and Physics* 10: 5951–5964.

Porcella, D. 1996. Protocol for estimating historic atmospheric mercury deposition. Electric Power Research Institute Report EPRI/TR-106768. Palo Alto, California.

Resh, V.H., and E.P. McElvary. 1993. Contemporary quantitative approaches to biomonitoring using benthic macroinvertebrates. In: Rosenberg, D.M., and V.H. Resh (Editors). *Freshwater biomonitoring and benthic macroinvertebrates.* Chapman and Hall, NY, pp. 159–194.

Rimmer, C., K. McFarland, D.C. Evers, E.K. Miller, Y. Aubry, D. Busby, and R. Taylor. 2005. Mercury levels in Bicknell's Thrush and other insectivorous passerine birds in montane forests of northeastern United States and Canada. *Ecotoxicology* 14: 223–240.

Roue-Legall, A., Lucotte, M., Carreau, J., Canuel, R., and Garcia, E. 2005. Development of an ecosystem sensitivity model regarding mercury levels in fish using a preference modeling methodology: Application to the Canadian boreal system. *Environmental Science and Technology* 39(24): 9412–9423.

Ryaboshapko, A., O.R. Bullock, J. Christensen, M. Cohen, A. Dastoor, I. Ilyin, G. Petersen, D. Syrakov, R.S. Artz, D. Davignon, R.R. Draxler, and J. Munthe. 2007a.

Intercomparison study of atmospheric mercury models: 1. Comparison of models with short-term measurements. *Science of the Total Environment* 376(1–3): 228–240.

Ryaboshapko, A., O.R. Bullock, J. Christensen, M. Cohen, A. Dastoor, I. Ilyin, G. Petersen, D. Syrakov, O. Travnikov, R.S. Artz, D. Davignon, R.R. Draxler, J. Munthe, and J. Pacyna. 2007b. Intercomparison study of atmospheric mercury models: 2. Modelling results vs. long-term observations and comparison of country deposition budgets. *Science of the Total Environment* 377(2–3): 319–333.

Ryaboshapko, A., O.R. Bullock, R. Ebinghaus, I. Ilyin, K. Lohman, J. Munthe, G. Petersen, C. Seigneur, and I. Wangberg. 2002. Comparison of mercury chemistry models. *Atmospheric Environment* 36(24): 3881–3898.

Saltman T., R. Harris, M.W. Murray, and R. Reash. 2007. An integrated framework for ecological mercury assessments. In: Harris, R., D.P. Krabbenhoft, R.P. Mason, M.W. Murray, R. Reash, and T. Saltman (Editors). *Ecosystem response to mercury contamination: indicators of change.* CRC Press, Boca Raton, FL, pp. 191–208.

Schmeltz D., D.C. Evers, C.T. Driscoll, R. Artz, M. Cohen, D. Gay, R. Haeuber, D.P. Krabbenhoft, R.P. Mason, K. Morris, and J.G. Weiner. 2011. MercNet: a national mercury monitoring network to assess responses to changing mercury emissions in the United States. *Ecotoxicology* 20: 1713–1725.

Schroeder, W.H. and J. Munthe. 1998. Atmospheric mercury— an overview. *Atmospheric Environment* 32(5): 809–822.

Seigneur, C., K. Vijayaraghavan, K. Lohman, P. Karamchandani, and C. Scott. 2004. Global source attribution for mercury deposition in the United States. *Environmental Science and Technology* 38: 555–569.

Seigneur, C., K. Vijayaraghavan, K. Lohman, and L. Levin. 2009. The AER/EPRI global chemical transport model for mercury (CTM-HG). In: Pirrone, N., and R.P. Mason (Editors). *Mercury fate and transport in the global atmosphere.* Springer, Dordrecht, the Netherlands, pp. 589–601.

Selin, N.E., D.J. Jacob, R.J. Park, R.M. Yantosca, S. Strode, L. Jaegle, and D. Jaffe. 2007. Chemical cycling and deposition of atmospheric mercury: Global constraints from observations. *Journal of Geophysical Research– Atmosphere* 112: DO2308, doi: 10.1029/2006JD007450.

Selin, N.E., D.J. Jacob, R.M. Yantosca, S. Strode, L. Jaegle, and E.M. Sunderland, 2008. Global 3-D land-ocean-atmosphere model for mercury: present-day vs. preindustrial cycles and anthropogenic enhancement factors for deposition. *Global Biogeochemical Cycles* 22: GB3099, doi: 10.1029/2008GB003282 .

Sellers, P., C.A. Kelly, and J.W.M. Rudd. 1995. Sources of methyl mercury to freshwater ecosystems: A review. *Water, Air and Soil Pollution* 80: 697–713.

Sheu, G.R., and R.P. Mason. 2001. An examination of methods for the measurements of reactive gaseous mercury in the atmosphere. *Environmental Science and Technology* 35(6): 1209–1216.

Skov, H., S.B. Brooks, M.E. Goodsite, S.E. Lindberg, T.P. Meyers, M.S. Landis, M.R.B. Larsen, B. Jensen, G. McConville, and J. Christensen et al. 2006. Fluxes of reactive gaseous mercury measured with a newly developed method using relaxed eddy accumulation. *Atmospheric Environment* 40(28): 5452–5463.

Slemr, F., E.G. Brunke, R. Ebinghaus, C. Temme, J. Munthe, I. Wangberg, W. Schroeder, A. Steffen, and T. Berg. 2003. Worldwide trend of atmospheric mercury since 1977. *Geophysical Research Letters* 30(10): doi: 10.5194/acp-11-4779-2011.

St. Louis, V.L., J.W.M. Rudd, C.A. Kelly, B.D. Hall, K.R. Rolfhus, K.J. Scott, S.E. Lindberg, and W. Dong. 2001. Importance of the forest canopy to fluxes of methyl mercury and total mercury to boreal ecosystems. *Environmental Science and Technology* 35(15): 3089–3098.

Sunderland, E.M., and R.P. Mason. 2007. Human impacts on open ocean mercury concentrations. *Global Biogeochemical Cycles* 21: GB4022, doi:10.1029/2006GB002876.

Travnikov, O., and I. Ilyin. 2009. The EMEP/MSC-E mercury modeling system. In: Pirrone, N., and R.P. Mason (Editors). *Mercury fate and transport in the global atmosphere,* Springer, Dordrecht, the Netherlands, pp. 571–587.

Trudel, M., and J.B. Rasmussen. 2006. Bioenergetics and mercury dynamics in fish: a modelling perspective. *Canadian Journal of Fisheries and Aquatic Sciences* 63(8): 1890–1902.

Tsao, D.C., A. K. Miles, J. Y. Takekawa, and I. Woo. 2009. Potential effects of mercury on threatened California black rails. *Archives of Environmental Contamination and Toxicology* 56: 292–301.

UNEP. 2009. Website. http://www.chem.unep.ch/MERCURY/ Sector-Specific-Information/Fate_and_Transport(1).htm (accessed September 23, 2009).

USEPA. 1996. Listing of fish and wildlife advisories. CD-ROM. EPA-823-C-97-005. Office of Water, Washington DC.

USEPA. 1997. Mercury study report to Congress. EPA Report 452-R-97-004. Office of Air Quality and Standards and Office of Research and Development, Washington DC.

USEPA. 2008. US EPA Mercury Homepage http://www.epa. gov/hg (accessed January 23, 2011).

Watras, C.J., R.C. Back, S. Halvorsen, R.J.M. Hudson, K.A. Morrison, and S.P. Wente. 1998. Bioaccumulation of mercury in pelagic freshwater food webs. *Science of the Total Environment* 219(2–3): 183–208.

Watras, C.J., N.S. Bloom, R.J.M. Hudson, S. Gherini, R. Munson, S.A. Claas, K.A. Morrison, J. Hurley, J.G. Wiener, W.F. Fitzgerald, R.P. Mason, G. Vandal, D. Powell, R. Rada, L. Rislov, M. Winfrey, J. Elder, D. Krabbenhoft, A.W. Andren, C. Babiarz, D.B. Porcella, and J.W. Huckabee. 1994. Sources and fates of mercury and methylmercury in Wisconsin lakes. In: Watras, C.J., and J.W. Huckabee (Editors). *Mercury pollution: Integration and synthesis.* Lewis, Boca Raton, FL, pp. 153–177.

Wiener J.G., D. Krabbenhoft, G.H. Heinz, and A.M. Scheuhammer. 2003. Ecotoxicology of mercury. In: Hoffman, R.B., G.A. Burton, and J. Cairns (Editors). *Handbook of ecotoxicology,* CRC Press, Boca Raton, FL, pp. 409–463.

Wiener, J.G., R.A. Bodaly, S.S. Brown, M. Lucotte, M.C. Newman, D.B. Porcella, R.J. Reash, and E.B. Swain. 2007. In: Harris, R., D.P. Krabbenhoft, R.P. Mason, M.W. Murray, R. Reash and T. Saltman (Editors). *Ecosystem response to mercury contamination: indicators of change.* CRC Press, Boca Raton, FL, pp. 87–122.

Wolfe, M.F., S. Schwarzbach, and R.A. Sulaiman. 1998. Effects of mercury on wildlife: A comprehensive review. *Environmental Toxicology and Chemistry* 17(2): 146–160.

Wolfe, M.F., T. Atkeson, W. Bowerman, K. Burger, D.C. Evers, M.W. Murray, and E. Zillioux. 2007. Wildlife indicators. In: Harris, R., D.P. Krabbenhoft, R.P. Mason, M.W. Murray, R. Reash, and T. Saltman (Editors). *Ecosystem response to mercury contamination: Indicators of change.* CRC Press, Boca Raton, FL, pp. 123–189.

Yates, D., D. Mayack, K. Munney, D.C. Evers, R.J. Taylor, T. Kaur, and A. Major. 2005. Mercury levels in mink and river otter in northeastern North America. *Ecotoxicology* 14: 263–274.

PART THREE

MERCURY IN TERRESTRIAL
AND AQUATIC ENVIRONMENTS

CHAPTER 7

The Role of Soils in Storage and Cycling of Mercury

ARIA AMIRBAHMAN and IVAN J. FERNANDEZ

Mercury (Hg) cycling in soils is critical to our understanding of Hg accumulation and loss in the environment. Soils have a large capacity to store Hg, and small changes in Hg dynamics can have large effects on ecosystem function and biologic exposure. In most watersheds, the terrestrial components receive and retain considerably more atmospheric Hg deposition than the associated freshwater bodies. This can be attributed to: (a) the typically larger areal extent of the watershed as compared with the water body, (b) the role of a vegetative canopy in expanding the effective surface area, and (c) soil's high capacity to store Hg. These characteristics cause soils to act as a long-term source of Hg to freshwater systems and can uncouple the temporal linkage between atmospheric deposition of Hg and its delivery to surface waters. Studies have estimated the present-time annual retention of atmospheric Hg deposition at 74% (Engstrom et al., 1994) and 78% (Driscoll et al., 1998; Lorey and Driscoll,

1999) in the upper Midwestern United States and the Adirondacks (New York) watersheds, respectively. The Hg content of forested watersheds in the United States is more than two orders of magnitude greater than the annual anthropogenic Hg emissions in this country. Approximately 90% of watershed Hg is in the soil rather than the aboveground vegetation, with the bulk of the Hg storage in the mineral soil (Grigal, 2003). Soils can also be a direct source of Hg to the associated surface waters (Swain et al., 1992; Lorey and Driscoll, 1999). It is estimated that 5–25% of atmospherically derived Hg reaches downstream lakes, and in some instances can account for up to 85% of the total Hg loading to these ecosystems (Mierle and Ingram, 1991; Swain et al., 1992; Krabbenhoft et al., 1995; Grigal, 2002; Shanley and Bishop, this book, chapter 8). In light of the ability of soils to store Hg, it might be argued that soils buffer downstream aquatic ecosystems against acute Hg contamination.

Soils play a large role in determining the fate and transport of Hg within a watershed. Cycling and speciation of Hg in watersheds is largely dependent on characteristics such as percentage of wetland, slope, soil thickness, vegetation type, pH, and carbon content (Branfireun et al., 1998). Hg retention can vary among watersheds having similar precipitation and discharge rates because of differences in watershed characteristics, especially soils (Mierle and Ingram, 1991). Hg retention in soils varies depending on the type of soil. That soil Hg is largely associated with the organic matter is now axiomatic (Grigal, 2003). Soil mineralogy, however, can have an influence on the fate of Hg (Andersson, 1979). Soils that consist largely of aluminosilicate minerals, such as those common in northern climates, behave differently from soils that are dominated by Al and Fe hydroxides, such as those found in tropical regions. Waterlogged or hydric soils, such as those found in wetlands, also behave differently from well-drained soils, such as those found in uplands, with respect to Hg cycling. In terrestrial environments, wet soils that develop anoxia are largely responsible for the methylation of Hg to its highly toxic form, methylmercury (MeHg), which is biomagnified in the food chain. In general, well-drained soils do not produce and export significant concentrations of MeHg (Grigal, 2003).

Soils act as a source of Hg for associated freshwater bodies: (a) via transport of soluble Hg-dissolved organic matter (DOM) complexes, and (b) as particulate matter due to mechanical soil erosion or in-stream mineral (Al and Fe hydroxides) formation, especially during high-discharge events. The extent of watershed Hg contribution to a lake depends on the nature of the lake; seepage lakes receive most of their Hg loading directly from the atmosphere or groundwater, whereas drainage lakes can receive a significant fraction of their Hg from the associated watershed.

There have been several review articles specifically devoted to the role of soils in Hg retention and cycling (Andersson, 1979; Schuster, 1991; Schlüter, 2000; Grigal, 2003; Gabriel and Williamson, 2004), with each study emphasizing different aspects of the issue. Andersson, Schuster, and Gabriel and Williamson (2004) reviewed geochemical processes involved in Hg-soil surface association, Schlüter (2000) reviewed Hg volatilization from soils, and Grigal (2003) reviewed the role of soils in Hg storage. In this chapter, the emphasis is on Hg storage and cycling in forest soils, particularly in the freely drained upland ecosystem compartments. Wetlands that are key areas to MeHg production in terrestrial environments are discussed by Shanley and Bishop (this book, chapter 8). We review the geochemical processes leading to the binding, transport, and volatilization of Hg. Hg transformation processes are reviewed mainly with respect to its reduction from the ionic to the elemental form, which is the species most amenable to volatilization. We present the existing data on soil MeHg storage, but since well-drained forest soils do not contribute significantly to MeHg production, methylation and demethylation processes are not emphasized. We also review the role of vegetation type and soil disturbance on soil Hg storage and cycling.

The Role of Soils in Mercury Species Budgets

Total Mercury

Given the dominance of soil pools for Hg in upland watersheds, it is critical to understand soil Hg dynamics when establishing watershed mass balance relationships for Hg cycling and speciation. There is a large body of literature that reports on Hg budgets for soils of temperate and equatorial regions. Reviews of this literature have been published by Roulet et al. (1998) and Grigal (2003). Grigal reported that the mean total Hg concentrations in 48 agricultural soils and 50 forest soils (pastures and peats included) were similar at 140 ng g^{-1}. He estimated that the mass of Hg in the forest floor (~1 mg m^{-2}), the mineral soil (~10 mg m^{-2}), and peat (~20 mg m^{-2}) are considerably larger than that in forest vegetation (~0.1 mg m^{-2}). In a survey of Flemish soils of various origins (agricultural, forest, and pasture soils, n = 494), Tack et al. (2005) observed median baseline concentrations for Hg of 100 ng g^{-1}, with the 90th percentile value of 300 ng g^{-1}. Hg content in parent materials is approximately estimated at <50 ng g^{-1} in igneous rocks and minerals, sandstones, and limestones, with somewhat higher concentrations in shales because of the presence of finer-grained materials (Andersson, 1979).

Total Hg concentrations in surface organic horizons (e.g., O horizons) are significantly higher than those in the mineral horizons. Nater and Grigal (1992) reported a mean total Hg concentration of 140 ng g^{-1} in the organic horizon and 20 ng g^{-1} in the mineral soil in forests across the north-central USA (n = 133). In the surface organic horizons, mean total Hg concentrations of 190 ng g^{-1} in Norway, 250 ng g^{-1} in Sweden, and 300–900 ng g^{-1} in Central Europe have been reported (Godbold, 1994; Schwesig et al., 1999; Grigal, 2003). These regional variations may be attributed to the historical loading to individual soils (Grigal, 2003). Hissler and Probst (2006) reported total Hg concentrations ranging from 16 to 399 ng g^{-1} in the mineral layer of 11 grasslands in a mountainous watershed in France. Their mean lithogenic Hg concentration of 32±9 ng g^{-1} corresponded to those of other studies in temperate environments (e.g., Gracey and Stewart, 1974; McKeague and Kloosterman, 1974; Dudas and Pawluk, 1976; Nater and Grigal, 1992; Grigal et al., 1994; Amirbahman et al., 2004).

In temperate soils, it is widely accepted that inorganic Hg and MeHg are largely associated with soil organic matter (SOM). SOM in an O horizon is composed of a combination of freshly deposited litter and partially decomposed and humified material, typically with a larger and highly variable particle size as compared with SOM in mineral horizons. This holds true, in general, when comparing O and mineral soils whole or after sieving. The larger average particle size of SOM in the O horizon provides less surface area and fewer sites available to bind Hg than the SOM in the mineral horizons (Andersson, 1979). Hissler and Probst (2006) found a strong positive correlation between soil Hg concentrations and SOM (slope, 13.3) in brown acidic and brown podzolic soils. Brown acidic soils with a lower SOM (<4%) had lower Hg concentrations (<100 ng g^{-1}), and podzolic soils with a higher SOM (>6%) had higher Hg concentrations (>100 ng g^{-1}). They showed that Hg enrichment in soil and stream sediments, estimated by normalizing with respect to the soil scandium (Sc) content (Shotyk et al., 2000) was proportional to SOM. They interpreted this to reflect that SOM binds with Hg deposited from the atmosphere. The measured Hg concentration in the deeper mineral horizon (30–60 cm) was three times higher than the lithogenic Hg, suggesting the downward transport of Hg in the soil column.

Grigal (2003) discussed the changing Hg:SOM stoichiometry with depth. Based on data reported in the literature, Grigal estimated an average of 0.7 mg Hg g^{-1} C in the O horizon and 1.5, 2.5, and 3.8 mg Hg g^{-1} C in the A, B, and C horizons, respectively. Other authors have also reported Hg and organic C concentrations by depth or morphologic increments. For example, Amirbahman et al. (2004) reported 0.3, 1.4, and 2.3 mg Hg g^{-1} C in the O, Bh, and Bs horizons, respectively. Aastrup et al. (1991) reported 2.7, 4.6, 4.3, and 3.4 mg Hg g^{-1} C in the O, upper B, lower B, and C horizons, respectively, and Nater and Grigal (1992) reported 0.29 and 0.44 mg Hg g^{-1} SOM (~0.58 and 0.88 mg Hg g^{-1} C) for the forest floor and 0–25 cm mineral horizon, respectively. The fact that the Hg:SOM ratio increases with depth from the organic horizon to the mineral horizon is largely a function of the higher mineralization rate of SOM in the organic horizon. It may also be partly attributed to the higher reactive surface area of the more humified OM in the mineral horizon that would enhance Hg retention per gram of C as compared with the OM in the organic horizon. The increases in Hg:SOM ratio with depth has also been attributed to the increasing Fe and Al hydroxide content with depth (Schlüter, 1997). As these minerals dissolve, soil pH increases, allowing for less competition with Hg from H$^+$ for available surface binding sites. It should be noted, however, that for spatially extensive soil data, little or no correlation between Hg concentrations and soil properties such as SOM, clay content, or pH can result because of confounding factors such as parent materials and deposition history (Tack et al. 2005). Grigal (2003) notes that factors such as historical Hg loading and the quality of SOM can affect variations in the Hg:SOM ratio in soils in the same landscape.

TOTAL MERCURY IN TROPICAL SOILS

Roulet et al. (1998) presented a comparison of Hg concentration and cycling between the tropical soils of the central Amazon and those of temperate environments. They reported total Hg concentrations in the range of 93–171 ng g^{-1} in the organic horizons, similar to those found in temperate soils, and 88–209 ng g^{-1} in mineral horizons, higher than those found in temperate soils. The concentrations reported by Roulet et al. were similar to those reported for other tropical soils (e.g., Aula et al., 1994; Roulet and Lucotte, 1995; Oliveira et al., 2001; Lacerda et al., 2004). As a result, the soils of the central and northeastern Amazon possess Hg burdens in the upper 60 cm of the mineral soil, ranging between 36 and 147 mg m^{-2} (Roulet et al., 1998; Fostier et al., 2000), up to 10 times the Hg burden in temperate and boreal forest soils (Aastrup et al., 1991; Grigal et al., 1994).

In tropical soils, the generally advanced stage of pedogenesis and accompanying Fe and Al enrichment results in elevated retention and accumulation of Hg. In these soils, relatively high temperatures and high litter quality of the deciduous forests results in rapid turnover of the SOM (Johnson, 1995), with little evidence for significant organic horizon development, which limits Hg accumulation in the forest floor. Depth distributions of Hg in mineral soils (SOM <10%) of oxisols were similar to those of extracted Fe and Al, suggesting that Hg accumulation is controlled by soil Fe and Al concentrations (Roulet and Lucotte, 1995; Roulet et al., 1998). As a result, soil Hg burdens in a given system with similar external Hg input may be predominantly a function of the degree of soil pedogenesis (Roulet et al., 1998). Roulet et al. reported that soil differences between the plateau and valley manifest in the progressive podzolization from oxisols to ultisols to spodosols and corresponds to the leaching of soil Fe and Al and, consequently, Hg. Emphasizing the role of ferrallitic soils in Hg sequestration and the degradation of these soils in Hg release into freshwaters, Roulet et al. (1999) have maintained that gold mining or deforestation through large-scale burning does not explain the high Hg concentrations in these waters. They indicated that >97% of the Hg burden in the surface of central Amazonian soils is natural and not due to anthropogenic activity. Deforestation is important insofar as its role in accelerating the degradation of ferrallitic soils is concerned (Oliveira et al., 2001). Gold-mining operations and artisanal gold extractions have important consequences for soil Hg at the local level. Soils in the vicinity of these operations show Hg concentrations considerably higher than those observed in tropical forests (Lacerda et al., 1991, 2004; Rodrigues and Maddock, 1997).

Methylmercury

Processes leading to MeHg production in freshwater and terrestrial environments are reviewed by Chen et al. (this book, chapter 9). In these environments, biotic Hg methylation is the most important process in MeHg production and is largely catalyzed by sulfate-reducing bacteria. As a result, Hg methylation requires the existence of anaerobic conditions. In forested watersheds, hydric soils and wetlands have been identified as methylation hot spots because of the predominance of anaerobic conditions (Branfireun et al., 1996; Gilmour et al., 1998; Heyes et al., 1998; Marvin-DiPasquale et al., 2003; McClain et al., 2003; Mitchell et al., 2008). High concentrations of dissolved MeHg have been observed in waters draining wetlands and poorly drained upland soils (Krabbenhoft et al., 1995; Rudd, 1995; Branfireun et al., 1996). Low MeHg concentrations and fluxes from well-drained soils indicate that the rate of methylation in these soils is insignificant, except for recently harvested forests (Porvari et al., 1993; Driscoll et al., 2007). In 2008, Mitchell et al. observed that there is a significant spatial heterogeneity in MeHg distribution in wetlands, with methylation hot spots concentrated close to the upland–peatland interface. They attributed this partly to the transport of sulfate and labile DOM from the adjacent upland to the peatland, enhancing methylation in the peatland interface zone. Seasonal variations in MeHg production and export have been observed, with the highest concentrations in the summer (Rudd, 1995; Branfireun et al., 1996; Babiarz et al., 1998), perhaps because of higher temperatures. Previous work has also suggested the input of MeHg from the riparian soils (Bishop et al., 1991; Hultberg et al., 1994; St. Louis et al., 1996). Direct atmospheric MeHg contributions to watersheds occur, but in most cases they are relatively small (Fitzgerald et al., 1991; Hultberg et al., 1994).

Grigal (2003) noted that the MeHg:total Hg ratio was ~1.5% in vegetation and <1% in upland soil, but poorly drained soils and wetlands showed higher MeHg percentages. Grigal (2002) has reported this ratio in soil water in a range of ~0.15–15%, even though values >20% have been observed in peatlands (Mitchell et al., 2008). Well-drained soils have considerably lower MeHg:total Hg ratios (<1%) than waterlogged soils (Schwesig et al., 1999; Amirbahman et al., 2004). Schwesig et al. observed maximum MeHg concentrations of well-drained soils in the forest litter. Below this layer, MeHg concentrations decreased significantly, down to 20–40 cm, where it increased again in correspondence with an increase in total Hg concentration. Amirbahman et al., however, did not observe any significant differences between MeHg concentrations in the O, Bh, and Bs (down to ~15 cm) horizons in two coastal Maine forested watersheds. Factors influencing MeHg production, such as differences in forest vegetation and soil disturbances, are discussed in the following sections.

Modes of Mercury Entry into Soil

In terrestrial environments, the ultimate fate of Hg may be controlled by the means of its introduction and incorporation into forest soils (Demers et al., 2007). Studies involving the application of enriched stable Hg isotopes in forested catchments have shed light on the fate and transport of Hg species in terrestrial ecosystems (Hintelmann et al., 2002; Branfireun et al., 2005; Harris et al., 2007). Following the application of enriched ^{202}Hg onto a boreal forest catchment, Hintelmann et al. observed that a high fraction is initially incorporated into plants, suggesting that atmospherically deposited Hg enters the soil via throughfall and litterfall. In a forest, soil is the dominant sink for old Hg, whereas the newly deposited Hg is primarily associated with living vegetation. They also observed that a higher fraction of the newly deposited Hg as compared with the old Hg was found in methylated form, and was reemitted at a faster rate than the old Hg. The newly deposited ^{202}Hg exhibited a high initial mobility, but mobility decreased with time as it was rapidly incorporated into the soil pool. Branfireun et al. (2005) applied ^{202}Hg to a boreal wetland plot and observed significant vertical (30 cm) and horizontal (9 m) transport in a wetland soil in 1 month. The average log K_D (bound:dissolved Hg ratio in L kg^{-1}) values for old and newly deposited Hg sampled over a 3-month period were 4.12 and 3.19, respectively, suggesting less partitioning

of the newly deposited Hg into the solid phase. The newly deposited ^{202}Hg showed at least the same availability with respect to methylation as compared with the native Hg. At one site after 1 day, 6% of the added Hg was found in the methylated form, suggesting that the recently deposited Hg could rapidly enter the food chain. The new MeHg was also highly mobile (Branfireun et al., 2005).

Some studies have shown high Hg concentrations in road dust (Liang et al., 2009; Lu et al., 2009). Lu et al. studied 38 road-dust samples in an industrialized setting in northwest China and found Hg concentrations ranging from 0.48 to 2.32 mg g^{-1}, with a mean of 1.11 mg g^{-1}. Liang et al. found that Hg concentrations in road dust from 20 different urban locations in coastal southeast China ranged from 0.034 to 1.4 mg g^{-1}, correlating to the topsoil Hg concentrations from the same locations. These concentrations are significantly higher than the background soil Hg concentration in China (0.065 mg g^{-1}), suggesting that the source of Hg is largely anthropogenic (Lu et al., 2009). These studies suggest that road dust may be an important carrier of Hg to topsoil and vegetation and should be taken into consideration, especially in industrialized and urban areas.

In soils, Hg is typically introduced as elemental Hg [Hg(0)] and divalent Hg [Hg(II)]. Hg(0) can be in the gaseous state or dissolved in wet precipitation. Hg(II) can be introduced as dissolved Hg(II), associated with particulate matter in both wet and dry deposition, or as the reactive gaseous Hg(II) (RGM). In forests, throughfall and litterfall can deliver several forms of Hg to the soil, with the form delivered influencing Hg fate and transport in the ecosystem (Demers et al., 2007). Mosbaek et al. (1998) proposed that Hg(0) is either reemitted or taken up by leaves through their stomata. Following litterfall, leaf Hg is incorporated into the forest floor. On the other hand, Hg(II), in particulate and dissolved forms, and RGM adsorb to the leaf or other vegetation surfaces, as observed with newly deposited dissolved Hg(II) (Hintelmann et al., 2002). This Hg can be incorporated into the forest soil via litterfall or throughfall (Iverfeldt, 1991; Rea et al., 2001). Demers et al. (2007) proposed that Hg that is delivered to the forest floor via litterfall is likely to be incorporated into the forest soil, whereas Hg that is delivered via throughfall can be either incorporated into the soil or volatilized into the atmosphere. They also proposed that fungi in the decomposing litter may translocate Hg from surface soil organic layers, providing an internal recycling mechanism that would increase Hg residence time in the forest floor. It should be noted that vegetation type also has an important role in soil Hg accumulation. Total soil Hg concentrations have been shown to increase by a factor of 2–7.3 in forested soils as compared with grassland soils (Lacerda et al., 2004; Biester et al., 2002a; Hissler and Probst, 2006), primarily as a result of the magnification of deposition by foliar surface areas in the varying vegetative communities. The role of vegetation in soil Hg cycling, especially with respect to deciduous versus coniferous vegetation, is discussed in more detail below.

Association of Mercury Species with Soils and Soil Constituents

Solid–Solution Interface

ASSOCIATION OF MERCURY SPECIES WITH SOIL ORGANIC MATTER

The association of Hg species with soils and individual soil constituents has been reviewed previously by several authors (Andersson, 1979; Schuster, 1991; Grigal, 2003; Gabriel and Williamson, 2004). It has been shown that under environmentally relevant concentrations, Hg and MeHg have a higher binding strength with organic matter than with soil minerals (Hintelmann et al., 1995; Amirbahman et al., 2002; Drexel et al., 2002; Haitzer et al., 2002; Karlsson and Skyllberg, 2003). In natural ecosystems, saturation of the soil Hg binding capacity is seldom reached.

In the natural environment, the Hg retention mechanism by organic matter is through the association of Hg with reduced sulfur functional groups of the organic matter. Spectroscopic evidence reported by Xia et al. (1999) and Qian et al. (2002) suggested the involvement of thiol (RSH) and disulfane (RSSH) functional groups as binding sites for inorganic Hg and MeHg. The disulfide group (RSSR') was also implicated as a possible binding site for inorganic Hg. Oxygen- and nitrogen- containing functional groups are also involved in the binding of inorganic Hg to SOM. The fraction of total sulfur present as reduced sulfur groups depends on the source of organic matter, with values ranging from 10% for a mineral soil sample to 46% of total sulfur for a stream humic acid sample (Xia et al., 1998). A reduced sulfur atom in organosulfides has been defined as sulfur with an electronic oxidation state ranging between 0 and 0.5 (Morra et al. 1997; Xia et al., 1998). Reduced sulfur in soils can also be found in amino acids that are either associated with, or part of, organic matter. In a humic acid sample isolated from forest soil, cysteine and methionine were measured at concentrations of 2.74 and 1.71 nmol mg^{-1}, respectively (Fan et al., 2000). In most soil environments, reduced sulfur groups with electronic oxidation states <1 exist at higher concentrations than Hg and MeHg (Morra et al., 1997; Xia et al., 1998). In the presence of exceedingly high concentrations of MeHg, oxygen and nitrogen atoms, instead of reduced sulfur, have been detected in the first metal coordination shell (Xia et al., 1999; Qian et al., 2002).

The extent of inorganic Hg and MeHg association with organic matter depends on the concentration of organic matter, pH, and the presence of other competing ligands such as dissolved sulfide [S(-II)] and Cl$^-$. Hg speciation in solution influences its adsorption, which is in turn controlled by pH and the presence of dissolved ligands. Equilibrium speciation calculations show that in the absence of DOM and in the presence of >10 ppm concentrations of the Cl$^-$ ligand, Hg–Cl complexes, specifically HgOCl and HgCl$_2^0$, would be dominant in the soil–water environment. In light of findings regarding the high Hg concentrations in road dust (Liang et al., 2009; Lu et al., 2009), it is expected that the presence of high Cl$^-$ concentrations in road salt facilitate Hg mobilization in road dust. In the presence of <10 ppm concentrations of Cl$^-$, Hg(OH)$_2^0$, and Hg(OH)$^+$ would be the dominant species in most soil–water environments. The presence of even low concentrations of DOM, however, changes Hg speciation in terrestrial and freshwater ecosystems. For example, Amirbahman et al. (2002) estimated that in the presence of 1 ppm of dissolved humic acid and 35 ppm NaCl, 20 ppt of MeHg is predominantly complexed by the humic acid at pH >5, whereas below this pH, Cl$^-$ dominates MeHg complexation. Higher DOM concentrations shift this transition to lower pH values. Using the inorganic Hg–DOM stability constants published by Haitzer et al. (2003), similar conclusions can be obtained for the dominance of inorganic Hg–DOM complexes. Higher organic matter and lower Cl$^-$ concentrations in soil and soil water environments favor Hg and MeHg complexation by organic matter. One would also expect that the quality of SOM would influence Hg sorption, especially in view of the fact that landscape conditions lead to differential SOM accumulation (Grigal, 2003). However, Skyllberg et al. (2000) observed no significant differences in the binding constants of Hg to different types of SOM with varying reduced sulfur content collected along a transect from upland to wetland. Differences in Hg binding constants due to differences in SOM quality might be detectable at higher Hg concentrations, which in most cases are not environmentally relevant.

In soils, metal adsorption is complicated by the presence of SOM, whose solubility depends on pH. Yin et al. (1996) observed maximum inorganic Hg removal from solution by several sandy and loamy soils at pH values between 3 and 5. At higher pH values, the extent of Hg removal decreased because of the enhanced dissolution of SOM. Yin et al. (1997a) observed an S-type isotherm for the association of inorganic Hg with soils with SOM >11 g C kg^{-1}, and an L-type isotherm with SOM <7.5 g C kg^{-1}. A similar behavior was also observed in other studies, in which inorganic Hg adsorption isotherms with O-horizon soils were of S-type (Schlüter, 1997; Amirbahman et al., 2004). This could be due to the presence of higher DOM concentrations in organic soils, and the fact that DOM can possess a higher binding constant than solid organic matter for inorganic Hg (Drexel et al., 2002; Amirbahman et al., 2004). Both of these studies observed a higher inorganic Hg binding to DOM than to the solids and explained the lower adsorption to the solid at low total Hg concentrations as the reactive sites on DOM out-competing those on the solid. Schlüter (1996) studied transport of labeled inorganic Hg and MeHg in intact soil columns collected from a well-drained Fe-humus podzol in a coniferous forest. The applied Hg concentrations ranged approximately between 50 and 500 ng g^{-1} and were typical of those found in most forest soils. The soil columns were subjected to leaching with different intensities and acidities. Schlüter observed that at the lower end of the inorganic Hg and MeHg loading range, Hg species were associated with SOM in the O horizon, and Hg transport was due to the DOM transport. At a higher loading, however, Hg species were less strongly associated with the SOM and changes in the chemistry of rain could potentially lead to their mobilization, prompting the author to suggest that in soil with a high level of Hg contamination, ion exchange with H^+ may lead to Hg mobilization. MeHg was consistently more mobile than inorganic Hg in this study.

Biester et al. (2002b) studied Hg speciation in soils downwind from chlor-alkali plants using a mercury-thermo-desorption (MTD) technique (Biester and Nehrke, 1997; Biester and Scholz, 1997), as well as with chemical extractions. They defined the Hg extracted in $NaBH_4$ as the reactive Hg fraction, distinguished from the organic-bound Hg fraction. The Hg desorption spectra for organic-rich (9–15% SOM) and sandy (average 0.5% SOM) soils resembled those of Hg-humic standard and Hg–Fe(III) hydroxide standard, respectively. In the organic-rich soils, water-soluble Hg was mainly associated with the DOM, whereas in the sandy soil, up to 50% of the water-soluble Hg was in the $NaBH_4$-extractable fraction (Biester et al., 2002b). Hg mobility was highest in soils with a high level of soluble SOM and low level of clayey material. Accordingly, they proposed that Hg mobility is not dominated solely by the DOM and that the clay content also plays a role. In the soil profiles, they observed a significant vertical Hg transport only in high-SOM samples. Hg in the low-SOM sample showed very little vertical transport because of the low vertical transport of DOM. Effect of pH on Hg mobility may be understood as its effect on the mobility of organic matter, and not on the binding of Hg to soil. They did not report the DOM concentrations in the leachate, however.

ASSOCIATION OF MERCURY SPECIES WITH SOIL MINERALS

Andersson (1979) reviewed the Hg adsorption literature, especially with respect to pure aluminosilicates and other minerals. Based on a set of experiments with organic soils and some pure minerals, Andersson classified SOM as the most efficient component in soils for Hg adsorption at acidic pH values, but mineral fractions as the most efficient component at circumneutral pH. Among soil minerals, illite and Fe_2O_3 were the most effective sorbents, followed by montmorillonite, kaolinite, and $Al(OH)_3$. Later reviews agreed with the conclusions of Andersson's work as to the effectiveness of soil minerals over organic matter in adsorbing Hg at circumneutral and higher pH (Schuster, 1991; Jackson, 1998). Because of the analytical challenges of low-level Hg measurements at the time of Andersson's research, the Hg concentrations used in these experiments were several orders of magnitude higher than those observed in the environment. The initial Hg concentration used in Andersson's experiments was 40.2 ppm, inevitably resulting in an extremely high Hg surface coverage and, especially in the case of mineral oxides, perhaps surface precipitation of $Hg(OH)_{2(s)}$ (Tiffereau et al., 1995). At such high Hg concentrations, organic matter's reduced sulfur groups would largely be saturated, and as such, depending on its amount, organic matter may not have the capacity for further sorption. Adsorption experiments conducted with high Hg concentrations may indeed result in a gross underestimation of the binding strength (Lövgren and Sjöberg, 1989; Skyllberg et al., 2000). Therefore, it is difficult to compare the behavior of different sorbents in the environment at such high Hg concentrations. Also, a pH increase results in enhanced SOM dissolution and Hg mobilization, which is a different mechanism than a loss in SOM binding strength as compared with the mineral constituents.

In tropical soils, Fe and Al hydroxide minerals play a very important role in binding Hg (Semu et al., 1987; Roulet et al., 1998; Lacerda et al., 2004). Weathered oxisols (laterites) contain high concentrations of Fe and Al hydroxides. Fadini and Jardim (2001) observed a strong positive correlation between Hg and the soil Fe and Al concentrations down to a depth of 1 m in the Negro River basin (Amazon), with soil Fe exhibiting a higher Hg adsorption efficiency (i.e., higher molar Hg:Fe ratios) than soil Al. A higher soil Al content, however, resulted in presumably equivalent or higher Hg adsorption to Al than to Fe minerals. Fadini and Jardim found a poor correlation between SOM and Hg, as also reported for other tropical soils (Aula et al., 1994; Roulet and Lucotte, 1995; Roulet et al., 1998). Roulet et al. (1998) observed a strong correlation between Hg and the reductively extractable Al in acidic equatorial soils. Since Al hydroxide is not known to strongly adsorb Hg (Andersson, 1979), Roulet et al. (1998) concluded that Hg adsorption may have been enhanced by Al substitution of the Fe hydroxide, resulting in an increase in the mineral-specific surface area. Semu et al. (1987) observed a strong correlation between Hg adsorption capacity and the cation exchange capacity for a Tanzanian oxisol, suggesting the importance of ion exchange in Hg adsorption in this soil. They also observed a negative correlation between kaolinite and inorganic Hg, confirming the observations by Andersson (1979) that kaolinite is indeed a weak sorbent for inorganic Hg.

In the absence of Cl^-, inorganic Hg(II) was shown to form an inner-sphere surface complex via two deprotonated surface oxygen atoms coordinated to two edge-sharing Fe atoms on goethite (a-FeOOH) (Collins et al., 1999). Using surface complexation theory, Tiffereau et al. (1995) modeled the adsorption of inorganic Hg onto a-SiO_2 and amorphous $Fe(OH)_{3(s)}$. The experimental data were from the work of MacNaughton (1973) and Avotins (1975). The modeled Hg binding constants were greater for $Fe(OH)_{3(s)}$ than a-SiO_2, as expected from the reactivity of these surfaces. For the a-SiO_2 system, the initial Hg:solid ratio was at 920 ng g^{-1}, where up to ~70% of the added Hg was removed by adsorption. In the absence of any Cl^- ions, the pH adsorption edge was constant, and highest from pH 4 to 9. Increasing Cl^- concentrations resulted in lower Hg adsorption and maximum adsorption peaks at progressively higher pH values. Adsorption of Hg onto a-SiO_2 was best modeled using ternary surface complexes involving the OH^- and Cl^- species, with the electric double-layer model to account for the electrostatic effect at the surface. For the $Fe(OH)_{3(s)}$ system, the initial Hg:solid ratio was at 136 mg g^{-1}, where up to ~50% of the added Hg was removed. The pH-adsorption edge for $Fe(OH)_{3(s)}$ looked similar to that of Hg sorption onto a-SiO_2. Likewise, increasing Cl^- concentrations resulted in a decrease in Hg removal. For Hg adsorption onto $Fe(OH)_{3(s)}$, the authors invoked ternary surface complexes involving the OH^- and Cl^- ligands, as well as direct adsorption of the Hg^{2+} species. Based on potentiometric titrations of millimolar levels of inorganic Hg(II), Gunneriusson and Sjöberg (1993) also proposed the involvement of OH^- and Cl^- ligands in the Hg(II) surface complexes on the goethite surface. These surface species dominated at pH >5. At pH <5, Hg(II) directly coordinated with the surface oxygen group as shown also by Collins et al. (1999).

Adsorption of Hg–Cl complexes onto goethite was also proposed by Barrow and Cox (1992), based on the correspondence between the $HgCl^+$ species in solution and Hg adsorption on the surface. At such a high Hg loading, surface precipitation of $Hg(OH)_2$-$Fe(OH)_3$ solid solution has been proposed by Tiffereau et al. (1995). Barrow and Cox (1992) observed that the Hg adsorption maximum onto goethite corresponded with the predominance of $HgOH^+$ and $HgCl^+$ species in solution, and Newton et al. (1976) observed that maximum inorganic Hg adsorption onto bentonite corresponded with the predominance of $HgOCl$ species in solution. At acidic pH values, the decrease in sorption capacity corresponded with the predominance of $Hg(Cl)_2$ species at the expense of $HgOCl$, as also shown by Gunneriusson and Sjöberg (1993). These observations prompted the authors to conclude that the sorbed Hg species were Hg–Cl complexes. It should be noted that adsorption of the Hg–Cl complexes onto Fe(III) (oxy)hydroxides was not observed by Kinniburgh and Jackson (1978) using $^{36}Cl^-$ in Hg sorption onto amorphous $Fe(OH)_3$ experiments.

pH EFFECT ON ASSOCIATION OF MERCURY SPECIES WITH SOIL

Adsorption of charged species to surfaces can be highly pH-dependent. Adsorption of metals, including Hg species, onto organic and inorganic surfaces generally decreases with a decreasing pH because of the competition of H^+ with the metal. At a high pH, the predominance of hydrolysis species for some metals, including Hg, may reduce the extent of adsorption onto negatively charged surfaces, thereby resulting in a pH range of optimal adsorption. Sorption behavior of a metal onto organic and mineral surfaces

with respect to pH is generally similar. The exact behavior of the pH-dependent adsorption (i.e., adsorption edge) of metals, including Hg, depends on the adsorbent:adsorbate ratio (Dzombak and Morel, 1990; Tiffereau et al., 1995; Amirbahman et al., 2002). Haitzer et al. (2003) and Amirbahman et al. (2002) observed an increase in the binding of inorganic Hg and MeHg, respectively, to aquatic humic substances with pH within a range of 4 to 7, with the behavior at higher pH values depending on the Hg:DOM ratio.

KINETICS OF MERCURY SPECIES ASSOCIATION WITH SOIL

Kinetics of inorganic Hg adsorption onto soils (sandy loam) were studied by Yin et al. (1997b). The Hg concentrations were in the milligrams per liter range. They used a simple reversible reaction scheme (second-order forward and first-order reverse) to model the adsorption and desorption kinetics. Even though the individual fits were very good, the rate constants varied for the same material but at different initial Hg concentrations, suggesting a more complex Hg adsorption process, such as the presence of surface sites with different degrees of reactivity or pore diffusion as the limiting step. Skyllberg et al. (2000) studied the adsorption kinetics of inorganic Hg onto upland soils at more environmentally relevant concentrations. Sorption was rapid in the absence of competing ligands at pH ~3.1 with almost all of Hg sorbing within 3 hr. In the presence of 0.38 M Br^-, however, complete adsorption took several hundred hours. The authors attributed this to the slow decomposition of dissolved Hg–Br complexes. Hg desorption in the absence of competing ligands was negligible, and its kinetics were slow. The addition of Br^- to solution resulted in a considerably higher and faster Hg desorption (Skyllberg et al., 2000).

Desauziers et al. (1997) studied the kinetics of MeHg adsorption to kaolinite, montmorillonite, goethite, and hausmanite (Mn_3O_4). MeHg initial concentration was at 1 mg L^{-1}, and the experiments were performed at pH 3 for clays and pH 9 for the oxides, resulting in surface coverage 4 to 5 orders of magnitude larger than those found in most soils. Adsorption equilibrium in all cases was reached in less than 10 min under vigorous agitation, suggesting the lack of significant sorption in the internal structure. Because of poor resolution of the time-series data in this study, the reported rate constants constitute minimum values. It should be noted that kinetic uptake data obtained from continuously mixed reactors should be applied to soils with caution, since these batch experiments are normally done at high agitation rates, at which the effect of surface boundary layer resistance is minimized.

Soil–Air Interface: Mercury Emission from Soils

Mercury distribution in soil is dynamic because of the atmospheric Hg input and emission, as well as its redox-sensitive nature (Zhang and Lindberg, 1999). Hg in the environment exists in three oxidation states, Hg(II), Hg(I), and Hg(0). In the atmosphere, Hg exists as Hg(0), particulate Hg, RGM, and dimethylmercury (Me$_2$Hg). Hg(0) is the dominant (>95%) form of all atmospheric species and is normally transported the farthest (Mason et al., 1994). For most soils with natural background Hg concentrations, atmospheric Hg(0) deposition is the most important input vector (Engle et al., 2001). Hg(0) is volatile and has a vapor pressure of 2.5×10^{-6} atm and a dimensionless Henry's law constant of 0.32 [Hg(0)$_{(g)}$:Hg(0)$_{(aq)}$ mass ratio] at 25°C (Schroeder et al., 1991). Given the volatile nature of Hg(0), its dissolved concentration in soil water is expected to influence its gaseous concentration, and vice versa. This behavior is consistent with Henry's law for gases and Fick's law of diffusion (Zhang and Lindberg, 1999). Hg(0) has a relatively large stability field in the environment, covering a wide range of pH and redox potentials (Andersson, 1979; Drever, 1997). From a thermodynamic point of view, the dominant Hg species in oxic environments is Hg(II). The presence of Hg(0) in oxic environments, however, indicates its kinetic stability. Even though Hg(0) can be emitted from a variety of natural surfaces (Mason et al., 1994), this chapter covers Hg emissions from soils only. Hg emissions from other natural surfaces, such as vegetation and surface waters, as well as emissions from the whole watersheds, are discussed by Shanley and Bishop (this book, chapter 8).

A large body of literature has been devoted to Hg emission from porous solid surfaces, especially uncontaminated and contaminated soils. Some of this literature has been reviewed by Zhang and Lindberg (1999), Schlüter (2000), Grigal (2002), and Gustin et al. (2008). Gustin et al. (2008) presented an update on the current estimates of global Hg emissions. Global natural (volcanic and geothermal) and anthropogenic emissions are in the range of ~800–3000, and ~2000–2400 Mg yr^{-1}, respectively. Based on a review of the published measurements, soil Hg emission flux ranges from −2 to 13 ng m^{-2} hr^{-1}. It should be noted that most of the published flux data are collected during the summer and in the daytime, and as such, are not a good representative of the diel or seasonal variations (Gustin et al., 2008).

Depending on the physical and chemical soil characteristics, as described below, and the ambient soil and air Hg(0) concentrations, soils can act as sources or sinks for atmospheric Hg(0) (Xin and Gustin, 2007). Soil Hg(0) reemission is an important process to consider when estimating the Hg budget of a watershed. In boreal forests, Grigal (2002) estimates the soil Hg efflux at 11 ng m^{-2} hr^{-1} during the growing season, sufficient to reemit most of the deposited Hg. Abbott et al. (2003) observed relatively low concentrations of Hg in the soils close to a calciner, a point source Hg emitter, and concluded that most of the deposited was reduced to Hg(0) in and reemitted from the soil. Biester et al. (2002b) studied Hg in soils downwind from chlor-alkali plants and found no Hg(0) in any of the soils that received atmospheric Hg deposition originating from the chlor-alkali plants, even

though most of the emitted Hg from these plants was in Hg(0) form. They proposed that most of the deposited Hg(0) would be reemitted before oxidation to Hg(II). Demers et al. (2007) mentioned Hg(0) reemission of throughfall input to a coniferous forest floor as a major Hg loss mechanism, and proposed that in such forests, a large fraction of the Hg litterfall input might indeed consist of throughfall Hg recycled by reemission from the forest floor. Gustin et al. (2008) proposed that only a relatively small percentage of Hg introduced into soils via wet and dry deposition is reemitted immediately. Instead, Hg reemission is brought about gradually and is controlled by the physical and chemical factors mentioned below (Xin and Gustin, 2007; Gustin et al., 2008).

Zhang and Lindberg (1999) suggested that depending on the dominance of Hg(0) or inorganic Hg(II) in soil, adsorption and desorption of Hg(0) or reduction of Hg(II) could be the rate-limiting steps for Hg emission. Schlüter (2000) also mentions the reduction step as the rate-limiting step in Hg emission from soil. This, of course, assumes that physical transport of Hg(0) from soil solution to soil air is not the rate-limiting step. The reported soil–air Hg(0) concentrations generally range between 1 and 53 ng m^{-3} (Johnson and Lindberg, 1995), whereas reliable data on soil water Hg(0) do not exist (Zhang and Lindberg, 1999). If such data are available, then using the Henry's law constant, the extent of departure from equilibrium between the two phases can be evaluated. If the estimated equilibrium soil–water Hg(0) concentration is significantly smaller than the measured soil–water Hg(0) concentration, then: (a) Hg(0) is produced in the soil environment, and (b) the rate of Hg(0) production in soil is greater than its rate of mass transfer into soil air. If the estimated and measured soil–water Hg(0) are close, then the rate-determining step would be the biotic/abiotic processes leading to Hg(0) production.

FACTORS THAT CONTROL MERCURY EMISSION FROM SOILS

Processes that control reduction of Hg(II) to Hg(0) in soils can take place in soil solution or on soil surfaces and can be biotic or abiotic. Only the abiotic processes involved in Hg(II) reduction will be reviewed in this chapter. Biotic processes in Hg(II) reduction, which may be dominant in some soils and sediments, are reviewed by Barkay and Wagner-Dobler (2005) and Swartzendruber and Jaffe (this book, chapter 1). Factors that control abiotic Hg reduction and emission from soils include chemical factors, such as SOM content, Hg(II) concentration, and the presence of oxidants, such as atmospheric ozone (Gustin et al., 1997; Schlüter, 2000; Engle et al., 2005; Xin and Gustin, 2007; Mauclair et al., 2008), and physical factors, such as soil moisture content and precipitation (Gustin et al., 1999; Gustin and Stamenkovic, 2005; Xin et al., 2007; Lindberg et al., 1999), sunlight (Gustin et al., 1996; Carpi and Lindberg, 1997; Zhang and Lindberg, 1999; Moore and Carpi, 2005;

Xin et al., 2007), temperature (Dudas and Cannon, 1983; Schroeder and Munthe, 1998; Ericksen et al., 2006), and wind velocity and other meteorologic conditions (Landa, 1978; Lindberg et al., 1979; Kim et al., 1995; Gustin et al., 1997; Zhang et al., 2001). Given the extreme spatial and temporal variability of these parameters, Hg emission from soils is also highly variable, and as such, global estimates are poorly constrained (Gustin et al., 2008).

Schlüter (2000) reviewed processes that lead to soil Hg(0) production and emission. In general, an increase in soil Hg(0) emission rate has been reported with decreasing SOM and clay content. This can be attributed to the favorable binding of Hg(II) to these soil constituents. A lower sorption affinity and capacity renders Hg(II) more available to biotic or abiotic reduction (Zhang and Lindberg, 1999). Relatively fast (on the order of several hours) desorption of inorganic Hg(II) from soil has been shown by Yin et al. (1997b), suggesting that Hg(II) may be readily available for reduction. However, the Hg(II) concentrations used by Yin et al. were in the parts per million range, as mentioned above. In most soil environments, since Hg concentrations are considerably lower than the parts per million range and Hg(II) is largely associated with the reduced sulfur groups of SOM, the Hg(II) desorption rate, and consequently its availability for reduction, is expected to be lower.

DOM, mainly in the form of humic and fulvic acids, has been shown to reduce Hg(II) to Hg(0) in the dark (Alberts et al., 1974; Allard and Arsine, 1991). Alberts et al. used a 5:1 DOM:Hg(II) ratio (on a gram-to-gram basis) at pH 6.7–8.2 and observed a first-order reduction of Hg(II). The reduction was attributed to the organic free radicals of the quinonelike moieties associated with the DOM. Based on previously published work, Schlüter (2000) proposed that the DOM-mediated reduction of Hg(II) depends on the DOM:Hg(II) ratio. At high ratios (>1000:1), Hg(II) would be stabilized via complexation with the reduced sulfur groups, and at low ratios (<0.5:1), Hg(II) reduction would be limited perhaps because of the consumption of the reductive potential of the DOM. A rapid initial Hg(II) reduction rate followed by a much slower rate by DOM has been observed and attributed to the consumption of the reductive potential and the effective binding by DOM at low Hg(II) concentrations (Alberts et al., 1974; Allard and Arsine, 1991; Schlüter et al., 1995a). The presence of quinonelike moieties in DOM (Cory and McKnight, 2005) and the redox-active character of hydroquinone–quinone couples with a wide range of redox potentials in DOM (Scott et al., 1998; Fimmen et al., 2007) have been shown using spectroscopic techniques. DOM has also been shown to reduce other metals, such as Cr(VI) and Fe(III) abiotically, and to enhance the microbially catalyzed reduction of Cr(VI) and U(VI) potentially via an electron shuttling mechanism (Nevin and Lovley, 2000; Gu and Chen, 2003). A similar mechanism may also be expected for reduction of Hg(II) in the presence of DOM.

Allard and Arsine (1991) observed a decrease in the production rate of Hg(0) with increasing Cl^- and Eu concentrations, prompting them to propose that Hg(II)–DOM complexes should be formed before electron transfer can take place. Presence of strong ligands for Hg(II), such as Cl^-, inhibits reduction by forming stable complexes such as $HgCl_4^{2-}$ (Amyot et al., 1997).

Provided that solar radiation results in the reduction of Hg(II) to Hg(0) in surface waters, Zhang and Lindberg (1999) suggested that it might also play a role in Hg(0) production in near-surface soils. They presented several scenarios by which sunlight could affect Hg(0) production. These include direct photolysis in the presence of OH^- and organic acids, production of superoxide that leads to Hg(II) reduction, photolysis of Fe(III)–organic acid complexes that produce reducing organic radicals, and surface-catalyzed reduction of adsorbed Hg(II). DOM-catalyzed Hg(0) reduction can be especially enhanced in the presence of sunlight, as observed by Allard and Arsine (1991). Xiao et al. (1995) suggested that Hg(0) production in the near-surface soil environment that is subject to UV irradiation can be enhanced because of the presence of SOM. Sunlight-mediated soil Hg(II) reduction and emission is perhaps least likely in closed-canopy forests, but more likely in open fields (Grigal, 2002).

Redox cycling of Hg is complicated by reduction and oxidation reactions in the same system (Zhang and Lindberg, 1999). For example, Hg(0) production in sunlight has been followed by its oxidation in the dark in organic-rich Florida Everglades water (Lindberg et al., 1999). Soil Hg(0) emission/uptake processes are also controlled by the ambient Hg(0) and soil Hg concentrations, as well as the presence of sunlight. Xin and Gustin (2007) observed that at low air Hg(0) concentrations (2.8 ± 0.8 ng m^{-3}), soils emitted Hg(0) in sunlight, but took up Hg(0) in the dark. At higher air Hg(0) concentrations, however, they observed soil Hg(0) uptake regardless of the light condition. It is generally accepted that soils with naturally high Hg concentrations emit Hg(0) (Gustin, 2003), whereas soils with generally <100 ng g^{-1} of Hg can act as sources or sinks depending on the physical environment (Xin and Gustin, 2007).

Increases in Hg emission from unsaturated soils following wetting events have been reported (Carpi and Lindberg, 1998; Frescholtz and Gustin, 2004; Gustin and Stamenkovic, 2005). Lindberg et al. (1999) attributed the enhancement of Hg emission by an increase in soil moisture to: (a) physical displacement of Hg(0) by water filling the pores, (b) Hg(0) desorption from the soil surface by a wetting fluid with a higher affinity to the soil surface, and (c) reduction of Hg(II) following Hg(II) mobilization in solution. Studies involving soil Hg(II) amendments have observed an increase in Hg(0) production with an increase in pH (Landa, 1978; Schlüter et al., 1995b). In the forest and pasture oxisols of the Amazon, Lacerda et al. (2004) observed a significant negative correlation between soil Hg and pH, and proposed that a higher soil pH favors Hg(II) reduction followed by Hg(0) emission. In the soil environment, a higher pH can bring about a higher degree of microbial activity that in some cases can enhance Hg(II) reduction.

Role of Vegetation in Mercury Accumulation in Forest Soils

The role of vegetation on soil Hg content is reviewed here within the context of differences in coniferous versus deciduous forests. Several studies have indicated the importance of litterfall and throughfall as the two most important vectors for delivering Hg to the forest floor (Iverfeldt, 1991; Rea et al., 1996; Lee et al., 2000; Grigal et al., 2000; St. Louis et al., 2001; Ericksen et al., 2003; Grigal, 2003). Hg mass balance in forested catchments suggests that vegetation type, the resulting differences in Hg delivery (litterfall vs. throughfall) as described above, and processes of incorporation into the soil determine the fate of Hg, especially with respect to its residence time and transport into surface waters (Demers et al., 2007).

Schwesig and Matzner (2000) studied the pools and fluxes of Hg and MeHg in a coniferous and deciduous catchment in southeastern Germany. Total Hg concentrations in wet deposition, throughfall, and litterfall were relatively similar between the two catchments. MeHg concentrations in wet deposition and throughfall were also similar between the two catchments, but litterfall contained twice as much MeHg in the coniferous as in the deciduous catchment. Despite nearly double the mass of litterfall in the deciduous as compared with the coniferous catchment, litterfall MeHg fluxes were similar in the two catchments. Litterfall contributed 55% of total deposition of total Hg and MeHg in the deciduous catchment, while it contributed 29% of total deposition of total Hg and 55% of MeHg in the coniferous catchment. The coniferous soil retained four times higher total Hg and seven times higher MeHg as the deciduous soil in the top 60 cm (total Hg = 89.1 vs. 19.3 mg m^{-2}; MeHg = 0.43 vs. 0.06 mg m^{-2}), with total Hg concentrations peaking in the Oa layer at ~500 and ~160 ng g^{-1} for the coniferous and deciduous catchments, respectively (Schwesig and Matzner, 2000). MeHg concentration, on the other hand, peaked in the Oi layer, but the concentrations in both catchments remained <1 ng g^{-1}. Even though the soil storage:annual input ratio was approximately five times larger in the coniferous as compared with the deciduous watershed, the authors attributed the higher Hg accumulation in the coniferous watershed primarily to the different history of Hg deposition in the two watersheds.

The deciduous and the coniferous catchments in this study retained 95% and 85% of the deposited Hg, respectively (Schwesig and Matzner, 2000). In the deciduous catchment, 2.8 and 0.01 g m^{-2} yr^{-1} of total Hg and MeHg, respectively, were exported via runoff. In the coniferous catchment, total Hg and MeHg export in the runoff were 6.8 and 0.05 g m^{-2} yr^{-1}, respectively (Schwesig and Matzner, 2000). These observations correspond to those

of Johnson et al. (2007), who observed higher Hg and MeHg fluxes in the runoff from the coniferous catchment than in that from the deciduous catchment. This could be partly attributed to the concentration and quality of DOM released from each watershed.

The findings by Schwesig and Matzner (2000) regarding the higher Hg accumulation in coniferous than in deciduous soils were corroborated by Biswas et al. (2007), who systematically studied the Hg content in adjacent coniferous, deciduous (aspen), and meadow plots in the Rocky Mountains (Wyoming). For coniferous soils, they observed Hg concentrations in the O horizon (0–4 cm) ranging from 58.4 to 208 ng g^{-1}, and in the mineral horizon (5–8 cm) ranging from 30.9 to 68.1 ng g^{-1}. In aspen and meadow plots, the O-horizon Hg concentrations ranged from 25.2 to 37.5 ng g^{-1}, and in the mineral horizon it ranged from 19.5 to 39.2 ng g^{-1}. Biswas et al. (2007) also observed significantly higher SOM concentrations in coniferous plots than in aspen and meadow plots in the O horizon. This may be attributed to the slower rate of litter decomposition in lignin-rich coniferous forests (Johnson, 1995).

Amirbahman et al. (2004) studied the distribution of Hg and MeHg in the soils of a burned and unburned forested watershed at Acadia National Park, Maine. Deciduous vegetation became the dominant forest type after an intense fire in 1947, and coniferous forest dominated the unburned watershed. As expected, total Hg concentrations were significantly higher in the O horizon of the coniferous watershed as compared with the deciduous watershed (134 ± 48 ng g^{-1} vs. 103 ± 23 ng g^{-1}), but there were no significant differences in total Hg concentrations in the mineral horizons between the two watersheds (lowest in the Bh layer at 60.2 ng g^{-1} to highest in the Bs layer at 79.6 ng g^{-1}). The three comparative studies of Hg in coniferous and deciduous soils cited above all report significantly higher soil Hg concentrations under coniferous vegetation. The study by Amirbahman et al. (2004) also showed a numerically higher Bs Hg in the coniferous forest, although it was not statistically significant. A lower Hg concentration in deciduous forests is expected because of the relatively high rates of organic matter turnover as compared with coniferous forests, which leads to a lower SOM and soil Hg content (Grigal, 2003). The more lignin-rich character of the coniferous vegetation renders its degradation kinetics slower (Johnson, 1995), and its lower nutrient concentrations contributes to this effect. In addition, atmospheric inputs of Hg under a coniferous forest are typically higher than in deciduous forests because of the relatively higher specific surface area and the generally longer persistence of needles as compared with the deciduous leaves (Rustad et al., 1994; Bailey et al., 1996; Grigal, 2002), and possibly other foliar surface characteristics such as high surface roughness and waxier cuticles noted for pine (Rea et al., 2002). Higher throughfall Hg concentrations in coniferous forests than deciduous forests have been reported by Johnson et al.

(2007). Coniferous canopies are especially efficient filters for the removal of atmospheric particulates and gases, exhibiting two to five times the scavenging efficiency as compared with deciduous canopies (Grigal et al., 2000).

Demers et al. (2007) studied Hg dynamics in a coniferous and a deciduous forested catchment in the Adirondacks region of New York and observed a net increase in the litterfall's total Hg content that could not be explained via throughfall inputs. They attributed this increase to Hg translocation from the forest organic horizon into the litter, thereby retarding Hg transport into the mineral horizon. The authors proposed that this Hg accumulation in the leaf litter may delay the recovery of surface waters by increasing the Hg residence time in the forest.

Throughfall and litterfall have been proposed to deliver different forms of Hg to the forest floor. Throughfall contains Hg that is primarily associated with the leaf surface during dry deposition in the form of particulate Hg or the RGM (Mosbaek et al., 1998) that may originate from local and regional sources (Demers et al. 2007). Litterfall Hg, on the other hand, is originally derived from elemental Hg that is taken up by stomata (Rea et al., 2000, 2001, 2002). Demers et al. (2007) argued that Hg delivered to the forest floor via litterfall is more likely incorporated into the soil than Hg delivered via throughfall, which may be largely volatilized. They observed larger Hg pools in both the whole pedon and the O horizon in the deciduous (22.2 and 4.45 mg m^{-2}, respectively) than in the coniferous (9.64 and 2.05 mg m^{-2}) forest despite the larger Hg flux to the forest floor in the deciduous forest. This difference was partly attributed to the larger litter mass and a larger litter Hg accumulation rate in the deciduous forest (Demers et al., 2007). To account for this difference, the authors proposed that since Hg input into the coniferous forest floor is primarily via throughfall, Hg (re)emission from the forest floor is likely an important loss mechanism, whereas in deciduous forests, Hg input to the forest floor is primarily due to the litterfall, which has a lower likelihood of Hg emission losses. The soil Hg concentrations in this study peaked in the Oe layer (~1–4 cm depth) with 394.6 ng g^{-1} and 413.4 ng g^{-1} in the deciduous and coniferous stands, respectively.

In the forest floor at Acadia National Park (Maine), Sheehan et al. (2006) found that coniferous vegetation had the highest Hg concentration (58.8±3.3 ng g^{-1}) followed by mixed (41.7±2.8 ng g^{-1}), scrub (40.6±2.7 ng g^{-1}), and deciduous (31.6±2.6 ng g^{-1}) vegetation types. Previously, Johnson (2002) had reported average litterfall Hg concentrations in the same coniferous and deciduous watersheds at 52.9 and 39.7 ng g^{-1}, respectively. In contrast to the study by Demers et al. (2007), however, the litter Hg flux estimated by Sheehan et al. was similar among all vegetation classes, which in this case was attributed to the higher softwood litter Hg concentration being balanced by the larger hardwood litter mass (Grigal, 2002; Sheehan et al., 2006).

Vegetation type could also affect the lability and reactivity of SOM in the O horizon, in turn influencing Hg cycling. Amirbahman et al. (2004) observed that SOM from the O horizon of the coniferous soil was more soluble than that of an adjacent deciduous soil, although this contrast could also have been influenced by the deciduous forest being burned a half century earlier. Laboratory experiments showed that DOM from the coniferous O horizon had a higher Hg binding strength than that of the deciduous O horizon. Taken together with the higher solubility of SOM from the coniferous versus the deciduous soil, Hg mobilization from the coniferous watershed has a higher potential than from the deciduous watershed. These differences could be related to differences in the average age of the SOM, as well as to contrasting vegetation composition in the two watersheds. In both cases, however, Hg showed a higher affinity for DOM than the insoluble SOM. This difference in Hg affinity has also been observed in Fe-humus podzol O horizon soils (Schlüter, 1997) and in peat soils from the Everglades (Florida), where DOM from peat exhibited higher Hg conditional stability constants than solid peat (Drexel et al., 2002).

Soils in deciduous forests generally possess a higher pH and litter quality than in the coniferous forests (Cronan and Reiners, 1983). Deciduous forests also have faster nutrient cycling and decomposition rates than coniferous forests, as observed by higher rates of N mineralization in the presence of deciduous species (Johnson, 1995; Hill and Shackleton, 1989; Nadelhoffer et al., 1995; Campbell et al., 2000). The higher MeHg concentrations observed by Amirbahman et al. (2004) and by Schwesig and Matzner (2000) in deciduous as compared with coniferous forest soils could be partly due to the faster rate of microbial metabolism and relatively higher pH, as microbial activity, especially that of sulfate-reducing bacteria, tends to increase with increased nutrient availability and decrease with decreasing pH (Maier et al., 2000). MeHg also binds more favorably to organic matter with increasing pH up to the circumneutral pH range (Amirbahman et al. 2002), which may partly explain a higher MeHg concentration in a deciduous forest soil.

Differences in soil MeHg contents between watersheds can also be attributed to temperature differences, as higher temperatures increase microbial activity, thereby enhancing Hg methylation rate (Korthals and Winfrey, 1987; King et al., 1999). Fernandez et al. (2007) observed consistently higher mean soil temperatures in all soil horizons for deciduous as compared with coniferous stands. Temperature differences by forest type increased with soil depth, and greatest differences were observed during spring and summer. Coniferous soils exhibited a slower rate of temperature change during spring and fall as compared with deciduous soils in all horizons, suggesting less heat accumulation in the former, which may be attributed to the lower light penetration and moisture differences in coniferous stands (Fernandez et al., 2007).

Role of Forest Fires and Other Disturbances

Forest Fires

Forest and agricultural fires together contribute to nearly 30% of the global atmospheric Hg (Brunke et al., 2001; Sigler et al., 2003; Wiedinmyer and Friedli, 2007). In the United States alone, this amounts to an estimated release of 19 to 64 metric tons of Hg yr^{-1} from burning of 2.7×10^6 ha of forest and shrubland, which represents 13 to 42% of the U.S. anthropogenic Hg emissions (Biswas et al., 2007). For the lower 48 states, Wiedinmyer and Friedli (2007) estimated that forest fires release 44 metric tons of Hg per year. Fire results in the emission of a large part of soil and biomass C and Hg to the atmosphere, the extent of which depends in part on the severity of fire (Friedli et al., 2003; Biswas et al., 2007, 2008; Burke et al., 2010; Woodruff and Cannon, 2010). Friedli et al. (2007), for example, showed that heating organic soil at 300°C for 5 min results in a nearly complete loss of Hg, whereas heating the same soil at 100°C for 45 min results in the release of only 10% of Hg. In a study of the effect of fire on the soil Hg budget at the Experimental Lakes Area in Northwestern Ontario, Canada, Mailman and Bodaly (2005) reported that complete burning resulted in the loss of 97% and 94% of total Hg and MeHg in plants, and 79% and 82% of total Hg and MeHg in the upland soil. The practice of suppressing forest fires in the United States has resulted in the accumulation of fuel load, as well as Hg, and may increase the future Hg release to the atmosphere (Biswas et al., 2007).

In addition to atmospheric Hg emissions, forest fires have significant consequences for soil Hg storage and cycling, and Hg release into the receiving water bodies. Following a disturbance, forest soils can continue to release Hg, as soil changes due to the disturbance can reduce their ability to retain stored Hg (Burke et al., 2010). Hg contained in ash is also more readily mobilized via wind and water erosion, resulting in high Hg concentrations in lake sediments (Caldwell et al., 2000). It has been suggested that even though soil erosion is generally enhanced because of fire, excessive erosion may occur only for several years immediately following the fire because of the presence of roots that stabilize the soil (Wright and Bailey, 1982). The extent of erosion depends on factors such as slope and vegetation, as well as soil properties such as texture and moisture content.

Considering that a substantially larger mass of Hg is stored in forest soil than in vegetation (Grigal, 2003), more Hg released by fire could originate from the soil, depending on fire severity. The postfire soil physical and chemical environments that in turn control the fate of Hg are affected by factors such as the extent of soil heating; the removal of vegetation, litter, and part of the O horizon; and increased soil hydrophobicity because of the formation of charcoal (Chandler et al., 1983). Burned soils also tend to be thinner and more discontinuous than unburned soils. Soil temperature during the fire is regulated partly by the fuel load, the existing vegetation, and soil moisture regimen. The latter factor is especially crucial in determining the areal and vertical extent of fire; soils subject to drought lead to severe fires, resulting in a relatively significant release of Hg, C and nutrients (Kasischke and Stocks, 2000). Burning of SOM also reduces the C:N ratio that is favorable for plant growth and results in the loss of thermally labile C and excess accumulation of ligninlike C in the soil (Harden et al., 2004). In most cases, fire promotes soil microbial N fixation and brings about a change in N speciation toward increasing soil NH_4^+, NO_2^- and NO_3^- concentrations that are more readily available for plant uptake (Chandler et al., 1983; Acea and Carballas, 1996). Soil cations, however, are stable at high temperatures, and their mass remains relatively constant after the fire. The burning of vegetation produces ash rich in cations, which increases soil fertility (Harden et al., 2004), especially in nutrient-poor soils such as those in the Amazon (Farella et al., 2006). Increased soil cation concentrations also promote microbial and fungal growth, which has direct implications for Hg methylation. Cations exchange with soil H^+, the extent of which depends on the soil cation exchange capacity. This leads to the observation that especially in the acidic forest soils, pH increases relatively significantly after a fire (Wright and Bailey, 1982; Chandler et al., 1983). A combination of higher pH and nutrient availability in postfire soils promotes soil microbial activity that may in turn result in a greater level of Hg methylation. Cation input into soils also exchange with soil Hg and mobilize it into receiving waters, as evidenced by the postfire increase in lake sediment Hg content (Garcia and Carignan, 1999; Caldwell et al., 2000).

Biswas et al. (2007) contrasted soil Hg contents in three recently burned sites and adjacent unburned sites. Chosen sites represented a range of fire severities from low to moderate to high in coniferous, deciduous (aspen), and meadow plots. The fire resulted in the loss of Hg and SOM down to a depth of 6–8 cm, which was attributed to the severity as well as the duration of the fire. Statistical analysis showed that down to a depth of 4 cm, fire severity and vegetation type were the primary factors controlling Hg release. In the coniferous plots, high-, moderate-, and low-severity fires released 75–87%, 62%, and 22% of the Hg soil, respectively. In the deciduous plots, moderate and low severity fires released 63% and 17% of soil Hg, respectively. Given the higher Hg content in the unburned coniferous as compared with the unburned deciduous soils as mentioned above, the coniferous soils released a significantly higher mass of Hg than the deciduous soils (7–28 vs. 4–13 g ha^{-1}; Biswas et al., 2007). Engle et al. (2006) estimated that forest soils in the Sierran forests (California) released 2–5 g ha^{-1} of soil Hg because of prescribed and wild fires, whereas a desert sagebrush fire released 0.36 g ha^{-1} of soil Hg. In all cases, the most important sources of the released Hg were the litter and vegetation.

In the forested watersheds studied by Amirbahman et al. (2004), soil pH was significantly higher in all horizons of the burned soils than in the unburned soils because of the incorporation of ash into the soil profile. This difference was especially significant in the O horizon, where on average, burned soils had a pH of approximately 0.40 unit higher than the unburned soils (3.41 ± 0.22 vs. 2.99 ± 0.13). Total Hg concentrations were higher in the O horizon of the unburned soils than in the burned soils, most likely as a result of the fire volatilizing the SOM-bound Hg. Methylmercury concentrations, with respect to both soil mass and C content, were higher in the burned versus the unburned soils, also most likely as a result of the fire, even though no statistically significant differences between MeHg concentrations in the O and mineral horizons within each soil were observed. The MeHg concentration in the O horizon for the burned and unburned soils were 0.2 ± 0.13 and 0.07 ± 0.07 ng g^{-1}, respectively. Higher MeHg concentrations are generally a result of the enhanced microbial, especially sulfate-reducing, activity. An enhancement in microbial activity in burned soils was attributed to the increased nutrient availability and decreased soil acidity (Maier et al., 2000). Even though soils studied by Amirbahman et al. (2004) were generally well drained, and as such, well oxygenated, soil anaerobic microsites are known to serve as Hg methylation hot spots (Compeau and Bartha, 1985). However, microbial Hg methylation is slower in unsaturated systems, such as well-drained forest soils, than in saturated systems, such as wetlands (Rudd, 1995). The higher MeHg concentrations in the burned soils could also be attributed to the more favorable binding of MeHg to SOM at a less acidic pH (Amirbahman et al., 2002). MeHg concentrations with respect to the C content were higher in the mineral horizons than in the O horizon, which is indicative of the smaller MeHg than C loss during SOM mineralization. This can also be attributed to the presence of more humified organic matter in the mineral horizons.

Other Disturbances

Forest harvesting, especially by clear-cutting, also has important implications for soil Hg budgets and cycling (Porvari et al., 1993). The impacts, however, would be different from those of a wildfire (Carignan and Steedman, 2000). Even though both harvesting and wildfires result in the release of nutrients from the watershed, harvesting can result in a larger release of DOM, whereas fire can result in a larger release of NO_3^- from the soil, and released nitrogen being predominantly organic in the case of harvesting and inorganic in the case of fire (Carignan and Steedman, 2000).

In the Amazon, land-use change, especially the conversion of forest into agricultural and pasture land, has been suggested as one of the most important causes of soil Hg mobilization (Lacerda et al., 2004). Deforestation results in the degradation of the organic horizon, which in turn can cause significant erosion of the mineral layer. Lacerda et al.

(2004) studied forest and deforested (pasture) soils with a similar composition and distance from any Hg source. They observed significantly higher Hg concentrations in forest soils (average, 61.9 ng g^{-1}) than in pasture soils (average, 33.8 ng g^{-1}), with a cumulative Hg burden in the former soils nearly double that of the latter soils in the top 10 cm, pointing to the importance of deforestation in soil Hg mobilization. However, they observed no significant differences in the soil Hg down to a depth of 10 cm in both undisturbed (forest) and disturbed (pasture) Amazon forest soils.

Soil Hg in the Amazon is either associated with the surface organic horizon or horizons dominated by Fe and Al minerals (Roulet et al., 1998; Fostier et al., 2000; Oliveira et al., 2001), and as such, can be mobilized by the oxidation of SOM or degradation of the mineral duricrust (Lacerda et al., 2004). Several studies have shown that deforestation in the Amazon enhances both processes, and hence, results in soil Hg mobilization (Roulet et al., 1998, 1999; Fostier et al., 2000; Oliveira et al., 2001).

Higher Hg concentrations in forested as compared with pasture soils can be attributed not only to significant soil erosion in the latter soils (Roulet et al., 1998, 1999; Fostier et al., 2000), but also to the interception of dry deposition via throughfall and litterfall by the canopy in forested watersheds. Soil exposure also results in higher Hg emission rates (Zhang and Lindberg, 1999), with pasture soils exhibiting an order of magnitude larger emission rates than forest soils (Lacerda et al., 2004). Increased solar exposure in deforested soils leads to elevated soil temperatures that can also increase the Hg emission rate (Zhang et al., 2001).

The effect of soil disturbance on receiving water quality can be complicated by characteristics of the watershed as well as the water body. As such, extrapolating water-body response to wildfire or deforestation, especially with respect to nutrient and DOM loading, may not be warranted for other water bodies with different watershed and physicochemical conditions (Carignan and Steedman, 2000). Enhanced transport of Hg from disturbed soils increases its loading to a water body. Hg loading is one of the key factors determining the extent of Hg methylation in waters (Winfrey and Rudd, 1990; St. Louis et al., 1994). Studies of the effect of forest harvesting on lakes in Québec, Canada, have shown elevated Hg concentrations in zooplankton and northern pike, which was attributed to the increase in the DOM export to the receiving lakes (Garcia and Carignan, 1999, 2000). In a study of a partially burned catchment, Kelly et al. (2006) observed up to a fivefold increase in the fish Hg concentration as compared with a reference catchment. They proposed that fire causes a significant but short-term release of Hg and MeHg into streams and lakes that enhances fish Hg accumulation. However, they also proposed that the major enhancement in fish Hg accumulation could be due to food-web restructuring brought about by increased nutrient concentrations in lakes and streams that supports primary production. Kelly et al. (2006) further suggested that the relative importance of limiting nutrients versus Hg release from burned catchments is due to fire characteristics, such as fire severity, proportion of catchment burned, and timing and intensity of runoff.

Mailman and Bodaly (2005) proposed that burning land before flooding it would limit the extent of methylation and MeHg release into water due to the drastic reductions in SOM and Hg. They suggested that loss of SOM would limit the availability of the organic substrate to methylating organisms, while loss of Hg would limit its availability for methylation. The remaining ash also possesses a higher adsorption capacity and a lower solubility that promotes the adsorption and hinders the release of Hg and MeHg (Amirbahman et al., 2004). In a later study using mesocosms with burned and unburned soil and plant samples, Mailman and Bodaly (2006) observed that even though burning reduced MeHg concentrations in the flooded water, it did not lower MeHg accumulation in the lower food web. They attributed this to the lower DOM concentrations in mesocosms containing burned soil and vegetation, and the fact that a lower DOM concentration brought about a higher biota:water MeHg ratio.

Conclusions

The large capacity of soils for binding Hg causes them to act as a long-term Hg reservoir and source for freshwater ecosystems. Grigal (2003) estimated that the mass of Hg in mineral soils was significantly larger than that in the forest floor and living vegetation. Given that atmospheric Hg deposition is the main input into the forest floor and that mineral horizons in forest soils are the dominant ecosystem storage compartment for Hg, it follows that soil Hg is indeed mobile between horizons because of the downward migration of organic matter following litter decomposition and pedogenic processes. Harris et al. (2007) suggested that whereas reductions in anthropogenic mercury emissions would result in a relatively rapid decrease in fish mercury content on the order of years, a full recovery in fish Hg content could take centuries because of the gradual release of Hg from upland and wetland soils.

Lorey and Driscoll (1999) showed that net retention of Hg in Adirondack forested watersheds has declined from 95% in 1850 to 78% in more recent years, as the anthropogenic Hg emission has increased. This has resulted in an increase in the sedimentary Hg flux in the studied lakes significantly during this period. The reason behind this trend is not understood, even though it has resulted in an increase in the level of Hg contamination in surface waters. This trend is perhaps rooted in the terrestrial Hg interactions involving soils and litterfall (Demers et al., 2007), and its elucidation is vital to understanding the response of watersheds to changes in Hg deposition as well as the climate.

The effect of climate change on Hg storage and cycling in soils deserves attention. It is difficult to predict with any certainty how the modern era of accelerated climate change will influence ecosystem function, let alone Hg dynamics specifically. There is consensus that we will experience climatic warming on a local and global scale (Intergovernmental Panel on Climate Change [IPCC], 2007). Regional predictions such as for the northeastern United States can suggest both increased annual average precipitation as well as increased frequency of soil moisture stress at certain times in the growing season (Hayhoe et al., 2006), along with an overall intensification of the hydrologic cycle (Huntington, 2006), including earlier ice out in lakes (Hodgkins et al., 2002). These trends do not define changes in Hg cycling but give us insight into places to look for the first signs of effects on Hg. Warmer growing-season temperatures are likely to decrease overall soil moisture, particularly during the late growing season, leading to lower water tables, perhaps increased rates of decomposition, Hg mobilization, and methylation. A warmer soil also leads to greater soil Hg emission, but on the other hand, DOM export from watersheds increases because of warming, enhancing Hg mobilization. Changing forest growth and composition over short and long timeframes can alter landscapes from coniferous to deciduous vegetation, leading to changing Hg deposition and cycling as discussed above. Sustained droughts brought about by warming trends together with the current practice of forest fire suppression lead to the accumulation of surface fuel, and result in an increase in the magnitude and frequency of forest fires. This would in turn result in the release of higher Hg levels into the atmosphere.

References

Aastrup, M., Johnson, J., Bringmark, E., Bringmark, I., and Iverfeldt, A. 1991. Occurrence and transport of mercury within a small catchment area. *Water, Air, and Soil Pollution* 56: 155–167.

Abbott, M.L., Susong, D.D., Olson, M., and Krabbenhoft, D.P. 2003. Mercury in soil near a long term air emission source in southern Idaho. *Environmental Geology* 43: 352–356.

Acea, M.J., and Carballas, T. 1996. Changes in physiological groups of microorganisms in soils following wildfire. *FEMS Microbiology Ecology* 20: 33–39.

Alberts, J.J., Schindler, J.E., Miller, R.W., and Nutter, D.E. 1974. Elemental mercury evolution mediated by humic acid. *Science* 184: 895–897.

Allard, B., and Arsine, I. 1991. Abiotic reduction of mercury by humic substances in aquatic systems—an important process for the mercury cycle. *Water, Air, and Soil Pollution* 56: 457–464.

Amirbahman, A., Reid, A.L., Haines, T.A., Kahl, J.S., and Arnold, C. 2002. Association of methylmercury with dissolved humic acids. *Environmental Science and Technology* 36: 690–695.

Amirbahman, A., Ruck, P.L., Fernandez, I.J., Haines, T.A., and Kahl, J.S. 2004. The effect of fire on mercury cycling in the soils of forested watersheds: Acadia National Park, Maine. *Water, Air, and Soil Pollution* 152: 315–331.

Amyot, M., Mierle, G., Lean, D., and McQueen, D.J. 1997. Effect of solar radiation on the formation of dissolved gaseous mercury in temperate lakes. *Environmental Science and Technology* 61: 975–987.

Andersson, A. 1979. Mercury in soils. In: J.O. Nriagu (Editor), *The biogeochemistry of mercury in the environment.* Elsevier/ North-Holland Biomedical Press, Amsterdam, pp. 79–122.

Aula, I., et al. 1994. Levels of mercury in the Tucuruí Reservoir and in surrounding area in Pará, Brazil. In: C.J. Watras and J.W. Huckabee (Editors), *Mercury pollution: integration and synthesis.* Lewis, Boca Raton, FL, pp. 21–40.

Avotins, P. 1975. Adsorption and coprecipitation studies of mercury on hydrous iron oxide, Ph.D. thesis, Stanford University, Palo Alto, CA.

Babiarz, C.L., et al. 1998. Seasonal influences on partitioning and transport of total and methylmercury in rivers from contrasting watersheds. *Biogeochemistry* 41: 237–257.

Bailey, S., Hornbeck, J., Driscoll, C., and Gaudette, H.E. 1996. Calcium inputs and transport in a base-poor forest ecosystem as interpreted by Sr isotopes. *Water Resources Research* 32: 707–719.

Barkay, T., and Wagner-Dobler, I. 2005. Microbial transformations of mercury: Potentials, challenges, and achievements in controlling mercury toxicity in the environment. *Advances in Applied Microbiology* 57: 1–52.

Barrow, N.J., and Cox, V.C. 1992. The effects of pH and chloride concentration on mercury sorption. I. By goethite. *Journal of Soil Science* 43: 295–304.

Biester, H., Muller, G., and Schöler, H.F. 2002a. Estimating distribution and retention of mercury in three different soils contaminated by emissions from chlor-alkali plants: Part I. *Science of the Total Environment* 284: 177–189.

Biester, H., Muller, G., and Schöler, H.F. 2002b. Binding and mobility of mercury in soils contaminated by emissions from chlor-alkali plants. *Science of the Total Environment* 284: 191–203.

Biester, H., and Nehrke, G. 1997. Quantification of mercury in soils and sediments—Acid digestion vs. pyrolysis. *Fresenius Journal of Analytical Chemistry* 358: 446–452.

Biester, H., and Scholz, C. 1997. Determination of mercury phases in contaminated soils—Hg-pyrolysis vs. sequential extractions. *Environmental Science and Technology* 31: 233–239.

Bishop, K., Lee, Y., Pettersson, C., and Allard, B. 1991. Terrestrial sources of methyl-mercury in surface waters: the importance of the riparian zone on the Svartberget Catchment. *Water, Air, and Soil Pollution* 80: 435–444.

Biswas, A., Blum, J.D., Klaue, B., and Keeler, G.J. 2007. Release of mercury from Rocky Mountain forest fires. *Global Biogeochemistry Cycles* 21: GB1002, doi:10.1029/2006GB002696.

Biswas, A., Blum, J.D., and Keeler, G.J. 2008. Mercury storage in surface soils in a central Washington forest and estimated release during the 2001 Rex Creek fire. *Science of the Total Environment* 404: 129–138.

Branfireun, B.A., Heyes, A., and Roulet, N.T. 1996. The hydrology and methylmercury dynamics of a precambrian shield headwater peatland. *Water Resources Research* 32: 1785–1794.

Branfireun, B.A., Hilbert, D., and Roulet, N.T. 1998. Sinks and sources of methylmercury in a boreal catchment. *Biogeochemistry* 41: 277–291.

Branfireun, B.A., et al. 2005. Speciation and transport of newly deposited mercury in a boreal forest wetland: A stable mercury isotope approach. *Water Resources Research* 41: W06016, doi:10.1029/2004WR003219.

Brunke, E.G., Labushabne, C., and Slemr, F. 2001. Gaseous mercury emissions from a fire in the Cape Peninsula, South Africa, during January 2000. *Geophysical Research Letters* 28: 1483–1486.

Burke, M.P., Hogue, T.S., Ferreira, M., Mendez, C.B., Navarro, B., Lopez, S., and Jay, J.A. 2010. The effect of wildfire on soil mercury concentrations in southern California watersheds. *Water, Soil, and Air Pollution* 212: 369–385.

Caldwell, C.A., Canavan, C.M., and Bloom, N.S. 2000. Potential effects of forest fire and storm flow on total mercury and methylmercury in sediments of an arid-lands reservoir. *Science of the Total Environment* 260: 125–133.

Campbell, J.L., Eager, C., McDowell, W.H., and Hornbeck, J.W. 2000. Analysis of nitrogen dynamics in the Lye Brook Wilderness Area, Vermont, USA. *Water, Air, and Soil Pollution* 122: 63–75.

Carignan, R., and Steedman, R.J. 2000. Impacts of major watershed perturbations on aquatic ecosystems. *Canadian Journal of Fisheries and Aquatic Science* 57 (Suppl. 2): 1–4.

Carpi, A., and Lindberg, S.E. 1997. Sunlight-mediated emission of elemental mercury from soil amended with municipal sewage sludge. *Environmental Science and Technology* 31: 2085–2091.

Carpi, A., and Lindberg, S.E. 1998. Application of a Teflon dynamic flux chamber for quantifying soil mercury flux: tests and results over background soil. *Atmospheric Environment* 32: 873–882.

Chandler, C., Cheney, P., Thomas, P., Trabaud, L., and Williams, D. 1983. *Fire in forestry, Volume I: Forest fire behavior and effects.* Wiley, New York.

Collins, C.R., Sherman, D.M., and Ragnarsdottir, K.V. 1999. Surface complexation of Hg^{2+} on goethite: mechanism from EXAFS spectroscopy and density functional calculations. *Journal of Colloid and Interface Science* 219: 345–350.

Compeau, G.C., and Bartha, R. 1985. Sulfate-reducing bacteria: Principal methylators of mercury in anoxic estuarine sediments. *Applied Environmental Microbiology* 50(2): 498–502.

Cory, R.M., and McKnight, D.M. 2005. Fluorescence spectroscopy reveals ubiquitous presence of oxidized and reduced quinones in dissolved organic matter. *Environmental Science and Technology* 39: 8142–8149.

Cronan, C.S., and Reiners, W.A. 1983. Canopy processing of acidic precipitation by coniferous and hardwood forests in New England. *Oecologia* 59: 216–223.

Demers, J.D., Driscoll, C.T., Fahey, T.J., and Yavitt, J.B. 2007. Mercury cycling in litter and soil in different forest types in the Adirondack Region, New York, USA. *Ecological Applications* 17: 1341–1351.

Desauziers, V., Castre, N., and LeCloirec, P. 1997. Sorption of methylmercury by clays and mineral oxides. *Environmental Technology* 18: 1009–1018.

Drever, J.I. 1997. *The geochemistry of natural waters*. Prentice Hall, Upper Saddle River, NJ.

Drexel, R.T., Haitzer, M., Ryan, J.N., Aiken, G.R., and Nagy, K.L. 2002. Mercury(II) sorption to two Florida Everglades peats: evidence for strong and weak binding and competition by dissolved organic matter released from the peat. *Environmental Science and Technology* 36: 4058–4064.

Driscoll, C.T., et al. 2007. Mercury contamination in forest and freshwater ecosystems in the Northeastern United States. *Bioscience* 57: 17–28.

Driscoll, C.T., Holsapple, J., Schofield, C.L., and Munson, R. 1998. The chemistry and transport of mercury in a small wetland in the Adirondack region of New York, USA. *Biogeochemistry* 40: 137–146.

Dudas, M.J., and Cannon, K. 1983. Seasonal changes in background levels of mercury in surface horizons of forested soils in Alberta. *Canadian Journal of Soil Science* 63: 397–400.

Dudas, M.J., and Pawluk, S. 1976. The nature of mercury in chernozemic and luvisolic soils of Alberta. *Canadian Journal of Soil Science* 56: 413–423.

Dzombak, D.A., and Morel, F.M.M. 1990. *Surface complexation modeling*. Wiley, New York.

Engle, M.A. et al. 2006. Mercury distribution in two sierran forest and one desert sagebrush steppe ecosystems and the effects of fire. *Science of the Total Environment* 367: 222–233.

Engle, M.A., Gustin, M.S., Lindberg, S.E., Gertler, A.W., and Ariya, P.A. 2005. The influence of ozone on atmospheric emissions of gaseous elemental mercury and reactive gaseous mercury from substrates. *Atmospheric Environment* 39: 7506–7517.

Engle, M.A., Gustin, M.S., and Zhang, H. 2001. Quantifying natural source mercury emissions from the Ivanhoe Mining District, North-Central Nevada, USA. *Atmospheric Environment* 35: 3987–3997.

Engstrom, D.R., Swain, E.B., Henning, T.A., Brigham, M.E., and Brezonik, P.L. 1994. Recent decline in atmospheric mercury deposition in the upper Midwest. In: L.A. Baker (Editor), *Environmental chemistry of lakes and reservoirs*. American Chemical Society, Washington, DC, pp. 33–66.

Ericksen, J.A. et al. 2003. Accumulation of atmospheric mercury in forest foliage. *Atmospheric Environment* 37: 1613–1622.

Ericksen, J.A., Gustin, M.S., Xin, M., Weisberg, P.J., and Fernandez, G.C.J. 2006. Air–soil exchange of mercury from background soils in the United States. *Science of the Total Environment* 366: 851–863.

Fadini, P.S., and Jardim, W.F. 2001. Is the Negro River Basin (Amazon) impacted by naturally occurring mercury? *Science of the Total Environment* 275: 71–82.

Fan, T.W.M., Higashi, R.M., and Lane, A.N. 2000. Chemical characterization of a chelator-treated soil humate by solution-state multinuclear two-dimensional NMR with FTIR and pyrolysis-GCMS. *Environmental Science and Technology* 34: 1636–1646.

Farella, N., Lucotte, M., Davidson, R., and Daigle, S. 2006. Mercury release from deforested soils triggered by base cation enrichment. *Science of the Total Environment* 368: 19–29.

Fernandez, I.J., Karem, J.E., Norton, S.A., and Rustad, L.E. 2007. Temperature, soil moisture, and streamflow at the Bear Brook Watershed in Maine (BBWM). 196, Maine Agricultural and Forest Experiment Station, University of Maine, Orono, ME.

Fimmen, R.L., Cory, R.M., Chin, Y.-P., Trouts, T.D., and McKnight, D.M. 2007. Probing the oxidation–reduction properties of terrestrially and microbially derived dissolved organic matter. *Geochimica et Cosmochimica Acta* 71: 3003–3015.

Fitzgerald, W.F., Mason, R.P., and Vandal, G.M. 1991. Atmospheric cycling and air-water exchange of mercury over midcontinental lacustrine regions. *Water, Air, and Soil Pollution* 56: 745–767.

Fostier, A.-H. et al. 2000. Mercury fluxes in a natural forested Amazonian catchment (Serra do Navio, Amapa State, Brazil). *Science of the Total Environment* 260: 201–211.

Frescholtz, T.F., and Gustin, M.S. 2004. Soil and foliar mercury emission as a function of soil concentration. *Water, Air, and Soil Pollution* 155: 223–237.

Friedli, H.R. et al. 2003. Mercury emissions from burning of biomass from temperate North American forests: laboratory and airborne measurements. *Atmospheric Environment* 37: 253–267.

Friedli, H.R. et al. 2007. Mercury in vegetation and organic soil at an upland boreal forest site in Prince Albert National Park, Saskatchewan, Canada. *Journal of Geophysical Research* 112: G01004, doi:10.1029/2005JG000061.

Gabriel, M.C., and Williamson, D.G. 2004. Principal biogeochemical factors affecting the speciation and transport of mercury through the terrestrial environment. *Environmental Geochemistry and Health* 26: 421–434.

Garcia, E., and Carignan, R. 1999. Impact of wildfire and clear-cutting in the boreal forest on methyl mercury in zooplankton. *Canadian Journal of Fisheries and Aquatic Science* 56: 339–345.

Garcia, E., and Carignan, R. 2000. Mercury Concentrations in Northern Pike (*Esox Lucius*) from boreal lakes with logged, burned, or undisturbed catchments. *Canadian Journal of Fisheries and Aquatic Science* 57 (Suppl. 2): 129–135.

Gilmour, C.C. et al. 1998. Methylmercury concentrations and production rates across a trophic gradient in the northern Everglades. *Biogeochemistry* 40: 327–345.

Godbold, D.L. 1994. Mercury in forest ecosystems: risk and research needs. In: C.J. Watras and J. Huckabee (Editors), *Hg pollution: Integration and synthesis*. Lewis, Boca Raton, FL, pp. 295–303.

Gracey, H.I., and Stewart, J.W.B. 1974. Distribution of mercury in Saskatchewan soils and crops. *Canadian Journal of Soil Science* 54: 105–108.

Grigal, D.F., Nater, E.A., and Homann, P.S. 1994. Spatial distribution patterns of mercury in an east-central Minnesota Landscape. In: C.J. Watras and J.W. Huckabee (Editors), *Mercury pollution: Integration and synthesis*. Lewis, Boca Raton, FL, pp. 305–312.

Grigal, D., Kolka, R., Fleck, J., and Nater, E. 2000. Mercury budget in an upland peatland watershed. *Biogeochemistry* 50: 95–109.

Grigal, D. 2002. Inputs and outputs of mercury from terrestrial watersheds: a review. *Environmental Reviews* 10: 1–39.

Grigal, D.F. 2003. Mercury sequestration in forests and peatlands: a review. *Journal of Environmental Quality* 32: 393–405.

Gu, B., and Chen, J. 2003. Enhanced microbial reduction of Cr(VI) and U(VI) by different natural organic matter fractions. *Geochimica et Cosmochimica Acta* 67: 3575–3582.

Gunneriusson, L., and Sjöberg, S. 1993. Surface complexation in the H⁺-goethite (a-FeOOH)-Hg(II)-chloride system. *Journal of Colloid and Interface Science* 156: 121–128.

Gustin, M.S. 2003. Are mercury emissions from geologic sources significant? a status report. *Science of the Total Environment* 304: 153–167.

Gustin, M.S., Lindberg, S.E., and Weisberg, P.J. 2008. An update on the natural sources and sinks of atmospheric mercury. *Applied Geochemistry* 23: 482–493.

Gustin, M.S., Rasmussen, P., Schroeder, W., and Kemp, J. 1999. Application of a laboratory gas exchange chamber for assessment of in situ mercury emissions. *Journal of Geophysical Research* 104: 21873–21878.

Gustin, M.S., and Stamenkovic, J. 2005. Mercury emissions from soils: effect of watering and soil water content. *Biogeochemistry* 76: 215–232.

Gustin, M.S., Tayler, G.E., Leonard, T.L., and Keislar, R.E. 1996. Atmospheric mercury concentrations associated with geologically and anthropologically enriched sites in central western Nevada. *Environmental Science and Technology* 30: 2572–2579.

Gustin, M.S., Taylor, G.E., and Maxey, R.A. 1997. Effect of temperature, wind velocity and concentration on the flux of elemental mercury from mill tailings to the atmosphere. *Journal of Geophysical Research* 102: 3891–3898.

Haitzer, M., Aiken, G.R., and Ryan, J.N. 2002. Binding of mercury(II) to dissolved organic matter: the role of the mercury(II) to DOM concentration ratio. *Environmental Science and Technology* 36: 3564–3570.

Haitzer, M., Aiken, G.R., and Ryan, J.N. 2003. Binding of mercury(II) to aquatic humic substances: influence of pH and source of humic substances. *Environmental Science and Technology* 37: 2436–2441.

Harden, J.W. et al. 2004. Chemistry of burning the forest floor during the FROSTFIRE experimental burn, interior Alaska 1999. *Global Biogeochemistry Cycles* 18: GB3014, doi:10.1029/2003GB002194.

Harris, R.C. et al. 2007. Whole-ecosystem study shows rapid fish-mercury response to changes in mercury deposition. *Proceedings of the National Academy of Sciences of the United States of America* 104: 16586–16591.

Hayhoe, K. et al. 2006. Past and future changes in climate and hydrological indicators in the US Northeast. *Climate Dynamics* 28: 381–407.

Heyes, A., Moore, T.R., and Rudd, J.W.M. 1998. Mercury and methylmercury in decomposing vegetation of a pristine and impounded wetland. *Journal of Environmental Quality* 27: 591–599.

Hill, A.R., and Shackleton, M. 1989. Soil N mineralization and nitrification in relation to nitrogen solution chemistry in a small forested watershed. *Biogeochemistry* 8: 167–184.

Hintelmann, H. et al. 2002. Reactivity and mobility of new and old mercury deposition in a boreal forest ecosystem during the first year of the METAALICUS study. *Environmental Science and Technology* 36: 5034–5040.

Hintelmann, H., Welbourn, P.M., and Evans, R.D. 1995. Binding of methylmercury compounds by humic and fulvic acids. *Water, Air, and Soil Pollution* 80: 1031–1034.

Hissler, C., and Probst, J.-L. 2006. Impact of mercury atmospheric deposition on soils and streams in a mountainous catchment (Vosges, France) polluted by chlor-alkali industrial activity: the important trapping role of the organic matter. *Science of the Total Environment* 361: 163–178.

Hodgkins, G.A., James, I.C., and Huntington, T.G. 2002. Historical changes in lake ice-out dates as indicators of climate change in New England, 1850–2000. *International Journal of Climatology* 22: 1819–1827.

Hultberg, H., Iverfeldt, A., and Lee, Y.H. 1994. Methylmercury input/output and accumulation in forested catchments and critical loads for lakes in southern Sweden. In: C.J. Watras and J. Huckabee (Editors), *Hg pollution: Integration and synthesis*. Lewis, Boca Raton, FL, pp. 313–322.

Huntington, T.G. 2006. Evidence for intensification of the global hydrologic cycle: review and synthesis. *Journal of Hydrology* 319: 83–95.

IPCC (Intergovernmental Panel on Climate Change) 2007. *Climate change 2007: The physical science basis.* http://www.ipcc.ch/publications_and_data/publications_ipcc_fourth_assessment_report_wg1_report_the_physical_science_basis.htm (accessed December 28, 2011).

Iverfeldt, A. 1991. Mercury in forest canopy throughfall water and its relation to atmospheric deposition. *Water, Air, and Soil Pollution* 56: 533–564.

Jackson, T.A. (Editor) 1998. *Mercury in aquatic ecosystems. Metal metabolism in aquatic environments.* Chapman and Hall, London, pp. 76–157.

Johnson, D.W. (Editor) 1995. *Role of carbon in the cycling of other nutrients in forested ecosystems: carbon forms and functions in forest soils.* SSSA, Madison, WI, pp. 299–328.

Johnson, D.W., and Lindberg, S.E. 1995. The biogeochemical cycling of Hg in forests: alternative methods for quantifying total deposition and soil emission. *Water, Air, and Soil Pollution* 80: 1069–1077.

Johnson, K.B. 2002. Fire and its effects on mercury and methylmercury dynamics for two watersheds in Acadia National Park, Maine. M.S. Thesis, The University of Maine, Orono.

Johnson, K.B., Haines, T. A., Kahl, J.S., Norton, S. A., Amirbahman, A., Sheehan, K.D. 2007. Controls on mercury and methylmercury deposition for two watersheds in Acadia National Park, Maine. *Environmental Monitoring and Assessment* 126: 55–67.

Karlsson, T., and Skyllberg, U. 2003. Bonding of ppb levels of methyl mercury to reduced sulfur groups in soil organic matter. *Environmental Science and Technology* 37: 4912–4918.

Kasischke, E.S., and Stocks, B.J. 2000. *Fire, climate change, and carbon cycling in the boreal forest.* Springer-Verlag, New York.

Kelly, E.N., Schindler, D.W., St. Louis, V.L., Donald, D.B., and Vladicka, K.E. 2006. Forest fire increases mercury accumulation by fishes via food web restructuring and increased mercury inputs. *Proceedings of the National Academy of Sciences of the United States of America* 103: 19380–19385.

Kim, K.H., Lindberg, S.E., Hanson, P.J., and Meyers, T.P. 1995. Micrometeorological measurements of mercury fluxes over background forest soils in eastern Tennessee. *Atmospheric Environment* 29: 267–282.

King, J.K., Saunders, F.M., Lee, R.F., and Jahnke, R.A. 1999. Coupling mercury methylation rates to sulfate reduction rates in marine sediments. *Environmental Toxicology and Chemistry* 18(7): 1362–1369.

Kinniburgh, D.G., and Jackson, M.L. 1978. Adsorption of mercury(II) by iron hydroxide gel. *Soil Science Society of America Journal* 42: 45–47.

Korthals, E.T., and Winfrey, M.R. 1987. Seasonal and spatial variations in mercury methylation and demethylation in an oligotrophic lake. *Applied Environmental Microbiology* 53(10): 2397–2404.

Krabbenhoft, D.P., Benoit, J.M., Babiarz, C.L., Hurley, J.P., and Andren, A.W. 1995. Mercury cycling in the Allequash Creek Watershed, Northern Wisconsin. *Water, Air, and Soil Pollution* 80: 425–433.

Lacerda, L.D., DeSouza, M., and Ribeiro, M.G. 2004. The effects of land use change on mercury distribution in soils of Alta Floresta, Southern Amazon. *Environmental Pollution* 129: 247–255.

Lacerda, L.D., Salomons, W., Pfeiffer, W.C., and Bastos, W.R. 1991. Mercury distribution in sediment profiles of remote High Pantanal Lakes, Central Brazil. *Biogeochemistry* 14: 71–77.

Landa, E.R. 1978. Soil water content and temperature as factors in the volatile loss of applied mercury(II) from soils. *Soil Science* 126: 44–48.

Lee, Y., Bishop, K., and Munthe, J. 2000. Do concepts about catchment cycling of methylmercury and mercury in boreal catchments stand the test of time? Six years of atmospheric inputs and runoff export at Svartberg, Northern Sweden. *Science of the Total Environment* 260: 11–20.

Liang, Y., Yuan, D., Lu, M., Gong, Z., Liu, X., and Zhang, Z. 2009. Distribution characteristics of total mercury and methylmercury in the topsoil and dust of Xiamen, China. *Journal of Environmental Science* 21: 1400–1408.

Lindberg, S.E., et al. 1979. Atmospheric emission and plant uptake if mercury from agricultural soils near the Almaden mercury mine. *Journal of Environmental Quality* 8: 572–578.

Lindberg S.E., et al. 1999. Increases in mercury emissions from desert soils in response to rainfall and irrigation. *Journal of Geophysical Research* 104: 21879–21888.

Lorey, P., and Driscoll, C.T. 1999. Historical trends of mercury deposition to Adirondack lakes. *Environmental Science and Technology* 33: 718–722.

Lövgren, L., and Sjöberg, S. 1989. Equilibrium approaches to natural water systems—7. Complexation reactions of copper(II), cadmium(II) and mercury(II) with dissolved organic matter in a concentrated bog water. *Water Research* 23: 327–332.

Lu, X., Li, L.Y., Wang, L., Lei, K., Huang, J., and Zhai, Y. 2009. Contamination assessment of mercury and arsenic in roadway dust from Baoji, China. *Atmospheric Environment* 43: 2489–2496.

MacNaughton, M.G. 1973. Adsorption of mercury(II) at the solid/water interface. Ph.D. thesis, Stanford University, Palo Alto, CA.

Maier, R.M., Pepper, I.L., and Gerba, C.P. 2000. *Environmental microbiology*. Academic Press, Boston.

Mailman, M., and Bodaly, R.A. 2005. Total mercury, methyl mercury, and carbon in fresh and burned plants and soil in northwestern Ontario. *Environmental Pollution* 138: 161–166.

Mailman, M., and Bodaly, R.A. 2006. The burning question: does burning before flooding lower methyl mercury production and bioaccumulation? *Science of the Total Environment* 368: 407–417.

Marvin–DiPasquale, M.C., Agee, J.L., Bouse, R.M., and Jaffe, B.E. 2003. Microbial cycling of mercury in contaminated pelagic and wetland sediments of San Pablo Bay, California. *Environmental Geology* 43: 260–267.

Mason, R.P., Fitzgerald, W.F., and Morel, F.M.M. 1994. The biogeochemical cycling of elemental mercury: Anthropogenic influences. *Geochimica et Cosmochimica Acta* 58: 3191–3198.

Mauclair, C., Layshock, J., and Carpi, A. 2008. Quantifying the effect of humic matter on the emission of mercury from artificial soil surfaces. *Applied Geochemistry* 23: 594–601.

McClain, M.E., et al. 2003. Biogeochemical hot spots and hot moments at the interface of terrestrial and aquatic ecosystems. *Ecosystems* 6: 301–312.

McKeague, J.A., and Kloosterman, B. 1974. Mercury in horizons of some soil profiles in Canada. *Canadian Journal of Soil Science* 54: 503–507.

Mierle, G., and Ingram, R. 1991. The role of humic substances in the mobilization of mercury from watersheds. *Water, Air, and Soil Pollution* 56: 349–357.

Mitchell, C.P.J., Branfireun, B.A., and Kolka, R.K. 2008. Spatial characteristics of net methylmercury production hot spots in peatlands. *Environmental Science and Technology* 42: 1010–1016.

Moore, C., and Carpi, A. 2005. Mechanisms of the emission of mercury from soil: the role of UV radiation. *Journal of Geophysical Research* 110: D24302.

Morra, M.J., Fendorf, S.E., and Brown, P.D. 1997. Speciation of sulfur in humic and fulvic acids using x-ray absorption near-edge structure (XANES) spectroscopy. *Geochimica et Cosmochimica Acta* 61(3): 683–688.

Mosbaek, H., Tjell, J.C., and Sevel, T. 1998. Plant uptake of airborne mercury in background areas. *Chemosphere* 17: 1227–1236.

Nadelhoffer, K.J. et al. 1995. The fate of 15N-labelled nitrate additions to a northern hardwood forest in eastern Maine, USA. *Oecologia* 103: 292–301.

Nater, E.A., and Grigal, D.F. 1992. Regional trends in mercury distribution across the Great Lakes states, north central U.S.A. *Nature* 358: 139–141.

Nevin, K.P., and Lovley, D.R. 2000. Potential for nonenzymatic reduction of Fe(III) via electron shuttling in subsurface sediments. *Environmental Science and Technology* 34: 2472–2478.

Newton, D.W., Ellis, R., and Paulsen, G.M. 1976. Effect of pH and complex formation in mercury (II) adsorption by bentonite. *Journal of Environmental Quality* 5: 251–254.

Oliveira, S.M.B. et al. 2001. Soils as an important sink for mercury in the Amazon. *Water, Air, and Soil Pollution* 126: 321–337.

Porvari, P., Vetra, M., Munthe, J., and Haapanen, M. 1993. Forestry practices increase mercury and methyl mercury output from boreal forest catchments. *Environmental Science and Technology* 37: 2389–2393.

Qian, J. et al. 2002. Bonding of methyl mercury to reduced sulfur groups in soil and stream organic matter as determined by x-ray absorption spectroscopy and binding affinity studies. *Geochimica et Cosmochimica Acta* 66: 3873–3885.

Rea, A.W., Keeler, G.J., and Scherbatskoy, T. 1996. The deposition of mercury in throughfall and litterfall in the Lake Champlain watershed: a short-term study. *Atmospheric Environment* 30: 3257–3263.

Rea, A.W., Lindberg, S.E., and Keeler, G.J. 2000. Assessment of dry deposition and foliar leaching of mercury and selected trace elements based on washed foliar and surrogate surfaces. *Environmental Science and Technology* 34: 2418–2425.

Rea, A.W., Lindberg, S.E., and Keeler, G.J. 2001. Dry deposition and foliar leaching of mercury and selected trace elements in deciduous forest throughfall. *Atmospheric Environment* 35: 3453–3462.

Rea, A.W., Lindberg, S.E., Scherbatskoy, T., and Keeler, G.J. 2002. Mercury accumulation in foliage over time in two northern mixed-hardwood forests. *Water, Air, and Soil Pollution* 133: 49–67.

Rodrigues, S., and Maddock, J.E.L. 1997. Mercury pollution in two gold mining areas of the Brazilian Amazon. *Journal of Geochemical Exploration* 58: 231–240.

Roulet, M., and Lucotte, M. 1995. Geochemistry of mercury in pristine and flooded ferralitic soils of a tropical rain forest in French Guiana, South America. *Water, Air, and Soil Pollution* 80: 1079–1088.

Roulet, M. et al. 1999. Effects of recent human colonization on the presence of mercury in Amazonian ecosystems. *Water, Air, and Soil Pollution* 112: 297–313.

Roulet, M. et al. 1998. The geochemistry of mercury in Central Amazonian soils developed on the Alter-do-Chão Formation of the Lower Tapajós River Valley, Pará State, Brazil. *Science of the Total Environment* 223: 1–24.

Rudd, J.W.M. 1995. Sources of methyl mercury to freshwater ecosystems: A review. *Water, Air, and Soil Pollution* 80: 679–713.

Rustad, L.E., Kahl, J.S., Norton, S.A., and Fernandez, I.J. 1994. Underestimation of dry deposition by throughfall in mixed northern hardwood forests. *Journal of Hydrology* 162: 319–336.

Schlüter, K. 1996. Translocation of ^{203}Hg labelled HgCl$_2$ and CH$_3$HgCl in an iron-humus podzol studied by radio-analytical techniques. *Zeitschrift für Pflanzenernähr Bodenk* 159: 215–226.

Schlüter, K. 1997. Sorption of inorganic mercury and monomethylmercury in an iron-humus podzol soil of southern Norway studied by batch experiments. *Environmental Geology* 30: 266–279.

Schlüter, K. 2000. Review: evaporation of mercury from soils: an integration and synthesis of current knowledge. *Environmental Geology* 39: 249–271.

Schlüter, K., Alstad, J., and Seip, H.M. 1995a. Mercury translocation in and evaporation from soil. I. Soil lysimeter experiments with ^{203}Hg-radiolabeled compounds. *Journal of Soil Contamination* 4(4): 327–353.

Schlüter, K., Seip, H.M., and Alstad, J. 1995b. Mercury translocation in and evaporation from soil. II. Evaporation of mercury from podzolized soil profiles treated with HgCl$_2$ and CH$_3$HgCl. *Journal of Soil Contamination* 4(4): 269–298.

Schroeder, W.H., and Munthe, J. 1998. Atmospheric mercury—An overview. *Atmospheric Environment* 32: 809–822.

Schroeder, W.H., Yarwood, G., and Niki, H. 1991. Transformation processes involving mercury species in the atmosphere—Results from a literature survey. *Water, Air, and Soil Pollution* 56: 653–666.

Schuster, E. 1991. The behavior of mercury in the soil with special emphasis on complexation and adsorption processes—A review of the literature. *Water, Air, and Soil Pollution* 56: 667–680.

Schwesig, D., Ilgen, G., and Matzner, E. 1999. Mercury and methylmercury in upland and wetland acid forest soils of a watershed in NE-Bavaria, Germany. *Water, Air, and Soil Pollution* 113: 141–154.

Schwesig, D., and Matzner, E. 2000. Pools and fluxes of mercury and methylmercury in two forested catchments in Germany. *Science of the Total Environment* 260: 213–223.

Scott, D.T., McKnight, D.M., Blunt-Harris, E.L., Kolesar, S.E., and Lovley, D.R. 1998. Quinone moieties act as electron acceptors in the reduction of humic substances by humics reducing microorganisms. *Environmental Science and Technology* 32: 2984–2989.

Semu, E., Singh, B.R., and Selmer-Olsen, A.R. 1987. Adsorption of mercury compounds by tropical soils. *Water, Air, and Soil Pollution* 32: 1–16.

Sheehan, K.D., Fernandez, I.J., Kahl, J.S., and Amirbahman, A. 2006. Litterfall mercury in two forested watersheds at Acadia National Park, Maine, USA. *Water, Air, and Soil Pollution* 170: 249–265.

Shotyk, W., Blaser, P., Grünig, A., and Cheburkin, A.K. 2000. A new approach for quantifying cumulative, anthropogenic, atmospheric lead deposition using peat cores from bogs: Pb in eight Swiss peat bog profiles. *Science of the Total Environment* 249: 281–295.

Sigler, J.M., Lee, X., and Munger, W. 2003. Emission and long-range transport of gaseous mercury estimates from a large-scale Canadian boreal forest fire. *Environmental Science and Technology* 37: 4343–4347.

Skyllberg, U., Xia, K., Nater, E.A., and Bleam, W.F. 2000. Binding of mercury(II) to reduced sulfur in soil organic matter along upland-peat soil transects. *Journal of Environmental Quality* 29: 855–865.

St. Louis, V., et al. 1996. Production and loss of total mercury from boreal forest catchments containing different types of wetlands. *Environmental Science and Technology* 30: 2719–2729.

St. Louis, V.L., et al. 1994. Importance of wetlands as sources of methyl mercury to boreal forest ecosystems. *Canadian Journal of Fisheries and Aquatic Science* 51: 1065–1076.

St. Louis, V.L., et al. 2001. Importance of the forest canopy to fluxes of methyl mercury and total mercury to boreal systems. *Environmental Science and Technology* 35: 3089–3098.

Swain, E.B., Engstrom, D.R., Brigham, M.E., Henning, T.A., and Brezonik, P.L. 1992. Increasing rates of atmospheric mercury deposition in midcontinental North America. *Science* 257: 784–787.

Tack, F.M.G., Vanhaesebroeck, T., Verloo, M.G., Van Rompaey, K., and Van Ranst, E. 2005. Mercury baseline levels in Flemish soils (Belgium). *Environmental Pollution* 134: 173–179.

Tiffereau, C., Lutzenkirchen, J., and Behra, P. 1995. Modeling the adsorption of Mercury(II) on (hydr)oxides. *Journal of Colloid and Interface Science* 172: 82–93.

Wiedinmyer, C., and Friedli, H. 2007. Mercury emission estimates from fires: an initial inventory for the United States. *Environmental Science and Technology* 41: 8092–8098.

Winfrey, M.R., and Rudd, J.H. 1990. Environmental factors affecting the formation of methylmercury in low pH lakes. *Environmental Toxicology and Chemistry* 9: 855–869.

Woodruff, L.G., and Cannon, W.F. 2010. Immediate and long-term fire effects on total mercury in forests soils of northeastern Minnesota. *Environmental Science and Technology* 44: 5371–5376.

Wright, H.A., and Bailey, A.W. 1982. Fire ecology, United States and southern Canada. Wiley, New York.

Xia, K., Bleam, W.F., Bloom, P.R., Skyllberg, U.L., and Helmke, P.A. 1998. XANES studies of oxidation states of sulfur in aquatic and soil humic substances. *Soil Science Society of America Journal* 62: 1240–1246.

Xia, K., et al. 1999. X-ray Absorption spectroscopic evidence for the complexation of Hg(II) by reduced sulfur in soil humic substances. *Environmental Science and Technology* 33: 257–261.

Xiao, Z.F., Strömberg, D., and Lindqvist, O. 1995. Influence of humic substances on photolysis of divalent mercury in aqueous solution. *Water, Air, and Soil Pollution* 80: 789–798.

Xin, M., and Gustin, M.S. 2007. Gaseous elemental Hg exchange with low Hg containing soils: investigation of controlling factors. *Applied Geochemistry* 22: 1451–1466.

Xin, M., Gustin, M., and Johnson, D. 2007. Laboratory investigation of the potential for re-emission of atmospherically derived Hg from soils. *Environmental Science and Technology* 41: 4946–4951.

Yin, Y., Allen, H.E., Li, Y., Huang, C.P., and Sanders, P.F. 1996. Adsorption of mercury(II) by soil: effects of pH, chloride, and organic Matter. *Journal of Environmental Quality* 25: 837–844.

Yin, Y., Allen, H.E., Huang, C.P., and Sanders, P.F. 1997a. Adsorption/desorption isotherms of Hg(II) by soil. *Soil Science* 162(1): 35–45.

Yin, Y., Allen, H.E., Huang, C.P., Sparks, D.L., and Sanders, P.F. 1997b. Kinetics of mercury(II) adsorption and desorption on soil. *Environmental Science and Technology* 31: 496–503.

Zhang, H., and Lindberg, S.E. 1999. Processes influencing the emission of mercury from soils: a conceptual model. *Journal of Geophysical Research* 104: 21889–21896.

Zhang, H., Lindberg, S.E., Marsik, F.J., and Keeler, G.J. 2001. Mercury air/surface exchange kinetics of background soils for the Tahquamenon River watershed in the Michigan upper peninsula. *Water, Air, and Soil Pollution* 126: 151–169.

Mercury Cycling in Terrestrial Watersheds

JAMES B. SHANLEY and KEVIN BISHOP

Long-range atmospheric transport of anthropogenic mercury (Hg) emissions has led to Hg deposition well in excess of natural levels throughout much of Europe, North America, and other areas (Iverfeldt, 1991; Mierle and Ingram, 1991; Fitzgerald et al., 1998; Slemr et al., 2003). This deposition has contributed to the accumulation of Hg in the aquatic food chain (Lindqvist et al., 1991; Kamman et al., 2005). It is now common for some species of fish to contain Hg near or above levels deemed harmful to human health, even in relatively remote areas such as boreal areas of Fenno-Scandia (Munthe

et al., 2004) and North America (Lucotte et al., 1995). High levels of Hg in freshwater fish have been a concern for more than three decades (Johnels et al., 1967; Håkansson et al., 1990). More recently, bio-accumulation in the terrestrial ecosystem has come to the fore (this book, chapter 16), and even the possibility that soil microbiota are directly affected (Bringmark and Bringmark, 2001). When the problem was originally addressed in the 1970s and 1980s, researchers focused on Hg deposition and the role that acidification might play in mobilizing Hg from catchment soils to surface waters (Johansson et al., 1991). This focus has since given way to an emerging awareness of the importance of catchment processes in controlling the loading of Hg to aquatic ecosystems, and especially loading of the most bio-available form of Hg, methylmercury (MeHg) (Rudd, 1995; St. Louis et al., 1996; Meili et al., 2003; Drevnick et al., 2007). As understanding has grown, so too has an appreciation of the magnitude of the Hg problem.

Some of the earliest investigations of Hg cycling in terrestrial watersheds were carried out in boreal landscapes, and many of the findings were presented in special issues of *Water, Air and Soil Pollution* in 1991 and 1995. These were followed by studies aimed at quantifying fluxes of Hg from the terrestrial landscape in small forested streams (Krabbenhoft et al., 1995; Lee et al., 1995; Allan and Heyes, 1998; Scherbatskoy et al., 1998; Schwesig and Matzner, 2000; Allan et al., 2001; Shanley et al., 2002) to larger rivers of mixed land use (Hurley et al., 1995; Babiarz et al., 1998; Balogh et al., 1998a, 2005). The majority of the literature is weighted toward midlatitudes and especially high latitudes in the northern hemisphere, primarily North America and Europe (Figure 8.1). The more limited literature on tropical systems and the southern hemisphere is nearly exclusively from mining-impacted areas of the Amazon (Hacon et al., 1995; Malm, 1998; Wasserman et al., 2003).

FIGURE 8.1   Global sites of terrestrial mercury cycling research cited in this chapter.

In general, more than 80% of annual atmospheric Hg deposition to terrestrial watersheds is retained in the soil (Aastrup et al., 1991; Lee et al., 1998; Hintelmann et al., 2002). Soil retention has protected the aquatic ecosystem from receiving the full load of anthropogenic Hg deposition. Conversely, however, soil Hg retention has increased the store of Hg in soils and vegetation, posing an uncertain but potentially large future risk (Harris et al., 2007). Annual losses of Hg through volatilization or streamflow represent only a minute fraction of the catchment store. Decreased Hg emissions and deposition appear to result in a direct reduction of Hg uptake in aquatic ecosystems (Evers et al., 2007; Harris et al., 2007), but decreased emissions may not be effective at reducing the terrestrial outputs of Hg and MeHg. Thus, management for Hg in freshwater ecosystems becomes a much more complex problem, in that not only direct atmospheric deposition of Hg, but the entire Hg-contaminated landscape, is a Hg source. Indeed, one of the paramount issues facing scientists and policymakers today is the ultimate fate of the large amount of "legacy Hg" that has accumulated in terrestrial soils and vegetation. Prudent land management can help to limit Hg in runoff.

Terrestrial Hg cycling is important for several reasons: (1) terrestrial vegetation enhances atmospheric Hg capture; Hg deposition to forests may be 3–4 times greater than Hg deposition to adjacent water bodies (Miller et al., 2005); (2) despite the high Hg retention in terrestrial landscapes, Hg "leakage" from land areas often results in terrestrial Hg being the dominant source to a water body; (3) a significant proportion of the MeHg in freshwaters forms in the terrestrial landscape, notably in wetlands but also in upland soils,

before its hydrologic transport to water bodies; (4) Hg export from watersheds tends to be episodic, and these high-Hg pulses may either stimulate methylation or comprise a major source of MeHg in their own right; and (5) there is increasing documentation of Hg bio-accumulation in terrestrial food webs (Evers et al., 2007) as well as the potential of direct effects on soil microbial communities.

Although inorganic total Hg (THg) is the main form of Hg in atmospheric deposition, the dominant form in fish is MeHg. The transformation of THg to MeHg occurs naturally in anoxic environments—that is, water-saturated zones in peatlands, riparian areas, and sediments (Meili, 1997; Holmes and Lean, 2006). Under humid hydrologic regimes, such zones are naturally abundant (e.g., wetlands in boreal and tropical regions), or they can be created/induced by land-use changes such as forest harvest or flooding from hydroelectric dams and reservoirs. Advances have been made in localizing and identifying processes in the forest floor and near-stream wetland areas that increase the loading of bio-available MeHg to the aquatic ecosystem (Lee et al., 2000; Branfireun and Roulet, 2002; Mitchell et al., 2008b). Water-table fluctuations may also stimulate the sulfur-reducing bacteria (SRB) which are particularly effective in methylating Hg (Sorensen et al., 2005; Selch et al., 2007). Sulfur (S) deposition may enhance methylation by SRB as well (Branfireun et al., 2001; Jeremiason et al., 2006; Drevnick et al., 2007; Mitchell et al., 2008a). These findings help to explain the observations that catchment disturbance, such as forestry operations and land development, increase the MeHg exported from catchments (Porvari et al., 2003) as well as the amount of Hg bio-accumulated in downstream fish (Garcia and Carignan, 2005).

In this chapter, we review and synthesize the current state of knowledge on inputs, outputs, and stores of THg and MeHg in the terrestrial landscape, including wetlands, as well as our current understanding of how Hg moves through catchments and its transformations en route. Wetlands have long been recognized as important methylation sites, but here we also present the emerging evidence for methylation in terrestrial uplands. Following the literature, our treatment is weighted toward forested landscapes in temperate and high latitudes, but we consider agricultural, urban, and tropical landscapes to the extent possible. In this context we also discuss the effect of disturbance (such as forest harvesting and urbanization) on Hg and MeHg fluxes. Finally, we consider the fate of this legacy Hg and its sensitivity to future changes in Hg emissions, land use, and climate.

Mercury Inputs

Hg is a global pollutant because atmospheric transport and deposition effectively connect anthropogenic emissions to the most remote areas of the globe. Some of this anthropogenic Hg is deposited directly to water bodies, but most falls on the surrounding terrestrial landscape, where it is a potential source to freshwater ecosystems via runoff. Moreover, deposition per unit area is greater to land than to water surfaces because the forest canopy and other vegetative surfaces tend to scavenge gaseous Hg from the atmosphere more effectively than water surfaces (Allan and Heyes, 1998; Miller et al., 2005).

Atmospheric deposition of Hg is treated thoroughly in chapter 6. Here we present the basic concepts relevant to terrestrial Hg cycling. Over the past decade, an important debate has taken place in the literature about whether freshly deposited atmospheric Hg ("new Hg") is more labile and biologically available than Hg that has been incorporated into soils and vegetation ("aged Hg") (Krabbenhoft et al., 2004). The implications are important, because if only new Hg bio-accumulates, reductions in Hg emissions would have an immediate ecologic benefit.

Atmospheric Hg enters watersheds via wet deposition, in rain or snow, or as dry deposition, by various processes, when it is not precipitating. Most Hg emissions from both natural and anthropogenic sources are in the form of gaseous Hg(0), which is relatively unreactive and has a 1-year average residence time in the atmosphere. A smaller portion is emitted as ionic Hg(II), either as reactive gaseous mercury (RGM) or particulate Hg (HgP). Hg(II) has a much shorter residence time; model results suggest that more than 60% of the RGM and more than 20% of HgP deposits within 1000 km of its emission source (Cohen et al., 2007). Wet deposition of Hg at a given site originates partly from the globally distributed Hg(0) pool and partly from regional emissions of Hg(II).

Atmospheric deposition of Hg, in contrast to most other elements, occurs primarily as dryfall in most landscapes.

Much of this dry deposition occurs by forest canopy scavenging of Hg(0), which enters leaf stomata at a fairly constant rate and binds to foliar tissue throughout the growing season (Rea et al., 2002; Miller et al., 2005). The leaf cuticle has been proposed as an alternative Hg(0) entry point (Stamenkovic and Gustin, 2009; Converse et al., 2010). In contrast, dry deposition of RGM and HgP occurs on external foliar surfaces (Krabbenhoft et al., 2005; Miller et al., 2005). Together, these mechanisms result in dry Hg deposition in forests that exceeds wet Hg deposition, in some cases by severalfold (Munthe et al., 1995; Lee et al., 1998; Kolka et al., 1999; St. Louis et al., 2001). Hg in litterfall appears to be primarily a new, not recycled, input of atmospheric Hg (Bushey et al., 2008; Graydon et al., 2009). Conversely, dry Hg deposition is lower in nonforested areas and smaller yet to water surfaces (Miller et al., 2005). Operationally, dry deposition of Hg(0) is commonly quantified as the Hg in litterfall, while dry deposition of Hg(II) is quantified as the Hg in net throughfall (throughfall Hg minus open precipitation Hg) (Driscoll et al., 1994; Miller et al., 2005; Risch et al., 2012). Enrichment of Hg in the snowpack under forest canopy shows that throughfall is important even in winter (Nelson et al., 2010).

MeHg in wet deposition is on the order of 1% of THg (Lee et al., 1998). In catchments without significant internal net MeHg generation, this input may be quantitatively sufficient to account for stream MeHg output, though it is unlikely that MeHg in deposition transits through a catchment conservatively. Dry deposition of MeHg also appears to be significant; St. Louis et al. (2004) found a twofold enrichment in annual MeHg under the forest canopy relative to open spaces. Nearly all of the excess MeHg was in litterfall, but it is not clear whether it is taken up by stomata or binds to external foliar surfaces. Schwesig and Matzner (2001) found that litterfall supplied only one third of the annual input of THg, but more than half of the annual input of MeHg.

Mercury Stocks

The affinity of Hg for organic matter governs its distribution on the landscape. We consider here Hg stores in vegetation and soils (forest floor and mineral soils), including peatlands.

Vegetation

In forested landscapes, a relatively small pool of Hg (~2% of the total soil pool) is retained by living vegetation and associated coarse woody debris (Grigal, 2003). This pool is about 4 times the annual Hg deposition, suggesting an average 4-year residence time of Hg in vegetation. However, more than half of this Hg is stored in tree boles and has a much longer residence time, while ~15% is present in foliage, with a much shorter residence time. In the METALLICUS study, where isotopically distinct Hg inputs could be directly tracked, 66% of new Hg input remained in aboveground vegetation after 1 year (Hintelmann et al.,

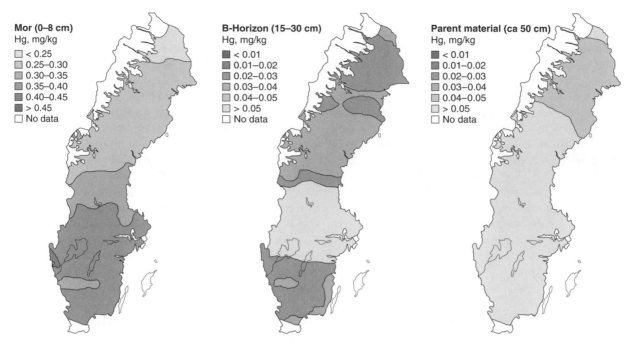

FIGURE 8.2 Spatial distribution of soil THg concentrations at three different depths in Sweden.

2002). In boreal wetlands Moore et al. (1995) found 4–160 ng g^{-1} THg and 0.1–139 ng g^{-1} MeHg, with the lowest values in shrubs and highest in mosses. For a given land area, the mass of Hg in vegetation was similar to the mass of Hg in porewater but was only a small fraction of the mass of Hg in peat. In general, THg and MeHg concentrations increased with increasing proximity of the plant's habitat to the water table, though some upland mosses also had high concentrations. Hall and St. Louis (2004) reported THg concentrations near 10 ng g^{-1} in needles/leaves, 5–30 ng g^{-1} in shrubs, 33 ng g^{-1} in lichen, and 50–100 ng g^{-1} in mosses.

Soils

Chapter 7 has a complete treatment of soil Hg, but we present here some contextual information to help in understanding terrestrial Hg cycling. Hg content in soils is typically on the order of 100 ng g^{-1}. As reported in Grigal (2003), Rundgren et al. (1992) compiled Hg concentrations in European soils and found nearly identical Hg of about 140 ng g^{-1} in natural (mostly forest, n = 50) and agricultural (n = 48) soils. Industrially contaminated soils can have much higher Hg concentrations, up to 1500 ng g^{-1} (Zhao et al., 2008). Nater and Grigal (1992) reported THg in humus of 100–250 ng g^{-1} and THg in mineral soil of 15–30 ng g^{-1} in forest soils of the upper midwestern United States. Wiener et al. (2006) reported THg averages of 324 ng g^{-1} in the O horizon, 126 ng g^{-1} in the A horizon, and 49 ng g^{-1} in the C horizon, as compared with <20 ng g^{-1} in bedrock (assumed to be geogenic Hg). Wiener et al. (2003) summarized the range of MeHg concentrations as 0.2–0.5 ng g^{-1} in organic soils and <0.05 ng g^{-1} in mineral soils, but stressed the lack of measurements in soils relative to aquatic systems. Skyllberg et al. (2003), working in a gradient from upland mineral soils to riparian peats and wetlands reported soil THg in Sweden ranging from 10 to 115 ng g^{-1} and soil MeHg ranging from <0.05 to 13.4 ng g^{-1}, with concentrations generally greatest toward the stream. Soil MeHg:THg ratios in this study ranged from 0.004 to 0.17. In stream sediment, THg concentration is commonly low because organic matter is poorly retained, but in lakes and oceans, sediments represent a large repository for Hg.

The recent era of anthropogenic emissions has increased Hg deposition by a factor of 3–4. Modern Hg concentrations in organic horizons of northern temperate and boreal soils (Figure 8.2) have increased by a similar factor (Johansson et al., 1995, 2001). Demers et al. (2007) found that forest litter accumulated THg over time. Hall and St. Louis (2004) and Heyes et al. (1998) found that THg was lost from decomposing litter over time, but at a slower rate than total litter mass loss. Indeed, Alriksson (2001) found higher Hg within the lower mor layer (which is older and more degraded), as compared with the upper mor layer at sites across Sweden, supporting the idea that Hg is retained as organic matter breaks down. THg concentrations are generally much higher in the forest floor relative to mineral soil (Grigal, 2003). However, given the greater thickness and higher bulk density of the mineral soil, the pool of Hg in the mineral soil can be several times to well over an order of magnitude greater than that in the forest floor. Analogously, peats commonly have lower THg concentrations than adjacent upland soils (Schwesig et al., 1999), but may hold a greater pool of Hg where deposits are deep. Grigal (2003) calculated that peatlands store 1000 times more Hg per unit area than annual atmospheric deposition of Hg.

Even in the mineral soil, Hg is presumed to be nearly exclusively associated with organic matter; Grigal (2003) used C content as a surrogate to estimate a national (U.S.) forest soil Hg inventory. Few measurements of MeHg in mineral soil exist, but it is generally less than 2% of THg (Grigal, 2003). Interestingly, while soil C content decreases sharply with depth from the forest floor to mineral soil, many investigators have found that the Hg:C ratios are higher in the mineral soil (Aastrup et al., 1991; Grigal et al., 1994; Schwesig et al., 1999).

The accumulations of Hg near the terrestrial–atmospheric interface, coupled with the known affinity of Hg for organic matter, leave little doubt that this surface Hg is predominantly atmospheric. But as one moves deeper into the mineral soil and Hg concentrations decrease, background geogenic Hg probably becomes increasingly important. Some of the Hg in mineral soil may have originated from natural atmospheric deposition of Hg that moved slowly downward over millennia. In Sweden, the Hg concentration in mineral soil at ~50 cm depth is uniform from south to north, despite a strong gradient in Hg deposition, which shows up clearly in the surface mor layer (Figure 8.2). Moreover, the total store of Hg in most soils is too great to be explained by recent anthropogenic emissions. In assessing the rate of Hg sequestration by soil and anthropogenic effects, it would be helpful to know how much of the Hg present is native (geogenic) and how much is atmospheric. Quantification of Hg in unweathered parent material may help estimate the geogenic Hg proportion.

Mercury Outputs

The two main pathways of Hg output from the terrestrial landscape are volatilization to the atmosphere and export in streamwater. Volatilization is difficult to quantify, and assessments of its importance in the terrestrial Hg cycle range widely. Streamwater Hg export is more readily quantified, and is typically only a small fraction of Hg in deposition, which itself is measured in parts per trillion. Yet this "small fraction of a trace amount" exported from terrestrial landscapes has profound ecologic significance. In this section, we examine the magnitude and processes controlling THg and MeHg outputs from catchments.

Volatilization

Terrestrial soils are a primary sink for atmospherically deposited mercury, but some of this Hg is volatilized back to the atmosphere. Estimates of Hg volatilized from soil or vegetation surfaces to the atmosphere vary widely and error bars on the estimates are large. Hg deposition and volatilization are both too small relative to the soil Hg pool to calculate volatilization from an annual mass balance approach. In a long-term mass balance, Grigal (2002) computed that soil Hg accretion since deglaciation accounted for only about one quarter of the soil Hg pool, and therefore

concluded that volatilization must be large. Some plot scale measurements in the Adirondack Mountains, United States, support volatilization fluxes approaching the magnitude of Hg wet deposition fluxes—for example, 7.0 $\mu g\ m^{-2}\ a^{-1}$ from a forest floor (Choi and Holsen, 2009b) and 4.6 $\mu g\ m^{-2}\ a^{-1}$ from a wetland (Selvendiran et al., 2008). Global Hg mass balance considerations likewise suggest that a sizable fraction of terrestrial Hg deposition is revolatilized to the atmosphere (Mason and Sheu, 2002).

Several watershed studies suggest lower Hg volatilization losses. In an unpolluted boreal forest in Canada, St. Louis et al. (2001) concluded that volatilization amounted to only about 10% of Hg deposition. In the METAALICUS study, volatilization was directly measured from isotopically distinct Hg input, and was found to occur only in the first few months after application (Lindberg et al., 2003), accounting for about 8% of the applied isotope (Hintelmann et al., 2002). In an overview of catchment Hg cycling, Krabbenhoft et al. (2005) concluded that volatilization from forest soils was a comparatively small flux. In montane grasslands, Fritsche et al. (2008) found net uptake of atmospheric Hg, while Converse et al. (2010) found a bidirectional flux dependent on season. Ultraviolet radiation is thought to be the primary driver of volatilization both from foliar surfaces (Graydon et al., 2006) and forest soils (Choi and Holsen, 2009a). Johnson et al. (2003) also showed that soil moisture and other factors affect Hg volatilization from soils and that it is not driven by diffusion. For more on Hg volatilization see chapter 7.

Stream Mercury Export

TOTAL MERCURY

Export by streamwater is the dominant loss pathway for THg in most catchments. Most streams have detectable levels of THg (>0.1 ng L^{-1}) at all times. At base flow, concentrations generally range from 0.5 to 2 ng L^{-1} (Hurley et al., 1995; Babiarz et al., 1998; Balogh et al., 1998a, 1998b, 2005; Hurley et al., 1998; Scherbatskoy et al., 1998), and are sustained by dissolved THg in groundwater. Nearly all Hg in streamwater occurs as Hg(II) in dissolved or particulate form. MeHg also occurs in dissolved or particulate form. Dissolved Hg is operationally defined as the Hg fraction that passes a filter membrane (pore size range, 0.2–0.7 μm), but Babiarz et al. (2001) showed that much of the <0.2-μm Hg fraction is colloidal. For this reason the term *filtered Hg* is preferable when referring to discrete samples. In addition to Hg(II), some dissolved gaseous Hg(0) is present but typically represents $<1\%$ of the aqueous Hg in streams. Dissolved gaseous Hg(0) is important in lakes and other water bodies because it regulates the amount of dry deposition of Hg to the water surface (O'Driscoll et al., 2004; Eckley et al., 2005).

Catchments release only a minute amount of their stored Hg to streamwater, but stream Hg flux tends to be focused in short episodes of high concentrations and loading (Bishop et al., 1995a, 1995b; Allan and Heyes, 1998; Hurley et al., 1998; Mason and Sullivan, 1998; Scherbatskoy et al., 1998; Whyte and Kirchner, 2000; Allan et al., 2001; Shanley et al., 2002, 2008; Schuster et al., 2008). The episodic loading of Hg during brief periods may exacerbate its toxicologic impact on downstream water bodies relative to the same load distributed more evenly in time. MeHg export may also be episodic, but its behavior is more variable.

During events, dissolved THg (and to some extent MeHg) is mobilized from surface soil by rising water tables and shallow hydrologic flow paths. Particulate THg and MeHg enter streams during events by erosion of soil organic matter or streambanks. Some particle Hg may also be resus-pended from streambed sediments (Hurley et al., 1998). Dissolved THg concentrations increase during storms by typically twofold to fivefold (Schuster et al., 2008; Shanley et al., 2008) and rarely exceed 20 ng L^{-1} in unpolluted landscapes. HgP concentrations, on the other hand, are negligible at base flow but increase more dynamically during storms, often exceeding 50 ng L^{-1} during high flow (Figure 8.3). Selected measured peak THg concentrations are presented in Table 8.1. Progress on unattended, automated sampling for Hg may help researchers collect important high-flow samples (Riscassi et al., 2010).

Landscape characteristics, to a much greater extent than Hg deposition, control the amount and form of stream Hg export (Schelker et al., 2011). Hg on the landscape is strongly associated with organic matter, and thus watershed features that regulate the accumulation and release of dissolved organic carbon (DOC) and particulate organic carbon (POC) will have a strong bearing on the mobility of Hg and MeHg. The mechanism of Hg–DOC and Hg–POC associations will be discussed later in the section "Role of Dissolved and Particulate Organic Carbon."

In a Vermont stream, Scherbatskoy et al. (1998) found that annual THg export was about two thirds particulate and one third dissolved. Particulate THg export occurred primarily during high-flow events. Dissolved THg export, though its concentration also increased with discharge, occurred primarily as cumulative release during low-flow periods. A single event may dominate the annual stream flux of particulate THg (Babiarz et al., 1998; Scherbatskoy et al., 1998). Hurley et al. (1995) found that THg export in agricultural and developed watersheds was dominated by particulate Hg, but 80% of the THg was in the dissolved fraction in a forested watershed with numerous wetlands.

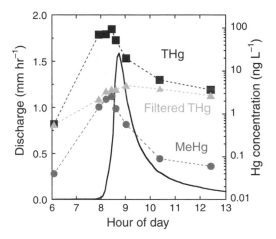

FIGURE 8.3 Hydrograph showing filtered and unfiltered THg and unfiltered MeHg in response to an intense rain storm (51 mm in 1 hr) at the 41-ha W-9 catchment at Sleepers River, Vermont, September 15, 2002. Modified from Schuster et al., 2008.

TABLE 8.1

Selected Maximum Stream Total Mercury Concentrations from Various Studies

Location	Land cover	Hydrologic condition	Peak THg (ng/L)	Source
Wisconsin	Forested	Snowmelt	21	Hurley et al., 1995
Vermont	Forested	Snowmelt	80	Scherbatskoy et al., 1998
Vermont	Forested	Summer storm	96	Schuster et al., 2008
Puerto Rico	Forested	Tropical downpour	112	Shanley et al., 2008
Georgia	Forested	Heavy rain	55	Shanley et al., 2008
Minnesota	Forest/agriculture	Summer storm	76	Balogh et al., 1998b
Wisconsin	Urban	Summer dam release	182	Hurley et al., 1998
Vermont	Urban	Summer storm	129	Shanley and Chalmers, 2012
Washington, D.C.	Urban	Spring rain storm	205	Mason and Sullivan, 1998
California	Mine area	Intense rain storm	1,040,000	Whyte and Kirchner, 2000

NOTE: All values are for unfiltered samples and reflect dominance by particulate mercury.

Babiarz et al. (1998) similarly reported high particulate THg export in agricultural watersheds. Mason and Sullivan (1998) found that both THg and MeHg export in an urban stream were dominated strongly by the particulate fraction except at base flow. Quemerais et al. (1999) found that nearly 75% of the THg load in the St. Lawrence River was particulate, with erosion of the bed and banks the single largest source of particles. THg concentrations and fluxes are low even in some high-relief catchments such as Loch Vale, Colorado (Mast et al., 2005) and Hubbard Brook, NH (Demers et al., 2010) because both POC and DOC export are low. In low-relief environments of boreal Fennoscandia, particulate Hg transport can be a minor flux as compared with dissolved THg, whose concentrations sometimes exceed 10 ng/L.

METHYLMERCURY

Hg may methylate and demethylate multiple times within a catchment, but stream export is still an important flux of MeHg in many landscapes. MeHg concentrations in groundwater are often elevated in peatlands and wetlands relative to better-drained soils, so streams draining these landscapes may have higher concentrations and fluxes of MeHg than those without wetlands (Krabbenhoft et al., 1995; Lee et al., 1995; Galloway and Branfireun, 2004; Schuster et al., 2008). In early research on the role of wetlands in MeHg cycling, St. Louis et al. (1994, 1996) found that wetlands in boreal Canada were consistently a net source of MeHg, whereas adjacent uplands were a sink. MeHg export from catchments varied with the amount and type of wetlands, and MeHg production in wetlands was of the same magnitude as MeHg production in the surrounding lakes. Krabbenhoft et al. (1995) and Bradley et al. (2011) likewise demonstrated that wetlands were a net source of MeHg.

Many authors have also documented a strong correlation between MeHg concentrations and fluxes in streams and the percentage of wetlands in a catchment in North American (Hurley et al., 1995; St. Louis et al., 1996; Shanley et al., 2005) and Fennoscandia (Lee et al., 2000; Porvari and Verta, 2003). Lee et al. (2000) interpreted 6 years of stream THg and MeHg dynamics at the Svartberget catchment in northern Sweden and concluded that the organic-rich riparian soils were also a significant source of MeHg, supporting the earlier findings of Bishop et al. (1995c). Within wetlands, hot spots of net methylation with higher MeHg levels are associated with the availability of sulfate and relatively fresh organic carbon (Branfireun et al., 1998; Mitchell et al., 2008a), which sustain methylation. Stoor et al. (2006) also documented elevated MeHg in groundwater at the upland–riparian transition, suggesting that this transition zone may contribute MeHg to groundwater.

MeHg tracks THg closely in many catchments and thus also exhibits episodic export (e.g., Schuster et al., 2008). MeHg has a greater tendency to occur in dissolved form, but catchments with high particulate THg also have high particulate MeHg. At Sleepers River, Vermont (Schuster et al., 2008) and other small catchments across the United States (Shanley et al., 2008), stream MeHg concentrations varied in step with THg concentrations. While stream MeHg: THg ratios varied markedly among the five sites from near 0 (undetectable MeHg) to 0.15, MeHg: THg within a site remained relatively constant during events and throughout the year. In an urban stream, Mason and Sullivan (1998) found that only 1–2 % of THg was methylated. Allan et al. (2001) found that THg and MeHg dynamics were linked at a given site on the Canadian shield, with MeHg showing greater variation.

In contrast to the above cases, in many catchment studies, THg and MeHg are not strongly linked. Eight small Finnish catchments showed little relation between THg and MeHg (Porvari and Verta, 2003). Schwesig and Matzner (2001) found that MeHg and THg in streams were uncoupled, as MeHg was not correlated to DOC. Lawson et al. (2001) found a strong relation of THg with stream discharge, but less so for MeHg. Allan et al. (2001) found high THg (~10 ng/L) in zero- and first-order catchments with thin soil cover, much higher than in nearby wetlands, but the pattern was reversed for MeHg.

In the Scandinavian spring flood MeHg concentration has been found to decline to its lowest levels of the year at the same time as DOC and THg increase to high levels (Bishop et al., 1995b; Porvari and Verta, 2003). But at other times of the year in these same catchments, MeHg sometimes increases in parallel with increasing flow, DOC, and THg concentrations (Bishop et al., 1995a). Because MeHg and THg sources should generally coincide on the landscape, this alternating coupled and decoupled behavior suggests that the supply of MeHg has a kinetic constraint (i.e., low production rate) that cannot keep pace with hydrologic flushing rates during spring flooding, when up to half of annual THg output flux occurs within 2 or 3 weeks. Low-flow periods have some of the highest MeHg and DOC concentrations in such wetland systems. Selvendiran et al. (2008) found a strong seasonal signal of MeHg concentration, peaking in the warm summer months.

Role of Dissolved and Particulate Organic Carbon

The mobility of Hg is strongly linked to the mobility of organic matter—DOC and POC (Figure 8.4). The association of Hg with DOC was recognized as early as the 1970s in marine sediments and pore waters (Lindberg and Harriss, 1974). In many regions, the Hg–DOC relation is colinear across diverse sites even with large differences in DOC (Grigal, 2002; Dittman et al., 2009). Sites receiving similar amounts of atmospheric Hg deposition may have very different amounts of stream Hg export, as the latter is so coupled to organic carbon export, which varies greatly among watersheds.

With respect to Hg binding and transport, not all DOC is created equal. Hg complexes primarily with DOC containing certain functional groups, particularly S-containing

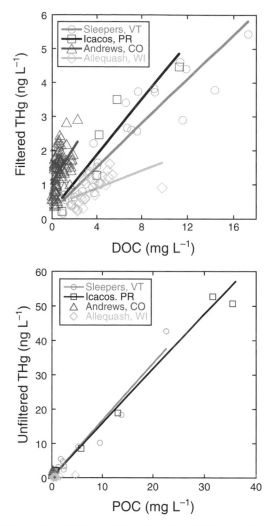

FIGURE 8.4 Filtered THg vs. DOC and unfiltered THg vs. POC at four U.S. catchments. Modified from Shanley et al., 2008.

Just as DOC drives filtered Hg export, POC drives particulate Hg export (Figure 8.4). The Hg–POC association originates in the vegetation (foliage) or soil, and particulate Hg in the stream reflects erosion of near-surface organic-rich soil particles into the channel—for example, during high flows, plus any direct deposition of litter in the channel. Particulate Hg in streamwater may also be resuspended from streambed sediment (Hurley et al., 1995; Quémerais et al., 1999) or form in situ from dissolved Hg, as there is greater affinity of Hg for the solid phase (log K_d from nine studies averaged 5.1; Grigal, 2002). Mason and Sullivan (1998) showed that the K_d for Hg increased as the organic content of particles increased in an urban stream. Streamwater typically displays a strong relation between particulate Hg and total suspended solids (TSS) (Balogh et al., 1998a; Shanley et al., 2008). For this reason, continuous monitoring of turbidity, a proxy for TSS, has enabled highly accurate calculation of stream Hg flux (Whyte and Kirchner, 2000; Wall et al., 2005).

The relation of dissolved MeHg to DOC is less straightforward, as seen in the studies cited earlier in which MeHg did not track DOC (Lee et al., 2000; Allan et al., 2001; Schwesig and Matzner, 2001). Export of MeHg may be controlled more by its net production rate than by the availability of DOC for transport.

In-Stream Mobility and Bio-availability

Once in the stream, THg and MeHg tend to remain mobile until they reach a larger water body. In support of in-stream mobility is the analysis by Grigal (2002) showing that Hg export per unit area of the landscape decreases only slightly with increasing watershed size. Particulate Hg may settle out of the water column to the streambed, particularly in response to lessening stream gradients with decreasing elevation. However, the Hg–DOC complex is stable and unlikely to be removed from the water column, although dissolved Hg may partition on to particles that ultimately settle. MeHg is subject to photooxidation and demethylation and may be less stable in streamwater (Bradley et al., 2011), but nonetheless there is net delivery of MeHg from the terrestrial landscape to downstream water bodies.

In-stream transport of particulate Hg and its susceptibility to settle out brings up the question of the bioavailability of particulate Hg, which dominates the Hg flux in some streams and rivers. Hurley et al. (1995) suggested that particulate Hg may be available for methylation, as organic matter is mineralized in shallow sediments. But in one assessment, Munthe et al. (2007) questioned the biologic significance of this fraction. The reconstruction of credible historic rates of Hg deposition and watershed Hg delivery from lake sediment Hg profiles with depth (Lorey and Driscoll, 1999; Kamman and Engstrom, 2002; Mast et al., 2010) points to sediment as the ultimate Hg repository, but that does not preclude some in-lake cycling prior to deposition. In fact, research from METAALICUS shows

thiol groups. The binding strength of Hg with thiols is orders of magnitude greater than that with inorganic anions, and there are generally far more thiol binding sites than Hg atoms present (Haitzer et al., 2002; Skyllberg et al., 2003). Hg associates primarily with aromatic, refractory DOC comprised of hydrophobic acids (HPOA), commonly known as the "humic fraction." At a stream in Vermont, filtered Hg correlated strongly with DOC ($r^2 = 0.96$), but even more strongly with HPOA ($r^2 = 0.99$) (Shanley et al., 2008). HPOA typically comprises about half of the DOC in natural waters, and its percentage tends to range narrowly (40–60%) (Aiken et al., 1992), thus most waters exhibit a high correlation between filtered Hg and DOC, even though the HPOA fraction is responsible for the Hg complexation. Analysis of Hg and HPOA are costly, but UV absorbance is a promising and inexpensive alternative to HPOA as a proxy for dissolved Hg concentration (Dittman et al., 2009, 2010). Using another approach, Petterson et al. (1995) also found a larger amount of MeHg associated with the humic fraction of organic matter in boreal streams.

that particulate matter formed within the lake and caught by sediment traps had been actively recycled and methylated in the hypolimnion (Chadwick et al., 2006).

Mercury Mass Balances

As a framework for interpreting terrestrial processes affecting Hg dynamics, we review the literature on watershed mass balances. Quantifying the inputs and outputs from the landscape establishes boundary conditions (Likens and Bormann, 1995) from which processes can be inferred and accumulation (or loss) rates can be determined and evaluated relative to catchment stocks. Watershed input–output budgets for THg and MeHg have been compiled previously (Allan and Heyes, 1998; Lee et al., 1998). Grigal (2002) performed a thorough synthesis of the available literature and condensed THg and MeHg inputs and outputs from more than 100 studies in the form of histograms. Here we build on these earlier efforts by tabulating and discussing specific Hg mass balance efforts from multiple landscapes, including several more recent studies. Finally, we demonstrate the value of applying Hg mass balances to specific components of the landscape (e.g., an individual wetland) within a given catchment.

Input–output budgets for THg are subject to inaccuracies because few studies determine dry deposition. To be fair to the earlier investigators, the importance of dry deposition has been widely recognized only in the past 10–15 years, beginning with the discovery of high Hg fluxes in throughfall and litterfall (Driscoll et al., 1994; Hultberg et al., 1995). We now know that, particularly in forested areas, dry deposition of THg generally dominates inputs, but measurements in conjunction with mass balance studies are still relatively infrequent and have considerable uncertainty. Most investigators continue the convention of reporting watershed Hg retention relative to wet deposition, recognizing that wet deposition may underestimate Hg input by a factor of 2–4. Quantification of stream Hg output is also hampered by fixed interval sampling schedules, which tend to underestimate stream Hg export because of its episodic nature (Bishop et al., 1995a, 1995b; Hurley et al., 1998; Shanley et al., 2008; Demers et al., 2010). Depending on individual stream Hg dynamics and frequency of the sampling program, actual Hg stream export could be two or more times the calculated flux. But even taking this underestimation into account does not alter the general finding that Hg export is small relative to inputs.

These caveats notwithstanding, in Table 8.2 we present a compilation of several Hg mass balance studies representing a diversity of landscape types. We have also synthesized typical values of inputs and outputs as well as internal THg and MeHg fluxes and stores as an aid to interpreting catchment Hg budgets (Figure 8.5). In Table 8.2, we have calculated watershed retention of THg and MeHg from published fluxes of the investigators, using measured or author-estimated dry deposition and stream fluxes as

presented in the original works. Some studies ignored dry deposition, so watershed retention is likely to be considerably underestimated. Overall retention averaged 84% (median, 89%) for THg (n = 23) and 58% (median, 79%) for MeHg (n = 9). In addition to all other uncertainties, this compilation does not account for volatilization, so some of the "retained THg" may have volatilized.

Watershed retention ranges from about 55% to 95% for THg and from –28% (net export) to 95% for MeHg (Table 8.2). The wide ranges reflect the importance of watershed features and processes, which tend to trump deposition as a control on THg and MeHg export (Driscoll et al., 2007; Evers et al., 2007). Some of the range is also attributed to uncertainties in or failure to account for dry deposition, and inaccurate stream Hg flux due to lack of event sampling. Watershed retention of MeHg is commonly less than that of THg, reflecting internal production of MeHg; MeHg is cyclically produced and degraded in the landscape, and MeHg inputs probably have little bearing on MeHg exports, although THg input (which affects the supply of Hg available to be methylated) may partly control MeHg export.

Studies that accounted for dry deposition generally showed the greatest THg inputs (>20 μg m^{-2} a^{-1}) and had near or above the median THg retention. The Lehstenbach and Steinkreuz catchments in Germany had among the highest wet and dry THg deposition, yet had 88% and 95% retention (Schwesig et al., 2000, 2001). At Río Icacos, Puerto Rico, where THg inputs were high and dry deposition was estimated as two times wet deposition, retention was much lower (54%), possibly due to an internal catchment source (a negligible factor in most watersheds) and/or the high erosion rate (Shanley et al., 2008). Allequash Creek, Wisconsin, had the greatest overall THg retention of nearly 99%, reflecting estimated dry THg input and low THg output in streamflow dominated by low-DOC groundwater discharge from a sandy aquifer, coupled with low erosion rates (Shanley et al., 2008). Erosion plays a role by physically removing Hg that would otherwise be bound indefinitely by sorption to or incorporation in organic matter.

Watershed Hg retention appears to be more complex than the simple retention of contemporary Hg deposition. Hg accumulation rates in lake sediment are consistent with watershed retention rates discussed earlier (Swain et al., 1992), but the sediment record suggests less watershed Hg retention during the more recent period of enhanced anthropogenic Hg deposition (Lorey and Driscoll, 1999; Kamman and Engstrom, 2002). Meili et al. (2003) suggested that the equilibration time of catchments to Hg deposition can be measured in centuries. Catchment characteristics play an important role in Hg retention. For example, Nelson et al. (2007) studied two forested catchments in Maine, one of which had been burned in the 1940s. Though receiving similar THg inputs as measured in throughfall, the burned catchment exports only about one third as much THg as the unburned catchment. One interpretation for the greater THg retention at the burned catchment

TABLE 8.2

Compilation of Annual Stream Total Mercury and Methylmercury Fluxes Computed from Watershed Studies

Site	Land cover	Citation	No. years
Europe			
Paroninkorpi, Finland	Boreal forest	Lee et al. 1998	3
Treated catchment, Finland	Conifer forest	Porvari et al. 2003	3
Svartberget, Sweden	Conifer/wetland	Lee et al. 2000	5
V. Dybäcken, Sweden	Conifer/wetland	Lee et al. 1998	3
Gårdsjön, Sweden F1 (control)	Conifer forest	Munthe and Hultburg 2004	9
Gårdsjön, Sweden G1 (roof)	Conifer forest	Munthe and Hultburg 2004	9
Langtjern, Norway	Conifer/wetland	Larssen et al. 2008	1
Lehstenbach, Germany	Conifer forest	Schwesig et al. 2001	1
Steinkreuz, Germany	Hardwood forest	Schwesig et al. 2000	1
Canada			
ELA Basin upland Ontario, CAN	Boreal forest	St. Louis et al. 1996	3
ELA Basin valley bottom wetland, Ontario, CAN	Boreal mire	St. Louis et al. 1996	3
ELA Basin riverine wetland, Ontario, CAN	Boreal mire	St. Louis et al. 1996	2
ELA Basin basin wetland, Ontario, CAN	Boreal mire	St. Louis et al. 1996	3
Harp 3A, Ontario, CAN	Hardwood forest	Mierle, 1990	1
Harp 5, Ontario, CAN	Conifer/wetland	Mierle, 1990	1
USA			
Loch Vale, CO	Alpine tundra	Shanley et al. 2008	2
Big Thompson River, CO	Conifer forest	Mast et al. 2006	1
Miississippi River at Anoka, MN	Mixed forest	Balogh et al. 2005	2
Minnesota river at Le Sueur, MN	Agricultural	Balogh et al. 2005	2
Allequash Creek, WI	Conifer/wetland	Krabbenhoft et al. 1995	2
Allequash Creek, WI	Conifer/wetland	Shanley et al. 2008	2
Hadlock Brook, ME	Conifer forest	Nelson et al. 2007	2
Cadillac Brook, ME	Hardwood (burned)	Nelson et al. 2007	2
Nettle Brook, VT	Hardwood forest	Scherbatskoy et al. 1998	2
Sleepers River, VT	Hardwood forest	Shanley et al. 2008	4
Archer Creek, NY	Hardwood forest	Selvendiran et al. 2008	2
Coweeta WS 18, NC	Hardwood forest	Allan and Heyes 1998	0.2
Coweeta WS 27, NC	Hardwood forest	Allan and Heyes 1998	0.2
Rio Icacos, Puerto Rico	Wet forest	Shanley et al. 2008	1

| Input fluxes (µg m^{-2} a^{-1}) | | | | | | | | Output fluxes (µg m^{-2} a^{-1}) | | | | % Retention | |
| THg | | | | MeHg | | | | THg | | MeHg | | THg | MeHg |
PRECIP	TFALL	LITTER	TOTAL	PRECIP	TFALL	LITTER	TOTAL	UNFILT.	FILT.	UNFILT.	FILT.		
5.1		59.5	64.6	0.10		0.64	0.74	3.2		0.09		95.0	87.8
								0.9		0.02			
7.0	15.0	18.0	33.0	0.08	0.17	0.30	0.47	1.6		0.07		95.2	85.1
5.0			5.0	0.10				1.4		0.16		72.0	
11.2	16.0	23.0	39.0	0.34	0.20	0.55	0.75	2.3		0.03		94.1	96.7
								1.1		0.02			
	6.7	2.7	9.4					2.5		0.04		73.4	
35.0	39.5	16.0	55.5	0.13	0.07	0.17	0.24	6.8	0.1	0.05	0.14	87.7	78.8
28.0	29.0	32.0	61.0	0.09	0.12	0.13	0.25	2.8	0.0	0.01	0.05	95.4	94.7
3.1		1.5	4.6	0.04			0.06	1.6		0.08		64.7	-28.3
3.1		1.5	4.6	0.04			0.06	2.1		0.06		54.5	3.3
3.1		1.5	4.6	0.04			0.06	0.7		0.02		85.3	63.3
3.1		1.5	4.6	0.04			0.06	1.4		0.19		69.7	
10.0			10.0					0.8				92.0	
10.0			10.0					1.6				83.7	
8.9			9.3					1.6		0.02		83.3	
6.6								1.0					
								0.5		0.05			
								4.9		0.09			
			10.0					0.8				91.6	
7.4			19.7					0.3	0.2	0.03	0.03	98.7	
	10.2		10.2			0.10	0.1	1.3		0.06		87.3	40.0
	9.4		9.4			0.05		0.4		0.04		95.7	
8.4			44.4					2.7	0.8			93.9	
8.2			25.1					3.3	1.2	0.06	0.02	87.0	
								2.3		0.09			
24.0			24.0	0.13				1.7		0.01		93.0	
31.5			31.5	0.15				3.5		0.05		89.0	
39.7			119.1					54.4	3.5	0.37	0.08	54.3	

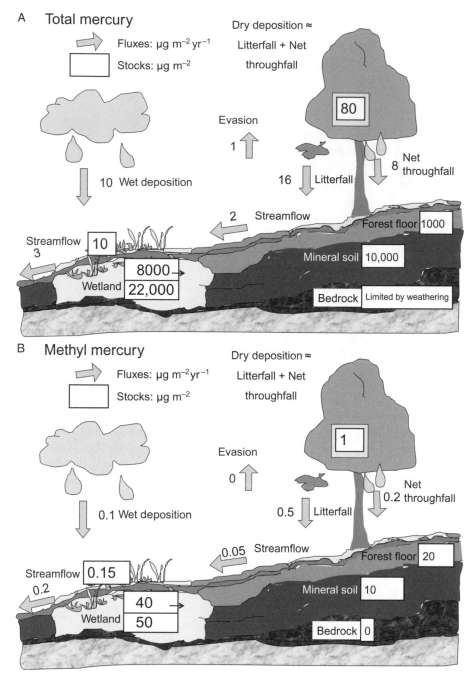

FIGURE 8.5 Typical values for stocks and annual fluxes in the northern temperate–boreal landscape for (a) THg and (b) MeHg.

is that it has a lower stock of Hg available for export and thus a high net accumulation, while the unburned catchment is closer to a steady-state condition. Presumably, aged Hg made up a considerable portion of Hg export from the unburned catchment (Hintelmann et al., 2002).

In another paired catchment study at Gårdsjön, Sweden, Munthe and Hultburg (2004) examined output of THg and MeHg from a small forested control catchment and a nearby experimental catchment with a roof constructed below the canopy. The roof excluded ambient throughfall, but the forest floor was irrigated with artificial throughfall of preindustrial composition. Although THg and MeHg stream flux per unit area in the control was about two times that in the roofed catchment before roof construction, this ratio did not change during 10 years of the roof experiment. This finding convincingly demonstrates that existing Hg stores and internal catchment processes, such as organic matter mineralization, can be more important to stream THg and MeHg export than ambient deposition at time scales at least up to a decade. The Gårdsjön results are supported by the METAALICUS study in Canada, where only a minute fraction of isotopically labeled Hg applied to an upland catchment was detected in streamwater; rather, Hg export was dominated by native Hg already present in the catchment (Harris et al., 2007). Also demonstrating the importance of catchment processes, Lee et al. (1995) showed that MeHg output at Svartberget in northern Sweden was comparable to that at Gårdsjön, despite two times higher MeHg deposition at Gårdsjön.

Wetland area and location is an important factor in THg and especially MeHg export and retention, as highlighted by St. Louis et al. (1996). Although their estimate of dry THg deposition as 50% of wet deposition may be low, THg and MeHg export from various wetland types on their Ontario landscape was relatively high, giving somewhat low THg retention values of 55% to 85%, with wetland type influencing the amount of retention. MeHg output from the various wetland types varied greatly, with at least one site showing net export of MeHg. Branfireun et al. (1996) and Selvendiran et al. (2008) have also found that THg and MeHg retention vary by wetland type, and Kramar et al. (2005) showed that wetland location relative to the stream network was a critical control on THg export.

Applying Hg mass balances to specific components of the landscape can help to pinpoint Hg sources, transformations, and retention mechanisms. In the few studies in which the areal export from wetland and nearby uplands could be identified (Figure 8.6), wetlands, including riparian organic soils, showed one to two orders of magnitude greater MeHg export than uplands. Even though there is considerable variability in the MeHg export from different types of peat and organic soils, the generally elevated MeHg export from organic soils relative to mineral soils may be a first-order control on some of the large differences in export and retention rates between catchments.

Mercury Mobility and Flow Paths

The high soil sequestration rate for Hg is explained by its strong preference for the solid phase. The log K_d for THg is on the order of 5.0 (Hurley et al., 1998; Brigham et al., 2009), consistent with an O-horizon soil Hg concentration of 100 ng g^{-1} in equilibrium with a soil solution Hg concentration of 1 ng L^{-1}, typical values for uncontaminated

sites. Log K_d's vary as the actual partitioning is controlled by the quantity and quality of organic matter in both phases. With Hg partitioning strongly favoring the solid phase, only DOC with strong binding sites successfully complexes and mobilizes Hg in solution. In the boreal and temperate ecosystems where Hg has been most studied, DOC concentrations are about six orders of magnitude greater than Hg concentrations (Bishop et al., 1995b; Driscoll et al., 1995; Schwesig and Matzner, 2001) The Hg:DOC ratio is often consistent across diverse sites (Grigal, 2002; Shanley et al., 2002; Åkerblom et al., 2008; Riscassi and Scanlon, 2011), but may vary at a single stream site (Schelker et al., 2011).

Uplands

Schwesig and Matzner (2001) found that about 20% of MeHg and 40% of THg in deposition pass through the forest floor to mineral soil. The THg–DOC relation was much stronger in the stream than in soil water, presumably because the stream integrates the various THg and DOC source areas in the catchment. In freely draining upland soils, the concentration of THg in soil solution tends to increase toward the soil surface, mirroring the patterns of DOC in soil solution and organic matter in the soil. MeHg is also more abundant in organic soils, and rising water tables facilitate transport of THg and MeHg to the stream.

In B-horizon soil water and in groundwater, DOC and THg concentrations decrease. In well-drained upland catchments, THg concentrations in groundwater are usually <1 ng L^{-1}, controlling the baseflow Hg concentrations in streams. Note that even these low THg concentrations are still controlled by DOC, as supported by the linearity of the THg–DOC relation (Figure 8.4). THg and MeHg typically are considerably higher in peatland groundwater (Selvendiran et al., 2008). Groundwater may transport Hg directly to a lake or coastal sea without any stream transport (Bone et al., 2007).

When considering THg and MeHg movement through catchments, debate has centered on "new" Hg, and its reactivity (Krabbenhoft et al., 2004). Researchers have hypothesized that newly deposited atmospheric Hg is more mobile and more biologically available to methylating bacteria than native or aged Hg, so that lowering of Hg emissions would have an immediate benefit. In the METAALICUS study, designed to directly test this idea, the hypothesis was supported for Hg applied directly to the lake (Harris et al., 2007). However, a surprisingly small amount of Hg (~1%) applied to uplands appeared in runoff in the first season of application, and most of the Hg export was preexisting "old" Hg (Hintelmann et al., 2002).

Wetlands

Wetlands are hot spots on the landscape for production of MeHg and for mobilization of THg and MeHg. Wetlands range from small pocket swamps or mires in otherwise steep and/or well-drained terrain, to large features

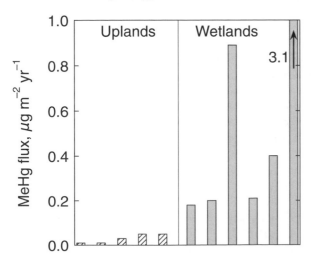

FIGURE 8.6 THg export per unit area reported from several upland and wetland areas in Europe and N. America. (*Sources:* St. Louis et al., 1994; Krabbenhoft et al., 1995; Bishop and Lee, 1997; Lee et al., 2000.)

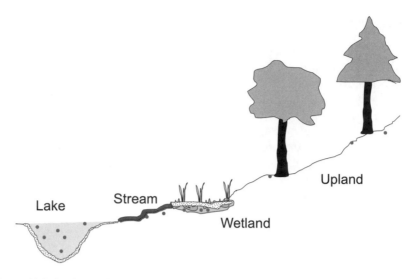

FIGURE 8.7 An upland forested-lake landscape showing methylation hot spots. The wetland and pond sediments (stippled areas) are favored sites for methylation. Dots indicate the possibility for localized methylation.

in more gentle terrain. Wetlands are generally, but not always, hydrologically connected to the stream network. Wetlands that are hydrologically connected to the stream system or lake play a disproportionately strong role in Hg and MeHg mobility on the landscape (Watras et al., 1995; Kramar et al., 2005). Wetlands along the margins of lakes have similar importance (Driscoll et al., 1995).

The importance of wetlands to Hg cycling was noted by Mierle and Ingram (1991), who showed that the mass of Hg exported from wetlands was an order of magnitude greater than that from other units of the landscape. St. Louis et al. (1994) and Branfireun et al. (1996) showed that different types of wetlands had differing effects on THg and MeHg export. Selvendiran et al. (2008) showed that a wetland created by a beaver dam was a net source of THg and MeHg, while a nearby riparian wetland, despite high porewater THg and MeHg concentrations, was not a source because it had low water throughput. In a broad landscape study, Balogh et al. (1998b) showed higher THg and MeHg in forested areas with wetlands relative to nearby agricultural areas that lacked wetlands.

Riparian Zones

Riparian zones are important to Hg and MeHg mobility for two reasons. First, they often have wetland-like character, with highly organic surface horizons and water tables near the surface, and they may be sources of MeHg production. Second, the proximity to the stream facilitates the ultimate movement of aqueous Hg to the channel, whether by shallow groundwater flow or saturation overland flow (Bishop et al., 1995c), or erosion of particulate Hg (Hurley et al., 1995; Schuster et al., 2008). Bradley et al. (2010) demonstrated that contrasting floodplain groundwater hydrology explained why only one of two adjacent South Carolina coastal streams— the one where upward hydraulic gradients transported MeHg to the stream—had elevated fish Hg levels.

Transformation/Methylation Processes

An early advance in the understanding of Hg cycling in terrestrial/freshwater ecosystems was the recognition of MeHg as the form responsible for most bio-accumulation of Hg. The abundance of MeHg is controlled by two counteracting microbiologic processes: Hg methylation (Jensen and Jernelov, 1969) and MeHg demethylation (Spangler et al., 1973). The pattern of net methylation in the landscape (i.e. the balance of these processes in space and time) determines the risk of biota to Hg bio-accumulation. Here we address terrestrial methylation, including wetlands. Until recently, Hg methylation was viewed primarily as an aquatic process affecting primarily the aquatic food web. However, aquatic MeHg finds its way into terrestrial food webs (Cristol et al., 2008), and high MeHg has been documented in songbirds nourished from purely terrestrial food webs (Rimmer et al., 2005, 2010), making it clear that terrestrial Hg methylation cannot be ignored (this book, chapter 16). The importance of terrestrial relative to aquatic methylation can be expected to vary with their relative areas on the landscape (e.g., the ratio of catchment to lake surface area), as well as the relative strength of the methylation sources (such as wetlands), as explored by Rudd (1995). Typical methylation sites on the landscape are depicted in Figure 8.7.

There is great variability in MeHg concentrations in soil water and groundwater (Åkerblom et al., 2008). They are generally low (up to a few tenths of a nanogram per liter) where there are low DOC concentrations and/or oxic conditions. However, in waters with more than a few milligrams per liter of DOC, MeHg concentrations are often higher, with concentrations of one to several nanograms per liter possible, but with considerable variations. These patterns, which reflect the local balance between methylation and demethylation, vary in space but are less well characterized in time.

The convergence of factors promoting high net methylation rates gives rise to the concept of hot spots for methylation in the landscape (Driscoll et al., 2007; Mitchell et al., 2008b).

Patterns of MeHg concentrations and methylation rates in soils also demonstrate the importance of wetlands. Skyllberg et al. (2003) found a progressive increase in the MeHg:THg ratio from soil to soil solution to the stream. They also found a greater MeHg:THg ratio in riparian soils as compared with upland soils, suggesting riparian soils as a source of MeHg. Schuster et al. (2008) demonstrated net MeHg production in riparian, wetland, and headwater stream sediment, with greater net methylation in summer as compared with snowmelt. Marvin-DiPasquale et al. (2009) explored controls on Hg methylation rates in stream sediments. In comparison to aquatic sediments and wetland and riparian soils, upland soils are a more limited source of MeHg. Allan et al. (2001) demonstrated in situ MeHg production in upland soils of the Canadian Shield.

Hg methylation is performed primarily by SRB, and the rates can vary markedly (Devereux et al., 1996; King et al., 2001). Some evidence suggests that other bacterial communities also methylate Hg (Warner et al., 2003). Demethylation is also carried out by microbes (Warner et al., 2003; Rodriguez Martin-Doimeadios et al., 2004; Marvin-DiPasquale et al., 2000, 2003), but may occur in part through abiotic processes. Methylation and demethylation often take place simultaneously. In boreal wetlands, Tjerngren et al. (2011) found that nutrient status and organic matter quality affected the relative extent of methylation and demethylation. Demethylation rates are generally less variable (Lambertsson and Nilsson, 2006), and as a result, methylation rates tend to control net methylation patterns.

The varying degree of correlation between THg and MeHg (Sunderland et al., 2004) suggests that the presence of Hg (Hg^{2+}), while essential (Benoit et al., 2003), is only one of several factors and conditions required for methylation. Other conditions include the availability of both sulfate (electron acceptor) and high-quality carbon (electron donor) and suitable redox conditions (Harmon et al., 2004; Jeremiason et al., 2006; Mitchell et al., 2008b). Finally, hydrology is an important control as well, both in supplying solutes, influencing redox, and ultimately transporting any MeHg produced to surface waters, or to soil environments where demethylation may occur.

The tight coupling of the sulfur and Hg biogeochemical cycles make the distribution of sulfur in the landscape a fundamental factor influencing net methylation. Current knowledge suggests that the increased deposition of sulfate, a component of acid rain, in northern boreal catchments and upland lake systems has boosted SRB activity and hence increased Hg methylation. Branfireun et al. (2001) came to this conclusion based on the immediate increase in Hg methylation in peat porewater following sulfate additions. A longer-term study of chronic S additions also found an MeHg response to several years of simulated increases in S deposition in peat mesocosms (Branfireun et al., 2001). More recently, Jeremiason et al. (2006) found that S addition to a wetland greatly stimulated methylation across the wetland. Mitchell et al. (2008a) have also elucidated how the common presence of high-quality carbon sources and sulfate interact to stimulate methylation. Drevnick et al. (2007) attributed a decrease in Hg bioaccumulation to a decrease in S deposition.

In constructed wetlands, Harmon et al. (2004) found that sulfate amendments led to significantly higher MeHg concentrations in porewater over the course of 1 year. Similarly, in a mesocosm experiment, Mitchell at al. (2008a) found that sulfate additions significantly increased MeHg porewater concentrations. Additions of different carbon substrates alone had no effect, but combined sulfate and C additions gave the largest increases, providing an explanation of why hot spots of MeHg appear in mires where there are inputs of both C and sulfate (Mitchell et al., 2008b).

Research has also revealed the role that neutral Hg sulfides have in transporting Hg across the cell membrane into bacteria where methylation can take place (Benoit et al., 1999). The presence of sulfide thus promotes uptake and methylation of Hg, provided sulfide concentrations remain low. High sulfide concentrations generate polysulfides, which form stable complexes with Hg, making it unavailable to the SRB (Benoit et al., 2001). This optimal or "just right" amount of sulfide for methylation has been called the "Goldilocks effect" (Gilmour et al., 1992). Research indicates that FeS(s) can strongly influence the concentration of dissolved sulfides [$Hg(SH)_2^0$, HgS^0, and CH_3HgSH^0] and thus further complicate the relationships among S, Hg, and MeHg (Drott et al., 2007). Studies from the marine environment suggest alternate views that methylation extent is controlled less by sulfur than by the amount of Hg present (Fitzgerald et al., 2007) or the organic matter concentration within the sediment (Lambertsson and Nilsson, 2006).

Given the significant stores of Hg in the terrestrial landscape from both natural and anthropogenic emissions, the most direct linkage between human society and Hg uptake by biota lies in how human activity may affect net methylation in the landscape through factors such as changes in land use, climate, and S deposition. This is especially true given the length of time (decades or centuries) before reductions in Hg emissions will lead to reduced Hg stores in the soil as a whole. The scope for controlling methylation is framed by the nature of the processes controlling methylation, though the complexity in relation to understanding makes it difficult to make simple prescriptions about how to control net methylation in the landscape. Another key question for controlling MeHg is whether contemporary deposition of Hg is more available for methylation, meaning that deposition reductions could reduce methylation in the landscape.

In a study to address this latter question, Branfireun et al. (2005) showed that in one wetland location in METAALICUS, 6% of newly applied ^{202}Hg was methylated within 1 day. After 90 days, up to 65% (average, 21%) of the applied Hg in porewater was methylated, as compared with a maximum of 50% (average, 36%) of native Hg, suggesting relatively rapid methylation of the newly applied spike Hg.

Methylation in the solid-phase peat was more limited but still rapid, with 2% of both applied and native Hg methylated after 90 days. Transport of spike Hg both laterally and vertically was quicker than expected. In an analogous study in METAALICUS uplands, Hintelmann et al. (2002) showed less methylation overall in soils but preferential methylation of spike Hg. In the upper 3 cm of forest floor, about 1.5% of spike Hg was methylated as compared with 0.4% of the native Hg. With the upland Hg spike, in contrast, most Hg stayed in vegetation and did not migrate far vertically into upland soils (Hintelmann et al., 2002). The preferential methylation of newly deposited Hg in wetlands suggests an immediate benefit of reduced Hg emissions. However, it is unclear whether differences in the availability of new and old Hg are sufficient for reduced deposition to translate into reduced Hg methylation and MeHg export, at least on a decadal scale.

Effects of Perturbation

The large pool of Hg in the surface soil leaves it vulnerable to release on perturbation. This release may be as particulate THg or MeHg, where disturbance causes surface erosion, as dissolved THg or MeHg where flow paths change, or as gaseous Hg in the case of fire. Perturbations may be natural (hurricanes, forest fires, tree throw) or human-induced (forest harvest, agriculture, land development).

Forestry is the predominant land use in much of the boreal zone, where elevated Hg in fish is widespread. In a synthesis of the literature, Bishop et al. (2009) estimated that between 10% and 25% of the Hg in the fish of high-latitude, managed forest landscapes can be attributed to forest harvesting. Specific catchment studies have demonstrated THg and MeHg mobilization as a result of forest disturbance. Munthe and Hultberg (2004) measured large and enduring releases of THg and MeHg when a logging road was constructed through a forested research catchment in Sweden. Porvari et al. (2003) documented increased Hg export from a logging operation in Finland.

These effects of forestry can be attributed to an increased net methylation of natural and anthropogenic Hg stored in soils. Removal of trees will raise the water table, and the disturbance associated with logging can also increase the hydrologic connectivity along superficial flow pathways as well as the output of DOC, which is associated with THg–MeHg. However, Sorensen et al. (2009) demonstrated that harvesting alone caused only a 20–30% increase in Hg flux and had an indeterminate effect on MeHg. They implicated soil disturbance in association with site preparation as the primary driver of Hg and MeHg release following logging. In any case, the evidence is clear that forest harvest can lead to both increased Hg outputs and increased net Hg methylation, but more work needs to be done to identify the degree of sensitivity of forested catchments to disturbance.

Forestry practices that release Hg and MeHg to surface waters have been linked to Hg bioaccumulation. In Canada, elevated concentrations of MeHg levels in zooplankton

(Garcia and Carignan, 1999) and THg levels in pike (Garcia and Carignan, 2000) were observed in adjacent waters after clear cutting. Desrosiers et al. (2006) found that logging decreased periphyton biomass in Canadian boreal lakes but increased its MeHg content by a factor of 2 to 10. Garcia and Carignan (2000, 2005) found elevated levels in fish after lake catchments were harvested, and Garcia et al. (2007) found significantly elevated MeHg in zooplankton in lakes with forest harvesting in their basins, correlated with increases in DOC. In all cases, the effect lasted for at least 3 years following the cessation of logging.

Although there are still relatively few studies of forestry effects on Hg cycling, they have raised awareness that forestry practices may contribute to Hg bio-accumulation in fish. Minimizing disturbances in riparian zones and peatlands, where much of the methylation potential lies, appears to be a prudent measure to try to reduce the impacts of forestry on methylation and export of Hg. With the information available today though, it is difficult to assess the magnitude of that eventual forestry contribution or the possibilities for mitigating that contribution through altered forestry practices.

Fire is another feature of the landscape that influences Hg. Garcia et al. (2007) found that increased MeHg in zooplankton after forest harvest had no significant effect on lakes whose basins had wildfires during the same time. Few studies have investigated Hg release from fire, though Hg release has been documented from western United States forest fires (Friedli et al., 2003). Watershed studies at Acadia National Park, Maine, were conducted on a watershed known to have burned in 1938. THg flux from the burned watershed was only about half of the THg flux from a nearby control watershed, possibly because of the loss of Hg volatilized during the fire, lower DOC release from the redeveloping forest floor, or both (Kahl et al., 2007; Nelson et al., 2007) (see also, this book, chapter 7).

Land-use changes alter Hg cycling not only during the initial conversion, but also in a more permanent way by changing land surface properties and land–atmosphere interactions. For example, forest removal causes a significant reduction in Hg inputs via dry deposition. Countering this factor, however, is a greater susceptibility to erosion in agricultural and developing landscapes, favoring Hg mobility. Thus, Hg export from agricultural streams is often greater than forested streams in the same region (Hurley et al., 1995, 1998; Babiarz et al., 1998; Balogh et al., 1997, 1998b). Urban runoff has some of the highest Hg export per unit area (Mason and Sullivan, 1998, Eckley and Branfireun, 2008; Shanley and Chalmers, 2012). However, MeHg export in urban landscapes is relatively small, presumably because of lack of landscape features that foster methylation.

Conclusions and Future Scenarios

Anthropogenic emission of Hg to the atmosphere and its subsequent deposition has increased the concentrations of THg and MeHg in the superficial soils of catchments.

The high proportion of Hg inputs that are retained have protected freshwater ecosystems from the full impact of Hg pollution. But society is confronted with a contaminated landscape where "legacy" Hg has accumulated preferentially in the organic fraction of soils, and especially wetlands. Relative to newly deposited Hg, the availability of this legacy Hg for transport and methylation remains in question. Even if the legacy Hg should prove to be less available for biotic uptake, there are still two major implications for the role of the terrestrial landscape as a source of THg and especially MeHg to freshwater ecosystems. The first implication is that reductions in the atmospheric inputs of Hg to catchments are unlikely to bring about a corresponding decrease in the output of THg and MeHg from catchments in the coming decades. This does not mean that deposition reductions will not bring some rapid benefits to freshwater ecosystems. For example, Hg deposition directly to lakes enters the aquatic food chain rapidly (Munthe et al., 2007). For lakes, the importance of this direct atmospheric loading relative to the catchment loading varies with factors such as catchment to lake area and the methylation potential of the landscape as compared with the lake (Rudd, 1995).

The second implication pertains to another component of atmospheric deposition, sulfate, which may regulate the rate of net methylation in the landscape. If the "sulfur rain" hypothesis is correct, then elevated S deposition in the latter half of the 20th century has stimulated the SRB responsible for much of the transformation of Hg to MeHg, the form that bio-accumulates most rapidly. If so, then the dramatic decrease in S deposition that has occurred since about 1990 across much of Europe and North America could lead to a decrease in net methylation in the landscape, and a corresponding decrease in the loading of MeHg to surface water ecosystems. At least one study, in the north-central United States, demonstrates a decrease in fish Hg from decreasing S deposition alone (Hg deposition was constant) (Drevnick et al., 2007). However, the lack of widespread declines in the Hg of freshwater biota suggest that this effect is either small, delayed, or has escaped detection because monitoring networks are too sparse. Alternatively, widespread trends of increasing DOC concentrations (Monteith et al., 2007) may be countering the effects of decreasing S. Increasing DOC will result in mobilizing additional Hg from terrestrial to aquatic systems.

While changing deposition inputs of Hg to the landscape appears unlikely to have a strong influence on Hg and MeHg outputs from catchments in the near future, changes in climate may act more rapidly. This climatic influence can work by changing hydrology and/or the pools of carbon in the soil. Since carbon binds most of the Hg in the soil, increasing those pools will increase the ability of catchments to hold Hg, while factors that reduce the C pool in the soil will increase the output of legacy Hg and reduce the ability to retain new inputs. The removal of Hg from catchments occurs either by volatilization of elemental Hg back to the atmosphere, or by flushing from the catchment in runoff. Thus, changes in hydrology, as are widely expected from climate change (Huntington, 2006), will likely affect the outputs of carbon and Hg. Changes in hydrology would also alter water-table levels and soil saturation and redox potential, another key control on the net methylation rates in the landscape.

In the long term, society will reduce the risk of contamination from terrestrial Hg if it reduces Hg emissions. In the short term, however, society must contend with the legacy of Hg on the landscape, and weigh its management options. Herein lies a conundrum. Some management activities that otherwise have strong environmental or societal benefits may exacerbate Hg contamination. These include wetland restoration and storm water retention, both of which create favorable sites for Hg methylation. Another example is managing nutrient runoff to reduce eutrophication. The resulting reduction in algal growth, while clearly desirable for restoring dissolved oxygen and for aesthetic values, actually increases Hg uptake in fish by concentrating available Hg into a more limited algal biomass that forms the base of the food web. Managing hydropower-generating facilities to limit water-table fluctuations may reduce Hg methylation in those water bodies, but these measures may be at odds with optimal power production. The one management strategy universally favorable, with the caveat that it will reduce the eutrophication that dilutes Hg, is erosion control. Management of human activities, including land development, agriculture, and forestry, to reduce sediment movement to streams, will help to keep the mercury on the terrestrial landscape and out of the water.

References

Aastrup, M., J. Johnson, E. Bringmark, I. Bringmark, and Å. Iverfeldt. 1991. Occurrence and transport of mercury within a small catchment area. *Water, Air and Soil Pollution* 56:155–167.

Aiken, G. R., D. M. McKnight, K. A. Thorn, and E. M. Thurman. 1992. Isolation of hydrophilic organic acids from water using nonionic macroporous resins. *Organic Geochemistry* 18:567–573.

Åkerblom, S., M. Meili, L. Bringmark, K. Johansson, D. Kleja, and B. Bergkvist. 2008. Partitioning of Hg between solid and dissolved organic matter in the humus layer of boreal forests. *Water, Air and Soil Pollution* 189:239–252.

Allan, C. J., and A. Heyes. 1998. A preliminary assessment of wet deposition and episodic transport of total and methyl mercury from low order Blue Ridge Watersheds, S.E. U.S.A. *Water, Air and Soil Pollution* 105:573–592.

Allan, C. J., A. Heyes, N. P. Roulet, V. L. St. Louis, and J. W. M. Rudd. 2001. Spatial and temporal dynamics of mercury in Precambrian Shield upland runoff. *Biogeochemistry* 52:13–40.

Alriksson, A. 2001. Regional variability of Cd, Hg, Pb and C concentrations in different horizons of Swedish forest soils. *Water, Air and Soil Pollution: Focus* 1:325–341.

Babiarz, C. L., J. M. Benoit, M. M. Shafer, A. W. Andren, J. P. Hurley, and D. A. Webb. 1998. Seasonal influences on partitioning and transport of total and methylmercury in rivers from contrasting watersheds. *Biogeochemistry* 41:237–257.

Babiarz, C. L., J. P. Hurley, S. R. Hoffmann, A. W. Andren, M. M. Shafer, and D. E. Armstrong. 2001. Partitioning of total mercury and methylmercury to the colloidal phase in freshwaters. *Environmental Science and Technology* 35:4773–4782.

Balogh, S. J., M.L. Meyer, and D. K. Johnson. 1997. Mercury and Suspended Sediment Loadings in the Lower Minnesota River. *Environmental Science and Technology* 31:198–202.

Balogh, S., M. Meyer, and D.K. Johnson. 1998a. Diffuse and point source mercury inputs to the Mississippi, Minnesota, and St. Croix Rivers. *Science of the Total Environment* 213:109–113.

Balogh, S. J., M. L. Meyer, and D. K. Johnson. 1998b. Transport of mercury in three contrasting river basins. *Environmental Science and Technology* 32:456–462.

Balogh, S. J., Y. H. Nollet, and H. J. Offerman. 2005. A comparison of total mercury and methylmercury export from various Minnesota watersheds. *Science of the Total Environment* 340:261–270.

Benoit, J. M., C. C. Gilmour, and R. P. Mason. 2001. The influence of sulfide on solid-phase mercury bioavailability for methylation by pure cultures of desulfobulbus propionicus (1pr3). *Environmental Science and Technology* 35:127–132.

Benoit, J. M., C. C. Gilmour, R. P. Mason, and A. Heyes. 1999. Sulfide controls on mercury speciation and bioavailability to methylating bacteria in sediment pore water. *Environmental Science and Technology* 33:951–957.

Benoit, J. M., C. G. Gilmour, A. Heyes, R. P. Mason, and C. L. Miller. 2003. Geochemical and biological controls over methylmercury production and degradation in aquatic ecosystems. ACS Symposium Series. American Chemical Society, Washington, DC, pp. 262–297.

Bishop, K., C. Allan, L. Bringmark, E. Garcia, S. Hellsten, L. Hogbom, K. Johansson, A. Lomander, M. Meili, J. Munthe, M. Nilsson, P. Porvari, U. Skyllberg, R. Sorensen, T. Zetterberg, and S. Akerblom. 2009. The effects of forestry on Hg bioaccumulation in nemoral/boreal waters and recommendations for good silvicultural practice. *Ambio: A Journal of the Human Environment* 38:373–380.

Bishop, K., Y. H. Lee, C. Pettersson, and B. Allard. 1995a. Methylmercury in runoff from the Svartberget Catchment in northern Sweden during a stormflow episode. *Water, Air and Soil Pollution* 80:221–224.

Bishop, K., Y. H. Lee, C. Pettersson, and B. Allard. 1995b. Methylmercury output from the Svartberget Catchment in northern Sweden during spring flood. *Water, Air and Soil Pollution* 80:445–454.

Bishop, K., Y. H. Lee, C. Pettersson, and B. Allard. 1995c. Terrestrial sources of methylmercury in surface waters: The importance of the riparian zone on the Svartberget Catchment. *Water, Air and Soil Pollution* 80:435–444.

Bishop, K. H., and Y. H. Lee. 1997. Catchments as a source of mercury/methylmercury in boreal surface waters. In: A. Sigel and H. Sigel, editors. *Metal ions in biological systems: Mercury and its effect on environment and biology.* Marcel Dekker, New York, pp. 113–127.

Bone, S. E., M. A. Charette, C. H. Lamborg, and M. E. Gonneea. 2007. Has submarine groundwater discharge been overlooked as a source of mercury to coastal waters? *Environmental Science and Technology* 41:3090–3095.

Bradley, P. M., C. A. Journey, F. H. Chapelle, M. A. Lowery, and P. A. Conrads. 2010. Flood Hydrology and Methylmercury Availability in Coastal Plain Rivers. *Environmental Science and Technology* 44:9285–9290.

Bradley, P. M., D. A. Burns, K. R. Murray, M. E. Brigham, D. T. Button, L. C. Chasar, M. Marvin-DiPasquale, M. A. Lowery, and C. A. Journey. 2011. Spatial and Seasonal Variability of Dissolved Methylmercury in Two Stream Basins in the Eastern United States. *Environmental Science and Technology* 45:2048–2055.

Branfireun, B. A., K. Bishop, N. T. Roulet, G. Granberg, and M. Nilsson. 2001. Mercury cycling in boreal ecosystems: The long-term effect of acid rain constituents on peatland pore water methylmercury concentrations. *Geophysical Research Letters* 28:1227–1230.

Branfireun, B. A., A. Heyes, and N. T. Roulet. 1996. The Hydrology and Methylmercury Dynamics of a Precambrian Shield headwater peatland. *Water Resources Research* 32:1785–1794.

Branfireun, B. A., D. Hilbert, and N. T. Roulet. 1998. Sinks and sources of methylmercury in a boreal catchment. *Biogeochemistry* 41:277–291.

Branfireun, B. A., D. P. Krabbenhoft, H. Hintelmann, R. J. Hunt, J. P. Hurley, and J. W. M. Rudd. 2005. Speciation and transport of newly deposited mercury in a boreal forest wetland: A stable mercury isotope approach. *Water Resources Research* 41:W06016.

Branfireun, B. A., and N. T. Roulet. 2002. Controls on the fate and transport of methylmercury in a boreal headwater catchment, northwestern Ontario, Canada. *Hydrology Earth System Sciences* 6:785–794.

Brigham, M. E., D. A. Wentz, G. R. Aiken, and D. P. Krabbenhoft. 2009. Mercury cycling in stream ecosystems. 1. Water column chemistry and transport. *Environmental Science and Technology* 43:2720–2725.

Bringmark, L. and E. Bringmark. 2001. Soil Respiration in relation to small-scale patterns of lead and mercury in Mor Layers of Southern Swedish Forest Sites. *Water, Air and Soil Pollution: Focus* 1:395–408.

Bushey, J. T., A. G. Nallana, M. R. Montesdeoca, and C. T. Driscoll. 2008. Mercury dynamics of a northern hardwood canopy. *Atmospheric Environment* 42:6905–6914.

Chadwick, S. P., C. L. Babiarz, J. P. Hurley, and D. E. Armstrong. 2006. Influences of iron, manganese, and dissolved organic carbon on the hypolimnetic cycling of amended mercury. *Science of the Total Environment* 368:177–188.

Choi, H.-D., and T. M. Holsen. 2009a. Gaseous mercury emissions from unsterilized and sterilized soils: The effect of temperature and UV radiation. *Environmental Pollution* 157:1673–1678.

Choi, H.-D. and T. M. Holsen. 2009b. Gaseous mercury fluxes from the forest floor of the Adirondacks. *Environmental Pollution* 157:592–600.

Cohen, M. D., R. S. Artz, and R. R. Draxler. 2007. Report to Congress: Mercury Contamination in the Great Lakes.

National Oceanic and Atmospheric Administration, Air Resources Laboratory, Silver Springs, Maryland. Presented to Congress May 14, 2007 http://www.arl.noaa.gov/data/web/reports/cohen/NOAA_GL_Hg.pdf

Converse, A. D., A. L. Riscassi, and T. M. Scanlon. 2010. Seasonal variability in gaseous mercury fluxes measured in a high-elevation meadow. *Atmospheric Environment* 44:2176–2185.

Cristol, D. A., R. L. Brasso, A. M. Condon, R. E. Fovargue, S. L. Friedman, K. K. Hallinger, A. P. Monroe, and A. E. White. 2008. The movement of aquatic mercury through terrestrial food webs. *Science* 320:335.

Demers, J. D., C. T. Driscoll, T. J. Fahey, and J. B. Yavitt. 2007. Mercury cycling in litter and soil in different forest types in the Adirondack region, New York, USA. *Ecological Applications* 17:1341–1351.

Demers, J. D., C. T. Driscoll, and J. B. Shanley. 2010. Mercury mobilization and episodic stream acidification during snowmelt: Role of hydrologic flow paths, source areas, and supply of dissolved organic carbon. *Water Resources Research* 46:W01511.

Desrosiers, M., D. Planas, and A. Mucci. 2006. Short-term responses to watershed logging on biomass mercury and methylmercury accumulation by periphyton in boreal lakes. *Canadian Journal of Fisheries and Aquatic Sciences* 63:1734–1745.

Devereux, R., M. R. Winfrey, J. Winfrey, and D. A. Stahl. 1996. Depth profile of sulfate-reducing bacterial ribosomal RNA and mercury methylation in an estuarine sediment. *FEMS Microbiology Ecology* 20:23–31.

Dittman, J. A., J. B. Shanley, C. T. Driscoll, G. R. Aiken, A. T. Chalmers, and J. E. Towse. 2009. Ultraviolet absorbance as a proxy for total dissolved mercury in streams. *Environmental Pollution* 157:1953–1956.

Dittman, J. A., J. B. Shanley, C. T. Driscoll, G. R. Aiken, A. T. Chalmers, J. E. Towse, and P. Selvendiran. 2010. Mercury dynamics in relation to DOC concentration and quality during high flow events in three northeastern USA streams. *Water Resources Research* 46:W07522.

Drevnick, P. E., D. E. Canfield, P. R. Gorski, A. L. C. Shinneman, D. R. Engstrom, D. C. G. Muir, G. R. Smith, P. J. Garrison, L. B. Cleckner, J. P. Hurley, R. B. Noble, R. R. Otter, and J. T. Oris. 2007. Deposition and cycling of sulfur controls mercury accumulation in Isle Royale fish. *Environmental Science and Technology* 41:7266–7272.

Driscoll, C. T., V. Blette, C. Yan, C. L. Schofield, R. Munson, and J. Holsapple. 1995. The role of dissolved organic carbon in the chemistry and bioavailability of mercury in remote Adirondack lakes. *Water, Air, and Soil Pollution* 80:499–508.

Driscoll, C. T., Y.-J. Han, C. Y. Chen, D. C. Evers, K. F. Lambert, T. M. Holsen, N. C. Kamman, and R. K. Munson. 2007. Mercury contamination in forest and freshwater ecosystems in the northeastern United States. *BioScience* 57:1–28.

Driscoll, C. T., C. Yan, C. L. Schofield, R. Munson, and J. Holsapple. 1994. The mercury cycle and fish in the Adirondack lakes. *Environmental Science and Technology* 28:136A–143A.

Drott, A., L. Lambertsson, E. Bjorn, and U. Skyllberg. 2007. Importance of dissolved neutral mercury sulfides for methyl mercury production in contaminated sediments. *Environmental Science and Technology* 41:2270–2276.

Eckley, C. S., and B. Branfireun. 2008. Gaseous mercury emissions from urban surfaces: Controls and spatiotemporal trends. *Applied Geochemistry* 23:369–383.

Eckley, C. S., C. J. Watras, H. Hintelmann, K. Morrison, A. D. Kent, and O. Regnell. 2005. Mercury methylation in the hypolimnetic waters of lakes with and without connection to wetlands in northern Wisconsin. *Canadian Journal of Fisheries and Aquatic Sciences* 62: 400–441.

Evers, D. C., Y.-J. Han, C. T. Driscoll, N. C. Kamman, M. W. Goodale, K. F. Lambert, T. M. Holsen, C. Y. Chen, T. A. Clair, and T. J. Butler. 2007. Biological mercury hotspots in the northeastern United States and southeastern Canada. *BioScience* 57: 29–43.

Fitzgerald, W. F., D. R. Engstrom, R. P. Mason, and E. A. Nater. 1998. The case for atmospheric mercury contamination in remote areas. *Environmental Science and Technology* 32:1–7.

Fitzgerald, W. F., C. H. Lamborg, and C. R. Hammerschmidt. 2007. Marine biogeochemical cycling of mercury. *Chemical Reviews* 107:641–662.

Friedli, H. R., L. F. Radke, J. Y. Lu, C. M. Banic, W. R. Leaitch, and J. I. MacPherson. 2003. Mercury emissions from burning of biomass from temperate North American forests: laboratory and airborne measurements. *Atmospheric Environment* 37:253–267.

Fritsche, J., D. Obrist, M. J. Zeeman, F. Conen, W. Eugster, and C. Alewell. 2008. Elemental mercury fluxes over a sub-alpine grassland determined with two micrometeorological methods. *Atmospheric Environment* 42:2922–2933.

Galloway, M. E., and B. A. Branfireun. 2004. Mercury dynamics of a temperate forested wetland. *Science of the Total Environment* 325:239–254.

Garcia, E., and R. Carignan. 1999. Impact of wildfire and clear-cutting in the boreal forest on methyl mercury in zooplankton. *Canadian Journal of Fisheries and Aquatic Sciences* 56:339–345.

Garcia, E., and R. Carignan. 2000. Mercury concentrations in northern pike (Esox lucius) from boreal lakes with logged, burned, or undisturbed catchments. *Canadian Journal of Fisheries and Aquatic Sciences* 57:129–135.

Garcia, E., and R. Carignan. 2005. Mercury concentrations in fish from forest harvesting and fire-impacted Canadian boreal lakes compared using stable isotopes of nitrogen. *Environmental Toxicology and Chemistry* 24:685–693.

Garcia, E., R. Carignan, and D. Lean. 2007. Seasonal and Inter-Annual Variations in Methyl mercury concentrations in zooplankton from boreal lakes impacted by deforestation or natural forest fires. *Environmental Monitoring and Assessment* 131:1–11.

Gilmour, C. C., E. A. Henry, and R. Mitchell. 1992. Sulfate stimulation of mercury methylation in freshwater sediments. *Environmental Science and Technology* 26:2281–2287.

Graydon, J. A., V. L. St. Louis, H. Hintelmann, S. E. Lindberg, K. A. Sandilands, J. W. M. Rudd, C. A. Kelly, M. T. Tate, D. P. Krabbenhoft, and I. Lehnherr. 2009. Investigation of uptake and retention of atmospheric Hg(II) by boreal forest plants using stable Hg isotopes. *Environmental Science and Technology* 43:4960–4966.

Graydon, J. A., V. L. St. Louis, S. E. Lindberg, H. Hintelmann, and D. P. Krabbenhoft. 2006. Investigation of mercury exchange between forest canopy vegetation and the atmosphere using a new dynamic chamber. *Environmental Science and Technology* 40:4680–4688.

Grigal, D. F. 2002. Inputs and outputs of mercury from terrestrial watersheds: a review. *Environmental Reviews* 10:1–39.

Grigal, D. F. 2003. Mercury Sequestration in Forests and Peatlands: A Review. *Journal of Environmental Quality* 32:393–405.

Grigal, D. F., E. A. Nater, and P. S. Homann. 1994. Spatial distribution patterns of mercury in an east-central Minnesota landscape. In: C. J. Watras and J. W. Huckabee, editors. *Mercury pollution: integration and synthesis*. Lewis, Boca Raton, FL, pp. 305–312.

Hacon, S., P. Artaxo, F. Gerab, M. A. Yamasoe, R. C. Campos, L. F. Conti, and L. D. De Lacerda. 1995. Atmospheric mercury and trace elements in the region of Alta Floresta in the Amazon Basin. *Water, Air, and Soil Pollution* 80:273–283.

Haitzer, M., G. R. Aiken, and J. N. Ryan. 2002. Binding of mercury(II) to dissolved organic matter: the role of the mercury-to-DOM concentration ratio. *Environmental Science and Technology* 36:3564–3570.

Håkansson, L., Å. Nilsson, and T. Andersson. 1990. Mercury in fish in Swedish lakes—linkages to domestic and European sources of emission. *Water, Air and Soil Pollution* 50:171–191.

Hall, B. D., and V. L. St. Louis. 2004. Methylmercury and total mercury in plant litter decomposing in upland forests and flooded landscapes. *Environmental Science and Technology* 38:5010–5021.

Harmon, S. M., J. K. King, J. B. Gladden, G. T. Chandler, and L. A. Newman. 2004. Methylmercury formation in a wetland mesocosm amended with sulfate. *Environmental Science and Technology* 38:650–656.

Harris, R. C., J. W. M. Rudd, M. Amyot, C. L. Babiarz, K. G. Beaty, P. J. Blanchfield, R. A. Bodaly, B. A. Branfireun, C. C. Gilmour, J. A. Graydon, A. Heyes, H. Hintelmann, J. P. Hurley, C. A. Kelly, D. P. Krabbenhoft, S. E. Lindberg, R. P. Mason, M. J. Paterson, C. L. Podemski, A. Robinson, K. A. Sandilands, G. R. Southworth, V. L. St. Louis, and M. T. Tate. 2007. Whole-ecosystem study shows rapid fish-mercury response to changes in mercury deposition. *Proceedings of the National Academy of Sciences of the United States of America* 104:16586–16591.

Heyes, A., T. R. Moore, and J. W. M. Rudd. 1998. Mercury and methylmercury in decomposing vegetation of a pristine and impounded wetland. *Journal of Environmental Quality* 27:591–599.

Hintelmann, H., R. Harris, A. Heyes, J. P. Hurley, C. A. Kelly, D. P. Krabbenhoft, S. Lindberg, J. W. M. Rudd, K. J. Scott, and V. L. St. Louis. 2002. Reactivity and mobility of new and old mercury deposition in a boreal forest ecosystem during the first year of the METAALICUS study. *Environmental Science and Technology* 36:5034–5040.

Holmes, J., and D. Lean. 2006. Factors that influence methylmercury flux rates from wetland sediments. *Science of the Total Environment* 368:306–319.

Hultberg, H., J. Munthe, and Åkeiverfeldt. 1995. Cycling of methyl mercury and mercury — Responses in the forest roof catchment to three years of decreased atmospheric deposition. *Water, Air and Soil Pollution* 80:415–424.

Huntington, T. G. 2006. Evidence for intensification of the global water cycle: Review and synthesis. *Journal of Hydrology* 319:83–95.

Hurley, J. P., J. M. Benoit, C. L. Babiarz, M. M. Shafer, A. W. Andren, J. R. Sullivan, R. Hammond, and D. A. Webb. 1995. Influences of watershed characteristics on mercury levels in Wisconsin rivers. *Environmental Science and Technology* 29:1867–1875.

Hurley, J. P., S. E. Cowell, M. M. Shafer, and P. E. Hughes. 1998. Partitioning and transport of total and methyl mercury in the Lower Fox River, Wisconsin. *Environmental Science and Technology* 32:1424–1432.

Iverfeldt, Å. 1991. Occurrence and turnover of atmospheric mercury over the Nordic countries. *Water, Air, and Soil Pollution* 56:251–265.

Jensen, S., and A. Jernelov. 1969. Biological methylation of mercury in aquatic organisms. *Nature* 223:753–754.

Jeremiason, J. D., D. R. Engstrom, E. B. Swain, E. A. Nater, B. M. Johnson, J. E. Almendinger, B. A. Monson, and R. K. Kolka. 2006. Sulfate addition increases methylmercury production in an experimental wetland. *Environmental Science and Technology* 40:3800–3806.

Johansson, K., M. Aastrup, A. Andersson, L. Bringmark, and A. Iverfeldt. 1991. Mercury in Swedish forest soils and waters — Assessment of critical load. *Water, Air and Soil Pollution* 56:267–281.

Johansson, K., A. Andersson, and T. Andersson. 1995. Regional accumulation pattern of heavy metals in lake sediments and forest soils in Sweden. *Science of the Total Environment* 160–161:373–380.

Johansson, K., B. Bergbäck, and G. Tyler. 2001. Impact of atmospheric long range transport of lead, mercury and cadmium on the Swedish forest environment. *Water, Air and Soil Pollution: Focus* 1:279–297.

Johnels, A. G., T. Westermark, W. Berg, P. I. Persson, and B. Sjostrand. 1967. Pike (Esox Lucius L.) and some other aquatic organisms in Sweden as indicators of mercury contamination in the environment. *Oikos* 18:323–333.

Johnson, D. W., J. A. Benesch, M. S. Gustin, D. S. Schorran, S. E. Lindberg, and J. S. Coleman. 2003. Experimental evidence against diffusion control of Hg evasion from soils. *The Science of the Total Environment* 304:175–184.

Kahl, J., S. Nelson, I. Fernandez, T. Haines, S. Norton, G. Wiersma, G. Jacobson, A. Amirbahman, K. Johnson, M. Schauffler, L. Rustad, K. Tonnessen, R. Lent, M. Bank, J. Elvir, J. Eckhoff, H. Caron, P. Ruck, J. Parker, J. Campbell, D. Manski, R. Breen, K. Sheehan, and A. Grygo. 2007. Watershed nitrogen and mercury geochemical fluxes integrate landscape factors in long-term research watersheds at Acadia National Park, Maine, USA. *Environmental Monitoring and Assessment* 126:9–25.

Kamman, N. C., N. M. Burgess, C. T. Driscoll, H. A. Simonin, W. Goodale, J. Linehan, R. Estabrook, M. Hutcheson, A. Major, A. M. Scheuhammer, and D. A. Scruton. 2005. Mercury in freshwater fish of northeast North America—A geographic perspective based on fish tissue monitoring databases. *Ecotoxicology* 14:163–180.

Kamman, N. C., and D. R. Engstrom. 2002. Historical and present fluxes of mercury to Vermont and New Hampshire lakes inferred from ^{210}Pb dated sediment cores. *Atmospheric Environment* 36:1599–1609.

King, J. K., J. E. Kostka, M. E. Frischer, F. M. Saunders, and R. A. Jahnke. 2001. A quantitative relationship that demonstrates mercury methylation rates in marine sediments are based on the community composition and activity of sulfate-reducing bacteria. *Environmental Science and Technology* 35:2491–2496.

Kolka, R. K., E. A. Nater, D. F. Grigal, and E. S. Verry. 1999. Atmospheric inputs of mercury and organic carbon into a forested upland/bog watershed. *Water, Air and Soil Pollution* 113:273–294.

Krabbenhoft, D., D. R. Engstrom, C. Gilmour, R. Harris, J. P. Hurley, and R. P. Mason. 2004. Monitoring and evaluating trends in sediment and water indicators. In: *SETAC North American workshop on mercury monitoring and assessment*. CRC Press, Pensacola, FL, pp. 47–86.

Krabbenhoft, D. P., J. M. Benoit, C. L. Babiarz, J. P. Hurley, and A. W. Andren. 1995. Mercury cycling in the Allequash Creek watershed, northern Wisconsin. *Water, Air and Soil Pollution* 80:425–433.

Krabbenhoft, D. P., B. A. Branfireun, and A. Heyes. 2005. Biogeochemical cycles affecting the speciation, fate and transport of mercury in the environment. In: M. B. Parsons and J. B. Percival, editors. *Mercury: Sources, measurements, cycles, and effects*. Mineralogical Association of Canada, Halifax, pp. 139–156.

Kramar, D., W. M. Goodale, L. M. Kennedy, L. W. Carstensen, and T. Kaur. 2005. Relating land cover characteristics and common loon mercury levels using Geographic Information Systems. *Ecotoxicology* 14:253–262.

Lambertsson, L., and M. Nilsson. 2006. Organic material: The primary control on mercury methylation and ambient methyl mercury concentrations in estuarine sediments. *Environmental Science and Technology* 40: 1822–1829.

Larssen, T. R., H. A. de Wit, M. Wiker, and K. Halse. 2008. Mercury budget of a small forested boreal catchment in southeast Norway. *Science of the Total Environment* 404:290–296.

Lawson, N. M., R. P. Mason, and J.-M. Laporte. 2001. The fate and transport of mercury, methylmercury, and other trace metals in Chesapeake bay tributaries. *Water Research* 35:501–515.

Lee, Y. H., K. Bishop, C. Pettersson, Å. Iverfeldt, and B. Allard. 1995. Subcatchment output of mercury and methylmercury at Svartberget in northern Sweden. *Water, Air and Soil Pollution* 80:455–465.

Lee, Y. H., K. H. Bishop, and J. Munthe. 2000. Do concepts about catchment cycling of methylmercury and mercury in boreal catchments stand the test of time? Six years of atmospheric inputs and runoff export at Svartberget, northern Sweden. *Science of the Total Environment* 260:11–20.

Lee, Y. H., K. H. Bishop, J. Munthe, å. Iverfeldt, M. Verta, H. Parkman, and H. Hultberg. 1998. An examination of current Hg deposition and export in Fenno-Scandian catchments. *Biogeochemistry* 40:125–135.

Likens, G. E., and F. H. Bormann. 1995. *Biogeochemistry of a forested ecosystem*. Springer-Verlag, New York.

Lindberg, S. E., and R. C. Harriss. 1974. Mercury-organic matter associations in estuarine sediments and interstitial water. *Environmental Science and Technology* 8:459–462.

Lindberg, S. E., G. Southworth, M. Peterson, H. Hintelmann, J. Graydon, V. L. St. Louis, M. Amyot, and D. Krabbenhoft. 2003. Quantifying reemission of mercury from terrestrial and aquatic systems using stable isotopes: Results from the experimental lakes area METAALICUS Study. *EOS, Transactions, American Geophysical Union, Fall Meeting* Suppl. 84: Abstract B31E-0364.

Lindqvist, O., K. Johansson, L. Bringmark, B. Timm, M. Aastrup, A. Andersson, G. Hovsenius, L. Håkanson, Å. Iverfeldt, and M. Meili. 1991. Mercury in the Swedish environment—Recent research on causes, consequences and corrective methods. *Water, Air and Soil Pollution* 55:xi–261.

Lorey, P., and C. T. Driscoll. 1999. Historical trends of mercury deposition in Adirondack lakes. *Environmental Science and Technology* 33:718–722.

Lucotte, M., A. Mucci, C. Hillaire-Marcel, P. Pichet, and A. Grondin. 1995. Anthropogenic mercury enrichment in remote lakes of northern Québec (Canada). *Water, Air and Soil Pollution* 80:467–476.

Malm, O. 1998. Gold mining as a source of mercury exposure in the Brazilian Amazon. *Environmental Research* 77:73–78.

Marvin-DiPasquale, M., J. Agee, R. Bouse, and B. Jaffe. 2003. Microbial cycling of mercury in contaminated pelagic and wetland sediments of San Pablo Bay, California. *Environmental Geology* 43:260–267.

Marvin-DiPasquale, M., J. Agee, C. McGowan, R. S. Oremland, M. Thomas, D. Krabbenhoft, and C. C. Gilmour. 2000. Methyl-mercury degradation pathways: A comparison among three mercury-impacted ecosystems. *Environmental Science and Technology* 34:4908–4916.

Marvin-DiPasquale, M., M. A. Lutz, M. E. Brigham, D. P. Krabbenhoft, G. R. Aiken, W. H. Orem, and B. D. Hall. 2009. Mercury Cycling in Stream Ecosystems. 2. Benthic Methylmercury Production and Bed Sediment — Pore Water Partitioning. *Environmental Science and Technology* 43:2726–2732.

Mason, R. P., and G.-R. Sheu. 2002. Role of the ocean in the global mercury cycle. *Global Biogeochemical Cycles* 16(4), 1093, doi:10.1029/2001GB001440.

Mason, R. P. and K. A. Sullivan. 1998. Mercury and methylmercury transport through an urban watershed. Water Research 32:321–330.

Mast, M. A., D. H. Campbell, D. P. Krabbenhoft, and H. E. Taylor. 2005. Mercury transport in a high-elevation watershed in Rocky Mountain National Park, Colorado. *Water, Air and Soil Pollution* 164:21–42.

Mast, M. A., D. J. Manthorne, and D. A. Roth. 2010. Historical deposition of mercury and selected trace elements to high-elevation National Parks in the Western U.S. inferred from lake-sediment cores. *Atmospheric Environment* 44:2577–2586.

Meili, M. 1997. Mercury in lakes and rivers. In: A. Sigel and S. H., editors. *Mercury and its effects on environment and biology*. Marcel Dekker, New York, pp. 21–51.

Meili, M., K. Bishop, L. Bringmark, K. Johansson, J. Munthe, H. Sverdrup, and W. de Vries. 2003. Critical levels of atmospheric pollution: criteria and concepts for operational modelling of mercury in forest and lake ecosystems. *Science of the Total Environment* 304:83–106.

Mierle, G. 1990. Aqueous inputs of mercury to precambrian shield lakes in Ontario. *Environmental Toxicology and Chemistry* 9:843–851.

Mierle, G., and R. Ingram. 1991. The role of humic substances in the mobilization of mercury from watersheds. *Water, Air and Soil Pollution* 56:349–357.

Miller, E. K., A. Vanarsdale, G. J. Keeler, A. Chalmers, L. Poissant, N. C. Kamman, and R. Brulotte. 2005. Estimation and mapping of wet and dry mercury deposition across northeastern North America. *Ecotoxicology* 14:53–70.

Mitchell, C. P. J., B. A. Branfireun, and R. K. Kolka. 2008a. Assessing sulfate and carbon controls on net methylmercury production in peatlands: An in situ mesocosm approach. *Applied Geochemistry* 23:503–518.

Mitchell, C. P. J., B. A. Branfireun, and R. K. Kolka. 2008b. Spatial characteristics of net methylmercury production hot spots in peatlands. *Environmental Science and Technology* 42:1010–1016.

Monteith, D. T., J. L. Stoddard, C. D. Evans, H. A. de Wit, M. Forsius, T. Hogasen, A. Wilander, B. L. Skjelkvale, D. S. Jeffries, J. Vuorenmaa, B. Keller, J. Kopacek, and J. Vesely. 2007. Dissolved organic carbon trends resulting from changes in atmospheric deposition chemistry. *Nature* 450:537–540.

Moore, T. R., J. L. Bubier, A. Heyes, and R. J. Flett. 1995. Methyl and total mercury in boreal wetland plants, experimental lakes area, Northwestern Ontario. *Journal of Environmental Quality* 24:845–850.

Munthe, J., R. A. Bodaly, B. A. Branfireun, C. T. Driscoll, C. C. Gilmour, R. Harris, M. Horvat, M. Lucotte, and O. Malm. 2007. Recovery of mercury-contaminated fisheries. *Ambio: A Journal of the Human Environment* 36:33–44.

Munthe, J., E. Fjeld, M. Meili, P. Porvari, S. Rognerud, and M. Verta. 2004. Mercury in Nordic freshwater fish: an assessment of spatial variability in relation to atmospheric deposition. In: 7th International Conference on Mercury as a Global Pollutant. RMZ, Ljubljana, pp. 1239–1242.

Munthe, J., and H. Hultberg. 2004. Mercury and methylmercury in runoff from a forested catchment – concentrations, fluxes, and their response to manipulations. *Water, Air and Soil Pollution: Focus* 4:607–618.

Munthe, J., H. Hultberg, and Å. Iverfeldt. 1995. Mechanisms of deposition of methylmercury and mercury to coniferous forests. *Water, Air and Soil Pollution* 80:363–371.

Nater, E. A., and D. F. Grigal. 1992. Regional trends in mercury distribution across the Great Lakes states, north central USA. *Nature* 358:139–141.

Nelson, S., K. Johnson, J. Kahl, T. Haines, and I. Fernandez. 2007. Mass balances of mercury and nitrogen in burned and unburned forested watersheds at Acadia National Park, Maine, USA. *Environmental Monitoring and Assessment* 126:69–80.

Nelson, S. J., I. J. Fernandez, and J. S. Kahl. 2010. A review of mercury concentration and deposition in snow in eastern temperate North America. *Hydrological Processes* 24:1971–1980.

O'Driscoll, N. J., D. R. S. Lean, L. L. Loseto, R. Carignan, and S. D. Siciliano. 2004. Effect of dissolved organic carbon on the photoproduction of dissolved gaseous mercury in lakes: Potential impacts of forestry. *Environmental Science and Technology* 38:2664–2672.

Pettersson, C., K. Bishop, Y. H. Lee, and B. Allard. 1995. Relations between organic carbon and methylmercury in humic rich surface waters from Svartberget catchment in northern Sweden. *Water, Air and Soil Pollution* 80:971–979.

Porvari, P., and M. Verta. 2003. Total and methyl mercury concentrations and fluxes from small boreal forest catchments in Finland. *Environmental Pollution* 123:181–191.

Porvari, P., M. Verta, J. Munthe, and M. Haapanen. 2003. Forestry practices increase mercury and methyl mercury output from boreal forest catchments. *Environmental Science and Technology* 37:2389–2393.

Quemerais, B., D. Cossa, B. Rondeau, T. T. Pham, P. Gagnon, and B. Fortin. 1999. Sources and fluxes of mercury in the St. Lawrence River. *Environmental Science and Technology* 33:840–849.

Rea, A. W., S. E. Lindberg, T. Scherbatskoy, and G. J. Keeler. 2002. Mercury accumulation in foliage over time in two northern mixed-hardwood forests. *Water, Air and Soil Pollution* 133:49–67.

Rimmer, C., E. Miller, K. McFarland, R. Taylor, and S. Faccio. 2010. Mercury bioaccumulation and trophic transfer in the terrestrial food web of a montane forest. *Ecotoxicology* 19:697–709.

Rimmer, C. C., K. P. McFarland, D. C. Evers, E. K. Miller, Y. Aubry, D. Busby, and R. J. Taylor. 2005. Mercury concentrations in Bicknell's Thrush and other insectivorous passerines in montane forests of northeastern North America. *Ecotoxicology* 14:223–240.

Riscassi, A. L., A. D. Converse, K. J. Hokanson, and T. M. Scanlon. 2010. Evaluation of automated streamwater sampling during storm events for total mercury analysis. *Journal of Environmental Monitoring* 12:1833–1839.

Riscassi, A. L., and T. M. Scanlon. 2011. Controls on stream water dissolved mercury in three mid-Appalachian forested headwater catchments. *Water Resources Research* 47, W12512, doi:10.1029/2011WR010977.

Risch, M. R., J. F. DeWild, D. P. Krabbenhoft, R. K. Kolka, and L. Zhang. 2012. Litterfall mercury dry deposition in the eastern USA. *Environmental Pollution* 161:284–290.

Rodriguez Martin-Doimeadios, R. C., E. Tessier, D. Amouroux, R. Guyoneaud, R. Duran, P. Caumette, and O. F. X. Donard. 2004. Mercury methylation/demethylation and volatilization pathways in estuarine sediment slurries using species–specific enriched stable isotopes. *Marine Chemistry* 90:107–123.

Rudd, J. W. M. 1995. Sources of methyl mercury to freshwater ecosystems: a review. *Water, Air and Soil Pollution* 80:697–713.

Rundgren, S., A. Ruehling, K. Schlueter, and G. Tyler. 1992. *Mercury in soil: distribution, speciation and biological effects.* Nordisk Ministerraad, Copenhagen.

Schelker, J., D. A. Burns, M. Weiler, and H. Laudon. 2011. Hydrological mobilization of mercury and dissolved organic carbon in a snow-dominated, forested watershed: Conceptualization and modeling. *Journal of Geophysical Research—Biogeosciences* 116, G01002, doi:10.1029/2010JG001330.

Scherbatskoy, T., J. Shanley, and G. Keeler. 1998. Factors controlling mercury transport in an upland forested catchment. *Water, Air and Soil Pollution* 105:427–438.

Schuster, P., J. Shanley, M. Marvin-DiPasquale, M. Reddy, G. Aiken, D. Roth, H. Taylor, D. Krabbenhoft, and J. DeWild. 2008. Mercury and organic carbon dynamics during runoff episodes from a northeastern USA watershed. *Water, Air and Soil Pollution* 187:89–108.

Schwesig, D., G. Ilgen, and E. Matzner. 1999. Mercury and methylmercury in upland and wetland acid forest soils of a watershed in NE-Bavaria, Germany. *Water, Air and Soil Pollution* 113:141–154.

Schwesig, D., and E. Matzner. 2000. Pools and fluxes of mercury and methylmercury in two forested catchments in Germany. *Science of the Total Environment* 260:213–223.

Schwesig, D., and E. Matzner. 2001. Dynamics of mercury and methylmercury in forest floor and runoff of a forested watershed in central Europe. *Biogeochemistry* 53:181–200.

Selch, T., C. Hoagstrom, E. Weimer, J. Duehr, and S. Chipps. 2007. Influence of fluctuating water levels on mercury concentrations in adult walleye. *Bulletin of Environmental Contamination and Toxicology* 79:36–40.

Selvendiran, P., C. T. Driscoll, J. T. Bushey, and M. R. Montesdeoca. 2008. Wetland influence on mercury fate and transport in a temperate forested watershed. *Environmental Pollution* 154:46–55.

Shanley J. B., and Chalmers, A. 2012. Streamwater fluxes of mercury and methylmercury into and out of Lake Champlain. *Environmental Pollution* 161, 311–320. doi:10.1016/j.envpol.2011.07.006.

Shanley, J. B., N. C. Kamman, T. A. Clair, and A. Chalmers. 2005. Physical controls on total and methylmercury concentrations in streams and lakes of the Northeastern USA. *Ecotoxicology* 14:125–134.

Shanley, J. B., M. A. Mast, D. H. Campbell, G. R. Aiken, D. P. Krabbenhoft, R. J. Hunt, J. F. Walker, P. F. Schuster, A. Chalmers, B. T. Aulenbach, N. E. Peters, M. Marvin-DiPasquale, D. W. Clow, and M. M. Shafer. 2008. Comparison of total mercury and methylmercury cycling at five sites using the small watershed approach. *Environmental Pollution* 154:143–154.

Shanley, J. B., P. F. Schuster, M. M. Reddy, D. A. Roth, H. E. Taylor, and G. R. Aiken. 2002. Mercury on the move during snowmelt in Vermont. *EOS Transactions* 83:45, 47–48.

Skyllberg, U., J. Qian, W. Frech, K. Xia, and W. F. Bleam. 2003. Distribution of mercury, methyl mercury and organic sulphur species in soil, soil solution and stream of a boreal forest catchment. *Biogeochemistry* 64:53–76.

Slemr, F., E. Brunke, R. Ebinghaus, C. Temme, J. Munthe, I. Wängberg, W. Schroeder, A. Steffen, and T. Berg. 2003. Worldwide trend of atmospheric mercury since 1977. *Geophysical Research Letters* 30.

Sorensen, J. A., L. W. Kallemeyn, and M. Sydor. 2005. Relationship between mercury accumulation in Young-of-the-Year Yellow Perch and water-level fluctuations. *Environmental Science and Technology* 39:9237–9243.

Sorensen, R., M. Meili, L. Lambertsson, C. von Bromssen, and K. Bishop. 2009. The effects of forest harvest operations on mercury and methylmercury in two boreal streams: Relatively small changes in the first two years prior to site preparation. *Ambio: A Journal of the Human Environment* 38:364–372.

Spangler, W. J., J. L. Spigarelli, J. M. Rose, and H. M. Miller. 1973. Methylmercury: Bacterial degradation in lake sediments. *Science* 180:192–193.

St. Louis, V. L., J. W. M. Rudd, C. A. Kelly, K. G. Beaty, N. S. Bloom, and R. J. Flett. 1994. Importance of wetlands as sources of methyl mercury to boreal forest ecosystems. *Canadian Journal of Fisheries and Aquatic Sciences* 51:1065–1076.

St. Louis, V. L., J. W. M. Rudd, C. A. Kelly, K. G. Beaty, R. J. Flett, and N. Roulet. 1996. Production and loss of methylmercury and loss of total mercury from boreal forest catchments containing different types of wetlands. *Environmental Science and Technology* 30:2719–2729.

St. Louis, V. L., J. W. M. Rudd, C. A. Kelly, B. D. Hall, K. R. Rolfhus, K. J. Scott, S. E. Lindberg, and W. Dong. 2001. Importance of the forest canopy to fluxes of methyl mercury and total mercury to boreal ecosystems. *Environmental Science and Technology* 35:3089–3098.

St. Louis, V. L., J. W. M. Rudd, C. A. Kelly, B. D. hall, K. R. Rolfhus, K. J. Scott, S. E. Lindberg, and W. Dong. 2004. Importance of the forest canopy to fluxes of methyl mercury and total mercury to boreal ecosystems. *Environmental Science and Technology* 35:3089–3098.

Stamenkovic, J., and M. S. Gustin. 2009. Nonstomatal versus stomatal uptake of atmospheric mercury. *Environmental Science and Technology* 43:1367–1372.

Stoor, R. W., J. P. Hurley, C. L. Babiarz, and D. E. Armstrong. 2006. Subsurface sources of methyl mercury to Lake Superior from a wetland-forested watershed. *Science of the Total Environment* 368:99–110.

Sunderland, E. M., F. A. P. C. Gobas, A. Heyes, B. A. Branfireun, A. K. Bayer, R. E. Cranston, and M. B. Parsons. 2004. Speciation and bioavailability of mercury in well-mixed estuarine sediments. *Marine Chemistry* 90:91–105.

Swain, E. B., D. R. Engstrom, M. E. Brigham, T. A. Henning, and P. L. Brezonik. 1992. Increasing rates of atmospheric mercury deposition in midcontinental North America. *Science* 257:784–787.

Tjerngren, I., T. Karlsson, E. Björn, and U. Skyllberg. 2011. Potential Hg methylation and MeHg demethylation rates related to the nutrient status of different boreal wetlands. *Biogeochemistry*. doi:10.1007/s10533-011-9603-1.

Wall, G. R., H. H. Ingleston, and S. Litten. 2005. Calculating mercury loading to the tidal Hudson River, New York, using rating curve and surrogate methodologies. *Water, Air and Soil Pollution* 165:233–248.

Warner, K. A., E. E. Roden, and J. C. Bonzongo. 2003. Microbial mercury transformation in anoxic freshwater sediments under iron-reducing and other electron-accepting conditions. *Environmental Science and Technology* 37:2159–2165.

Wasserman, J. C., S. Hacon, and M. A. Wasserman. 2003. Biogeochemistry of mercury in the Amazonian environment. *Ambio: A Journal of the Human Environment* 32:336–342.

Watras, C. J., K. A. Morrison, J. S. Host, and N. S. Bloom. 1995. Concentrations of mercury species in relationship to other site-specific factors in the surface waters of northern Wisconsin lakes. *Limnology and Oceanography* 40:556–565.

Whyte, D. C., and J. W. Kirchner. 2000. Assessing water quality impacts and cleanup effectiveness in streams dominated by episodic mercury discharges. *Science of the Total Environment* 260:1–9.

Wiener, J. G., B. C. Knights, M. B. Sandheinrich, J. D. Jeremiason, M. E. Brigham, D. R. Engstrom, L. G. Woodruff, W. F. Cannon, and S. J. Balogh. 2006. Mercury in soils, lakes, and fish in Voyageurs National Park (Minnesota): Importance of atmospheric deposition and ecosystem factors. *Environmental Science and Technology* 40:6261–6268.

Wiener, J. G., D. P. Krabbenhoft, G. H. Heinz, and A. M. Scheuhammer. 2003. Ecotoxicology of mercury. In: D. J. Hoffman, G. A. Burton, B. A. Rattner, and J. Cairns, editors. *Handbook of ecotoxicology*. Lewis, Boca Raton, FL, pp. 409–464.

Zhao, Y., X. Xu, W. Sun, B. Huang, J. Darilek, and X. Shi. 2008. Uncertainty assessment of mapping mercury contaminated soils of a rapidly industrializing city in the Yangtze River Delta of China using sequential indicator co-simulation. *Environmental Monitoring and Assessment* 138:343–355.

CHAPTER 9

Mercury Hotspots in Freshwater Ecosystems

Drivers, Processes, and Patterns

CELIA Y. CHEN, CHARLES T. DRISCOLL, and NEIL C. KAMMAN

MECHANISMS THAT CONTROL MERCURY SENSITIVITY

Supply or Inputs and Transport
Bio-Availability and Transformation
Bio-Accumulation and Trophic Transfer

MERCURY HOT SPOT CASE STUDIES

Everglades
The Adirondacks
Reservoirs
Large Lake Ecosystems: Lake Michigan
The Nyanza Superfund Site on the Sudbury River, Massachusetts

CONCLUSIONS

The transformations and fate of the global, regional, and local contaminant mercury (Hg) have been studied extensively in freshwater ecosystems for the past 15 years (Watras et al., 1998; Driscoll et al., 2007; Evers et al., 2007). Much is known about the processes involved in methylmercury (MeHg) production and flux and MeHg bio-accumulation and trophic transfer in lakes, ponds, and reservoirs. Moreover, studies conducted in a wide range of freshwater ecosystems have revealed specific suites of attributes that predispose certain systems to being hot spots of MeHg bio-accumulation. Evers et al. (2007) defines a biologic Hg hotspot as "a location on the landscape that, compared to the surrounding landscape, is characterized by elevated concentrations of Hg in biota (e.g., fish, birds, mammals) that exceed established human or wildlife health criteria." Here, the definition is based on bio-accumulation in a biotic end point rather than levels of emission or deposition at a particular location. Based on this definition and a dataset of over 7000 observations of Hg concentrations in yellow perch and common loon blood, five confirmed and nine suspected hot spots were identified in the northeast United States and southeastern Canada (Figure 9.1 and Table 9.1)

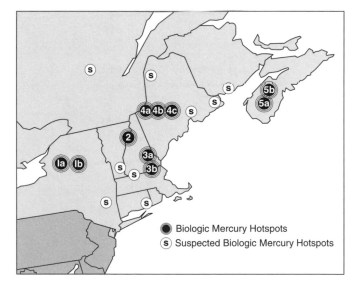

FIGURE 9.1 Mercury hot spots in the northeastern United States and southeastern Canada. (*Source:* Adapted from Evers et al., 2007.)

(Evers et al., 2007). These 14 areas encompass great variation in the types of ecosystems and mechanisms that create Hg hot spots.

Although elevated inputs of ionic Hg (Hg^{2+}) to ecosystems are generally thought to result in high concentrations in fish, there are many factors that mediate the ultimate fate and trophic transfer of Hg in the environment. Elevated MeHg bio-accumulation in fish and piscivorous birds and mammals results from a complex sequence of biotic and abiotic mechanisms that control the transport and availability of Hg^{2+}, MeHg production, bio-accumulation, or biomagnification. These mechanisms occur at critical points in the transfer of Hg in the environment (Figure 9.2) which include: (1) Hg supply and inputs to the ecosystem (e.g., deposition to the landscape); (2) transport to aquatic ecosystems (e.g.,

TABLE 9.1

TABLE 9.1
Mercury Levels in Biological Hotspots

Biological hotspot	State/ Province	Yellow Perch		Common Loon		
		Average (ppm)	Range (ppm)	Average (ppm)	Range (ppm)	% of loons > adverse effect level
1a. Adirondack Mountains – west	NY	0.73	0.57–0.96	1.5	1.1–2.1	0%
1b. Adirondack Mountains – central	NY	0.54	0.39–0.80	2.0	0.3–4.1	25%
2. Upper Connecticut River	NH, VT	0.35	0.14–0.58	1.1	0.1–2.9	0%
3a. Merrimack River – middle	NH	0.78	0.05–5.03	2.6	0.7–7.1	28%
3b. Merrimack River – lower	MA, NH	0.65	0.23–3.81	No data		
4a. Upper Androscoggin River	ME, NH	0.44	0.21–1.25	1.9	0.15–5.5	14%
4b. Upper Kennebec River – west	ME	0.40	0.24–0.52	3.1	0.6–14.2	43%
4c. Upper Kennebec River – east	ME	0.38	0.14–0.72	2.2	0.6–4.1	26%
5a. Kejimkujik National Park	NS	0.50	0.14–0.85	5.5	2.9–7.8	93%
5b. Central, Nova Scotia	NS	0.58	0.14–3.79	No data		

SOURCE: Evers et al., 2007.

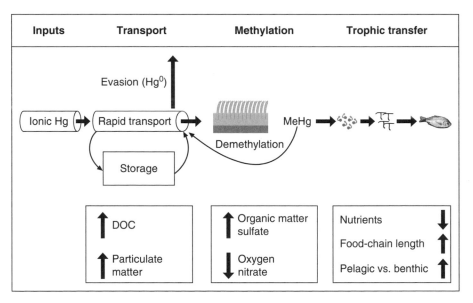

FIGURE 9.2 Conceptual model of important transformation and transfer points in the Hg cycle.

from terrestrial watersheds); (3) transformation in wetlands and sediments to MeHg; and finally, (4) bio-accumulation and trophic transfer in aquatic food webs. Moreover, the effect of each of these processes can be enhanced or diminished depending on environmental conditions.

In this chapter, we discuss each of these mechanisms as they pertain to a range of aquatic ecosystems, including natural lakes and ponds, reservoirs, wetlands, and rivers. To illustrate how these processes co-occur and enhance one another in natural and human impacted systems, we also describe in detail several case studies in which Hg concentrations in biotic end points are known to be elevated. These case examples are summarized from many past and ongoing studies published in government reports and peer reviewed papers and include: (1) the Everglades; (2) lakes in the Adirondack mountains; (3) reservoirs and their formation and management; (4) a large lake ecosystem (Lake Michigan); and (5) a point source of Hg (the Nyanza Superfund site on the Sudbury River, Massachusetts).

Mechanisms That Control Mercury Sensitivity

Supply or Inputs and Transport

Elevated inputs of Hg^{2+} to ecosystems are generally thought to result in high concentrations in fish, which ultimately control the exposure of humans and wildlife to this toxic element. Mercury inputs to ecosystems largely occur as Hg^{2+}, which enters aquatic ecosystems via atmospheric deposition or from point sources such as wastewater and storm drainage discharges or contaminated industrial sites (Driscoll et al., 2007). Inputs of Hg can be retained in soil or sediments, reduced to gaseous elemental mercury (GEM) and emitted to the atmosphere, or transported via drainage water to sites of net methylation (Grigal, 2003). This transport is often facilitated by an Hg carrier, generally either dissolved organic matter or suspended particulate matter. Note that hydrologic flow paths are a critical factor controlling Hg transport. Concentrations of total Hg in streams typically increase with discharge. These increases typically occur through both the dissolved and particulate fractions of total Hg. Increases in particulate Hg with discharge are undoubtedly due to increases in sediment transport with flow. Increases in the dissolved fraction of total Hg are generally associated with increases in DOC, particularly the hydrophobic fraction of DOC (Dittman et al., 2009). This change likely reflects increased transport of Hg^{2+} due to shifts toward more shallow hydrologic flow paths during high discharge. A critical factor concerning the response of ecosystems to changes in Hg inputs is ecosystem storage. Upland soils and lake sediments are large and important net sinks of Hg inputs. This Hg could be permanently buried and sequestered or could be remobilized and become available for methylation and trophic transfer in downstream aquatic ecosystems.

Bio-Availability and Transformation

An important factor controlling concentrations of Hg to fish and other biota is net methylation. Methylation is the process by which microbes convert Hg^{2+} to MeHg. This process is important because MeHg is the form that readily bio-accumulates in the terrestrial and aquatic food chain resulting in potential exposure to wildlife and humans. Although methylation can be mediated by a variety of microbes, the most important of these is sulfate-reducing bacteria (Benoit et al., 2003). Sulfate-reducing bacteria flourish in reducing environments, such as wetlands and lake and river sediments. As a result, zones of high methylation activity occur only at restricted locations on the landscape. Conditions that promote the methylation of Hg^{2+} are low oxygen, high inputs of labile organic carbon, and a supply of sulfate and Hg^{2+}. Inputs of oxygen or nitrate inhibit sulfate reduction and therefore methylation of Hg^{2+} (Todorova et al., 2009). In the presence of elevated concentrations of sulfide, methylation of Hg^{2+} is also restricted because the sulfide binds Hg^{2+}, making it unavailable for methylation and because of the formation of charged Hg-sulfide complexes, which cannot be readily assimilated by sulfate-reducing bacteria (Gilmour et al., 1992; Benoit et al., 2003). MeHg can be demethylated by oxidative or reductive processes, resulting in the formation of either Hg^{2+} or GEM. Therefore, the net production of MeHg is the result of two processes: methylation and demethylation.

Bio-Accumulation and Trophic Transfer

The final process in the sequence is bio-accumulation (uptake from food and water) and trophic transfer of Hg^{2+} and MeHg. MeHg and Hg^{2+} are bioconcentrated (from water) and assimilated by phytoplankton. MeHg in phytoplankton is assimilated more efficiently by zooplankton than Hg^{2+}, resulting in an enrichment in MeHg content (Mason et al., 1996). Phytoplankton in the water column exhibit the largest bioconcentration step in aquatic food webs resulting in log bio-accumulation factors of 5–6 (Driscoll et al., 2007). A bio-accumulation factor is the ratio of the concentration of a contaminant (e.g., MeHg) in the organism to the value in water. A number of mechanisms influence the bio-accumulation of MeHg in phytoplankton, including bio-availability of MeHg to algal uptake and phytoplankton growth. Phytoplankton bio-accumulate both Hg^{2+} and MeHg from water but partition the MeHg to the cytoplasm, leaving Hg^{2+} bound to the cell wall (Mason et al., 1996). Zooplankton appear to assimilate the MeHg inside algal cells and egest the Hg^{2+} with the cell walls (Mason et al., 1995). Fish also obtain MeHg from ingestion of food and take up far less directly from water (Hall et al., 1997). Enrichment of MeHg continues up the food chain to top consumers, who are found to have virtually all their Hg occurring as MeHg (Driscoll et al., 2007). Several factors influence this trophic transfer of MeHg in aquatic ecosystems. Elevated inputs of growth-limiting nutrients (e.g., P, N) increase biomass, resulting in a decrease in the Hg concentration of individual organisms; this phenomenon is called biodilution (Pickhardt et al., 2002; Chen and Folt, 2005). Higher growth rates in individuals also result in lower mass-specific concentrations in their tissues because of growth dilution (Karimi et al., 2007; Ward et al., 2009). Growth dilution has been hypothesized as the mechanism explaining lower MeHg concentrations in fish and shellfish from the more productive lakes (Beckvar et al., 2000; Essington and Houser, 2003).

Differences in food-web structure and type affect the fate of MeHg as well. Several studies have found chain length to be positively related to MeHg concentrations in top-trophic-level fish, suggesting that the increased number of trophic levels results in greater biomagnification of MeHg (Cabana et al., 1994; Stemberger and Chen, 1998). Finally the Hg concentration of fish is greater for those species feeding from a pelagic food chain rather than a benthic food chain (Becker and Bigham, 1995; Power et al., 2002; Gorski et al., 2003; Kamman et al., 2005). Some studies have shown that bio-accumulation of MeHg also occurs along the terrestrial food chain (Rimmer et al., 2005).

Mercury Hot Spot Case Studies

The following five case studies have been chosen in part because they represent systems that have been extensively studied for their Hg dynamics and also to illustrate the importance of the specific mechanisms and transfer points shown in Figure 9.2. Each system has been the subject of many peer-reviewed studies and government reports, and the findings therein have been summarized here. They represent large and small lakes and reservoir ecosystems (Adirondack lakes, reservoirs, and Great Lakes) as well as complex flowing ecosystems as found in the Everglades in Florida and the Sudbury River in Massachusetts. Here, we discuss the specific mechanisms and processes in each of these systems that result in Hg hotspots.

Everglades

Since the early 1990s, Hg contamination has been recognized as a critical health issue for humans and wildlife that consume fish from the Everglades. The state of Florida has advisories that either ban or restrict consumption of nine species of fish from over 0.8 million ha in the Everglades (USEPA, 2007b). Advisories include a ban on consumption of largemouth bass that exceed 36 cm. These conditions do not allow for a consumable fishery, and as a result fishing for consumption is not advised in the Everglades. In addition to human health impacts, there is concern over elevated exposure of Hg to piscivorous birds and the Florida panther, which may impact breeding success.

In many respects, the Everglades is an ideal environment to promote the transport, transformation, and trophic transfer resulting in elevated concentrations of MeHg in fish. Warm conditions, wet and dry seasons and abundant rainfall contribute to elevated wet deposition of Hg in south Florida, among the highest levels found in regions monitored in the United States (National Air Deposition Program [NADP], 2008). In the Everglades, more than 95% of the Hg inputs are from atmospheric deposition (Landing et al., 1995; USEPA, 1996; Guentzel et al., 1998, 2001). Because of the wetland environment, the Everglades are characterized by elevated concentrations of dissolved organic carbon (DOC), with particularly high concentrations in the Everglades Agricultural Areas and values decreasing downgradient to the south (Figure 9.3). This DOC binds Hg, enhancing its transport (Aiken et al., 2003) but may also likely influence its bioavailability. The warm water temperatures, the large supply of labile organic carbon, and the reducing conditions of the Everglades promote the net methylation of Hg^{2+}. Alternating dry and wet hydrologic conditions promote mineralization and methylation cycles. Finally, the Everglades is an oligotrophic ecosystem, which limits biodilution of MeHg.

SPATIAL PATTERNS

There are intriguing spatial patterns in fish Hg concentrations across the Everglades. The Everglades ecosystem is comprised of several contiguous but varied land-use areas: Everglades Agricultural Areas (EAA), Loxahatchee National Wildlife Refuge (LNWR), Water Conservation Areas (WCA), Big Cypress Swamp, and Everglades National Park (ENP) (see Figure 9.3). In 2005, 71% of the largemouth bass sampled in the WCAs and 100% sampled in Shark Slough in the ENP exceeded the fish-tissue criterion for Hg of 0.3 µg/g (Axelrad et al., 2007). Mosquitofish have been used as an indicator of Hg contamination because they are abundant and widely distributed in the Everglades. They have a relatively short lifespan and spatial range, so tissue Hg concentrations reflect local conditions over the period for which they are sampled. They are an important food source for game fish and piscivorous birds so they have relevance to both human and wildlife health. The United States Environmental Protection Agency (USEPA), Regional Environmental Monitoring and Assessment Program (REMAP) indicated that Hg concentrations in mosquitofish in the Everglades are highest in remote portions of WCA-3A extending into Shark Slough (Figure 9.4a; USEPA, 2007). This spatial distribution is consistent with the pattern observed for largemouth bass, discussed above, as well as that of great egrets (Axelrad et al., 2007) and alligators (Rumbold et al., 2002). The United States Fish and Wildlife Service has suggested a level of 0.1 µg/g wet weight (ww) in prey fish to protect top predators from exposure to elevated Hg levels (Eisler, 1987). It appears that great egrets, bald eagles, and wood storks foraging in the northern portion of the ENP likely experience exposures that exceed an acceptable dose (above the level of no observed adverse effect; Rumbold et al., 2008).

The spatial pattern in fish Hg concentrations does not correspond with water-column Hg concentrations. During 2005, the highest surface water concentrations of total Hg (THg) and MeHg were in the northern Everglades, with concentrations decreasing southward (Figure 9.4b; USEPA, 2007b). There are marked spatial gradients in water quality in the Everglades. These gradients are driven by the relative solute concentrations of precipitation, groundwater, and storm water and by land-cover/land-use considerations. The highest concentrations of constituents generally occur in WCA-2 due to its location near the EAA and storm water discharges (Figure 9.3). The transport and transformations of THg and MeHg in storm water treatment areas are variable. In general, storm water treatment areas appear to be a net sink for inputs of THg and MeHg (Miles and Fink, 1998). However, the drying and rewetting of organic deposits in storm water treatment areas can result in elevated concentrations of MeHg (Rumbold and Fink, 2006; see their Reservoirs case study for the mechanism behind this phenomenon).

The highest concentrations of THg and MeHg occur in WCA-2 and the northern Everglades, while the highest concentrations in mosquitofish are found in WCA-3A and ENP (Figure 9.4a). The bio-accumulation factor for MeHg in mosquitofish vary by about one order of magnitude across the Everglades, with the highest values in the south corresponding with the highest concentrations in mosquitofish. This pattern is undoubtedly due to several factors, but suggests that some process is restricting biologic uptake of MeHg.

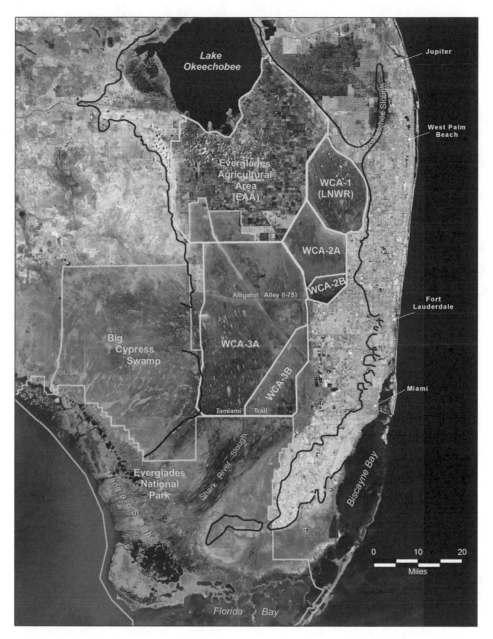

FIGURE 9.3 Satellite image of South Florida, circa 1995, with light outline representing areas sampled: Everglades Agricultural Area (EAA); Arthur R. Marshall Loxahatchee National Wildlife Refuge (LNWR); Everglades Water Conservation Area 2 (WCA-2); Everglades Water Conservation Area 3 north of Alligator Alley (WCA-3A); Everglades Water Conservation Area 3 south of Alligator Alley (WCA-3A); the eastern portion of Big Cypress Swamp National Preserve, and the freshwater portion of Everglades National Park (ENP). Light areas on the east are urban development. The black line approximates the extent of the historic (pre-1900) Everglades marsh. The Everglades watershed extends north of Lake Okeechobee.

A logical mechanism to partially explain this spatial pattern in fish mercury is DOC. Naturally occurring organic solutes bind Hg^{2+} and MeHg (Aiken et al., 2003), likely reducing bio-availability (Hudson et al., 1994; Driscoll et al., 1995). The northern Everglades, which are strongly influenced by the EAA storm water have higher concentrations of DOC and are more reactive with Hg than southern areas of ENP (Figure 9.5; Aiken et al., 2006). Mercury in mosquitofish is correlated with DOC-normalized MeHg but not total MeHg in surface water (USEPA, 2007b).

Sulfur supplies and concentrations have important environmental implications for the Everglades. Sulfur is a critically important driver of MeHg production and exposure (Benoit et al., 2003). Elevated concentrations of sulfate can also enhance the supply of phosphorus from wetland soils to surface waters, and high concentrations of sulfide may be toxic to plants (Lamars et al., 1998; Smolders et al., 2006). As a result, the Comprehensive Everglades Restoration Plan recommends that sulfate (SO_4-S) concentrations be decreased or maintained to concentrations of 1 mg/L or

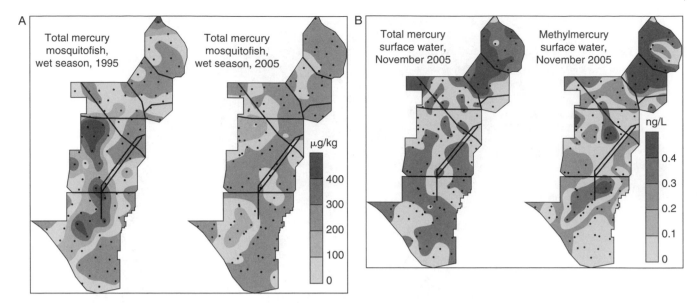

FIGURE 9.4   (a) Spatial patterns of mercury concentrations in mosquitofish during wet season sampling 1995 and 2005. (b) Spatial patterns in total mercury concentrations in surface water during November 2005 (left) and MeHg concentrations in surface water (right) for the Everglades. (*Source:* Data were obtained from the United States Environmental Protection Agency REMAP [USEPA, 2007b]).

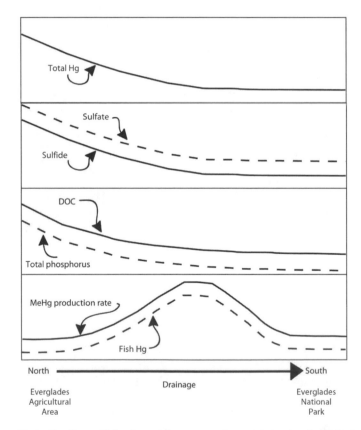

FIGURE 9.5   Conceptual diagram illustrating the spatial patterns in mercury and associated water chemistry in the Everglades. There is a north to south gradient in total mercury, sulfate, porewater sulfide, total phosphorus, and dissolved organic carbon (DOC). The sulfate, total phosphorus, and DOC largely originate from the Everglades Agricultural Area. High porewater sulfide and/or DOC may limit the formation of methylmercury in the north. Lower concentrations of porewater sulfide and DOC toward the south may allow the formation of methylmercury in the central Everglades. A peak in fish mercury concentrations in the center of the Everglades and into the Everglades National Park may be due to this spatial pattern of methylmercury production coupled with decreases in phosphorus, which limits fish production and increases mercury concentrations.

less throughout the Everglades (Restoration, Coordination and Verification, 2007). However, sulfur is applied to EAA soils to decrease pH and improve nutrient availability for agricultural use. Using sulfur-stable isotope measurements, it appears that sulfur applied for agriculture is a major contributor to the excess sulfate concentrations in the Everglades (Bates et al., 2002). The relative contribution of recent versus legacy sulfur additions to sulfate concentrations in the Everglades is not clear.

Sulfate concentrations vary spatially throughout the Everglades depending on the proximity to the EAA and the relative contribution of water sources from precipitation, storm water, and groundwater. The highest sulfate concentrations >100 mg/L are observed in canals within the EAA and in WCA-2A (USEPA, 2007b). The storm water treatment areas remove modest and variable quantities of sulfate, ranging from 5% to 67% (USEPA, 2007). From this source, concentrations of sulfate in the Everglades decrease toward the south and west. Sulfur dynamics appear to be an important spatial controller of MeHg production. In the northern Everglades, the high supply of sulfate coupled with reducing conditions result in high concentrations of sulfide in wetland porewaters, often exceeding 1 mg/L (USEPA, 2007b). Sulfide concentrations >0.3 mg/L appear to restrict the production of MeHg (Benoit et al., 2003). The elevated production of sulfide may limit MeHg concentrations in the northern Everglades. With decreases in sulfate and sulfide concentrations, there is an increase in MeHg production rate in WCA-2B and WCA-3A, with subsequent decreases through the ENP toward the south (see Figure 9.4; Gilmour et al., 2007).

An additional factor that likely influences the spatial patterns in fish Hg in the Everglades is phosphorus supply. Water concentrations of phosphorus exhibit a distinct decreasing gradient north to south due to inputs from the EAA (see Figure 9.5; USEPA, 2007b). This elevated supply of phosphorus increases aquatic productivity, which may result in the biodilution discussed above (Pickhardt et al., 2002; Chen and Folt, 2005). However, to our knowledge this hypothesis has never been tested for the Everglades.

TEMPORAL PATTERNS

An ambitious REMAP plan is in place to track changes in Hg contamination in south Florida (Axelrad et al., 2007; USEPA, 2007). The major sources of Hg emissions in south Florida in the early 1990s were municipal and medical-waste incinerators. Since that time there has been an approximately 90% decline in these sources due to reductions in the waste stream and emission controls (Atkeson et al., 2005). Wet Hg deposition decreased from 1994 to 2002. Since that time, deposition has been highly variable, with high deposition from early 2003 to mid-2004 due to elevated precipitation (Axelrad et al., 2007).

The REMAP study (USEPA, 2007) showed slight changes in concentrations of THg and MeHg in water from 1995 to 2005. Mercury concentrations of largemouth bass in the

WCA have decreased 30–70% from concentrations observed in the late 1980s and early 1990s. However, concentrations have not changed appreciably since 1998 to the present (Lange, 2006). The REMAP study showed declines in the Hg concentrations of mosquitofish from 1995 to 2005 in the Everglades. In contrast, concentrations of Hg in largemouth bass have increased in the ENP since 1999. It is not clear what is driving these complex changes in fish Hg concentrations across the Everglades. The recent declines in fish Hg in the WCAs do not appear to coincide with decreases in atmospheric deposition of Hg. Rather, it is hypothesized that decreases in fish Hg in the WCAs, that formerly exhibited very high concentrations, are due to restoration associated water flow increases resulting in a decrease in sulfate concentrations to below values that were optimum for MeHg production by sulfate-reducing bacteria (Axelrad et al., 2005).

In summary Hg contamination is widespread in the Everglades. Concentrations of Hg in fish widely exceed established criteria for the health of humans and wildlife. The extent of this contamination is likely due to elevated inputs of Hg from atmospheric deposition coupled with the high sensitivity of the Everglades ecosystem (due to extensive wetlands, elevated sulfate inputs, warm conditions and low productivity). There are distinct spatial patterns of Hg contamination across the Everglades due to variations in source waters, and the supply of sulfate, DOC, and possibly phosphorus. There have also been temporal variations in fish Hg concentrations across the Everglades. Declines in fish Hg from the 1980s through 1990s were probably driven by controls on local incinerator sources. Since the late 1990s, changes in fish Hg have not coincided with changes in atmospheric deposition of Hg. Rather, it is likely that recent changes in Hg dynamics are due to changes in sulfate concentrations, and possibly changes in other constituents that affect Hg transport and trophic transfer. One pattern that emerges from this synthesis of Hg in the Everglades is that land use is central to the Hg problem in south Florida because it influences the supply of critical chemical constituents (i.e., sulfate, DOC, nitrate, and total phosphorus) and possibly alters the pathways of water that transport Hg and the critical chemical constituents influencing Hg transformation. These spatial and temporal patterns are indicative of the complexity of Hg dynamics and the myriad factors that influence the extent of contamination in the Everglades. Future management of Hg contamination will need to consider these factors that control Hg transport, methylation, bio-availability, and bio-accumulation, and not solely Hg inputs.

The Adirondacks

The Adirondack region of New York is one of the biologic Hg hot spots identified by Evers et al. (2007), with consistently widespread contamination of Hg in fish and wildlife as compared with other areas in the region. It is located in northern New York state and encompasses a large (~2.4 million ha) predominantly forested portion of the Canadian Shield underlaid by metasedimentary rocks and granite gneisses. The soils of the Adirondacks are largely Spodosols developed from glacial surficial materials that cover much of the region (Driscoll et al., 1994; Sullivan et al., 2006). There are approximately 2800 lakes in the Adirondack Park (Driscoll et al., 1991). Moreover, wetlands are a prominent feature of the Adirondack landscape, covering about 5% of the land area. An important characteristic of the Adirondacks is that it receives elevated acidic deposition and contains sensitive watersheds and surface waters that have been impacted by acidic deposition (Driscoll et al., 1991). Inputs of acidic deposition have been decreasing in recent years resulting in limited recovery of surface water acidity (Driscoll et al., 2003).

Wet Hg deposition has been monitored at the Mercury Deposition Network (MDN) site at the Huntington Forest in the central Adirondacks (48.98°N, 74.23°W) since 2000, with an annual mean value of 6.7 µg m^{-2} yr^{-1}. Levels of wet Hg deposition in the Adirondacks are modest compared to other regions of the United States (http://nadp.sws.uiuc.edu/mdn). Unfortunately, there are no long-term measurements of Hg deposition. However, paleolimnologic measurements of lake sediments provide a record of historical changes in Hg deposition. Studies of the sediment record of eight lakes in the Adirondacks suggest that preindustrial Hg deposition to the region was approximately 3 µg m^{-2} yr^{-1} (Lorey and Driscoll, 1999). Around 1900, there was a marked increase in Hg deposition to about six times background levels. Mercury deposition peaked around the 1970s–1980s and has declined about 25% in more recent decades.

Mercury contamination in the region is widespread; New York has issued 66 fish-consumption advisories for elevated Hg in the Adirondacks. Considerable research has been conducted on the deposition, transport, and effects of Hg in the Adirondack region of New York. In particular there have been detailed process-level studies of Hg dynamics at the Huntington Forest in the central Adirondacks, which includes Arbutus Lake and its watershed at Archer Creek, and at Sunday Lake watershed in the western Adirondacks (43.85°N, 74.10°W). These detailed studies have been complemented by regional surveys. A synthesis of this research is provided in this case study.

ATMOSPHERIC DEPOSITION, THROUGHFALL, AND LITTERFALL

Air concentrations of Hg in the Adirondacks are typical of remote regions and relatively low as compared with values reported for more urban and industrial regions (Choi et al., 2008a). Significant diurnal patterns were apparent in warm seasons for all Hg species, whereas diurnal patterns were weak in cold seasons. These diurnal patterns of Hg species may be due to reemissions of GEM from the forest floor, which largely occur during the daylight period in the sum-

mer (see below), and oxidation of GEM largely by ozone, which is also more prominent in the summer months. Choi et al. (2008a) used potential source contribution function analysis and back trajectory analysis to determine potential Hg sources to the Adirondacks. Their analysis showed that regional source areas, including Pennsylvania, West Virginia, Ohio, Kentucky, Indiana, and Texas, were important in contributing Hg deposition to the Adirondacks.

Studies from the Adirondacks and other remote forest ecosystems have shown that the canopy can greatly enhance atmospheric Hg deposition (Rea et al., 2002; Miller et al., 2005). Throughfall is the water leached from the forest canopy that enters the forest floor. Choi et al. (2008b) observed a slight enrichment in throughfall Hg in comparison with wet Hg deposition (11.6 µg Hg m^{-2} yr^{-1} vs. 12.0 µg Hg m^{-2} yr^{-1}) from a hardwood site at Huntington Forest in the central Adirondacks. Similar levels of throughfall enrichment were evident for a hardwood stand in the western Adirondacks (Sunday Lake watershed; Demers et al., 2007). In contrast, much greater enrichment in throughfall Hg fluxes occurred from a conifer stand. These increases were attributed to a greater leaf area index and the year-round canopy of the coniferous vegetation (Demers et al., 2007).

Plant litter is an also important pathway of Hg inputs to forest ecosystems. At the Huntington Forest, the THg concentration of leaf tissue increased approximately 10-fold over the growing season for three hardwood species, from 4.4 ± 2.7 to 37.3 ± 12.4 ng g^{-1} (Bushey et al., 2008). This linear increase in concentration over the growing season suggests that accumulation in leaves is regulated by mass transfer processes between the atmosphere and leaf tissue. Conversely, the MeHg concentration of leaf tissue (0.17 ± 0.18 ng g^{-1}) and accumulation were low. Annual litterfall Hg at Huntington Forest was 17.2 µg m^{-2} yr^{-1}, representing the largest input of Hg to this forest ecosystem. Litter input of MeHg was 0.12 µg m^{-2} yr^{-1}. Demers et al. (2007) observed comparable rates of litterfall Hg from the hardwood stand at Sunday Lake (14.9 µg m^{-2} yr^{-1}) but much lower rates at the conifer stand (9.7 µg m^{-2} yr^{-1}). Modeling estimates of transpiration uptake and GEM deposition suggest that Hg in leaf tissue is largely derived from atmospheric sources (Bushey et al., 2008). Thus, litterfall Hg probably represents largely a new, rather than recycled, input to the forest ecosystem. The pattern that emerges from this work is that the forest canopy greatly amplifies Hg deposition. Dry deposition (estimated as the sum of net throughfall plus litterfall Hg) is the predominant pathway of Hg inputs to the forest floor, representing 72% for the hardwood stands and 82% at the conifer stand (Demers et al., 2007). In addition, the mechanism of dry inputs appears to vary with forest vegetation type. Total Hg inputs were greater at the conifer stand (35.5 µg m^{-2} yr^{-1} vs. 22.3 µg m^{-2} yr^{-1} in deciduous stands), and Hg inputs occurred largely as throughfall, while for the hardwood stands litterfall is the major Hg input pathway.

TRANSPORT OF MERCURY FROM SOILS

Evasion is an important Hg loss from upland forests. However, this flux varies highly with space and time and is difficult to quantify. Soil Hg evasion fluxes have been measured at the Huntington Forest, with values ranging between -2.5 ng m^{-2} hr^{-1} (i.e., deposition) and 27.2 ng m^{-2} hr^{-1} and positively correlated with temperature and solar radiation (Choi and Holsen, 2009). The measured GEM emission flux was highest in spring and summer, and lowest in winter. During leaf-off periods, the GEM emission flux was highly dependent on solar radiation and less dependent on temperature. During leaf-on periods, the Hg emission flux was fairly constant because of canopy shading of the forest floor. The annual GEM emission flux was estimated to be 7.0 µg GEM m^{-2} yr^{-1}. Note that this value is comparable to throughfall Hg fluxes.

Understanding mobilization/immobilization processes from upland soils is important in assessing the fate of Hg. Upland soils represent the largest Hg ecosystem pool that could potentially supply large quantities of Hg to the atmosphere and/or to downstream aquatic ecosystems. At the Huntington Forest, THg concentrations in upland forest soil decreased with depth, coinciding with decreases in soil organic matter (Driscoll et al., unpublished data). Soil solution THg concentrations, measured using lysimeters, also decreased from 8.0 ng L^{-1} to 1.9 ng L^{-1} from the forest floor to the lower mineral soil, respectively, and were significantly correlated with DOC concentrations. The stoichiometric pattern of Hg and DOC within soil solutions suggest that Hg retention/mobilization is controlled by the dynamics of soil organic matter. Conversely, soil water concentrations of MeHg were relatively constant, near the analytical detection limit (0.05–0.06 ng L^{-1}) and were not correlated significantly with DOC. While annual drainage losses from upland soil (THg, 2.3 µg m^{-2} yr^{-1}; MeHg, 0.039 µg m^{-2} yr^{-1}) were a small fraction of the soil pool remaining in soil (THg, 73 mg m^{-2}; MeHg, 0.29 mg m^{-2}), these values were comparable to measured fluxes in the stream watershed, demonstrating the potential importance of the mobilization of upland Hg species in watershed budgets.

ROLE OF WETLANDS

The fluxes and pools of THg and MeHg were also evaluated for two northern temperate forest wetlands at the Huntington Forest in the Adirondacks: an abandoned beaver meadow and a riparian wetland (Selvendiran et al., 2008a). Mass balance calculations reveal that the wetlands were net sources of THg and MeHg, although the magnitude of the source is a function of wetland connectivity to stream water. The storage of THg and MeHg in wetland soil is a large pool that appears coupled with organic carbon and sulfur accumulation. In the current scenario of decreasing Hg emissions and atmospheric deposition, the large "active" soil pool in wetlands is a potential short-term and long-term source of Hg and MeHg to downstream aquatic ecosystems.

The two wetlands studied at the Huntington Forest intercept a majority of the upland runoff to the Arbutus Lake watershed and have a significant impact on downstream MeHg fluxes (Selvendiran et al., 2008b). The percent of THg as MeHg (%MeHg) in the upland runoff increased 2–6% from the inlet to the outlet of the wetlands. The average concentration of MeHg in the upland stream above the wetlands was near quantifiable limits (0.04 ng/L) and much lower than in the stream below the wetland (0.17 ng/L). MeHg in the stream below was strongly driven by seasonal processes. During the growing season, MeHg concentrations were three times higher (0.27 ng/L) as compared with the nongrowing season (0.10 ng/L). There was also a strong coupling of increases in MeHg with decreases in sulfate concentrations during the growing season, suggesting the linkage of sulfate reduction to MeHg production in wetlands. Moreover, transport of Hg species from the wetlands was facilitated by DOC, as indicated by its significant positive relations with THg and MeHg. Both wetlands were net sources of THg to the downstream lake ecosystem. The calculated annual fluxes of THg and MeHg draining the wetlands at the outlet of the watershed were 2.3 µg m^{-2} yr^{-1} and 0.092 µg m^{-2} yr^{-1}, respectively.

Routine monthly sampling at Huntington Forest indicated that hydrologic conditions influence THg concentrations in upland and wetland streams. Detailed sampling of Hg species during elevated discharge events confirmed that concentrations of Hg species increased during storm events (Bushey et al., 2008; Dittman et al., 2009). Event sampling also showed that relationships of Hg with DOC and total suspended solids (TSS) were not simple and varied over storm events. Marked increases in Hg^{2+} were evident during the rising limb of the hydrograph, suggesting wash-off of Hg from the canopy or the near-stream channel (i.e., riparian area) early in the storm event. Positive relationships of THg and DOC were not evident until later in the hydrograph, likely associated with soil flushing of DOC and THg and a shift in water hydrology to more shallow hydrologic flow paths.

MERCURY FATE IN ADIRONDACK LAKES

Compared to field studies in the Adirondacks of larger organisms (namely, fish), those investigating concentrations of Hg in seston are limited. The Hg concentrations of water and seston were measured in nine lakes in the Adirondacks exhibiting a range of physical and chemical characteristics (Adams et al., 2009). Consistent with other studies of remote temperate region lakes with forested watersheds (Driscoll et al., 1994), dissolved (<0.45 µm) Hg concentrations from the mid-epilimnion of the study lakes was $88 \pm 16\%$ of THg, and ranged from 1.15 to 5.42 ng L^{-1}. Dissolved Hg concentration was strongly related to lake DOC. Mercury concentrations in each seston size class were proportional to the dissolved surface water Hg concentration of each lake. Increased dissolved surface water Hg resulted in increased Hg concentrations in each of four seston size classes (0.2–2, 2–20, 20–200, and >153 μm), suggesting that the supply of Hg to lake ecosystems is important to Hg partitioning at the base of the food web. Mercury concentrations in sestons varied among the lakes and among the three size fractions of the microbial planktonic food web. Picoseston (0.2–2 μm) made up the majority of the particulate Hg pool in each lake and had the highest average Hg concentrations (mean 361 ± 319 ng g^{-1} dry weight [dw]). Mean Hg concentrations for the nanoseston (2–20 μm) and microseston (>20–200 μm) size classes were lower than the picoseston size class and ranged from 114 ± 79 ng g^{-1} to 135 ± 61 ng g^{-1} dw, respectively. Seston density across all size fractions was negatively correlated with seston Hg concentrations and significantly predicted Hg concentrations in the 0.2–2 μm size class. Note that seston Hg was not related to chlorophyll concentration, suggesting that bacterial production is an important carbon source at the base of the food chain in these unproductive lakes. Mercury in bulk zooplankton (>153 μm) ranged from 105 to 613 ng g^{-1} with an average 38 ± 18% of THg as MeHg (Adams et al., 2009).

Over the past two decades, fish with elevated concentrations of Hg have been observed in remote lake districts, including the Adirondacks (Driscoll et al., 1995). Studies across eastern North America have shown that fish Hg concentrations increase with decreases in lake pH. Controls in emissions of sulfur dioxide have resulted in some improvement in the acid–base status of Adirondack lakes. In addition, decreases in atmospheric Hg deposition have also occurred. In 1992–1993 and again in 2005–2006, 25 Adirondack lakes were surveyed to analyze patterns of Hg in the water column and yellow perch (*Perca flavescens*) and changes in these patterns (Dittman and Driscoll, 2009). During the 1992–1993 survey 64% of the yellow perch surveyed (n = 725) exceeded the United States Environmental Protection Agency action limit for fish Hg of 0.3 μg g^{-1} (ww). The percentage of yellow perch exceeding the 0.3 μg g^{-1} (ww) action limit decreased to 49% in the 2005–2006 survey (n = 1154). Twelve lakes exhibited a decrease in perch Hg, six lakes showed an increase, and seven lakes had no change. Four key variables influenced the change in perch Hg concentrations in the Adirondacks: watershed area, elevation, change in pH, and change in fish condition. Dittman and Driscoll (2009) speculated that as the acidity in lakes is attenuated, the lakes may become more productive and water-quality conditions less stressful to fish, leading to improved fish conditions. As fish body conditions and growth rates improve, fish can exhibit "growth dilution" of tissue contaminants, leading to lower fish Hg levels, as seen in other studies (Karimi et al., 2007; Ward et al., 2009).

In summary, Hg contamination is widespread in the Adirondacks, despite its remote location and moderate inputs of wet Hg deposition. These characteristics point to the Hg sensitivity of the region. The forest cover facilitates enhanced deposition due to the scavenging of GEM and Hg^{2+} by the canopy. The shallow surficial deposits facilitate the transport of Hg^{2+} from uplands to downstream wetlands and lakes, particularly through the mobilization of DOC during high-flow events. Wetlands are a prominent feature of the Adirondack landscape and important zones of MeHg production. Adirondack lakes are nutrient-poor and unproductive. This condition limits plankton and fish biomass and likely enhances fish Hg concentration. Finally, there is an important linkage between Hg contamination and elevated acidic deposition in the Adirondacks. Sulfate input from acidic deposition is a critical substrate for sulfate-reducing bacteria, which produce MeHg. Also there is the widespread relationship between increases in fish Hg with decreases in pH. The mechanism driving this relationship is unclear, but trends in fish Hg suggest that acidification may limit fish growth, resulting in associated high concentrations of Hg in fish tissue; improvements in fish growth may cause decreases in fish Hg concentrations.

Reservoirs

The impoundment of reservoirs for hydroelectric generation, flood control, recreation, waste management, and other purposes continues to increase worldwide, modifying global carbon cycling and exacerbating local Hg contamination (Kelly et al., 1997; St. Louis et al., 2000). Mercury sources in reservoirs are largely identical to those of natural water bodies: atmospheric deposition of Hg from local and distant sources due to combustion of fossil fuels, waste incineration, and other combustion processes; and, wastewater and industrial point source discharges (Arnason and Fletcher, 2003; Abbott and Kotchenruler, 2006; Driscoll et al., 2007; Park et al., 2008). Despite this commonality, Hg concentrations in biota are universally elevated in reservoirs relative to other freshwater aquatic environments (Evers et al., 2007), a finding that has prompted increasing research and management attention at the international (e.g., World Commission on Dams, 2000) and regional levels (e.g., Mason and Sveinsdottir, 2003). The United States Federal Energy Regulatory Commission now routinely addresses Hg contamination in their relicensing documents for U.S. hydroelectric facilities. Mercury contamination in reservoirs is a particular concern from the perspectives of human health and ecologic integrity, as many of these systems are vast in scale and support large fisheries and complex ecologic communities. In a general sense, elevated biotic Hg concentrations in reservoirs stem from two major effects: the creation of the reservoirs; and the ongoing management of those reservoirs (Evers et al., 2007). In this section, we describe factors within these two general aspects that result in elevated Hg in biota due to enhanced MeHg production.

THE RESERVOIR EFFECT

In every case, creation of new reservoirs begins by the impoundment of waters in low-lying terrain, with resultant reservoirs ranging in size from small "flowage" ponds to major projects such as the Three Gorges Dam (China), Tucurui Reservoir (Brazil), or the Bourassa–La Grande complex (James Bay, Quebec). The initial impoundment of a new reservoir yields a large flux of organic and inorganic material to the water in the form of decomposing plants, woody material, and organic and mineral soils (Figure 9.6a). This material includes legacy Hg from prior atmospheric deposition or legacy Hg from industrial sources. This occurs in a decompositional environment characterized by high organic loading and low dissolved oxygen, which favors methylation. Muresan et al., (2006) describe a newly constructed reservoir in simple terms as a "reactor" that creates favorable conditions for MeHg production, both at the sediment–water interface, and on organic particles in water. This pattern is known colloquially as the "reservoir effect," which is well described by current and emerging literature. For example, in the reservoirs of the Bourassa–La Grande project, aqueous MeHg concentrations increased to 1.3 times their initial values within the first 13 years after reservoir creation (Shetagne and Verdon, 1999). Much higher increases have been observed in one experimental reservoir system (up to 13 times, Bodaly et al., 2004; see also, St. Louis et al., 2004). Reservoir systems with intermediate increases in MeHg have been described in Amazonia (Albuquerque Palermo et al., 2006a: Niklasson et al., 2006; Muresan et al., 2006) and in chains of reservoirs in the Wujiang River, China (e.g., Guo et al., 2006). The typical increase in aqueous MeHg concentrations in reservoirs is 2–4 times those observed before flooding.

Organic Matter and Methylation

The single most important factor controlling the increase in MeHg in reservoir waters is the organic content of the impounded soils and detrital material. While the relationship between the organic content of sediment and water and methylation potential is well described in the literature (see the review in Driscoll et al., 2007), this simple relationship is more nuanced in reservoir systems. In a study of an experimentally impounded wetland/pond system in Ontario (the ELARP project, Kelly et al., 1997; St. Louis et al., 2004), the methylation promoted by the initial flooding peaked in intensity 2–3 years after the flood. These high MeHg concentrations began to decline thereafter because of increased demethylation (St. Louis et al., 2004), likely by active demethylation via the "mer" detoxification pathway used by sulfate-reducing bacteria (Marvin-DiPasquale et al., 2000).

Similarly, Bodaly et al. (2004, the FLUDEX project) describe the creation of three experimental impoundments in watersheds characterized by low, medium, and high concentrations of soil organic content. In these watersheds,

MeHg production was not significantly different between the middle- and high-carbon reservoirs, but was considerably elevated in these relative to the low-carbon reservoir. In the FLUDEX project, MeHg also peaked at year 3 of the study. The FLUDEX study indicated that lability of the carbon was a more important driver of methylation than the simple presence of higher quantities of organic carbon. In both the ELARP and FLUDEX projects, MeHg photoreduction (Sellers et al., 1996) was likely limited because of decreased light penetration from increases in dissolved organic matter in the water column. The limitation of this pathway of MeHg loss would serve to perpetuate higher MeHg concentrations.

Similar findings were noted from experimental studies of soils of varying types in the Three Gorges Dam project area (Zhang et al., 2006; Yu et al., 2007). Paradoxically, while the highest methylation potential was observed in the highest-carbon cambisols (e.g., paddy soils) the second-highest methylation potential was observed in well-drained soils primosols, which are low in carbon, but may allow for more movement of soil-based DOC. This finding further emphasizes not only the importance of soil carbon content of parent soil material, but also the subsequent lability of the organic ligands that are produced by that soil.

METHYLATION SITES WITHIN RESERVOIRS

As with lakes and rivers, the processes by which MeHg in reservoirs is incorporated into biota is governed by factors described in this chapter, as well as those summarized by Evers et al. (2007) and Driscoll et al. (2007). There is little about the existence or operation of a reservoir alone that results in a differential uptake of Hg into biota, at least within the reservoirs themselves. However, the sources of the MeHg may indeed differ. In reservoir systems, as has also been shown for natural lakes, methylation can occur in marginal wetlands and littoral soils (Branfireun et al., 1996, 2006), upon particles within open waters (St. Louis et al., 2004) or at the sediment–water interface (e.g., Kuwabara et al., 2003; Albuquerque-Palermo et al., 2006a; Malm, 2006). Verta et al. (1986) initially attributed high fish-tissue Hg concentrations to MeHg production in marginal peats. While the supply of MeHg from marginal wetlands to natural lakes is well documented (e.g., Branfireun et al., 1996), the importance of these wetlands in open-water reservoirs remains the topic of considerable research (Branfireun et al., 2006).

In the ELARP, the production of MeHg in both open waters and marginal peatlands was studied. Despite generally higher rates of MeHg production in the wetlands, the predominant source of MeHg in biota was that produced in the open water areas of the pond on the suspended organic matter, which served as a methylation substrate. Because of alteration of hydrology and depositional environments, ongoing erosion of soil material to open waters can perpetuate the supply of substrates for methylation, prolonging the so-called reservoir effect (St. Louis et al.,

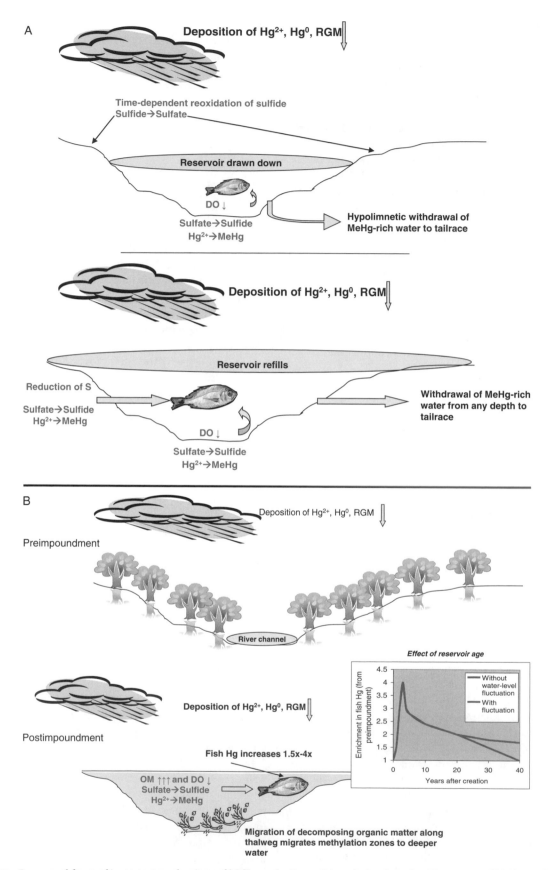

FIGURE 9.6   Conceptual figure of important mechanisms of MeHg production and transfer in reservoirs: (a) processes of MeHg production during reservoir creation and temporal pattern of enrichment in fish afterwards, and (b) processes of MeHg production during reservoir fluctuation.

2004). Erosion control in reservoirs and their associated watersheds is therefore one management option that can mitigate prolonged MeHg production and bio-accumulation. He et al. (2008) also described open water methylation as the predominant source of MeHg to the large and highly eutrophic Hongfeng Reservoir, Guizhou Province, China.

In many reservoirs, methylation at the sediment–water interface is the major source of bio-available MeHg. In the Baihua Reservoir, China, and in some large Amazonian reservoirs, migration and focusing of sediments toward the deepest reservoir forebay areas have resulted in a migration of the most active MeHg-producing zones. (Han and Feng, 2006; Malm, 2006). Kuwabara et al. (2003) also found the greatest methylation potential along the thalweg sediments of Camp Far West Reservoir.

RESERVOIRS: A SOURCE OF DOWNSTREAM METHYLMERCURY

The production of MeHg near the sediment–water interface of forebay waters presents a particular problem where reservoir discharges are from hypolimnetic depth zones. In this instance, the MeHg that is produced in one reservoir becomes immediately available to downstream biota in the receiving tailraces. This idea is well supported by the ELARP and FLUDEX projects (Bodaly et al., 2004; St. Louis et al., 2004) and from several cascading reservoir systems studied in Brazil and China. In the ELARP and FLUDEX projects, the reservoir systems became sources of MeHg for downstream receiving waters for periods of several years. The same phenomenon has been observed by He et al. (2008) in the Hongfeng Reservoir. In the Tucurui Reservoir system of Brazil, fishes of several trophic guilds were found Hg levels that were elevated by a factor of 3 in downstream receiving waters over in-reservoir fishes of similar trophic position (Albuquerque Palermo et al., 2006b).

RESERVOIR AGE AND FISH MERCURY

The enhanced production of MeHg in reservoirs is readily bio-accumulated in fishes and other piscivorous biota. This effect is an unavoidable consequence of creating a reservoir, but one with a finite lifespan. The age of the reservoir has a large influence on net MeHg production. In the Bourassa–La Grande project, increases in fish Hg concentrations of 1.5 to 4 times natural lake background levels were observed, with concentrations peaking ~10–15 years postconstruction and declining thereafter (Shetagne and Verdon, 1999). Where reservoirs are not further manipulated or managed, fish Hg concentration typically declines to background levels between 20 and 40 years after construction (Anderson et al., 1995; Shetagne and Verdon, 1999). In a series of Amazonian reservoirs, Malm (2006) observed a 2–3 times decreases in fish Hg concentrations during the period of 6–21 years after construction.

THE ROLE OF WATER-LEVEL FLUCTUATIONS

Water-level fluctuation also influences fish Hg concentrations (Figure 9.6b). In reservoirs, reservoir managers fluctuate water stage primarily for hydropower generation or flood control, but also for irrigation and, in limited instances, recreation. Bodaly et al. (1994) and Verta et al. (1986) identified water-level fluctuation in Manitoba and Finnish Reservoirs, respectively, as the key variable explaining high fish-tissue Hg concentrations. In the Finnish study, the elevated fish Hg concentrations were attributed to the expulsion of MeHg-rich waters from marginal peats due to pressing by ice following winter drawdown. Numerous studies since have also implicated water-level fluctuations. For example, depth and hydroperiod have been shown to be strongly associated with increased fish Hg concentrations in depression wetland ponds of the Southeastern United States (Snodgrass et al., 2000). In an experimental study, fish-tissue Hg concentrations were significantly elevated in manipulated reservoirs in Maine (annual drawdown, 3–7 m) relative to control lakes (annual fluctuation, 1–1.2 m), and the MeHg:Hg ratio in sediments was shown to increase considerably, then remain elevated, after the onset of reservoir fluctuation (Haines and Smith, 1998). Tissues of fishes and avian piscivores nesting on large open water impoundments with large dewatered and reinundated littoral areas have also been shown to display elevated Hg concentrations, particularly where littoral sediment substrates are more enhanced in organic matter (Evers et al., 2007).

A study of 14 Minnesota lakes subject to varying water-level manipulation regimens provides the best empirical evidence of the role played by water-level fluctuation (Sorensen et al., 2005). In that study, variation in the seasonal magnitude and timing of fluctuations was highly and positively correlated to Hg concentrations in young-of-year yellow perch. The work of these authors, along with findings of ELARP, clarify the importance of redox cycling at the dewatered and re-inundated sediment–water interface in reservoirs. During periods when reservoirs are at full capacity, methylation proceeds in sediments until the available sulfate has been reduced to sulfides. Upon drawdown, the sulfides within the interstitial soils of exposed littoral areas undergo reoxidation to sulfate. When the water level increases again, this newly "re-available" sulfate, in addition to atmospherically deposited sulfate and Hg, facilitate the reestablishment of the methylation cycle. Assuming that the transformation of sulfide to sulfate is not instantaneous, then the amount of time the exposed littoral surface is dry will also enhance methylation potential in the next reinundation cycle, due to the presence of progressively more available sulfate. Therefore, where drawdowns are longer and/or affect greater area, ongoing water-level fluctuations in systems subject to continuing Hg deposition or stream inputs explain why Hg concentrations in fish and other biota often remain elevated in "old" reservoirs.

In countries that rely on both coal and hydropower for a significant component of their energy use, the "footprint" of the Hg can reflect a dynamic balance between Hg emissions associated with coal combustion, and Hg contamination that is exacerbated by reservoir creation and operation. The current pace of reservoir construction in the Peoples Republic of China may be particularly problematic, given the vast land areas involved. Estimates suggest that construction of the Three Gorges Dam alone would offset coal-based emissions of carbon dioxide and sulfur dioxide by 100 metric tons and 2 metric tons, respectively (China Three Gorges Project Corporation, 2002). Yet because of increased energy demands, coal use continues to increase in China, despite the additional generating capacity of the Three Gorges project and its upstream reservoirs. Major upstream erosion at the Three Gorges project will sustain continuing methylation. Therefore, the construction of new reservoir facilities upstream of the Three Gorges project and elsewhere in China will certainly, because of the reservoir effect and ongoing water-level manipulation, exacerbate the impacts of an already Hg-contaminated landscape. The situation described here for the People's Republic of China is occurring worldwide. Yet, in areas where Hg emissions from coal and other sources are limited to the maximum extent, and reservoir operations are conducted in a fashion that mitigates methylation (e.g., appropriate drawdown regimen, reducing upstream sediment supply), the environmental problems of Hg within reservoirs can be controlled.

Large Lake Ecosystems: Lake Michigan

The Great Lakes are freshwater systems that are physically much like marine ecosystems and therefore have much to tell us about Hg transformation, bio-accumulation, and trophic transfer in much larger and physically complex systems. Several characteristics predispose these lakes to potentially higher levels of bio-accumulation in fish. First, the watersheds of these lakes are vast, as are the surface areas for receiving high Hg deposition. Second, the lakes are relatively oligotrophic, which results in higher bioconcentration of Hg in particulates and lower growth rates in fish, which is likely to result in higher fish concentrations. Moreover, the food webs in these ecosystems contain invertebrate predators and numerous piscivorous species, both of which lengthen the food chain and increase biomagnification of MeHg. In the Great Lakes basin, MeHg bio-accumulation in fish has resulted in numerous fish-consumption advisories. Great Lakes sediments are the primary sink for contaminants, including Hg, which can be subsequently resuspended and redistributed. Persistent contaminants in the Great Lakes have been studied since the 1960s prior to and since mitigative binational strategies were taken to reduce environmental impacts (Cahill, 1981; Painter et al., 2001; Rossmann, 2002; Marvin et al., 2002, 2004a, 2004b; Gewurtz et al., 2008).

TABLE 9.2

Concentrations of Total Mercury in Great Lakes Sediments and Probable Effect Level (PEL) Exceedances

Lake	Lakewide average (μg/g)	% Exceeding PEL (0.486 μg/g)
Michigan	0.077	0
Superior	0.088	0
Huron	0.043	0
St. Clair	0.196	0
Erie	0.187	6
Ontario	0.586	62

SOURCE: USEPA (2006) and Marvin et al. (2004).

All the Great Lakes (Lake Superior, Lake Huron, Lake Michigan, Lake Erie, and Lake Ontario) are large and physically complex and have large watersheds and long residence times. Spatial and temporal patterns of Hg and other contaminants reflect sources, lake sedimentology and bathymetry, and circulation patterns (Marvin et al., 2004b). Lakes Superior, Michigan, and Huron generally have lower concentrations of Hg in their sediments than Lake Ontario and Lake Erie (Table 9.2). In all the lakes, Hg concentrations decline from shallow near-shore coarser sediments to deep-water depositional basin sediment of silts and clays (Marvin et al., 2004a, 2004b). Despite lower sediment concentrations, fish concentrations of MeHg are highest in Lake Superior (greater than 0.3 ppm).

Although there is considerable information on the spatial distribution of Hg in Great Lakes sediments, concentrations of Hg in biota are less available and not linked to sources of MeHg in sediments. Thus, Hg fate in these aquatic food webs is poorly understood, just as it is in large marine systems (Chen et al., 2008). Organic contaminants are known to bio-accumulate in Great Lakes biota and the long food webs, which include invertebrate predators such as *Mysis* enhance biomagnification of these persistent contaminants (Swackhamer et al., 1998). The fish consumption advisories for Hg and other contaminants in the Great Lakes are established on a state-by-state (Illinois, Indiana, Michigan, Minnesota, New York, Ohio, Pennsylvania, and Wisconsin) or province-by-province basis (Ontario and Quebec) and differ for each fish species, lake, and political entity (USEPA http://www.great-lakes.net/humanhealth/fish/advisories.html). The consumption advisories due to Hg comprise a small percentage of the total advisories for each of the Great Lakes (Superior 4%, Huron 9%, Erie 2%, Ontario 7%). However, they represent a greater proportion (93%) of the advisories in inland lakes in the Great Lakes basin, reflecting both the broader range of contaminants and their respective advisories in the Great Lakes and the fact that the highest concentrations of Hg in fish are from smaller, shallower lakes than the Great Lakes themselves. In fact, the largest fisheries in the Great Lakes, especially Lake Erie, produce lower Hg than typical commercially available fish.

LAKE MICHIGAN MASS BALANCE STUDY

Among the Great Lakes, Lake Michigan is one of the most thoroughly studied for a whole array of contaminants (organics and metals), chemicals (e.g., nutrients, carbon, dissolved oxygen), and biologic and meteorologic characteristics through the Lake Michigan Mass Balance Study (LMMBS; USEPA, 2004). Hg and MeHg were among the contaminants measured in the open-lake water column, tributaries, fish, lower pelagic food web, sediments, and atmosphere (Figure 9.7). The results of the LMMBS are documented in a series of papers and a USEPA report (Mason and Sullivan, 1997; Hurley et al., 1998a, 1998b; Sullivan and Mason, 1998; Landis and Keeler, 2002; Rossmann, 2002; Vette et al., 2002; Marvin et al., 2004a, 2004b; USEPA, 2004). The LMMBS objectives for Hg were to estimate the loading rates, establish a baseline, predict benefits of loading reductions, and understand the processes governing Hg cycling and availability in Lake Michigan (USEPA, 2004). Although vast amounts of data have been collected, the links between atmospheric deposition, Hg cycling, and Hg bio-accumulation in biotic end points in Lake Michigan have not been made.

Hg inputs to the Lake Michigan system were characterized by measurements in atmospheric components and via tributaries and the development of a deposition model. Given its large lake surface area and low watershed:lake area ratio, the model identified atmospheric deposition as the primary pathway for Hg input to the lake, accounting for 84% of the estimated total annual input of 1403 kg (Landis and Keeler, 2002). However, the particulate and vapor-phase Hg at the urban sampling site near Chicago were higher than other more rural stations, a pattern seen in other regional studies of Hg sources and sinks (Keeler, 1994; Mason et al., 2000). The deposition model estimated that the Chicago/Gary urban area contributed about 20% of the total annual input, suggesting that Hg controls in that region could significantly decrease Hg inputs to the lake (Landis et al., 2002). Moreover, meteorologic analysis determined that this urban area also impacted all other LMMBS sampling sites, making it a major point source of deposition for the entire lake (Landis et al., 2002). Inputs to Lake Michigan from tributaries, although a lesser component of the total annual inputs, were also highest in urban and industrialized watersheds and lower in forested and wetland-dominated watersheds. In contrast, MeHg concentrations were highest in tributaries draining agricultural and forested areas and lowest in the Chicago/Gary urban area.

Despite differences in tributary inputs of Hg, water-column concentrations of particulate and dissolved Hg were homogeneous across 15 sampling stations, again suggesting that the primary source of Hg is atmospheric rather than riverine. Moreover, concentrations were lower than in the smaller and shallower lakes studied in the region (Watras et al., 1998), which may be related to lower DOC and particulate matter concentrations in Lake Michigan. Unlike other studies of smaller, shallower lakes, Hg concentration in the epilimnion is higher in Lake Michigan than in the hypolimnion, which may be more characteristic of larger, deeper lakes in which sediment resuspension is minimal and atmospheric inputs dominate.

SPATIAL TRENDS

Mercury concentrations in Great Lake sediments vary greatly (see Table 9.1) with the highest concentrations in Lake Ontario (0.586 mg kg^{-1}), in which 63% of sites exceed the probable effect level (0.486 µg g^{-1}) for Hg in sediments (Canadian Council of Ministers of the Environment [CCME], 1999). As compared with the other Great Lakes, surficial sediments in the main bay of Lake Michigan are relatively uncontaminated with Hg (mean concentration, 0. 078 mg kg^{-1}). However, Green Bay, an embayment of Lake Michigan, is contaminated as compared with the other Great Lakes (Rossmann and Edgington, 2000). The distribution of Hg in sediments in the main bay of Lake Michigan is largely driven by the lake bathymetry and physical currents, and is highest in

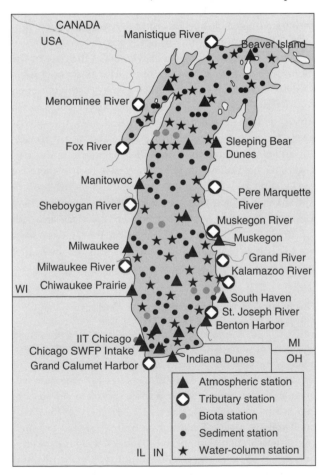

FIGURE 9.7 Map of sampling locations and sample types in Lake Michigan. IIT = Illinois Institute of Technology; SWFP = South Water Filtration Plant.

depositional basins (Rossmann, 2002). When comparing these depositional basins throughout the lake, the mean Hg concentrations ranged between 120 and 160 ng g^{-1} and did not differ significantly among depositional areas. Hg fluxes measured across sampling sites also did not differ from basin to basin except for Green Bay, which was much higher largely because of riverine sources (Rossmann and Edgington, 2000). Regional atmospheric Hg deposition accounts for about 50% of the total Hg flux to Lake Michigan surficial sediments, with the remainder coming from tributary inputs (Rossmann, 2002).

MERCURY BIO-ACCUMULATION

Based on the longer food chains in Lake Michigan and the other Great Lakes, one might expect higher Hg concentrations in the food web; however, this is not the case. Bio-accumulation of Hg in plankton and fish in Lake Michigan have been studied, and total Hg concentrations in phytoplankton and zooplankton averaged 35.0 ng g^{-1} and 54.3 ng g^{-1}, respectively, with a biomagnification factor (BMF) of 1.55 between them. Bioaccumulation factors for phytoplankton and zooplankton (log Bioaccumulation factor (BAF), 5.03 and 5.22, respectively) are higher than for other lakes in the region, but fish concentrations are lower (Watras and Bloom, 1992; Monson and Brezonik, 1998; USEPA, 2004). Hg concentrations measured in adult coho salmon and lake trout averaged 69 ng g^{-1} and 139 ng g^{-1}, values well below Food and Drug Administration action levels of 1000 ng g^{-1}, but these fish Hg values still warrant restrictions on fish consumption based on EPA guidance for fish advisories. In fact, only 3% of lake trout and 9% of coho salmon fall into the unrestricted consumption category. Thus, fish Hg concentrations in Lake Michigan, although lower than those in smaller lakes in the region still pose a risk to human health.

TEMPORAL TRENDS

Sediment cores and comparisons of sediment concentrations at particular sites through time provide a temporal record of Hg deposition in the Great Lakes. Across most of the lakes, there have been declines in Hg deposition since peak Hg loads in the 1970s–1980s (USEPA, 2006). In Lake Michigan, there were peak Hg concentrations between 1930 and 1950 and a consistent decrease in Hg concentration between 1969 and 1975 that continued through 1981 (Cahill, 1981; Pirrone et al., 1998; USEPA, 2004). However, temporal trends differ in other Great Lakes. For example, surficial concentrations of Hg measured in Superior and Huron in 2001–2002 are similar to those measured in the 1960s–1970s, which is not consistent with emissions patterns (Gewurtz et al., 2008). Despite the declines in emissions over the past 10–20 years in the Great Lakes region, there has not been a concurrent decline in Hg in fish, bald eagles, and herring gulls. However, one analysis shows

slight declines in the Hg concentrations of salmon from Lake Ontario (French et al., 2006), and there have also been declines in fish Hg in lakes on Isle Royale in Lake Superior that have been attributed to decreases in sulfate deposition (Drevnick et al., 2007). However, concentrations remain high in Lake Michigan, and it is not clear what factors are responsible for this pattern. These findings suggest that there is not a direct linkage between atmospheric Hg deposition and biotic Hg contamination, possibly due to other controls or sources of MeHg to the food web and that perhaps legacy Hg in sediments is supplying MeHg to benthic and pelagic fauna (USEPA, 2006).

In summary, the linkages between Hg sources and biotic end points are poorly characterized in the Great Lakes, even in Lake Michigan, for which there has been a detailed research effort as part of the LMMBS. In Lake Michigan, atmospheric sources are considered to be extremely important relative to tributary inputs except for in Green Bay, where point sources are more important. Despite the locations of river inlets, the spatial distribution of Hg in water is homogeneous and in sediments appears highest in depositional basins associated with fine sediments. The source of MeHg to the food web is possibly methylation in the sediments; however, given the depths and stratification of the Great Lakes, it is possible that methylation in lake sediments is not closely linked to bio-accumulation processes in the epilimnion. Perhaps there are other zones of Hg transformation, such as methylation at the base of the thermocline, where an oxygen minimum exists because of decay of particulates, as has been proposed for the open ocean (Lamborg et al., 2002; Sunderland et al., 2009). Given the vast sizes and depths of these lakes, the mechanisms and processes controlling Hg fate and transfer in abiotic and biotic components are different from smaller, shallower lake ecosystems in the Great Lakes basin, where Hg methylation and bio-accumulation result in higher concentrations in the food web. Thus, despite the relatively long food chains, low productivity, and large surface areas for capturing deposition in the Great Lakes, the Hg concentrations in fish are generally not as high as those in the nearby smaller lakes or other smaller lake ecosystems in the region.

The Nyanza Superfund Site on the Sudbury River, Massachusetts

The earliest known hot spots of Hg contamination have been in the receiving waters of industrial point sources of Hg. Probably the most well known site was Minamata Bay in Japan, where the population was exposed to elevated Hg in a nearby fishing village (Harada, 1995). Other sites with point sources have often involved industrial facilities such as chlor-alkali plants that have discharged Hg into nearby surface or coastal waters. The Sudbury River in Massachusetts has been the receiving body for many organic and inorganic chemicals, including Hg from a number of companies that operated from 1917 to 1978 at the Nyanza site in Ashland, Massachusetts (Weiner and Shields, 2000). Hg was used as a catalyst in the production of dyes and approximately 2.3 metric tons of Hg were used per year at the site from 1940 to 1970. The disposed chemical wastes at the Nyanza site migrated via overland flow into nearby wetlands and eventually into the Sudbury River, about 330 m from the industrial site. The facility was closed in 1978, and in 1982 the site was placed on the National Priorities List. The EPA completed remediation, including excavation and capping of the contaminated soils at the site, in 1991. The EPA has since removed contaminated sediments from wetlands and drainage streams near the site, however Sudbury River sediments remain significantly contaminated with inorganic Hg for many miles downstream of the site.

The fate of Hg discharged at the Nyanza site has been complex both spatially and temporally (Beckvar et al., 2000; Frazier et al., 2000; Weiner and Shields, 2000; Waldron et al., 2000; Haines et al., 2003). Studies in 1989–1995 revealed that Hg sediment concentrations were highest in impoundments and slow-flowing reaches within a few miles downstream of the site, decreased with distance from the source, yet remained somewhat elevated above regional background concentrations even in Fairhaven Bay 30 km downstream (Figure 9.8). For study purposes, the river was divided into 10 distinct reaches, representing impoundments, flowing reaches, and reaches with wide bordering wetlands. Included in the 10 reaches of the river affected by the contamination are two former drinking-water reservoirs and the Great Meadow National Wildlife Refuge (GMNWR), named for the extensive wet meadow and scrub-shrub wetlands bordering the river channel in this reach. The reservoirs are located a short distance downstream of the source, and the sediment in these reservoirs has high concentrations of ionic Hg (average, 15 mg/kg dw). Within the GMNWR, located 25 km downstream of the source, Hg^{2+} in sediment is found in relatively low concentrations (average, ~1 mg kg^{-1} dw), but is broadly distributed across the bordering wetlands as a result of downstream flow from the site at seasonal high water when the wetlands are flooded. The exported Hg^{2+} has fueled methylation processes in the contaminated wetland 25 km downstream, where the Hg^{2+} is transformed into MeHg and bio-accumulated in the food web. In contrast, Hg^{2+} in the reservoirs that are closer to the original source appears to be far less available to methylation because of natural burial processes.

SPATIAL DISCONTINUITY

The Sudbury River system provides an interesting example of the source of Hg^{2+} being spatially disconnected from the major site of methylation, thus representing two of the mechanisms responsible for the transformation and fate of MeHg (see Figure 9.2). As a result, the concentrations of Hg^{2+} are not spatially correlated with the concentrations of MeHg in sediments (US Geological Survey [USGS], 2001).

In a study of stream discharge and concentration measurements (Waldron et al., 2000), Hg budgets were calculated and the annual mean load for total Hg increased sixfold in the river reaches just below the point source while the MeHg load did not increase. In the two reservoirs directly downstream of the source, net MeHg production was similar to levels in natural lakes. However, in the riparian wetland reach 25 km downstream, the calculated net MeHg production was 15 times greater than that reported in other studies in which there were no point sources of Hg. Since the total Hg loads in the reach immediately upstream of the wetland reach do not appear elevated, it appears that the increases in the wetlands were not related to current releases from the source or to mobilization from the contaminated sediments in the upstream reservoirs, but rather from Hg previously deposited in the wetland from the Nyanza site (Weiner and Shields, 2000). The differences in MeHg transport to the water column from the reservoirs as compared with the wetlands may be due to the diffusive processes in the reservoirs in comparison with periodic flooding in the wetlands (Waldron et al., 2000).

The spatial heterogeneity of Hg and McHg flux from sediments and water in the Sudbury River system also resulted in spatial discontinuities in MeHg bio-accumulation in biotic compartments. Haines et al. (2003) investigated Hg and MeHg in fish and their prey from four sites, including two reference sites upstream (Whitehall Reservoir and Cedar Street Bridge) and two downstream sites (Reservoir 2 and Sherman Bridge within the GMNWR) (see Figure 9.8). As expected, the THg concentrations in largemouth bass fillets were higher in Reservoir 2 than from Whitehall, and whole-body concentrations were higher at Sherman Bridge and Reservoir 2 than the two reference sites. However, the THg concentrations in large mouth bass in Reservoir 2 were lower than those measured in earlier studies from 1989–1990. Whole-body Hg concentrations in yellow perch were also highest in Reservoir 2 and lowest at Whitehall (Figure 9.9), as expected, but in the benthic feeding brown bullhead, Hg concentrations were not different between Whitehall and Reservoir 2. In smaller prey fish species, MeHg concentrations were significantly related to total Hg concentration in large mouth bass, although concentrations in prey and bass were not higher than those in other studies in uncontaminated sites, suggesting that the bio-availability of Hg to the aquatic food webs has declined (Haines et al., 2003).

The relative MeHg bio-availability in reservoirs versus the downstream wetlands was tested in earlier studies using mayfly nymphs in laboratory exposures and freshwater mussels in situ as bio-indicators of accumulation. The final concentrations of MeHg were the highest in nymphs exposed to wetland sediments, intermediate in reservoir sediments, and lowest in reference sediments (Naimo et al., 2000), again suggesting greater bio-accumulation potential in the contaminated wetlands. Mussel-tissue Hg concentrations were greatest in stations closest to the Nyanza site and decreased downstream (Beckvar et al., 2000). These contrasting results may be due to the difference between benthic and pelagic exposures. More

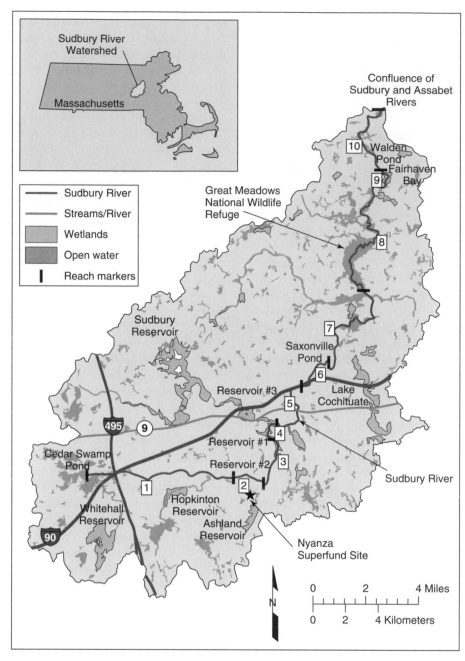

FIGURE 9.8 Map of the Sudbury River system in Massachusetts, showing study reaches in relation to the Nyanza chemical waste dump site, a point source of mercury to the river. (*Source:* Map created by USEPA Region 1 by Bart Hoskins and Gordon Hamilton.)

recent measurements of sediment and fish tissues have shown that this pattern has persisted for 10 years after the original studies. Hg in fish tissue within the reservoirs (approximately 5 km from the Nyanza site) remains elevated, is lower in the flowing reaches downstream, and increases as the river flows through the wetlands in the GMNWR 25 km from the site (see Figure 9.9). Note there is a lack of direct correlation between Hg in sediment and in fish tissues.

TEMPORAL PATTERNS AND ECOLOGIC RISK

The temporal change in Hg bio-accumulation and trophic transfer in the Sudbury River system illustrates the dynamic nature of contaminant fate in lotic systems. Just as in the case of polychlorinated biphenyls (PCBs) in the Hudson River, the transport of contaminant from a point source can create new source regions downstream (Connolly et al., 2000). In this case, the methylation in the wetland 25 km downstream of the Nyanza site is a new source region for MeHg to sites further downstream. Moreover, burial of contaminated sediments in the reservoirs upstream appear to be diminishing the Hg flux from those originally contaminated sites, as evidenced by the reductions in MeHg bio-accumulated by resident fish.

An Environmental Risk Assessment has been conducted based upon numerous water, sediment, avian, mammal,

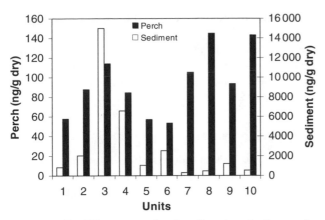

FIGURE 9.9 Total Hg concentrations in sediments and yellow perch across Reaches 2–10 in the Sudbury River, showing the elevated levels in fish 30 km downstream from the Hg source. (*Source:* Data from Bart Hoskins, USEPA Region 1.)

fish, and invertebrate endpoints (USEPA, 2007). Across the 10 sampled reaches of the river, the peak sediment Hg concentrations did not coincide with peak Hg concentrations in predator fish, suggesting that Hg in sediments is not spatially linked with bio-accumulation in the food web (see Figure 9.9). For each reach of the river, multiple end points were evaluated to assess risk using a weight–of-evidence approach. Despite the history of Hg contamination known to exist in the Sudbury River and the high risk posed by the contamination still existing in the sediments, most of the biotic end points, particularly the piscivore species, which are commonly targeted in mercury uptake studies, did not show any population-level risk in any of the reaches of the river. Based on this assessment, it appears that Hg contamination resulting from the Nyanza site discharges is not substantially impacting ecologic resources residing in or using the Sudbury River drainage. Note that

blood concentrations of Hg from insectivorous marsh birds inhabiting the wetlands in GMNWR were generally higher than blood from piscivorous birds (hooded mergansers and kingfishers) sampled in this area. It also appears that the potential for population-level risk for birds may be greatest at the end of the summer, when the adult birds have accumulated dietary Hg throughout the summer. At some sites with higher Hg loads, this may affect the ability of some adults to successfully return to the area and breed in the spring. This potential risk has been noted in the South River in Virginia, where tree swallows have been studied in relation to a point source of Hg (Brasso and Cristol, 2008).

Thus, Hg from point sources in river ecosystems can be transported downstream and result in the formation of new sediment hot spots in habitats that are more favorable to the methylation of Hg than the original source area. The Sudbury River is no longer a system in which Hg bio-accumulation is highest near the source. Transport and methylation downstream have resulted in a "moving target" of contamination and a much more complex remediation challenge. Nonetheless, Hg bio-accumulation and exposure have not resulted in any discernable enduring ecologic risk to aquatic and terrestrial organisms in the watershed.

Conclusions

The fate of Hg and MeHg in aquatic ecosystems has been studied in a wide range of ecosystem types, revealing that there are multiple mechanisms that facilitate elevated exposure of humans and wildlife to MeHg (Table 9.3). In some cases, the sources of Hg (via high deposition over large surface areas or point sources) are most significant; in other cases, conditions promoting Hg methylation in

TABLE 9.3
A Summary of Sources and Strength of Each Mercury Enhancement Mechanism for Each of the Case Study Systems Discussed in This Chapter

System	Hg sources	Transformation/ bio-availability	Bio-accumulation	Trophic transfer
Adirondacks	High atmospheric deposition	Strong	High	High (low productivity)
Everglades	High atmospheric deposition	Spatially variable	Spatially variable	Variable
Reservoirs	Atmospheric, point sources	Strong because of reservoir formation and fluctuation	High after reservoir formation	Variable
Great Lakes	Large area for receiving atmospheric deposition, also point sources	Major sources poorly known	Low	Potentially high because of long food chains
Sudbury River	Major point source	Spatially variable	Low	Low

sediments are optimal, such as in newly created and fluctuating reservoirs and in acidic environments. In still other cases, enhanced Hg supply and transformation processes are compounded by low productivity in the pelagic zone, resulting in increased bio-accumulation in the food web. The links between Hg methylation in sediments and uptake by aquatic organisms are poorly understood, particularly since Hg concentrations in sediments are often not spatially linked to bio-accumulation in fish, as seen in the Everglades and the Sudbury River. These linkages are perhaps best understood in small, shallow aquatic systems such as the Adirondack lakes but difficult to decipher in large physically complex systems such as the Great Lakes or complex flowing systems. Hg methylation has been most extensively studied in sediment, but there are systems in which water-column methylation processes may be equally important, as in some eutrophic reservoirs and

potentially in systems such as the Great Lakes. Studies of these greatly varied ecosystems in which Hg hot spots have been created by both natural and anthropogenic processes help us to understand and predict the conditions under which there might be ecologic and human risk due to Hg exposure.

Acknowledgments

This book chapter was supported by funds from the United States Department of Defense Strategic Environmental Research and Development Program (SERDP) Project ER-1503 and by National Institutes of Health Grant P42 ESO7373 from the National Institute of Environmental Health Sciences. Support was also provided by the New York State Energy Research and Development Authority and the National Science Foundation.

References

Abbot, M., and R. Kotchenruther. 2006. Atmospheric mercury inputs at Salmon Falls Creek Reservoir, Idaho—Where is the mercury coming from? *Proceedings of the Eighth International Conference on Mercury as a Global Pollutant*. DEStech Publications, Inc., Madison, WI.

Adams, R. M., M. R. Twiss, and C. T. Driscoll. 2009. Patterns of mercury accumulation among seston in lakes of the Adirondack Mountains, New York. *Environmental Science and Technology* 43: 4836–4842.

Aiken, G., M. Haitzer, J. N. Ryan, and K. Nagy. 2003. Interactions between dissolved organic matter and mercury in the Florida Everglades. *Journal De Physique IV* 107:29–32.

Aiken, G., D. P. Krabbenhoft, W. H. Orem, and C. C. Gilmour. 2006. Dissolved organic matter and mercury in the Everglades: implications for ecosystem restoration. In: *2006 Greater Everglades Ecosystem Restoration Conference*, p. 5. http://sofia.usgs.gov/geer/2006/index.html (accessed January 2012).

Albuquerque Palermo, E. F., D. Kasper, C. Castelo Branco, and O. Malm. 2006a. Inorganic and organic mercury in Fish upstreams and downstream of the dam at Tucurui Reservoir, Brazil. In: *Proceedings of the Eighth International Conference on Mercury as a Global Pollutant*. DEStech Publications, Inc., Madison, WI.

Albuquerque Palermo, E. F., D. Kasper, C. Castelo Branco, and O. Malm. 2006b. Trophic transfer of inorganic and organic mercury in fish from four reservoirs of the Paraiba Do Sul—Guandu River System, Brazil,—Conclusions. In: *Proceedings of the Eighth International Conference on Mercury as a Global Pollutant*. DEStech Publications, Inc., Madison, WI.

Anderson, M. R., D. A. Scruton, U. P. Williams, and L. R. Curtis. 1995. Mercury in the fish in the Smallwood Reservoir, Labrador, 21 years after impoundment. *Water, Air, and Soil Pollution* 80: 927–930.

Arnason, J. G., and B. Fletcher. 2003. A 40+ year record of Cd, Hg, Pb, and U deposition in sediments of Patroon Reservoir, Albany County, NY, USA. *Environmental Pollution* 123:383–91.

Atkeson, T. D., C. D. Pollman, and D. M. Axelrad. 2005. Recent trends in Hg emissions, deposition, and biota in the Florida Everglades: A monitoring and modeling analysis. In: N. Pirrone and K. Mahaffey, editors. *Dynamics of mercury pollution on regional and global scales: Atmospheric processes, human exposure around the world*. Springer, Norwell, MA, pp. 637–656.

Axelrad, D. M., T. D. Atkeson, T. Lange, C. C. Gilmour, C. D. Pollman, W. H. Orem, I. A. Mendelssohn, P. C. Frederick, D. P. Krabbenhoft, G. R. Aiken, D. G. Rumbold, D. J. Scheidt, and P. I. Kalla. 2007. Mercury monitoring, research and environmental assessment in South Florida. In: *2007 South Florida Environmental Report*. South Florida Water Management District, West Palm Beach, FL, chapter 3B.

Axelrad, D. M., T. D. Atkeson, C. D. Pollman, T. Lange, D. G. Rumbold, and K. Weaver. 2005. Mercury monitoring, research and environmental assessment in South Florida. In: G. Redfield, editor. *2005 South Florida Environmental Report*, Volume I. South Florida Water Management District, West Palm Beach, FL, chapter 2B.

Bates, A. L., W. H. Orem, J. W. Harvey, and E. C. Spiker. 2002. Tracing sources of sulfur in the Florida Everglades. *Journal of Environmental Quality* 31:287–299.

Becker, D. and G. N. Bigham. 1995. Distribution of mercury in the aquatic food-web of Onondaga Lake, New York. *Water, Air, and Soil Pollution*. 80: 563–571.

Beckvar, N., S. Salazar, M. Salazar, and K. Finkelstein. 2000. An in situ assessment of mercury contamination in the Sudbury River, Massachusetts, using transplanted freshwater mussels (Elliptio complanata). *Canadian Journal of Fisheries and Aquatic Science* 57:1103–1112.

Benoit, J. M., C. Gilmour, A. Heyes, R. P. Mason, and C. Miller. 2003. Geochemical and biological controls over methylmercury production and degradation in aquatic ecosystems. In: Y. Chai and O. C. Braids, editors. *Biogeochemistry of environmentally important trace elements*. ACS Symposium Series 835. American Chemical Society, Washington, DC, pp. 262–297.

Bodaly, R., K. Beaty, L. Hendzel, A. Majewski, M. Peterson, K. Rolfus, A. Penn, V. St. Louis, B. Hall, C. Matthews, K. Cherewyk, M. Mailman, J. Hurley, S. Schiff, and J. Venkiteswaran. 2004. Experimenting with hydroelectric reservoirs. *Environmental Science and Technology* 38:346A–352A.

Bodaly, R. A., R. E. Heckey, and R. J. P. Fudge. 1994. Increases in fish mercury in lakes flooded by the Churchill River diversion, northern Manitoba. *Canadian Journal of Fisheries and Aquatic Science* 41:682–691.

Branfireun, B., A. Heyes, and N. Roulet. 1996. The hydrology and methylmercury dynamics of a Precambrian Shield headwater peatland. *Water Resources Research* 32:1785–1794.

Branfireun, B., D. Krabbenhoft, D. Fowle, C. Mitchell, L. Neudhall, and J. Iraci. 2006. Does reservoir water-level fluctuation affect mercury methylation and transport in surrounding wetlands? *Proceedings of the Eighth International Conference on Mercury as a Global Pollutant.* DEStech Publications, Inc., Madison, WI.

Brasso, R. L., and D. A. Cristol. 2008. Effects of mercury exposure on the reproductive success of tree swallows (*Tachycineta bicolor*). *Ecotoxicology* 17:133–141.

Bushey, J. T., A. G. Nallana, M. R. Montesdeoca, and C. T. Driscoll. 2008. Mercury dynamics of a northern hardwood canopy. *Atmospheric Environment* 42:6905–6914.

Cabana, G., A. Tremblay, J. Kalff, and J. B. Rasmussen. 1994. Pelagic food-chain structure in Ontario lakes—a determinant of mercury levels in lake trout (*Salvelinus namaycush*). *Canadian Journal of Fisheries and Aquatic Science* 51:381–389.

Cahill, R. S. 1981. *Geochemistry of recent Lake Michigan sediments.* Illinois Institute of Natural Resources, Illinois State Geological Survey, Circular 517. Champaign, IL.

CCME (Canadian Council of Ministers of the Environment). 1999. *Canadian environmental quality guidelines.* Canadian Council of Ministers of the Environment. Winnipeg, MB.

Chen, C. Y., and C. L. Folt. 2005. High plankton biomass reduces mercury biomagnification. *Environmental Science and Technology* 39:115–121.

Chen, C. Y., A. Amirbahman, N. Fisher, G. Harding, C. Lamborg, D. Nacci, and D. Taylor. (2008). Methylmercury in marine ecosystems: spatial patterns and processes of production, bioaccumulation, and biomagnification. *Ecohealth* 5:399–408.

China Three Gorges Project Corporation. 2002. *Environmental benefit of Three Gorges Project.* http://www.ctgpc.com/ environmental/environmental_a.php (accessed August 21, 2008).

Choi, H. D., T. M. Holsen, and P. K. Hopke. 2008a. Atmospheric mercury (Hg) in the Adirondacks: Concentrations and sources. *Environmental Science and Technology* 42:5644–5653.

Choi, H. D., T. M. Holsen, and T. J. Sharac. 2008b. Mercury deposition in the Adirondacks: A comparison between precipitation and throughfall. *Atmospheric Environment* 42:1818–1827.

Choi, H. D., and T. M. Holsen. 2009. Gaseous mercury emissions from forest floor of the Adirondacks. *Environmental Pollution* 157:592–600.

Connolly, J. P., Zahakos, H. A., J. Benaman, C. K. Ziegler, J. R. Rhea, and K. Russell. 2000. A model of PCB fate in the upper Hudson River. *Environmental Science and Technology* 34:4076–4087.

Demers, J. D., C. T. Driscoll, T. J. Fahey, and J. B. Yavitt. 2007. Mercury cycling in litter and soil in different forest types in the Adirondack region, New York, USA. *Ecological Applications* 17:1341–1351.

Dittman, J. A., and C. T. Driscoll. 2009. Factors influencing changes in mercury concentrations in yellow perch (*Perca flavescens*) in Adirondack lakes. *Biogeochemistry* 93:179–196.

Dittman, J. A., J. B. Shanley, C. T. Driscoll, G. R. Aiken, A. T. Chalmers, and J. E. Towse. 2009. Ultraviolet absorbance as a proxy for total dissolved mercury in streams. *Environmental Pollution* 157:1953–1956. doi:10.1016/j.envpol. 2009. 01. 031.

Drevnick, P. E., D. E. Canfield, P. R. Gorski, A. L. C. Shinneman, D. R. Engstrom, D. C. Muir, G. R. Smith, P. J. Garrison, L. B. Cleckner, J. P. Hurley, R. B. Noble, R. R. Otter, and J. T. Oris. 2007. Deposition and cycling of sulfur controls mercury accumulation in Isle Royale fish. *Environmental Science and Technology* 41:7266–7272.

Driscoll, C. T., R. M. Newton, C. P. Gubala, J. P. Baker, and S. W. Christensen. 1991. Adirondack Mountains. In: D. F. Charles, editor. *Acidic deposition and aquatic ecosystems: Regional case studies.* Springer-Verlag, New York, pp. 133–202.

Driscoll, C. T., S. W. Effler, and S. M. Doerr. 1994. Changes in inorganic carbon chemistry and deposition of Onondaga Lake, New York. *Environmental Science and Technology* 28:1211–1218.

Driscoll, C. T., V. Blette, C. Yan, C. L. Schofield, R. Munson, and J. Holsapple. 1995. The role of dissolved organic carbon in the chemistry and bioavailability of mercury in remote Adirondack lakes. *Water, Air, and Soil Pollution* 80:499–508.

Driscoll, C. T., K. M. Driscoll, K. M. Roy, and M. J. Mitchell. 2003. Chemical response of lakes in the Adirondack region of New York to declines in acidic deposition. *Environmental Science and Technology* 37:2036–2042.

Driscoll, C. T., Y. -J. Han, C. Y. Chen, D. C. Evers, K. F. Lambert, T. M. Holsen, N. C. Kamman, and R. K. Munson. 2007. Mercury contamination in forest and freshwater ecosystems in the Northeastern United States. *BioScience* 57:17–28.

Eisler, R. 1987. Mercury hazards to fish, wildlife, and invertebrates: A synoptic review. *U. S. Fish and Wildlife Service Biological Report* 85 (1.10).

Essington, T. E. and J. N. Houser. 2003. The effect of whole-lake nutrient enrichment on mercury concentration in age-1 yellow perch. *Transactions of the American Fisheries Society* 132:57–68.

Evers, D. C., Y. -J. Han, C. T. Driscoll, N. C. Kamman, W. M. Goodale, K. F. Lambert, T. M. Holsen, C. Y. Chen, T. A. Clair, and T. J. Butler. 2007. Biological mercury hotspots in the Northeastern United States and Southeastern Canada. *BioScience* 57:1–15.

Frazier, B. E., J. G. Wiener, R. G. Rada, D. R. Engstrom. 2000. Stratigraphy and historic accumulation of mercury in recent depositional sediments in the Sudbury River, Massachusetts, U. S. A. *Canadian Journal of Fisheries and Aquatic Science* 57: 1062–1072.

French, T. D., L. M. Campbell, D. A. Jackson, J. M. Casselman, W. A. Scheider, and A. Hayton. 2006. Long-term changes in legacy trace organic contaminants and mercury in Lake Ontario salmon in relation to source controls, trophodynamics, and climatic variability. *Limnology and Oceanography* 51:2794–2807.

Gewurtz, S. B., L. Shen, P. A. Helm, J. Waltho, E. J. Reiner, S. Painter, I. D. Brindle, and C. H. Marvin. 2008. Spatial distributions of legacy contaminants in sediments of Lakes Huron and Superior. 2008. *Journal of Great Lakes Research* 34:153–168.

Gilmour, C., W. Orem, D. Krabbenhoft, S. Roy, and I. Mendelssohn. 2007. Preliminary assessment of sulfur sources, trends and effects in the Everglades. *2007 South Florida Environmental Report*. South Florida Water Management District, West Palm Beach, FL, appendix 3B-3.

Gilmour, C. C., E. A. Henry, and R. Mitchell. 1992. Sulfate stimulation of mercury methylation in freshwater sediments. *Environmental Science and Technology* 26:2281–2287.

Gorski, P. R., L. B. Cleckner, J. P. Hurley, M. E. Sierszen, and D. E. Armstrong. 2003. Factors affecting enhanced mercury bioaccumulation in inland lakes of Isle Royale National Park, USA. *Science of the Total Environment* 304:327–348.

Grigal, D. F. 2003. Mercury sequestration in forests and peatlands: a review. *Journal of Environmental Quality* 32: 393–405.

Guentzel, J. L., W. M. Landing, G. A. Gill, and C. D. Pollman. 1998. Mercury and major ions in rainfall, throughfall, and foliage from the Florida Everglades. *Science of the Total Environment* 213:43–51.

Guentzel, J. L., W. M. Landing, G. A. Gill, and C. D. Pollman. 2001. Processes influencing rainfall deposition of mercury in Florida. *Environmental Science and Technology* 35:863–873.

Guo, Y., X. Feng, H. Yan, and J. Guo. 2006. Effects of hydroelectric reservoirs on mercury transport in the Wujiang River. In: *Proceedings of the Eighth International Conference on Mercury as a Global Pollutant*. DEStech Publications, Inc., Madison, WI.

Haines, T. A., T. W. May, R. T. Finlayson, and S. E. Mierzykowski. 2003. Factors affecting food chain transfer of mercury in the vicinity of the Nyanza site, Sudbury River, Massachusetts. *Environmental Monitoring and Assessment* 86:211–232.

Haines, T. and A. M. Smith. 1998. Determination of the influence of impounds on bioavailability of mercury to fish, wildlife, and humans in the Penobscot River watershed, Maine. University of Maine, Orono, ME.

Hall, B. D., R. A. Bodaly, R. J. P. Fudge, J. W. M. Rudd, and D. M. Rosenberg. 1997. Food as the dominant pathway of methylmercury uptake by fish. *Water, Air, and Soil Pollution* 100:13–24.

Han, Y. and X. Feng. 2006. Total mercury in sediment profiles from a historical Hg-contaminated reservoir: Baihua Reservoir, Guizhou, China. In: *Proceedings of the Eighth International Conference on Mercury as a Global Pollutant*. DEStech Publications, Inc., Madison, WI.

Harada, M. 1995. Minamata disease—Methylmercury poisoning in Japan caused by environmental pollution. *Critical Reviews in Toxicology* 25:1–24.

He, T. X. Feng, Y. Guo, G. Qiu, Z. Li, L. Liang, and J. Lu. 2008. The impact of eutrophication on the biogeochemical cycling of mercury species in a reservoir: A case study from Hongfeng Reservoir, Guizhou. *China Environmental Pollution* 154:56–67.

Hudson, R. J. M., S. A. Gherini, C. J. Watras, and D. B. Porcella. 1994. Modeling the biogeochemical cycle of mercury in lakes: The mercury cycling model (MCM) and its application to the MTL study lakes. In: C. J. Watras and J. W. Huckabee, editors. *Mercury pollution: Integration and synthesis*. Lewis, Boca Raton, F, pp. 473–523.

Hurley, J. P., W. E. Cowell, M. M. Shafer, and P. E. Hughes. 1998a. Partitioning and transport of total and methyl mercury in the lower Fox River, Wisconsin. *Environmental Science and Technology* 32:1424–1432.

Hurley, J. P., W. E. Cowell, M. M. Shafer, and P. E. Hughes. 1998b. Tributary loading of mercury to Lake Michigan: importance of seasonal events and phase partitioning. *Science of the Total Environment* 213:129–137.

Kamman, N. C., N. M. Burgess, C. T. Driscoll, H. A. Simonin, W. Goodale, J. Linehan, R. Estabrook, M. Hutcheson, A. Major, A. M. Scheuhammer, and D. A. Scruton. 2005. Mercury in freshwater fish of northeast North America—A geographic perspective based on fish tissue monitoring databases. *Ecotoxicology* 14:163–180.

Karimi, R., C. Y. Chen, P. C. Pickhardt, N. S. Fisher, and C. L. Folt. 2007. Stoichiometric controls of mercury dilution by growth. *Proceedings of the National Academy of Sciences of the United States of America* 1104:7477–7482.

Keeler, G. 1994. Lake Michigan Urban Air Toxics Study. USEPA Atmospheric Research and Exposure Assessment Laboratory EPA/600/SR-94/191. USEPA, Research Triangle Park, NC.

Kelly, C. A., J. W. M. Rudd, R. A. Bodaly, N. T. Roulet, V. L. St. Louis, A. Heyes, T. R. Moore, S. Schiff, R. Aravena, K. J., B. Dyck, R. Harris, B. Warner, and G. Edwards. 1997. Increases in fluxes of greenhouse gases and methylHg following flooding of an experimental reservoir. *Environmental Science and Technology* 31:1334–1344.

Kuwabara, J. S., C. N. Alpers, M. Marvin-DiPasquale, B. Topping, J. Carter, A. R. Stewart, S. Fend, F. Parchaso, G. Moon, and D. P. Krabbenhoft. 2003. Sediment-water interactions affecting dissolved-mercury distributions in Camp Far West Reservoir, California. USGS Water Resources Investigations Report 03-4140. USGS, Reston, VA.

Lamars, L. P. M., H. B. M. Tomassen, and J. G. M. Roelofs. 1998. Sulfate-induced eutrophication and phytotoxicity in freshwater wetlands. *Environmental Science and Technology* 32:199–205.

Lamborg, C. H., W. F. Fitzgerald, J. O'Donnell, and T. Torgersen. 2002. A non-steady-state compartmental model of global-scale mercury biogeochemistry with interhemispheric atmospheric gradients. *Geochimica et Cosmochimica Acta* 66: 1105–1118.

Landing, W. M., J. J. Perry, J. L. Guentzel, G. A. Gill, and C. D. Pollman. 1995. Relationships between the atmospheric deposition of trace-elements, major ions, and mercury in Florida—the Fams Project (1992–1993). *Water, Air, and Soil Pollution* 80:343–352.

Landis, M. S., and G. J. Keeler. 2002. Atmospheric mercury deposition to Lake Michigan during the Lake Michigan Mass Balance Study. *Environmental Science and Technology* 36:4518–4517.

Landis, M. S., A. F. Vette, and G. J. Keeler. 2002. Atmospheric mercury in the Lake Michigan Basin: influence of the Chicago/Gary urban area. *Environmental Science and Technology* 36:4508–4517.

Lange, T. 2006. Trends in mercury in Everglades fish. Report from Florida Fish and Wildlife Conservation Commission (FFWCC).

Lorey, P., and C. T. Driscoll. 1999. Historical trends of mercury deposition in Adirondack lakes. *Environmental Science and Technology* 33:718–722.

Malm, O. 2006. Mercury in different Amazon reservoirs, Brazil. In: *Proceedings of the Eighth International Conference on Mercury as a Global Pollutant*. DEStech Publications, Inc., Madison, WI.

Marvin, C. H., M. N. Charlton, E. J. Reiner, T. Kolic, K. MacPherson, G. A. Stern, E. Braekevelt, J. F. Estenik, L. Thiessen, and S. Painter. 2002. Surficial sediment contamination in Lakes Erie and Ontario: A comparative analysis. *Journal of Great Lakes Research* 28:437–450.

Marvin, C., S. Painter, and R. Rossman. 2004a. Spatial and temporal patterns in mercury contamination in sediments of the Laurentian Great Lakes. *Environmental Research* 95:351–362.

Marvin, C., S. Painter, D. Williams, V. Richardson, R. Rossman, P. Van Hoof. 2004b. Spatial and temporal trends in surface water and sediment contamination in the Laurentian Great Lakes. *Environmental Pollution* 129:131–144.

Marvin-DiPasquale, M., J. Agee, C. McGowan, R. Oremland, M. Thomas, D. Krabbenhoft, and C. Gilmour. 2000. Methyl-mercury degradation pathways: A comparison among three mercury-impacted ecosystems. *Environmental Science and Technology* 34:4908–4916.

Mason, R. P., N. M. Lawson, and G. R. Sheu. 2000. Annual and seasonal trends in mercury deposition in Maryland. *Atmospheric Environment* 34:1691–1701.

Mason, R. P., J. R. Reinfelder, and F. M. M. Morel. 1996. Uptake, toxicity, and trophic transfer of mercury in a coastal diatom. *Environmental Science and Technology* 30:1835–1845.

Mason, R. P., K. R. Rolfhus, and W. F. Fitzgerald. 1995. Bioaccumulation of mercury and methylmercury. *Water, Air, and Soil Pollution* 80:915–919.

Mason, R. P., and K. A. Sullivan. 1997. Mercury in Lake Michigan. *Environmental Science and Technology* 31:942–947.

Mason, R. P., and A. Y. Sveinsdottir. 2003. Mercury and methylmercury concentrations in water and largemouth bass in Maryland reservoirs. Maryland Department of Natural Resources. Annapolis, MD. http://www.dnr.state.md.us/streams/pubs/ad-03-1_Hg_bass.pdf (accessed August 21, 2008).

Miles, C. J., and L. E. Fink. 1998. Monitoring and mass budget for mercury in the Everglades Nutrient Removal Project. *Archives of Environmental Contamination and Toxicology* 35:549–557.

Miller, E. K., A. Vanarsdale, G. J. Keeler, A. Chalmers, L. Poissant, N. C. Kamman, and R. Brulotte. 2005. Estimation and mapping of wet and dry mercury deposition across northeastern North America. *Ecotoxicology* 14:53–70.

Monson, B. A. and P. L. Brezonik. 1998. Seasonal patterns of mercury species in water and plankton from softwater lakes in northeastern Minnesota. *Biogeochemistry* 40:147–162.

Muresan, B., D. Cossa, and S. Richard. 2006 Monomethylmercury in an artificial tropical reservoir. In: *Proceedings of the Eighth International Conference on Mercury as a Global Pollutant*. DEStech Publications, Inc., Madison, WI.

Naimo, T. J., J. G. Wiener, W. G. Cope, and N. S. Bloom. 2000. Bioavailability of sediment-associated mercury to Hexagenia mayflies in a contaminated floodplain river. *Canadian Journal of Fisheries and Aquatic Science* 57:1092–1102.

National Air Deposition Program. 2008. http://nadp.sws.uiuc.edu/mdn (accessed January 2012).

Niklasson, T., L. Tuomola, E. de Castro e Silva, O. Malm, and L. Hylander. 2006. Mercury accumulation in fish in relation to abiotic characteristics and carbon source in a five-year old Brazilian Reservoir. In: *Proceedings of the Eighth International Conference on Mercury as a Global Pollutant*. DEStech Publications, Inc., Madison, WI.

Painter, S., C. Marvin, F. Rosa, T. B. Reynoldson, M. N. Charlton, M. Fox, P. A. L. Thiessen, and J. F. Estenik. 2001. Sediment contamination in Lake Erie: A 25-year retrospective analysis. *Journal of Great Lakes Research* 27:434–448.

Park, J., S. Oh, Mi. Shin, M. Kim. 2008. Seasonal variation in dissolved gaseous mercury and total mercury. *Environmental Pollution* 154:12–20.

Pickhardt, P. C., C. L. Folt, C. Y. Chen, B. Klaue, and J. D. Blum. 2002. Algal blooms reduce the uptake of toxic methylmercury in freshwater food webs. *Proceedings of the National Academy of Sciences of the United States of America* 99:4419–4423.

Pirrone, N., I. Allegrini, G. J. Keeler, J. O. Nriagu, R. Rossman, and J. A. Robbins. 1998. Historical records of mercury pollution in North America. *Atmospheric Environment* 32:929–940.

Power, M., G. M. Klein, K. R. R. A. Guiguer, and M. K. H. Kwan. 2002. Mercury accumulation in the fish community of a sub-Arctic lake in relation to trophic position and carbon sources. *Journal of Applied Ecology* 39: 819–830.

Rea, A. W., S. E. Lindberg, T. Scherbatskoy, and G. J. Keeler. 2002. Mercury accumulation in foliage over time in two northern mixed-hardwood forests. *Water, Air, and Soil Pollution* 133:49–67.

Restoration Coordination and Verification. 2007. *Comprehensive Everglades Restoration Plan System-wide Performance Measures.* http://www.evergladesplan.org/pm/recover/eval_team_perf_measures.aspx (accessed January 2012).

Rimmer, C. C., K. P. McFarland, D. C. Evers, E. K. Miller, Y. Aubry, D. Busby, and R. J. Taylor. 2005. Mercury concentrations in Bicknell's Thrush and other insectivorous passerines in montane forest of northeastern North America. *Ecotoxicology* 14:223–240.

Rossmann, R. 2002. Lake Michigan 1994–1996 surficial sediment mercury. *Journal of Great Lakes Research* 28:65–76.

Rossmann, R., and D. N. Edgington. 2000. Mercury in 1987–1990 Green Bay, Lake Michigan surficial sediments. *Journal of Great Lakes Research* 26:323–339.

Rumbold, D. G., and L. E. Fink. 2006. Extreme spatial variability and unprecedented methylmercury concentrations within a constructed wetland. *Environmental Monitoring and Assessment* 112:115–135.

Rumbold, D. G., L. E. Fink, K. A. Laine, S. L. Niemczyk, T. Chandrasekhar, S. D. Wankel, and C. Kendall. 2002. Levels of mercury in alligators (*Alligator mississippiensis*) collected along a transect through the Florida Everglades. *Science of the Total Environment* 297:239–252.

Rumbold, D. G., T. R. Lange, D. M. Axelrad, and T. D. Atkeson. 2008. Ecological risk of methylmercury in Everglades National Park, Florida, USA. *Ecotoxicology* 17:632–641.

Sellers, P., C. Kelly, J. Rudd, and A. MacHutchon. 1996. Photodegradation of Methylmercury in Lakes. *Nature* 380:694–696.

Selvendiran, P., C. T. Driscoll, M. R. Montesdeoca, and J. T. Bushey. 2008a. Inputs, storage and transport of total and methyl mercury in two temperate forest wetlands. *Journal of Geophysical Research* 113:G00C01, doi:10. 1029/2008JG000739.

Selvendiran, P., C. T. Driscoll, J. T. Bushey, and M. R. Montesdeoca. 2008b. Wetland influence on mercury fate and transport in a temperate forested watershed. *Environmental Pollution* 154:46–55, doi:10.1016/j.envpol.2007.12.005.

Shetagne, R., and Verdon, R. Post-impoundment evolution of fish mercury levels at the La Grande Complex, Quebec, Canada (from 1978–1996). 1999. In: Lucotte, M. R. Schetagne, N. Therien, C. Langlois, and A. Tremblay, eds. *Mercury in the biogeochemical cycle: Natural environments and hydroelectric reservoirs of northern Quebec.* Springer-Verlag, Berlin.

Smolders, A. J. P., L. P. Lamars, C. H. Lucassen, G. van der Velde, and J. G. Roelofs. 2006. Internal eutrophication: how it works and what to do about it—a review. *Chemistry and Ecology* 22:93–111.

Snodgrass, J. W., C. H. Jagoe, A. L. Bryan, H. A. Brant, and J. Burger. 2000. Effects of trophic status and wetland morphology, hydroperiod, and water chemistry on mercury concentration in fish. *Canadian Journal of Fisheries and Aquatic Science* 57:171–180.

Sorenson, J. A., L. Kallemyn, and M. Sydor. 2005. Relationship between mercury accumulation in young-of-the-year yellow perch and water level fluctuations. *Environmental Science and Technology* 39:9237–9243.

Stemberger, R. S., and C. Y. Chen. 1998. Fish tissue metals and zooplankton assemblages of northeastern US lakes. *Canadian Journal of Fisheries and Aquatic Sciences* 55:339–352.

St. Louis, V., C. A. Kelly, E. Duchemin, J. Rudd, and D. Rosenburg. 2000. Reservoir surfaces as sources of greenhouse gases to the atmosphere: A global estimate. *BioScience* 50:766–775.

St. Louis, V., J. Rudd, C. Kelly, R. Bodaly, M. Peterson, K. Beaty, R. Hesslein, A. Heyes, and A. Majewski. 2004. The rise and fall of mercury methylation in an experimental reservoir. *Environmental Science and Technology* 38:1348–1358.

Sullivan, K. A., and R. P. Mason. 1998. The concentration and distribution of mercury in Lake Michigan. *Science of the Total Environment* 213:213–228.

Sullivan, T. J., I. J. Fernandez, A. T. Herlihy, C. T. Driscoll, T. C. McDonnell, K. U. Snyder, and J. W. Sutherland. 2006. Acid-base characteristics of soils in the Adirondack Mountains, New York. *Soil Science Society of America Journal* 70:141–152.

Sunderland, E. M., D. P. Krabbenhoft, J. W. Moreau, S. A. Strode, and W. M. Landing. 2009. Mercury sources, distribution, and bioavailability in the North Pacific Ocean: Insights from data and models. *Global Biogeochemical Cycles* 23: GB2010, doi:10. 1029/2008GB003425.

Swackhamer, D. L., R. F. Pearson, and S. P. Schottler. 1998. Toxaphene in the Great Lakes. *Chemosphere* 37:2545–2561.

Todorova, S. G., C. T. Driscoll, D. A. Matthews, S. W. Effler, M. E. Hines, and E. A. Henry. 2009. Evidence for regulation of monomethyl mercury by nitrate in a seasonally stratified, eutrophic lake. *Environmental Science and Technology* 43:6572–6578.

USEPA. 1996. South Florida ecosystem assessment interim report: Monitoring for adaptive management: Implications for ecosystem restoration. Region 4 Science and Ecosystem Support Division and office of Research and Development. EPA-904-96-008. U.S. Environmental Protection Agency, Washington, DC. http:www.epa.gov/region4/sesd/sflea/sfleair.pdf (accessed January 2008).

USEPA. 2004. *Results of the Lake Michigan Mass Balance Study: Mercury data report.* EPA 905 R-01-012. Great Lakes National Program Office, Chicago, IL.

USEPA. 2006. *Great Lakes binational toxics strategy management assessment for mercury.* Great Lakes National Program Office, Chicago, IL.

USEPA. 2007a. *Draft supplemental baseline ecological risk assessment: Nyanza Superfund Site operable unit IV Sudbury River mercury contamination.* Avatar work order number 0023.001.02.

USEPA. 2007b. *Everglades ecosystem assessment, water management and quality, eutrophication, mercury contamination, soils and habitat: Monitoring for adaptive management.* R-EMAP status report EPA 904-R-07-001, August 2007. US-EPA, Region 4, Athens, GA.

USGS. 2001. *A national pilot study of mercury contamination of aquatic ecosystems along multiple gradients: Bioaccumulation in fish.* Biological Science Report UGSG/BRD/BSR-2001–0009 September 2001.

Verta, M., S. Rekolainen, and K. Kinnunen. 1986. *Causes of increased fish mercury levels in Finnish reservoirs.* Publications of the Water Research Institute, National Board of Waters, Finland, No. 65.

Vette, A. F., M. S. Landis, and G. J. Keeler. 2002. Deposition and emission of gaseous mercury to and from Lake Michigan during the Lake Michigan mass balance study (July, 1994—October, 1995). *Environmental Science and Technology* 36:4525–4532.

Waldron, M. C., J. A. Colman, and R. F. Breault. 2000. Distribution, hydrologic transport, and cycling of total mercury and methyl mercury in a contaminated river-reservoir-wetland system (Sudbury River, eastern Massachusetts). *Canadian Journal of Fisheries and Aquatic Science* 57:1080–1091.

Ward, D. M., K. H. Nislow, C. Y. Chen, and C. L. Folt. 2010. Rapid, efficient growth reduces mercury concentrations in stream-dwelling Atlantic salmon. *Transactions of the American Fisheries Society* 139:1–10.

Watras, C. J., and N. S. Bloom. 1992. Mercury and methylmercury in individual zooplankton: implications for bioaccumulation. *Limnology and Oceanography* 37:1313–1318.

Watras, C. J., R. C. Back, S. Halrvosen, R. J. M. Hudson, K. A. Morrison, and S. P. Wente. 1998. Bioaccumulation of mercury in pelagic freshwater food webs. *Science of the Total Environment* 219:183–208.

Weiner, J. G. and P. J. Shields. 2000. Mercury in the Sudbury River (Massachusetts, U. S. A.): pollution history and a synthesis of recent research. *Canadian Journal of Fisheries and Aquatic Science* 57:1053–1061.

World Commission on Dams. 2000. Case Study: Tucuruí Hydropower Complex, Brazil. Final Report: November 2000. World Commission on Dams. Cape Town, South Africa. http://www.dams.org/docs/kbase/studies/csbrmain.pdf (accessed August 22, 2008).

Yu, D., X. Shi, H. Wang, W. Sun, E. Warner, and Q. Liu. 2007. National scale analysis of soil organic carbon storage in China based on Chinese soil taxonomy. *Pedosphere* 17:11–18.

Zhang, J., D. Wang, and L. He. 2006. Species transformations of mercury in wet-dry alteration soils in the drawdown zone of the Three Gorges Reservoir, China In: *Proceedings of the Eighth International Conference on Mercury as a Global Pollutant.* DEStech Publications, Inc., Madison, WI.

CHAPTER 10

Mercury in the Marine Environment

FRANK J. BLACK, CHRISTOPHER H. CONAWAY,
and A. RUSSELL FLEGAL

The study of mercury in marine ecosystems is necessary to understand and minimize the chronic, sublethal toxicity due to exposure to organomercury in the marine environment and marine resources. The combination of the complex biogeochemical cycling of mercury with similarly complex marine ecologic processes make this study challenging, requiring a multitude of scientific approaches to answer specific questions about mercury in marine ecosystems. Some of these questions relate to fish consumption, with the most obvious being "Which fish are the healthiest to eat" and "Is there a limit to how much is healthy?" Other questions relate to the source of mercury in the marine environment and the degree to which the mercury found in fish is from anthropogenic versus natural sources. These questions, in turn, are related to our ability to mitigate mercury contamination in

the marine environment and potential increases in mercury concentrations in fish. In addition, there is a need to understand how long-term and large-scale trends in marine ecosystems affect the biogeochemical cycling of mercury. In this chapter, we discuss some of these questions and summarize information on mercury in marine ecosystems, including the sources of mercury in marine environments, the transformation and methylation of mercury, its uptake into biological systems, and its biomagnification in marine food webs.

Environmental and Human Health Concerns

The primary motivations for researching mercury in the environment are related to its toxicity. The majority of the human population lives within 100 km of the ocean, and the benefits from marine ecosystems are greater than those from all other ecosystems combined (Costanza et al., 1997). Those benefits include the consumption of seafood, which has many health benefits. However, the consumption of marine fish and shellfish accounts for more than 90% of the population-wide mercury intake in the United States (Sunderland, 2007), as is true in much of the world. Accordingly, the study of mercury biogeochemistry and environmental toxicology in marine systems is of great importance for both human and environmental health.

While mercury has long been recognized as a potent toxin, full appreciation of the threat of mercury contamination from environmental exposures has occurred only within the latter half of the past century (Clarkson and Magos, 2006). The environmental mercury problem was first documented in the 1950s in Minamata Bay, Japan (Harada, 1995), where many individuals suffered severe mercury poisoning from their consumption of seafood with elevated levels of methylmercury (5–35 µg g^{-1}). That contamination was traced to wastewater discharges of monomethylmercury to the bay from a chemical plant producing acetaldehyde and vinyl chloride. Since then, other cases of mercury poisoning have been chronicled, including in native populations of Arctic and sub-Arctic regions who consume relatively high amounts of fish, marine mammals, and marine birds (Burger et al., 2007; Van Oostdam et al., 2005). More recently, the focus has shifted to the potential sublethal or long-term toxicity of mercury to individuals consuming relatively large amounts of marine fish, and in a few cases marine mammals (National Research Council, 2000).

The greatest concern for human health related to environmental mercury pollution is the consumption of fish by the most susceptible populations, specifically pregnant women and children (Clarkson and Magos, 2006; Mergler et al., 2007). The National Research Council (2000) estimated that ~60,000 children born in the United States each year are at risk of neurodevelopmental problems associated with their in utero exposure to mercury from their mother's consumption of fish, while the Centers for Disease Control and Prevention (2001) reported that as a result of fish consumption nearly 1 in 10 women in the United States could have blood mercury levels that are hazardous for a developing fetus. As a result, fish consumption advisories have been issued by government agencies for numerous species of fish in areas of Canada, Europe, and all 50 states in the United States (e.g., US Environmental Agency [US EPA], 2007). Thus, while fish represent an important protein source for large segments of the population, and the consumption of fish has many health benefits, it is also the pathway responsible for most human exposure to mercury.

The growing awareness of mercury's sublethal toxicity in humans has increased concerns about mercury's adverse effects on other organisms. Ecosystems can be threatened by elevated environmental mercury levels, with higher trophic-level organisms considered most at risk. These include top predator fish, as well as piscivorous birds and mammals, which can have high body burdens of mercury (often described as "potentially toxic") because of the biomagnification of mercury in aquatic food chains (Brookens et al., 2008; Scheuhammer et al., 2007; Sonne et al., 2007). Some of the adverse effects associated with these elevated mercury concentrations are reduced reproductive success in fish and birds, altered behavioral traits or neurologic effects in marine mammals, and immunotoxic effects in birds and marine mammals (Scheuhammer et al., 2007).

Mercury in Saline Waters

Mercury is a naturally occurring element, and is released to the environment by a variety of natural and anthropogenic processes (this book, chapter 2). It is then distributed and redistributed by various processes, including atmospheric exchange with both terrestrial and oceanic compartments, export from terrestrial and freshwater systems to the ocean, and deposition and burial in sediments (Sunderland and Mason, 2007). Mercury concentrations in the ocean are typically in the picomolar to subpicomolar range, making quantification of this element an analytical challenge.

There are four principal forms of mercury found in the marine environment: elemental mercury, inorganic Hg(II), monomethylmercury (MMHg) and dimethylmercury (DMHg). Analytically, the sum of all of these forms is referred to as "total mercury." Dissolved gaseous mercury (DGM) is a combination of volatile forms (elemental and dimethylmercury) but is often measured only as dissolved elemental mercury because of the relatively low concentration of DMHg. Reactive mercury is an operationally defined fraction of easily reducible mercury under acidic conditions that includes some fraction of inorganic Hg(II) and perhaps some organomercury. Depth profiles for various mercury species in the North Pacific and the equatorial and South Atlantic are shown in Figures 10.1–10.3.

Elemental mercury, Hg(0), is volatile and in seawater usually exists as a dissolved gas at subpicomolar concentrations. In rare cases, Hg(0) may be present as a liquid, which can occur in association with marine geothermal metal-bearing fluids (Dekov, 2007; Stoffers et al., 1999) or anthropogenic discharges to the ocean, such as the amphoras of Sharm El Sheikh in the Red Sea or the wreck of the German U-boat U-864 off the coast of Fedje, Norway.

Inorganic Hg(II) exists as a variety of dissolved complexes in saline aquatic environments. Ligands important in binding mercury include chloride, inorganic reduced sulfur species, and dissolved organic matter (including thiol functional groups), with binding to colloidal and particulate matter also being important (Dyrssen and Wedborg, 1991; Han and Gill, 2005; Lamborg et al., 2004). The complexation of Hg(II) in aquatic environments (both oxic and anoxic) has been reviewed previously, and a more thorough treatment of the subject can found elsewhere (Dyrssen and Wedborg, 1991; Mason et al., 1996; Fitzgerald et al., 2007; Skyllberg, 2008).

Organic mercury species include MMHg and DMHg. MMHg is only detectable in open ocean waters at very low concentrations, and is likely present in saline water as a dissolved complex bound to chloride, organic matter, or reduced sulfur species

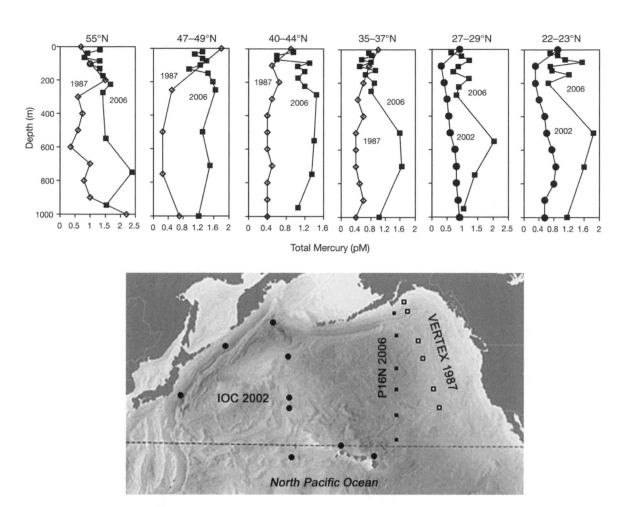

FIGURE 10.1 Total Hg depth profiles and map showing sample locations in the North Pacific for the VERTEX cruise (July–August, 1987), the IOC cruise (May–June, 2002), and the P16N cruise (March 2006). (*Source:* Reprinted/adapted from Sunderland et al., 2009, with permission from the American Geophysical Union.)

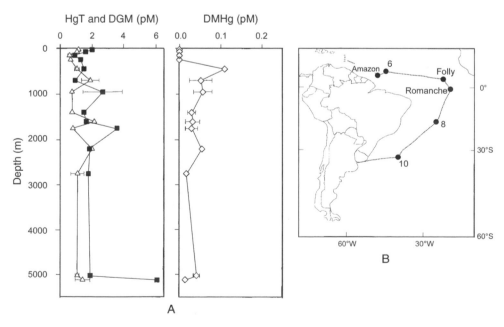

FIGURE 10.2 Depth profiles of DGM (open triangles), total Hg (HgT; solid squares), and DMHg (open diamonds) at Station 8 in the equatorial Atlantic measured in 1996 (Mason and Sullivan, 1999). The cruise track and station locations are shown on the accompanying map. (Reprinted/adapted, with permission, from Elsevier.)

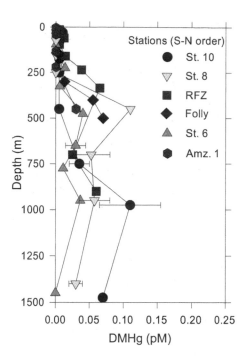

FIGURE 10.3 Depth profiles of DMHg to 1500 m in the South and equatorial Atlantic measured in 1996 (Mason and Sullivan, 1999). See figure 10.2 for map with station locations. RFZ = Romanche Fracture Zone; Amz. = Amazon. (Reprinted, with permission, from Elsevier.)

(Dyrssen and Wedborg, 1991; Mason et al., 1996; Amirbahman et al., 2002). DMHg is present as a dissolved gas in saline waters, and it is the predominant methylated form of mercury in much of the open ocean below the thermocline (Cossa et al., 1994, 1997; Horvat et al., 2003; Mason and Fitzgerald, 1993; Mason et al., 1995, 1998; Mason and Sullivan, 1999; St. Louis et al., 2007). Exceptions to this trend are in surface waters, many coastal environments, and the Mediterranean Sea, all areas where MMHg concentrations are generally greater than DMHg concentrations. DMHg is found at depth in the water column at femtomolar to subpicomolar concentrations, but is rarely detectable in the mixed layer (Pongratz and Heumann, 1998). Depth profiles for DMHg in the equatorial and South Atlantic are shown in Figures 10.2 and 10.3. DMHg has generally not been detected in the coastal zone waters, with the exception of high Arctic marine surface waters (St. Louis et al., 2007; Kirk et al., 2008) and upwelled coastal waters off California (Conaway et al., 2009). Water column concentrations of DMHg and MMHg, and the percentage of mercury existing in a methylated form, are summarized in Table 10.1 for various oceanic locations.

Mercury in Estuarine and Coastal Waters

Mercury concentrations are higher in coastal and estuary waters than in the open ocean, with unfiltered total mercury concentrations in the nearshore typically within the range 1–40 pM (Baeyens et al., 1998; Benoit et al., 1998; Coquery et al., 1997; Cossa et al., 1997; Laurier et al., 2003a; Leermakers et al., 1995, 2001; Mason et al., 1999; Rolfhus and Fitzgerald, 2001; Stordal et al., 1996). Considerably

higher total mercury concentrations are found in contaminated coastal and estuary environments, where they can exceed 500 pM (Balcom et al., 2008; Conaway et al., 2003; Faganeli et al., 2003; Heyes et al., 2004). Such trends are not surprising, given that estuaries and coastal zones are highly influenced by industrial and other human activities, including mercury pollution.

The higher mercury concentrations in the nearshore are also the result of the greater importance of terrestrial runoff as a source of mercury to coastal waters relative to the open ocean, and are thus controlled by sediment transport and resuspension. Inorganic mercury in the water column tends to be associated with particulate matter, with particle distribution coefficients (K_d) typically in the range 10^5–10^6 for estuary and coastal waters (Baeyens et al., 1998; Balcom et al., 2008; Benoit et al., 1998; Choe et al., 2003; Conaway et al., 2003; Coquery et al., 1997; Laurier et al., 2003a; Leermakers et al,. 1995, 2001; Stordal et al., 1996). As a consequence, most transport of mercury within aquatic systems occurs via the particulate phase, and approximately 90% of the riverine inputs of mercury to the ocean are deposited in coastal sediments (Sunderland and Mason, 2007). Estuaries are sinks for inorganic, particle-associated mercury, but can be net sources of MMHg (Benoit et al., 1998; Faganeli et al., 2003; Macleod et al., 2005; Mason et al., 1999).

Mercury in the Open Ocean

The distribution and mass balance of total mercury in the water column of the oceans have been reviewed elsewhere (Lamborg et al., 2002; Mason and Sheu, 2002; Laurier et al., 2004; Fitzgerald et al., 2007; Strode et al., 2007; Sunderland and Mason, 2007; Selin et al., 2008). Typical depth profiles of total mercury in the North Pacific and tropical South Atlantic are shown in Figures 10.1 and 10.2, respectively. They illustrate vertical variations and the distribution of total mercury in the open ocean, which are controlled by the magnitude of different sources and sinks at the boundaries of the marine environment, as well as water column processes. These include particle scavenging, remineralization of sinking particles, sediment diagenesis, water-column stratification, vertical mixing, ventilation, and horizontal advection along isopycnals (Laurier et al., 2004).

The principle sources and transport processes of total mercury to the open ocean are: (1) atmospheric deposition and (2) runoff from coastal and freshwater systems followed by advection offshore (Lamborg et al., 2002; Mason and Sheu, 2002; Sunderland and Mason, 2007). Mercury from hydrothermal vents, submarine volcanic activity, and weathering of oceanic crust and other submarine geologic structures are additional potentially important natural sources, but their contributions are not well known. A global mass balance developed by Sunderland and Mason (2007) estimating the magnitude of important fluxes of total mercury between environmental reservoirs for both preindustrial times and the present is shown in Figure 10.4

Preindustrial budget

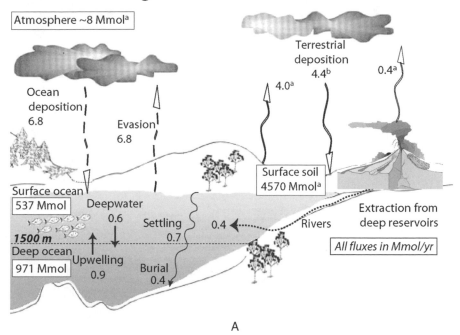

Present-day budget

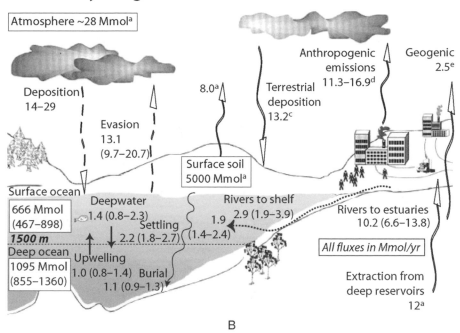

FIGURE 10.4 Global total mercury budget estimated under preindustrial and current conditions. In the present-day budget, river fluxes shown refer to the amounts of mercury deposited in each region (estuaries, shelf, open ocean), not the total flux (sum >14 Mmol). [a]From Mason and Sheu (2002). [b]Calculated by assuming the preindustrial atmosphere is at steady state. [c]Estimated from sediment core data showing that contemporary atmospheric deposition to terrestrial systems is approximately 3 times greater than preindustrial deposition (Fitzgerald et al., 1998). [d]Lower end of range is year 2000 global anthropogenic emissions from Pacyna et al. (2006). Upper limit of anthropogenic emissions were used in GEOS-Chem simulations and include additional sources described by Selin et al. (2007). [e]Estimate derived by Selin et al. (2007). 90% confidence intervals are given in parentheses. (*Source:* Reprinted from Sunderland and Mason, 2007, with permission from the American Geophysical Union.)

TABLE 10.1

Concentrations of Monomethylmercury, Dimethylmercury, and Total Methylated Mercury for Various Locations and Depths in the Ocean

Location	Depth (m)	MMHg (fM)[a]	DMHg (fM)	Σ Methylated Hg (fM)[b]	%HgT as Σ methylated[a]	References
North Pacific	Surface (<150)	NA	NA	100 ± 50 (<50–280)	10 ± 5 (2–24)	Sunderland et al., 2009
	Deep (>150)	NA	NA	260 ± 110 (60–470)	19 ± 6 (5–29)	
	All	NA	NA	170 ± 120 (<50–470)	15 ± 7 (2–29)	
Equatorial Pacific	Surface (<150)	≤50	<5	nd	nd	Mason and Fitzgerald, 1990
	Deep (≥150)	100 ± 130 (<50–580)	200 ± 170 (30–670)	240 ± 230 (30–900)	18 ± 14 (<1–61)	Mason and Fitzgerald, 1991
	All	90 ± 120 (<50–580)	160 ± 170 (<5–670)	200 ± 230 (nd–900)	15 ± 15 (<1–61)	Mason and Fitzgerald, 1993
North Atlantic	Surface (<200)	—[c]	30 ± 30 (<10–80)	30 ± 30 (<10–80)[c]	0–7[d]	Mason et al., 1998
	Deep (>200)	—[c]	130 ± 80 (10–320)	130 ± 80 (10–320)[c]	1–23[d]	
	All	—[c]	80 ± 70 (<10–320)	80 ± 70 (<10–320)[c]	3 ± 4 (0–23)[d]	
South, equatorial Atlantic	Surface (<150)	<50	<10	nd	0	Mason and Sullivan, 1999
	Deep (>150)	<50–200	<10–110	nd–240	<1–10	
Mediterranean Sea	Surface (<~150)	NA	NA	<15–240	NA	Cossa et al., 2009
	Deep (>150)	NA	NA	100–430	NA	
	All	NA	NA	150 ± 110 (<15–430)	14 ± 10 (<1–37)	
	Surface (≤60)	180 ± 100 (50–520)	0.3 ± 0.6 (<0.4–2.6)	180 ± 100 (50–520)	17 ± 10 (3–35)	Kotnik et al., 2007
	Deep (>60)	240 ± 120 (60–660)	2 ± 3 (<0.4–12)	240 ± 120 (60–660)	22 ± 11 (6–49)	
	All	220 ± 120 (50–660)	1 ± 2 (<0.4–12)	220 ± 120 (50–660)	20 ± 11 (3–49)	
	Surface (≤20)	280 ± 50 (190–390)	0.2 ± 0.4 (<0.9–1)	280 ± 50 (190–390)	20 ± 8 (5–39)	Horvat et al., 2003
	Deep (≥100)	290 ± 30 (260–330)	4 ± 4 (1–11)	290 ± 30 (260–330)	20 ± 6 (10–32)	
	All	280 ± 40 (190–330)	1 ± 3 (<0.9–11)	280 ± 40 (190–330)	20 ± 8 (5–39)	

	Surface (<60)	<150	3 ± 10 (<20–20)	3 ± 10 (nd–20)	1 ± 1 (0–3)	Cossa et al., 1997
	Deep (>60)	<150	90 ± 100 (<20–290)	90 ± 100 (nd–290)	4 ± 5 (0–15)	
	All	<150	60 ± 90 (<20–290)	60 ± 90 (nd–290)	3 ± 5 (0–15)	
Black Sea	Surface (≤60)	38 ± 46 (<25–110)	6.3 ± 7.5 (<4–20)	40 ± 47 (nd–120)	2 ± 2 (0–4)	Lamborg et al., 2008
	Deep (>60)	110 ± 205 (<25–1040)	4.6 ± 8.9 (<4–41)	120 ± 210 (nd–1040)	3 ± 4 (0–14)	
	All	100 ± 190 (<25–1040)	5.0 ± 8.5 (<4–41)	100 ± 190 (nd–1040)	3 ± 3 (0–14)	
San Francisco Bay	Surface	450 ± 460 (<50–2300)	NA	450 ± 460 (<50–2300)[d]	2 ± 3 (0–14)[e]	Conaway et al., 2003; Choe and Gill, 2003
New York/New Jersey Harbor	Surface	430 ± 310 (240–1170)	NA	430 ± 310 (240–1170)[e]	0.8 ± 0.7 (<1–2)[e]	Balcom et al., 2008
	Bottom	550 ± 630 (130–2390)	NA	550 ± 630 (130–2390)[e]	0.6 ± 0.4 (≤1)[e]	
	All	520 ± 560 (130–2390)	NA	520 ± 560 (130–2390)[e]	0.6 ± 0.5 (<1–2)[e]	
Chesapeake Bay[f]	All	<25–3700	NA	<25–3700[e]	0–26[e]	Mason et al., 1999; Benoit et al., 1998
North Sea, Scheldt Estuary	Surface	70–3600	NA	80–3600[c]	<1–17[e]	Leermakers et al., 2001; Baeyens et al., 1998; Leermakers et al., 1995

NOTE: Values are reported as the mean ± standard deviation, with range given in parentheses when also available. NA = not available/not measured; nd = below detection limit.

a. Unfiltered.

b. Σ methylated = sum of MMHg and DMHg.

c. Analyte measured but quality of data subsequently questioned and considered suspect.

d. Includes only DMHg.

e. Includes only MMHg.

f. Including Baltimore Harbor and Patuxent River estuary.

The open ocean serves as a large source *and* sink for atmospheric mercury (Figure 10.4). Inorganic Hg(II) in the ocean can be reduced to elemental mercury, Hg(0), via photochemical reactions and biologically mediated pathways (Lalonde et al., 2004; Mason et al., 2001; Rolfhus and Fitzgerald, 2004; Monperrus et al., 2007; Poulain et al., 2007; Whalin et al., 2007). Most marine surface waters are supersaturated with volatile Hg(0), resulting in its evasion to the atmosphere. Concentrations of DGM in surface waters (which is primarily Hg(0)) and fluxes of DGM to the atmosphere for various coastal and open ocean environments are summarized in Table 10.2. The net flux of Hg(0)

TABLE 10.2

Concentrations and Fluxes of Dissolved Gaseous Mercury, Primarily Hg(0), Measured
for Various Surface Waters in the Marine Environment

Location	Surface water DGM[a] (fM)	DGM flux to atmosphere[a] (nmol $m^{-2} d^{-1}$)	References
Arctic Ocean	220 ± 110 (25–670)[b]	0.29 (−0.19–11.8)	Andersson et al., 2008
Subtropical North Pacific	60 ± 30	0.10 ± 0.09	Laurier et al., 2003b
Tropical North Pacific	130 ± 70	0.30 ± 0.25	Laurier et al., 2003b
Equatorial Pacific	160 ± 110 (40–360)[c]	0.16–1.44	Mason and Fitzgerald, 1993
Subtropical North Atlantic	650 ± 390[d]	1.9 ± 1.3	Mason et al., 1998
Tropical North Atlantic (Bermuda Atlantic Time-Series)	80–30[c]	0.20–0.66	Mason et al., 2001
South, equatorial Atlantic	1200 ± 790 (200–4100)[e]	9.6	Lamborg et al., 1999; Mason and Sullivan, 1999
Mediterranean Sea	160 ± 110 (20–520)[e]	0.27 (0.22–0.60)	Gårdfeldt et al., 2003b; Horvat et al., 2003; Kotnik et al., 2007; Rajar et al., 2007; Žagar et al., 2007
San Francisco Bay	900 ± 880 (10–2700)[b]	0.3–5.5	Conaway et al., 2003; Macleod et al., 2005
Long Island Sound	200 ± 130 (40–550)[b]	0.32 (0.01–0.53)	Rolfhus and Fitzgerald, 2001
Chesapeake Bay	100–250[b]	0.13 (0.05–0.20)	Mason et al., 1999
Scheldt Estuary	360 (100–650)[b]	0.42 ± 0.17 (0.23–0.70)	Baeyens and Leermakers, 1998; Baeyens et al., 1998
North Sea	60–800[b]	0.47 ± 0.35 (0.06–1.11)	Baeyens and Leermakers, 1998
Atlantic Ocean, Irish coast	110 ± 40 (70–200)[b]	0.33 ± 0.22 (0.05–0.72)	Gårdfeldt et al., 2003b
Seine River estuary	140–450[b]	0.07–0.14	Coquery et al., 1997
Loire River estuary	60–120[b]	0.02–0.09	Coquery et al., 1997

NOTE: Values reported as the mean ± standard deviation, with range given in parentheses when also available.
a. Primarily as Hg^0.
b. ≤2 m.
c. ≤50 m.
d. ≤100 m.
e. ≤20 m.

to the atmosphere is perhaps marginally higher in the open ocean than in coastal and estuarine waters, but it is not clear whether this is due to higher rates of mercury reduction or lower rates of its oxidation in the open ocean relative to coastal environments. Current mass balance models suggest that this gaseous exchange of Hg(0) represents the largest sink or loss of mercury from the oceans, with the next most important loss term being deposition and burial in sediments, often following the scavenging of mercury by particles in the water column that then sink to depth (Lamborg et al., 2002; Mason and Sheu, 2002; Sunderland and Mason, 2007; Žagar et al., 2007).

Hg(0) constitutes over 90% of the total atmospheric mercury pool, and the average residence time of Hg(0) in the troposphere has been estimated to be on the time scale of 3–24 months (Bergan and Rodhe, 2001; Radke et al., 2007; Selin et al., 2007, 2008). Atmospheric Hg(0) can be deposited directly to the oceans, with gross dry deposition thought to be greatest in areas where temperatures are low and wind speeds high, such as the Southern Ocean (Selin et al., 2008). However, atmospheric deposition of mercury commonly involves Hg(II) following the oxidation of Hg(0). Hg(0) can be oxidized to Hg(II) in the atmosphere by ozone and numerous radical species, including hydroxyl,

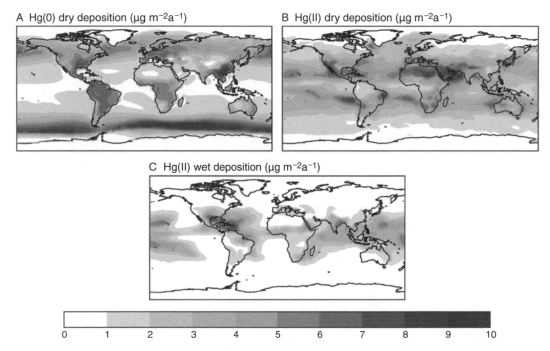

FIGURE 10.5   Estimated annual mean mercury deposition fluxes under preindustrial conditions. (a) Hg(0) dry deposition. (b) Hg(II) dry deposition. (c) Hg(II) wet deposition. All fluxes reported as $\mu g\ m^{-2}\ yr^{-1}$. (*Source:* Adapted/reprinted from Selin et al., 2008, with permission from the American Geophysical Union.)

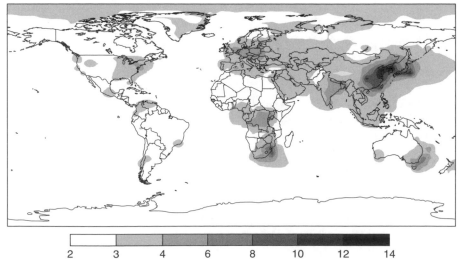

FIGURE 10.6   Increase in the atmospheric deposition of mercury in the present-day relative to preindustrial times expressed as an enrichment factor (i.e., a value of 4 denotes a fourfold increase). (*Source:* Reprinted from Selin et al., 2008, with permission from the American Geophysical Union.)

halogen, and nitrogen oxide radicals (Lin et al., 2006; Lindberg et al., 2002, 2007; Pal and Ariya, 2004; Seigneur et al., 2006). This ionic Hg(II), often referred to as reactive gaseous mercury (RGM), is presumed to exist as $HgCl_2$, $HgBr_2$, and HgOBr and is very particle-reactive and commonly becomes associated with aerosols or other particles (Lin et al., 2006; Holmes et al., 2009). As a result, the average residence time of RGM in the atmosphere is only hours to weeks (Holmes et al., 2009; Lin and Pehkonen, 1999; Lindberg et al., 2007). The preindustrial spatial distribution of wet and dry deposition of Hg(0) and Hg(II) to surface waters of the ocean, as estimated by Selin et al. (2008), is shown in Figure 10.5, and their modeled anthropogenic increase in that deposition is shown in Figure 10.6.

Although earlier studies largely suggested that •OH and O_3 were the most important oxidizers of Hg(0) in the atmosphere (Bergan and Rodhe, 2001; Pal and Ariya, 2004), this has been questioned more recently, as have the rate constants typically used to model the reactions involved (Carlvert and Lindberg, 2005 ; Seigneur et al., 2006). Based on modeling results for the marine boundary layer (MBL), the oxidation of Hg(0) by Br and O_3, along with entrainment of RGM-rich air from the free troposphere, appear to account for the majority of RGM present in the MBL. RGM concentrations in the MBL are highly diurnal, with a lifetime on the order of hours, with scavenging onto sea-salt aerosols and subsequent deposition to surface waters as the dominant source of Hg(II) to the surface ocean (Holmes et al., 2009). However, scavenged RGM is also deposited to the ocean via wet deposition, a process most important in the subtropics, where global scale atmospheric downwelling occurs alongside abundant precipitation (Selin et al., 2008). The reduction of Hg(II) and the reoxidation of Hg(0) in surface waters and the MBL is exceedingly rapid, and mercury deposited to the oceans can be quickly reemitted and recycled (Mason and Sheu, 2002; Mason et al., 2001; Pal and Ariya, 2004; Selin et al., 2007; Strode et al., 2007; Whalin et al., 2007).

The distribution of mercury in the ocean and profiles of mercury concentrations in different oceanic basins (Figures 10.1 and 10.2) vary as the result of differences in the relative size of mercury sources and sinks, as well as variations in ocean circulation. Open ocean concentrations of unfiltered total mercury are lower than in estuary and coastal regions, and generally fall within the range 0.4–4.0 pM. However, concentrations greater than 7 pM have been reported for multiple locations and depths in the ocean (Mason et al., 1998, 2001; Laurier et al., 2004).

The dominant source of mercury to the open ocean is atmospheric deposition; therefore, concentrations of total mercury are often highest in the mixed layer and decrease with depth because particle scavenging (Mason and Fitzgerald, 1993; Mason et al., 1995, 2001; Mason and Sullivan, 1999; Horvat et al., 2003; Laurier et al., 2004; Cossa and Coquery, 2005; Kotnik et al., 2007; Sunderland

et al., 2009). Concentrations of mercury in some areas of the ocean increase slightly in intermediate or bottom waters, presumably because of remineralization of sinking particles or sediment resuspension. The obvious exception to this otherwise "scavenged type" profile for total mercury is found in the Arctic Ocean, where large areas are covered with ice for much of the year and inputs of mercury from rivers are believed to be more important than atmospheric deposition (Outridge et al., 2008).

Importance of Monomethylmercury in the Marine Environment

Methylated forms of mercury are the most toxic and readily biomagnified in aquatic food chains, with MMHg being the most important for both ecologic and human health implications. MMHg is bioaccumulated and biomagnified much more efficiently than inorganic Hg(II) (Mason et al., 1996; Pickhardt and Fisher, 2007; Wang and Wong, 2003; Watras and Bloom, 1992). Phytoplankton bioaccumulate MMHg to concentrations ~10,000 times greater than the natural waters in which they live (Pickhardt and Fisher, 2007; Watras et al. 1998). This transfer from natural waters to phytoplankton represents the single greatest bioconcentration of MMHg that occurs at any trophic level in aquatic food chains. This process is important because most of the MMHg in fish at higher trophic levels comes from dietary sources (Pickhardt et al., 2006; Wang and Wong, 2003). As a result, two of the more important steps in the biogeochemical cycling of mercury responsible for its toxicity involve: (1) the methylation of inorganic mercury to form the more toxic form MMHg, and (2) the subsequent biomagnification of MMHg up the food chain to potentially dangerous levels in large predatory fish consumed by humans and wildlife. This section will focus on the sources and sinks of MMHg in ocean ecosystems, while subsequent sections will describe MMHg bioaccumulation in marine organisms and its biomagnification in marine food webs.

Sources and Sinks of Monomethylmercury in the Marine Environment

Concentrations of MMHg in the compartments comprising the marine environment (i.e., surface waters, deep waters, suspended particles, sediments, sediment pore waters, etc.) are the net result of its biotic and abiotic production and decomposition and its partitioning or movement between different reservoirs. Because the *in situ* production and decomposition of MMHg occur simultaneously in aquatic and sedimentary environments (Heyes et al., 2006; Monperrus et al., 2007; Rodríguez Martín-Doimeadios et al., 2004), concentrations of MMHg reflect the net result of these competing processes in conjunction with the transport of MMHg into or out of the world's oceans. Concentrations of MMHg and DMHg in marine waters are summarized in Table 10.1.

Although there are numerous sources of MMHg and pathways for its production in the marine environment, the relative importance of these has yet to be completely elucidated. MMHg production by sulfate-reducing, and potentially iron reducing, bacteria in sediments is considered to be the predominant source of MMHg to both sediments and overlying surface waters in freshwater, estuary, and coastal environments (Benoit et al., 2003; Compeau and Bartha, 1985; Fleming et al., 2006; Gilmour et al., 1992; Kerin et al., 2006; King et al., 2001). However, in the open ocean, the dominant source of MMHg has yet to be conclusively demonstrated, so the source of the MMHg found in marine fish is unclear. As a result, the effects of past or future changes in anthropogenic mercury emission on mercury levels in seafood are uncertain.

Although there have been a number of mass balances and models developed to quantify sources, sinks, and the biogeochemical cycling of total mercury in both the marine environment as a whole as well as in regional seas (Balcom et al., 2004, 2008; Cossa and Coquery, 2005; Horvat et al., 1999; Lamborg et al., 2002; Macleod et al., 2005; Mason and Sheu, 2002; Mason et al., 1994; Outridge et al., 2008; Rajar et al., 2007; Selin et al., 2008; Strode et al., 2007; Sunderland and Mason, 2007; Žagar et al., 2007), there has been a decided lack of quantitative models of the biogeochemical cycling of MMHg in the world's oceans (Mason and Gill, 2005). Efforts to develop mass balances for MMHg in small coastal areas (Balcom et al., 2004, 2008; Bloom et al., 2004a; Macleod et al., 2005; Mason et al., 1999) represent the first step to this end. Below we discuss the importance of different sources and sinks of MMHg in marine ecosystems and present a preliminary mass balance for MMHg in the oceans.

External Sources of Monomethylmercury to the Marine Environment

ATMOSPHERIC DEPOSITION

The presence of MMHg in precipitation has been reported, with MMHg concentrations in precipitation measured in open ocean areas (≤ 0.05 pM) (Lamborg et al., 1999; Mason et al., 1992) being lower than those along the coast or inland (0.1–3.0 pM) (Balcom et al., 2004; Bloom et al., 2004; St. Louis et al., 2005). The sources of MMHg in rainwater are unknown, but may include the abiotic gas or aqueous-phase methylation of inorganic mercury in the atmosphere (Hammerschmidt et al., 2007) by acetate (Gårdfeldt et al., 2003a) or other organic compounds (Hall et al., 1995), or the biotic methylation of Hg(II) by microbes present in atmospheric aerosols or cloud droplets (Jones and Harrison, 2004). Other potential sources of MMHg in precipitation include the volatilization of MMHg complexes from surface waters (Iverfeldt and Lindqvist, 1982; Mester and Sturgeon, 2002) or landfill gas (Lindberg et al., 2005) or the atmospheric degradation of DMHg (Niki et al., 1983a, 1983b) originating from landfill gas (Lindberg

et al., 2005), mangrove sediment (Quevauviller et al., 1992), coastal upwelling (Conaway et al., 2009), or arctic ice leads and polynyas (St. Louis et al., 2005, 2007).

Although MMHg generally represents only a few percent of the total Hg in precipitation, it is possible that this MMHg is more labile than MMHg from other sources, and may more easily be assimilated into aquatic food webs. The wet deposition of MMHg may also be more ecologically important over the time scale of storm events, when it might represent a pulse of bioavailable mercury to ecosystems. Nevertheless, precipitation does not represent a predominant source of MMHg to the marine environment. Assuming that MMHg makes up 0.2% of the mercury in marine precipitation (Mason et al., 1992; Lamborg et al., 1999), and using estimates of wet deposition of total mercury (Lamborg et al., 2002; Mason and Sheu, 2002), the wet depositional flux of MMHg to the ocean is estimated to be only 0.02 Mmol yr^{-1}.

There is limited evidence suggesting that marine aerosols are a source of MMHg in the subarctic areas (Constant et al., 2007). Evaporation of cloud droplets containing MMHg and reports of MMHg in the atmosphere and its volatilization from surface waters (Iverfeldt and Lindqvist, 1982; Lee et al., 2002; Mester and Sturgeon, 2002) suggest that dry deposition of MMHg is possible. However, dry deposition is not believed to be an importance source of MMHg to the oceans.

SURFACE AND SUBSURFACE MONOMETHYLMERCURY INPUTS FROM TERRESTRIAL SOURCES

RIVERINE AND ESTUARINE INPUTS

Riverine and estuarine inputs of total mercury to coastal waters can be substantial, both in areas affected by local anthropogenic sources of mercury (Balcom et al., 2004, 2008; Conaway et al., 2003; Mason et al., 1999) and in remote regions where human-related inputs of mercury are limited to atmospheric deposition (Leitch et al., 2007). Although riverine inputs of total mercury can be important locally, and are similar in size to the net burial of mercury in marine sediments, they are small relative to atmospheric inputs of total mercury to the oceans. Conversely, the flux of MMHg to coastal environments via surface waters of terrestrial origin is poorly quantified for all but the most extensively studied areas (e.g., Long Island Sound, Chesapeake Bay, San Francisco Bay, and the Gulf of Trieste).

Rivers and estuaries could play a more important role as a source of MMHg to the ocean than they do for total mercury because the largest sources of total mercury to the ocean are wet and dry atmospheric deposition (Figure 10.4), whereas atmospheric deposition of MMHg is relatively inconsequential. The importance of riverine MMHg inputs to coastal waters is illustrated by estimates that fluvial inputs account for 55% of the MMHg fluxes to the New York/New Jersey Harbor Estuary (Balcom et al., 2008) and 18% of the MMHg fluxes to the water column of Long Island Sound (Balcom et al., 2004).

Dissolved and particulate MMHg concentrations reported for estuaries are often less than 0.3 pM, and MMHg generally represents less than 4% of the total mercury pool (Balcom et al., 2004, 2008; Benoit et al., 1998; Choe and Gill, 2003; Conaway et al., 2003; Cossa and Gobeil, 2000; Leermakers et al., 1995, 2001; Mason et al., 1993, 1999). Substantially higher MMHg concentrations may exist, but values >2 pM are only rarely reported for estuary waters (Baeyens et al., 1998; Conaway et al., 2003; Mason et al., 1993, 1999).

Much of this riverine and estuarine MMHg is transported bound to particles. MMHg has a high affinity for particles, with particle distribution coefficients (K_d) generally in the range 10^4—10^5 in estuarine and coastal waters (Baeyens et al., 1998; Balcom et al., 2008; Benoit et al., 1998; Choe and Gill, 2003; Horvat et al., 1999; Leermakers et al., 2001; Hammerschmidt and Fitzgerald, 2006a). In addition, a substantial portion of the operationally defined "dissolved" MMHg can be associated with colloids in both estuary and open ocean environments, as is also true for total Hg (Choe and Gill, 2003; Mason and Sullivan, 1999; Mason et al., 1995, 1998; Stordal et al., 1996).

Evaluating the importance of rivers, or any other input, as a source of MMHg to the marine environment requires an estimate of the amount of MMHg in the oceans. Unfortunately, data on MMHg levels in many regions of the ocean are scarce. Outside of coastal regions, MMHg concentrations in the water column of the ocean are generally less than 0.2 pM (Cossa et al., 1997; Horvat et al., 2003; Kotnik et al., 2007; Lamborg et al., 2008; Mason and Fitzgerald, 1993; Mason and Sullivan, 1999), and it is not uncommon for them to be less than detection limits, which until very recently were ~0.05 pM for seawater. Using an estimate of the total amount of mercury in the oceans of 1760 Mmol (Sunderland and Mason, 2007) and assuming that MMHg comprises, on a weighted average basis, roughly 4% of the total oceanic mercury pool (Cossa and Coquery, 2005; Cossa et al., 1997; Horvat et al., 2003; Kotnik et al., 2007; Lamborg et al., 2008; Mason and Fitzgerald, 1993; Mason and Sullivan, 1999), then the total amount of MMHg in the oceans (water column only) is estimated to be ~70 Mmol (equivalent to a mean MMHg concentration of ~50 fM). Using a global riverine flux of total mercury to the open ocean of 1.9 Mmol yr^{-1} (Sunderland and Mason, 2007) and assuming that MMHg constitutes 1.5% of this, the input of MMHg to the open oceans from rivers would be ~0.03 Mmol yr^{-1}. This fluvial flux is ~0.03% of the estimated standing stock of MMHg in the ocean, and is similar to the estimated wet depositional flux of MMHg.

This calculation of riverine inputs includes only dissolved and particulate MMHg making it to the open ocean. As described above, roughly 90% of the total mercury riverine inputs are deposited in coastal and nearshore sediments, and the overall flux of total mercury to coastal waters from rivers is ~14 Mmol yr^{-1} (Sunderland and Mason, 2007). MMHg is not as particle-reactive as total mercury (lower K_d), and a larger fraction of MMHg likely makes it to the open ocean than for total mercury. Nonetheless, if

MMHg again constitutes ~1.5% of this 14 Mmol yr^{-1}, then the riverine flux of MMHg to coastal areas would be ~0.21 Mmol yr^{-1}. Because such fluxes are concentrated in nearshore regions, riverine inputs represent a more important source of MMHg to coastal regions than for the entire oceanic reservoir.

Estuaries represent an important source of MMHg to the coastal ocean both as vectors for transporting MMHg from upstream terrestrial environments and as sites of MMHg production. This behavior is in contrast to the ability of estuaries to attenuate the flux of total mercury to coastal oceans through the formation and evasion of Hg(0) out of surface waters and the scavenging of total Hg by estuarine sediments (Benoit et al., 1998; Macleod et al., 2005; Mason et al., 1999). The contrasting behavior of total Hg and MMHg result in the estuaries of the Patuxent River (Benoit et al., 1998), Chesapeake Bay (Mason et al., 1999), Gulf of Trieste (Faganeli et al., 2003), and San Francisco Bay (Macleod et al., 2005) all acting as sinks for total mercury but net sources of MMHg to adjacent coastal waters.

Despite difficulties in determining the relative importance of internal versus upstream sources of MMHg in estuaries, estuary sediments are known to be a source of MMHg, and their efficient production of MMHg is due to a number of factors unique to these ecosystems. The oxic–anoxic oscillations and alternating episodes of sedimentation and resuspension experienced by tidally influenced estuary sediments can facilitate both the production and export of MMHg (Catallo, 1999; Tseng et al., 2001; Sunderland et al., 2004). In addition to mercury methylation and demethylation, the export of MMHg from estuaries is highly dependant upon hydrologic and transport processes, and at times can be controlled largely by flow conditions and the transport of organic carbon and particulate material to and through an estuary (Mason et al., 1999).

WASTEWATER

Municipal and industrial wastewater or sludge can be a source of MMHg when discharged directly or indirectly to coastal waters (Balcom et al., 2004; Balogh and Nollet, 2008; Bodaly et al., 1998). The most infamous example of this occurred in Minamata, Japan, and was one of the few cases of environmental mercury contamination in which the mercury was methylated before it entered the environment. Most developed countries now regulate mercury levels in wastewater effluent, and various technologies have been used to remove Hg from the waste stream (Bodaly et al., 1998; Wagner-Dobler, 2003; Balogh and Nollet, 2008). As a result, wastewater discharges do not represent an important source of MMHg to the marine environment at large, although they may in isolated coastal environments.

SUBMARINE GROUNDWATER DISCHARGE

Studies of mercury dynamics in subterranean estuaries in Massachusetts (Bone et al., 2007), northern France (Laurier et al., 2007), and central California (Black et al., 2009b) have indicated that the flux of total mercury to the ocean via groundwater discharge is more important than previously believed. Elevated MMHg concentrations in groundwater in some areas (Stoor et al., 2006) suggest that submarine groundwater discharge (SGD) may also represent a previously unidentified source of MMHg to coastal waters. To date there has been only one report on MMHg transport in SGD (Black et al., 2009b).

Fluxes of SGD will usually be greatest within a few kilometers of the coastline. As a result, SGD may be an important local source of MMHg to some coastal areas, but is unlikely to be an important source to the ocean at large. This point is demonstrated by extrapolating measured fluxes of MMHg in SGD along the central California coast to coastlines globally. Using the mean MMHg flux in SGD of 10 nmol m^{-1} d^{-1} (Black et al., 2009b) and assuming a relevant global coastline of 1×10^6 km (Crossland et al., 2005) after reducing the length to exclude barrier islands, coast covered with ice, and other areas unlikely to have active MMHg fluxes in SGD, it is estimated that the annual flux of MMHg to the ocean via SGD is 0.004 Mmol.

MARINE HYDROTHERMAL SYSTEMS

Submarine hydrothermal vents, fluids, deposits, fumaroles, mud volcanoes, midocean ridges, and other marine geothermal features are sources of inorganic and elemental mercury to both nearshore regions and the deep ocean (Crespo-Medina et al., 2009; Dekov, 2007; Lamborg et al., 2006; Stoffers et al., 1999; Tomiyasu et al., 2007). But only one study to date has reported species-specific measurements and quantified methylmercury concentrations at a marine hydrothermal system (Lamborg et al., 2006); it identified methylmercury as the dominant form of mercury present, although much higher total Hg concentrations have been measured in waters at marine vents elsewhere (Crespo-Medina et al., 2009). Methylmercury concentrations as high as 16 pM were reported for the hydrothermal vent fluids at Gorda Ridge (Lamborg et al., 2006), although it is not clear whether that methylmercury was the result of biotic or abiotic methylation. Chemosynthetic microbes abundant at these deep-sea hydrothermal systems might be responsible for Hg methylation, or the high temperatures and pressures characterizing these environments might be conducive to the abiotic methylation of Hg by methane or other organic compounds, as both Hg and methane are also elevated in these hydrothermal systems. Alternatively, Fein and Williams-Jones (1997) noted that crustal fluids can have elevated concentrations of carboxylic acids, including acetate, which has been shown to methylate inorganic mercury (Gårdfeldt et al., 2003a).

Using measurements made at one marine hydrothermal system and extrapolating to hydrothermal systems elsewhere, the total input of dissolved mercury to the oceans was estimated to be 0.1–0.4 Mmol yr^{-1} (Lamborg et al., 2006). This flux of mercury is, at least initially at this one site, nearly all in a methylated form. However, based on the low MMHg concentrations in the deep ocean and the high concentrations of mercury in sediments near this marine geothermal system, it was hypothesized that much of this methylmercury was deposited nearby and/or rapidly demethylated. As a result, it was predicted that submarine hydrothermal systems are not a dominant source of MMHg to the oceans. It is possible that the elevated concentrations of total Hg in marine hydrothermal waters has led to the adaptation of microbes at deep-sea hydrothermal vents to high Hg levels (Crespo-Medina et al., 2009; Vetriani et al., 2005), and to the rapid demethylation of MMHg by microbes here via the *mer* operon, as has been suggested for Hg-contaminated freshwater aquatic systems (Schaefer et al., 2004).

Internal Sources of Monomethylmercury

INTERNAL ABIOTIC MONOMETHYLMERCURY PRODUCTION

Abiotic mechanisms for the methylation of mercury in aquatic environments that have been demonstrated in the laboratory include transfer of a methyl radical or carbanion to inorganic Hg(II) by methylcobalamin (Filippelli and Baldi, 1993; Nobumasa et al., 1971) and methylated tin species (Cerrati et al., 1992). The importance of these compounds in this role in the marine environment is questionable, however, because of their low concentration in natural waters and sediments, and because their potential for interacting with Hg(II) is likely minimal because of Hg(II) complexation by organic and inorganic ligands (Benoit et al., 1999, 2001b; Dyrssen and Wedborg, 1991; Haitzer et al., 2003; Han and Gill, 2005; Lamborg et al. 2004). A more plausible abiotic methylating agent in the environment is humic substances, based on laboratory studies that have shown the ability of humic matter to methylate Hg(II) to MMHg (Lee et al., 1985; Nagase et al., 1982) and because of the substantial concentration of humics that can complex Hg(II) in natural aquatic systems (Benoit et al., 2001b; Haitzer et al., 2003).

Studies have reported abiotic photochemical production of MMHg in laboratory (Akagi and Takabatake, 1973; Akagi et al., 1976) and field studies (Siciliano et al. 2005). The work by Akagi and colleagues demonstrated the abiotic photomethylation of aqueous Hg^{2+} in the presence of acetate, which is commonly found in aquatic systems. Alternatively, studies by Gårdfeldt et al. (2003a) have demonstrated the ability of acetate to abiotically methylate Hg(II) in the dark. They reported that when using millimolar concentrations of acetic acid, the reaction proceeded via mercury acetate complexes (most likely $Hg(CHCOO)_3^-$), and the reaction rate was first order with respect to inorganic mercury concentration and not affected by pH or the concentration of acetate or other ions, as long as acetate complexes dominated the Hg(II) speciation. While marine waters and sediment pore waters can have low micromolar and low millimolar concentrations of acetate, respectively (Albert et al., 1995; Wu et al., 1997), acetate will not play a role in the complexation of Hg(II) in surface waters or sediment pore waters because of the strong binding of Hg(II) by chloride, inorganic sulfide, polysulfides, and thiols associated with dissolved organic matter (DOM) (Benoit et al., 1999, 2001b; Dyrssen and Wedborg, 1991; Haitzer et al., 2003; Han and Gill, 2005; Lamborg et al., 2004). Consequently, it is unlikely that acetate plays a dominant role in MMHg production in marine waters.

DEGRADATION OF DIMETHYLMERCURY AS A SOURCE OF MONOMETHYLMERCURY

DMHg is prevalent in the intermediate and deep waters throughout the oceans (Figure 10.3), and it is often the dominant methylated form of mercury at depth in the open ocean (Cossa et al., 1994, 1997; Horvat et al., 2003; Mason and Fitzgerald, 1993; Mason and Sullivan, 1999; Mason et al., 1995). It is not clear exactly where or how this DMHg is formed, but it has long been hypothesized that DMHg production occurs in the water column and is associated with heterotrophic activity and carbon remineralization at intermediate depths (Cossa and Coquery, 2005; Cossa et al., 1994, 1997; Mason and Fitzgerald, 1990, 1993; Mason and Sullivan, 1999; Mason et al., 1995). An exception to this may be in the Arctic Ocean, where DMHg has been detected in surface waters under sea ice (St. Louis et al., 2007). The link between organic carbon remineralization and DMHg production has been suggested based upon: (1) mass balance calculations, (2) elevated DMHg levels observed in low-oxygen intermediate waters or recently formed deep waters below regions with high primary productivity, and (3) correlations between DMHg (or "methylated Hg") concentrations and apparent oxygen utilization, carbon remineralization rates, and nutrient concentrations.

Two of the most recent studies to have investigated relationships between methylated Hg distributions and measurements of organic carbon utilization, nutrient concentrations, and hydrographic parameters were carried out by Cossa et al. (2009) in the Mediterranean Sea and Sunderland et al. (2009) in the North Pacific Ocean. DMHg and MMHg concentrations were not measured separately in either study; instead, samples were acidified prior to MMHg analysis, converting DMHg to MMHg (Black et al., 2009a). Thus, these studies could report only concentrations of "methylated Hg," the sum of DMHg and MMHg. While both studies showed correlations between methylated Hg and apparent oxygen utilization and different measures of organic carbon utilization and remineralization in intermediate waters, it is unclear whether this relationship applies to DMHg, MMHg, or both species. Other studies measuring both DMHg and MMHg separately have shown that DMHg is often in excess of MMHg in intermediate and deep waters of the ocean (Cossa and Coquery, 2005; Cossa et al., 1994, 1997; Mason and Fitzgerald, 1990, 1993; Mason and Sullivan, 1999; Mason et al., 1995). Studies from the Mediterranean are mixed on this point, with some reporting relatively high (100–300 fM) DMHg concentrations at depth (Cossa and Coquery, 2005; Cossa et al., 1994, 1997) but others reporting lower (≤100 fM) DMHg concentrations that are less than MMHg concentrations (Horvat et al., 2003; Kotnick et al., 2007; Monperrus et al., 2007). Despite the apparently conflicting data from the Mediterranean, the general trends suggest that "methylated Hg" is MMHg in surface waters but primarily DMHg in intermediate and deep waters. Consequently, the link between particulate organic carbon remineralization in intermediate waters and methylated Hg in the North Pacific (Sunderland et al., 2009) most likely attests to DMHg, rather than MMHg, production in the water column at those depths.

Despite uncertainties as to the source of DMHg in the ocean, it is well established that DMHg is generally absent above the thermocline. Processes that could act to keep DMHg levels low in surface waters include evasion of DMHg to the atmosphere, photodegradation, thermal decomposition, and/or biotic degradation. Photodegradation has widely been perceived to be the most important of these processes based upon incubation experiments during which DMHg losses were observed, as well as estimated degradation rates required to offset calculated diffusive fluxes between different oceanic compartments (Mason and Fitzgerald, 1993; Mason and Sullivan, 1999; Mason et al., 1995).

However, a study investigating the potential photodegradation of DMHg in seawater detected no loss of DMHg in dark controls or light-exposed seawater samples exposed to ambient sunlight for 1 day (Black et al., 2009a). Photodegradation of DMHg still might have occurred, but at a sufficiently slow rate that it was within the analytical error of that study. Still, the upper limit of DMHg photodegradation in that study would be substantially lower than rates of MMHg photodegradation measured in seawater (Monperrus et al., 2007). Therefore, even if DMHg is photodegraded in seawater and MMHg is the dominant product, the steady-state concentration of MMHg from this reaction will be relatively low because MMHg is itself rapidly photodegraded. Other processes, such as evasion of DMHg to the atmosphere, are therefore likely responsible for the low levels of DMHg measured in the surface mixed layer.

Even if DMHg is not rapidly photodegraded, calculations indicate that degradation of DMHg does occur in the ocean, and this may represent a source of MMHg to the marine environment (Mason and Fitzgerald, 1993; Mason and Sullivan, 1999; Mason et al., 1995). Indeed, it has been suggested that the degradation of DMHg alone might account for all of the MMHg in the ocean (Mason and Fitzgerald, 1993). The fact that DMHg levels are highest in intermediate and deep waters suggests either that rates of DMHg production are highest there and/or that DMHg is more stable under conditions characterizing the subsurface than those at the surface. Upwelling of deep waters containing DMHg could represent an important mechanism for increasing MMHg levels in surface waters if DMHg was then degraded to MMHg (Niki et al., 1983a, 1983b).

If the upwelling and subsequent degradation of DMHg were an important source of MMHg to surface waters, one would expect MMHg levels to be highest in areas with strong upwelling, such as along the equator or along the western margins of North America, South America, and Africa (Mittelstaedt, 1986). Unfortunately, data for MMHg levels in upwelling regimes are sparse. MMHg concentrations in the equatorial Pacific and Monterey Bay are not anomalously high relative to nearby waters without upwelling, and instead, MMHg concentrations in these regions are often below detection limits (Black et al., 2009a; Mason and Fitzgerald, 1990, 1993).

INTERNAL BIOTIC MONOMETHYLMERCURY PRODUCTION

SULFATE- AND IRON-REDUCING BACTERIA

The factors controlling the microbially mediated methylation of mercury and the biochemical mechanisms of MMHg production have been reviewed elsewhere (Barkay et al., 2003; Benoit et al., 2003). Briefly described, the production of MMHg is most controlled by factors that influence: (1) the bioavailability of Hg(II), and (2) the activity of microbes responsible for the methylation of Hg. Although many microbes have been shown to have the ability to methylate Hg in the laboratory, research using natural sediments and specific metabolic inhibitors suggests that sulfate-reducing bacteria are the principal Hg methylators in natural marine ecosystems, with iron-reducing bacteria in sediments and heterotrophic bacteria in the water column receiving more recent attention.

Because of the abundance of sulfate in seawater, most organic carbon utilization in coastal and some deep sea sediments is attributed to microbial sulfate reduction (Canfield, 1989). Numerous species of sulfate-reducing bacteria and other microbes have been shown to be capable of methylating mercury in pure culture or in natural sediments (Compeau and Bartha, 1985; Dias et al., 2008; King et al., 2001), but at widely variable rates (King et al., 2000). It is currently unknown which species of bacteria are most responsible for MMHg production in natural marine sediments, and there exists substantial diversity in sulfate-reducing microbial communities between different locations in nearshore, shelf, and deep-sea sediments (Liu et al., 2003).

Some iron-reducing bacteria are also able to methylate mercury (Fleming et al., 2006; Kerin et al., 2006). Because utilization of organic carbon in sediments in some coastal regions is largely carried out via iron reduction (Aller et al., 1986; Canfield et al., 1993; Taillefert et al., 2007), iron-reducing bacteria could be important in MMHg production in some coastal sediments, although to date there is only indirect evidence of this (Mitchell and Gilmour, 2008).

Although the biotic formation and degradation of MMHg is controlled by a number of chemical, biologic, and physical factors, many studies have focused on the role of only a small number of these. For example, some studies attempting to understand MMHg distribution and production have explored the relationship between total mercury and MMHg in sediments (Kelly et al., 1995), the importance of the chemical speciation of Hg(II) on its uptake and subsequent methylation (Benoit et al., 1999, 2001a; Drott et al., 2007; Jay et al., 2002; Mason et al., 1996), or the potential role of cobalt speciation and limitation in MMHg production (Ekstrom and Morel, 2008). Yet other studies focusing on only a few factors have suggested that either DOM (Mason and Lawrence, 1999; Lambertsson and Nilsson, 2006) or sulfate-reduction rates and microbial community (King et al., 2001) are the most important controls on MMHg production or distribution. These studies have proved very valuable in demonstrating the importance of different individual factors in controlling net MMHg production. There has at times, however, been a propensity to use results from such limited studies to make far-reaching generalizations about what most controls MMHg production in large regions based on a small number of relationships measured at a few sites and a few points in time. A more holistic view of MMHg production or abundance realizes that numerous processes and factors are important (e.g., Benoit et al., 2003; Marvin-DiPasquale and Agee, 2003; Heyes et al., 2006), but their relative importance differs substantially both spatially and temporally.

DISTINGUISHING BETWEEN DIFFERENT SITES OF MICROBIAL MONOMETHYLMERCURY PRODUCTION

Based on data currently available, the microbial production of MMHg is the principle source of MMHg in marine ecosystems. Distinguishing between the different locations where this can be carried out to determine the source of MMHg in the ocean is a topic of ongoing debate (Fitzgerald et al., 2007; Kraepiel et al., 2003 Sunderland et al., 2009). Unequivocally identifying the predominant regions of MMHg production will provide insight into the source of MMHg to marine fish, which in turn will help answer the question of whether the mercury found in marine organisms is predominantly derived from natural or anthropogenic sources.

Knowing the dominant source or location of MMHg production in the oceans is also necessary to predict how changes in sediment, organic carbon, nutrient, and total mercury loads will affect MMHg production and accumulation by marine biota. For example, in freshwater systems the atmospheric flux of inorganic Hg(II) plays an important role in both MMHg production and bioaccumulation (Hammerschmidt and Fitzgerald, 2006c; Harris et al., 2007; Orihel et al., 2006, 2007; Paterson et al., 2006). These studies suggest that newly deposited Hg(II) is more labile and bioavailable to sediment microbes and is thus more easily methylated than mercury from other internal or external sources.

Conversely, the atmospheric deposition of mercury would not likely play an important role in MMHg levels and bioaccumulation in the ocean if MMHg production was carried out primarily in deep-sea sediments. Were this the case, the historical increase in mercury emissions due to anthropogenic activity would be unlikely to have resulted in a substantial increase in MMHg levels in marine fish during the past 200 years, although such an assertion is also debatable (Fitzgerald et al., 2007; Sunderland and Mason, 2007). Alternatively, if MMHg in the oceans is produced primarily in intermediate waters or coastal sediments, then the increased atmospheric load of mercury from anthropogenic emissions would be much more likely to have increased MMHg production and bioaccumulation in marine organisms, as observed in freshwater systems.

COASTAL WETLANDS, SALT MARSHES, AND MANGROVE SWAMPS

The high rates of nutrient and organic matter deposition and cycling in wetlands drive high microbial respiration rates in wetland sediments, including sulfate reduction linked to MMHg production (Benoit et al., 2003; Compeau and Bartha, 1985; Gilmour et al., 1992). It is, therefore, not surprising that salt marshes and coastal wetlands are sites of elevated MMHg production (Marvin-DiPasquale et al., 2003; Choe et al., 2004; Canário et al., 2007b; Heim et al., 2007; Hall et al., 2008; Mitchell and Gilmour, 2008).

Microbial methylation of mercury and MMHg concentrations in sediments are generally highest at or near the oxic/anoxic interface (Choe et al., 2004; Covelli et al., 2008; Hammerschmidt et al., 2004; Han et al., 2007; Hines et al., 2000; King et al., 2001, Marvin-DiPasquale and Agee, 2003; Ouddane et al., 2008). Because of the abundance of rooted macrophytes in wetlands that facilitate and mediate the exchange of oxygen and other compounds in the rhizosphere–ectorhizosphere zone (Grosse et al., 1996), the size of this oxic–suboxic boundary layer in salt marshes and other wetlands is much greater than in pelagic sediments. These plants increase the volume of sediment potentially involved in MMHg production per unit area relative to other areas, and they may be responsible for the higher MMHg concentrations and Hg methylation rates commonly reported in marsh sediments colonized by plants as compared with nonvegetated areas (Choe et al., 2004; Marvin-DiPasquale et al., 2003; Canário et al., 2007b; Heim et al., 2007; Windham-Myers et al., 2009). Seasonal changes in MMHg production and degradation in wetlands likely reflect temporal changes in temperature and inputs of organic carbon and nutrients (Marvin-DiPasquale and Agee, 2003; Stoichev et al., 2004), which can influence Hg(II) speciation and microbial respiration rates, and changes in plant growth and physiology, which influence microbial community composition and activity (Hines et al., 1999).

Bioturbation and bioirrigation by microbenthos and macrobenthos abundant in coastal wetlands are also responsible for increasing the size of the oxic–anoxic boundary layer and the continual reoxidation of surficial sediments, resulting in heterogeneity in microbial populations and redox zonation, in addition to increasing rates of iron reduction (Koretsky et al., 2005; Kostka et al., 2002a,

2002b). The vertical and lateral movement of the oxic–suboxic boundary caused by tidal pumping and the alternating patterns of wetting and drying may also contribute to the high MMHg production rates in coastal and salt-marsh sediments compared to nearshore or shelf sediments (Catallo, 1999; Tseng et al., 2001; Taillefert et al., 2007).

There are concerns of increased mercury methylation and bioaccumulation related to efforts to restore wetlands following their degradation over the past two centuries. Because wetlands are hot spots for MMHg production, wetland restoration may exacerbate existing mercury problems of biomagnification and toxicity in aquatic food chains. However, not all wetlands produce or release copious amounts of MMHg. MMHg concentrations in sediments of a mangrove in Brazil were only slightly greater than those in an adjacent estuary (Kehrig et al., 2003), and a comparison found that MMHg levels were lower in Venice Lagoon in Italy than in Lavaca Bay in Texas, despite roughly 30% of Venice Lagoon's margin consisting of various types of intertidal wetlands, as compared with less than 5% for Lavaca Bay (Bloom et al., 2004b).

NEARSHORE SEDIMENTS

In situ production of MMHg in nearshore sediments is the greatest source of MMHg to coastal waters, and studies of the production, export, and biogeochemical cycling of MMHg in surficial estuary and coastal sediments make nearshore sediments the most widely studied source of MMHg in the marine environment. Sediment concentrations of MMHg in the solid phase, pore waters, and estimates of benthic fluxes of MMHg for various estuary and coastal areas are listed in Table 10.3. Concentrations of MMHg in the majority of coastal sediments range from 0.01 to 50 ng g^{-1} dry weight (dw). MMHg in pore waters of coastal sediments range from 0.02 to 25 ng L^{-1}. MMHg typically constitutes less than 1.5% of the total mercury pool in the solid phase of sediments, but comprises a much larger portion in pore waters, where it can be the dominant form of mercury present. Solid-phase MMHg concentrations in sediments generally correlate to mercury methylation potential (Benoit et al., 2003; Gilmour et al., 1998 ; Heyes et al., 2004, 2006; Hines et al., 2006; Sunderland et al, 2004), although the nature of this relationship varies by site and season.

Measurements of MMHg benthic fluxes generally quantify either fluxes due only to diffusion and bioirrigation (using concentration gradients between pore waters and overlying waters or with laboratory-based flux chambers using sediment cores) or fluxes due to the combination of diffusive and advective processes (using *in situ* benthic flux chambers). Because the diffusive fluxes of MMHg out of sediments that have been measured (0–34 ng m^{-2} d^{-1}) are generally much smaller than advective fluxes (−330 to +2370 ng m^{-2} d^{-1}), diffusive fluxes usually represent a relatively minor portion of MMHg benthic fluxes from coastal sediments (Choe et al., 2004; Covelli et al., 1999, 2008; Gill et al., 1999). However, this is unlikely to be true

Monomethylmercury Concentrations and Fluxes for Estuary, Coastal and Deep Sea Sediments and Associated Pore Waters

Location	Sediment MMHg (ng g^{-1}, dry weight)	% Hg as MMHg in solid phase	Pore water MMHg (ng L^{-1})	% Hg as MMHg in pore water	MMHg benthic flux (ng m^{-2} day^{-1})	References
Venice Lagoon (Italy)	0.3–3.0	0.01–0.4	0.05–15	0.3–60		Bloom et al., 2004a, 2004b; Han et al., 2007
Pialassa Baiona Lagoon (Italy)	0.13–45	0.01–0.3				Trombini et al., 2003
Grado Lagoon (Italy)	<1–22	0.001–0.2	0.9–7.9	0.15–15	−2–1490	Covelli et al., 2008
Gulf of Trieste (Italy/Slovenia)			0.1–10.4	4–58	−105–2370	Covelli et al., 1999
Isonzo River Estuary and Gulf of Trieste (Italy/Slovenia)	0.1–60	0.01–1.0	<0.1–25	<0.5–>100		Hines et al., 2000, 2006
Krka estuary (Croatia)	0.4–3.0	0.1–2.7				Kwokal et al., 2002
Kaštela Bay (Croatia)	2.0–37	0.04–1.4				Kwokal et al., 2002; Mikac et al., 1985
Loire estuary (France)	0.05–0.3	0.05–0.3				Coquery et al., 1997
Adour River Estuary (France)	<0.5–8.0	0–1.8				Stoichev et al., 2004
Thau Lagoon (France)	0.8–2.8	0.02–0.8	0.02–0.5	3–15	0.9[a]	Muresan et al., 2007
Seine Estuary (France)	0.1–6.0	0.1–2.0	<2–10	<1–5		Mikac et al., 1999; Ouddane et al., 2008
Tagus Estuary (Portugal)	<0.3–200	0.01–18				Canário et al., 2005, 2007a, 2007b
Lagoon of Bizerte (Tunisia)	<0.1–3.1	<0.01–5.8				Mzoughi et al., 2002
Southwest England estuaries	<0.4–4.0	0.03–4.5				Craig and Moreton, 1986
Clyde River Estuary (Scotland)	<0.5–17	0.4–7.2				Craig and Moreton, 1986
Mersey River Estuary (England)	<0.5–24	0.03–3.0				Craig and Moreton, 1986

(continued)

TABLE 10.3 (continued)

Location	Sediment MMHg (ng g^{-1}, dry weight)	% Hg as MMHg in solid phase	Pore water MMHg (ng L^{-1})	% Hg as MMHg in pore water	MMHg benthic flux (ng m^{-2} day^{-1})	References
Medway River Estuary (England)	0.02–4.3	0.1–1.0				Ouddane et al., 2008
Scheldt Estuary (Belgium)	0.8–22	0.4–0.8				Baeyens et al., 1998
Öre Estuary (Sweden)	0.2–1.0	0.7–1				Kwokal et al., 2002
Öre Estuary (Sweden)	0.1–13	0.1–13				Lambertsson and Nilsson, 2006
Baltic Sea	0.08–2.0	0.02–2.3				Kannan and Falandysz, 1998
Saguenay Fjord and St. Lawrence Estuary (Canada)	<0.1–34	0.1–1.4	<0.3–10	0.5–30		Gagnon et al., 1996; Cossa and Gobeil, 2000
Bay of Fundy (Canada)	0.05–1.7	0.1–1.6	0.5–1.5	1.7–9		Sunderland et al., 2004, 2006
Continental shelf of southern New England	0.01–0.3	0.5–1.0	0.3–2.7	7–62	1.4–2.6[a]	Hammerschmidt and Fitzgerald, 2006b
Long Island Sound (CT/NY)	0.1–3.9	0.2–1.4	1.7–8.3	2–80	5.2–38[a]	Hammerschmidt and Fitzgerald, 2004 Hammerschmidt et al., 2004
New York/New Jersey Harbor	0.4–12	0.2–1.9	0.8–16	10–65	1.7–27[a]	Hammerschmidt and Fitzgerald, 2008 Hammerschmidt et al., 2008
Hudson River estuary (New York)	0.4–2.5	0.07–0.3	<0.01–0.4	0.2–16		Heyes et al., 2004
Chesapeake Bay (Maryland)	0.04–10.5	0.05–4.0				Heyes et al., 2006; Mason and Lawrence, 1999
Baltimore Harbor (Maryland)	1500	0.2			0–11[a]	Mason et al., 2006

(continued)

TABLE 10.3 *(continued)*

Location	Sediment MMHg (ng g^{-1}, dry weight)	% Hg as MMHg in solid phase	Pore water MMHg (ng L^{-1})	% Hg as MMHg in pore water	MMHg benthic flux (ng m^{-2} day^{-1})	References
Putuxent River Estuary (Maryland)	0.1–0.8	0.1–0.5	<0.03–0.2	<0.5–6		Benoit et al., 1998
South Florida coast and estuaries	<0.001–0.5	0.01–6.1				Kannan et al., 1998
Lavaca Bay (Texas)	0.03–13	0.01–2.8	0.7–250	1.5–92	−330–1500	Bloom et al., 1999; Gill et al., 1999
San Francisco Bay (California)	0.06–2.4	0.03–1.2				Conaway et al., 2003; Marvin-DiPasquale et al., 2003
San Francisco Bay Delta (California)	0.02–14	0.1–10	0.1–13	<0.5–>100	−20–180	Choe et al., 2004; Heim et al., 2007
Bering Sea	0.06–0.6	0.02–0.7				Kannan and Falandysz, 1998
Guanabara Bay (Brazil)	1.1–11	0.2–6.3				Kehrig et al., 2003
South China Sea	0.01–0.05	0.02–0.27				Kannan and Falandysz, 1998
Deep sea sediments of Mediterranean Sea	0.08–3.2	0.2–4.2	2.2–64.7	5–25	0.6–6.9[a]	Ogrinc et al., 2007

NOTE: Values were estimated visually from plots when data were not provided explicitly in a table or in the text.

a. Only diffusive component of benthic fluxes were calculated and reported.

in off-axis deep-sea sediments, where advective fluxes are generally minor (Wolf and Chilingarian, 1992).

Benthic fluxes of MMHg, like sediment MMHg concentrations and % total mercury as MMHg, display seasonal and diurnal patterns. Bioirrigation, bioturbation, and other sediment processes play an important role in controlling rates of MMHg release to overlying waters (Covelli et al., 2008; Gill et al., 1999; Hammerschmidt and Fitzgerald, 2008; Hammerschmidt et al., 2004). MMHg fluxes from sediments are sometimes higher when overlying waters are low in oxygen, potentially because of increased MMHg production at the sediment–water interface (Covelli et al., 1999, 2008; Gill et al., 1999; Mason et al., 1999). However, the opposite has been reported in other cases, presumably due to decreased bioirrigation and bioturbation by infauna during low oxygen conditions (Hammerschmidt and Fitzgerald, 2008; Hammerschmidt et al., 2004, 2008; Hines et al., 2006; Mason et al., 2006).

Benthic fluxes of MMHg reported for estuary and nearshore sediments are listed in Table 10.3. These fluxes range from −330 to +2370 ng m^{-2} d^{-1}, demonstrating that sediments can act as a source or sink for MMHg, although they are most often an important source of MMHg to overlying waters. For areas where data on the different sources of MMHg to coastal environments exist and allow for a comparison, the production and flux of MMHg from coastal sediments represents the largest source of MMHg to coastal waters (Balcom et al., 2008; Hammerschmidt et al., 2004; Horvat et al., 1999). For example, benthic fluxes are estimated to represent ~67% of MMHg inputs to the water column of Long Island Sound (Hammerschmidt et al., 2004) and 25% in the New York/New Jersey Harbor Estuary (Balcom et al., 2008). Similarly, in the San Francisco Bay Delta the efflux of MMHg from sediment was estimated to be roughly equal to riverine inputs of MMHg during the dry season and one third of riverine inputs during the wet season (Choe et al., 2004).

Scaling a mean MMHg benthic flux of 50 pmol m^{-2} d^{-1} in coastal areas (see Table 10.3) and 9 pmol m^{-2} d^{-1} for the continental shelf (Hammerschmidt and Fitzgerald, 2006b) to the area of the ocean covered by these two respective regions globally (Ryther, 1969), coastal and shelf sediments together might be responsible for a MMHg flux to the ocean of 0.18 Mmol yr^{-1}. This is substantially greater than the riverine inputs of MMHg to the open ocean estimated above (0.03 Mmol yr^{-1}), but less than inputs from the deep-sea sediments estimated below (0.6 Mmol yr^{-1}).

Most MMHg in coastal sediments is found associated with the solid phase. Partition coefficients (K_d) for MMHg generally range from 10^2 to $10^{3.5}$ in coastal sediments, which is approximately 1 to 2 orders of magnitude lower than typical K_d values for both total mercury in sediments and MMHg in surface waters (Benoit et al., 1998; Black et al., 2009b; Bloom et al., 1999; Choe et al., 2004; Covelli et al., 2008; Hammerschmidt and Fitzgerald, 2004, 2006b; Hammerschmidt et al., 2004, 2008; Heyes et al., 2004; Hines et al., 2006; Sunderland et al., 2004). The benthic flux and partitioning of MMHg between the dissolved and sediment solid phase are affected by the mineral and organic matter composition and content of sediments, sediment grain size, redox state, the abundance of iron and manganese oxyhydroxides, and sulfide concentrations in the dissolved and solid phases (Benoit et al., 1998; Covelli et al., 2008; Gill et al., 1999; Hammerschmidt and Fitzgerald, 2004, 2006b; Hammerschmidt et al., 2008; Heim et al., 2007; Lambertsson and Nilsson, 2006; Mason and Lawrence, 1999; Stoichev et al., 2004). Research by Liu et al. (2009) has highlighted the potential importance of sediment disturbance on Hg biogeochemistry in nearshore sediments. The redistribution of sediment and organic carbon associated with hurricanes in the Gulf of Mexico was accompanied by changes in sediment Hg concentrations and speciation, which in some cases included increases in Hg methylation potentials and %MMHg.

Although the factors capable of controlling the microbially mediated production and decomposition of MMHg in coastal sediments are largely known (e.g., Benoit et al., 2003; Heyes et al., 2006), the complex interplay between these factors in determining MMHg net production, concentrations, and distribution remain poorly understood. For example, some studies of coastal sediments have concluded that both sulfide and organic matter inhibit MMHg production (Hammerschmidt and Fitzgerald, 2004; Hammerschmidt et al., 2008), while other studies have concluded that sulfide and organic matter increase MMHg production and accumulation (Lambertsson and Nilsson, 2006; Ouddane et al., 2008; Sunderland et al., 2006). These seemingly contradictory results highlight the ability of sulfur chemistry and organic matter to influence MMHg production in multiple ways, depending upon ambient concentrations and conditions—e.g., as substrates for respiration, sulfate and organic matter can increase MMHg production by increasing sulfate reduction, while as ligands capable of binding Hg(II), both sulfide and organic matter can reduce MMHg production by making Hg(II) less bioavailable to microbes. But more importantly, such contrasting results underscore the complexity of net MMHg production, accumulation, and distribution in coastal sediments and the need to consider the multitude of factors that simultaneously play roles in the processes involved and how the importance of these varies spatially and temporally.

DEEP SEA SEDIMENTS

While sulfate reduction in surficial deep-sea sediments is not as important in the oxidation of organic matter as it is in nearshore sediments (Canfield, 1989), sulfate reduction associated with underlying microbial methane production in buried (>2 m below the seafloor) deep-sea sediments can be substantial (D'Hondt et al., 2002). Thus, it is not unreasonable to expect mercury to be methylated in deep-sea sediments via the same processes observed elsewhere. Appreciable concentrations of mercury exist in surficial layers of deep sea sediments (Cossa and Coquery, 2005; Gobeil et al,. 1999; Ogrinc et al., 2007), which could act as a substrate for methylation. It remains to be seen, however, whether microbial activity results in substantial net production of MMHg and appreciable benthic fluxes of MMHg to overlying deep waters of the open ocean.

Because concentrations of MMHg in deep waters of the open ocean are not systematically much greater than those in the rest of the water column, the importance of deep-sea sediments as a source of MMHg to both the ocean and marine fish has been questioned (Fitzgerald et al., 2007). Given the much larger surface area of sediments in the open ocean relative to nearshore and shelf environments, MMHg production and fluxes could be much lower in deep-sea sediments and still overwhelm nearshore sedimentary sources of MMHg. Even if this were the case, in order for MMHg produced in deep-sea sediments to make its way into epipelagic or mesopelagic food webs, it would first have to be transported from the deep ocean toward the surface and coastal zones. The time required for such transport may allow for substantial demethylation or particle scavenging of MMHg, and as mentioned earlier, depth profiles of MMHg in different regions of the ocean are not completely consistent with the deep ocean being a dominant source of MMHg.

We are aware of only one study that has measured MMHg concentrations, MMHg methylation potential, and/or MMHg efflux in deep sea sediments (Ogrinc et al., 2007). That study showed that potential rates of mercury methylation in deep-sea sediments of the Mediterranean Sea ranged from 0.16 to 0.71% d^{-1}. Those rates are relatively low compared to those in estuary or coastal sediments, where potential methylation rates typically range from 0.5 to 10% d^{-1} (Hammerschmidt and Fitzgerald, 2004; Lambertsson and Nilsson, 2006; Monperrus et al., 2007). However, the proportion of solid-phase mercury existing as MMHg (mean of ~2%) was higher than in coastal or estuary sediments, as were MMHg concentrations in the pore waters of these deep-sea sediments in the Mediterranean. In addition, the highest methylation potentials, MMHg concentrations in both the solid phase and pore water, and ratios of MMHg to total mercury all occurred near the sediment–water interface, potentially allowing for greater fluxes of MMHg to overlying waters than if the peak in these parameters occurred at depth in the sediments. As a result, diffusive benthic fluxes of MMHg out of these deep-sea sediments (range, 0.7–7.0 ng m^{-2} d^{-1}) were similar to those calculated for estuary and nearshore sediments (Table 10.3). Although this suggests that deep-sea sediments may be an important source of MMHg to the marine environment, both the higher MMHg concentrations and higher %MMHg in the water column of the Mediterranean as compared with other open ocean waters (Cossa and Coquery, 2005; Horvat et al., 2003; Kotnik et al., 2007) suggest that the MMHg benthic fluxes measured in the Mediterranean are likely higher than those from other deep-sea sediments.

Using a benthic flux on the low end of those calculated for deep-sea sediments of the Mediterranean Sea (5 pmol m^{-2} d^{-1}) by Ogrinc et al. (2007) and scaling to deep-sea sediments globally, which cover an estimated area of 3.26×10^{14} m^2 (Ryther, 1969), we estimate that the flux of MMHg from deep-sea sediments is 0.6 Mmol yr^{-1}. Again, it is quite likely that the MMHg flux from deep-sea sediments in the Mediterranean is higher than elsewhere in the open ocean, and depth profiles of MMHg do not show a consistent increase in MMHg concentration near the sediment–water interface in the deep ocean of the magnitude that would be expected if deep-sea sediments were the predominant source of MMHg. However, it is possible that large fluxes of MMHg do occur out of deep-sea sediments, but are accompanied by relatively high rates of MMHg demethylation in bottom waters.

SUBOXIC AND OXIC WATER MASSES

Elevated concentrations of MMHg have been reported in the pycnocline of the Pettaquamscutt River estuary (Mason et al., 1993) and in the water column of the Black Sea at the oxic–suboxic boundary (Lamborg et al., 2008). Such distributions suggest that MMHg is being produced in the water column by sulfate-reducing or other bacteria at this interface, and below this depth sulfate-reduction rates are high but Hg(II) bioavailability is low because of high sulfide concentrations and the dominance of less bioavailable, negatively charged complexes HgS$_2^{2-}$ and HgHS$_2^-$ (Benoit et al., 1999). Elevated MMHg levels have also been reported for the low-oxygen bottom waters of the Chesapeake Bay (Mason et al., 1999), which is similar to the high MMHg concentrations found in the anoxic hypolimnions of freshwater lakes (Mauro et al., 2002; Regnell et al., 1997). The high MMHg levels in such suboxic bottom waters of lakes are likely due, at least to some extent, to diffusion and advection of MMHg from sediments to overlying waters, and those benthic fluxes may be enhanced when the overlying water is hypoxic (Covelli et al., 2008). However, that does not discount the microbial methylation of mercury in suboxic regions of the water column.

MMHg produced in the marine water column may be more readily incorporated into marine food webs than MMHg produced in marine sediments if it more easily diffuses or is advected to adjacent oxygenated waters where it can then be taken up by organisms. This could occur where oceanic water masses of substantial size experience hypoxia on a seasonal or persistent basis. These include stratified and stagnant basins and fjords along the coast of Scandinavia, California, British Columbia, Japan, and Venezuela, as well as the Black Sea, Caspian Sea, and the "dead zones" that form annually at the mouths of the Mississippi, Yangtze, and other rivers (Diaz, 2001). The microbial methylation of mercury in these nearshore and shelf water masses has yet to be the focus of substantial scientific exploration, but it warrants greater attention given the high biologic productivity and human utilization of these regions, some of which are also areas of local mercury pollution.

In addition to the biotic production of MMHg in suboxic regions of the water column, the biotic methylation of mercury has been measured in incubations of oxic surfaces waters of the Mediterranean, where mercury methylation rates as high as 6.3% d^{-1} were reported (Monperrus et al., 2007). Concentrations of methylated Hg are sometimes greatest in the open ocean at intermediate depths, where apparent oxygen utilization is high (Cossa et al., 2009; Sunderland et al., 2009), a phenomenon related to the remineralization of sinking organic carbon by heterotrophic bacteria. However, much of this methylated Hg, at least in the Pacific, is likely to be DMHg. The importance of Hg methylation across the entire oxic water column, and the need to identify the predominant organo-form created (DMHg or MMHg), clearly deserves further study.

PARTICLES

MMHg is particle-reactive, and scavenging by particles that then sink to depth likely plays a part in maintaining the low MMHg levels measured in oceanic surface waters. Conversely, these sinking particles may also be sites of MMHg production, and thus a source of MMHg to intermediate and deep waters. Particle partitioning coefficients (K_d) for inorganic Hg(II) in open ocean waters are generally in the range $10^5–10^6$ (Mason and Fitzgerald, 1993; Mason et al., 1998), and vertical movement of total mercury in the open ocean is thought to occur primarily via particle transport (Mason and Fitzgerald, 1993). Thus, persistent or sinking particles and fecal pellets that are rich in organic carbon and substrates for heterotrophic bacterial respiration are also enriched in inorganic Hg(II) that could be methylated by the consortium of microbes colonizing these particles. Marine snow, aggregates, and other particles are rich in microbes and are hot spots of bacterial metabolism and enzymatic activity (Simon et al., 2002). It is not certain whether these heterotrophic microbes are capable of methylating mercury, and even if they can, it is unclear whether this process would produce substantial amounts of MMHg.

The existence of suboxic microenvironments in larger aggregates or biofilm-coated particles (Kühl and Jørgensen, 1992; Ploug et al., 1997) may allow for limited microbial sulfate reduction, which is linked to MMHg production. In addition, MMHg production rates are substantially higher in biofilms than in planktonic sulfate-reducing cells (Lin and Jay, 2007). Any MMHg produced in particle micro-environments would have to diffuse out of particles or be released as the aggregates are remineralized in order to be a direct source of MMHg to the water column. Any MMHg retained in sinking particles will be exported to surface sediments, although this could be subsequently remobilized to overlying deep waters.

The importance of sinking particles as sites of MMHg production may be limited because the impact of fluid flow on the diffusion and exchange of gases and solutes between aggregates and the surrounding solution (Kiorboe et al., 2001) makes substantial sulfate reduction unlikely in small or rapidly sinking, loosely consolidated particles (Ploug et al., 1997). Exceptions to this could be in oxygen minimum zones and other intermediate waters where the remineralization of particulate organic carbon results in low oxygen concentrations that may allow for sulfate reduction in particle microenvironments as particles pass through these waters. Elevated levels of DMHg and methylated Hg have been measured in such intermediate waters at depths associated with organic matter mineralization and low oxygen concentrations (Cossa and Coquery, 2005; Cossa et al., 1994, 1997, 2009; Mason and Fitzgerald, 1990, 1993; Mason and Sullivan, 1999; Mason et al., 1995; Sunderland et al., 2009). It is not known how much of this methylated Hg is MMHg, nor whether the Hg methylation at these depths occurs primarily in sinking particles or in the bulk water column.

Sinks for Monomethylmercury in the Marine Environment

MONOMETHYLMERCURY PHOTODECOMPOSITION

Studies indicate that the photodecomposition of MMHg is likely the dominant mechanism of MMHg degradation or loss in the photic zone of aquatic environments (Bergquist and Blum, 2007; Sellers et al., 1996; Monperrus et al., 2007). This may be an indirect process mediated by reactive oxygen species or other reactive intermediates generated by photochemistry, such as singlet oxygen and the hydroxyl radical (Chen et al., 2003; Suda et al., 1993).

It has been proposed that rates of MMHg photodemethylation are substantially lower in seawater as compared with freshwater (Whalin et al., 2007). However, MMHg photodegradation rates as high as 25% d^{-1} have been reported for marine surface waters (Monperrus et al., 2007), and when normalized to light levels and exposure duration, photodemethylation rates in seawater are likely to be less than

those in freshwater by a factor of 2–3. Photodegradation of MMHg would be limited to the upper 50 m of oligotrophic oceanic waters because of the attenuation of sunlight with water depth (Smith and Baker, 1981), and this would be considerably shallower in coastal waters and other areas with appreciable dissolved and particulate organic matter that absorb light, especially in the UV region (Morris et al., 1995).

We estimate that 0.7 Mmol of MMHg is photodegraded in the photic zone of the ocean annually, assuming a MMHg concentration of 0.05 pM in surface waters, a MMHg photodegradation rate constant of 0.12 d^{-1} for the uppermost layer of the water column during a cloudless summer day at a latitude of 38°N (Monperrus et al., 2007; Whalin et al., 2007), and extrapolating to the rest of the ocean by accounting for typical DOM concentrations and light-absorbing properties for neritic and open ocean waters (Hansell and Carlson, 2002), the attenuation of light at depth from absorption and scattering by water and DOM (Smith and Baker, 1981; Morris et al., 1995), and latitudinal differences and seasonal changes in sunlight irradiance and cloud cover. Although there are many potential sources of error in such a calculation, one of the more conspicuous is the value chosen for the concentration of MMHg in the mixed layer, which is poorly known and often below detection limits.

VOLATILIZATION TO THE ATMOSPHERE

The volatilization of MMHg from surface waters and its presence in the atmosphere has been reported (Iverfeldt and Lindqvist, 1982; Lee et al., 2002; Mester and Sturgeon, 2002). However, this topic has been little studied, and it is not clear whether all of the analytical methods used to date have actually measured MMHg rather than gaseous form(s) of inorganic or elemental mercury.

Any volatilization of MMHg that does occur from seawater would likely involve the species CH_3HgCl^0. CH_3HgCl^0 is predicted to be the dominant inorganic complex under the oxic saline conditions found in the ocean. However, organic material, sulfide, or other ligands in seawater are capable of binding MMHg and dominating its complexation (Amirbahman et al., 2002; Dyrssen and Wedborg, 1991). Such complexation would diminish the importance of chloride in binding MMHg, and thus decrease rates of MMHg volatilization because of lower levels of CH_3HgCl^0. The exception to this would be if sulfide were present at low nanomolar concentrations, as has been reported (Cutter et al., 1999; Luther and Tsamakis, 1989), then the dominant complex could be CH_3HgSH^0 (Dyrssen and Wedborg, 1991). This neutrally charged complex could be sufficiently volatile to result in the loss of MMHg to the atmosphere as reported for $MMHgCl^0$, although this has yet to be demonstrated.

BIOTIC DEMETHYLATION OF MONOMETHYLMERCURY

The biotic demethylation of MMHg has been reviewed elsewhere (Barkay et al., 2003; Misra, 1992); therefore, it is not discussed in detail here. Many strains of bacteria are capable of demethylating MMHg, and this can occur in either the water column or sediment (Barkay et al., 2003; Monperrus et al., 2007). The microbially mediated decomposition of MMHg in the aquatic environment can proceed via oxidative or reductive pathways (Marvin-DiPasquale et al., 2000; Schaefer et al., 2004). In oxidative demethylation, MMHg decomposition is believed to be unintended and is related to C1 metabolic pathways. The more widely studied microbial reductive demethylation pathway involves the inducible *mer* operon used in mercury detoxification (Misra, 1992; Barkay et al., 2003). The gene *mer*B, found in the plasmid-borne *mer* operon, encodes a organomercury lyase enzyme that degrades MMHg to methane and inorganic Hg(II), with the Hg(II) then reduced to Hg(0) by mercuric reductase (Misra, 1992).

Both microbial demethylation pathways have been observed under aerobic and anaerobic conditions in freshwater, estuarine water, and marine sediments (Barkay et al., 2003; Benoit et al., 2003; Hines et al., 2000, 2006; Marvin-DiPasquale et al., 2000). In mercury-contaminated areas the *mer* operon is more prevalent and plays an important role in controlling MMHg levels (Marvin-DiPasquale et al., 2000; Schaefer et al., 2004). However, there are relatively few locations in the marine environment with sufficiently high total mercury levels that induction of the *mer* operon is likely to be the predominant control on MMHg concentrations. Such mercury-contaminated locations would be limited to some estuaries (e.g., San Francisco Bay), coastal environments (e.g., Gulf of Trieste), and areas influenced by geothermal activity (e.g., hydrothermal vents), and would represent only a small percentage of the oceans. As a result, both the absolute rates and the relative importance of the oxidative and reductive pathways for microbial degradation of MMHg in the water column or sediments of the ocean are poorly understood. Nonetheless, biologically mediated degradation could be one of the largest sinks for MMHg in the marine environment, especially if it were to occur throughout the entire water column at rates suggested by some studies (Monperrus et al., 2007; Whalin et al., 2007).

PARTICLE SCAVENGING AND SEDIMENT BURIAL

The low, or nondetectable, levels of MMHg in waters of the open ocean may be attributed to some degree to scavenging by particles that then sink, being remineralized at depth or buried in sediments. This includes increased scavenging during phytoplankton blooms, which can reduce dissolved Hg(II) and MMHg levels in the water column due to uptake into the cell and scavenging onto cell surfaces (Luengen and Flegal, 2009). When the bloom subsequently crashes or decays, the associated export of cellular components to bottom sediments could act to export substantial amounts of the scavenged Hg(II) and MMHg with it. However, the longer-term effects of phytoplankton blooms on MMHg dynamics is unknown, in part because the Hg(II) in phytoplankton is associated primarily with cell-wall material, while MMHg is associated more with the cytoplasmic components (Mason et al., 1996). The cytoplasm is more likely to be remineralized and released back into solution before sediment burial than cell-wall material, so the MMHg is less likely to undergo sediment burial than Hg(II) following an algal bloom. In addition, the export of Hg(II) with the fresh organic matter during the decay of a phytoplankton bloom may lead to a pulse in microbial respiration and MMHg production in sediments. Some of this newly produced MMHg could make its way into overlying waters, in which case algal blooms may prove to be a source of MMHg to the water column in the longer term.

Estimates for sediment burial of total mercury (Balcom et al., 2004, 2008; Fitzgerald et al., 2007; Horvat et al. 2003) are much more abundant than for MMHg burial in marine sediments. This difference is, in part, due to uncertainties in MMHg cycling and its nonconservative behavior in sediments. Despite this, it is estimated that sediment burial comprises 8% of all sinks for MMHg in the Chesapeake Bay (Mason et al., 1999), and particle scavenging and burial is an important sink for MMHg in the Pettaquamscutt Estuary (Mason et al., 1993).

We estimate sediment burial of MMHg in nearshore regions to be ~0.19 Mmol yr^{-1}, assuming that the riverine transport of MMHg to the oceans is 0.21 Mmol yr^{-1} and 90% of that MMHg is buried in nearshore sediments, as suggested for total mercury (Sunderland and Mason, 2007). Sediment burial of total Hg outside of coastal areas is estimated to be approximately 1–2 Mmol yr^{-1} (Lamborg et al., 2002; Mason and Sheu, 2002; Sunderland and Mason, 2007). Because of the lower concentrations and lower particle partition coefficients for MMHg as compared with Hg(II), MMHg likely represents only ~2% of the total Hg lost to sedimentation in the ocean, which would give a burial sink for MMHg of ~0.02 Mmol yr^{-1} outside coastal areas. Thus, the loss of MMHg from the oceanic water column due to particle scavenging and sediment burial for both nearshore and deep sea sediment is ~0.21 Mmol yr^{-1}.

REMOVAL VIA FISHING

Many mass balances of MMHg in marine ecosystems include an estimate of the MMHg production required to balance uptake by biota, often derived from concentrations of MMHg in biota and estimates of primary production. While these estimates are useful, it is unclear whether such uptake of MMHg represents a true sink for MMHg in the ocean or merely internal cycling. Much of this MMHg may be recycled both because the trophic transfer of MMHg is less than 100% at any step in the food chain, and eukaryotes excrete MMHg as a detoxification mechanism, although rates of MMHg depuration are much slower than rates of accumulation (Rouleau et al., 1998; Tsui and Wang, 2004; Wang and Wong, 2003). And although some birds and mammals can demethylate MMHg, there is little evidence

TABLE 10.4
Concentrations of Total Mercury in Fish and Other Marine Organisms Representing the 32 Largest Fisheries Globally by Wet Weight, Which Together Comprise 40% of the Global Catch from Marine Ecosystems

Species		Mean annual catch, 2001–2006 (millions of tons)[a]	% of global marine catch	Mean total Hg (μg g^{-1} wet weight)	Total Hg range (μg g^{-1} wet weight)
Common name	Scientific name				
Anchoveta (Peruvian anchovy)	*Engraulis ringens*	8.76	9.42	NA (~0.04)[b,c]	NA
Alaska pollock (walleye pollock)	*Theragra chalcogramma*	2.78	2.99	0.05[c,d,e,f,g]	nd–0.78
Skipjack tuna	*Katsuwonus pelamis*	2.23	2.40	0.20[c,h,i,j]	0.08–0.85
Blue whiting	*Micromesistius poutassou*	2.10	2.26	0.18[k,l,m]	0.02–0.59
Atlantic herring	*Clupea harengus*	2.08	2.24	0.03[c,n,o]	nd–0.77
Chub mackerel (Spanish mackerel)	*Scomber japonicus*	1.88	2.03	0.08[c,p]	0.03–0.19
Japanese anchovy	*Engraulis japonicus*	1.81	1.94	0.03[q]	NA
Chilean jack mackerel	*Trachurus murphyi*	1.75	1.88	0.16[r]	0.11–0.31
Largehead hairtail (cutlassfish)	*Trichiurus lepturus*	1.50	1.61	0.12[s,t,u,v]	0.02–0.50
Yellowfin tuna	*Thunnus albacares*	1.31	1.41	0.26[c,h,i,w,x]	nd–1.32
European pilchard (sardine)	*Sardina pilchardus*	1.04	1.12	0.09[c,m,y,z]	0.01–0.40
Atlantic cod	*Gadus morhua*	0.86	0.93	0.08[c,A,B,C,D]	nd–0.60
Akiami paste shrimp	*Acetes japonicus*	0.66	0.71	NA (~0.02)[b,c,v,E,F]	nd–0.08
European sprat	*Sprattus sprattus*	0.66	0.71	0.06[z]	nd–0.14
Atlantic mackerel	*Scomber scombrus*	0.66	0.71	0.06[c,k]	0.02–0.36
Jumbo flying squid	*Dosidicus gigas*	0.64	0.69	NA	NA
California pilchard (sardine)	*Sardinops caeruleus*	0.64	0.69	0.02[c]	0.01–0.04
European anchovy	*Engraulis encrasicolus*	0.56	0.60	0.07[m,G]	0.04–0.09
Gulf menhaden	*Brevoortia patronus*	0.47	0.50	0.01[H]	0.005–0.02
Round sardinella	*Sardinella aurita*	0.45	0.49	0.08[c,m,y,z]	0.01–0.30
Japanese flying squid	*Todarodes pacificus*	0.45	0.48	0.09[I]	NA
Argentine shortfin squid	*Illex argentinus*	0.44	0.48	NA (~0.07)[b,c,I]	NA
Saithe (pollock)	*Pollachius virens*	0.43	0.46	0.10[J,K]	0.01–0.30
Bigeye tuna	*Thunnus obesus*	0.43	0.46	0.62[c,h,q,L,M]	0.20–1.04
Argentine hake	*Merluccius hubbsi*	0.42	0.45	0.10[N,O]	0.07–0.10
Pacific saury	*Cololabis saira*	0.40	0.43	0.04[P]	nd–0.07

TABLE 10.4 *(continued)*

Species		Mean annual catch, 2001–2006 (millions of tons)[a]	% of global marine catch	Mean total Hg (μg g^{-1} wet weight)	Total Hg range (μg g^{-1} wet weight)
Common name	Scientific name				
Northern prawn	*Pandalus borealis*	0.40	0.43	0.30[B,C]	0.10–0.55
Gazami crab	*Portunus trituberculatus*	0.37	0.39	NA (0.05–0.40)[b,c,j,v,E]	NA
Southern rough shrimp	*Trachypenaeus curvirostris*	0.36	0.38	NA (~0.02)[b,c,v,E,F]	NA
Araucanian herring	*Strangomera bentincki*	0.35	0.37	NA (~0.04)[b,c]	NA
Chum salmon	*Oncorhynchus keta*	0.34	0.37	0.05[Q,R,S,T]	0.01–0.13
Daggertooth pike conger	*Muraenesox cinereus*	0.33	0.35	0.31[U]	0.14–0.46

NA = data not available; nd = below detection limit

a. UN FAO (2007)

b. Expected Hg concentration based on related species with similar feeding habits and trophic level

Hg concentration data references:

c. US FDA (2006)	r. Cortes and Fortt (2007)	G. Falcó et al. (2006)
d. Burger et al. (2007)	s. Costa et al. (2009)	H. Senn et al. (personal communication)
e. Knowles et al. (2003)	t. Kehrig et al. (2004)	I. Ichihashi et al. (2001)
f. Legrand et al. (2005)	u. Mol et al. (2000)	J. Haines and Bauer (2001)
g. Plessi et al. (2001)	v. Chen and Chen (2006)	K. Zauke et al. (1999)
h. Kaneko and Ralston (2007)	w. Adams (2004)	L. Boush and Thieleke (1983)
i. Kojadinovic et al. (2006)	x. Kraepiel et al. (2003)	M. Brooks (2004)
j. Andersen and Depledge (1997)	y. Joiris et al. (1999)	N. Jókai et al. (2005)
k. Perugini et al. (2009)	z. Storelli et al. (2003a)	O. Kütter et al. (2008)
l. Storelli et al. (2003b)	A. Green and Knutzen (2003)	P. Nakagawa et al. (1997)
m. Arcos et al. (2002)	B. Jardine et al. (2009)	Q. Foran et al. (2005)
n. Braune et al. (1987)	C. Joiris et al. (1997a)	R. Jewett and Duffy (2007)
o. Dixon and Jones (1994)	D. Cossa and Gobeil (2000)	S. Kelly et al. (2008)
p. Keskin et al. (2007)	E. Bloom (1992)	T. Zhang et al. (2001)
q. Yamashita et al. (2005)	F. Burger et al. (2005)	U. Cheng et al. (2009)

of demethylation by phytoplankton, invertebrates, or lower-trophic-level fish (Eagles-Smith et al., 2009b; Palmisano et al., 1995; Scheuhammer et al., 2007; Wagemann et al., 1998). Consequently, a substantial portion of the MMHg taken up at the base of the food chain may eventually be released back into the marine environment. This internal cycling is in contrast to MMHg removed by the harvesting of marine products, which would represent a true sink for oceanic MMHg.

Mass balances of mercury in the Mediterranean Sea (Rajar et al., 2007) and Arctic Ocean (Outridge et al., 2008) have shown that the amount of mercury in fish and the amount of mercury removed by fishing are very small relative to the total reservoir of mercury in these marine environments. Because MMHg constitutes only a small percentage of the total mercury pool in oceanic waters but represents most of the mercury in fish, fishing may be more important in the biogeochemical cycling of MMHg in the marine environment than for total mercury.

That importance is indicated by our estimate that fishing removes approximately 0.04 Mmol of MMHg from the ocean each year. This estimate is based on: (1) 93 million metric tons of marine fish being harvested each year since 2000 (United Nations Food and Agricultural Organization [UN FAO], 2007), (2) a weighted average mercury concentration in muscle tissue of commercially caught marine fish of 120 ng g^{-1} wet weight (Table 10.4, and references therein), (3) whole-fish mercury concentrations being 25% lower than those in muscle tissue (Goldstein et al., 1996; Peterson et al., 2005), and (4) MMHg comprising 90% of the mercury in fish (Andersen and Depledge, 1997; Baeyens et al., 2003; Bank et al., 2007; Bloom, 1992; Hammerschmidt and Fitzgerald, 2006a; Storelli et al., 2003a). This estimate of MMHg removed by fishing is similar to the estimated annual flux of MMHg to the open ocean via rivers presented above, but less than the overall riverine input of MMHg to coastal waters and sediment.

Mass Balance of Monomethylmercury in the Oceans

Using estimates and calculations presented above for the various MMHg fluxes of interest, we present a preliminary mass balance for MMHg in the oceans in Figure 10.7. We have not attempted to quantify the errors associated with each of these fluxes because in many cases the MMHg data are so limited in number or extent as to preclude our doing so. That said, uncertainties associated with the estimated fluxes are unquestionably quite large, likely approaching an order of magnitude in some cases. We, therefore, present this mass balance not as an authoritative model of MMHg biogeochemical cycling in the marine environment, but rather as a first attempt at a comprehensive estimate for the ocean that can be revised in the future, as will certainly be necessary. We do not provide estimates for fluxes for which insufficient data prevent their calculation, but include them in Figure 10.7 to illustrate areas requiring more research in order to improve our understanding of MMHg cycling in marine ecosystems.

As summarized in Figure 10.7, the *in situ* production and flux of MMHg out of deep-sea sediments is estimated to be the dominant source of MMHg to the marine environment (0.6 Mmol yr^{-1}). We acknowledge that this value was estimated by extrapolation from near the lower limit of MMHg fluxes measured for deep-sea sediments in the Mediterranean Sea (Ogrinc et al., 2007), and that fluxes from deep-sea sediments elsewhere are likely to be considerably smaller. Even if this were the case, and MMHg fluxes from deep-sea sediments were only one third those measured in the Mediterranean, the export of MMHg from open ocean sediments would be ~0.2 Mmol yr^{-1}, and still constitute one of the largest sources of MMHg to the oceans. Recent research has suggested that the microbial methylation of Hg in the water column may be one of the largest sources of methylated Hg to the open ocean water column, although this may well be DMHg, not MMHg. Thus, the production of MMHg in deep-sea sediments and intermediate waters of the open ocean are potentially the largest sources of MMHg to the oceans, but these are also two of the least understood and studied.

Other important sources of MMHg to the ocean include geothermal activity (0.2 Mmol yr^{-1}, much of which may be quickly demethylated), nearshore sediments (0.18 Mmol yr^{-1}), and riverine and estuarine inputs (0.21 yr^{-1}, much of which is deposited in nearshore sediments). Minor sources include atmospheric deposition (0.02 Mmol yr^{-1}) and submarine groundwater discharge (0.004 Mmol yr^{-1}). Additional potential sources include export from coastal wetlands, the degradation of DMHg, and the abiotic methylation of mercury in the water column.

The sinks for MMHg in the marine environment are even less well understood than the sources. Photodemethylation (0.7 Mmol yr^{-1}) and sediment burial (0.21 Mmol yr^{-1}) appear to be the most important sinks that can currently be estimated,

with fishing (0.04 Mmol yr^{-1}) being of lesser importance. The dark biotic and/or abiotic degradation of MMHg in the water column and volatilization to the atmosphere are other potential, but poorly quantified, sinks for MMHg.

The sum of all identified and estimated sources for MMHg in the mass balance is ~1.2 Mmol yr^{-1}, while the sum of all identified and estimated sinks is ~1.0 Mmol yr^{-1}. If correct, this disparity indicates that the ocean is not at steady state with respect to MMHg concentrations and that levels of MMHg are on the rise, as is true for total mercury. However, this difference (0.2 Mmol yr^{-1}) is well within the error of this preliminary mass balance, and a number of potentially important sources and sinks (e.g., production in the water column) cannot yet be accurately estimated. In addition, the magnitude of some of the sinks for MMHg in the ocean may be substantially greater than estimated here, while some of the sources of MMHg are quite possibly significantly smaller. Such discrepancies and uncertainties further highlight the need for additional research in these areas if we are to better understand the biogeochemical cycling and bioaccumulation of MMHg in marine ecosystems.

Based on our estimated standing stock of MMHg in the ocean (70 Mmol) and the annual sources and sinks for MMHg (1–1.2 Mmol yr^{-1}), the residence time of MMHg in the oceans would be on the order of 60–70 years. As is true of most of the MMHg fluxes estimated above, this value is a preliminary estimate based on limited data, which are themselves subject to large errors. Thus, the uncertainty associated with this residence time is likely at least a factor of 5.

Mercury in Marine Organisms

Mercury concentrations systematically increase with increasing trophic level in freshwater, estuary, and marine food chains (Figure 10.8 and Table 10.5). Mercury levels in apex predators in the marine environment may be more than 1 million–fold higher than in surrounding waters. This enrichment underlies mercury's persistent and bioaccumulative nature as a toxicant, representing a serious environmental and human health concern. Table 10.5 summarizes data from various marine ecosystems, illustrating the general trend of increasing total mercury concentrations and increasing %MMHg with trophic level.

Central to mercury's biomagnification is that only MMHg, not Hg(II), is biomagnified in marine food webs. The preferential bioaccumulation of MMHg, due to its relatively low elimination rate and relatively high assimilation efficiency, has been shown in kinetic models, laboratory studies, and field studies of mercury uptake by aquatic organisms (Baeyens et al. 2003; Bargagli et al., 1998; Francesconi and Lenanton, 1992; Hammerschmidt and Fitzgerald, 2006a; Lawson and Mason, 1998; Mason et al., 1996; Mathews and Fisher, 2008; Moye et al., 2002; Pickhardt and Fisher, 2007; Tsui and Wang, 2004; Wang

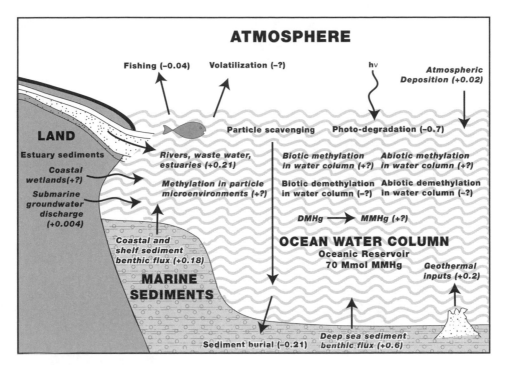

FIGURE 10.7 Preliminary mass balance of MMHg in the ocean. Estimates of all sources and sinks are derived and presented in the text. Many of the fluxes are estimated from very limited data of direct measurements, and thus uncertainties for some fluxes are likely to be as great as an order of magnitude. This is particularly true of the deep sea MMHg fluxes, the magnitude of which is inconsistent with field measurements, which do not show particularly elevated MMHg concentrations in the deep ocean.

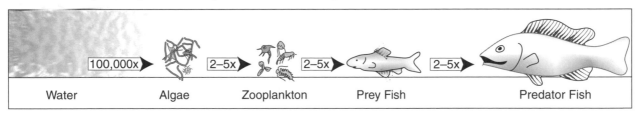

FIGURE 10.8 Typical magnitude of mercury bioaccumulation and biomagnification in a stylized aquatic food chain.

and Wong, 2003; Watras and Bloom, 1992). Those reports demonstrate that in most cases MMHg is the only form of mercury biomagnified and that MMHg constitutes a larger fraction of the overall body burden of mercury in aquatic organisms with increasing trophic level.

Mercury in Phytoplankton

Numerous studies have demonstrated the important role that phytoplankton play in the introduction of mercury into aquatic food chains. These include laboratory (Mason et al., 1996; Moye et al., 2002), mesocosm (Pickhardt et al., 2002), and field studies (Chen and Folt, 2005; Kainz and Mazumder, 2005; Watras and Bloom, 1992). Those studies have shown that phytoplankton generally concentrate MMHg 10^4–10^5 above ambient water concentrations (Moye et al., 2002; Pickhardt and Fisher, 2007; Watras et al. 1998), and this accumulation represents the largest relative increase in MMHg levels at any point in a food web. Because most of the MMHg in phytoplankton is in the cytoplasm, rather than sorbed onto the surface, it is more

effectively transferred to, and bioaccumulated by, zooplankton and planktivorous fish than inorganic mercury (Mason et al., 1996; Pickhardt and Fisher, 2007).

Because of their efficacy in sequestering MMHg from surface waters, it has been proposed that mercury concentrations in phytoplankton, on a per-cell basis, decrease during algal blooms (Chen and Folt, 2005; Pickhardt et al., 2002), potentially leading to reduced bioaccumulation of mercury to higher trophic levels during blooms. Such studies were initially conducted in freshwaters, but a study in San Francisco Bay found similar results (Luengen and Flegal, 2009).

Mercury concentrations in those and other *in situ* phytoplankton populations are not usually measured directly because of the concurrent presence of bacteria, detritus, and suspended sediments also collected in phytoplankton tows. Instead, concentrations of mercury in phytoplankton are often derived by normalizing mercury levels to other parameters (e.g., aluminum as a measure of suspended sediments; chlorophyll as a measure of primary productivity and standing biomass). While such methods enable calculations

TABLE 10.5

Total Mercury and Monomethylmercury Biomagnification in Various Marine Food Webs

Arctic and Antarctic Ecosystems

Test substance	Baffin Bay[a,b] TOTAL Hg (μg g⁻¹ wet wt)	% MMHg	Barents Sea[c,d] TOTAL Hg (μg g⁻¹ wet wt)	% MMHg	Lancaster Sound[e] TOTAL Hg (μg g⁻¹ wet wt)	% MMHg	Terra Nova Bay/Ross Sea[f] TOTAL Hg (μg g⁻¹ wet wt)	% MMHg
Surface waters	0.0000006[g]	4 ± 3	NA	NA	NA	NA	NA	NA
Algae or microseston	≤0.003	nd	NA	NA	<0.005	NA	0.01 ± 0.002	NA
Zooplankton	0.015 ± 0.015	43 ± 40	0.03	6	0.02 ± 0.01	NA	0.02 ± 0.01	NA
Molluscs	NA	NA	NA	NA	0.03 ± 0.01	NA	0.06 ± 0.03	NA
Prey (small) fish	0.023 ± 0.015	100	<0.01	nd	0.06 ± 0.1	NA	0.03 ± 0.02	NA
Piscivorous (large) fish[h]	NA	NA	0.06 ± 0.02	35 (9–100)	NA	NA	0.15 ± 0.11	NA
Piscivorous birds[h]	1.7 ± 1.1	79 ± 20	0.22 ± 0.09	62 ± 21[i]	0.5 ± 0.2	NA	0.17	NA
Seals[h]	0.68 ± 0.29	79 ± 14	NA	NA	0.3 ± 0.3	NA	1.9	NA

Coastal Ecosystems

Test substance	Long Island Sound[j] TOTAL Hg (μg g⁻¹ wet wt)	% MMHg	Princess Royal Harbor[k] TOTAL Hg (μg g⁻¹ wet wt)	% MMHg	North Sea[l] TOTAL Hg (μg g⁻¹ wet wt)	% MMHg	South San Francisco Bay[m,n,o,p,q,r,s] TOTAL Hg (μg g⁻¹ wet wt)	% MMHg
Surface waters	0.000001[g]	3	NA	NA	0.000000009[g]	<1–17	0.0000005[g]	2 ± 3
Algae or microseston	0.006	9	0.03 (0.02–0.04)	10 (5–13)	0.044	3	0.024	(1–2)
Zooplankton	NA	NA	0.28 (0.13–0.42)	65 (25–89)	NA	NA	NA	NA
Molluscs	NA	NA	0.37 (0.11–1.2)	48 (18–72)	0.022 ± 0.009	35 ± 17	0.06 ± 0.02	NA
Prey (small) fish	0.03	92	0.48 (0.37–0.60)	93 (91–95)	0.12 ± 0.12	96 ± 6	0.15 ± 0.10	NA
Piscivorous (large) fish[h]	0.14	98	2.3 (0.62–4.8)	>95	0.16 ± 0.19	94 ± 4	0.45 ± 0.20	NA
Piscivorous birds[h]	NA	NA	NA	NA	NA	NA	1.0 ± 0.7	NA
Seals[h]	NA	NA	NA	NA	NA	NA	0.34 ± 0.09[t,u]	NA

NA = not available/not measured, nd = below detection limit.

a. Campbell et al. (2005), b. Kirk et al. (2008), c. Jaeger et al. (2009), d. Joiris et al. (1997a, 1997b), e. Atwell et al. (1998), f. Bargagli et al. (1998), g. total Hg in water in μg mL−1, h. muscle tissue, i. liver, j. Hammerschmidt and Fitzgerald (2006), k. Francesconi and Lenanton (1992), l. Baeyens et al. (2003), m. Conaway et al. (2003), n. Davis et al. (2006), o. Hunt et al. (2008), p. Eagles-Smith et al. (2009a), q. Luengen and Flegal (2009), r. NOAA (2007), s. Brookens et al. (2008), t. blood, u. juveniles and adults.

of mercury concentrations per mass of phytoplankton, it is unclear how much of this is intracellular versus simply sorbed onto the outside of cell surfaces.

Using those normalizations, estimated values of total mercury concentrations (dry weight) in particles likely to be phytoplankton in the Arctic Ocean are less than 20 ng g^{-1} (Atwell et al., 1998; Campbell et al., 2005). These are substantially lower than mercury levels for similar sized particles and sestons in estuaries and coastal areas such as the Seine estuary in France (40–170 ng g^{-1}; Laurier et al., 2003a), Monterey Bay (100–600 ng g^{-1}; Martin and Knauer, 1973), San Francisco Bay (500–3700 ng g^{-1}, mean = 1200 ± 1000 ng g^{-1}; Flegal, 1977), South San Francisco Bay (80–420 ng g^{-1}, mean = 250 ± 90 ng g^{-1}; Luengen and Flegal, 2009), or those (60–100 ng g^{-1}) estimated for an estuarine mesocosm experiment (Kim et al., 2004). The higher concentration of mercury in phytoplankton-sized particles in coastal waters reflects the greater mercury contamination here; also, these operationally defined size fractions are likely to include a larger percentage of more mercury-contaminated inorganic particles and resuspended sediment in estuary and coastal environments. These mercury concentrations are well within the range, although slightly on the lower end, of particulate concentrations of total mercury on all suspended material in estuary and coastal waters (Baeyens et al., 1998; Balcom et al., 2008; Benoit et al., 1998; Choe et al., 2003; Conaway et al., 2003; Coquery et al., 1997; Laurier et al., 2003a; Leermakers et al., 1995, 2001; Stordal et al., 1996). Thus, it appears that the partitioning of total mercury onto phytoplankton is similar to that for inert particles, as also suggested by laboratory experiments (Pickhardt and Fisher, 2007).

MMHg concentrations estimated for phytoplankton in the Seine estuary in France (5 ± 3.6 ng g^{-1}; Laurier et al., 2003a) and the San Francisco Bay estuary (0.6–2.2 ng g^{-1}; Luengen and Flegal, 2009) are similar to those measured by Kim et al. (2004) in an estuarine mesocosm experiment (1.0–6.5 ng g^{-1}). These values are noticeably higher than particulate MMHg concentrations of microseston and suspended particulate matter in these waters and other estuaries and coastal waters (Baeyens et al., 1998, 2003; Balcom et al., 2008; Benoit et al., 1998; Choe and Gill, 2003; Conaway et al., 2003; Hammerschmidt and Fitzgerald, 2006a; Horvat et al., 1999; Leermakers et al., 2001). This disparity reflects the preferential bioaccumulation of MMHg by phytoplankton compared with inorganic Hg(II).

Mercury in Zooplankton

There have been fewer studies of mercury in zooplankton in saline waters than for zooplankton in freshwaters or phytoplankton in saline waters. Despite this, the processes controlling the uptake and trophic transfer of mercury by zooplankton in freshwater and saline environments are probably similar. Mercury levels in particles of comparable size to zooplankton as high as 25 µg g^{-1} (dw) have been reported in coastal and estuarine waters (Pereira et al., 2007), but concentrations are generally in the range 0.5–200 ng g^{-1} (Al-Majed and Preston, 2000; Atwell et al., 1998; Campbell et al., 2005; Hammerschmidt and Fitzgerald, 2006a; Joiris et al., 1997b; Outridge et al., 2008; Pereira et al., 2007; Stern and MacDonald, 2005). These mercury concentrations in marine zooplankton are slightly lower than those for zooplankton from freshwater systems (10–500 ng g^{-1}; Kainz and Mazumder, 2005; Tremblay et al., 1995; Watras and Bloom, 1992; Watras et al., 1998). This disparity presumably reflects the lower concentrations of MMHg in microseston of marine environments, but may also be due to differences in zooplankton community and associated differences in diet or MMHg assimilation efficiencies.

The ratio of MMHg to Hg(II) in zooplankton is highly variable (Al-Majed and Preston, 2000; Campbell et al., 2005; Francesconi and Lenanton, 1992; Joiris et al., 1997b; Stern and MacDonald, 2005) and is not consistently as great as in higher trophic levels. Even when the majority of the mercury in zooplankton is not MMHg, the %MMHg is still consistently greater than in phytoplankton from the same environment because of the higher assimilation efficiency of MMHg by zooplankton relative to inorganic mercury (Lawson and Mason, 1998). Mercury levels tend to be 2–6 times higher in zooplankton than in phytoplankton or microseston, demonstrating bioaccumulation. In laboratory studies, the assimilation efficiency by herbivorous copepods (*Acartia tonsa*, *Temora longicornis*, and *Centropages* sp.) feeding on the diatom *Thalassiosira weissflogii* for MMHg, which was accumulated in the cytoplasm of the phytoplankton, was fourfold greater than it was for inorganic Hg(II), which was principally bound to membranes (Mason et al., 1996).

The uptake of Hg(II) and MMHg by zooplankton varies with taxonomic, morphometric, and ontogenic differences, but in general zooplankton bioconcentrate both inorganic Hg(II) and MMHg from the surrounding medium. However, most accumulated mercury comes from their food (Mason et al., 1996; Mathews and Fisher, 2008; Monson and Brezonik, 1999; Pickhardt et al., 2006; Watras et al., 1998). As a result, zooplankton mercury levels display spatial and seasonal variability that reflect differences in diet, phytoplankton community dynamics, factors affecting phytoplankton uptake of MMHg, and changes in DOM and suspended particle load (Chen and Folt, 2005; Joiris et al., 1997b; Laurier et al., 2003a; Lawson and Mason, 1998; Mathews and Fisher, 2008; Monson and Brezonik, 1999; Pereira et al., 2007; Pickhardt et al., 2002; Stern and MacDonald, 2005).

Mercury in Macroinvertebrates

Analyses of a large number of marine invertebrates have shown that most contain relatively low concentrations of mercury and MMHg in contrast to larger, piscivorous fish. Average total mercury concentrations in oysters, clams, squid, octopus, scallops, and crabs consumed in the United States range from only 0.01 to 0.12 μg g^{-1} wet weight (ww), as compared with an average concentration of 0.95–1.3 μg g^{-1} ww in swordfish and shark muscle (US EPA, 1997; US FDA, 2006). The ratio of MMHg to total mercury is also generally substantially lower in marine invertebrates (<60%) than it is in edible marine fish (60–100%) (Lasora and Allen-Gil, 1995; Andersen and Depledge, 1997). Some exceptions are marine shrimp, crabs, and lobsters, for which mercury burdens in muscle tissue are more consistently 80–100% MMHg (Andersen and Depledge, 1997; Bloom, 1992; Campbell et al., 2005; Francesconi and Lenanton, 1992; Hammerschmidt and Fitzgerald, 2006a; Joiris et al., 1997b). A substantial amount of that mercury in lobsters (*Nephrops norvegicus*) is in the tail, which is the part principally consumed by humans (Canli and Furness, 1995; Hammerschmidt and Fitzgerald, 2006a; Perugini et al., 2009).

One reason for interest in mercury concentrations in marine invertebrates, primarily mussels and oysters, has been because of their applicability as biomonitors of pollutants in coastal waters. These organisms are used because they are widespread, numerous, convenient to collect, sessile, and tend to bioaccumulate pollutants, including mercury, to levels that are easily measured. Consequently, a national "mussel watch" program was started in the United States more than three decades ago (Goldberg et al., 1978), and comparable programs now exist in most of the world's coastal waters (Laurier et al., 2007; Nakhlé et al., 2006; National Oceanographic and Atmospheric Administration [NOAA], 2007). Cubadda et al. (2006) have reported that variations of mercury concentrations in mussels (*Mytilus galloprovincialis*) ranged from 0.02 to 0.07 μg g^{-1} (ww) and revealed spatial gradients in anthropogenic pollution in the Venice Lagoon. The use of mussels as biosentinels is not as well suited for quantifying differences in mercury pollution across ecosystems or time as for other pollutants if only total Hg is measured, because there is high variability in the ratio of MMHg to total Hg in the bivalves used.

Documentation of differences in mercury concentrations and speciation both within and between invertebrate species has catalyzed a number of studies on the abiotic and biotic factors that account for those differences (Baeyens et al., 1998; Canli and Furness, 1995; Gagnon and Fisher, 1997; Mason and Lawrence, 1999). These have generally shown that MMHg is more readily bioaccumulated than inorganic Hg(II) in marine invertebrates, ranging from small deposit-feeding polychaetes (*Nereis succinea* and *N. diversicolor*), amphipods (*Leptocheirus plumulosus*), and mussels (*Mytilus edulis*) to macroinvertebrates, including scavenging Norway lobsters (*Nephrops norvegicus*). In contrast, Laporte et al. (2002) determined that inorganic Hg(II) and MMHg were accumulated by the blue crab (*Callinectes sapidus*) at similar rates, albeit by different mechanisms.

Finally, there have been varying accounts of anomalously high levels of mercury in marine invertebrates at some submarine hydrothermal vent systems. These vents emit fluids enriched in mercury, resulting in anomalously high mercury levels (e.g., 7 μg g^{-1} dw) in mussels (*Bathymodiolus azoricus*) and ascidians (*Polydistoma azorensis*) living in those chemotrophic systems (Kádár et al., 2007). Several studies have investigated factors influencing the bioavailability, bioaccumulation, biomagnification, compartmentalization, and toxic effects of mercury in hydrothermal vent invertebrates (Colaço et al., 2006; Cunha et al., 2008; Kádár et al., 2005, 2007; Martins et al., 2001; Ruelas-Inzunza et al., 2005). For example, Kádár et al. (2005) determined that the bioaccumulation factor for inorganic Hg(II) in the hydrothermal mussel *Bathymodiolus azoricus* was 10^4, while Colaço et al. (2006) found no clear evidence of mercury biomagnification in seven different species of invertebrates (worms, mussel, shrimp and crabs) in food chains of Mid-Atlantic Ridge hydrothermal vent systems. In a related study, Martins et al. (2006a) found levels of mercury in fish (0.6–1.9 μg g^{-1} ww) caught at the Mid-Atlantic hydrothermal vent fields that were relatively high compared with previously published values for deep-sea fish "with identical diets, but caught in other areas."

Mercury in Fish

Interest in mercury levels in fish has been catalyzed by concerns of mercury toxicity to humans and other animals, whose principal source of mercury contamination is from the consumption of fish. Most studies of mercury in marine fish have, therefore, focused on species commonly preyed upon by marine mammals and birds, or more often, on fish of commercial importance. This anthropocentric orientation has been of great value in evaluating human exposure to mercury via fish consumption and developing guidelines for protecting public health (Burger et al., 2005; Mergler et al., 2007; Mozaffarian and Rimm, 2006; Sunderland, 2007). However, it may have inadvertently skewed common perceptions of the cycling of mercury in the marine biosphere.

Reviews and public reports on mercury concentrations in fish often focus on those with the highest mercury concentrations (e.g., shark and swordfish) and those commonly eaten by affluent Western and Asian populations (e.g., tuna and halibut). Although these are appropriate for assisting people in evaluating the risk of mercury levels in the fish they most often eat, such fish do not represent the majority of fish in marine ecosystems, nor even the majority of species harvested by global fisheries. So while tuna represents the most important source of mercury to the average American (Sunderland, 2007), all tuna combined accounts for less than 5% of the global fish catch each year (UN FAO, 2007) and comprise a much smaller percentage of the total fish biomass in the oceans. Table 10.4 provides mercury concentrations for the 32 leading marine organisms harvested globally (by fresh weight), which together account for over 40% of all fish harvested from the oceans. Of these 32, only 4 have mean mercury concentrations in muscle tissue in excess of 0.2 μg g^{-1} ww. Many of the ecologically important smaller fish found in Table 10.4, as well as other organism low in the food web, typically have lower total mercury concentrations and lower percentages of MMHg.

Even when only comparing mercury levels in axial muscle tissue, large differences in the percentage of total Hg existing as MMHg in marine fish exist and can be influenced by numerous variables. These include factors that can be readily measured (e.g., species, sex, size, age, trophic level, life histories, and physiologic condition), and others that cannot be as easily documented (e.g., metabolic rate, elimination rate, ecophysiologic activity, variations in trophic structure, prey dynamics, feeding location, and time spent in proximity to pollution). Consequently, addressing all of those variables to determine the factors regulating mercury and MMHg concentrations in marine fish can be quite daunting.

One approach to resolve the relative importance of factors has been to investigate mercury concentrations, along with $\delta^{13}C$, $\delta^{15}N$, and other measures of trophic level in similar species from the same location. Using this approach, it was concluded that most of the differences in the bioaccumulation of two sympatric snapper species (*Lutjanus campechanus* and *L. griseus*) in the Gulf of Mexico could be accounted for by "modest differences in their trophic position, and, to a lesser degree, carbon sources, which had low variation and high overlap among species" (Bank et al., 2007). This study concluded that even small differences in trophic position and food habits of similar species could result in relatively large differences in their bioaccumulation of mercury.

Another difficulty with assessing the role of fish in the cycling of mercury within an ecosystem is that many fish move from one ecosystem to another. Fish transport contaminants, including mercury, with them via bio-advection (Blais et al., 2005, 2007; Krummel et al., 2003). This transport is most evident for long-lived anadromous fish that accumulate and concentrate MMHg in oceanic waters and then return to spawn and die in freshwater systems (Zhang et al., 2001). For example, mass balance calculations by Sarica et al. (2004) indicated that: (1) salmon are an important source of mercury in a Lake Ontario spawning stream, and (2) invertebrates and vertebrates that feed on the salmon detritus in that stream are important vectors for the transport of that mercury to terrestrial ecosystems.

Biotransport is not limited to lateral movement. It has been reported that fish spending more of their time feeding in deep waters have higher Hg concentrations than epipelagic fish feeding primarily in surface waters at the same location (Monteiro et al., 1996). A consequence of those deep-water fish migrating to surface waters is that mercury concentrations in seabirds were found to depend upon whether they were feeding on mesopelagic or epipelagic fish, rather than on their trophic level (Monteiro and Furness, 1997; Monteiro et al., 1998; Thompson et al., 1998).

Mercury in Marine Mammals

Mercury in the flesh of marine mammals can be exceptionally high. For example, Atwell et al. (1998) reported

average total mercury concentrations ($\mu g\ g^{-1}$ dw) of 0.41 ± 0.08 in walruses (*Odobenus rosmartus*), 0.84 ± 0.17 in polar bears (*Ursus maritimus*), 1.07 ± 0.11 in ringed seals (*Phoca hispida*), 2.25 ± 0.97 in beluga whales (*Delphinapterus leucas*), and 2.32 in narwhal (*Monodon monoceros*). Of special concern are the high levels of mercury in pilot whales (*Globicephalus meleanus*), because they are an important part of the human diet in the Faroe Islands (Andersen et al., 1987).

Mercury concentrations in most marine mammals are typically higher than those of their prey. One exception is polar bears, whose muscle tissue is lower than that of their principal prey, ringed seals. This inconsistency has been explained by polar bears' preferential consumption of ringed seal tissues (skin and blubber) that have relatively low mercury concentrations (Atwell et al., 1998). In a human parallel, the skin of narwhal and beluga whales, which have mercury concentrations ranging from 0.3 to 1.5 $\mu g\ g^{-1}$, are considered a delicacy by native Canadian and Greenland people (Wagemann and Kozlowska, 2005; Wagemann et al., 1998).

In contrast to most measurements of mercury in fish, which generally focus on muscle, most measurements of mercury concentrations in marine mammals have been conducted on several different tissues (Dehn et al., 2006; Dietz et al., 2006b; Johansen et al., 2007; Lockhart et al., 2005; Outridge et al., 2005; Riget and Dietz, 2000; Riget et al., 2007a; Sonne et al., 2007; Wagemann et al., 1998; Wagemann and Kozlowska, 2005). These include tissues consumed by other marine organisms and humans (e.g., skin, muscle, fat, liver, and kidney) and tissues that may be used to chronicle temporal changes of mercury concentrations in those organisms (e.g., hair, teeth, and baleen). The rationale for these multiple analyses is that: (1) marine mammals are too large for whole body measurements, (2) the distribution of mercury in tissues of marine mammals is a better measure of the potential toxicity of mercury for them, (3) other marine mammals and people typically consume only certain tissues of marine mammals, and (4) some preserved marine mammal tissues (e.g., teeth and baleen) may be used as biomonitors of historic mercury concentrations in those organisms and their environment.

Riget et al. (2005) reported that spatial variations in mercury content of the liver and kidney of ringed seals were consistent with those observed in previous studies of ringed seals, beluga whales, and polar bears (Wagemann et al., 1998; Muir et al., 1999) that showed the highest concentrations in the western Canadian Arctic. The reason for this geographic variation was tentatively attributed to regional differences in geology, but this has yet to be resolved (Riget et al., 2005), and regional differences in diet or natural and anthropogenic fluxes of mercury may also play roles.

Mercury in Marine Birds

As with marine mammals, mercury concentrations in some marine birds are high because of their position at or near the top of their food web, while concentrations in other seabirds are relatively low (Campbell et al., 2005; Jarman et al., 1996). This variability was illustrated in a study by Borga et al. (2006), who found that average total mercury levels in the muscle tissue of seven species of Arctic seabirds ranged from 0.05 μg g^{-1} (ww) in the black guillemot (*Cepphus grylle*) to 0.8 μg g^{-1} (ww) in the glaucous-winged gull (*Larus hyperboreus*). Higher concentrations have been reported for other species of marine birds (Eagles-Smith et al., 2009a, 2009b; Ruelas-Inzunza et al., 2009).

Because of the high levels of mercury in some marine birds, there are concerns that mercury may pose a health threat both to the birds (Scheuhammer et al., 2007) and humans that consume the birds and their eggs. For example, Burger et al. (2007) found that 95% of the pigeon guillemot (*Cepphus columba*) muscles sampled in the Aleutians had Hg concentrations greater than 0.3 μg g^{-1} and 43% were greater than 0.5 μg g^{-1}, and therefore they represented a potential health risk to indigenous peoples of the Aleutians. In a follow-up study, Burger and Gochfeld (2007) found that 100% of glaucous-winged gull (*Larus glaucescens*) eggs in that region were above 0.3 μg g^{-1}, 62% were above 0.5 μg g^{-1}, and 8% were above 1.0 μg g^{-1}. Nearly all of the mercury in bird eggs is MMHg, which is easily transferred from mother to egg (Heinz and Hoffman, 2004; Scheuhammer et al., 2001). In fact, deposition of mercury into eggs is an important elimination route in birds for MMHg, as is incorporation of MMHg into growing feathers (Braune and Gaskin, 1987; Monteiro and Furness, 2001).

The elevated mercury levels in marine birds are of concern because, as in eggs and feathers, most of the mercury in seabird muscle is MMHg. For example, Joiris et al. (1997c) determined that mercury in muscle tissues of five seabird species ranged from 0.8 to 4.1 μg g^{-1} (dw), and the corresponding MMHg concentrations ranged from 0.7 to 4.1 μg g^{-1} (dw), with MMHg accounting for 85–100% of the mercury measured in those samples. In contrast, they found that MMHg constituted a relatively low percentage of the total mercury burden in two other species of seabirds: 63% in black scoters (*Melanitta nigra*) and 39% in black-legged kittiwakes (*Rissa tridactyla*). These anomalously low values may have reflected the poor health of the birds that were collected after they had been beached.

Variations in mercury concentrations in various tissues from various water birds in the San Francisco Estuary were associated with differences in foraging areas, time spent in the estuary, and the onset of breeding (Ackerman et al., 2007; Eagles-Smith et al., 2009a). Some of the highest mercury concentrations in the bird species studied were found in colonies that fed in the southern reach of the estuary, where mercury concentrations in sediments and surface waters were anomalously high because of contamination from historic mercury mining (Conaway et al., 2004). This is consistent with observations that mercury levels increase in birds that migrate there from less-contaminated areas. Moreover, mercury levels in some birds in this estuary,

including the endangered California clapper rail (*Rallus longirostris obsoletus*), are believed to reduce their reproductive success (Schwarzbach et al., 2006).

Mercury in Marine Ecosystems

Mercury in Arctic Marine Ecosystems

There is great interest in mercury contamination in Arctic marine ecosystems because of concerns that: (1) the Arctic may serve as a global "sink" for global industrial mercury emissions due to springtime atmospheric mercury depletion events (AMDEs) that are unique to polar regions (Schroeder et al., 1998), (2) some native Arctic people are exposed to unusually high amounts of mercury through their consumption of marine mammals, birds, and fish with unusually high levels of mercury (Burger and Gochfeld, 2007; Burger et al., 2007; Johansen et al., 2007), and (3) high levels of mercury are potentially toxic to the marine organisms themselves (Burger and Gochfeld, 2007; Lockhart et al., 2005; Sonne et al., 2007). These concerns have been amplified by measurements of relatively low mercury concentrations in numerous preindustrial archived Arctic marine organisms, including beluga whales, ringed seals, polar bears, and a variety of seabirds, as well as humans, as compared with those found in contemporary organisms in the Arctic. Mercury levels in these contemporary organisms are reportedly as much as an order of magnitude greater than their prehistoric baseline levels (Outridge et al., 2005; Dietz et al., 2006a, 2006b).

There are several reviews of mercury in Arctic marine food webs. These include general summaries of mercury concentrations in different trophic levels (Campbell et al., 2005; Dehn et al., 2006; Outridge et al., 2008; Riget and Dietz, 2000; Riget et al., 2007b), as well as more specific studies that address the role of trophic level or feeding ecology on mercury concentrations in a single species or group of species (Borga et al., 2006; Joiris et al., 1997a, 1997b; Lockhart et al., 2005; Outridge et al., 2005; Riget et al., 2005; Wagemann and Kozlowska, 2005). While all of the preceding studies have focused on organisms at or near the top of Arctic marine food webs, a few studies have focused on mercury concentrations in primary consumers (e.g., zooplankton and shrimp) in the Arctic (e.g., Joiris et al., 1997b; Stern and Macdonald, 2005).

Results from those studies attest to the complexity of tracing mercury in Arctic marine food webs. For example, Burger and Gochfeld (2007) tentatively attributed differences in mercury concentrations in various species of marine birds in the Arctic to differences in their diets, while acknowledging that the diets of birds within the same species can be highly variable. They also noted that mercury concentrations in the eggs of common eiders (*Somateria mollissima*) and glaucous-winged gulls (*Larus glaucescens*), which averaged 0.43 ± 0.22 and 0.68 ± 0.97 μg g^{-1} (ww) respectively, were above the levels of sublethal toxicity (0.2

and 0.5 µg g^{-1} ww) reported by Thompson (1996) and Eisler (1987). These observations were consistent with those of previous studies by Joiris et al. (1997c) of migratory common guillemots (*Uria aalge*) in the North Sea, and by Borga et al. (2006) of a suite of Arctic seabirds. The latter studies also attested to the importance of spatial and temporal variations on mercury concentrations in those Arctic birds.

Some of the reasons for that variability have been resolved with complementary measurements of δ^{15}N values to more accurately establish trophic level(s) of organisms in Arctic food webs (Michener and Schell, 1994). For example, Atwell et al. (1998) measured both δ^{15}N and mercury in 27 species in an Arctic food web, from invertebrates to polar bears, and determined that mercury concentrations were biomagnified in muscle tissue throughout that food web with one exception—the polar bears. Average mercury levels in their muscle (0.84 ± 0.17 µg g^{-1} dw) were found to be lower than those (1.07 ± 0.11 µg g^{-1} dw) of their principal prey, ringed seals. This anomaly was attributed to the bears preferentially consuming seal blubber, which is relatively low in mercury compared with other tissues (Brookens et al., 2008). It has also been noted that polar bears are able to store unusually high amounts of mercury in their kidneys (Dietz et al., 1990), which would further reduce the amount of mercury in their muscle tissue, and may be related to demethylation of MMHg in the liver, as observed in other mammals and birds.

Finally, mass balance calculations of mercury fluxes through the Arctic Ocean (Outridge et al., 2008) suggest that the system is near steady state (net annual increase in mercury of ~0.3%). Sustained reductions in emissions of industrial mercury would be required to measurably reduce mercury contamination of marine organisms in the Arctic. Any such declines are projected to be slower there than in most other marine ecosystems because of the large reservoir of mercury in the Arctic relative to inputs, resulting in a longer residence time of mercury in the Arctic Ocean compared with most other oceans (Mason and Sheu, 2002; Outridge et al., 2008; Sunderland and Mason, 2007). Moreover, dramatic climate change in the Arctic is further compounding difficulties with already complicated models of mercury in the Arctic environment (Macdonald et al., 2005; Outridge et al., 2008).

Mercury in Antarctic Ecosystems

There are many similar concerns regarding the biogeochemical cycling, biomagnification, and potential toxicity of mercury in the two polar regions. Mercury depletion events were first reported (Schroeder et al., 1998) shortly after Arctic springtime; Antarctic AMDE s were also detected (Ebinghaus et al., 2002). And while there are no indigenous peoples in Antarctica who are subject to mercury exposure from the consumption of local species, fish and large marine mammals from the Antarctic, like from the Arctic, are caught and shipped to markets globally.

Consequently, the cycling of mercury in Antarctic marine food webs is of both basic and applied scientific interest.

Most of the data on mercury in Antarctic marine organisms are relatively limited or preliminary (e.g., Ancora et al., 2002; Bocher et al., 2003; de Moreno et al., 1997; dos Santos et al., 2006; Honda et al., 2006; McArthur et al. 2003; Riva et al., 2004), but some studies have begun to address mercury in Antarctic food webs. Nygård et al. (2001) investigated metal concentrations in the Antarctic petrel (*Thalassoica antarctica*), Antarctic krill (*Euphausia superba*) in petrel stomach contents, and in the petrel's predator, the South Polar skua (*Catharacta maccormicki*). The average mercury concentration of the krill (40 ng g^{-1} dw) was comparable to that of copepods (*Calanus hyperboreus*) (20 ng g^{-1} dw) from the Beaufort and Chukchi Seas in the Arctic (Stern and Macdonald, 2005), as well as that of zooplankton elsewhere. While mercury was biomagnified in that simple food chain, mercury concentrations in the birds were found to vary substantially, indicative of variations associated with age, sex, and diet. This was consistent with the more extensive study of variations of mercury in feathers of 13 species of seabirds in the Southern Ocean (Becker et al., 2002), as well as that of terrestrial and marine birds elsewhere.

Bargagli et al. (1998) conducted a more extensive analysis of the biomagnification of mercury in an Antarctic marine coastal food web, extending from phytoplankton to seals (Table 10.5). They also measured mercury concentrations in soils at the site (12 ng g^{-1} dw), which they reported to be the lowest ever reported for a coastal location. They attributed the "slightly lower" mercury concentrations in primary producers and consumers in that food web, as compared with related species elsewhere, to the low natural background levels of mercury and minimal contamination in the Antarctic. However, a comparison with data in Table 10.5 suggests that their results are consistent with mercury concentrations at those same trophic levels in the Arctic. Similarly, they noted that mercury concentrations in piscivorous birds and mammals in the Antarctic food web were comparable to those observed in similar species in the northern hemisphere, but attributed that enrichment "to enhance natural biomagnification processes of Hg in the pristine Antarctic coastal environment."

Mercury in Open Oceanic Ecosystems

While anthropogenic mercury contamination has occurred in the Arctic and appears to have occurred in the Antarctic, the extent of mercury contamination in open oceanic food webs—where most industrial atmospheric emissions have been deposited—is unknown. This surprising gap in knowledge was emphasized by Fitzgerald et al. (2007) in their review on the marine biogeochemical cycling of mercury.

Despite a lack of appreciable data on mercury in open ocean food webs, there is limited data suggesting that mercury concentrations in biota may vary as a function of depth in the open ocean. Total mercury concentrations in small prey fish in the North Atlantic with similar diet and trophic status were reported to be correlated with median daytime depth, with greater mercury concentrations in fish that forage primarily in intermediate waters as compared with those spending most of their time in surface waters (Monteiro et al., 1996). Similarly, in the North Atlantic, total mercury concentrations in feathers and food were up to fourfold higher in seabirds feeding on mesopelagic prey than for those feeding predominantly on epipelagic prey (Monteiro and Furness, 1997; Monteiro et al., 1998; Thompson et al., 1998). Such a trend of increasing total mercury concentrations in biota with depth may reflect the greater concentrations of DMHg and methylated Hg in intermediate waters as compared with surface waters in the open ocean. However, linking the reportedly higher concentrations of mercury in biota in intermediate waters of the open ocean with the potential production of DMHg and methylated Hg (most of which is likely to be DMHg) would require the conversion of DMHg into MMHg at depth prior to its uptake into the food web because only MMHg is biomagnified.

Mercury in Nearshore and Coastal Ecosystems

Studies of mercury in coastal food webs have primarily focused on the effect of local anthropogenic discharges on mercury levels in seafood. This concern is based on measurements of high mercury levels in some commercial species of shellfish and fish (Baeyens et al., 2003; Bank et al., 2007; Davis et al., 2008; Kawaguchi et al., 1999; Ruelas-Inzunza et al., 2008) that have been correlated with point source discharges of mercury to those waters. While it is difficult to establish whether the correlations are causal, a few studies have documented decreases of mercury concentrations in coastal species following the termination of point source discharges of industrial mercury (e.g., Francesconi et al., 1997).

However, the attenuation of mercury pollution in coastal embayments and estuaries can be quite slow. For example, Francesconi et al. (1997) noted that mercury concentrations in fish within Princess Royal Harbour in Australia declined by ~50% over a 10-year period after the discharge of industrial wastewater to the harbor was terminated. They noted that most of that decrease occurred during the first few years and that elevated concentrations of mercury in the fish could persist for many more years. Their observations were consistent with the results of others using time-series analyses of persistent mercury contamination elsewhere. This includes Lavaca Bay, Texas, where fishing remained closed more than 20 years after a chemical plant ceased discharging mercury to the bay (Palmer et al., 1993), and Minamata Bay, Japan, where the resumption of fishing was not allowed for more than 30 years after industrial mercury discharges into that bay were terminated (Harada, 1995). Moreover, there is no evidence that mercury concentrations in fish in San Francisco Bay have decreased despite decades of extensive efforts to reduce anthropogenic discharges of mercury into that estuarine system (Greenfield et al., 2005).

Most of the preceding studies focused exclusively on mercury concentrations in seafood (i.e., large fish and macroinvertebrates), but a few studies have attempted a more comprehensive analysis of the accumulation of mercury in estuarine and coastal food chains. One study of this type was by Hammerschmidt and Fitzgerald (2006a), who measured MMHg concentrations in representative species from different trophic levels in Long Island Sound. They found a systematic bioaccumulation of MMHg from water to microseston ($10^{4.2}$) and then from microseston to zooplankton (2.3). MMHg concentrations in four species of fish (alewife, *Alosa pseudoharengus*, a pelagic planktivore; winter flounder, *Pseudopleuronectes americanus*, a demersal omnivore; tautog, *Tautoga onitis*, a benthic invertivore; and bluefish, *Pomatomus saltatrix*, a piscivore) were positively correlated with their size and tended to correspond with their trophic structure. There were, however, considerable differences in mercury concentrations among some of the larger individuals within a species, which they tentatively attributed to differences in dietary histories, migratory patterns, and physiologic condition. One surprising observation was that the durophagous tautog, which feeds primarily on lower-trophic-level organisms (e.g., bivalves and small decapod crustaceans), had the highest mean MMHg concentration of the four fish species sampled, including the piscivorous bluefish that was calculated to bioaccumulate MMHg 3–5 times faster than the tautog. Consequently, they attributed the anomalously high MMHg levels in the tautog to the accumulation of mercury over their relatively long life span (30+ years), as compared with that of the younger bluefish.

Other researchers have tried to circumvent questions in variable and changing diets of higher-trophic-level organisms by using stable isotope ratios ($\delta^{13}C$ and $\delta^{15}N$), along with measurements of mercury concentrations in marine biota (Bank et al., 2007; Ikemoto et al., 2008). These stable isotopic composition measurements can provide a measure of individual trophic position and community-wide structure, as described by Layman et al. (2007).

An alternative for investigating the bioaccumulation and biomagnification of mercury is to conduct microcosm or mesocosm studies. This approach enables one to control and/or measure processes that may be influencing the transfer of mercury, including food characteristics (quantity, quality, nutrient stoichiometry, metal concentration), physicochemical species involved in sequestration (metal-rich granules, sulfide, protein levels), homeostasis (body burden, pre-exposure, adaptation/tolerance) or detoxification and digestive/feeding physiology (prey selectivity, digestive enzyme/partitioning, ingestion rate, gut passage, optimal foraging). Some microcosm and mesocosm studies have incorporated the use of stable and radiogenic mercury isotopes (Mathews and Fisher, 2008; Pickhardt et al., 2002; Wang and Wong, 2003).

Mercury in Coastal Wetland Ecosystems

Distributed at the middle and high latitudes along shores worldwide, salt marshes are among the most highly productive ecosystems in the world—comparable to subsidized agriculture (Mitsch and Gosselink, 2000). Ecosystem function in salt marshes is dominated by belowground production, anaerobic conditions, and detrital food webs. Studies of MMHg in salt marshes attest to the importance of its belowground production (Canário et al., 2007b). In contrast to this, scientific study of these ecosystems often focuses on birds and other organisms living predominantly above ground. Those birds often have relatively high concentrations of total Hg and MMHg, and can have varied diets covering a broad range of habitat types (Ackerman et al., 2007; Eagles-Smith et al., 2009a). The export of MMHg from tidal wetlands, either flushed out tidally, or via bioadvection due to fish or bird migration, is a potentially important source of MMHg to adjacent ecosystems (Hall et al., 2008; Heim et al., 2007; Mitchell and Gilmour, 2008).

Most studies on mercury and primary producers in salt marshes have been on macrophytes, although algal production in these coastal wetlands can be as high or higher (Zedler, 1980). Indeed, direct grazing by consumers on macrophytes is thought to be minor compared to grazing on algae (Mitsch and Gosselink, 2000). Nonetheless, certain plants or plant assemblages create or take up more mercury than others, and the decay of these plant materials by microbial consumers can play an important role in MMHg production (Rajan et al., 2008).

Best et al. (2007) found that uptake of inorganic Hg(II) and MMHg by plants differed substantially among vegetation types in a salt march, with cordgrass (*Spartina foliosa*) accumulating more of both types of mercury than pickleweed (*Sarcocornia pacifica*, formerly *Salicornia virginica*). Using stable isotope ratios ($\delta^{13}C$ and $\delta^{15}N$) and marsh vegetation structure, Best et al. (2007) found no relationship between trophic level (based on $\delta^{15}N$) and MMHg concentration and only a weak relationship between MMHg bioaccumulation and the defined habitat types. But they did find that plant detritus was enriched in mercury relative to live plants—consistent with the plant litter experiments by Windham et al. (2004) and Zawislanski et al. (2001)—and suggested that detritivores would have a higher mercury exposure than herbivores. This and other studies (Rajan et al., 2008) have also showed that the rates and timing of MMHg production during plant decay differed substantially under aerobic and anaerobic conditions.

Some studies have highlighted the importance of predator macroinvertebrates with high percentages of MMHg as a key source of MMHg in salt marsh food webs, consistent with similar observations in freshwater and terrestrial systems (Cristol et al., 2008). Song sparrows (*Melospiza melodia samuelis*) had the highest mercury concentrations in the Best et al. (2007) survey, at 1.7 μg g^{-1}, with 80% as MMHg. These birds are thought to feed primarily on insects, spiders, and amphipods, which is supported by their $\delta^{13}C$ and $\delta^{15}N$ values. The percentage of mercury as MMHg in amphipods (*Orchestia traskiana*) and beetles (*Cicindela* sp.) was relatively high (83–94%) in this study, and the exceptionally high values of mercury in sparrows are likely a result of this MMHg-rich diet. In a study of bird colonies in coastal salt pans in Portuguese coastal wetlands, Tavares et al. (2008) found that mercury concentrations in blackwinged stilt (*Himantopus himantopus*) chicks correlated with mercury concentrations in some macroinvertebrate groups (Corixidae, Chironomidae, and Hydrophilidae). Surprisingly, they found that mercury levels in the chicks did not correlate with trophic levels as predicted by $\delta^{15}N$ values. This disparity was attributed to spatial and temporal differences in prey availability between colony sites.

Long-Term Changes of Mercury in Marine Ecosystems

One of the key reasons for studying mercury in ecosystems has been to determine whether, and how, humans have influenced mercury concentrations in fish. Unfortunately, these are not simple questions to answer. Although there has clearly been an increase in mercury concentrations in many environmental compartments, there are few reliable long-term data sets on mercury concentrations in marine organisms. Another difficulty is that marine ecosystems are not static, and in most cases they have been fundamentally changed by human activity. In addition, the way humans have used these ecosystems has changed markedly through time, and will continue to do so in the future.

Measuring Human Impact on Mercury Concentrations in Biota

The importance of attributing some fraction of the mercury in fish to human activity lies in how we perceive and manage mercury contamination. A great deal of money, legislation, and research has been focused on linking the atmospheric deposition of mercury from industrial discharges to mercury concentrations in fish. The combustion of fossil fuels, primarily coal, now accounts for the largest anthropogenic emission of mercury to the atmosphere globally (Pacyna et al., 2006). Regulation of coal combustion is already an environmentally and politically charged topic because of rising atmospheric CO_2 levels and the uncertain supply of crude oil. It is inevitable that coal use will rise, but regulation of mercury from this source globally is not assured. Linking the bulk of mercury in marine biota to human contamination would provide a human health incentive to enact such regulation. Evidence for such a link in freshwater systems has been rapidly accumulating in recent years, with multiple studies demonstrating that the atmospheric deposition of mercury is linked to the production and accumulation of MMHg in aquatic ecosystems (Hammerschmidt and Fitzgerald, 2006c; Harris et al., 2007; Orihel et al., 2006, 2007; Paterson et al., 2006).

In addition to affecting controls on mercury emissions, linking mercury in fish to human activities has implications for how mercury concentrations in fish are perceived and regulated. Risk perception likely changes depending on whether one considers mercury in fish as natural or instead as an insidious by-product of human industrial activity. The former description is far less likely to arouse a call for government regulation. And indeed, the proposed link between human activity and mercury concentrations in fish has been the basis of litigation for health warnings on some seafood.

Long-Term Changes of Mercury in the Marine Environment

Humans have undeniably had a measurable and profound effect on mercury in the environment (see previous chapters). Mercury depth profiles in lake sediment, peat, and ice cores demonstrate global and regional increases in mercury deposition from human activity (Biester et al., 2002; Gobeil et al., 1999; Roos-Barraclough and Shotyk, 2003; Vandal et al., 1993). Lake sediments appear to provide the most reliable archive of past mercury deposition (Biester et al., 2007), and these studies collectively show a threefold to fivefold increase in atmospheric deposition of mercury since the advent of the Industrial Revolution. The observed increases in mercury in these sediment records are consistent with human uses of mercury and estimated losses to the environment (as also discussed in previous chapters), and generally reflect the change in the magnitude of the atmospheric mercury reservoir since preindustrial times.

Nearshore and estuarine sediment cores near urbanized areas show similar or greater temporal increases in mercury contamination, demonstrating more local and regional effects of human pollution. In San Francisco Bay, for example, a tidal salt marsh downstream of a mercury mine showed mercury concentrations that had increased 10 times over preindustrial values, peaking after the 1950s, then returning to 5 times above baseline levels in modern-day sediments (Conaway et al., 2004). Mercury deposition histories recorded in Connecticut wetlands and Long Island Sound sediments exhibit similar temporal trends of enrichment, generally with an increase of threefold to fivefold. However, in these areas mercury contamination appears to be caused by both local point sources and regional atmospheric fluxes (Varekamp et al., 2003).

Models of Mercury Cycling

While the increase in atmospheric mercury levels and deposition due to human activity is well documented, it is less clear how mercury concentrations in the ocean have changed since preindustrial times. Because there have been no global measurements of mercury over the past 150 years, models must be used to reconstruct human-caused changes in the global distribution of mercury. Some recent models include Mason, Fitzgerald, and Morel's

"MFM" model (Mason et al., 1994), the Global/Regional Interhemispheric Mercury Model "GRIMM" (Lamborg et al., 2002), the Mason and Sheu (2002) global mercury cycle model, the Strode et al. (2007) GEOS-Chem global mercury atmospheric/mixed slab ocean model, the Sunderland and Mason (2007) multicompartment open ocean box model, and the Selin et al. (2008) GEOS-Chem global 3-D ocean-atmosphere-land model. Based on measured changes in sources, reservoir size, concentrations, and knowledge of reaction rates and exchange processes, these models attempt to recreate past and current concentrations in various reservoirs over time and predict future trends in mercury concentrations and fluxes. Table 10.6 presents results from those six models related to past and current increases in total mercury concentrations in surface and deep waters of the ocean.

The predominance of atmospheric exchange with the ocean is a key feature of global mercury cycling models (Lamborg et al., 2002; Mason and Sheu, 2002; Mason et al., 1994; Selin et al., 2008; Strode et al., 2007; Sunderland and Mason, 2007). However, Sunderland and Mason's model suggests that for surface waters of the North Pacific, Mediterranean, and Atlantic Oceans, the input of mercury via rivers is substantially more important than estimated in previous models. While vertical mixing and exchange with the deep ocean was previously assumed to be unimportant and was sometimes excluded from older models (e.g., Mason et al., 1994), more recent models of mercury in the ocean consider both deep ocean exchange and lateral movement (e.g., Sunderland and Mason, 2007).

The global mass budget of Sunderland and Mason (2007) suggests that reservoirs of mercury in the surface ocean (to a depth of 1500 m) and deep ocean have increased on average by ~25% and ~11%, respectively, compared with preindustrial values. They note that global mean values obscure regional-scale changes. For example, mercury concentrations in surface waters of the Mediterranean have increased by ~68% relative to preindustrial values, whereas those in surface waters of the North Pacific have increased by only ~9% in their model.

However, these estimates differ in both absolute and relative amounts from those made by others (Lamborg et al., 2002; Selin et al., 2008; Strode et al., 2007), with respect to surface waters in some cases and deep waters in others (Table 10.6), and their accuracy has been questioned (Fitzgerald et al., 2007). Despite these differences, there is generally agreement that the marine environment is no longer in steady state with respect to mercury fluxes, and the ocean is now a net sink for mercury, with a current rate of accumulation of between 2.4 and 9.2 Mmol yr^{-1}, representing an increase of 0.1–0.5% per year when averaged across the entire ocean. Calculations predict that at current rates of anthropogenic emissions, concentrations of mercury in the oceans will continue to increase: up to ~80% of current levels in surface oceans and ~170% in deep oceans in one model (Sunderland and Mason, 2007). Such

TABLE 10.6
Numerical Model and Mass Balance Results for Cycling of Total Mercury in the Ocean

Study	Increase in Hg since preindustrial times (Mmol)	Current rate of increase in Hg (Mmol yr^{-1})	Past rate of increase in Hg (Mmol yr^{-1})[a]
	Surface Waters		
Mason et al., 1994 (MFM)	36 (200%)[b]	<0.5 (≤0.9% yr^{-1})[b]	0.24 (1.3% yr^{-1})[b]
Lamborg et al., 2002a (GRIMM)	25 (86%)[b]	0.8 (1.5% yr^{-1})[b]	0.17 (0.57% yr^{-1})[b]
Mason and Sheu, 2002	<15 (<5%)[d,e]	<0.1 (<0.03% yr^{-1})[d]	<0.1 (<0.03% yr^{-1})[d,e]
Strode et al., 2007	NA	0[f]	NA
Sunderland and Mason, 2007			
Entire Ocean	129 (25%)[g]	7.7 (1.2% yr^{-1})[g]	0.86 (0.17% yr^{-1})[g]
Atlantic	(58%)[g]	NA	(0.39% yr^{-1})[g]
Pacific/Indian	(56%)[g]	NA	(0.37% yr^{-1})[g]
Selin et al., 2008	22 (1800%)[f]	0[f]	0.15 (12% yr^{-1})[f]
	Deep Waters		
Mason et al., 1994 (MFM)	NA	0.7 (0.07% yr^{-1})[c]	NA
Lamborg et al., 2002a (GRIMM)	178 (20%)	4.0 (0.40% yr^{-1})	1.2 (0.13% yr^{-1})
Mason and Sheu, 2002	120 (11%)[e]	2.4 (0.22% yr^{-1})	0.8 (0.07% yr^{-1})[e]
Strode et al., 2007	NA	7.7 (0.70% yr^{-1})	NA
Sunderland and Mason, 2007			
Entire Ocean	124 (11%)	1.5 (0.14% yr^{-1})	0.83 (0.07% yr^{-1})
Atlantic	(32%)	NA	(0.21% yr^{-1})
Pacific/Indian	(<1%)	NA	(<0.01% yr^{-1})
Selin et al., 2008	249 (17%)	8.5 (0.49% yr^{-1})	1.7 (0.11% yr^{-1})

NOTE: Total Hg amounts are reported in Mmol, with percent change given in parentheses. Fluxes are reported as Mmol yr^{-1}, with percent change per year given in parentheses. NA = not available.

a. Averaged over the past 150 years, assuming simple linear increase.

b. ≥100 m.

c. Assumes subthermocline total Hg pool of 1000 Mmol.

d. ≥500 m.

e. Assumes past increases in oceanic Hg were primarily limited to the deep ocean, consistent with the mass balance described for the present day.

f. Variable mixed layer depth, mean of 53 m, g. ≥1500 m.

increases are not predicted to occur quickly, with the system requiring decades to millennia to reach steady state, but time scales will vary as a function of both depth and location in the ocean (Selin et al., 2008; Sunderland and Mason, 2007). Such differences reflect the spatial heterogeneity of total Hg inputs to the ocean, which occur primarily to surface waters via atmospheric deposition, and to a lesser extent to coastal waters via runoff. Spatial differences and increases in Hg atmospheric deposition are displayed in Figures 10.5 and 10.6. Figure 10.5 shows the mean annual atmospheric deposition of Hg globally by species and flux during preindustrial times, while Figure 10.6 shows the increase in net Hg atmospheric deposition in the present-day relative to preindustrial times, both as estimated by Selin et al. (2008).

Mercury models have also been created for local and regional scales. Macleod et al. (2005) developed a multispecies model describing the distribution of mercury in the San Francisco Bay Area, a region contaminated by both historic mining and contemporary industrial activities. Riverine inputs and resuspension of contaminated sediment dominate the mercury cycle in that estuary. Their model suggests that the response time of mercury concentrations to changes in mercury loads is on the order of decades—a result that is supported by long-term monitoring of temporal changes of mercury concentrations in surface sediments in the Bay (Conaway et al., 2007).

Measuring Changes in Biota

Are measured and modeled mercury changes in abiotic compartments of the ocean reflected in changes in biota in marine ecosystems? This is an important question, but difficult to answer because most studies have not focused on measuring how mercury concentrations in fish or other populations change with geographic location and time. Nonetheless, a few approaches have been taken to detect temporal changes and human influence on mercury in biota, including the use of museum archive samples and long-term monitoring datasets. The use of stable mercury isotopes in "fingerprinting" human influence on mercury concentrations represents an emerging tool for such studies, and it is discussed in other chapters.

Museum collections have been used in studies of environmental mercury contamination of fish and birds (Martins et al., 2006b; Monteiro and Furness, 1997; Thompson et al., 1992, 1993, 1998). The veracity of these data, however, has been questioned because collection and storage techniques gave little foresight to future mercury analysis (Fitzgerald et al., 2007). As a result, the limitations associated with the use of historic material to document temporal changes in mercury concentrations in biota require consideration (Martins et al., 2006b; Renaud et al., 1995). Potential problems include: (1) sample contamination or loss of mercury via volatilization after sample collection, (2) changes in Hg speciation (e.g., MMHg demethylation) during storage or preparation, (3) limited information on the health, sex, developmental state, and age of the organisms, and (4) temporal changes in trophic structure and size of prey that would affect the amount and speciation of mercury consumed during different periods.

Kraepiel et al. (2003) compared mercury concentrations in yellowfin tuna (*Thunnus albacares*) collected near Hawaii in 1971 and 1998. They concluded that there was no apparent temporal increase in mercury levels in the tuna from the region, and that their results would be inconsistent (with 95% confidence) with any increase of more than 6% (i.e., 0.2% per year). Using this value as a constraint, Kraepiel et al. (2003) developed a multispecies box model to describe the distribution of mercury in the ocean, concluding that MMHg formed in the deep sea was a potential source of mercury to yellowfin tuna.

An examination of mercury content in the mesopelagic glacier lanternfish (*Benthosema glaciale*) from the Atlantic (39°N, 70°W) showed no long-term change for 1936–1993, although there was apparently an increase in mercury contamination in the Atlantic Ocean during World War II

(Martins et al., 2006b). The lack of change in mercury concentrations in lanternfish is in contrast to the Sunderland and Mason model (2007), which suggests a ~38% anthropogenic enrichment of total mercury in waters to a depth of 1500 m in that region over such a period, but is more consistent with the other models, which suggest a smaller change in mercury concentrations in subthermocline–mesopelagic waters over that time (0.1–0.2% per year over the past 150 years; Table 10.6). Such differences in modeled increases in oceanic Hg concentrations and measured Hg concentrations in biota over time is, in part, due to the global models of mercury cycling created to date only including total mercury, whereas most of the mercury bioaccumulated by marine organisms is MMHg. Because of the complex nature of MMHg production and bioaccumulation, temporal and spatial trends in total Hg fluxes in many cases do not directly parallel MMHg production and uptake into the food web.

The use of bird feathers appears to have emerged as a more sound approach for monitoring changes in mercury exposure over time (Fitzgerald et al., 2007). Feathers are typically cleaned for surficial contamination (including mercury used as a preservative) and then analyzed solely for MMHg, which comprises the majority of mercury in feathers (Monteiro and Furness, 1997; Thompson et al., 1998). Furness and Camphuysen (1997) summarized the applicability of using bird feathers as biomonitors of mercury contamination in the marine environment. Since then, feathers from museum collections have been used to chronicle increases in mercury contamination of marine seabirds over the past 150 years, as well as to trace spatial variations of this contamination (Ancora et al. 2002; Burger and Gochfeld, 1995; Monteiro and Furness, 1997; Thompson et al., 1992, 1998).

A study of mercury in bird feathers by Dietz et al. (2006a) documented significant ($p < 0.05$) temporal increases in mercury concentrations in three species of west Greenland birds of prey from 1851–2003, and attributed that increase to anthropogenic contamination. Similarly, a study of museum bird specimens collected from the North Atlantic (primarily the Azores archipelago) by Thompson et al. (1998) showed mean increases of 65–100% from pre-1931 to post-1979 in three seabirds feeding predominantly in the epipelagic zone. This translates to an increase in mercury in those birds of 0.7–1.4% yr^{-1}, which is in agreement with the predictions of the MFM model (Mason et al., 1994) for past increases in surface waters, but smaller than the 12% yr^{-1} estimated for that time period by the Selin et al. (2008) model. The other four models summarized in Table 10.6 estimate that total Hg concentrations in surface waters increased during the past at a rate of <0.6% yr^{-1} when averaged over the past 150 years, but some estimate current increases in Hg concentrations in surface waters to be substantially greater (Lamborg et al., 2002; Sunderland and Mason, 2007). In contrast, the two mesopelagic feeders Bulwer's petrel (*Bulweria bulwerii*) and the band-rumped storm petrel (*Oceanodroma castro*), also from the North Atlantic, showed Hg increases of 260% and 394%, respectively, which translates to a change of 2.9–4.1% per year. This increase is greater than the change suggested by any of the models for subthermocline–mesopelagic waters for past or current situations (0.1–0.7% yr^{-1}; Table 10.6).

There has been a spate of reports on temporal variations of mercury concentrations in Arctic biota (Dietz et al., 2006a, 2006b; Lockhart et al., 2005; Outridge et al., 1997, 2005; Riget and Dietz, 2000; Riget et al., 2005, 2007a). Results from investigations of recent temporal variations have been mixed (contrasting and/or not statistically significant) for numerous reasons, as noted in those reports and summarized in an article by Bignert et al. (2004). They assessed the statistical power of existing data sets of mercury in Arctic biota and determined that most data sets were insufficient to detect temporal trends over the past few centuries, for several reasons. These included small sample size and interannual variations in season of collection, specimen size, sex, and maturity. Even if a statistically significant change in mercury content of the organisms occurs, that change may reflect natural variations (e.g., change in diet), rather than a response to anthropogenic mercury fluxes to the Arctic (Riget and Dietz, 2000).

Results of the longer time-series analyses of mercury concentrations in Arctic biota are more straightforward—albeit still subject to questions about the accuracy of mercury measurements in historic samples. These long-term studies consistently show measurable increases of mercury concentrations in organisms at or near the top of Arctic marine food webs over the past century. For example, mercury levels in the hair of contemporary polar bears were found to be an order of magnitude higher that those of preindustrial polar bears in Greenland—suggesting that ~90% of the mercury at the top of that Arctic marine food web was due to anthropogenic contamination (Dietz et al., 2006b).

There are a limited number of studies that have attempted to determine temporal changes of mercury concentrations in marine biota in the Antarctic. Efforts to do so by comparing samples collected over the past few decades have had mixed results (e.g., Honda et al., 2006; Scheifler et al., 2005). One of the more recent of those studies (Sun et al., 2006) shows a systematic increase of mercury in seal hair over the past century, relative to samples from the preceding two millennia, which correlates with temporal increases in mercury observed in a peat bog in southern Chile over the same period. In addition, earlier increases of mercury concentrations in the seal hair and peat bog appear to correlate with anthropogenic emissions of mercury.

The development of long-term, high-quality monitoring programs to detect changes in marine ecosystems is an essential part of detecting ecologic impacts of mercury emissions from human activities, and such programs have been suggested and outlined (Evers et al., 2008). Unfortunately, few of these monitoring programs currently exist, and the changes that they must detect over the course of a few decades are likely small—on the order of a few percent. The Regional Monitoring Program for Water Quality in the San Francisco Estuary is one such program (Flegal et al., 2005). Despite a measured decrease of mercury in parts of the estuary, sportfish in San Francisco Estuary have shown no apparent trend in mercury concentration over 1970–2000 (Greenfield et al., 2005). However, there are interannual variations in fish mercury concentrations, which are tentatively linked to changes in migration patterns, diets, populations sampled, or to variation in freshwater discharge to the estuary.

Conclusion

Globally, mercury inputs to the atmosphere have decreased in the European region, but continue to increase in areas such as Asia (Pacyna et al., 2006). Models of mercury cycling suggest that oceanic reservoirs of total mercury have not yet reached steady state with current inputs, and will not do so for decades to centuries (Selin et al., 2008; Sunderland and Mason, 2007). As a result, mercury concentrations can be expected to rise in some marine reservoirs. Conversely, in regions with extensive point source or legacy contamination, total mercury concentrations can be expected to decrease over many decades as mercury is lost by burial and natural attenuation (Macleod et al., 2005). Ecosystems, however, are in a dynamic state, with multiple influences on interannual, decadal, and multidecadal time scales. The detection of small yearly changes (a few percent) predicted by mercury cycling models might not be measured as easily as changes in mercury accumulation by organisms. The unambiguous identification of such small changes is made all the more problematic by the complex nature of MMHg cycling, bioaccumulation, and biomagnification in marine ecosystems.

In summary, there are many areas that need to be investigated to increase our knowledge of mercury in marine ecosystems and improve our understanding of how humans have influenced its biogeochemical cycling in the marine environment. These include: (1) further research on the mechanisms, rates, and locations of MMHg production and degradation in the ocean, (2) the establishment of monitoring programs to capture small changes in mercury and MMHg concentrations over time scales of interest, and (3) an improvement in our understanding of the structure and function of marine ecosystems and how they affect the bioaccumulation and biomagnification of mercury. Such efforts will require substantial effort by scientists from many different disciplines.

References

Ackerman, J.T., Eagles-Smith, C.A., Takekawa, J.Y., Demers, S.A., Adelsbach, T.L., Bluso, J.D., Miles, A.K., Warnock, N., Suchanek, T.H. and Schwarzbach, S.E. 2007. Mercury concentrations and space use of pre-breeding American avocets and black-necked stilts in San Francisco Bay. *Science of the Total Environment*, 384: 452–466.

Adams, D.H. 2004. Total mercury levels in tunas from offshore waters of the Florida Atlantic coast. *Marine Pollution Bulletin*, 49: 659–663.

Akagi, H. and Takabatake, E. 1973. Photochemical formation of methylmercuric compounds from mercuric acetate. *Chemosphere*, 2: 131–133.

Akagi, H., Fujita, Y., and Takabatake, E. 1976. Photochemical transformation of mercuric sulfide into methylmercury in aqueous solutions. *Chemistry Letters*, 1976: 1–4.

Albert, D.B., Taylor, C., and Martens, C.S. 1995. Sulfate reduction rates and low-molecular-weight fatty-acid concentrations in the water column and surficial sediments of the Black Sea. *Deep Sea Research, Part I, Oceanographic Research Papers*, 42: 1239–1260.

Aller, R.C., Mackin, J.E., and Cox, R.T. 1986. Diagenesis of Fe and S in Amazon inner shelf muds: apparent dominance of Fe reduction and implications for the genesis of ironstones. *Continental Shelf Research*, 6: 263–289.

Al-Majed, N.B., and Preston, M.R. 2000. An assessment of the total and methyl mercury content of zooplankton and fish tissue collected from Kuwait territorial waters. *Marine Pollution Bulletin*, 40: 298–307.

Amirbahman, A., Reid, A.L., Haines, T.A., Kahl, J.S., and Arnold, C., 2002. Association of methylmercury with dissolved humic acids. *Environmental Science and Technology*, 36: 690–695.

Ancora, S., Volpi, V., Olmastrom, S., Focardi, S., and Leonizo, C. 2002. Assumption and elimination of trace elements in Adélie penguins from Antarctica: a preliminary study. *Marine Environmental Research*, 54: 341–344.

Andersen, A., Julshamn, K., Ringdal, O., and Morkore, J. 1987. Trace element intake in the Faroe Islands II. Intake of mercury and other elements by consumption of pilot whales (*Globicephalus meleanus*). *Science of the Total Environment*, 65: 63–68.

Andersen, J.L., and Depledge, M.H. 1997. A survey of total mercury and methyl mercury in edible fish and invertebrates from Azorean waters. *Marine Environmental Research*, 44: 331–350.

Andersson, M.E., Sommar, J., Gårdfeldt, K., and Lindqvist, O. 2008. Enhanced concentrations of dissolved gaseous mercury in the surface waters of the Arctic Ocean. *Marine Chemistry*, 110: 190–194.

Arcos, J.M., Ruiz, X., Bearhop, S., and Furness, R.W. 2002. Mercury levels in seabirds and their fish prey at the Ebro Delta (NW Mediterranean): the role of trawler discards as a source of contamination. *Marine Ecology Progress Series*, 232: 281–290.

Atwell, L., Hobson, K.A., and Welch, H.E., 1998. Biomagnification and bioaccumulation of mercury in an arctic marine food web: insights from stable nitrogen isotope analysis. *Canadian Journal of Fish and Aquatic Science*, 55: 114–1121.

Baeyens, W., and Leermakers, M. 1998. Elemental mercury concentrations and formation rates in the Scheldt estuary and the North Sea. *Marine Chemistry*, 60: 257–266.

Baeyens, W., Leermakers, M., Papina, T., Saprykin, A., Brion, N., Noyen, J., De Gieter, M., Elskens, M., and Goeyens, L. 2003. Bioconcentration and biomagnification of mercury and methylmercury in North Sea and Scheldt estuary fish. *Archives of Environmental Contamination and Toxicology*, 45: 498–508.

Baeyens, W., Meuleman, C., Muhaya, B., and Leermakers, M. 1998. Behaviour and speciation of mercury in the Scheldt estuary (water, sediments and benthic organisms). *Hydrobiologia*, 366: 63–79.

Balcom, P.H., Fitzgerald, W.F., Vandal, G.M., Lamborg, C.H., Rolfhus, K.R., Langer, C.S., and Hammerschmidt, C.R. 2004. Mercury sources and cycling in the Connecticut River and Long Island Sound. *Marine Chemistry*, 90: 53–74.

Balcom, P.H., Hammerschmidt, C.R., Fitzgerald, W.F., Lamborg, C.H., and O'Connor, J.S. 2008. Seasonal distributions and cycling of mercury and methylmercury in the waters of New York/New Jersey Harbon Estuary. *Marine Chemistry*, 109: 1–17.

Balogh, S.J., and Nollet, Y.H. 2008. Methylmercury input to the Mississippi River from a large metropolitan wastewater treatment plant. *Science of the Total Environment*, 406: 145–153.

Bank, M.S., Chesney, E., Shine, J.P., Maage, A., and Senn, D.B. 2007. Mercury bioaccumulation and trophic transfer in sympatric snapper species from the Gulf of Mexico. *Ecological Applications*, 17: 2100–2110.

Bargagli, R., Monaci, F., Sanchez-Hernandez, J.C., and Cateni, D. 1998. Biomagnification of mercury in an Antarctic marine coastal food web. *Marine Ecological Progress Series*, 169: 65–76.

Barkay, T., Miller, S.M., and Summers, A.O. 2003. Bacterial mercury resistance from atoms to ecosystems. *FEMS Microbiology Reviews*, 27: 355–384.

Becker, P.H., González-Solís, J., Behrends, B., and Croxall, J. 2002. Feather mercury levels in seabirds at South Georgia: influence of trophic position, sex and age. *Marine Ecology Progress Series*, 243: 261–269.

Benoit, J.M., Gilmour, C.C., Heyes, A. Mason, R.P., and Miller, C.L., 2003. Geochemical and biological controls over methylmercury production and degradation in aquatic environments. In: Cai, Y. and Braids, O.C., (Editors), *Biogeochemistry of Environmentally Important Trace Elements*. ACS Symposium Series No. 835. American Chemical Society, Washington DC, pp. 262–297.

Benoit, J.M., Gilmour, C.C., Mason, R.P., Riedel, G.S., and Riedel, G.F., 1998. Behavior of mercury in the Patuxent River estuary. *Biogeochemistry*, 40: 249–265.

Benoit, J.M., Gilmour, C.C., Mason, R.P., and Heyes, A. 1999. Sulfide controls on mercury speciation and bioavailability to methylating bacteria in sediment pore waters. *Environmental Science and Technology*, 33: 951–957.

Benoit, J.M., Gilmour, C.C., and Mason, R.P., 2001a. The influence of sulfide on solid-phase mercury bioavailability for methylation by pure cultures of *Desulfobulbus propionicus* (1pr3). *Environmental Science and Technology*, 2001, 35: 127–132.

Benoit, J.M., Mason, R.P., Gilmour, C.C., and Aiken, G.R. 2001b. Constants for mercury binding by dissolved organic matter isolates from the Florida Everglades. *Geochimica et Cosmochimia Acta*, 65: 4445–4451.

Bergan, T., and Rodhe, H. 2001. Oxidation of elemental mercury in the atmosphere; Constraints imposed by global scale modeling. *Journal of Atmospheric Chemistry*, 40: 191–212.

Bergquist, B.A., and Blum, J.D. 2007. Mass-dependent and -independent fractionation of Hg isotopes by photo-reduction in aquatic systems. *Science*, 318: 417–420.

Best, E.P.H., Fredrickson, H.L., Hintelmann, H., Clarisse, O., Dimock, B., Lutz, C.H., Lotufo, G.R., Millward, R.N., Bednar, A.J. and Furey, J. 2007. Pre-construction biogeochemical analysis of mercury in wetlands bordering the Hamilton Army Airfield wetlands restoration site, part 2. ERDC/EL TR-05-15, U.S. Army Corps of Engineers, San Francisco.

Biester, H., Kilian, R., Hertel, C., Woda, C., Mangini, A., and Schöler, H.F. 2002. Elevated mercury concentrations in peat bogs of south Patagonia, Chile - An anthropogenic signal. *Earth and Planetary Science Letters*, 201: 609–620.

Biester, H., Bindler, R., Martinez-Cortizas, A., and Engstrom, D.R. 2007. Modelling past atmospheric deposition of mercury using natural archives. *Environmental Science and Technology*, 41: 4851–4860.

Bignert, A., Riget, F., Braune, B., Outridge, P., and Wilson, S., 2004. Recent temporal trend monitoring of mercury in Arctic biota – how powerful are the existing data sets? *Journal of Environmental Monitoring*, 6: 351–355.

Black, F.J., Conaway, C.H., and Flegal, A.R. 2009a. Stability of dimethyl mercury in seawater and its conversion to monomethyl mercury. *Environmental Science and Technology*, 43: 4056–4062.

Black, F.J., Paytan, A., Knee, K.L., de Sieyes, N.R., Ganguli, P.M., Gray, E., and Flegal, A.R. 2009b. Submarine groundwater discharge of total mercury and monomethylmercury to central California coastal waters. *Environmental Science and Technology*, 43: 5652–5659.

Blais, J.M., Kimpe, L.E., McMahon, D., Keatley, B.E., Mallory, M.L., Douglas, M.S.V., and Smol, J.P. 2005. Arctic seabirds transport marine-derived contaminants. *Science*, 309: 445.

Blais, J.M., Macdonald, R.W., MacKay, D., Webster, E., Harvey, C., and Smol, J.P., 2007. Biologically mediated transport of contaminants to aquatic systems. *Environmental Science and Technology*, 41: 1075–1084.

Bloom, N.S. 1992. On the chemical form of mercury in edible fish and marine invertebrate tissue. *Canadian Journal of Fisheries and Aquatic Science*, 49: 1010–1017.

Bloom, N.S., Gill, G.A., Cappellino, S., Dobbs, C., McShea, L., Driscoll, C., Mason, R., and Rudd, J. 1999. Speciation and cycling of mercury in Lavaca Bay, Texas, sediments. *Environmental Science and Technology*, 33: 7–13.

Bloom, N.S., Moretto, L.M., Scopece, P., and Ugo, P., 2004a. Seasonal cycling of mercury and monomethylmercury in the Venice Lagoon (Italy). *Marine Chemistry*, 91: 85–99.

Bloom, N.S., Moretto, L.M., and Ugo, P. 2004b. A comparison of the speciation and fate of mercury in two contaminated coastal marine ecosystems: The Venice Lagoon (Italy) and Lavaca Bay (Texas). *Limnology and Oceanography*, 49: 367–375.

Bocher, P., Caurant, F., Miramand, P., Cherel, Y., and Bustamante, P. 2003. Influence of the diet on the bioaccumulation of heavy metals in zooplankton-eating petrels at the Kerguelen archipelago, Southern Indian Ocean. *Polar Biology*, 26: 759–767.

Bodaly, R.A., Rudd, J.W.M., and Flett, R.J. 1998. Effect of urban sewage treatment on total and methyl mercury concentrations in effluents. *Biogeochemistry*, 40: 279–291.

Bone, S.E., Charette, M.A., Lamborg, C.H., and Gonneea, M.E. 2007. Has submarine groundwater discharge been overlooked as a source of mercury to coastal waters? *Environmental Science and Technology*, 41: 3090–3095.

Borga, K., Campbell, L., Gabrielsen, G.W., Norstrom, R.J., Muir, D.C.G., and Fisk, A.T. 2006. Regional and species specific bioaccumulation of major and trace elements in Arctic seabirds. *Environmental Toxicology and Chemistry*, 25: 2927–2936.

Boush, M., and Thieleke, J.R., 1983. Total mercury content in yellowfin and bigeye tuna. *Bulletin of Environmental Contamination and Toxicology*, 30: 291–297.

Braune, B.M. 1987. Mercury accumulation in relation to size and age of Atlantic Herring (*Clupea harengus harengus*) from the Southwestern Bay of Fundy, Canada. *Archives of Environmental Contamination and Toxicology*, 16: 311–320.

Braune, B.M., and Gaskin, D.E. 1987. Mercury levels in Bonapart's gulls (*Larus Philadelphia*) during autumn molt in the Quoddy region, New Brunswick, Canada. *Archives of Environmental Contamination and Toxicology*, 16: 539–549.

Brookens, T.J., O'Hara, T.M., Taylor, R.J., Bratton, G.R., and Harvey, J.T. 2008. Total mercury body burden in Pacific harbor seal, *Phoca vitulina richardii*, pups from central California. *Marine Pollution Bulletin*, 56: 27–41.

Brooks, B. 2004. Mercury levels in Hawaiian commercial fish. Presentation at the U.S. EPA Forum on Contaminants in Fish. January, 2004, San Diego, CA. http://www.epa.gov/waterscience/fish/forum/2004.

Burger, J., and Gochfeld, M. 1995. Biomonitoring of heavy metals in the Pacific Basin using avian feathers. *Environmental Toxicology and Chemistry*, 14: 1233–1239.

Burger, J., Stern, A.H., and Gochfeld, M. 2005. Mercury in commercial fish: Optimizing individual choices to reduce risk. *Environmental Health Perspectives*, 113: 266–271.

Burger, J., and Gochfield, M. 2007. Metals and radionuclides in birds and eggs from Amchitka and Kiska Islands in the Bering Sea/Pacific Ocean ecosystem. *Environmental Monitoring and Assessment*, 127: 105–117.

Burger, J., Gochfeld, M., Jeitner, C., Burke, S., Stamm, T., Snigaroff, R., Snigaroff, D., Patrick, R., and Weston, J. 2007. Mercury levels and potential risk from subsistence foods from the Aleutians. *Science of the Total Environment*, 384: 93–105.

Calvert, J.G. and Lindberg, S.E., 2005. Mechanisms of mercury removal by O_3 and OH in the atmosphere. *Atmospheric Environment*, 39: 3355–3367.

Campbell, L.M., Nordstrom, R.J., Hobson, K.A., Muir, D.C.G., Backus, S., and Fisk, A.T. 2005. Mercury and other trace elements in a pelagic Arctic marine food web (North Water Polyna, Baffin Bay). *Science of the Total Environment*, 351–352: 247–263.

Canário J., Vale, C., and Caetano, M. 2005. Distribution of monomethylmercury and mercury in surface sediments of the Targus Estuary (Portugal). *Marine Pollution Bulletin*, 50: 1121–1145.

Canário J., Branco, V., and Vale, C. 2007a. Seasonal variation of monomethylmercury concentrations in surface sediments of the Tagus Estuary (Portugal). *Environmental Pollution*, 148: 380–383.

Canário J., Caetano, M., Vale, C., and Cesário, R. 2007b. Evidence for elevated production of methylmercury in salt marshes. *Environmental Science and Technology*, 41: 7376–7382.

Canfield, D.E. 1989. Sulfate reduction and oxic respiration in marine sediments: implications for organic carbon preservation in euxinic environments. *Deep-Sea Research*, 36: 121–138.

Canfield, D.E., Thamdrup, B., and Hansen, J.W. 1993. The anaerobic degradation of organic matter in Danish coastal sediments: iron reduction, manganese reduction, and sulfate reduction. *Geochemica et Cosmochimica Acta*, 57: 3867–3883.

Canli, M., and Furness, R.W. 1995. Mercury and cadmium uptake from seawater and from food by the Norway lobster *Nephrops norvegicus*. *Environmental Toxicology and Chemistry*, 14: 819–828.

Catallo, W.J. 1999. *Hourly and daily variation of sediment redox potential in tidal wetland sediments*. US Geological Survey, Biological Science Report USGS/BRD/BRS-1999–0001.

Centers for Disease Control and Prevention, 2001. Blood and hair mercury levels in young children and women of childbearing age—United States, 1999. *Morbidity and Mortality Weekly Report*, 50: 140–143.

Cerrati, G., Bernhard, M., and Webber, J.H. 1992. Model ractions for abiotic mercury(II) methylation: Kinetics of methylation of mercury(II) by mono-, di-, and trimethytin in seawater. *Applied Organometallic Chemistry*, 6: 587–595.

Chen, C.Y., and Folt, C.L. 2005. High plankton densities reduce mercury biomagnification. *Environmental Science and Technology*, 39: 115–121.

Chen J., Pehkonen, S.O., and Lin, C.J., 2003. Degradation of monomethylmercury chloride by hydroxyl radicals in simulated natural waters. *Water Research*, 37: 2496–2504.

Chen, Y.C., and Chen, M.H., 2006. Mercury levels of seafood commonly consumed in Taiwan. *Journal of Food and Drug Analysis*, 14: 373–378.

Cheng, J., Gao, L., Zhao, Wenchang, Liu, Z., Sakamoto, M., and Wang, W. 2009. Mercury levels in fisherman and their household members in Zhoushan, Chinga: Impact of public health. *Science of the Total Environment*, 407: 2625–2630.

Choe, K.Y., and Gill, G.A. 2003. Distribution of particulate, colloidal, and dissolved mercury in San Francisco Bay estuary. 2. Monomethylmercury. *Limnology and Oceanography*, 48: 1547–1556.

Choe, K.Y., Gill, G.A., and Lehman, R. 2003. Distribution of particulate, colloidal, and dissolved mercury in San Francisco Bay estuary. 1. Total mercury. *Limnology and Oceanography*, 48: 1535–1546.

Choe K.Y., Gill G.A., Lehman R.D., Han S., Heim W.A., and Coale K.H. 2004. Sediment-water exchange of total mercury and monomethylmercury in the San Francisco Bay-Delta. *Limnology and Oceanography*, 49:1512–1527.

Clarkson T.W. and Magos, L. 2006. The toxicology of mercury and its chemical compounds. *Critical Reviews in Toxicology*, 36: 609–662.

Colaço, A., Bustamante, P., Fouquet, Y., Sarradin, P.M., and Serrão-Santos, R., 2006. Bioaccumulation of Hg, Cu, and Zn in the Azores triple junction hydrothermal vent fields food web. *Chemosphere*, 65: 2260–2267.

Compeau G., and Bartha, R. 1985. Sulfate-reducing bacteria: Principal methylators of mercury in anoxic estuarine sediment. *Applied and Environmental Microbiology*, 50: 498–502.

Conaway, C.H., Squire, S., Mason, R.P., and Flegal, A.R. 2003. Mercury speciation in the San Francisco Bay estuary. *Marine Chemistry*, 80: 199–225.

Conaway, C.H., Watson, E.B., Flanders, J.R., and Flegal, A.R. 2004. Mercury deposition in a tidal marsh of south San Francisco Bay downstream of the historic New Almaden mining district, California. *Marine Chemistry*, 90: 175–184.

Conaway, C.H., Ross, J.R.M., Looker, R., Mason, R.P., and Flegal, A.R. 2007. Decadal mercury trends in San Francisco Estuary sediments. *Environmental Research*, 105(1): 53–66.

Conaway, C.H., Black, F.J., Gault-Ringold, M., Pennington, J.T., Chavez, F.P., and Flegal, A.R. 2009. Dimethylmercury in coastal upwelling waters, Monterey Bay, California. *Environmental Science and Technology,* 43: 1305–1309.

Constant, P., Poissant, L., Vellemur, R., Yumvihoze, E., and Lean, D. 2007. Fate of inorganic mercury and methyl mercury within snow cover in the low arctic tundra on the shore of Hudson Bay (Quebec, Canada). *Journal of Geophysical Research*, 112, D08309, doi:10.1029/2006JD007961.

Coquery, M., Cossa, D., and Sanjuan, J. 1997. Speciation and sorption of mercury in two macro-tidal estuaries. *Marine Chemistry*, 58:213–227.

Cortes, S., and Fortt, A. 2007. Mercury content in Chilean fish and estimated intake levels. *Food Additives and Contaminants*, 24: 955–959.

Cossa, D., Averty, B., and Pirrone, N. 2009. The origin of methylmercury in open Mediterranean waters. *Limnology and Oceanography*, 54: 837–844.

Cossa, D., and Coquery, M. 2005. The Mediterranean mercury anomaly, a geochemical or biological issue. *Handbook of Environmental Chemistry*, Vol. 5, Part K: 177–208.

Cossa, D., and Gobeil, C, 2000. Mercury speciation in the Lower St. Lawrence Estuary. *Canadian Journal of Fisheries and Aquatic Science*, 57: 138–147.

Cossa, D., Martin, J.M., and Sanjuan, J. 1994. Dimethylmercury formation in the Alboran Sea. *Marine Pollution Bulletin*, 28: 381–384.

Cossa, D., Martin, J.M., Takayanagi, K., and Sanjuan, J. 1997. The distribution and cycling of mercury species in the western Mediterranean. *Deep-Sea Research II*, 44: 721–740.

Costa, M.F., Barbosa, S.C.T., Barletta, M., Dantas, D., Kehrig, H.A., Seixas, T.G., and Malm, O. 2009. Seasonal differences in mercury accumulation in *Trichiurus lepturus* (Cutlassfish) in relation to length and weight in a Northeast Brazilian estuary. *Environmental Science and Pollution Research*, 16: 423–430.

Costanza, R., d'Arge, R., deGroot, R., Farber, S., Grasso, M., Hannon, B., Limburg, K., Naeem, S., O'Neill, R.V., Paruelo, J., Raskin, R.G., Sutton, P., and van den Belt, M. 1997. The value of the world's ecosystem services and natural capital. *Nature*, 387: 253–260.

Covelli, S., Faganeli, J., Horvat, M., and Brambati, A. 1999. Benthic fluxes of mercury and methylmercury in the Gulf of Trieste. *Estuarine, Coastal and Shelf Science*, 48: 415–428.

Covelli, S., Faganeli, J., De Vittor, C., Predonzani, S., Acquavita, A., and Horvat, M. 2008. Benthic fluxes of mercury species in a lagoon environment (Grado Lagoon, Northern Adriatic Sea, Italy). *Applied Geochemistry*, 23: 529–546.

Craig, P.J., and Moreton, P.A. 1986. Total mercury, methyl mercury and sulphide levels in British estuarine sediments-III, 1986. *Water Resources*, 20: 1111–1118.

Crespo-Medina, M., Chatziefthimiou, A.D., Bloom, N.S., Luther, G.W., Wright, D.D., Reinfelder, J.R., Vetriani, C., and Barkay, T. 2009. Adaptation of chemosynthetic microorganisms to elevated mercury concentration in deep-sea hydrothermal vents. *Limnology and Oceanography*, 54: 41–49.

Cristol, D.A., Brasso, R.L., Condon, A.M., Fovargue, R.E., Friedman, S.L., Hallinger, K.K., Monroe A.P., and White, A.E. 2008. The movement of aquatic mercury through terrestrial food webs. *Science*, 320: 335.

Crossland, C.J., Kremer, H.H., Lindeboom, H.J., Marshall Crossland, J.I., and Le Tissier, M.D.A. (Eds.). 2005. *Coastal Fluxes in the Anthropocene*. Global Change—The IGBP Series, Springer, Berlin.

Cubadda, F., Raggi, A., and Coni, E. 2006. Elemental fingerprinting of marine organisms by dynamic reaction cell inductively coupled plasma mass spectrometry. *Analytical and Bioanalytical Chemistry*, 384: 887–896.

Cunha, L., Amaral, A., Medeiros, V., Martins, G.M., Wallenstein, F.F., Couto, R.P., Neto, A.I., and Rodriques, A., 2008. Bioavailable metals and cellular effects in the digestive gland of marine limpets living close to shallow water hydrothermal vents. *Chemosphere*, 71: 1356–1362.

Cutter, G.A., Walsh, R.S., and Silva de Echols, C., 1999. Production and speciation of hydrogen sulfide in surface waters of the high latitude North Atlantic Ocean. *Deep-Sea Research, Part II*, 46: 991–1010.

Davis, J.A., Hunt, J.A., Greenfield, B.K., Fairey, R., Sigala, M., Crane, D.B., Regalado, K., and Bonnema, A. 2006. Contaminant concentrations in sport fish from San Francisco Bay, 2006. SFEI Contribution #432. San Francisco Estuary Institute, Oakland, CA.

Davis, J.A., Greenfield, B.K., Ishikawa, G., and Stephenson, M. 2008. Mercury in sport fish from the Sacramento-San Joaquin Delta region, California, USA. *Science of the Total Environment*, 391: 66–75.

Dehn, L.-A., Follmann, E.H., Thomas, D.L., Sheffield, G.G., Rosa, C., Duffy, L.K., and O'Hara, T. 2006. Trophic relationships in an Arctic food web and implications for trace metal transfer. *Science of the Total Environment*, 362: 103–123.

Dekov, V.M., 2007. Native Hg-liq in the metalliferous sediments of the East Pacific Rise (21 degrees S). *Marine Geology*, 238: 107–113.

de Moreno, J.E.A., Gerpe, M.S., Moreno, V.J., and Vodopivez, C., 1997. Heavy metals in Antarctic organisms. *Polar Biology*, 17: 131–140.

D'Hondt, S., Rutherford, S., and Spivack, A.J. 2002. Metabolic activity of subsurface life in deep-sea sediments. *Science*, 295: 2067–2070.

Dias, M., Salvado, J.C., Monperrus, M., Caumette, P., Amouroux, D., Duran, R., and Guyoeaud, R. 2008. Characterization of *Desulfomicrobium salsuginis* sp. nov. and *Desulfomicrobium aestuarii* sp. nov., two new sulfate-reducing bacteria isolated from the Adour estuary (French Atlantic coast) with specific mercury methylation potentials. *Systematic and Applied Microbiology*, 31: 30–37.

Diaz, R.J. 2001. Overview of hypoxia around the world. *Journal of Environmental Quality*, 30: 275–281.

Dietz, R., Nielsen, C.O., Hansen, M.M., and Hansen, C.T. 1990. Organic mercury in Greenland birds and mammals. *Science of the Total Environment*, 95: 41–51.

Dietz, R., Riget, F.F., Boerrtmann, D., Sonne, C., Olsen, M.T., Fjeldsa, J., Falk, K., Kirkegaard, M., Egevang, C., Asmund, G., Wille, F., and Moller, S. 2006a. Time trends of mercury in feathers of west Greenland birds of prey during 1851–2003. *Environmental Science and Technology*, 40: 5911–5916.

Dietz, R., Riget, F., Born, E.W., Sonne, C., Grandjean, P., Kirkegaard, M. Olson, M.T., Asmund, G., Benzoni, A., Baagoe, H., and Andreason, C. 2006b. Trends in mercury in hair of Greenlandic polar bears (*Ursus maritimus*) during 1892–2001. *Environmental Science and Technology*, 40: 1120–1125.

Dixon, R., and Jones, B. 1994. Mercury concentrations in stomach contents and muscle of five fish species from the north east coast of England. *Marine Pollution Bulletin*, 28: 741–745.

dos Santos, I.R., Silva-Filho, E.V., Schaefer, C., Sella, S.M., Silva, C.A., Gomes, V., Passos, M.J. de A.C.R., and Ngan, P.V. 2006. Baseline mercury and zinc concentrations in terrestrial and coastal organisms of Admiralty Bay, Antarctica. *Environmental Pollution*, 140: 304–311.

Drott, A., Lambertsson, L., Bjorn, E., and Skyllberg, U. 2007. Importance of dissolved neutral mercury sulfides for methyl mercury production in contaminated sediments. *Environmental Science and Technology*, 41: 2270–2276.

Dyrssen, D., and Wedborg, M., 1991. The sulfur-mercury(II) system in natural waters. *Water, Air and Soil Pollution*, 56: 507–519.

Eagles-Smith, C.A., Ackerman, J.T., De La Cruz, S.E.W., and Yakekawa, J.Y. 2009a. Mercury bioaccumulation and risk to three waterbird foraging guilds is influenced by foraging ecology and breeding stage. *Environmental Pollution*, 157: 1993–2002.

Eagles-Smith, C.A., Ackerman, J.T., Yee, J., and Adelsbach, T.L. 2009b. Mercury demethylation in waterbird livers: dose-response thresholds and differences among species. *Environmental Toxicology and Chemistry*, 28: 568–577.

Ebinghaus, R., Koch, H.H., Temme, C., Einax, J.W., Lowe, A.G., Richter, A., Burrows, J.P., and Schroeder, W.H. 2002. Antarctic springtime depletion of atmospheric mercury. *Environmental Science and Technology*, 36: 1238–1244.

Eisler, R. 1987. Mercury hazards to fish, wildlife, and invertebrates: A synoptic review. *Biology of Reproduction*, 85: 85–90.

Ekstrom, E., and Morel., F.M.M. 2008. Cobalt limitation of growth and mercury methylation in sulfate reducing bacteria. *Environmental Science and Technology*, 42: 93–99.

Evers, D.C., Mason, R.P., Kamman, N.C., Chen, C.Y., Logomolni, A.L., Taylor, D.L., Hammerschmidt, C.R., Jones, S.H., Burgess, N.M., Munney, K., and Parsons, K.C. 2008. Integrated mercury monitoring program for temperate estuarine and marine ecosystems on the North American coast. *EcoHealth*, 5: 426–441.

Faganeli, J., Horvat, M., Covelli, S., Fajon, V., Logar, M., Lipej, L., and Cermelj, B. 2003. Mercury and methylmercury in the Gulf of Trieste (northern Adriatic Sea). *Science of the Total Environment*, 304: 315–326.

Falcó, G., Llobet, J.M., Bocio, A., and Domingo, J.L. 2006. Daily intake of arsenic, cadmium, mercury, and lead by consumption of edible marine species. *Journal of Agricultural and Food Chemistry*, 54: 6106–6112.

Fein, J.B., and Williams-Jones, A.E. 1997. The role of mercury-organic interactions in the hydrothermal transport of mercury. *Economic Geology*, 92: 20–28.

Filippelli, M., and Baldi, F. 1993. Alkylation of ionic mercury to methylmercury and dimethylmercury by methylcobalamin: simultaneous determination by purge-and-trap GC in-line with FTIR. *Applied Organometallic Chemistry*, 7: 487–493.

Fitzgerald, W.F., Lamborg, C.H., and Hammerschmidt, C.R., 2007. Marine biogeochemical cycling of mercury. *Chemical Reviews*, 107: 641–662.

Flegal, A.R. 1977. Mercury in the seston of the San Francisco Bay estuary. *Bulletin of Environmental Contamination and Toxicology*, 17: 273–277.

Flegal, A.R., Conaway, C.H., Scelfo, G.M., Hibdon, S., and Sañudo-Wilhelmy, S. 2005. Factors influencing measurements of decadal variations in metal contamination in San Francisco Bay, California. *Ecotoxicology*, 14: 645–660.

Fleming, E.J., Mack, E.E., Green, P.G., and Nelson, D.C. 2006. Mercury methylation from unexpected sources: molybdate-inhibited freshwater sediments and an iron-reducing bacterium. *Applied and Environmental Microbiology*, 72: 457–464.

Foran, J.A., Good, D.H., Carpenter, D.O., Hamilton, M.C., Knuth, B.A., and Schwager, S.J. 2005. Quantitative analysis of the benefits and risks of consuming farmed and wild salmon. *Journal of Nutrition*, 135: 2639–2643.

Francesconi K., and Lenanton, R.C.J. 1992. Mercury contamination in a semi-enclosed marine embayment: organic and inorganic mercury content of biota, and factors influencing mercury levels in fish. *Marine Environmental Research*, 33: 189–212.

Francesconi, K.A., Lenanton, R.C.J., Caputi, N., and Jones, S. 1997. Long-term study of mercury concentrations in fish following cessation of a mercury-containing discharge. *Marine Environmental Research*, 43: 27–40.

Furness, R.W., and Camphuysen, K.C.J. 1997. Seabirds as monitors of the marine environment. *ICES Journal of Marine Science*, 54: 726–737.

Gagnon, C., and Fisher, N.S., 1997. Bioavailability of sediment-bound methyl and inorganic mercury to a marine bivalve. *Environmental Science and Technology*, 31: 993–998.

Gagnon, C., Pelletier, E., Mucci, A., and Fitzgerald, W.F. 1996. Diagenetic behavior of methylmercury in organic-rich coastal sediments. *Limnology and Oceanography*, 41: 428–434.

Gårdfeldt, K., Munthe, J., Strömberg, D., and Lindqvist, O. 2003a. A kinetic study on the abiotic methylation of divalent mercury in the aqueous phase. *Science of the Total Environment*, 304: 127–136.

Gårdfeldt, K., Sommar, J., Rerrara, R., Ceccarini, C., Lanzillotta, E., Munthe, J., Wängberg, I., Lindqvist, O., Perrone, N., Sprovieri, F., Pesenti, E., and Stömberg, D. 2003b. Evasion of mercury from coastal and open waters of the Atlantic Ocean and the Mediterranean Sea. *Atmospheric Environment*, 37: S73–S84.

Gill, G.A., Bloom, N.S., Cappellino, S., Driscoll, C.T., Dobbs, C., McShea, L., Mason, R., and Rudd, J.W.M. 1999. Sediment-water fluxes of mercury in Lavaca Bay, Texas. *Environmental Science and Technology*, 33: 663–669.

Gilmour, C.C., Henry, E.A., and Mitchell, R. 1992. Sulfate stimulation of mercury methylation in fresh-water sediments. *Environmental Science and Technology*, 26: 2281–2287.

Gilmour, C.C., Riedel, G.S., Ederington, M.D., Bell, J.T., Benoit, J.M., Gill, G.A., and Stordal, M.C., 1998. Methylmercury concentrations and production rates across a trophic gradient in the northern Everglades. *Biogeochemistry*, 40: 327–345.

Gobeil, C., MacDonald, R.W., and Smith, J.N. 1999. Mercury profiles in sediments of the Arctic Ocean basins. *Environmental Science and Technology*, 33: 4194–4198.

Goldberg, E.D., Bowen, V.T., Farrington, J.W., Harvey, G., Martin, J.H., Parker, P.L., Risebrough, R.W., Robertson, W., Schneider, E., and Gamble, E. 1978. The mussel watch. *Environmental Conservation*, 5: 101–125.

Goldstein, R.M., Brigham, M.E., and Stauffer, J.C. 1996. Comparison of mercury concentrations in liver, muscle, whole bodies, and composites of fish from the Red River of the North. *Canadian Journal of Fisheries and Aquatic Sciences*, 53: 244–252.

Green, N.W., and Knutzen, J, 2003. Organohalogens and metals inmarine fish and mussels and some relationships to biological variables at reference localities in Norway. *Marine Pollution Bulletin*, 46: 362–377.

Greenfield, B.K., Davis, J.A., Fairey, R., Roberts, C., Crane, D. and Ichikawa, G. 2005. Seasonal, interannual, and long-term variation in sport fish contamination, San Francisco Bay. *Science of the Total Environment*, 336: 25–43.

Grosse, W., Armstrong, J., and Armstrong, W., 1996. A history of pressurised gas-flow studies in plants. *Aquatic Botany*, 54: 87–100.

Haines, T., and Bauer, S. 2001. Geographic differences in mercury concentration among in-shore populations of Pollock (*Pollachius virens*) and Atlantic mackerel (*Scomber scombus*) in Maine, USA. Presentation at the 22nd Society of Environmental Toxicology and Chemistry (SETAC) Annual Meeting, November, 2001, Baltimore, Maryland.

Haitzer, M., Aiken, G.R., and Ryan, J.N. 2003. Binding of mercury(II) to aquatic humic substances: Influence of pH and source of humic substances. *Environmental Science and Technology*, 37: 2436–2441.

Hall, B., Bloom, N.S., and Munthe, J. 1995. An experimental study of two potential methylation agents of mercury in the atmosphere: CH_3I and DMS. *Water, Air, and Soil Pollution*, 80: 337–341.

Hall, B.D., Aiken, G.R., Krabbenhoft, D.P., Marvin-DiPasquale, M., and Swarzenski, C.M. 2008. Wetlands as principal zones of methylmercury production in southern Louisiana and the Gulf of Mexico region. *Environmental Pollution*, 154: 124–134.

Hammerschmidt, C.R., and Fitzgerald, W.F. 2004. Geochemical controls on the production and distribution of methylmercury in near-shore marine sediments. *Environmental Science and Technology*, 38: 1487–1495.

Hammerschmidt, C.R., and Fitzgerald, W.F. 2006a. Bioaccumulation and trophic transfer of methylmercury in Long Island Sound. *Archives of Environmental Contamination and Toxicology*, 51: 416–424.

Hammerschmidt, C.R., and Fitzgerald, W.F. 2006b. Methylmercury cycling in sediment on the continental shelf of southern New England. *Geochimica et Cosmochimica Acta*, 70: 918–930.

Hammerschmidt, C.R., and Fitzgerald, W.F. 2006c. Methylmercury in freshwater fish linked to atmospheric mercury deposition. *Environmental Science and Technology*, 40(24): 7764–7770.

Hammerschmidt, C.R., Fitzgerald, W.F., Lamborg, C.H., Balcom, P.H., and Visscher, P.T. 2004. Biogeochemistry of methylmercury in sediments of Long Island Sound. *Marine Chemistry*, 90: 31–52.

Hammerschmidt, C.R., Lamborg, C.H., and Fitzgerald, W.F., 2007. Aqueous phase methylation as a potential source of methylmercury in wet deposition. *Atmospheric Environment*, 41: 1663–1668.

Hammerschmidt, C.R., and Fitzgerald, W.F. 2008. Sediment-water exchange of methylmercury determined from shipboard benthic flux chambers. *Marine Chemistry*, 109: 86–97.

Hammerschmidt, C.R., Fitzgerald, W.F., Balcom, P.H., and Visscher, P.T. 2008. Organic matter and sulfide inhibit methylmercury production in sediments of New York/New Jersey Harbor. *Marine Chemistry*, 109: 165–182.

Han, S., and Gill, G.A., 2005. Determination of mercury complexation in coastal and estuarine waters using competitive ligand exchange method. *Environmental Science and Technology*, 39, 6607–6615.

Han, S., Obraztsova, A., Pretto, P., Choe, K.Y., Gieskes, J., Deheyn, D.D., and Tebo, B.M. 2007. Biogeochemical factors affecting mercury methylation in sediments of the Venice Lagoon, Italy. *Environmental Toxicology and Chemistry*, 26: 655–663.

Hansell, D.A. and Carlson, C.A., 2002. *Biogeochemistry of Marine Dissolved Organic Matter*. Academic Press, San Diego.

Harada, M., 1995. Minamata disease: methylmercury poisoning in Japan caused by environmental pollution. *Critical Reviews in Toxicology*, 25: 1–24.

Harris, R.C., Rudd, J.W.M., Almyot, M., Babiarz, C.L., Beaty, K.G., Blanchfield, P.J., Bodaly, R.A., Branfireun, B.A., Gilmour, C.C., Graydon, J.A., Heyes, A., Hintelmann, H., Hurley, J.P., Kelly, C.A., Krabbenhoft, D.P., Lindberg, S.E., Mason, R.P., Paterson, M.J., Podemski, C.L., Robinson, A., Sandilands, K.A., Southworth, G.R., Louis, V.L.S., and Tate, M.T. 2007. Whole-ecosystem study shows rapid fish-mercury response to changes in mercury deposition. *Proceedings of the National Academy of Sciences*, 104: 16586–16591.

Heim, W.A., Coale, K.H., Stephenson, M., Choe, K.-Y., Gill, G.A., and Foe, C. 2007. Spatial and habitat-based variations in total and methyl mercury concentrations in surficial sediments in the San Francisco Bay-Delta. *Environmental Science and Technology*, 41(10): 3501–3507.

Heinz, G.H., and Hoffman, D.J. 2004. Mercury accumulation and loss in mallard eggs. *Environmental Toxicology and Chemistry*, 23: 222–224.

Heyes, A., Miller, C., and Mason, R.P., 2004. Mercury and methylmercury in Hudson River sediment: impact of tidal resuspension on partitioning and methylation. *Marine Chemistry*, 90: 75–89.

Heyes, A. Mason, R.P., Kim, E.H., and Sunderland, E. 2006. Mercury methylation in estuaries: Insights from using measuring rates using stable mercury isotopes. *Marine Chemistry*, 102: 134–147.

Hines, M.E., Evans, R.S., Genthner, B.R.S., Willis, S.G., Friedman, S., Rooney-Varga, J.N., and Devereux, R., 1999. Molecular phylogenetic and biogeochemical studies of sulfate-reducing bacteria in the rhizosphere of *Spartina alterniflora*. *Applied and Environmental Microbiology*, 65: 2209–2216.

Hines, M.E., Faganeli, J., Adatto, Isaac, and Horvat, M. 2006. Microbial mercury transformation in marine, estuarine, and freshwater sediment downstream of the Idrija Mercury Mine, Slovenia. *Applied Geochemistry*, 21: 1924–1939.

Hines, M.E., Horvat, M., Faganeli, J., Bonzongo, J.C.J., Barkay, T., Major, E.B., Scott, K.J., Bailey, E.A., Warwick, J.J., and Lyons, W.B. 2000. Mercury biogeochemistry in the Idrija River, Slovenia, from above the mine into the Gulf of Trieste. *Environmental Research Section A*, 83: 129–139.

Holmes, C.D., Jacob, D.J., Mason, R.P., and Jaffe, D.A. 2009. Sources and deposition of reactive gaseous mercury in the marine atmosphere. *Atmospheric Environment*, 43: 2278–2285.

Honda, K., Aoki, M., and Fujise, Y. 2006. Ecochemical approach using mercury accumulation of Antarctic minke whale, *Balaenoptera bonaerensis*, as tracer off historical change in Antarctic marine ecosystem during 1980–1999. *Bulletin of Environmental Contamination and Toxicology*, 76: 140–147.

Horvat, M., Covelli, S., Faganeli, J., Logar, M., Mandić, V., Rajar, R., Širca, A., and Žagar, D. 1999. Mercury in contaminated coastal environments; a case study: the Gulf of Trieste. *Science of the Total Environment*, 238: 43–56.

Horvat, M., Kotnik, J., Logar, M., Fajon, V., Zvonarić, T., and Pirrone, N. 2003. Speciation of mercury in surface and deep-sea waters of the Mediterranean Sea. *Atmospheric Environment*, 37: S93–S108.

Hunt, J.A., Davis, J.A., Greenfield, B.K., Melwani, A., Fairey, R., Sigala, M, Crane, D.B., Regalado, K, and Bonnema, A. 2008. Contaminant concentrations in sport fish from San Francisco Bay, 2006. SFEI Contribution #544. San Francisco Estuary Institute, Oakland, CA.

Ikemoto, T., Tu, N.P.C., Okuda, N., Iwanta, A., Omori, K., Tanabe, S., Tuyen, B.C., and Takeuchi, I. 2008. Biomagnification of trace elements in the aquatic food web in the Mekong Delta, South Vietnam using stable carbon and nitrogen isotope analysis. Archives of *Environmental Contamination and Toxicology*, 54: 504–515.

Ichihashi, H., Nakamura, Y., Kannan, K., Tsumura, A., and Yamasaki, S. 2001. Multielemental concentrations in tissues of Japanese common squid (*Todarodes pacificus*). *Archives of Environmental Contamination and Toxicology*, 41:483–90.

Iverfeldt, A., and Lindqvist, O. 1982. Distribution equilibrium of methyl mercury chloride between water and air. *Atmospheric Environment*, 16: 2917–2925.

Jardine, L.B., Burt, M.D.B., Arp, P.A., and Diamond, A.W.,2009. Mercury comparisons between farmed and wild Atlantic salmon (*Salmo salar L.*) and Atlantic cod (*Gadus morhua L.*). *Aquaculture Research*, 40: 1148–1159.

Jarman, W.M., Hobson, K.A., Sydeman, W.J., Bacon, C.E., and McLaren, E.B., 1996. Influence of trophic position and feeding location on contaminant levels in the Gulf of the Farallones food web revealed by stable isotope analysis. *Environmental Science and Technology*, 30: 654–660.

Jay, J.A., Murray, K.J., Gilmour, C.C., Mason, R.P., Morel, F.M.M., Roberts, A.L., and Hemond, H.F. 2002. Mercury methylation by *Desulfovibrio desulfuricans* ND132 in the presence of polysulfides. *Applied and Environmental Microbiology*, 68: 5741–5745.

Jewett, S.C., and Duffy, L.K. 2007. Mercury in fishes of Alaska, with emphasis on subsistence species. *Science of the Total Environment*, 387: 3–27.

Johansen, P., Mulvard, G., Pedersen, H.S., Hansen, J.C., and Riget, F. 2007. Human accumulation of mercury in Greenland. *Science of the Total Environment*, 377: 173–178.

Joiris, C.R., Ali, I.B., Holsbeek, L., Kanuya-Kinokti, M., and Tekele-Michael, Y. 1997a. Total and organic mercury in Greenland and Barents Seas demersal fish. *Bulletin of Environmental Contamination and Toxicology*, 58, 101–107.

Joiris, C.R., Moatemri, N.L., and Holsbeeek, L. 1997b. Mercury and polychlorinated biphenyls in zooplankton and shrimp from the Barents Sea and the Spitsbergen area. *Bulletin of Environmental Contamination and Toxicology*, 59: 472–478.

Joiris, C.R., Tapia, G., and Holsbeek, L. 1997c. Increase of organochlorines and mercury levels in common guillemots Uria aalge during winter in the southern North Sea. *Marine Pollution Bulletin*, 34: 1049–1057.

Joiris, C.R., Holsbeek, L., and Moatemri, N.L. 1999. Total and methylmercury in sardines *Sardinella aurita* and *Sardina pilchardus* from Tunisia. *Marine Pollution Bulletin*, 38: 188–192.

Jókai, Z., Abrankó, L., and Fodor, P. 2005. SPME-GC-pyrolysis-AFS determination of methylmercury in marine fish products by alkaline sample preparation and aqueous phase phenylation derivatization. *Journal of Agricultural and Food Chemistry*, 53: 5499–5505.

Jones, A.M., and Harrison, R.M. 2004. The effects of meteorological factors on atmospheric bioaerosol concentrations: a review. *Science of the Total Environment*, 326: 151–180.

Kádár, E., Costa, V., Santos, R.S., and Lopes, H. 2005. Behavioral response to the bioavailability of inorganic mercury in the hydrothermal mussel *Bathymodiolus azoricus*. *Journal of Experimental Biology*, 208: 505–513.

Kádár, E., Costa, V., and Segonzac, M. 2007. Trophic influences of metal accumulation in natural pollution laboratories at the deep-sea hydrothermal vents of the Mid-Atlantic Ridge. *Science of the Total Environment*, 373: 464–472.

Kainz, M., and Mazumder, A. 2005. Effect of algal and bacterial diet on methyl mercury concentrations in zooplankton. *Environmental Science and Technology*, 39: 1666–1672.

Kaneko, J.J., and Ralston, N.V.C. 2007. Selenium and mercury in pelagic fish in the central North Pacific near Hawaii. *Biological Trace Element Research*, 119: 242–254.

Kannan, K., and Falandysz, J., 1998. Speciation and concentrations of mercury in certain coastal marine sediments. *Water, Air, and Soil Pollution*, 103: 129–136.

Kannan, K., Smith, R.G. Jr., Lee, R.F., Windom, H.L., Heitmuller, P.T., Macauley, J.M., and Summers, J.K. 1998. Distributions of total mercury and methyl mercury in water, sediment, and fish from South Florida estuaries. *Archives of Environmental Contamination and Toxicology*, 34: 109–118.

Kawaguchi, T., Porter, D., Bushek, D., and Jones, B. 1999. Mercury in the American oyster *Crossostrea virginica* in South Carolina, USA, and public health concerns. *Marine Pollution Bulletin*, 38: 324–327.

Kehrig, H.A., Pinto, F.N., Moreira, I., and Malm, O. 2003. Heavy metals and methylmercury in a tropical coastal estuary and a mangrove in Brazil. *Organic Geochemistry*, 34: 661–669.

Kehrig, H.A., Brito, J.L., Malm, O., and Moreira, I. 2004. Methyl and total mercury in the food chain of a tropical estuary-Brazil. *RMZ– Materials and Geoenvironment*, 51: 1099–1102.

Kelly, C.A., Rudd, J.W.M., Louis, V.L., and Heyes, A. 1995. Is total mercury concentration a good predictor of methyl mercury concentration in aquatic systems? *Water, Air, and Soil Pollution*, 80: 715–724.

Kelly, B.C., Ikonomu, M.G., Higgs, D.A., Oakes, J., and Dubetz, C., 2008. Mercury and other trace elements in farmed and wild salmon from British Columbia, Canada. *Environmental Toxicology and Chemistry*, 27: 1361–1370.

Kerin, E.J., Gilmour, C.C., Roden, E., Suzuki, M. T., Coates, J. D., and Mason, R. P. 2006. Mercury methylation by dissimilatory iron-reducing bacteria. *Applied and Environmental Microbiology*, 72: 7919–7921.

Keskin, Y., Baskaya, R., Özyaral, O., Yurdun, T., Lüleci, N.E., and Hayran, O. 2007. *Bulletin of Environmental Contamination and Toxicology*, 78: 258–261.

Kim, E.H., Mason, R.P., Porter, E.T., and Soulen, H.L. 2004. The effect of resuspension on the fate of total mercury and methyl mercury in a shallow estuarine ecosystem: a mesocosm study. *Marine Chemistry*, 86: 121–137.

King, J.K., Kostka, J.E., Frischer, M.E., and Saunders, F.M., 2000. Sulfate-reducing bacteria methylate mercury at variable rates in pure culture and in marine sediments. *Applied and Environmental Microbiology*, 66: 2430–2437.

King, J.K., Kostka, J.E., Frischer, M.E., Saunders, F.M., and Jahnke, R.A. 2001. A quantitative relationship that demonstrates mercury methylation rates in marine sediments are based on community composition and activity of sulfate-reducing bacteria. *Environmental Science and Technology*, 35: 2491–2496.

Kiorboe, T., Ploug, H., and Thygesen, U.H. 2001. Fluid motion and solute distribution around sinking aggregates. I. Small-scale fluxes and heterogeneity of nutrients in the pelagic environment. *Marine Ecology-Progress Series*, 211: 1–13.

Kirk, J.L., St. Louis, V.L., Hintelmann, H., Lehnherr, I., Else, B., and Poissant, L. 2008. *Environmental Science and Technology*, 42: 8367–8373.

Knowles, T.G., Farrington, D., and Kestin, S.C. 2003. Mercury in UK imported fish and shellfish and UK-farmed fish and their products. *Food Additives and Contaminants*, 20: 813–818.

Kojadinovic, J., Potier, M., Le Corre, M., Cosson, R.P., and Bustamante, P. 2006. Mercury content in commercial pelagic fish and its risk assessment in the western Indian Ocean. *Science of the Total Environment*, 366: 688–700.

Koretsky, C.M., Van Cappellen, P., DiChristina, T.J., Kostka, J.E., Lowe, K.L., Moore, C.M., Roychoudhury, A.N., and Viollier, E. 2005. Salt marsh pore water geochemistry does not correlate with microbial community structure. *Estuarine, Coastal and Shelf Science*, 62: 233–251.

Kostka, J., Gribsholt, B., Petrie, E., Dalton, D., Skelton, H., and Kristensen, E. 2002a. The rates and pathways of carbon oxidation in bioturbated saltmarsh sediments. *Limnology and Oceanography*, 47: 230–240.

Kostka, J.E., Roychoudhury, A., and Van Cappellen, P. 2002b. Rates and controls of anaerobic microbial respiration across spatial and temporal gradients in saltmarsh sediments. *Biogeochemistry*, 60: 49–76.

Kotnik, J., Horvat, M., Tessier, E., Ogrinc, N., Monprerrus, M., Amouroux, D., Fajon, V., Gibičar, D., Žižek, S., Sprovieri, F., and Pirrone, N. 2007. Mercury speciation in surface and deep waters of the Mediterranean Sea. *Marine Chemistry*, 107: 13–30.

Kraepiel, A.M.L., Keller, K., Chin, H.B., Malcolm, E.G., and Morel, F.M.M. 2003. Sources and variations of mercury in tuna. *Environmental Science and Technology*, 37: 5551–5558.

Krümmel, E.R., Macdonald, R.W., Kimpe, L.E., Gregory-Eaves, I., Demers, M.J., Smol, J.P., Finney, B., and Blais, J.M. 2003. Delivery of pollutants by spawning salmon. *Nature*, 425: 255–256.

Kühl, M., and Jørgensen, B.B. 1992. Microsensor measurements of sulfate reduction and sulfide oxidation in compact microbial communities of aerobic biofilms. *Applied and Environmental Microbiology*, 58: 1164–1174.

Kütter, V.T., Mirlean, N., Baisch, P.R.M., Kütter, M.T., and Silva-Filho, E.V. 2008. Mercury in freshwater, estuarine, and marine fishes from Southern Brazil and its ecological implication. *Environmental Monitoring and Assessment*, DOI 10.1007/s10661-008-0610-1.

Kwokal, Ž., Frančiŝković-Bilinski, S., Bilinski, H., and Branica, M. 2002. A comparison of anthropogenic mercury pollution in Kaŝtela Bay (Croatia) with pristine estuaries in Öre (Sweden) and Krka (Croatia). *Marine Pollution Bulletin*, 44: 1152–1169.

Lalonde, J.D., Amyot, M., Orvoine, J., Morel, F.M.M., and Ariya, P.A. 2004. Photoinduced oxidation of $Hg^0_{(aq)}$ in the waters from the St. Lawrence estuary. *Environmental Science and Technology*, 38: 508–514.

Lambertsson, L., and Nilsson, M. 2006. Organic material: The primary control on mercury methylation and ambient methyl mercury concentrations in estuarine sediments. *Environmental Science and Technology*, 40: 1822–1829.

Lamborg, C.H., Fitzgerald, W.F., O'Donnell, J., and Torgersen, T. 2002. A non-steady-state compartmental model of global-scale mercury biogeochemistry with interhemispheric atmospheric gradients. *Geochimica et Cosmochimica Acta*, 66: 1105–1118.

Lamborg, C.H., Fitzgerald, W.F., Skoog, A., and Visscher, P.T. 2004. The abundance and source of mercury-binding organic ligands in Long Island Sound. *Marine Chemistry*, 90: 151–163.

Lamborg, C.H., Rolfhus, K.R., Fitzgerald, W.F., and Kim, G. 1999. The atmospheric cycling and air-sea exchange of mercury species in the South and equatorial Atlantic Ocean. *Deep-Sea Research, Part II*, 46: 957–977.

Lamborg, C.H., Von Damm, K.L., Fitzgerald, W.F., Hammerschmidt, C.R., and Zierenberg, R. 2006. Mercury and monomethylmercury in fluids from Sea Cliff submarine hydrothermal field, Gorda Ridge. *Geophysical Research Letters*, 33: L17606, 1–4.

Lamborg, C.H., Yiğiterhan, O., Fitzgerald, W.F., Balcom, P.H., Hammerschmidt, C.R., and Murray, J. 2008. Vertical distribution of mercury species at two sites in the Western Black Sea. *Marine Chemistry*, 111: 77–89.

Laporte, J.-M., Andres, S., and Mason, R.P., 2002. Effect of ligands and other metals on the uptake of mercury and methylmercury across the gills and intestine of the blue crab (*Callinectes sapidus*). *Comparative Biochemistry and Physiology Part C*, 131: 185–196.

Lasora, B., and Allen-Gil, S. 1995. The methylmercury to total mercury ratio in selected marine, freshwater, and terrestrial organisms. *Water, Air, and Soil Pollution*, 80: 905–913.

Laurier, F.J.G., Cossa, D., Beucher, C., and Brévière, E. 2007. The impact of groundwater discharges on mercury partitioning, speciation and bioavailability to mussels in a coastal zone. *Marine Chemistry*, 104: 143–155.

Laurier, F.J.G., Cossa, D., Gonzalez, J.L., Breviere, E., and Sarazin, G. 2003a. Mercury transformations and exchanges in a high turbidity estuary: The role of organic matter and amorphous oxyhydroxides. *Geochimica et Cosmochimica Acta*, 67: 3329–3345.

Laurier, F., Mason, R.P., Gill, G.A., and Whalin, L. 2004. Mercury distribution in the North Pacific Ocean: 20 years of observations. *Marine Chemistry*, 90: 3–19.

Laurier, F.J.G., Mason, R.P., Whalin, L., and Kato, S. 2003b. Reactive gaseous mercury formation in the North Pacific Ocean's marine boundary layer: A potential role of halogen chemistry. *Journal of Geophysical Research*, 108(D17), 4529, doi:10.1029/2003JD003625, 2003.

Lawson, N.M., and Mason, R.P. 1998. Accumulation of mercury in estuarine food chains. *Biogeochemistry*, 40: 235–247.

Layman, C.A., Arrington, D.A., Montaña, C.G., and Post, D.M. 2007. Can stable isotope ratios provide for community-wide measures of trophic structure. *Ecology*, 88: 42–48.

Lee, Y.H., Hultberg, H., and Andersson, I. 1985. Catalytic effect of various metal ions on the methylation of mercury in the presence of humic substances. *Water, Air, and Soil Pollution*, 25: 391–400.

Lee, Y.H., Wängberg, I., and Munthe, J. 2002. Sampling and analysis of gas phase methylmercury in ambient air. *Science of the Total Environment*, 304: 107 113.

Leermakers, M., Galletti, S., De Galan, S., Brion, N., and Baeyens, W. 2001. Mercury in the southern North Sea and Scheldt estuary. *Marine Chemistry*, 75: 229–248.

Leermakers, M., Meuleman, C., and Baeyens, W. 1995. Mercury speciation in the Scheldt Estuary. *Water, Air, and Soil Pollution*, 80: 641–652.

Legrand, M., Arp, P., Ritchie, C., and Chan, H.M. 2005. Mercury exposure in two coastal communities of the Bay of Fundy, Canada. *Environmental Research*, 98: 14–21.

Leitch, D.R., Carrie, J., Lean, D., Macdonald, R.W., Stern, G.A., and Wang, F. 2007. The delivery of mercury to the Beaufort Sea of the Arctic Ocean by the Mackenzie River. *Science of the Total Environment*, 373: 178–195.

Lin C., and Pehkonen, S.O. 1999. The chemistry of atmospheric mercury: a review. *Atmospheric Environment*, 33: 2067–2079.

Lin, C.C. and Jay, J.A. 2007. Mercury methylation by planktonic and biofilm cultures of *Desulfovibrio desulfuricans*. *Environmental Science and Technology*, 41: 6691–6697.

Lin, C.J., Pongprueksa, P., Lindberg, S.E., Pehkonen, S.O., Byun, D., and Jang, C. 2006. Scientific uncertainties in atmospheric mercury models I: model science evaluation. *Atmospheric Environment*, 40: 2911–2928.

Lindberg, S.E., Brooks, S., Lin, C.-J., Scott, K.J., Landis, M.S., Stevens, R.K., Goodsite, M., and Richter, A. 2002. Dynamic oxidation of gaseous mercury in the arctic troposphere at polar sunrise. *Environmental Science and Technology*, 36: 1245–1256.

Lindberg, S., Bullock, R., Ebinghaus, R., Engstrom, D., Feng, X., Fitzgerald, W., Pirrone, N., Prestbo, E., and Seigneur, C. 2007. A synthesis of progress and uncertainties in atributing the sources of mercury in deposition. *Ambio*, 36: 19–32.

Lindberg, S.E., Southworth, G., Prestbo, E.M., Wallschlager, D., Bogle, M.A., and Price, J. 2005. Gaseous methyl- and inorganic mercury in landfill gas from landfills in Florida, Minnesota, Delaware, and California. *Atmospheric Environment*, 39: 249–258.

Liu, X.D., Bagwell, C.E., Wu, L.Y., Devol, A.H., and Zhou, J.H. 2003. Molecular diversity of sulfate-reducing bacteria from two different continental margin habitats. *Applied and Environmental Microbiology*, 69: 6073–6081.

Liu, B., Schaider, L.A., Mason, R.P., Bank, M.S., Rabalais, N.N., Swarzenski, P.W., Shine, J.P., Hollweg, T., and Senn, D.B. 2009. Disturbance impacts on mercury dynamics in northern Gulf of Mexico sediments. *Journal of Geophysical Research*, 114, G00C07, doi:10.1029/2008JG000752.

Lockhart, W.L. Stern, G.A., Wagmann, R., Hunt, R.V., Menter, D.A., DeLaronde, J., Dunn, B., Stewart, R.E.A., Hyatt, C.K., Harwood, L., and Mount, K. 2005. Concentrations of mercury in tissues of beluga whales (*Delphinapterus leucas*) from several communities in the Canadian Arctic from 1981 to 2002. *Science of the Total Environment*, 351–352: 391–412.

Luengen, A.C.,. and Flegal, A.R. 2009. Role of phytoplankton in mercury cycling in the San Francisco Bay estuary. *Limnology and Oceanography*; 54: 23–40.

Luther, F.W., and Tsamakis, E. 1989. Concentration and form of dissolved sulfide in the oxic water column of the ocean. *Marine Chemistry*, 27: 165–177.

Macdonald, R.W., Harner, T., and Fyfe, J. 2005. Recent climate change in the Arctic and its impact on contaminant pathways and interpretation of temporal trend data. *Science of the Total Environment*, 342: 5–86.

Macleod, M., Mckone, T.E., and Mackay, D., 2005. Mass balance for mercury in the San Francisco Bay Area. *Environmental Science and Technology*, 39: 6721–6729.

Martin, J.H., and Knauer, G.A. 1973. The elemental composition of phytoplankton. *Geochimica et Cosmochimica Acta*, 37: 1639–1653.

Martins, I., Costa, V., Porteiro, F., Cravo, A., and Santos, R.S. 2001. Mercury concentrations in invertebrates from Mid-Atlantic Ridge hydrothermal vent fields. *Journal of the Marine Biological Association of the United Kingdom*, 81: 913–915.

Martins, I., Costa, V., Porteiro, F., Colaço, A., and Santos, R.S. 2006a. Mercury concentrations in fish species caught at the Mid-Atlantic Ridge hydrothermal vent fields. *Marine Ecology Progress Series*, 320: 253–258.

Martins, I., Costa, V., Porteiro, F.M., and Santos, R.S. 2006b. Temporal and spatial changes in mercury concentrations in the North Atlantic as indicated by museum specimens of glacier lanternfish *Benthosema glaciale* (Pisces : Myctophidae). *Environmental Toxicology*, 21: 528–532.

Marvin-DiPasquale, M.C., and Agee, J. 2003. Microbial mercury cycling in sediments of the San Francisco Bay-Delta. *Estuaries*, 26: 1517–1528.

Marvin-DiPasquale, M.C., Agee, J., Bouse, R.M., and Jaffe, B.E., 2003. Microbial cycling of mercury in contaminated pelagic and wetland sediments of San Pablo Bay, California. *Environmental Geology*, 43: 26–267.

Marvin-DiPasquale, M.C., Agee, J., McGowan, C., Oremland, R.S., Thomas, M., Krabbenhoft, D., and Gilmour, C.C. 2000. Methylmercury degradation pathways: a comparison among three mercury-impacted ecosystems. *Environmental Science and Technology*, 34: 4908–4917.

Mason, R.P., and Fitzgerald, W.F. 1990. Alkylmercury species in the Equatorial Pacific. *Nature*, 347: 457–459.

Mason, R.P. and Fitzgerald, W.F., 1991. Mercury speciation in open ocean waters. *Water, Air, and Soil Pollution*, 56: 779–789.

Mason, R.P., and Fitzgerald, W.F. 1993. The distribution and biogeochemical cycling of mercury in the equatorial Pacific Ocean. *Deep-Sea Research, Part I*, 40: 1897–1924.

Mason, R.P., Fitzgerald, W.F., and Vandal., G.M. 1992. The sources and composition of mercury in Pacific Ocean rain. *Journal of Atmospheric Chemistry*, 14: 489–500.

Mason, R.P., Fitzgerald, W.F., Hurley, J., Hanson, A.K., Donaghay, P.L., and Sieburth, J.M. 1993. Mercury biogeochemical cycling in a stratified estuary. *Limnology and Oceanography*, 38: 1227–1241.

Mason, R.P., Fitzgerald, W.F., and Morel, F.M.M. 1994. The biogeochemical cycling of elemental mercury: Anthropogenic influences. *Geochimica et Cosmochimica Acta*, 58(15): 3191–3198.

Mason, R.P., Kim, E.H., Cornwell, J., and Heyes, D. 2006. An examination of the factors influencing the flux of mercury, methylmercury and other constituents from estuarine sediment. *Marine Chemistry*, 102: 96–110.

Mason, R.P., and Lawrence, A.L. 1999. Concentration, distribution, and bioavailability of mercury and methylmercury in sediments of Baltimore Harbor and Chesapeake Bay, Maryland, USA. *Environmental Toxicology and Chemistry*, 18: 2438–2447.

Mason, R.P., Reinfelder, J.R., and Morel, F.M.M. 1996. Uptake, toxicity, and trophic transfer of mercury in a coastal diatom. *Environmental Science and Technology*, 30: 1835–1845.

Mason, R.P., Lawson, N.M., Lawrence, A.L., Leaner, J.J., Lee, J.G., and Sheu, G.R. 1999. Mercury in the Chesapeake Bay. *Marine Chemistry*, 65: 77–96.

Mason, R.P., Lawson, N.W., and Sheu, G.R. 2001. Mercury in the Atlantic Ocean: factors controlling the air-sea exchange of mercury and its distribution in the upper waters. *Deep-Sea Research Part II*, 48: 2829–2853.

Mason, R.P., Rolfhus, K.R., and Fitzgerald, W.F. 1995. Methylated and elemental mercury cycling in surface and deep ocean waters of the North Atlantic. *Water, Air and Soil Pollution*, 80: 665–677.

Mason, R.P., Rolfhus, K.R., and Fitzgerald, W.F. 1998. Mercury in the North Atlantic. *Marine Chemistry*, 61: 37–53.

Mason, R.P., and Sheu, G.R. 2002. Role of the ocean in the global mercury cycle. *Global Biogeochemical Cycles*, 16 (4), 1093, doi:10.1029/2001GB001440.

Mason, R.P., and Sullivan, K.A. 1999. The distribution and speciation of mercury in the South and equatorial Atlantic. *Deep-Sea Research II*, 46: 937–956.

Mason, R.P., and Gill, G.A. 2005. Mercury in the marine environment, in *Mercury: Sources, Measurements, Cycles and Effects*, M.B. Parsons and J.B. Percival, Eds., pp. 179–216. Short Course Series, Vol. 34, Mineralogical Association of Canada, Halifax, Nova Scotia, Canada.

Mauro, J.B.N., Gimaraes, J.R.D., Hintelmann, H., Watras, C.J., Haack, E.A., and Coelho-Souza, S.A. 2002. Mercury methylation in macrophytes, periphyton, and water – comparative studies with stable and radio-mercury additions. *Analytical and Bioanalytical Chemistry*, 374: 983–989.

Mathews, T., and Fisher, N.S. 2008. Evaluating the trophic transfer of cadmium, polonium, and methylmercury in an estuarine food chain. *Environmental Toxicology and Chemistry*, 27: 1093–1101.

McArthur, T., Butlerand, E.C., and Jackson, G.D. 2003. Mercury in the marine food chain in the Southern Ocean at Macquarie Island: an analysis of the top predator, Patagonian toothfish (*Dissostichus eleginoides*) and a mid-trophic species, the warty squid (*Moroteuthis ingens*). *Polar Biology*, 27: 1–5.

Mergler, D., Anderson, H.A., Chan, L.H.M., Mahaffey, K.R.. Murray, M., Sakamoto, M., and Stern, A.H., 2007. Methylmercury exposure and health effects in humans: A worldwide concern. *Ambio*, 36: 3–11.

Mester, Z., and Sturgeon, R.E. 2002. Detection of volatile organometal chloride species in model atmospheric above seawater and sediment. *Environmental Science and Technology*, 36: 1198–1201.

Michener, R.H., and Schell, D.M. 1994. Stable isotope ratios as tracers in marine aquatic food webs. In: *Stable isotope tracers in ecology and environmental science*. Lathja, K., and Michener, R.H. (Eds.). Blackwell Scientific, Oxford, U.K., pp. 138–186.

Mikac, N., Picer, M., Stegnar, P., and Tusekznidaric, M., 1985. Mercury distribution in a polluted marine area, ration of total mercury, methyl mercury and selenium in sediments, mussels and fish. *Water Research*, 19: 1387–1392.

Mikac, N., Biessen, S., Ouddane, B., and Wartel, M., 1999. Speciation of mercury in sediments of the Seine Estuary (France). *Applied Organometallic Chemistry*, 13: 715–725.

Misra, T.K. 1992. Bacterial resistance to inorganic mercury salts and organomercurials. *Plasmid*, 27: 4–16.

Mitchell, C.P.J., and Gilmour, C.C. 2008. Methylmercury production in a Chesapeake Bay salt marsh. *Journal of Geophysical Research*, 13, G00C04, doi:10.1029/2008JG000765.

Mitsch, W.J., and Gosselink, J.G. 2000. *Wetlands*. Wiley, New York.

Mittelstaedt, E. 1986. Upwelling regions. In: *Oceanography*, Jürgen Sündermann, Ed. Springer-Verlag, Berlin, Germany, pp. 135–166.

Mol, J.H., Ramlal, J.S., Lietar, C., and Verloo, M. 2000. Mercury contamination in freshwater, estuarine and marine fishes in relation to small-scale gold mining in Suriname, South America. *Environmental Research*, 86: 183–187.

Monperrus, M., Tessier, E., Amouroux, D., Leynaert, A., Huonnic, P., and Donard, O.F.X. 2007. Mercury methylation, demethylation and reduction rates in coastal and marine surface waters of the Mediterranean Sea. *Marine Chemistry*, 107: 49–63.

Monson, B.A., and Brezonik, P.L., 1999. Influence of food, aquatic humus, and alkalinity on methylmercury uptake by *Daphnia magna*. *Environmental Toxicology and Chemistry*, 18: 560–566.

Monteiro, L.R., Costa, V., Furness, R.W., and Santos, R.S. 1996. Mercury concentrations in prey fish indicate enhanced bioaccumulation in mesopelagic environments. *Marine Ecology Progress Series*, 141: 21–25.

Monteiro, L.R., and Furness, R.W. 1997. Accelerated increase in mercury contamination in North Atlantic mesopelagic food chains as indicated by time series of seabird feathers. *Environmental Toxicology and Chemistry*, 16: 2489–2493.

Monteiro, L.R., and Furness, R.W. 2001. Kinetics, dose-response, and excretion of methylmercury in free-living adult Cory's shearwaters. *Environmental Science and Technology*, 35: 739–746.

Monteiro, L.R., Granadeiro, J.P., and Furness, R.W. 1998. Relationship between mercury levels and diet in Azores seabirds. *Marine Ecology Progress Series*, 166: 259–265.

Morris, D.P., Zagarese, H., Williamson, C.E., Balseiro, E.G., Hargreaves, B.R., Modenutti, B., Moeller, R., and Queimalinos, C. 1995. The attenuation of solar UV radiation in lakes and the role of dissolved organic carbon. *Limnology and Oceanography*, 40: 1381–1391.

Moye, H. A., Miles, C. J., Phlips, E. J., Sargent, B., and Merritt, K. K. 2002. Kinetics and uptake mechanisms for monomethylmercury between freshwater algae and water. *Environmental Science and Technology*, 36: 3550–3555.

Mozaffarian, D., and Rimm, E.B. 2006. Fish intake, contaminants, and human health - Evaluating the risks and the benefits. *JAMA-Journal of the American Medical Association*, 296: 1885–1899.

Muir, D., Braune, B., de March, B., Nordstrom, R., Wagemann, R., Lockhart, L., Hargrave B., Bright, D., Addison, R., Payne, J., and Reimer, K. 1999. Spatial and temporal trends and effects of contaminants in the Canadian Arctic marine ecosystem: a review. *Science of the Total Environment*, 230: 83–144.

Muresan, B., Cossa, D., Jezequel, D, Prevot, F, and Kerbellec, S. 2007. The biogeochemistry of mercury at the sediment-water interface in the Thau lagoon. 1. Partition and speciation. *Estuarine, Coastal and Shelf Science*, 72: 472–484.

Mzoughi, N., Stoichev, T., Dachraoui, M., El Abed, A., Amouroux, D., and Donard, O.F.X. 2002. Inorganic mercury and methylmercury in surface sediments and mussel tissues from a microtidal lagoon (Bizerte, Tunisia). *Journal of Coastal Conservation*, 8:141–145.

Nagase, H., Ose, Y., Sato, T., and Ishikawa, T. 1982. Methylation of mercury by humic substances in an aquatic environment. *Science of the Total Environment*, 24: 133–142.

Nakagawa, R., Yumita, Y., and Hiromoto, M. 1997. Total mercury intake from fish and shellfish by Japanese people. *Chemosphere*, 35: 2909–2913.

Nakhlé, K.F., Cossa, D., Khalaf, G., and Beliaeff, B. 2006. *Brachidontes variabilis* and *Patella* sp. as quantitative biological indicators for cadmium, lead and mercury in the Lebanese coastal waters. *Environmental Pollution*, 142: 73–82.

National Oceanographic and Atmospheric Administration (NOAA), 2007. Mussel Watch, National Centers for Coastal Ocean Science, http://www8.nos.noaa.gov/cit/nsandt/download/mw_monitoring.aspx.

National Research Council, 2000. *Toxicological Effects of Methylmercury*. National Academy Press, Washington, DC.

Niki, H., Maker, P.D., Savage, C.M., and Brietenbach, L.P., 1983a. A long-path Fourier transform infrared study of the kinetics and mechanism for the reaction Cl + dimethylmercury. *Journal of Physical Chemistry*, 24: 3722–2724.

Niki, H., Maker, P.D., Savage, C.M., and Brietenbach, L.P., 1983b. A long-path Fourier transform infrared study of the kinetics and mechanism for the HO-radical initiated oxidation of dimethylmercury. *Journal of Physical Chemistry*, 24: 4978–4981.

Nobumasa, I., Eiji, S., Shoe-Kung, P., Kiyoshi, N., Jong-Yoon, K., Kwan, T., and Ukita, T. 1971. Chemical methylation of inorganic mercury with methylcobalamin, a vitamin B12 analog. *Science*, 172: 1248–1249.

Nygård, T., Lie, E., Røv, N., and Steinnes, E., 2001. Metal dynamics in an Antarctic food chain. *Marine Pollution Bulletin*, 42: 598–602.

Ogrinc, N., Monperrus, M., Kotnik, J., Fajon, V., Vidimova, K., Amouroux, D., Kocman, D., Tessier, E., Žižek, S., and Horvat, M. 2007. Distribution of mercury and methylmercury in deep-sea surficial sediments of the Mediterranean Sea. *Marine Chemistry*, 107: 31–48.

Orihel, D.M., Paterson, M.J., Blanchfield, P.J., Bodaly, R.A., Hintelmann, H., 2007. Experimental evidence of a linear relationship between inorganic mercury loading and methylmercury accumulation by aquatic biota. *Environmental Science and Technology*, 41: 4952–4958.

Orihel, D.M., Paterson, M.J., Gilmour, C.C., Bodaly, R.A., Blanchfield, P.J., Hintelmann, H., Harris, R.C., and Rudd, J.W.M. 2006. Effect of loading rate on the fate of mercury in littoral mesocosms. *Environmental Science and Technology*, 40: 5992–6000.

Ouddane, B., Mikac, N., Cundy, A.B., Quillet, L., and Fischer, J.C., 2008. A comparative study of mercury distribution and methylation in mudflats from two macrotidal estuaries: The Seine (France) and the Medway (United Kingdom). *Applied Geochemistry*, 23: 618–631.

Outridge, P.M., Evans, R.D., Wagemann, R., and Stewart, R.E.A. 1997. Historical trends of heavy metals and stable lead isotope in beluga (*Delphinapterus leucas*) and walrus (*Odobenus rosmarus rosmarus*) in the Canadian Arctic. *Science of the Total Environment*, 203: 209–219.

Outridge, P.M., Hobson, K.A., and Savelle, J.M. 2005. Changes in the mercury and cadmium concentrations and feeding behavior of beluga (*Delphinapterus leucas*) near Somerset Island, Canada during the 20th Century. *Science of the Total Environment*, 350: 106–118

Outridge, P.M., Macdonald, R.W., Wang, F., Stern, G.A., and Dastoor, A.P. 2008. A mass balance inventory of mercury in the Arctic Ocean. *Environmental Chemistry*, 5: 89–111.

Pacyna, E.G., Pacyna, J.M., Steenhuisen, F., and Wilson, S. 2006. Global anthropogenic mercury emission inventory for 2000. *Atmospheric Environment*, 40: 4048–4063.

Pal, B., and Ariya, P.A. 2004. Gas-phase HO-initiated reactions of elemental mercury: Kinetics, product studies, and atmospheric implications. *Environmental Science and Technology*, 38: 5555–5566.

Palmer, S.J., Presley, B.J., Taylor, R.J., and Powell, E.N. 1993. Field studies using the oyster *Crossostrea virginica* to determine mercury accumulation and depuration rates. *Bulletin of Environmental Contamination and Toxicology*, 51: 464–470.

Palmisano, F., Cardellicchio, N., and Zambonin, P.G. 1995. Speciation of mercury in dolphin liver: A two-stage mechanism for the demethylation accumulation process and role of selenium. *Marine Environmental Research*, 40: 109–121.

Paterson, M.J., Blanchfield, P., Podemski, C., Hintelmann, H.H., Gilmour, C.C., Harris, R., Ogrinc, N., Rudd, R.W.M., and Sandilands, K.A. 2006. Bioaccumulation of newly-deposited mercury by fish and invertebrates: an enclosure study using stable mercury isotopes. *Canadian Journal of Fisheries and Aquatic Science*, 66: 2213–2224.

Pereira, M.E., Abreu, S., Pato, P., Coelho, J.P., Azeiteiro, U.M., Pardal, M.A., and Duarte, A.C. 2007. Seasonal mercury concentrations in plankton-net material from a contaminated coastal lagoon (Ria de Aveiro, Portugal). *Fresenius Environmental Bulletin*, 16: 1442–1450.

Perugini, M., Visciano, P., Manera, M., Zaccaroni, A., Plivieri, V., and Amorena, M. 2009. Levels of total mercury in marine organisms from Adriatic Sea, Italy. *Bulletin of Environmental Contamination and Toxicology*, 83: 244–248.

Peterson, S.A., Van Sickle, J., Hughes, R.M., Schacher, J.A., and Echols, S.F. 2005. A biopsy procedure for determining filet and predicting whole-fish mercury concentration. *Archives of Environmental Contamination and Toxicology*, 48: 99–107.

Pickhardt, P.C., and Fisher, N.S. 2007. Accumulation of inorganic and methylmercury by freshwater phytoplankton in two contrasting water bodies. *Environmental Science and Technology*, 41: 125–131.

Pickhardt, P.C., Folt, C.L., Chen, C.Y., Klaue, B., and Blum, J.D. 2002. Algal blooms reduce the uptake of toxic methylmercury in freshwater food webs. *Proceedings of the National Academy of Sciences of the United States of America*, 99: 4419–4423.

Pickhardt, P.C., Stepanova, M., and Fisher, N.S. 2006. Contrasting uptake routes and tissue distributions of inorganic and methylmercury in mosquitofish (*Gambusia affinis*) and redear sunfish (*Lepomis microlophus*). *Environmental Toxicology and Chemistry*, 25: 132–2142.

Plessi, M., Bertelli, D., and Monzani, A. 2001. Mercury and selenium content in selected seafood. *Journal of Food Composition and Analysis*, 14: 461–467

Ploug, H., Kühl, M., Buchholz-Cleven, B., and Jørgensen, B.B. 1997. Anoxic aggregates: an ephemeral phenomenon in the pelagic environment? *Aquatic Microbial Ecology*, 13: 285–294.

Pongratz, R., and Heumann, K.G. 1998. Determination of concentration profiles of methyl mercury compounds in surface waters of polar and other remote oceans by GC-AFD. *International Journal of Envirnomental Analytical Chemistry*, 71: 41–56.

Poulain, A.J., Garcia, E., Amyot, M., Campbell, P.G.C., Raofie, F., and Ariya, P.A. 2007. Biological and chemical redox transformations of mercury in fresh and salt waters of the high arctic during spring and summer. *Environmental Science and Technology*, 41: 1883–1888.

Quevauviller, P., Donard, O.F.X., Wasserman, J.C., Martin, F.M., and Schneider, J. 1992. Occurrence of methylated tin and dimethylmercury-compounds in a mangrove core from Sepetiba Bay, Brazil. *Applied Organometallic Chemistry*, 6(2): 221–228.

Radke, L. F., Friedli, H. R., and Heikes, B. G. 2007. Atmospheric mercury over the NE Pacific during ITCT2K2: Gradients, residence time, stratosphere-troposphere exchange, and long-range transport. *Journal of Geophysical Research*, 112 (D19305).

Rajan, M., Darrow, J., Hua, M., Barnett, B., Mendoza, M., Greenfield, B.K, and Andrews, J.C. 2008. Hg L$_3$ XANES study of mercury methylation in shredded *Eichhornia crassipes*. *Environmental Science and Technology*, 42: 5568–5573.

Rajar, R., Četina, M., Horvat, M., and Žagar, D. 2007. Mass balance of mercury in the Mediterranean Sea. *Marine Chemistry*, 107: 89–102.

Regnell, O., Ewald, G., and Lord, E. 1997. Factors controlling temporal variation in methyl mercury levels in sediment and water in a seasonally stratified lake. *Limnology and Oceanography*, 42: 1784–1795.

Renaud, C.B., Nriagu, J.O., and Wong, H.K.T. 1995. Trace-metals in fluid-preserved museum fish specimens. *Science of the Total Environment*, 159: 1–7.

Riget, F., and Dietz, R., 2000. Temporal trends of cadmium and mercury in Greenland marine biota. *Science of the Total Environment*, 245: 49–60.

Riget, F., Muir, D., Kwan, M., Savinova, T., Nyman, M., Woshner, V., and O'Hara, T. 2005. Circumpolar pattern of mercury and cadmium in ringed seals. *Science of the Total Environment*, 351–352: 312–322.

Riget, F., Dietz, R., Born, E.W., Sonne, C., and Hobson, K.A., 2007a. Temporal trends of mercury in marine biota of west and northwest Greenland. *Marine Pollution Bulletin*, 54: 72–80.

Riget, F., Muller, R., Nielsen, T.G., Asmund, G., Strand, J., Larsen, M.M., and Hobson, K.A. 2007b. Transfer of mercury in the marine food web of West Greenland. *Journal of Environmental Monitoring*, 9: 877–883.

Riva, S.D., Abelmoschi, M.L., Magi, E., and Soggia, F. 2004. The utilization of the Antarctic environmental specimen bank (BCAA) in monitoring Cd and Hg in an Antarctic coastal area in Terra Nova (Ross Sea—Northern Victoria Land). *Chemosphere*, 56: 59–69.

Rodríguez Martín-Doimeadios, R.C., Tessier, E., Amouroux, D., Guyoneaud, R., Duran, R., Caumette, P., and Donard, O.F.X. 2004. Mercury methylation/demethylation and volatilization pathways in estuarine sediment slurries using species-specific enriched stable isotopes. *Marine Chemistry*, 90: 107–123.

Rolfhus, K.R., and Fitzgerald, W.F. 2001. The evasion and spatial/temporal distribution of mercury species in Long Island Sound, CT-NY. *Geochemica et Cosmochimica Acta*, 65: 407–418.

Rolfhus, K.R., and Fitzgerald, W.F. 2004. Mechanisms and temporal variability of dissolved gaseous mercury production in coastal seawater. *Marine Chemistry*, 90: 125–136.

Roos-Barraclough, F., and Shotyk, W. 2003. Millennial-scale records of atmospheric mercury deposition obtained from ombrotrophic and minerotrophic peatlands in the Swiss Jura mountains. *Environmental Science and Technology*, 37: 235–244.

Rouleau, C., Cobeil, C., and Tjälve, H. 1998. Pharmacokinetics and distribution of dietary tributyltin compared to those of methylmercury in the American plaice Hippoglossoides platessoides. *Marine Ecology Progress Series*, 171: 275–284.

Ruelas-Inzunza, J., Páez-Osuna, F., and Soto, L.A. 2005. Bioaccumulation of Cd, Co, Cr, Cu, Few, Hg, Mn, Ni, Pb and Zn in trophosome and vesmentum of the tube worm *Riftia pachyptila* from Guaymas basin, Gulf of California. *Deep-Sea Research I*, 5: 1319–1323.

Ruelas-Inzunza, J., Meza-López, G., and Páez-Osuna, F. 2008. Mercury in fish that are of dietary importance from coasts of Sinaloa (SE Gulf of California). *Journal of Food Composition and Analysis*, 21: 211–218.

Ruelas-Inzunza, J., Hernández-Osuna, J., and Páez-Osuna, F. 2009. Organic and total mercury in muscle tissue of five aquatic birds with different feeding habits from the SE Gulf of California, Mexico. *Chemosphere*, 76: 415–418.

Ryther, J.H. 1969. Photosynthesis and fish production in the sea. *Science*, 166: 72–76.

Sarica, J., Amyot, M. Hare, L., Doyon, M.-R., and Stanfield, L.W. 2004. Salmon-derived mercury and nutrients in a Lake Ontario spawning stream. *Limnology and Oceanography*, 49: 891–899.

Schaefer, J.K., Yagi, J., Reinfelder, J., Cardona-Marek, T., Ellickson, K., Tel-Or, S., and Barkay, T. 2004. The role of the bacterial organomercury lyase (MerB) in controlling methylmercury accumulation in mercury contaminated natural waters. *Environmental Science and Technology*, 34: 4304–4311.

Scheifler, R., Gauthier-Clerc, M., Le Bohec, C., Crini, N., Cœurdassier, M., Badot, P.-M., Giraudoux, P., and Le Maho, T. 2005. Mercury concentrations in king penguin (*Aptenodytes patagonicus*) feathers at Crozet Islands (Sub-Antarctic): comparison between contemporary (2000–2001) and historical (1966–1974) samples. *Environmental Toxicology and Contamination*, 24: 125–128.

Scheuhammer, A.M., Perrault, J.A., and Bond, D.E., 2001. Mercury, methylmercury, and selenium concentrations in eggs of common loons (*Gavia immer*) from Canada. *Environmental Monitoring and Assessment*, 72: 79–84.

Scheuhammer, A.M., Meyer, M.W., Sandheinrich, M.B., and Murray, M.W. 2007. Effects of environmental methylmercury on the health of wild birds, mammals, and fish. *Ambio*, 36: 12–18.

Schroeder, W.H., Anlauf, K.G., Barrie, L.A., Lu, J.Y., Steffen, A., Schneeberger, D.R., and Berg, T. 1998. Arctic springtime depletion of mercury. *Nature*, 394: 331–332.

Schwarzbach, S.E., Albertson, J.D., and Thomas, C.M. 2006. Effects of predation, flooding, and contamination on reproductive success of California clapper rails (*Rallus longirostris obsoletus*) in San Francisco Bay. *Auk*, 123: 45–60.

Seigneur, C., Vijayaraghavan, K., and Lohman, K. 2006. Atmospheric mercury chemisty: sensitivity of global model simulation to chemical reactions. *Journal of Geophysical Research*, 111, D22306, doi:10.1029/2005JD006780.

Selin, N.E., Jacob, D.J., Park, R.J., Yantosca, R.M., Strode, S., Jaegle, L., and Jaffe, D. 2007. Chemical cycling and deposition of atmospheric mercury: Global constraints from observations. *Journal of Geophysical Research-Atmospheres*, 112(D2).

Selin, N.E., Jacob, D.J., Yantosca, R.M., Strode, S., Haegle, L., and Sunderland, E.M., 2008. Global 3-D land-oceanatmosphere model for mercury: Present-day versus preindustrial cycles and anthropogenic enrichment factors for deposition. *Global Biogeochemical Cycles*, 22, GB2011, doi:10.1029/2007GB003040.

Sellers, P., Kelly, C.A., Rudd, J.W.M., and MacHutchon, A.R. 1996. Photodegradation of methylmercury in lakes. *Nature*, 380: 694–697.

Senn, D.B., Chesney, E.J., Blum, J.D., Bank, M.S., Maage, A., and Shine, J.P. (personal communication). Stable isotope (N, C, Hg) study of methylmercury sources and trophic transfer in the northern Gulf of Mexico.

Siciliano, S.D., O'Driscoll, N.J., Tordon, R., Hill, J., Beauchamp, S., and Lean, D.R.S. 2005. Abiotic production of methylmercury by solar radiation. *Environmental Science and Technology*, 39: 1071–1077.

Simon, M., Grossart, H.P., Schweitzer, B., and Ploug, H. 2002. Microbial ecology of organic aggregates in aquatic systems. *Aquatic Microbial Microbiology Ecology*, 28: 175–211.

Skyllberg, U., 2008. Competition among thiols and inorganic sulfides and polysulfides for Hg and MeHg in wetland soils and sediments under suboxic conditions: Illumination of controversies and implications for MeHg net production. *Journal of Geophysical Research*, 113, G00C03, doi:10.1029/2008JG000745.

Smith, R.C., and Baker, K.S. 1981. Optical properties of the clearest natural waters (200–800 nm). *Applied Optics*, 20: 177–184.

Sonne, C., Dietz, R., Leifsson, P.S., Asmund, G., Born, E.W., and Kirkegaard, M., 2007. Are liver and renal lesions in East Greenland polar bears (*Ursus maritimus*) associated with high mercury levels? *Environmental Health*, 6: 11.

St. Louis, V.L., Sharp, M.J., Steffen, A., May, A., Barker, J., Kirk, J.L., Kelly, D.J.A., Arnott, S.E., Keatley, B., and Smol, J.P. 2005. Some sources and sinks of monomethyl and inorganic mercury on Ellesmere Island in the Canadian high arctic. *Environmental Science and Technology*, 39: 2686–2701.

St. Louis, V.L., Hintelmann, H., Graydon, J.A., Kirk, J.L., Barker, J., Dimock, B., Sharp, M.J., and Lehnherr, I. 2007. Methylated mercury species in Canadian high arctic marine surface waters and snowpacks. *Environmental Science and Technology*, 41: 6433–6441.

Stern, G.A., and Macdonald, R.W. 2005. Biogeographic provinces of total and methylmercury in zooplankton from the Beaufort and Chukchi Seas: Results from the SHEBA drift. *Environmental Science and Technology*, 39: 4707–4713.

Stoffers, P., Hannington, M., Wright, I., Herzig, P., de Ronde, C., and Party, S.S. 1999. Elemental mercury at submarine hydrothermal vents in the Bay of Plenty, Taupo volcanic zone, New Zealand. *Geology*, 27: 931–934.

Stoichev, T., Amouroux, D., Wasserman, J.C., Point, D., De Diego, A., Bareille, G., and Donard, O.F.X. 2004. Dynamics of mercury species in surface sediments of a macrotidal estuarine-coastal system (Adour River, Bay of Biscay). *Estuarine, Coastal and Shelf Science*, 59: 511–521.

Stoor, R.W., Hurley, J.P., Babiarz, C.L., and Armstrong, D.E. 2006. Subsurface sources of methyl mercury to Lake Superior from a wetland-forested watershed. *Science of the Total Environment*, 368: 99–110.

Stordal, M.C., Gill, G.A., Wen, L.S., and Santschi, P.H. 1996. Mercury phase speciation in the surface waters of three Texas estuaries: Importance of colloidal forms. *Limnology and Oceanography*, 41: 52–61.

Storelli, M.M., Giacominelli-Stuffler, R., Storelli, A., D'Addabbo, R., Palermo, C., and Marcotrigiano, G.O., 2003a. Survey of total mercury and methylmercury levels in edible fish from the Adriatic Sea. *Food Additives and Contaminants*, 20: 1114–1119.

Storelli, M.M., Stuffler, R.G., Storelli, A. and Marcotrigiano, G.O. 2003b. Total mercury and methylmercury content in edible fish from the Mediterranean Sea. *Journal of Food Protection*, 66: 300–303.

Strode, S.A., Jaegle, L., Selin, N.E., Jacob, D.J., Park, R.J., Yantosca, R.M., Mason, R.P., and Slemr, F. 2007. Air-sea exchange in the global mercury cycle. *Global Biogeochemical Cycles*, 21, GB1017, doi:10.1029/2006GB002766.

Suda, I., Suda, M., and Hirayama, K., 1993. Degradation of methyl and ethyl mercury by singlet oxygen generated from sea water exposed to sunlight or ultraviolet light. *Archives of Toxicology*, 67: 365–368.

Sun, L., Yin, X., Liu, X., Zhu, R., Xie, Z., and Wang, Y. 2006. A 2000-year record of mercury and ancient civilizations in seal hairs from King George Island, West Antarctica. *Science of the Total Environment*, 368: 236–247.

Sunderland, E.M. 2007. Mercury exposure from domestic and imported estuarine and marine fish in the US seafood market. *Environmental Health Perspectives*, 115: 235–242.

Sunderland, E.M., Gobas, F.A.P.C., Heyes, A., Branfireun, B.A., Bayer, A.K., Cranston, R.E., and Parsons, M.B. 2004. Speciation and bioavailability of mercury in well-mixed estuarine sediments. *Marine Chemistry*, 90: 91–105.

Sunderland, E.M., Gobas, F.A.P.C., Branfireun, B.A., and Heyes, A. 2006. Environmental controls on the speciation and distribution of mercury in coastal sediments. *Marine Chemistry*, 102: 111–123.

Sunderland, E.M., and Mason, R.P., 2007. Human impacts on open ocean mercury concentrations. *Global Biogeochemical Cycles*, 21: GB4022, 1–15.

Sunderland, E.M., Krabbenhoft, D.P., Moreau, J.W., Strode, S.A., and Landing, W.M. 2009. Mercury sources, distribution, and bioavailability in the North Pacific Ocean: Insights from data and models. *Global Biogeochemical Cycles*, 23, GB2010, doi:10.1029/2008GB003425.

Taillefert, M., Neuhuber, S., and Bristow, G. 2007. The effect of tidal forcing on biogeochemical processes in intertidal salt marsh sediments. *Geochemical Transactions*, 8: 6.

Tavares, P.C., Kelly, A., Maia, R., Lopes, R.J., Santos, R.S., Pereira, M.E., Duarte, A.C. and Furness, R.W. 2008. Variation in the mobilization of mercury into Black-winged Stilt *Himantopus himantopus* chicks in coastal saltpans, as revealed by stable isotopes. *Estuarine Coastal and Shelf Science*, 77: 65–76.

Thompson, D.R. 1996. Mercury in birds and terrestrial mammals. *In*: W.N. Beyer, G.H. Heinz and A.W. Redmon-Morwood (Eds.), *Environmental contaminants in wildlife: Interpreting tissue concentrations*. (pp. 341–356). SETAC Special Publications. Boca Raton, FL, Lewis Publishers.

Thompson, D.R., Bearhop, S., Speakman, J.R., and Furness, R.W. 1998. Feathers as a means of monitoring mercury in seabirds: insights from stable isotope analysis. *Environmental Pollution*, 101: 193–200.

Thompson, D.R., Furness, R.W., and Walsh, P.M. 1992. Historical changes in mercury concentrations in the marine ecosystem of the North and North-East Atlantic Ocean as indicated by seabird feathers. *Journal of Applied Ecology*, 29: 79–84.

Thompson, D.R., Becker, P.H., and Furness, R.W. 1993. Long-term changes in mercury concentrations in herring gulls *Larus argentatus* and common terns *Sterna hirundo* from the German North Sea coast. *Journal of Applied Ecology*, 30: 316–320.

Thompson, D.R., Furness, R.W., and Monteiro, L.R. 1998. Seabirds as biomonitors of mercury inputs to epipelagic and mesopelagic marine food chains. *Science of the Total Environment*, 213: 299–305.

Tomiyasu, T., Eguchi, T., Yamamoto, M., Anazawa, K., Sakamoto, H., Ando, T., Nedachi, M., and Marumo, K. 2007. Influence of submarine fumaroles on the distribution of mercury in the sediment of Kagoshima Bay, Japan. *Marine Chemistry* 107: 173–183.

Tremblay, A., Lucotte, M., and Rowan, D.,1995. Different factors related to mercury concentration in sediments and zooplankton of 73 Canadian lakes. *Water, Air, and Soil Pollution*, 80: 961–970.

Trombini, C., Fabbri, D., Lombardo, M., Vassura, I., Zavoli, E., and Horvat, M., 2003. Mercury and methylmercury contamination in surficial sediments and clams of a coastal lagoon (*Pialassa Baiona*, Ravenna, Italy). *Continental Shelf Research*, 23: 1821–1831.

Tseng, C.M., Amouroux, D., Abril, G., Tessier, E., Etcheber, H., Donard, O.F.X. 2001. Speciation of mercury in a fluid mud profile of a highly turbid macrotidal estuary (Gironde, France). *Environmental Science and Technology*, 35: 2627–2633.

Tsui, M.T.K., and Wang, W.X. 2004. Uptake and elimination routes of inorganic mercury and methylmercury in *Daphnia magna*. *Environmental Science and Technology*, 38: 808–816.

United States Environmental Protection Agency (US EPA), 1997. *Mercury Study Report to Congress*, EPA-452/R-97-003, U.S. Environmental Protection Agency, Washington, DC.

United States Environmental Protection Agency (US EPA), 2007. *National listing of fish advisories technical fact sheet*, EPA-823-F-07-003. U.S. Environmental Protection Agency, Washington, DC.

United Nations Food and Agricultural Organization (UN FAO), 2007. *The State of World Fisheries and Aquaculture 2006*. Food and Agriculture Organization of the United Nations, Rome, 2007.

United States Food and Drug Administration (US FDA). 2006. *Mercury levels in commercial fish and shellfish, February, 2006*. Center for Food Safety and Applied Nutrition, http://www.cfsan.fda.gov/~frf/sea-mehg.html.

Vandal, G.M., Fitzgerald, W.F., Boutron, C.F., and Candelone, J.P., 1993. Variations in mercury deposition to Antarctica over the past 34,000 years. *Nature*, 362: 621–623.

Van Oostdam, J., Donaldson, S.G., Feeley, M. Arnold, D., Ayotte, P., Bondy, G., Chan, L., Dewaily, E., Furgal., C.M., Kuhnlein, H., Loring, E., Muckle, G., Myles, E., Receveur, O., Tracey, B., Gill, U., and Kalhok, S., 2005. Human health implications of environmental contaminants in Arctic Canada: a review. *Science of the Total Environment*, 351–352: 165–246.

Varekamp, J.C., Kreulen, B., ten Brink, M.R.B., and Mecray, E.L. 2003. Mercury contamination chronologies from Connecticut wetlands and Long Island Sound sediments. *Environmental Geology*, 43: 268–282.

Vetriani, C., Chew, Y.S., Miller, S.M., Yagi, J., Coombs, J., Lutz, R.A., and Barkay, T. 2005. Mercury adaptation among bacteria from a deep-sea hydrothermal vent. *Applied and Environmental Microbiology*, 71: 220–226.

Wagemann, R., Trebacz, W., Boila, G., and Lockhart, W.L. 1998. Methylmercury and total mercury in tissues of arctic marine mammals. *Science of the Total Environment*, 218: 352–358.

Wagemann, R., and Kozlowska, H., 2005. Mercury distribution in the skin of beluga (*Delphinapterus leucas*) and narwhal (*Monodon monoceros*) from the Canadian Arctic and mercury burdens and excretion by moulting. *Science of the Total Environment*, 351–352: 333–343.

Wagner-Dobler, I., 2003. Pilot plant for bioremediation of mercury-containing industrial wastewater. *Applied Microbiology and Biotechnology*, 62: 124–133.

Wang, W.X., and Wong, R.S.K. 2003. Bioaccumulation kinetics and exposure pathways of inorganic mercury and methylmercury in a marine fish, the sweetlips *Plectorhinchus gibbosus*. *Marine Ecology Progress Series*, 261: 257–268.

Watras, C.J., and Bloom, N.S.,1992. Mercury and methylmercury in individual zooplankton: Implications for bioaccumulation. *Limnology and Oceanography*, 37: 1313–1318.

Watras, C.J., Back, R.C., Halvorsen, S., Hudson, R.J.M., Morrison, K.A., and Wente, S.P. 1998. Bioaccumulation of mercury in pelagic freshwater food webs. *Science of the Total Environment*, 219: 183–208.

Whalin, L., Kim, E.H., and Mason, R.P. 2007. Factors influencing the oxidation, reduction, methylation and demethylation of mercury species in coastal waters. *Marine Chemistry*, 107: 278–294.

Windham, L., Weis, J.S. and Weis, P. 2004. Metal dynamics of plant litter of Spartina alterniflora and Phragmites australis in metal-contaminated salt marshes. Part 1: Patterns of decomposition and metal uptake. *Environmental Toxicology and Chemistry*, 23(6): 1520–1528.

Windham-Myers, L., Marvin-DiPasquale, M., Krabbenhoft, D.P., Agee, J.L., Cox, M.H., Heredia-Middleton, P., Coates, C., and Kakouros, E. 2009. Experimental removal of wetland emergent vegetation leads to decreased methylmercury production in surface sediment. *Journal of Geophysical Research*, 114, G00C05, doi:10.1029/2008JG000815.

Wolf, K.H., and Chilingarian, G.V. (Eds.). 1992. *Diagenesis, III*. Developments in Sedimentology 47. Elsevier, Amsterdam.

Wu, H., Green, M., and Scranton, M.I.,1997. Acetate cycling in the water column and surface sediment of Long Island Sound following a bloom. *Limnology and Oceanography*, 42: 705–713.

Yamashita, Y., Omura, Y., and Okazaki, E. 2005. Total mercury and methylmercury levels in commercially important fishes in Japan. *Fisheries Science*, 71: 1029–1035.

Žagar, D., Petkovsek, G., Rajar, R., Sirnik, N., Horvat, M., Voudouri, A., Kallos, G., and etina, M. 2007. Modelling of mercury transport and transformations in the water compartment of the Mediterranean Sea. *Marine Chemistry*, 107: 64–88.

Zauke, G.P., Savinov, V.M., Ritterhoff, J., and Savinova, T. 1999. Heavy metals in fish from the Barents Sea (summer 1994). *Science of the Total Environment*, 227: 161–173.

Zawislanski, P.T., Chau, S., Mountford, H., Wong, H.C. and Sears, T.C. 2001. Accumulation of selenium and trace metals on plant litter in a tidal marsh. *Estuarine Coastal and Shelf Science*, 52(5): 589–603.

Zedler, J.B. 1980. Algal mat productivity: Comparisons in a salt marsh. *Estuaries*, 3: 122–131.

Zhang, X., Naidu, A.S., Kelley, J.J., Jewett, S.C., Dasher, D., and Duffy, L.R. 2001. Baseline concentrations of total mercury and methylmercury in salmon returning via the Bering Sea. *Marine Pollution Bulletin*, 42: 993–997.

PART FOUR

TOXICOLOGY, RISK ANALYSIS, HUMANS, AND POLICY

CHAPTER 11

Ecotoxicology of Mercury in Fish and Wildlife

Recent Advances

ANTON M. SCHEUHAMMER, NILADRI BASU, DAVID C. EVERS,

GARY H. HEINZ, MARK B. SANDHEINRICH, and MICHAEL S. BANK

EFFECTS OF METHYLMERCURY IN FISH

MERCURY IN AMPHIBIANS AND REPTILES

Amphibians
Reptiles

EFFECTS OF METHYLMERCURY IN WILD BIRDS AND MAMMALS

Effects on Neurochemistry
Reproductive Effects in Birds (Egg-Injection Studies)
Reproductive Effects in Birds (Field-Based Studies)
Mercury–Selenium Relationships

CONCLUSIONS

The toxic effects of mercury (Hg) in fish and wildlife have been extensively reviewed (e.g., Scheuhammer, 1987; Heinz, 1996; Thompson, 1996; Wiener and Spry, 1996; Wiener et al., 2003; Scheuhammer et al., 2007). However, some research on the subtle effects of methylmercury (MeHg) on brain chemistry, hormones, and reproductive success and the implications for population-level effects in certain at-risk species, such as the common loon (*Gavia immer*) have not been reviewed previously. A number of the newer studies demonstrate that current levels of environmental MeHg exposure are sufficient to cause significant biological impairment, both in individuals and in whole populations, in some ecosystems. In addition, there has historically been a lack of published research or critical review on the accumulation and toxicity of Hg in amphibians and reptiles. Here, we review recent findings on the ecotoxicology of Hg (primarily MeHg) in fish and wildlife (herptiles, birds, and mammals).

Effects of Methylmercury in Fish

Early toxicologic studies of MeHg exposure in fish examined survival and growth of different saltwater and freshwater species with relatively high tissue concentrations of MeHg (skeletal muscle typically greater than 5 µg g^{-1} wet weight) derived from point-source industrial pollution (see reviews by Wiener and Spry, 1996; Wiener et al., 2003). Although point sources of environmental Hg contamination are still of concern in some locations, increasing emphasis is being placed on Hg-sensitive habitats, such as low-alkalinity lakes and flooded impoundments, where a major proportion of the annual Hg load derives from atmospheric deposition, and where physical and chemical conditions facilitate methylation and incorporation of MeHg into the food chain. In these systems, the long-term effects of lower, but substantive, concentrations of MeHg are of greatest interest. A survey of Hg (primarily MeHg) concentrations in freshwater fish of northeast North America reported that mean Hg concentrations in fillets of standard-length fish of 13 species ranged from 0.19 µg g^{-1} (white sucker, *Catostomus commersoni*) to 0.98 µg g^{-1} wet weight (muskellunge, *Esox masquinongy*; Kamman et al., 2005). Mercury concentrations of about 0.06–2.5 µg g^{-1} dry weight (0.02–0.63 µg g^{-1} wet weight) in zooplankton, benthic invertebrates, and small fish that serve as prey for fish in low-alkalinity lakes and newly flood reservoirs are not atypical (Hammerschmidt et al., 2002).

Laboratory and field studies provide convincing evidence that environmentally relevant concentrations of MeHg in fish tissues, and in their diets, cause oxidative stress through the formation of reactive oxygen species (ROS). Both enzymatic and nonenzymatic antioxidants, such as superoxide dismutase (SOD), glutathione, and compounds associated with glutathione metabolism, are important in regulating free radicals in cells (Hayes and McLellan, 1999; Valavanidis et al., 2006). Unregulated ROS may cause tissue damage, including lipid peroxidation, resulting in biochemical and structural changes in various tissues of diverse species of aquatic organisms (Livingstone, 2001). These biochemical changes may serve as biomarkers of oxidative stress

(Valavanidis et al., 2006), including that caused by MeHg. For example, Berntssen et al. (2003) fed diets containing 0.03 (control), 4.35 (medium), or 8.48 (high) µg MeHg g^{-1} dry weight to juvenile Atlantic salmon (*Salmo salar*) for 4 months. Dietary MeHg had no effect on growth, body condition, or mortality of the salmon parr. However, induction of redox defense enzymes and lipid peroxidation of tissues due to MeHg exposure was apparent. The activity of SOD increased twofold in the brains of fish fed the medium-MeHg diet. In the brains of fish fed the high-MeHg diet, levels of SOD and glutathione peroxidase (GSH-Px) decreased significantly, which suggested failure of the redox defense system, and there was a sevenfold increase in the concentration of thiobarbituric acid reactive substances, a product of lipid peroxidation. The high-MeHg diet also significantly inhibited cerebral monoamine oxidase in the brain, an observation that was associated with reduced behavioral activity by the fish. Brains of fish exposed to the medium- and high-MeHg diet had Hg concentrations of 1.16 and 0.68 µg g^{-1} wet weight, respectively, and exhibited severe vacuolization and cell necrosis. Increased activity of SOD and GSH-Px was also measured in livers of fish receiving the high-MeHg diet. The apparent decline in brain Hg accumulation at the high (10 µg g^{-1}) compared with the medium (5 µg g^{-1}) MeHg diet was related to gross brain edema in the highest-dose group, which decreased apparent tissue Hg concentration on a wet weight basis. (Berntssen et al., 2003).

Altered histology in liver and other internal organs of fish may occur as a result of oxidative stress due to MeHg exposure. Mela et al. (2007) fed adult *Hoplias malabaricus*, a neotropical species, control or MeHg-contaminated diets at a dosage equivalent to 0.075 µg MeHg g^{-1} wet body weight for 70 days; subsequent Hg concentrations in the muscle of the fish were 0.67 (control diet) and 1.45 µg g^{-1} wet weight (treatment diet). An increased number of melano-macrophage centers were among the numerous cellular changes observed in liver and head kidney of exposed fish. These groups or aggregations of macrophages contain yellow or black pigments and collect components of damaged cells, including those damaged by oxidation and lipid peroxidation (Wolke, 1992). Moreover, there were increased numbers of dead and abnormal cells and necrotic tissues in fish receiving the MeHg-contaminated diet.

Changes in biochemistry and tissue histology associated with oxidative stress occur in wild populations of fish subject to non–point source contamination by Hg. Larose et al. (2008) reported altered glutathione metabolism among yellow perch (*Perca flavescens*) and walleye (*Sander vitreus*) from four boreal lakes in Canada. The activity of selenium-dependent glutathione peroxidase and glutathione S-transferase (GST) were negatively related to MeHg in the liver of yellow perch from the lake with the highest mean Hg concentration in the fish. In the lake with the highest mean concentration of MeHg in the walleye, activity of GST and glutathione reductase were related to liver size,

which, in turn, was negatively related to the concentration of MeHg in the liver. A decrease in the size of the liver may have been due, in part, to MeHg causing oxidative stress and lipid peroxidation (Larose et al., 2008).

Drevnick et al. (2008) reported that liver damage due to lipid peroxidation and poor body condition were correlated to Hg concentration in northern pike (*Esox lucius*) from eight inland lakes of Isle Royale, a relatively pristine and remote U.S. National Park in Lake Superior. Liver color (absorbance of liver homogenate at 400 nm) and total Hg (range 0.048–3.074 µg g^{-1} wet weight) were positively correlated; concentration of total Hg in the liver was positively related to that in the axial fillet (range, 0.069–0.622 µg g^{-1} wet weight). Lipofuscin was subsequently identified as the pigment responsible for altered liver color. An analysis of covariance revealed that lipofuscin accumulation was primarily associated with Hg exposure, and this association was independent of any normal accumulation of lipofuscin due to aging (Drevnick et al., 2008). Lipofuscin is formed as a result of lipid peroxidation of membranous organelles and is a pigment frequently found in melano-macrophage centers (Wolke, 1992). Raldúa et al. (2007) found higher concentrations of Hg and a greater prevalence of melano-macrophage centers and lipofuscin in livers of fish downstream from a chlor-alkali plant than in fish collected upstream from the plant. Schwindt et al. (2008) examined the relationship between melano-macrophage centers and Hg concentrations in salmonids (lake trout, *Salvelinus namaycush*; brook trout, *S. fontinalis*; cutthroat trout, *Oncorhynchus clarkii*; and rainbow trout, *O. mykiss*) obtained from 14 lakes in eight U.S. national parks or preserves. Independent of fish age, the number of melano-macrophage centers in the kidney and spleen were positively related to whole-body concentrations of MeHg. Although more than 90 pesticides and other chemical compounds were measured in brook trout, Hg alone explained more than one third of the variability in macrophage aggregates in the spleen.

Alterations in gene transcription can be used to detect the induction of antioxidant defenses and other effects following MeHg exposure, to provide additional insight into MeHg's mode of toxicity. Moran et al. (2007) compared levels of gene expression in livers of cutthroat trout from high-altitude lakes of western Washington state that had low (Skymo Lake) and high (Wilcox Lake) levels of Hg contamination. Of the 147 genes evaluated in the fish, the expression of 45 was significantly different between the two lakes, including those associated with cell maintenance, immune function, stress response, metabolism and growth, reproduction, and response to xenobiotics. For example, expression of glutathione peroxidase in high-Hg trout from Wilcox Lake was more than 1300% that in low-Hg trout from Skymo Lake. Although low concentrations of organic contaminants (e.g., dichlorodiphenyldichloroethylene [DDE] and polychlorinated biphenyls [PCBs]) were also present in the trout, differences in transcriptional responses of fish were attributed to differences in

Hg contamination between the two lakes. Gonzalez et al. (2005) found that expression of genes associated with oxidative stress (including SOD), mitochondrial metabolism, and apoptosis was up-regulated in the skeletal muscle and liver of adult male zebrafish (*Danio rerio*) 21 to 63 days after dietary exposure to 5 μg MeHg g^{-1} dry weight. Genes associated with DNA repair were down-regulated in the skeletal muscle. However, there was no change in gene expression in the brains of the exposed fish, including those genes associated with antioxidant defense, suggesting that a lack of transcriptional response to MeHg in the brain may contribute to its neurotoxic effects.

Oxidative stress due to MeHg may also affect gonadal tissue and subsequently inhibit the production of sex hormones and reproductive success of fish. Manipulative laboratory experiments and mensurative field studies have documented effects of MeHg on gonadal development and histology, sex hormone production, and reproduction in fish. Friedmann et al. (1996) fed juvenile walleye for 6 months with diets naturally contaminated with 0.04 (control), 0.137 (low-Hg diet) or 0.987 (high-Hg diet) μg MeHg g^{-1} wet weight. Mercury concentrations in the carcass of the walleye (whole body minus viscera) were 0.06 (control), 0.254 (low-Hg diet), and 2.37 (high-Hg diet) μg g^{-1} wet weight. Gonadal development of the male walleye was suppressed and multifocal cell atrophy and hypertrophy of cells adjacent to atrophied cells was evident in the gonads.

Hammerschmidt et al. (2002) reported that dietary MeHg reduced gonad size, delayed spawning, and reduced reproductive effort of female fathead minnows (*Pimephales promelas*). Relative to control fish, there was a 39% reduction in spawning success of fish fed diets with 0.88 μg Hg g^{-1} dry weight. Mean carcass concentrations of the male and female fish fed this diet were 0.71 and 0.86 μg Hg g^{-1} wet weight. In a similar study with fathead minnows, Drevnick and Sandheinrich (2003) found that dietary MeHg suppressed plasma testosterone and estradiol as well as reduced reproduction. Male fathead minnows fed control diets had plasma testosterone concentrations 20% and 106% greater than those fed diets with 0.87 (low) and 3.93 μg (medium) Hg g^{-1} dry weight. Control female fish had estradiol concentrations about 150% and 400% greater than those fed low- and medium-MeHg diets, respectively. Klaper et al. (2006) reported suppression of genes related to endocrine function—up-regulation in vitellogenin mRNA in individual Hg-exposed males and a significant decline in vitellogenin gene expression in female fish with increasing Hg concentrations—as well as changes in expression of other genes, including those associated with egg fertilization and development, sugar metabolism, apoptosis, and electron transport. Altered reproductive behavior of male fathead minnows caused by suppressed levels of testosterone (Sandheinrich and Miller, 2006) also occurred as a result of MeHg exposure. The synthesis of sex steroid hormones in fish occurs in the Leydig cells of testes and follicular cells of the ovaries (Fostier et al., 1983). Drevnick et al. (2006) found that dietary MeHg significantly increased the number of apoptotic cells in ovarian follicles of female fathead minnows. The size of the ovaries and levels of plasma estradiol were inversely related to the number of apoptotic follicular cells. Oxidative stress from MeHg exposure was proposed as the cause of follicular-cell apoptosis and subsequent suppression of estradiol and reproductive success in these fish. Crump and Trudeau (2009) thoroughly reviewed Hg-induced reproductive impairment in fish.

Suppressed concentrations of sex hormones have also been found in wild fish with elevated concentrations of Hg. There was a significant negative correlation between concentrations of Hg in the muscle of male white sturgeon (*Acipenser transmontanus*) in the lower Columbia River and concentrations of plasma testosterone and 11-ketotestosterone (Webb et al., 2006). An inverse relationship between the relative size of the testes and concentrations of Hg suggested that MeHg may have been responsible for suppression of sex-steroid production in immature male fish. Similarly, there was a negative correlation between concentrations of Hg in the liver of female fish and plasma estradiol. There was also a significant negative correlation between concentrations of Hg in the gonad and liver and the condition factor and relative weight of the fish. Conversely, a positive correlation between Hg in the axial fillet and plasma 11-ketotestosterone in male largemouth bass (*Micropterus salmoides*) from three lakes in New Jersey was reported by Friedmann et al. (2002). However, there was no significant relationship between Hg in the muscle of the largemouth bass and plasma testosterone concentration. Tan et al. (2009) have reviewed the endocrine effects of Hg in humans, fish, and wildlife.

In summary, environmentally relevant concentrations of MeHg resulting from non–point source pollution are sufficient to cause oxidative stress in fish. Evidence of oxidative stress is manifested at the molecular, biochemical, cellular, and organismal levels of biologic organization. Future studies should seek to determine specific links between biomarkers of MeHg exposure and oxidative stress to effects on reproduction and population change in wild fish populations and more clearly define the deleterious effects of low-level Hg exposure.

Mercury in Amphibians and Reptiles

Despite their overall biomass and importance to aquatic and terrestrial ecosystems, Hg and MeHg bioaccumulation dynamics and toxicity in amphibians and reptiles are not well studied, especially as compared with other vertebrate taxa such as birds, mammals, and fish. However, various studies have reported Hg concentrations in tissues of a number of amphibian and reptiles species. Population declines in amphibians are well documented and are likely caused by multiple stressors, including climate change, exotic species introductions, fungal pathogens, habitat loss and degradation, and exposure to toxic pollutants, including Hg. Reptile declines have also been reported (Gibbons et al., 2000).

Amphibians

A variety of terrestrial habitat types, including uplands, wetlands, riparian areas, and headwater streams and other surface waters are important to the breeding ecology and overall life history of herpetofauna. These habitats receive atmospheric Hg inputs, and some (especially wetlands) may be important for net MeHg production within watersheds. Mercury from atmospheric deposition can accumulate in amphibians and reptiles species inhabiting wetlands and their associated riparian and upland habitats, and likely poses a serious threat to the overall population performance of species with life history characteristics that make them sensitive to Hg bioaccumulation (Birge et al., 1979; Cooke, 1981; Hall and Mulhern, 1984; Bank et al., 2005, 2007).

Stream salamanders are often long-lived as compared with invertebrates and freshwater fishes (Moyle, 1976). These organisms are often suitable eco-indicators of environmental Hg and MeHg in lotic ecosystems (Bank et al., 2005). Their high trophic position in headwater streams, complex life histories, and sensitivity to perturbations make them reliable indicators of stream and watershed condition (Welsh and Ollivier, 1998; Rocco and Brooks, 2000; Jung et al., 2000; Southerland et al., 2004; Bank et al., 2005).

Bank et al. (2005) reported elevated levels of total Hg in two-lined salamander (*Eurycea bislineata*) larvae (73–97% MeHg) from streams in Acadia National Park, Maine. These larvae may serve as an indicator of stream and watershed Hg and MeHg contaminant levels, since larvae are strictly aquatic, fairly easy to sample (in comparison to fish), have low vagility, and have a diet that is comprised of a wide variety of invertebrate taxa (Petranka, 1984, 1998; Bank et al., 2005). In terrestrial habitats, red-backed salamanders (*Plethodon cinereus*), or similar species, may reflect local atmospheric Hg deposition. In addition, tail clip levels and regression algorithms may be used as a nonlethal method to estimate internal tissue mercury exposure (Bergeron et al., 2010a, 2010b). Unfortunately, no ecotoxicologic studies to explicitly investigate the possible impacts of Hg or MeHg have yet been conducted on these widespread species.

Mercury bio-accumulation in bullfrogs (*Rana catesbeiana*) and other common *Ranidae* species (Chang et al., 1974) has been investigated across a variety of wetland types in different geographical regions and in the laboratory (Yorio and Bentley, 1973; Terhivuo et al., 1984; Mudgall and Patil, 1988; Burger and Snodgrass, 1998; Gerstenberger and Pearson, 2002; Loumbourdis and Danscher, 2004; Bank et al., 2007; Hothem et al., 2008, 2010). The wide distribution of *Ranidae,* ease of field identification, and apparent changes in response to local contaminant levels make species of this group useful as bioindicators of Hg pollution in a variety of wetland ecosystem types. Although the link

between the occurrence of amphibian disease in tadpoles and Hg exposure has been reported (Bank et al., 2007), the primary mechanisms of this relationship remain unknown.

Byrne et al. (1975) documented Hg levels in a variety of amphibian species inhabiting sites with varying levels of Hg contamination in Yugoslavia; they reported that *Rana temporia* from contaminated sites had higher levels of Hg. Power et al. (1989) and Sparling et al. (2010) provide extensive reviews of the amphibian toxicologic literature, and although numerous studies exist on short-term toxicity, little is known about Hg exposure and its effects on amphibians. Kanamadi and Saidapur (1992) reported that sublethal mercuric chloride exposure inhibited spermatogenesis in *Rana cyanophlyctis* and studies by Punzo (1993a, 1993b) suggest that Hg, especially from local sources, can negatively affect the reproductive physiology of amphibians, including impairment of fertilization, ova maturation, and postembryonic development, and disruption of neuroendocrine regulation. Other amphibian species have also been studied. Chang et al. (1976) evaluated dose–response effects of MeHg on limb regeneration in *Triturus viridescens* and reported delayed limb regeneration at 8 μg/L MeHg in water, and death of this species was observed at ≥300 μg/L. Dial (1976) used *Rana pipiens* embryos at varying stages of development to study the effects of methylmercuric chloride (0.5–200 μg/L). Concentrations ≥40 μg/L were lethal to embryos treated at the cleavage stage of development. Embryos in other stages (blastula, gastrula, and neural-plate) were exposed for 5 days to concentrations of 5–30 μg/L. At 5 μg/L, tadpoles showed negligible effects; however 10, 15, or 20 μg/L caused various negative effects, including exogastrulae, and poor tail development and poor overall development. Tadpole deaths increased with exposure time and concentration. At 30 μg/L, tadpole defects were commonly observed within 24 hours and all tadpoles died within 3 days (Dial, 1976). Traditional toxicologic profile data for Hg, and other metals in amphibians and reptiles is reported in Sparling et al. (2010); however, data on several amphibian and reptile species is either limited or nonexistent.

Bergeron et al. (2010a, 2010b) described relationships between Hg, MeHg, and selenium (Se) in three amphibian species (*Plethodon cinereus, Eurycea bislineata,* and *Bufo americanus*) along a contamination gradient in Virginia. Mercury concentrations in amphibians varied and were generally associated with food habits and habitat selection. *Eurycea bislineata* had the highest Hg levels, and adults (3.45 ± 0.196 μg g^{-1} dry mass) had higher concentrations than larvae (2.48 ± 0.171 μg g^{-1} dry mass). *Bufo americanus* tadpoles had higher concentrations (2.13 ± 0.60 μg g^{-1} dry mass) than the more terrestrial adults (0.598 ± 0.117 μg g^{-1} μg g^{-1} dry mass) and *Plethodon cinereus* (0.583 ± 0.178 μg g^{-1} dry mass) had the lowest concentrations. Bergeron et al. (2010a) also reported a strong correlation between carcass levels of Hg and blood Hg in *Bufo americanus*) and tail tissue Hg for

Euryeca bislineata, suggesting that blood and tail tissue, respectively, for these species are useful sublethal indicators for estimating Hg exposure in amphibians. Bergeron et al. (2010b) also reported that female *Bufo americanus* transfer Hg and Se to their eggs, and they discussed the implications for amphibian population performance. Hopkins et al. (2006) also reported maternal transfer of Se and Hg in eastern narrowmouth toads (*Gastrophryne carolinensis*).

Investigations of Hg speciation, population decline, and Hg ecosystem setting (Bank et al., 2006, 2007), Hg spatial distribution (Ugarte et al., 2005) and dietary studies (Unrine and Jagoe, 2004, Unrine et al., 2004, 2005) in a variety of *Ranidae* species have collectively suggested that habitats contaminated by atmospheric Hg deposition have the potential to cause negative effects on amphibian larvae. These investigations also suggest that the observed highly variable Hg bio-accumulation rates across relatively small spatial scales may be a function of water chemistry attributes and trophic gradients, as well as the level of Hg contamination. Therefore, Hg pollution, in conjunction with other stressors, likely has important effects on the structure and function of the terrestrial, riparian, and aquatic ecosystems where many amphibians reside.

In general, determinants of Hg bioaccumulation, exposure and potential ecotoxicologic risk include species body mass, Hg source, habitat use, trophic position, and ecosystem methylation potential. Future investigations should evaluate whether Hg, MeHg, other contaminants, or other abiotic conditions (i.e., drought or warm water temperatures) potentially increase the susceptibility of amphibian populations to disease, such as chytrid fungus (*Batrachochytrium dendrobatidis*), which is common throughout much of the world and has caused dramatic population declines and extinctions of amphibian species. We also recommend that ecotoxicologic studies use realistic MeHg exposure regimens that reflect natural surface water and overall ecosystem conditions, and examine the long-term and sublethal effects of this contaminant with the synergistic or cumulative effects of stress from the presence of predators and/or predator cues (Relyea and Mills, 2001). Moreover, relating amphibian development and population performance to MeHg genotoxicity (de Flora et al., 1994), immunotoxicity, and endocrine disruption deserves further study.

Amphibian population declines on a worldwide basis are suggestive of serious environmental degradation. Monitoring population trends with regard to the degree and extent of contamination by Hg may aid in evaluating amphibian responses to co-occurring anthropogenic stressors (Semlitsch, 2003. Sparling et al., 2010). However, monitoring will only track the degree of the contamination problem. Direct reduction of Hg accumulation in the environment is likely dependent on improvements in air and water quality, which are accelerated by sound environmental policies

to reduce point source and non–point source Hg (and other) emissions (Bank et al., 2005).

Reptiles

Turtle and terrapin species inhabiting brackish waters have been successfully used for MeHg research and biomonitoring using nonlethal sampling techniques (Helwig and Hora, 1983; Golet and Haines, 2001; Bergeron et al., 2007; Blanvillain et al., 2007). The long-term exposure of these species to the ambient aquatic environment make them ideal candidates for studies involving contaminated, remediated, and reference sites. Blood samples from reptiles and other organisms are presumed to reflect recent dietary Hg exposure and can also be used to estimate trophic position and energy flow via stable isotope analyses. The relationship between blood Hg levels and other tissues has also been studied in other turtle species, alligators, and snakes. Blood mercury measurements for some turtles from contaminated reaches of the South River, reported by Bergeron et al. (2007), were considered elevated (≤ 3.6 μg g^{-1}), illustrating the need to evaluate the potential adverse effects of MeHg on turtles and reptiles in general. Research on Hg bio-accumulation in red-headed river turtles (*Podocnemis erythrocephala*), a species commonly consumed by humans in the Rio Negro region of the Amazon basin of Brazil, showed that average Hg levels were 0.00164 μg g^{-1} in blood, 0.033 μg g^{-1} wet weight in the muscles, 0.470 μg g^{-1} wet weight in the liver, and 0.068 μg g^{-1} fresh weight in the carapace (Sneider et al., 2009). In addition, Hg in each of the tissue types was not related to any of the measured water chemistry parameters (Schneider et al., 2009). Further work by Schneider et al. (2010) in the Rio Negro region reported that total Hg in muscle tissue varied among six turtle species in the Amazon basin of Brazil. Total Hg was greatest in *Chelus fimbriatus*, a piscivorous species, and averaged 0.432 μg g^{-1} wet weight, suggesting a substantial risk to humans who consume these organisms. Although interspecific differences in Hg levels were reported, no differences in sex or size (i.e., body mass or carapace length) were found (Schneider et al., 2010).

Research on alligators (Yanochko et al., 1997; Jagoe et al., 1998; Kahn and Tansel, 2000; Rumbold et al., 2002; Xu et al., 2006), crocodiles (Rainwater et al., 2002, 2007), and snakes (Burger et al., 2005) has also been undertaken. Xu et al. (2006) investigated body partitioning of total Hg (and other heavy metals) in endangered Chinese alligators (*Alligator sinensis*) and reported that liver (mean, 0.559 μg g^{-1} dry weight) and kidney (mean, 0.905 μg g^{-1} dry weight) had the highest concentrations. Yanochko et al. (1997) conducted a broad-scale survey of Hg bio-accumulation in American alligators (*Alligator mississippiensis*), including habitats in Savannah River Site (South Carolina) and the Florida Everglades. Their study determined that alligators can bio-accumulate significant amounts of Hg and that location, age-specific feeding habits, and size of individuals were important factors contributing to the observed variability in Hg levels. Moreover, Kahn and Tansel (2000) reported that in the Florida Everglades, where atmospheric deposition of inorganic Hg is believed to be a major source of Hg contamination, Hg bioconcentration factors (relative to Hg in the water column) for adult American alligators were extremely high (39.9×10^7 for liver, and 32.9×10^7 for kidney), whereas in juveniles they were lower (liver, 10.55×10^7; kidney, 9.34×10^7). Although Hg bioaccumulation studies in American alligators have been published, the long-term toxicity of Hg in this species (e.g., possible reproductive impairment) is unknown.

Although the use of snakes as bioindicators of environmental contaminants, such as pesticides, was proposed over 30 years ago (Bauerle, 1975; Stafford, 1976; Burger, 1992), very little is known about Hg bio-accumulation and short-term or low-level long-term MeHg toxicity in snakes (Heinz et al., 1980.) Burger et al. (2005) measured Hg in a variety of water snake eggs, testes, kidney, liver, muscle, and skin and blood samples. This study also evaluated the use of skin and blood as nonlethal indicators of Hg contamination and reported that this species was a reliable indicator because they are widely distributed top-level predators and because skin was shown to be predictive of internal exposure in this species.

In conclusion, amphibian and reptile Hg ecotoxicology has focused primarily on exposure studies, whereas, in general, studies of mechanistic effects are still lacking. In addition, the effects of Hg exposure in the context of multiple stressors, such as exposure to metal mixtures, the presence or absence of predators, varying food web structure, and spatiotemporal habitat complexities related to ecosystem sensitivity to Hg methylation are in need of further study. Future Hg ecotoxiciology research should focus on the mechanistic effects of MeHg at molecular, individual, and population scales and should use ecologically realistic concentrations and routes of exposure to reflect actual environmental conditions.

Effects of Methylmercury in Wild Birds and Mammals

The toxic effects of MeHg ingestion in wild birds and mammals have been studied for many years, and much research has been published relative to most other taxa, such as fish, amphibians, and invertebrates. Major advances in MeHg toxicology in birds and mammals have focused on early neurochemical changes, *in ovo* toxicity (birds), and effects on reproductive success in wild populations. In addition, new information on the important interactions between Hg and Se in various tissues has been published.

Effects on Neurochemistry

The central nervous system (CNS) has long been known as a major target organ for MeHg toxicity, and numerous studies have demonstrated overt neurotoxicity in fish-eating

wildlife following MeHg exposure. In an early account, cats, birds, and fish exhibited a range of neurologic symptoms in the vicinity of MeHg-contaminated Minamata Bay, Japan, in the 1950s (Harada, 1995; Eto 1997). From the 1960s through the 1980s, several reports of MeHg-associated neurobehavioral toxicity were reported in various species of wildlife, including mink (*Mustela vison*), river otter (*Lontra canadensis*), and predatory and seed-eating birds, across Europe and North America (Borg et al., 1967; Wobeser and Swift, 1976; Fimreite, 1979; Wren, 1985). Most of these cases of MeHg intoxication resulted from short-term exposures to high dietary levels of MeHg derived from point sources of contamination. Although legacy Hg contamination around some industrial sites remains problematic, many of the once-common sources of environmental Hg contamination (e.g., releases to the environment from the chlor-alkali industry; and organomercurials used as antifungal seed dressings) have been eliminated or greatly restricted. Currently, fish and wildlife are much less often exposed to MeHg under short-term exposure scenarios that were more common in the past, but are instead exposed to lower levels of dietary MeHg on a more continual basis over the long term. Nevertheless, tissue Hg concentrations in several wildlife species continue to be within an order of magnitude of levels associated with overt toxicity (USEPA, 1997; Basu et al., 2007a). New analytical tools and biomarker strategies are being developed to characterize the subclinical and early health effects associated with such environmentally relevant exposures.

Prior to the onset of toxicant-induced structural and functional damage to the nervous system, significant changes in brain neurochemistry occur (Manzo et al., 1996). "Brain neurochemistry" refers to neurotransmitters, receptors, enzymes, and transporters that mediate neuronal signaling throughout the nervous system. In experimental studies using laboratory rodents, MeHg was shown to affect several neurochemical receptors, enzymes, and transporters (e.g., Brookes and Kristt, 1989, Castoldi et al., 1996). Monitoring specific changes in brain chemistry (neurochemical biomarkers) thus represents a novel method to identify early CNS effects associated with MeHg exposure.

Measurement of neurochemical biomarkers has proven successful in recent years for characterizing early CNS effects of MeHg on several fish-eating wildlife species. In one of the earliest studies, brain tissues were obtained from wild mink trapped across Canada (Yukon Territory, Ontario, and Nova Scotia), and a significant positive correlation was found between levels of brain MeHg and the density of muscarinic cholinergic receptors (Basu et al., 2005a). In a subsequent study on these same wild mink, a significant negative correlation was found between brain MeHg and levels of N-methyl-D-aspartate (NMDA) receptor densities (Basu et al., 2007b). Studies of fish-eating birds (common loons and bald eagles) reported similar associations—positive correlations between brain MeHg and density of muscarinic cholinergic receptors and negative correlations between brain MeHg and density of NMDA receptors (Scheuhammer et al., 2008). A study of lower-brain stem-tissue from 87 Greenlandic polar bears found surprisingly low brain Hg concentrations in this top Arctic predator; nevertheless, a significant negative association between brain total Hg and NMDA receptor concentration was observed (Basu et al., 2009). Currently, studies are underway to examine similar neurochemical end points in a variety of other fish and wildlife species, including sharks, dolphins, and seals. The demonstrated associations between Hg and neurochemical changes are of physiologic importance because muscarinic cholinergic and NMDA receptors play important roles in normal memory, learning, and locomotion (Ozawa et al., 1998; Wess, 2004), all of which are essential to normal neurobehavioral development, survival, and reproduction. Taken together, these findings indicate that ecologically relevant levels of MeHg may be exerting subtle neurologic damage in a diverse group of fish-eating wildlife species, the long-term consequences of which are not yet understood.

Some of the correlations between brain Hg concentrations and neurochemical changes reported in wild animals have been verified using controlled feeding studies in which juvenile male mink were fed diets containing 0, 0.1, 0.5, 1, and 2 μg g^{-1} MeHg for 89 days (Basu et al., 2006a, 2007b, 2008). Overt histologic lesions were found only in the brains of mink exposed to the highest dietary MeHg concentrations (1 and 2 μg g^{-1} MeHg) (Lyn Ferns DVM, Nova Scotia Department of Agriculture, Veterinary Services Section, personal communication); and similar dietary levels of MeHg caused brain lesions and neurobehavioral toxicity in captive mink in other studies (Wobeser et al., 1976; Wren et al., 1987). At lower, more ecologically relevant exposure levels (0.1–0.5 μg g^{-1} dietary MeHg), histologic changes were not seen, but significant changes in neurochemistry were observed. At dietary MeHg concentrations as low as 0.1 μg g^{-1}—a level commonly found or exceeded in many North American fish species (Kamman et al., 2005)—Hg-dependent increases in muscarinic cholinergic receptor levels (total receptors and specific receptor subtypes) and cholinesterase activity (Basu et al., 2006a, 2008), and striking decreases in NMDA receptor levels (Basu et al., 2007b) were observed in several brain regions. The cellular mechanisms underlying these neurochemical changes are discussed in the references provided. Relationships between tissue Hg accumulation and neurochemical changes observed in captive mink not only validate the results of field studies, but also help establish a continuum of MeHg neurotoxicity whereby uptake of MeHg is followed first by neurochemical changes, and then neurobehavioral toxicity, neurologic impairment, reproductive dysfunction, and ultimately death at higher levels of exposure (Basu et al., 2007a). The monitoring of neurochemical changes is an emerging tool for assessing the early subclinical effects of MeHg exposure in wildlife.

Reproductive Effects in Birds (Egg-Injection Studies)

Among wildlife, some bird species seem to be particularly sensitive to MeHg, and the developing embryo is especially sensitive to Hg exposure in birds (Scheuhammer, 1987; Thompson, 1996; Wiener et al., 2003). Consequently, much research has been devoted to determining how much MeHg in the diet of breeding birds, or in their eggs, represents a threshold for reproductive harm. Field studies have implicated MeHg as a cause of reproductive impairment in common loons (Burgess and Meyer, 2008; Evers et al., 2008), common terns (*Sterna hirundo*) (Fimreite, 1974), California clapper rails (*Rallus longirostris obsoletus*) (Schwarzbach et al., 2006), white ibises (*Eudocimus albus*) (Heath and Fredrick, 2005), and snowy egrets (*Egretta thula*) (Hill et al., 2008). However, results from field studies are always complicated by the complex assemblage of environmental factors that may accompany changing levels of Hg contamination. It is desirable to study the effects of MeHg on bird reproduction within the context of the natural environment in which these effects are occurring, but the complexity of field conditions often makes it difficult to isolate the effects of Hg from those of other stressors. Factors such as disease, food shortage, predation, and weather may cause reduced reproduction or interact in unknown ways with MeHg exposure. In one field study, Hill et al. (2008) reported that MeHg seemed to reduce the reproductive success of snowy egrets, but only during drought years. In another study, the relative contributions of lake acidity and MeHg exposure to reduced reproductive success in common loons were initially unclear (Meyer et al., 1998). Field studies, by their labor-intensive nature, also tend to be very time consuming and expensive.

To overcome the complexities of field studies, and to determine how much MeHg in the diet of breeding birds or in their eggs is needed to impair reproduction, researchers sometimes turn to captive breeding studies. In these controlled studies, a colony of breeding birds is established and randomly selected groups are fed either a control diet or diets containing various concentrations of MeHg. The obvious advantage of these controlled breeding studies is that all variables, except the dietary concentration of MeHg, are equivalent for all groups. Therefore, there should be no confounding effects (disease, food supply, predation, or weather) on the outcome. Such controlled studies have yielded very useful information about dietary and egg levels of Hg that are associated with reproductive impairment in birds (Tejning, 1967; Fimreite, 1971; Finley and Stendell, 1978; Heinz 1979; Albers et al., 2007).

Unfortunately, controlled breeding studies suffer from their own set of weaknesses. Perhaps the most obvious is that, in controlling for all other factors that might affect reproduction, interactions of Hg with other environmental stressors are generally not tested. For example, it is unlikely that the interaction between drought and methylmercury exposure that Hill et al. (2008) reported for snowy egrets would have been uncovered in a controlled breeding study with snowy egrets. Another serious problem is that it is generally very difficult to bring wild birds into captivity and increase the number of breeding pairs to a point at which a statistically valid study can be done. Such studies, like their field study counterparts, tend to be long term, labor intensive, and expensive. Consequently, controlled breeding studies are usually conducted with commercially available game farm species such as mallards and ring-necked pheasants (*Phasianus colchicus*); however, this reliance on game farm birds calls into question how applicable the findings from these species might be to unrelated wild species. For example, can results from an MeHg feeding study on a duck species, such as the mallard, be confidently extrapolated to a fish-eating species like the common loon?

Egg injections represent a third approach to investigating the harmful effects of MeHg on avian reproduction. The biggest advantages of the egg-injection approach are that many wild bird species can be tested that might otherwise never be studied, neither in the field nor in controlled feeding studies, and that the studies are relatively fast and inexpensive. Heinz et al. (2006) developed a procedure by which graded doses of MeHg could be injected into the eggs of birds and embryonic survival measured. Briefly, the egg-injection procedure involves obtaining eggs from wild birds in the field, under appropriate federal and state collecting permits, and from places believed to be free of heavy contamination by Hg. The eggs are incubated in a laboratory incubator and injected when the embryos reach a standardized appearance (when embryonic development appears to be at the same stage as a 3-day-old chicken embryo). During the development of the egg-injection protocol, it was verified that nearly all of the MeHg that was dissolved in the corn-oil vehicle and injected into the air cell of the egg passed through the inner shell membrane and into the albumen of the egg (Heinz et al., 2006). One group of eggs, the controls, always receives pure corn oil without any added MeHg. Because artificially incubated wild bird eggs, including controls, generally show high survival up to within a day or two of hatching but often do not hatch as well as when incubated by the parents, actual hatching success may not be the best end point to measure in egg-injection studies. Therefore, Heinz et al. (2006) used as an end point the number of embryos that survived through 90% of the incubation period.

Heinz et al. (2009) injected the eggs of 26 avian species with MeHg and calculated the median lethal concentration (LC_{50}) for each species. Eggs were injected with doses of MeHg chloride that resulted in 0, 0.05, 0.1, 0.2, 0.4, 0.8, 1.6, 3.2 or 6.4 µg Hg g^{-1} (wet weight) in the egg. The most important finding was that there were large differences in sensitivity of the embryos of different species to MeHg. Some species, such as the American kestrel (*Falco sparverius*), osprey (*Pandion haliaetus*), white ibis, snowy egret, and tricolored heron (*Egretta tricolor*) were very sensitive and had

LC_{50}s that were <0.25 µg Hg g^{-1}, whereas other species such as the mallard, hooded merganser (*Lophodytes cucullatus*), lesser scaup (*Aythya affinis*), Canada goose (*Branta canadensis*), double-crested cormorant (*Phalacrocorax auritus*), and laughing gull (*Larus atricilla*) were comparatively insensitive and had LC_{50}s of 1 µg Hg g^{-1} or higher.

Scientists and risk assessors have often used embryotoxicity thresholds for Hg derived from breeding studies with captive mallards (Heinz, 1979) and ring-necked pheasants (Fimreite, 1971) as default values to predict possible harm in a wide range of wild bird species (Eisler, 2000; Henny et al., 2002; Meyer et al., 1998; Scheuhammer et al., 2001; Thompson, 1996; Wiemeyer et al., 1984; Wolfe et al., 1998). However, there is no reason to believe that the embryos of all bird species are equally sensitive to the harmful effects of MeHg. Based on egg-injection studies, Heinz et al. (2009) concluded that the threshold value for impaired reproduction of 0.8–1.0 µg Hg g^{-1} in eggs, derived from controlled breeding studies with game farm mallards (Heinz, 1979; Heinz and Hoffman, 2003), may not provide adequate protection for many species of wild birds that are more sensitive to Hg than the mallards. When MeHg was injected into the egg, among 26 species tested, only the double-crested cormorant, with an LC_{50} of 2.42, was less sensitive than the mallard (LC_{50}, 1.79).

One shortcoming discovered by Heinz et al. (2009) in their egg-injection studies was that injected MeHg was more toxic than maternally deposited MeHg. In nature, when MeHg is deposited into eggs by the female, it binds to sulfhydryl groups on proteins, which in eggs is mainly albumen (Simpson et al., 1973; Nishimura and Urakawa, 1976). This albumen-bound MeHg probably expresses its toxicity when the albumen is used as a food source by the embryo. In contrast, when MeHg is dissolved in corn oil and injected into eggs, MeHg-contaminated corn oil likely expresses its toxicity when droplets of corn oil come in contact with the embryo (Heinz et al., 2006). As an example of this enhanced toxicity of injected MeHg, a 48% reduction in hatching was observed at a level as low as 1.6 µg Hg g^{-1} when mallard eggs were injected with MeHg (Heinz et al., 2009). However, in feeding studies with mallards, a level of about 5.5 µg g^{-1} maternally deposited Hg was required to bring about a 55% reduction in hatching of eggs as compared with controls (Heinz, 1974); and in another feeding study, 16 µg g^{-1} maternally deposited Hg was needed to cause a 75% reduction in hatching success as compared with controls (Heinz and Hoffman, 1998). Heinz et al. (2009) suggested that it would be inappropriate to calculate a simple, single correction factor to convert the concentration of injected Hg at which a given species begins to experience embryo mortality into the concentration of maternally deposited Hg at which the same degree of harm would occur. Therefore, although the egg-injection procedure provides a good relative ranking among different wild bird species regarding the sensitivity of their embryos to MeHg, it is not clear what absolute levels of MeHg, maternally deposited in wild bird eggs, would be a threshold for harm in each species.

When one examines the strengths and weaknesses of field studies, captive feeding studies, and egg-injection studies it becomes clear that a combination of approaches will continue to be needed to fully assess the risk of environmental Hg to avian reproduction. Ideally, field studies will stimulate the design of companion laboratory studies, and vice versa. This interactive combination of approaches will gradually reveal the true range of sensitivities of many wild birds to the embryotoxic effects of MeHg.

Reproductive Effects in Birds (Field-Based Studies)

The deleterious effects of Hg in aquatic ecosystems due to biomagnification of MeHg are well documented (e.g., Scheuhammer et al., 2007; Wolfe et al., 2007). Studies of environmental Hg impacts on common loons are particularly robust, making the loon one of the more important indicator species for biologic effects of Hg in aquatic ecosystems (Evers, 2006; Scheuhammer et al., 2007). Earlier studies described the extent of Hg exposure in free-living common loons across much of their breeding range (Meyer et al., 1995, 1998; Evers et al., 1998, 2003; Scheuhammer et al., 1998, 2001; Burgess et al., 2005; Champoux et al., 2006) and provided indirect evidence of potential negative impacts to populations (Nocera and Taylor, 1998; Counard, 2001; Evers et al., 2003; Scheuhammer et al., 2008). Some interpretations of long-term datasets comparing reproductive success and MeHg availability and accumulation demonstrate clear negative impacts on wild, breeding common loon populations at currently realistic levels of environmental exposure (Burgess and Meyer, 2008; Evers et al., 2008). In Maine and New Hampshire, Evers et al. (2008) identified MeHg toxicity as the main factor responsible for a 41% decline in average reproductive success over an 11-year period. Here, individual loons were marked, monitored, and regularly resampled over an 18-year period. Mercury concentrations from multiple tissues (eggs and blood) and age/sex classes were converted into standard female loon unit equivalents to produce a dataset of over 5500 Hg concentrations. The lowest observed adverse effect levels (LOAELs) were identified as 3.0 µg g^{-1} (wet weight) in blood and 40 µg g^{-1} (wet weight) in feathers. Documented declines in reproductive success were partly explained by behavioral, physiologic, and survival variables. Based on over 1500 hours of observation, adult loons with high body burdens of Hg (or those individuals exceeding the established LOAELs) spent significantly less time in high-energy behaviors, such as foraging for themselves and their chicks, preening, and interacting with conspecifics as compared with loons having lower Hg body burdens. Loon pairs with low Hg body burdens left nests with eggs unattended for <1% of the time, whereas loons pairs with individuals having high Hg body burdens left eggs unattended an average of 14% of the time. Comparing developmental stability using differences in mean weights of right and left second secondary feathers, it was observed that loons with high Hg body burdens had significantly greater asymmetry than loons in four lower feather Hg categories. Lastly, the recapture of 441 adult loons over time documented an annual average increase of 8.4% in feather Hg concentrations, demonstrating that loons, especially those breeding in Hg-sensitive environments with elevated MeHg availability, tend to show increasing Hg body burdens as they age, which could possibly influence lifetime reproductive success and alter a breeding population's age structure toward younger individuals. Further efforts to better understand the relationships between population sinks and sources for such negatively impacted breeding populations are underway. Based on comparable findings from two parallel studies using similar field protocols in New England (Evers et al., 2008) and in Wisconsin and the Canadian Maritimes (Burgess and Meyer, 2008), the maximum productivity observed for breeding loon pairs declined by about 50% when Hg in prey fish reached about 0.2 µg g^{-1} (wet weight, whole body), an Hg level that is common for small fish of various species in many locations; thus, MeHg exposure may be limiting loon reproduction in some environments, and the presence of population sinks due to Hg exposure across the loon's breeding range may be more prevalent than formerly believed.

Although studies of Hg cycling in terrestrial ecosystems are more limited than those in aquatic ecosystems, wetland soils have considerable capacity to store and potentially methylate large quantities of inorganic Hg (Driscoll et al., 2007). New and compelling evidence connects MeHg production in floodplain forest and associated wetlands with uptake into certain terrestrial invertivore food webs. Cristol et al. (2008) reported that blood Hg concentrations in some terrestrial songbird species equaled or exceeded those of aquatic-based songbirds and even those of piscivorous species such as the belted kingfisher (*Megaceryle alcyon*). Previous studies have generally reported low (<0.5 µg ml^{-1}) average Hg concentrations in blood of a variety of passerine species; however, considerable interspecies variability exists, and a few species (e.g., red-winged blackbird; *Agelaius phoeniceus*) had mean blood Hg concentrations of ~0.6 µg ml^{-1} in environments not highly contaminated with Hg (Evers et al., 2005; Evers and Duron, 2008). The terrestrial habitats studied by Cristol et al. (2008) were adjacent to aquatic environments heavily contaminated with industrial mercuric sulfate. In these habitats, the highest blood Hg concentrations were observed in two terrestrial species—red-eyed vireos (*Vireo olivaceus*) and Carolina wrens (*Thryothorus ludovicianus*)—both of which had mean blood Hg >4 µg ml^{-1}, higher than levels found in aquatic-feeding species in the same study and sufficiently high to be of toxicologic concern, based on a reproductive impairment threshold estimated for common loons (2.87 µg ml^{-1} in the blood of breeding females) (Scheuhammer et al., 2007). A major dietary source of MeHg for these terrestrial birds was spiders, which had MeHg concentrations similar to fish preyed upon by kingfishers (Cristol et al., 2008). Spiders apparently have a particularly influential impact on the biomagnification of MeHg in terrestrial invertivore food webs. Such findings may have important ramifications for the health of some terrestrial songbird, bat and other invertivorous populations in some habitats. Although LOAELs for invertivorous birds have not been broadly developed, there is evidence that songbirds can be relatively sensitive to MeHg exposure *in ovo* (Heinz et al., 2008). Such sensitivity combined with the wide diversity of invertivorous species raises concern for the potential effects of Hg exposure on songbird conservation in the northeastern United States and elsewhere (Evers and Duron, 2008). Brasso and Cristol (2008) reported decreased reproductive success in tree swallows (*Tachycineta bicolor*), especially in young breeding females, nesting near an Hg-contaminated river; and Wada et al. (2009) reported suppressed adrenocortical responses in tree swallow nestlings from this same area. Franceschini et al. (2009) suggested that Hg exposure depressed resting plasma corticosterone levels in tree swallows. Future studies should better characterize the food-chain transfer of MeHg in critical terrestrial systems, identify the main at-risk species, and further investigate possible reproductive and other effects in these species.

Mercury–Selenium Relationships

Se is generally considered to protect against MeHg poisoning in vertebrates (Cuvin-Aralar and Furness, 1991; Sumino et al., 1977). It has long been postulated that demethylation of MeHg in tissues, and the subsequent sequestration of inorganic Hg with Se in an approximate 1:1 molar ratio, represents a detoxification mechanism for at least some animal species that are exposed to relatively elevated dietary concentrations of MeHg, including predatory marine mammals such as polar bears (Dietz et al., 2000), seals (Smith and Armstrong, 1978), and toothed whales (Caurant et al., 1996; Palmisano et al., 1995), as well as a variety of seabirds and other predatory aquatic birds (Scheuhammer et al., 1998; Thompson and Furness, 1989). Henny et al. (2002) reported an apparent threshold-dependant tolerance to MeHg by double-crested cormorants, black-crowned night herons (*Nycticorax nycticorax*), and snowy egrets from the Carson River, Nevada. In these birds, demethylation of MeHg seemed to increase at higher levels of MeHg intake, resulting in lower percentages of MeHg in the liver and kidney as total Hg concentrations increased. Similar findings have been reported in seabirds (Thompson and Furness, 1989), osprey (Hopkins et al., 2007), and common loons and common mergansers (Scheuhammer et al., 1998). In addition, Henny et al. (2002) reported a nearly perfect correlation ($r^2 = 0.98$) between inorganic Hg concentrations and Se concentrations in the livers of cormorants, night herons, and egrets, suggesting Se was important in sequestering inorganic Hg following demethylation. Wiemeyer et al. (2007) noted a similar inverse relationship between MeHg and total Hg concentrations, and a similar correlation between Hg and Se, in

the livers of American white pelicans (*Pelecanus erythrorhynchos*) from Pyramid Lake, Nevada. Eagles-Smith et al. (2009) reported that demethylation occurred when total Hg concentrations rose above about 8.5 µg g^{-1} dry weight in the livers of American avocets (*Recurvirostra americana*), black-necked stilts (*Himantopus mexicanus*), Caspian terns (*Hydroprogne caspia*), and Forster's terns (*Sterna forsteri*) in San Francisco Bay. Above the demethylation threshold, Se concentrations were significantly correlated with inorganic Hg concentrations in the liver. A similar threshold (~9–10 µg g^{-1} dry weight) was suggested by Scheuhammer et al. (2008) for common loons, above which hepatic Hg and Se concentrations became closely correlated. Similarly, for a number of marine mammal species, the inflection point below which the majority of hepatic Hg is organic (MeHg), and above which the proportion of inorganic Hg increases, was estimated to be about 2.2 µg g^{-1} wet weight (or ~9 µg g^{-1} dry weight) (Dietz et al., 1990).

As discussed in the section on egg-injection studies, some bird species appear to be much more sensitive than others to MeHg exposure *in ovo* (Heinz et al., 2009), a finding that raises questions regarding the molecular basis for interspecies differences in sensitivity to MeHg. Scheuhammer et al. (2008) reported significant differences between common loons and bald eagles with respect to Hg and Se accumulation in brain tissue. Although both species, by virtue of their high trophic status in aquatic ecosystems, can be exposed to relatively high dietary MeHg concentrations, their patterns of total Hg, MeHg, and Se accumulation in brain tissue were significantly different. Eagles showed a highly significant co-accumulation of Se with Hg and efficient demethylation of MeHg in brain as compared with loons. For loons, but not eagles, the molar ratio of Hg:Se in the brain often exceeded 1:1. Ralston et al. (2007) suggested that the ratio of Hg to Se is an important determinant of MeHg toxicity. Certain seleno-enzymes (e.g., thioredoxin reductase) are highly sensitive to inhibition by low nanomolar concentrations of Hg and may be primary targets of MeHg toxicity at the molecular level (Carvalho et al., 2008). The relative inability of the loon brain to demethylate MeHg and/or to increase the accumulation of Se as Hg concentrations rise may indicate a greater sensitivity to the toxic effects of MeHg in loons as compared with eagles. Similarly, river otters appear to demethylate MeHg (Basu et al., 2005b) and accumulate Se in their brain more efficiently than mink (Haines et al., 2004), findings that may help explain why MeHg-associated neurochemical changes in the brains of wild river otters (Basu et al., 2005b, 2006b) were different than those in wild mink. Additional studies are needed to better explain interspecies differences in sensitivity to MeHg exposure and the neurotoxic mechanisms of action of MeHg, including the role of Se.

All of the above studies support the concept that Se protects animals against MeHg poisoning, but in a controlled dosing study in which breeding pairs of mallard ducks were fed a diet containing a combination of 10 µg g^{-1} Hg as MeHg and 10 µg g^{-1} Se as selenomethionine, reproductive success was worse than when only MeHg or only Se was administered (Heinz and Hoffman, 1998). Thus, toxicity to the developing embryo, at least in birds, may be additive in response to a combination of elevated dietary MeHg plus Se, in spite of a protective effect of Se in adults. More research with various combinations of MeHg and Se are warranted.

Conclusions

The uptake, metabolism, and effects of Hg in fish and wildlife have been studied for more than 50 years, and much has been learned regarding the dynamics of Hg in the environment, its food-chain transfer, and its toxic effects. Some research has documented subtle, yet potentially important effects of Hg on behavior, neurochemistry, and endocrine function in fish and wildlife at currently realistic levels of environmental exposure. Given that substantial anthropogenic Hg emissions on a global scale will almost certainly continue well into the 21st century, the need for new research on the ecotoxicology of Hg, and continued monitoring of Hg in fish and wildlife in various natural environments, will undoubtedly continue as well.

It is recommended that future toxicologic studies focus on a number of key issues:

- Linking biomarkers of MeHg exposure and oxidative stress to effects on reproduction and population change in wild fish populations.
- Linking environmentally realistic levels of MeHg exposure or Hg accumulation in amphibian and reptile species with toxic effects on reproduction, neurochemistry, or other important physiologic processes.
- Determining the genetic (or other) basis for the species differences in sensitivity to MeHg toxicity observed in comparative egg-injection and other studies, including the role of MeHg demethylation and Hg–Se interactions.
- Linking changes at the level of the transcriptome or proteome with reproductive dysfunction, neurotoxicity, or other toxic effects of MeHg in at-risk fish and wildlife species.
- Linking toxic effects of MeHg exposure in individual animals to population-level changes in at-risk species.

References

Albers, P.H., M.T. Koterba, R. Rossmann, W.A. Link, J.B. French, R.S. Bennett, and W.C. Bauer. 2007. Effects of methylmercury on reproduction in American kestrels. *Environmental Toxicology and Chemistry* 26: 1856–1866.

Bank, M.S., J. Crocker, B. Connery, and A. Amirbahman. 2007. Mercury bioaccumulation in green frog and bullfrog tadpoles from Acadia National Park, Maine, USA. *Environmental Toxicology and Chemistry* 26: 118–125.

Bank, M.S., J. Burgess, D. Evers, and C.S. Loftin. 2007. Mercury contamination in biota from Acadia National Park, Maine, USA: a review. *Environmental Monitoring and Assessment* 126: 105–115.

Bank, M.S., J.B. Crocker, S. Davis, D. Brotherton, R. Cook, J. Behler, and B. Connery. 2006. Population decline of Northern Dusky Salamanders at Acadia National Park, Maine, USA. *Biological Conservation* 130: 230–238.

Bank, M.S., C.S. Loftin, and R.E. Jung. 2005. Mercury bioaccumulation in northern two-lined salamanders from streams in the Northeastern United States. *Ecotoxicology* 14: 181–191.

Basu, N., K. Klenavic, M. Gamberg, M. O'Brien, R.D. Evans, A.M. Scheuhammer, and H.M. Chan. 2005a. Effects of mercury on neurochemical receptor binding characteristics in wild mink. *Environmental Toxicology and Chemistry* 24: 1444–1450.

Basu, N., A.M. Scheuhammer, N.M. Grochowina, K. Klenavic, R.D. Evans, M. O'Brien, and H.M. Chan. 2005b. Effects of mercury on neurochemical receptors in wild river otters (*Lontra canadensis*). *Environmental Science and Technology* 39: 3585–3591.

Basu, N., A.M. Scheuhammer, K. Rouvinen-Watt, N. Grochowina, K. Klenavic, R.D. Evans, and H.M. Chan. 2006a. Methylmercury impairs components of the

cholinergic system in captive mink (*Mustela vison*). *Toxicological Sciences* 91: 202–209.

Basu, N., A.M. Scheuhammer, R.D. Evans, M. O'Brien, H.M. Chan. 2006b. Cholinesterase and monoamine oxidase activity in relation to mercury levels in the cerebral cortex of wild river otters. *Human and Experimental Toxicology* 26: 213–220.

Basu, N., A.M. Scheuhammer, Bursian, S.J., Elliott, J., Rouvinen-Watt, K. and H.M. Chan. 2007a. Mink as a sentinel species in environmental health. *Environmental Research* 103: 130–144.

Basu, N., A.M. Scheuhammer, K. Rouvinen-Watt, N. Grochowina, R.D. Evans, M. O'Brien, and H.M. Chan. 2007b. Decreased N-methyl-d-aspartic acid (NMDA) receptor levels are associated with mercury exposure in wild and captive mink. *Neurotoxicology* 28: 587–593.

Basu, N., A.M. Scheuhammer, K. Rouvinen-Watt, R.D. Evans, N. Grochowina, and H.M. Chan. 2008. The effects of mercury on muscarinic cholinergic receptor subtypes (M1 and M2) in captive mink. *Neurotoxicology* 29: 328–334.

Basu, N., A.M. Scheuhammer, C. Sonne, R.J. Letcher, E.W. Born, and R. Dietz. 2009. Is dietary mercury of neurotoxicological concern to polar bears (*Ursus maritimus*)? *Environmental Toxicology and Chemistry* 28: 133–140.

Bauerle, B. 1975. The use of snakes as pollution indicator species. *Copeia* 1975: 367–368.

Bergeron, C.M., C.M.. Bodinof, J.M. Unrine, and William A. Hopkins. 2010a. Mercury accumulation along a contamination gradient and nondestructive indices of exposure in amphibians. *Environmental Toxicology and Chemistry* 29: 980–988.

Bergeron, C.M., C.M.. Bodinof, J.M. Unrine, and W. A. Hopkins. 2010b. Bioaccumulation and maternal transfer of mercury and selenium in amphibians. *Environmental Toxicology and Chemistry* 29: 989–997.

Bergeron, C.M., J.F. Husak, J.M. Unrine, C.S. Romanek, W.A. Hopkins. 2007. Influence of feeding ecology on blood mercury concentrations in four species of turtles. *Environmental Toxicology and Chemistry* 26: 1733–1741.

Berntssen, M.H.G., A. Aatland, and R.D. Handy. 2003. Chronic dietary mercury exposure causes oxidative stress, brain lesions, and altered behavior in Atlantic salmon (*Salmo salar*) parr. *Aquatic Toxicology* 65: 55–72.

Birge, W.J., J.A. Black, A.G. Westerman and J.E. Hudson. 1979. The effects of mercury on reproduction of fish and amphibians. In: J.O. Nriagu (Ed.). *The Biogeochemistry of Mercury in the Environment*. Elsevier, New York.

Blanvillain, G., J.A. Schwenter, R.D. Day, D. Point, S.J. Christopher, W.A. Roumillat, and D.W. Owens. 2007. Diamondback terrapins, Malaclemys terrapin, as a sentinel species for monitoring mercury pollution of estuarine systems in South Carolina and Georgia, USA. *Environmental Toxicology and Chemistry* 26: 1441–1450.

Borg, K., H. Wanntorp, K. Erne, and H. Hanko. 1967. Alkyl mercury poisoning in terrestrial Swedish wildlife. *Viltrevy* 6: 302–377.

Brasso, R.L., and D.A. Cristol. 2008. Effects of mercury exposure on the reproductive success of tree swallows (*Tachycineta bicolor*). *Ecotoxicology* 17: 133–141.

Brookes, N., and D.A. Kristt. 1989. Inhibition of amino acid transport and protein synthesis by HgCl$_2$ and methylmercury in astrocytes: selectivity and reversibility. *Journal of Neurochemistry* 53: 1228–1237.

Burger, J. 1992. Trace element levels in Pine Snake hatchlings. Tissue and temporal differences. *Archives of Environmental Contamination and Toxicology* 22: 209–213.

Burger, J., K.R. Campbell, T.S. Campbell, T. Shulka, C. Jeitner, and M. Gochfeld. 2005. Use of skin and blood as nonlethal indicators of heavy metal contamination in northern water snakes (Nerodia sipedon). *Archives of Environmental Contamination and Toxicology* 49: 232–238.

Burger, J., and J. Snodgrass. 1998. Heavy metals in bullfrog (*Rana catesbeiana*) tadpoles: effects of depuration before analysis. *Environmental Toxicology and Chemistry* 17: 2203–2209.

Burger, J. 1992. Trace element levels in pine snake hatchlings: Tissue and temporal differences. *Archives of Environmental Contamination and Toxicology* 22: 209–213.

Burgess, N.M., D.C. Evers, and J.D. Kaplan. 2005. Mercury and other contaminants in Common Loons breeding in Atlantic Canada. *Ecotoxicology* 14: 241–252.

Burgess, N.M., and M.W. Meyer. 2008. Methylmercury exposure associated with reduced productivity in common loons. *Ecotoxicology* 17: 83–91.

Byrne, A.R., L. Kosta, and P. Stegnar. 1975. The occurrence of mercury in amphibian. *Environmental Letters* 8: 147–155.

Carvalho, C.M.L., E.-H. Chew, S.I. Hashemy, J. Lu, and A. Holmgren. 2008. Inhibition of the human thioredoxin system: a molecular mechanism of mercury toxicity. *Journal of Biological Chemistry* 283: 11913–11923.

Castoldi, A.F., S.M. Candura, P. Costa, L. Manzo, and L.G. Costa. 1996. Interaction of mercury compounds with muscarinic receptor subtypes in the rat brain. *Neurotoxicology* 17: 735–741.

Caurant, F., M. Navarro, and J.C. Amiard. 1996. Mercury in pilot whales: possible limits to the detoxification process. *Science of the Total Environment* 186: 95–104.

Champoux, L., D. Masse, D. Evers, O. Lane, M. Plante, and S.T.A. Timmerman. 2006. Assessment of mercury exposure and potential effects on Common Loons (*Gavia immer*) in Quebec. *Hydrobiologia* 567: 263–274.

Chang, L.W., K.R. Reuhl, and A.W. Dudley, Jr. 1974. Effects of methylmercury chloride on *Rana pipiens* tadpoles. *Environmental Research* 8: 82–91.

Chang, L.W., L.L.M. Mak, and A.H. Martin. 1976. Dose-dependent effects of methylmercury on limb regeneration of newts (*Triturus viridescens*). *Environmental Research* 11: 305–309.

Cooke, A.S. 1981. Tadpoles as indicators of harmful levels of pollution. *Environmental Pollution* (Series A) 25: 123–133.

Counard, C.J. 2001. Mercury exposure and effects on Common Loon (*Gavia immer*) behavior in the Upper Midwestern United States. MS thesis, University of Minnesota, St. Paul, MN.

Cristol, D.A., R.L. Brasso, A.M. Condon, R.E. Fovargue, S.L. Friedman, K.K. Hallinger, A.P. Monroe, and A.E. White. 2008. The movement of aquatic mercury through terrestrial food webs. *Science* 320: 335.

Crump, K.L., and V.L. Trudeau. 2009. Mercury-induced reproductive impairment in fish. *Environmental Toxicology and Chemistry* 28: 895–907.

Cuvin-Aralar, M.L.A., and R.W. Furness. 1991. Mercury and selenium interaction: a review. *Ecotoxicology and Environmental Safety* 21: 348–364.

de Flora, S., C. Bennicelli, and M. Bagnasco. 1994. Genotoxicity of mercury compounds: a review. *Mutation Research* 317: 57–79.

Dial, N.A. 1976. Methylmercury: teratogenic and lethal effects in frog embryos. *Teratology* 13: 327–334.

Dietz R, F. Riget, and E.W. Born. 2000. An assessment of selenium to mercury in Greenland marine animals. *Science of the Total Environment* 245: 15–24.

Dietz, R., C.O. Nielsen, M.M. Hansen, and C.T. Hansen. 1990. Organic mercury in Greenland birds and mammals. *Science of the Total Environment* 95: 41–51.

Drevnick, P. E., and M.B. Sandheinrich. 2003. Effects of dietary methylmercury on reproductive endocrinology of fathead minnows. *Environmental Science and Technology* 37: 4390–4396.

Drevnick, P.E., M.B. Sandheinrich, and J.T. Oris. 2006. Increased ovarian follicular apoptosis in fathead minnows (*Pimephales promelas*) exposed to dietary methylmercury. *Aquatic Toxicology* 79: 49–54.

Drevnick, P.E., A.P. Roberts, R.R. Otter, C.R. Hammerschmidt, R. Klaper, and J.T. Oris. 2008. Mercury toxicity in livers of northern pike (*Esox lucius*) from Isle Royale, USA. *Comparative Biochemistry and Physiology Part C* 147: 331–338.

Driscoll, C.T., Y.J. Han, C.Y. Chen, D.C. Evers, K.F. Lambert, T.M. Holsen, N.C. Kamman, and R. Munson. 2007. Mercury contamination in remote forest and aquatic ecosystems in the northeastern U.S.: Sources, transformations and management options. *Bioscience* 57: 17–28.

Eagles-Smith, C.A., J.T. Ackerman, J. Yee, and T.L. Adelsbach. 2009. Methylmercury demethylation in waterbird livers:

dose-response thresholds and differences among species. *Environmental Toxicology and Chemistry* 28: 568–577.

Eisler, R. 2000. *Handbook of chemical risk assessment: Health hazards to humans, plants, and animals.* Volume 1, *Metals.* Lewis, Boca Raton, FL.

Eto, K. 1997. Pathology of Minamata disease. *Toxicological Pathology* 25: 614–623.

Evers, D.C. 2006. Loons as biosentinels of aquatic integrity. *Environmental Bioindicators* 1: 18–21.

Evers, D.C., and M. Duron. 2008. Developing an exposure profile for mercury in breeding birds of New York and Pennsylvania, 2005-2006. Report BRI 2008-15 submitted to the Nature Conservancy and New York State Energy Research Development Authority. BioDiversity Research Institute, Gorham, ME.

Evers, D.C., J.D. Kaplan, M.W. Meyer, P.S. Reaman, W.E. Braselton, A. Major, N. Burgess, and A.M. Scheuhammer. 1998. Geographic trend in mercury measured in Common Loon feathers and blood. *Environmental Toxicology and Chemistry* 17: 173–183.

Evers, D.C., K.M. Taylor, A. Major, R.J. Taylor, R.H. Poppenga, and A. M. Scheuhammer. 2003. Common Loon eggs as indicators of methylmercury availability in North America. *Ecotoxicology* 11: 69–81.

Evers, D.C., N.M. Burgess, L. Champoux, B. Hoskins, A. Major, W. Goodale, R. Taylor, R. Poppenga, and T. Daigle. 2005. Patterns and interpretation of mercury exposure in freshwater avian communities in Northeastern North America. *Ecotoxicology* 14: 193–221.

Evers, D.C., L. Savoy, C.R. DeSorbo, D. Yates, W. Hanson, K.M. Taylor, L. Siegel, J.H. Cooley, M. Bank, A. Major, K. Munney, H.S. Vogel, N. Schoch, M. Pokras, W. Goodale, and J. Fair. 2008. Adverse effects from environmental mercury loads on breeding common loons. *Ecotoxicology* 17: 69–81.

Fimreite, N. 1971. Effects of dietary methylmercury on ring-necked pheasants. Canadian Wildlife Service Occasional Paper no. 9, Ottawa, Canada.

Fimreite, N. 1974. Mercury contamination of aquatic birds in northwestern Ontario. *Journal of Wildlife Management* 38: 120–131.

Fimreite, N. 1979. Accumulation and effects of mercury on birds. In: J.C. Niragu (Ed.). *The biochemistry of mercury in the environment.* Elsevier, Amsterdam, pp. 601–627.

Finley, M.T., and R.C. Stendell. 1978. Survival and reproductive success of black ducks fed methylmercury. *Environmental Pollution* 16: 51–64.

Fostier, A., B. Jalabert, R. Billard, B. Breton, and Y. Zohar. 1983. The gonadal steroids. In: W.S. Hoar, D.J. Randall, and E.M. Donaldson (Eds.). *Fish physiology, vol. IX, Reproduction, part a, endocrine tissues and hormones.* Academic Press, New York pp.277–372.

Franceschini, M.D., O.P. Lane, D.C. Evers, J.M. Reed, B. Hoskins, and L.M. Romero. 2009. The corticosterone stress response and mercury contamination in free-living tree swallows, *Tachycineta bicolour. Ecotoxicology* 18: 514–521.

Friedmann, A.S., M.C. Watzin, T. Brinck-Johnsen, and L.C. Leiter. 1996. Low levels of methylmercury inhibit growth and gonadal development in juvenile walleye (*Stizostedion vitreum*). *Aquatic Toxicology* 35: 265–278.

Friedmann, A.S., E.K. Costain, D.L. MacLatchy, W. Stansley, and E.J. Washuta. 2002. Effect of mercury on general and reproductive health of largemouth bass (*Micropterus salmoides*) from three lakes in New Jersey. *Ecotoxicology and Environmental Safety* 52: 117–122.

Gerstenberger, S., and R. Pearson. 2002. Mercury concentrations in bullfrogs (*Rana catesbeiana*) collected from a southern Nevada, USA, Wetland. *Bulletin of Environmental Contamination and Toxicology* 69: 210–218.

Gibbons, J.W., D.E. Scott, T.J. Ryan, K.A. Buhlmann, T.D. Tuberville, B.S. Metts, J.L. Greene, T. Mills, Y. Leiden, D. Poppy, and C.T. Winne. 2000. The global decline of reptiles, déjà vu amphibians. *BioScience* 50: 653–666.

Golet, W.J. and T.A. Haines, 2001. Snapping turtles (*Chelydra serpentina*) as monitors for mercury contamination of aquatic environments. *Environmental Monitoring and Assessment* 71: 211–20.

Gonazalez, P., Y. Dominique, J.C. Massabuau, A. Boudou, and J.P. Bourdineaud. 2005. Comparative effects of dietary methylmercury on gene expression in liver, skeletal muscle, and brain of the zebrafish (*Danio rerio*). *Environmental Science and Technology* 39: 3972–3980.

Haines, K.J.R., R.D. Evans, and M. O'Brien 2004. Relationship between mercury and selenium in the brain of river otter (*Lutra canadensis*) and wild mink (*Mustela vison*) from Nova Scotia, Canada. *RMZ Materials and Geoenvironment* 51: 1028–1030.

Hall, R.J., and B.M. Mulhern. 1984. Are anuran amphibians heavy metal accumulators? In: R.A. Siegel L.E. Hunt, J.L. Knoght, L. Malaret, and N.L. Zuschlag (Eds.). *Vertebrate ecology and systematics: a tribute to Henry S. Fitch.* University of Kansas Press, Lawrence, Kansas, pp 123–133.

Hammerschmidt, C.R., M.B. Sandheinrich, J.G. Wiener, and R.G. Rada. 2002. Effects of dietary methylmercury on reproduction of fathead minnows. *Environmental Science and Technology* 36: 877–883.

Harada, M. 1995. Minamata disease: Methylmercury poisoning in Japan caused by environmental pollution. *Critical Reviews in Toxicology* 25: 1–25.

Hayes, J., and L. McLellan. 1999. Glutathione and glutathione-dependent enzymes represent a co-ordinately regulated defence against oxidative stress. *Free Radical Research* 31: 273–300.

Heath, J.A., and P.C. Frederick. 2005. Relationships among mercury concentrations, hormones, and nesting effort of white ibises (*Eudocimus albus*) in the Florida Everglades. *Auk* 122: 255–267.

Heinz, G. 1974. Effects of low dietary levels of methyl mercury on mallard reproduction. *Bulletin of Environmental Contamination and Toxicology* 11: 386–392.

Heinz, G.H. 1979. Methylmercury: reproductive and behavioral effects on three generations of mallard ducks. *Journal of Wildlife Management* 43: 94–401.

Heinz, G.H., S.D. Haseltine, R.J. Hall, and A.J. Krynitsky. 1980. Organochlorine and mercury residues in snakes from Pilot and Spider Islands, Lake Michigan, 1978. *Bulletin of Environmental Contamination and Toxicology* 25: 738–743.

Heinz, G.H. 1996. Mercury poisoning in wildlife. In: A. Fairbrother, L.N. Locke, and G.L. Hoff (Eds.). *Noninfectious diseases of wildlife*, 2nd ed. Iowa State University Press, Ames, pp. 118–127.

Heinz, G.H., and D.J. Hoffman. 1998. Methylmercury chloride and selenomethionine interactions on health and reproduction in mallards. *Environmental Toxicology and Chemistry* 17: 139–145.

Heinz, G.H., and D.J. Hoffman. 2003. Embryotoxic thresholds of mercury: Estimates from individual mallard eggs. *Archives of Environmental Contamination and Toxicology* 44: 257–264.

Heinz, G.H., D.J. Hoffman, S.L. Kondrad, and C.A. Erwin. 2006. Factors affecting the toxicity of methylmercury injected into eggs. *Archives of Environmental Contamination and Toxicology* 50: 264–279.

Heinz, G.H., D.J. Hoffman, J.D. Klimstra, K.R. Stebbins, S.L. Kondrad, and C.A. Erwin. 2009. Species differences in the sensitivity of avian embryos to methylmercury. *Archives of Environmental Contamination and Toxicology* 56: 129–138.

Helwig, D.D. and M.E. Hora. 1983. Polychlorinated biphenyl, mercury, and cadmium concentrations in Minnesota snapping turtles. *Bulletin of Environmental Contamination and Toxicology* 30: 186–190.

Henny, C.J., E.F. Hill, D.J. Hoffman, M.G. Spalding, and R.A. Grove. 2002. Nineteenth century mercury: Hazard to wading birds and cormorants of the Carson River, Nevada. *Ecotoxicology* 11: 213–231.

Hill, E.F., C.J. Henny, and R.A. Grove. 2008. Mercury and drought along the lower Carson River, Nevada: II. Snowy egret and black-crowned night-heron reproduction on Lahontan Reservoir, 1997-2006. *Ecotoxicology* 17: 117–131.

Hopkins, W.A., S.E. DuRant, B.P. Staub, C.L. Rowe, and B.P. Jackson. 2006. Reproduction, embryonic development, and maternal transfer of contaminants in an amphibian *Gastrophryne carolinensis*. *Environmental Health Perspectives* 114: 661–666.

Hopkins, W.A., L.B. Hopkins, J.M. Unrine, J. Snodgrass, and J. Elliot. 2007. Mercury concentrations in tissues of osprey from the Carolinas, USA. *Journal of Wildlife Management* 71: 1891–1829.

Hothem, R.L., B.S. Trejo, M.L. Bauer, and J.J. Crayon. 2008. Cliff swallows, Petrochelidon pyrrhonota, as bioindicators of mercury, Cache Creek watershed, California. *Archives of Environmental Contamination and Toxicology* 55: 111–121.

Hothem, R.L., M.R. Jennings, and J.J. Crayon. 2010. Mercury contamination in three species of anuran amphibians from the Cache Creek Watershed, California, USA. *Environmental Monitoring and Assessment* 163: 433–448.

Jagoe, C.H., B. Arnold-Hill, G.M. Yanochko, P.V. Winger, and I.L. Brisbin, Jr. 1998. Mercury in alligators (*Alligator mississippiensis*) in the southeastern United States. *Science of the Total Environment* 213: 255–262.

Jung, R.E., S. Droege, J.R. Sauer, and R.B. Landy. 2000. Evaluation of terrestrial and streamside salamander monitoring techniques at Shenandoah National Park. *Environmental Monitoring and Assessment* 63: 65–79.

Kamman, N.C., N.M. Burgess, C.T. Driscoll, H.A. Simonin, W. Goodale, J. Linehan, R. Estabrook, M. Hutcheson, A. Major, A. M. Scheuhammer, and D. A. Scruton. 2005. Mercury in freshwater fish of northeast North America—a geographic perspective based on fish tissue monitoring databases. *Ecotoxicology* 14: 163–150.

Kahn, B., and B. Tansel. 2000. Mercury bioconcentration factors in American Alligators (*Alligator mississippiensis*) in the Florida Everglades. *Ecotoxicology and Environmental Safety* 47: 54–58.

Kanamadi, R.D., and S.K. Saidapur. 1992. Effects of exposure to sublethal mercuric chloride on the testis and fat body of the frog *Rana cyanophlyctis*. *Journal of Herpetology* 26: 499–501.

Klaper, R., C.B. Rees, P. Drevnick, D. Weber, M. Sandheinrich, and M. J. Caravan. 2006. Gene expression changes related to endocrine function and decline in reproduction in fathead minnow (*Pimephales promelas*) after dietary methylmercury exposure. *Environmental Health Perspectives* 11: 1337–1343.

Larose, C., R. Canuel, M. Lucotte, and R.T. Di Giulio. 2008. Toxicological effects of methylmercury on walleye (*Sander vitreus*) and perch (*Perca flavescens*) from lakes of the boreal forest. *Comparative Biochemistry and Physiology Part C* 147: 139–149.

Livingstone, D.R. 2001. Contaminant-stimulated reactive oxygen species production and oxidative stress in aquatic organisms. *Marine Pollution Bulletin* 42: 656–666.

Loumbourdis, N.S., and G. Danscher. 2004. Autometallographic tracing of mercury in frog liver. *Environmental Pollution* 129: 299–304.

Manzo, L., F. Artigas, E. Martinez, A. Mutti, E. Bergamaschi, P. Nicotera, M. Tonini, S.M. Candura, D.E. Ray, and L.G. Costa. 1996. Biochemical markers of neurotoxicity: a review of mechanistic studies and applications. *Human and Experimental Toxicology* 15: S20–S35.

Mela, M., M.A.F. Rand, D.F. Ventura, C.E.V. Carvalho, E. Pelletier, and C.A. Oliveira Ribeiro. 2007. Effects of dietary methylmercury on liver and kidney histology in the neotropical fish *Hoplia malabaricus*. *Ecotoxicology and Environmental Safety* 6: 426–435.

Meyer, M.W., D.C. Evers, T. Saulton, and W.E. Braselton. 1995. Common Loons (*Gavia immer*) nesting on low pH lakes in northern Wisconsin have elevated blood mercury content. *Water, Air and Soil Pollution*. 80: 871–880.

Meyer, M.W., D.C. Evers, J.J. Hartigan, and P.S. Rasmussen. 1998. Patterns of common loon (*Gavia immer*) mercury exposure, reproduction, and survival in Wisconsin, USA. *Environmental Toxicology and Chemistry* 17: 184–190.

Moran, P., N. Alur, R. W. Black, and M. M. Vijayan. 2007. Tissue contaminants and associated transcriptional response in trout liver from high elevation lakes of Washington. *Environmental Science and Technology* 41: 6591–6597.

Moyle, P. B. 1976. Inland fishes of California. University of California Press, Berkeley.

Mudgall, C.F., and S.S. Patil. 1988. Toxicity of lead and mercury to frogs *Rana cyanophlyctis* and *Rana tigerina*. *Environment and Ecology* 6: 506–508.

Nishimura, M., and N. Urakawa. 1976. A transport mechanism of methyl mercury to egg albumen in laying Japanese quail. *Japanese Journal of Veterinary Science* 38: 433–444.

Nocera, J and P. Taylor. 1998. *In situ* behavioral response of common loons associated with elevated mercury exposure. *Conservation Ecology [now Ecology and Society, online]* 2: 10. (URL: http://www.ecologyandsociety.org/vol2/iss2/art10/).

Ozawa, S., H. Kamiya, and K. Tsuzuki. 1998. Glutamate receptors in the mammalian central nervous system. *Progress in Neurobiology* 54: 581–618.

Palmisano, F., N. Cardellicchio, and P.G. Zambonin. 1995. Speciation of mercury in dolphin liver: a two-stage mechanism for the demethylation accumulation process and role of selenium. *Marine Environmental Research* 40: 109–121.

Petranka, J.W. 1984. Ontogeny of the diet and feeding behavior of *Eurycea bislineata* larvae. *Journal of Herpetology* 18: 48–55.

Petranka, J.W. 1998. *Salamanders of the United States and Canada*. Smithsonian Institution Press, Washington, D.C., 576 pp.

Power T., K.L. Clark, A. Harfenist and D.B. Peakall. 1989. A review and evaluation of the amphibian toxicological literature. Ottawa Ontario Canada: Canadian Wildlife Service. *Technical Report Series* 61: 222.

Punzo, F. 1993a. Effect of mercuric chloride on fertilization and larval development in the river frog, *Rana heckscheri* (Wright) (Anura: Ranidae). *Bulletin of Environmental Contamination and Toxicology* 51: 575–581.

Punzo, F. 1993b. Ovarian effects of a sublethal concentration of mercuric chloride in the river frog, *Rana heckscheri* (Anura: Ranidae). *Bulletin of Environmental Contamination and Toxicology* 50: 385–391.

Rainwater, T.R., B.M. Adair, S.G. Platt, T.A. Anderson, G.P. Cobb, and S.T. McMurry. 2002. Mercury in Morelet's crocodile eggs from northern Belize. *Archives of Environmental Contamination and Toxicology* 42: 319–324.

Rainwater, T.R., T.H. Wu, A.G. Finger, J.E. Cañas, L. Yu, K.D. Reynolds, G. Coimbatore, B. Barr, S.G. Platt, G.P. Cobb, T.A. Anderson, and S.T. McMurry. 2007. Metals and organochlorine pesticides in caudal scutes of crocodiles from Belize and Costa Rica. *Science of the Total Environment* 373: 146–156.

Raldúa, D., S. Diez, J.M. Bayona, and D. Barceló. 2007. Mercury levels and liver pathology in feral fish living in the vicinity of a mercury cell chlor-alkali factory. *Chemosphere* 66: 1217–1225.

Ralston, N.V., J.L. Blackwell, and L.J. Raymond. 2007. Importance of molar ratios in selenium-dependent protection against methylmercury toxicity. *Biological Trace Element Research* 119: 255–68.

Relyea, R.A. and N. Mills. 2001. Predator-induced stress makes the pesticide carbaryl more deadly to gray treefrog tadpoles (*Hyla versicolor*). *Proceedings of the National Academy of Sciences*, 98: 2491–2496.

Rocco, G.L., and R.P. Brooks. 2000. Abundance and distribution of a stream plethodontid salamander assemblage in 14 ecologically dissimilar watersheds in the Pennsylvania Central Appalachians. Final Report. Report No. 2000-4. Penn State Cooperative Wetlands Center, Forest Resources Laboratory, Pennsylvania State University.

Rumbold, D.G., L.E. Fink, K.A. Laine, S.L. Niemczyk, T. Chandrasekhar, S.D. Wankel, and C. Kendall. 2002. Levels of mercury in Alligators (*Alligator mississippiensis*) collected along a transect through the Florida Everglades. *Science of the Total Environment* 297: 239–252.

Sandheinrich, M.B., and K.M. Miller. 2006. Effects of dietary methylmercury on reproductive behavior of fathead minnows (*Pimephales promelas*). *Environmental Toxicology and Chemistry* 25: 3053–3057.

Scheuhammer, A.M. 1987. The chronic toxicity of aluminum, cadmium, mercury, and lead in birds: a review. *Environmental Pollution* 46: 263–295.

Scheuhammer, A.M., A.H.K. Wong, and D.E. Bond. 1998. Mercury and selenium accumulation in common loons (*Gavia immer*) and common mergansers (*Mergus merganser*) from eastern Canada. *Environmental Toxicology and Chemistry* 17: 197–201.

Scheuhammer, A.M., J.A. Perrault, and D.E. Bond. 2001. Mercury, methylmercury, and selenium concentrations in eggs of common loons (*Gavia immer*) from Canada. *Environmental Monitoring and Assessment* 72: 79–94.

Scheuhammer, A.M., M.W. Meyer, M.B. Sandheinrich, and M.W. Murray. 2007. Effects of environmental methylmercury on the health of wild birds, mammals, and fish. *Ambio* 36: 12–19.

Scheuhammer, A.M., N. Basu, N.M. Burgess, J.E. Elliott, G.D. Campbell, M. Wayland, L. Champoux, and J. Rodrigue. 2008. Relationships among mercury, selenium, and neurochemical parameters in common loons (*Gavia immer*) and bald eagles (*Haliaeetus leucocephalus*). *Ecotoxicology* 17: 93–101.

Schnieder, L., L. Belger, J. Burger, R.C. Vogt, and C.R. Ferrara. 2010. Mercury levels in muscle of six species of turtles eaten by people along the Rio Negro of the Amazon Basin. *Archives of Environmental Contamination and Toxicology* 58: 444–450.

Schnieder, L., L. Belger, J. Burger, and R.C. Vogt. 2009. Mercury bioaccumulation in four tissues of *Podocnemis erythrocephala* (Podocnemididae: Testudines) as a function of water parameters. *Science of the Total Environment* 407: 1048–1054.

Schwarzbach, S.E., J.D. Albertson, and C.M. Thomas. 2006. Effects of predation, flooding, and contamination on reproductive success of California clapper rails (*Rallus longirostris obsoletus*) in San Francisco Bay. *Auk* 123: 45–60.

Schwindt, A.R., J.W. Fournie, D.H. Landers, C.B. Schreck, and M.L. Kent. 2008. Mercury concentrations in salmonids from western U.S. national parks and relationships with age and macrophage aggregates. *Environmental Science and Technology* 42: 1365–1370.

Semlitsch, R.D. 2003. *Amphibian conservation*. Smithsonian Institution Press, Washington, D.C., 336 pp.

Simpson, P.G., T.E. Hopkins, and R. Haque. 1973. Binding of methylmercury chloride to the model peptide, N-Acetyl-L-cysteine: a proton magnetic study. *Journal of Physical Chemistry* 77: 2282–2285.

Smith, T.G., and F.A.J. Armstrong. 1978. Mercury and selenium in ringed and bearded seal tissues from Arctic Canada. *Arctic* 31: 75–84.

Southerland, M.T., R.E. Jung, D.P. Baxter, I.C. Chellmann, G. Mercurio, J.H. Volstad. 2004. Stream salamanders as indicators of stream quality in Maryland, USA. *Applied Herpetology* 2: 23–46.

Sparling, D.W., G.L. Linder, C.A. Bishop, and S. Krest. 2010. *Ecotoxicology of amphibians and reptiles*, 2nd ed. CRC Press. Boca Raton, FL.

Stafford, D.P., F.W. Platt Jr., and R.R. Fleet. 1976. Snakes as indicators of environmental contamination: relation of detoxifying enzymes and pesticide residues to species occurrence in three aquatic ecosystems. *Archives of Environmental Contamination and Toxicology* 15: 15–27.

Sumino, R., R. Yamamoto, and S. Kitamura. 1977. A role of selenium against methylmercury toxicity. *Nature* 268: 73–74.

Tan, S.W., J.C. Meiler, and K.R. Mahaffey. 2009. The endocrine effects of mercury in humans and wildlife. *Critical Reviews in Toxicology* 39: 228–269.

Tejning, S. 1967. Biological effects of methyl mercury dicyandiamide-treated grain in the domestic fowl. *Gallus gallus L. Oikos (Suppl 8)*.

Terhivuo, J., M. Ldenius, P. Nuorteva, and E. Tulisalo. 1984. Mercury content of common frogs (*Rana temporaria* L.) and common toads (*Bufo bufo* L.) collected in southern Finland. *Annales Zoologici Fennici* 21: 41–44.

Thompson, D.R. 1996. Mercury in birds and terrestrial mammals. In: W.N. Beyer, G.H. Heinz, and A.W. Redmond-Norwood (Eds.), *Environmental contaminants in wildlife: interpreting tissue concentrations.* Lewis, Boca Raton, FL, pp 341–356.

Thompson, D.R., and R.W. Furness. 1989. The form of mercury stored in south Atlantic seabirds. *Environmental Pollution* 60: 305–317.

Ugarte, C.A., K.G. Rice, and M.A. Donnelly. 2005. Variation of total mercury concentrations in pig frogs (Rana grylio) across the Florida Everglades, USA. *Science of the Total Environment* 345: 51–59.

Unrine, J.M., C.H. Jagoe, A.C. Brinton, H.A. Brant, and N.T. Garvin. 2005. Dietary mercury exposure and bioaccumulation in amphibian larvae inhabiting Carolina bay wetlands. *Environmental Pollution* 135: 245–253.

Unrine, J.M., and C.H. Jagoe. 2004. Dietary mercury exposure and bioaccumulation in southern leopard frog (*Rana sphenocephala*) larvae. *Environmental Toxicology and Chemistry* 23: 2956–2963.

Unrine, J.M., C.H. Jagoe, W.A. Hopkins, and H.A. Brant. 2004. Adverse effects of ecologically relevant dietary mercury exposure in southern leopard frog (*Rana sphenocephala*) larvae. *Environmental Toxicology and Chemistry* 23: 2964–2970.

USEPA. 1997. *Mercury study report to Congress. Vol. VII: Characterization of human health and wildlife risks from mercury exposure in the United States.* Washington DC: Office of Research and Development.

Valavanidis, A., T. Vlahogianni, M. Dassenakis, and M. Scoullos. 2006. Molecular biomarkers of oxidative stress in aquatic organisms in relation to toxic environmental pollutants. *Ecotoxicology and Environmental Safety* 64: 178–189.

Wada, H., D.A. Cristol, F.M.A. McNabb, and W.A. Hopkins. 2009. Suppressed adrenocortical responses and triiodothyronine levels in tree swallow (*Tachycineta bicolor*) nestlings near a Hg-contaminated river. *Environmental Science and Technology* 43: 6031–6038.

Webb, M.A.H., G.W. Feist, M.S. Fitzpatrick, E.P. Foster, C.B. Schreck, M. Plumlee, C. Wong, and D.T. Gundersen. 2006. Mercury concentrations in gonad, liver, and muscle of white sturgeon *Acipenser transmontanus* in the lower Columbia River. *Archives of Environmental Contamination and Toxicology* 50: 443–451.

Welsh, H. H., Jr., and L.M. Ollivier. 1998. Stream amphibians as indicators of ecosystem stress: a case study from California's redwoods. *Ecological Applications* 8: 1118–1132.

Wess, J. 2004. Muscarinic acetylcholine receptor knockout mice: novel phenotypes and clinical implications. *Annual Reviews of Pharmacology and Toxicology* 44: 423–450.

Wiemeyer, S.N., T.G. Lamont, C.M. Bunck, C.R. Sindelar, F.J. Gramlich, J.D. Frazer, and M.A. Byrd. 1984. Organochlorine pesticide, polychlorobiphenyl, and mercury residues in bald eagle eggs (1969-79) and their relationships to shell thinning and reproduction. *Archives of Environmental Contamination and Toxicology* 13: 529–549.

Wiemeyer, S.N., J.F. Miesner, P.L. Tuttle, E.C. Murphy, L. Sileo, and D. Withers. 2007. Mercury and selenium in American white pelicans breeding at Pyramid Lake, Nevada. *Waterbirds* 30: 284–295.

Wiener, J.G., and D.J. Spry. 1996. Toxicological significance of mercury in freshwater fish. In: W.N. Beyer, G.H. Heinz, and A.W. Redmon-Norwood (Eds.), *Environmental contaminants in wildlife: interpreting tissue concentrations,* CRC Press, Boca Raton, FL, pp. 297–339.

Wiener, J.G., D.P. Krabbenhoft, G.H. Heinz, and A.M. Scheuhammer. 2003. Ecotoxicology of mercury. In: D.J. Hoffman, B.A. Rattner, G.A. Burton, and J. Cairns, eds. *Handbook of ecotoxicology,* 2nd ed. CRC Press, Boca Raton, FL, pp. 409–463.

Wobeser, G., N.O. Nielsen, and B. Schiefer. 1976. Mercury and mink. II. Experimental methyl mercury intoxication. *Canadian Journal of Comparative Medicine* 40: 34–45.

Wobeser, G., and M. Swift. 1976. Mercury poisoning in a wild mink. *Journal of Wildlife Diseases* 12: 335–340.

Wolfe, M.F., S. Schwarzbach, and R.A. Sulaiman. 1998. The effects of mercury on wildlife: a comprehensive review. *Environmental Toxicology and Chemistry* 17: 146–160.

Wolfe, M.F., T. Atkeson, W. Bowerman, J. Burger, D.C. Evers, M.W. Murray, and E. Zillioux. 2007. Wildlife indicators. In: R. Harris, D.P. Krabbenhoft, R. Mason, M.W. Murray, R. Reash and T. Saltman (Eds.), *Ecosystem response to mercury contamination: indicators of change,* CRC Press, Webster, NY, pp. 123–189.

Wolke, R.E. 1992. Piscine macrophage aggregates: a review. *Annual Review of Fish Diseases* 2: 91–108.

Wren, C.D. 1985. Probable case of mercury poisoning in a wild otter, *Lutra canadensis,* in northwestern Ontario. *Canadian Field Naturalist* 99: 112–114.

Wren, C.D., D.B. Hunter, J.F. Leatherland, and P.M. Stokes. 1987. The effects of polychlorinated biphenyls and methylmercury, single and in combination, on mink. I: Uptake and toxic responses. *Archives of Environmental Contamination and Toxicology* 16: 441–447.

Yanochko, G.M., C.H. Jagoe, and I.L. Brisbin Jr. 1997. Tissue mercury concentrations in Alligators (*Alligator mississippiensis*) from the Florida Everglades and the Savannah River site, South Carolina. *Archives of Environmental Contamination and Toxicology* 32: 323–328.

Yorio, T., and P.J. Bentley. 1973. The effects of methylmercury compounds on the skin (in vitro) of the leopard frog (*Rana pipiens*). *Comparative and General Pharmacology* 4: 167–174.

Xu, Q., S. Fang, and Z. Wang. 2006. Heavy metal distribution in tissues and eggs of Chinese Alligator (Alligator sinensis). *Archives of Environmental Contamination and Toxicology* 50: 580–586.

CHAPTER 12

Risk Evaluation of Mercury Pollution

JOANNA BURGER and MICHAEL GOCHFELD

Increasingly the public, governmental agencies, and public policy makers, as well as health professionals and ecologists, want to understand the risks that derive from mercury in the environment. The risks are to individuals of a species, including humans, and to populations, communities, and ecosystems. The risks can be sublethal as well as lethal, resulting in altered behavior, impaired reproductive success and/or lower survival, and eventually decreases in populations. Toxic effects can be at the biochemical, cellular, or organ level. High levels of methylmercury in individual organisms can lead both to detrimental effects on the individuals themselves, and also to other organisms that consume them, such as birds and mammals (including humans) that are higher on the food chain (WHO, 2007). Many people are familiar with fish consumption as the most common route of exposure for methylmercury (Rice et al., 2000; Gochfeld and Burger, 2005; Mahaffey et al., 2009; chapters 13 and 14), but this is not the only issue of concern for mercury contamination, nor is it the only route of exposure for people or ecoreceptors. (An ecoreceptor is any species [microbial, plant, or animal] in an ecosystem, and usually excludes humans.) There is an abundance of information on mercury hazards and risks, including extensive summaries by the United States Environmental Protection Agency (USEPA, 1997), the Agency for Toxic Substances and Disease Registry (ATSDR, 1999), and the New Jersey Mercury Task Force (NJDEP, 2001). The EPA's Integrated Risk Information System (USEPA, 1995, 2001a) provides an extensive review as background for developing its Reference Dose for methylmercury and other mercury species.

In this chapter, we describe the methods that are available for assessing the levels and effects of contaminants on humans and ecoreceptors, including both risk evaluations and formal risk assessment, relate these methods to mercury pollution and risk, provide examples of such evaluations, and discuss future research and information needs. Information needs, however, partly depend on changing stakeholder interests and concerns (Rowe and Frewer, 2000; Greenberg et al., 2005; Burger, 2007; USEPA, 2009a; Burger et al., 2010). Our intent is to provide the information needed to understand how to evaluate risk (or potential harm) from mercury to humans and ecoreceptors, to provide the basis for understanding and evaluating possible management options (including cleanup levels), and for making public policy issues.

Risk evaluations are necessary to determine potential damage to humans and ecosystems, and their associated species, to provide early warning of potential harm, and to allow managers, regulators, public policy makers, and the public to respond quickly and decisively (Gochfeld and Burger, 2007). Risk evaluation is the process that governmental agencies use to gain understanding of the degree of injury or harm that may result from human activities, particularly pollutants (Ruckelshaus, 1985). In this chapter, we make a distinction between risk evaluation (all methods of evaluating any potential risk from a hazard) and risk assessment (a structured, formal approach). Risk assessment is a formal, quantitative process that crosses many disciplines, from bridge construction to toxicology and food safety. Thus, risk assessment is a type of risk evaluation. Today, risk evaluations are also being used to assess siting of new energy facilities and the potential threat of genetically engineered products and plants, as well as terrorist threats (Burger, 2007; Williams and Magsumbol, 2007). Risk evaluations are intended to provide objective, at least semiquantitative information useful for public-policy decisions (Burger et al., 2001a), and they are often used to facilitate individual decisions as well (i.e. whether or not to engage in a particular activity, such as skydiving, riding a motorcycle, or eating fish).

Although mercury enters the environment from both natural and anthropogenic (human-generated sources; this book, chapter 3), it is the anthropogenic sources that are of greatest concern because of both historic and recent changes and the increasing demand for electric power generation, which releases mercury to the atmosphere, resulting in both local and regional pollution through atmospheric transport and deposition. Anthropogenic activities account for up to 80% of the annual emission to the environment (Sunderland et al., 2008), varying by time and place, as well as method. For many areas of the world, atmospheric deposition, both regional and global, is the primary source of mercury in terrestrial and aquatic systems (Fitzgerald and Mason, 1996; Driscoll et al., 2006; Selin et al., 2010). The global release of mercury to the atmosphere is unevenly distributed, and largely related to coal combustion. The Asian countries contribute about 54% of the mercury to total atmospheric sources. China

alone contributes 28% to the total emissions, followed by Africa (18%), and Europe (11%) (Pacyna et al., 2006).

Mercury is a persistent toxicant that bio-accumulates (Nichols, 2001), making it critical to understand the risk it poses to humans and the environment. Armed with knowledge, managers and regulators can lower mercury emissions to a level that reduces adverse effects on individuals and populations. For example, in the Everglades of south Florida, knowledge of the high levels of mercury in predatory fish led to enacting controls on emissions by local power plants and other industries, which ultimately led to a drastic reduction in the levels in the fish eaten by birds and mammals, including people (Davis and Ogden, 1994; Lange et al., 1994; SFWMD, 2007), although levels remain high in some species (SFWMD, 2010).

Risk Evaluations Versus Formal Risk Assessment

Risk Evaluation

Many disciplines have examined the risks of chemical, physical, or biologic stressors to human and nonhuman populations and the environment. These studies are done by health professionals, ecologists, wildlife and land managers, toxicologists, and, more recently, restoration ecologists and ecologic engineers. Risk evaluations assess the potential risk to target organisms (including humans) or systems from chemical, physical or other environmental stressors (hazards). Even before the formal risk assessment paradigm was widely applied (National Research Council [NRC], 1983), scientists, health professionals, and managers were examining the effects of chemicals and other stressors on individuals. The risk methods and assumptions varied among and even within agencies and others examining harm to humans and the environment. Therefore, it was difficult to assess general health and well-being over time and space, to evaluate competing risks (past, present, and future), and to evaluate risks from different stressors (e.g. mercury vs. lead, eating fish vs. eating red meat, pollutants vs. development). The lack of consistency among methods led to confusion not only on the part of managers and decision makers, but also for the public. This lack of clarity created a need for a formal risk-assessment paradigm that could be applied uniformly, regardless of the nature of the stressor or the target organisms. In a time of competing needs for money, time, and other resources, formal risk-assessment paradigms can provide agencies, managers, public policy makers, and the public with a framework for evaluating risks, and prioritizing them for funding and action.

Formal Risk Assessment

For decades, agencies and organizations conducted risk evaluations using different methods. Evaluating the effect of chemicals on humans became particularly critical because

TABLE 12.1
Terms Used in National Research Council's (1983, 1993) Formal Human Health Risk Assessment (HRA),
as Well as Other Risk Evaluation Paradigms

NRC's risk assessment paradigm for humans
Hazard identification: Specification of the hazards (or stressors) that potentially can cause adverse effects).
Dose–response assessment: Establishing a relationship (through laboratory, field, or epidemiologic studies) between dose and the magnitude of adverse effects.
Exposure assessment: Assessing the contaminant levels in various media and biota, including in target organs, as well as pathways from contaminants to target species (and organs).
Risk characterization: Estimating the probability of an adverse outcome, or the threshold below which the probability of an adverse outcome is negligible.

Additional terms used for both human and ecologic risk assessment to broaden it to include stakeholders and public policy
Data acquisition, verification, and monitoring: Collecting field data on either contaminant levels or exposures, verifying the accuracy of the data, and monitoring (media or biota) to determine the potential for continued risk.
Problem-formulation (or scoping): Defining the problem that requires examining the potential risk to humans and the environment (including specific ecoreceptors or ecosystem processes.
Risk management: Discussion between risk assessors, risk managers, and scientists (health professionals, ecologists) about how to reduce or manage the potential risk to humans or the environment.
Stakeholder identification: Identifying the interested and affected parties (includes government agencies, nongovernmental organizations, and the interested public).

NOTE: Also see Burger and Gochfeld (1997b), and Gochfeld and Burger (2007). These methods are used for assessing risk for any stressor, including mercury pollution.

of the need for evaluating the effects of new chemicals, especially beginning in the 1960s. Agencies and companies used various methods. However, in, 1983, the National Research Council (NRC, 1983, 1993) formalized the human health risk assessment (HRA) paradigm to include four parts: hazard identification, dose–response assessment, exposure assessment, and risk characterization (Table 12.1, Figure 12.1). HRA has also been called "environmental risk assessment," but the term *human risk assessment* is more useful to distinguish it from *ecological risk assessment* (ERA).

Hazard identification is identifying any agent (or condition) that has the potential to cause harm (Rasmussen, 1981). This includes determining whether a substance is a carcinogen. Dose–response assessment evaluates the toxicologic (and in some cases, epidemiologic or pharmacologic) literature to estimate the parameters of the dose–response curve, including a threshold (if any can be determined). It examines the relationship between the amount of the chemical and the response. Exposure assessment is determining the pathways and routes of exposure and estimating dose, both to the receptor (plants, animals, or humans) and to target organs (liver, kidney, muscle). Finally, risk characterization combines the results of the dose–response and exposure assessment to assign probabilities for certain outcomes to certain doses, or to determine a "safe" level below which no harm is anticipated.

Most risk assessments are deterministic, and consider one point in time when examining exposure and toxicity inputs, but more recently probabilistic risk assessment has moved to the fore. Probabilistic risk assessments use probability distributions of toxicity and exposure variables and can consider several points in time and an array of exposure scenarios to provide more realistic exposure estimates. These often use Monte Carlo simulations in combination with various shaped distributions (e.g. normal, log-normal, triangular). Probabilistic risk assessment is designed to capture the distribution or range of exposures and environmental conditions, and can be used for both HRA and ERA (Constantinou et al., 1995; Barron et al., 2004; Tran et al., 2004; Rumbold, 2005; Brain et al., 2006; USEPA 2010). Distributions, rather than point values, can also be useful for identifying benchmark levels, allowing the user to select a tissue concentration that is associated with the protection of a specific percentage of organisms (Steevens et al., 2005). Probabilistic assessments can be used for determining mercury dose from a range of samples (Stern, 2005) and for determining environmental dynamics and regional mercury cycles as well. This approach encompasses the variability in environmental characteristics, as well as dose-related variables (Seigneur et al., 2006).

HRA thus involves identifying hazardous agents (such as mercury), establishing the effects of the hazardous agent

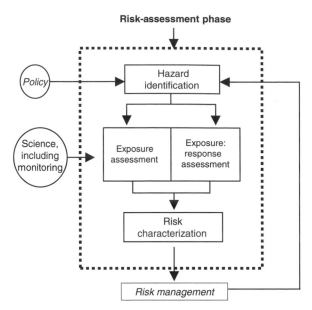

Risk-assessment phase

FIGURE 12.1 The National Research Council's modified model of Human Risk Assessment to include both human health and ecosystems. (*Source:* Adapted from NRC, 1983, 1993.)

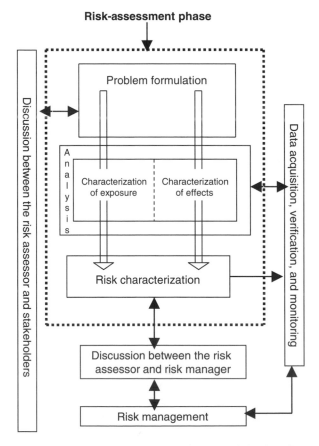

Risk-assessment phase

FIGURE 12.2 The Environmental Protection Agency's (EPA) ecologic risk evaluation model. (*Source:* Adapted from Norton et al., 1992.)

(from epidemiologic or laboratory studies), establishing the relationship between levels and effects (dose–response), establishing how people are exposed (pathways and routes), and identifying the target or at-risk populations. All of

these apply as well to individual species in an ecosystem, but even the simplest ecosystem has several species. The NRC's risk publications for HRA (1983, 1993) were followed by three major modifications: (1) the adaptation and modification of the HRA to fit the needs of different agencies, (2) the adaptation of the risk-assessment paradigm to ecoreceptors and ecosystems, and (3) the inclusion of stakeholders and public policy (NRC, 1986, 2009; Norton et al., 1992; Bachman et al., 1998).

ERA evolved from the convergence of human health risk assessment, ecology, and ecotoxicology to provide data for environmental management, decision makers, and the public. Generally, ERA estimates the effects of stressors (e.g. chemical, biologic, physical) on ecologic end points to support decision making (Barnthouse, 1994; Suter, 2001). ERA is inherently more difficult than HRA because of the complexity of ecosystems. HRA evaluates the risk to humans, while ERA must consider the potential risk to every population or species in an ecosystem, which can range from hundreds to thousands (if one considers microbes). An ecosystem is a spatial entity consisting of abiotic (e.g. air, soil, sediment, water) and biotic (e.g. bacteria, fungi, plants, animals) components through which energy flows, nutrients move, and matter is cycled (Odum, 1957; Payne, 1966; Sheehan, 1984; Wilson, 1986; Hunsaker et al. 1990). Ecosystems involve complex food webs through which contaminants can move. Further, ecosystems have both structure (e.g. species and populations, different levels and types of vegetation) and function (e.g. energy flow, nutrient flow), and these aspects must also be evaluated. Evaluating the risks to ecosystems from contaminants such as mercury is monumental, and it requires the careful selection of indicators and measurement end points assessment endpoints.

One key feature of the NRC (1983, 1993) HRA paradigm was the separation of the public, public policy, and cost considerations from the risk-assessment process, which was meant to be pure science. Excluding stakeholders often led to skepticism and rejection of risk estimates. This failure to include a range of stakeholders in the risk-assessment process was emphasized by the Presidential/Congressional Commission on Risk Assessment and Risk Management (PCCRARM, 1997), and led to myriad risk-assessment approaches tailored to fit the needs of particular agencies, many of which dealt with the problem of mercury in the environment (USDOI, 1986; USEPA, 1986; Bascietto et al., 1990; NRC, 1994, 2009; USACOE, 1996; USEPA, 1997; Washburn et al., 1998; Burger and Gochfeld, 1997a) (Figures 12.2 to 12.4). The PCCRARM (1997) report encouraged managing risks in a broader context, using an iterative approach rather than merely a formalized risk assessment paradigm (Figure 12.5). Thus, the NRC (1983, 1993) paradigm was adapted and modified to fit the particular environmental concerns of each agency. In the NRC (1983) formulation, risk assessment was isolated from risk management so that stakeholder and cost–benefit concerns were not superimposed on the "pure science" of

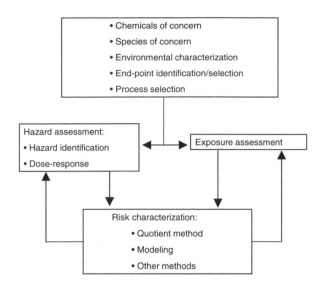

FIGURE 12.3 Toxic Substance Control Act view of ecologic risk assessment. (*Source:* Adapted from Zeeman and Gilford, 1993.)

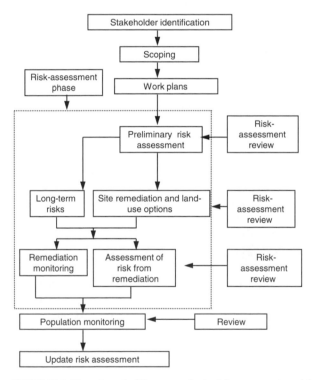

FIGURE 12.4 Department of Energy ecologic risk assessment model, with stakeholder participation. (*Source:* Adapted from NRC, 1994.)

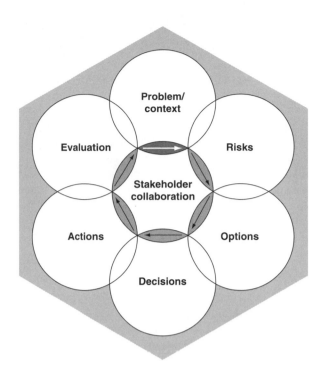

FIGURE 12.5 President/Congressional Commission on Risk Assessment and Management approach that includes stakeholders. (*Source:* President/Congressional Commission on Risk Assessment and Risk Management [PCCRARM], 1997).

1992; Zeeman and Gilford, 1993). The risk-evaluation process changed to include risk assessment and risk management, making it more responsive to the needs of the public, regulators, and public policy makers. Still, it is important to clearly distinguish between the roles of science and policy; science plays the key role in risk assessment and evaluations, but not in risk management and public policy (Power and McCarty, 1997).

Commonalities of Different Risk-Evaluation Methods

Regardless of whether the risks to humans and ecoreceptors are examined using formal risk-assessment paradigms, or less formal evaluation methods, there are some common steps. These include problem formulation, hazard assessment, exposure assessment, and relating exposure levels to potential harm for either humans or ecoreceptors (see Table 12.1). HRAs are generally divided into cancer and noncancer risk assessments. The former is generally accomplished by fitting toxicologic data (usually from rodents) on tumor numbers at various doses to a linearized multistage model, which allows a back extrapolation to the dose that would produce a particular level of excess cancer mortality, usually a 10^{-4}, 10^{-5} or 10^{-6} risk. The EPA has published cancer slope values (increase in cancer rate per unit increase in dose) for many chemicals in its Integrated Risk Information System (USEPA, 2009b).

However, although some studies implicate mercury as a carcinogen, there is currently no definitive evidence regarding the carcinogenicity of mercury. The EPA considers it

risk estimate. By the mid-1990s, the importance of stakeholder involvement gained acceptance and risk assessment became integrated as part of an overall risk management process (PCCRARM, 1997; NRC, 2009).

In nearly all cases, a wide range of stakeholders is involved at several different points in the risk-assessment and risk-management phases, but particularly at the beginning during the problem-formulation phase (Norton et al.,

Class D, "not classifiable" (USEPA, 2001a). All further discussion will focus on approaches for applying noncancer risk estimates to the management of environmental mercury. Methylmercury is classified as class C (USEPA, 1995). This follows the general form of establishing a denominator value, either a reference dose (RfD from the EPA), a minimal risk level (MRL from the ATSDR), an allowable daily intake (ADI from the Food and Drug Administration [FDA]), or a provisional tolerable daily or weekly intake (PTDI or PTWI from the World Health Organization (WHO) (FAO [Food and Agriculture Organization]/WHO, 2003). If the daily exposure is lower than the denominator value, the hazard quotient (HQ) is less than 1. If the HQ exceeds 1, then exposure is considered excessive.

PROBLEM FORMULATION

The problem-formulation stage for risk evaluation is critical because it determines the scope and extent of the problem in terms of the pollutants of concern (or mixtures of contaminants), species of concern, and habitats of concern. Considerable care is required for this phase, and it is at this stage that the widest range of stakeholders should be involved (PCCRARM, 1997). Further, stakeholders should and can be included in other stages of the risk assessment, especially if further data are required to evaluate pathways and levels of exposure (Burger et al., 2007a,b).

HAZARD ASSESSMENT AND SOURCES

One of the key features of risk assessment is the determination of the hazard and, where possible, the sources. A hazard can be defined as a pollutant or activity that has a disruptive effect on defined end points (e.g. extinction of an endangered species, declines of populations, lowering of reproductive success or survival). Obtaining data on contaminant levels in air, water, soil, and sediment is critical to this process, and is referred to as "defining the source term." The source of mercury is usually either point-source pollution (e.g. a chemical plant) or atmospheric deposition, which can be regional or global.

EXPOSURE ASSESSMENT

Exposure assessment is critical for both HRAs and ERAs because it is during this phase that the routes and pathways of exposure and actual exposure of target species (or target organs) is established. Formal risk assessments require information on all of these aspects, while other methods of risk evaluation may require only some of this information. For example, knowing the levels of a contaminant in fish allows health professionals to evaluate the possible risk to humans from consuming known quantities of fish.

Contaminants such as mercury can be at a steady state (no new increase in tissues regardless of exposure) or may bio-accumulate (accumulate over time in tissues). Bio-accumulation results in bio-amplification at each step in a food chain. In aquatic organisms, bio-accumulation is typically expressed using a ratio of chemical concentration in the organism's tissue (often whole body) relative to chemical exposure concentrations in water or food organisms. These bio-accumulation factors are highly variable among organisms, and they usually vary inversely with exposure concentration in the medium (DeForest et al., 2007).

In addition to directly examining levels of contaminants such as mercury in organisms and their tissues, scientists can use other organisms as bioindicators or they can place sentinels (or surrogate species) in the contaminated environment and periodically measure contamination or effect (Van der Schalie et al., 1999). In the former case, risk evaluators use organisms at the same trophic level to assess exposure; top-level predatory fish, birds, or mammals might indicate the potential exposure of people to the same fish (see below). In the latter case, other species are placed in the environment to assess effects. For example, in urban environments cats can be used as sentinels of exposure or effects of contaminants, and in mines canaries were placed to assess the presence of toxic gases. Earthworms of various species are often used as sentinels for soil ecotoxicity evaluation (He et al., 2006).

RISK ASSESSMENT AND ENVIRONMENTAL JUSTICE

Environmental justice is the fair treatment and meaningful involvement of all people, regardless of race, color, national origin, or income with respect to the development, implementation, and enforcement of environmental laws, regulations, and policies (USEPA, 2009a; USDOE [Department of Energy], 2009). Executive Order 12898, signed by President Clinton, states that communities should have the right to have their opinions and perceptions heard and to be part of the decision-making process on matters that affect their well-being. Federal agencies were directed to take action to address disparities leading to environmental injustice.

All phases of risk evaluation and risk assessment are mandated to take into account environmental justice communities, and the special exposures they face because of lifestyles, proximity, or other factors (Corburn, 2002). Matrices developed to capture exposures should take into account Native American, Alaskan Native, and minority and low-income populations and the special exposures they face (Donatuto and Harper, 2008; Burger et al., 2010; Burger and Gochfeld, 2011).

Relating Exposure to Possible Harm to Humans and Ecoreceptors

Once concentrations in food or organisms (whole body or tissues) are reported, the next step is to develop estimates of daily exposure that can be compared with some benchmarks, such as the RfDs, PTDIs, or MRLs for humans, the HQs (for both), or a toxicity reference value for biota. Benchmarks are numerical values used to guide risk assessors at various decision points in the risk process. Screening-level risk evaluations, used to decide whether a full risk assessment is necessary, often involve media-specific benchmarks, while

TABLE 12.2
Definitions for Human and Ecological Risk Assessment

Acceptable daily intake (ADI): The amount of a food additive that could be consumed daily for an entire life span without appreciable risk. Often determined by measuring the highest dose of the substance that has no effect on experimental animals, then dividing by a safety factor of 100. Substances that are not given an ADI are regarded as having no adverse effect at any level of intake. Set by the U.S. Food and Drug Administration Office of Food Additive Safety.

Benchmark dose: The lower confidence limit on a dose that produces an effect in some percent (10% or less) of the animals in a laboratory study.

Bioindicator: Species used as an indicator of overall exposure or effects of a stressor, such as mercury.

Biomarker: Indicators of internal dose or effect; can include alterations in enzyme activity disturbances to cell structure or function. Biomarkers are most useful when they are specific to a contaminant and quantifiable.

Biomonitoring: Periodic and regular measurement of contaminant levels in bioindicator species or of biomarkers of exposure or effects.

Ecological screening quotient (ESQ): A quotient used to assess risk in which protective assumptions are used. Generally, the numerator is the reasonable worst-case concentration at the point of exposure and the denominator is the no-adverse-effects–based toxicity reference value.

Hazard quotient (HQ): Chemical-specific HQ risk characterization is used in both HRAs and ERAs, It is a ratio of an exposure estimate to a toxicity reference value or benchmark. An HQ less than or equal to a value of 1 indicates that adverse impacts to human and ecologic receptors are considered unlikely.

Lowest observable adverse effects level (LOAEL): The lowest level tested in animals studies that resulted in an adverse effect. A threshold is presumed to exist between the NOAEL and LOAEL.

Minimal risk level (MRL): Health guidance values developed by Agency for Toxic Substances and Disease Registry (CDC-ATSDR) in its Toxicological Profiles. "An MRL is an estimate of the daily human exposure to a hazardous substance that is likely to be without appreciable risk of adverse noncancer health effects over a specified duration of exposure." Long-term MRLs assumes a lifetime exposure. "Conceptually equivalent" to the EPA RfD, the FDA ADI, and the WHO PTWI. The uncertainty values convey the impression of a margin of safety that may be real or illusory.

No observable adverse effect level (NOAEL): The highest level of a toxicant that appears to cause no adverse effect in animal studies. Whether a NOAEL is detected depends on the dosages chosen for a study.

No observable effect level (NOEL): The level of a toxicant that appears to cause no effect of any kind in animal studies; not usually used in risk assessment.

Provisional tolerable weekly intake (PTWI): Set by the United Nations Food and Agriculture Organization and World Health Organization through its, FAO/WHO Joint Expert Committee on Food Additives (JECFA).

Reference dose (RfD): The daily dose that a human can be exposed to every day (usually for a 50-year life span) without experiencing an adverse effect. Established by the Environmental Protection Agency based on cancer and noncancer end points.

Screening level: Level of a contaminant, such as mercury, that is known to produce adverse effects in humans or ecologic receptors.

Total maximum daily load (TMDL): A calculation of the maximum amount of a pollutant that a body of water can receive and still meet water-quality standards.

SOURCE: Compiled from Bartell et al., 1992; Peakall, 1992; Tardiff and Goldstein, 1992; Sorensen et al., 2004; Burger, 2006; Gochfeld and Burger, 2007.
NOTE: For additional definitions, see USEPA (2010).

higher-tier risk evaluations require receptor-specific toxicology. These values can apply specifically to humans or to a given species of animal (Clark et al., 1999; Hays et al., 2007). More specifically, a benchmark dose is the lower confidence limit on a dose that produces an effect in some percent of animal trials (Table 12.2). It thus relies on animal models for extrapolation to humans (and sometimes to other animals). It assumes that some level of illness in humans is tolerable.

Thus, benchmark doses need to incorporate some level of exposure uncertainty, which is sometimes accomplished by adding a safety factor of 10 (Gochfeld and Burger, 2007).

Several methods have been used to evaluate potential harm, including benchmark doses, no observed effect or no adverse effect levels (NOELs and NOAELs), and lowest observed adverse effect levels (LOAELs). These in turn can be used to calculate RfDs, MRLs, or ADIs used for human health guidelines to calculate HQs. NOELs, NOAELs, and LOAELs, mainly rely on animal models, whereby different doses of a chemical, such as mercury, are given to laboratory animals to determine the highest dose that produces no detectable effect of any type (NOEL) or no adverse effect (NOAEL). These are the highest nonzero (or noncontrol) dose at which there is no measurable or detectable effect. In many studies, even the lowest dose tried may produce an effect, thus there is no NOEL or NOAEL, and the lowest dose becomes the LOAEL, the lowest level at which adverse effects were detected. Although the NOAEL may be a "safe" dose, the LOAEL obviously is not. If an adverse response is related directly to dose, it is sometimes difficult to determine the dose at which the chemical is "safe". A threshold is presumed to exist between the NOAEL and the LOAEL. Thus, toxicologists use safety factors (also called uncertainty factors [UFs]) to account for uncertainties in the tests species differences, and individual susceptibilities.

Hazard Quotient Risk Characterization

One of the tools for ERA, which is used either as part of formal ERA or alone with risk management, is the chemical-specific HQ risk characterization. Chemical-specific HQ risk characterization is a ratio of an exposure estimate to a toxicity reference value or benchmark. An HQ less than a value of 1 indicates that adverse impacts to ecologic receptors are considered unlikely (USEPA, 1997, 2001b). Managers and others find HQs useful because they provide a risk number, which allows comparisons between and among sites, between and among species, and between and among chemicals. However, there are a number of uncertainties with HQs that can be masked by the apparent precision of having a number. Another difficulty with chemical-specific HQs is that they deal with species, and not with the many effects that subtle changes may produce at the population, community, and ecosystem level (Tannenbaum et al., 2003; Sorensen et al., 2004). Other methods have also been used, including compensatory restoration, performance-based ecologic monitoring, ecologic significance criteria, and net environmental benefit analysis (Sorensen et al., 2004). These methods, however, are more applicable to communities and ecosystems than to the analysis of a single chemical, such as mercury.

Screening Levels

Another, simpler, method of evaluating risk is to compare levels of contaminants in biota with field-validated risk-based screening levels. Such screening levels are the concentrations of contaminants in tissues (e.g. liver, muscle, heart, feathers, hair) that are associated with adverse effects in laboratory studies and have been found to result in similar adverse effects in wild animals (see Burger, 1997a; Burger and Gochfeld, 1997b). Developing these screening levels requires controlled laboratory experiments with a particular toxicant, such as mercury, and validation under field conditions. Such validation can include either dosing animals in the wild to achieve certain tissue levels and observing adverse effects, or observing adverse effects and collecting tissues to determine levels.

Total Maximum Daily Load

Another important determination that affects risk of a contaminant is the total maximum daily load (TMDL) that is allowed by the U.S. Clean Water Act. A TMDL is a calculation of the maximum amount of a pollutant that a body of water can receive and still meet water-quality standards. The USEPA has set water quality criteria based on methylmercury concentrations in fish at 0.3 µg/g (0.3 ppm; USEPA, 2001c), which has been adopted as a mercury freshwater quality standard of 0.3 ppm methylmercury in fish for most states. This was set to recognize the important fact that levels of mercury in water do not relate directly to the levels of mercury in fish. And, it is the levels of mercury in fish that are the important end point in terms of mercury risk. Some states have more stringent standards. Maine and Minnesota have water-quality standards of 0.2 µg/g. When fish mercury levels exceed the water-quality standard, the Clean Water Act requires the calculation of how much mercury loading must be reduced.

Risk Evaluations and Mercury

The general risk-evaluation methods discussed above are used to evaluate the potential risk from mercury to humans and ecosystems, including their component species, populations, and communities. Before addressing specific risk-evaluation methods for mercury, there are two differences between HRA and ERA that impact risk evaluations with mercury: (1) HRA focuses on the health of individual people, while ERA focuses on the health of populations (except in the case of endangered species), and (2) HRA mainly focuses on chemical toxicity and exposure, while ERA also focuses on the ecologic characteristics of a site. The focus on chemical toxicity resulted from emphasis on the Resource Conservation and Recovery Act (RCRA) and the Comprehensive Environmental Response, Compensation, and Liability Act (CERCLA) and other environmental protection laws that require chemical measurement of site conditions and not ecologic conditions, and was a function of focusing on humans (Sorensen et al., 2004). These two differences affect how we evaluate the risk from mercury because it creates a dichotomy between how risk is evaluated for humans and ecosystems. Many people have advocated that this barrier can partially be removed by selecting indicators that can be used to assess both human and ecologic health (DiGuillio and Monosson, 1996; Burger and Gochfeld, 2001, 2004a; Suter et al., 2003). Further, the ecologic risk caused by remediation to protect human health is a concern, since sometimes soil removal or other physically disruptive activities destroy functioning ecosystems with very little improvement in human health (Burger, 1999, 2007).

Assessment End Points and Measurement End Points

For most risk evaluations or assessments for mercury, the quality that stakeholders wish to understand cannot be easily measured. That is, managers, regulators, public policy makers and the public may be interested in whether the quality of a particular ecosystem is increasing or decreasing and whether mercury is contributing to the decline of the ecosystem or the populations within these ecosystem (the assessment end points). Overall ecosystem health, however, cannot be easily measured. Instead, we define measurement end points, which provide information about the overall assessment end points. Assessment end points are the valued properties of the environment (or of individual species) that are susceptible to the stressors of concern, such as mercury. It is the measurement end point (or metric) that can be quantified over some temporal and spatial scale and that can be used by managers and public policy makers. Measurement end points usually involve indicator species (Burger and Gochfeld, 2001; Suter, 2001). For example, one might measure mercury concentrations in the muscle of bass (*Micropterus salmoides*). In this case, bass are the indicators and mercury concentration in muscle is the measurement end point. Managers then use the measurement end point as an indication of the overall health of bass populations. Ecologists can use this measurement end point as an indicator of possible harm to organisms higher on the food chain that consume the bass (such as egrets [*Egretta* species], alligators [*Alligator mississippiensis*], and panthers [*Puma concolor*]), and human health professionals can use the same measurement end point as an indicator of potential risk to human consumers of this fish (see Bioindicators).

Mercury, Methylmercury, and Their Effects

For mercury, the risk from elemental, inorganic (mainly divalent mercuric compounds), and organic (methylmercury) forms needs to be considered separately (Schoeny, 1996). For biota, including humans, ingestion of methylmercury provides the greatest risk. Inorganic mercury poses a problem mainly for workers. Elemental mercury poses a problem through both occupational and community/residential inhalation exposure near gold mines and mercury-processing plants, as well as spills from mercury-containing instruments and devices (Hylander et al., 1994; USEPA, 1997; ATSDR, 1999; Ehrlich, 2001; NJDEP, 2001;

Eisler, 2003; Loredo et al., 2003; Mueezzinoglu, 2003; Goldblum et al., 2006). In some artisinal gold mining areas, elemental mercury is mixed with gravel to amalgamate gold dust. This is followed by heating the resultant pellets to drive off the gaseous mercury, leaving behind gold. This heated elemental mercury can pose a significant direct human health risk, including from mercury vapor (Beate et al., 2010). This occurs during both the initial handling of the mercury and the heating of the amalgam pellets. Much of this gold extraction involves alluvial deposits in streams and rivers. Some of the mercury that escapes from this process reaches the aquatic sediments, where it becomes biomethylated, which renders it accessible for bio-amplification up the food chain as methylmercury (Marins et al., 2000; Castilhos et al., 2006; Swain et al., 2007; Paruchuri et al., 2010). Incomplete information regarding the various chemical forms of mercury exposure, and the need to target the information provided to gold mining and subsistence communities, prevents the development of consistent public health policies (Dorea, 2010). Exposure to elemental mercury can also occur during building demolition from mercury-bearing fluorescent and high-intensity discharge lamps (Sheridan et al., 2000), from dental fillings (Fung and Molvar, 1992), and from cultural practices (Wendroff, 1995; Riley et al., 2001).

Methylmercury affects neurobehavioral development, and causes deficits in cognitive function, as well as nephrologic, immunologic, cardiac, motor, reproductive, and even genetic effects (ATSDR, 1999; NRC, 2000a). However, the analytical procedures for measuring methylmercury are more costly and complex than the analysis of total mercury, hence total mercury is usually measured. Thus, it has been necessary to develop conversion factors for fish. On average, across a variety of fish species and studies, about 90% of the mercury in edible fish muscle is methylmercury (Bloom, 1991; Lansens et al. 1991; Jewett et al. 2003). Such conversion factors, which require testing in different kinds of fish and under different conditions, allow laboratories to measure total mercury as a surrogate for methylmercury. However, some agencies simply assume that all the measured mercury is methylmercury (JECFA, 2006).

Acceptable Risk for Mercury

Ultimately, the question facing health professionals, ecologists, regulators, and the general public is: What risk from mercury is acceptable? It is a common goal of both HRA and ERA to identify whether a particular exposure scenario or toxicant level will lead to unacceptably high consequences, but whether this risk is "acceptable" to society. This is clearly a public policy, not at scientific, decision. The decision about acceptability is fraught with difficulties, since even within humans there is great variation is what risks are considered acceptable. Some people may accept the risks of riding motorcycles, bungee-jumping, and skydiving, while others may find them unacceptable. Similarly, some people may consider the risks of eating fish with mercury levels of 0.5 ppm

TABLE 12.3
Exposure Matrix for Mercury Compounds for Humans

Exposure route	Air	Water	Soil	Food	Products and processes
Inhalation	Elemental mercury	Some mercury volatilizes in showers	Fine, respirable dusts		Mercury mining, gold mining, battery reclamation, dental amalgams, instrument manufacture and breakage, cultural practices, and emissions from incinerators and coal-fired power plants
Ingestion		Drinking water	Eating soil (toddlers)	Eating fish high in methylmercury	Recreational and commercial fish
Dermal					Dimethylmercury in laboratory
Injection					Thimerosal in vaccines: cultural practices

NOTE: Mercury can be present in environmental media: air, water, soil, and food. **Airborne mercury** deposits on land and water surfaces. **Mercury on land** can wash into waterways. **Mercury in water bodies** can become biomethylated by bacteria in sediment. Mercury can **bio-accumulate and bio-amplify** in the aquatic food chain. **Inhalation** of airborne mercury is a significant route for elemental mercury in both workplaces and residences. **Ingestion of mercury from soil** is a pathway mainly for toddlers and adults who work with soil. **Foodborne mercury** is present mainly in fish.

acceptable, even for consumption every week, while others may not. Finally, people with occupational exposure to mercurial compounds or products may find the risks acceptable because of their economic gain, while others living nearby who have no financial interest, may not appreciate air or water emissions. Determining the risk from mercury in foods is generally based on epidemiologic studies coupled with fate and effects of mercury in humans, and the results of toxicological studies in animals, allowing for uncertainties relating to interspecific differences, human variability and susceptibility, and uncertainties in these measurements.

Human Health Risk Assessment for Mercury

Exposure Assessment

People are exposed to mercury through multiple pathways: air, water, food, cosmetic products, dental amalgams, cultural practices, and even from the thimerosal preservative in vaccines (NJDEP, 2001). Exposure assessment for mercury is a critical phase; it involves examining not only the routes of exposure, but also the form of the mercury. Table 12.3 summarizes the exposure pathways for various forms of mercury in environmental media (air, water, soil, and food) taken into the body by inhalation, ingestion, injection, or through the skin.

Methylmercury is one of the few toxicants for which exposure data are available from either consumption studies or unintentional poisoning exposures to derive a guideline intake for methylmercury, based on the most sensitive stage (the fetus). The consumption of fish poses the greatest risk to the public, making it essential to have accurate exposure assessments before risk can be evaluated (Hughner et al., 2008), as well as information on mercury levels in fish (Burger, 2009). For most risk assessments for exposure to methylmercury, fish consumption is the primary pathway (Boischio and Henshel, 1996; Rice et al., 2000; Burger and Gochfeld, 2006a), and farm-raised fish are not exempt if they have been fed fish meal high in mercury (Dorea, 2009). However, data from China (Zhang et al., 2010) shows that for some people rice ingestion is the major source of methylmercury.

In general, agencies often use average or default assumptions when computing risk. However, these assumptions are not suitable for people who consume a lot of fish—for example, Native Americans, subsistence peoples, some recreational fishers, or for those who eat a lot of fish for taste or health reasons. Sunderland (2007) has reported that per capita mercury intake rates using FDA mercury data differed significantly from those calculated based on site-specific mercury data for each area. Thus, site-specific information on mercury levels in fish, site-specific information on consumption patterns, and ethnic exposure patterns are desirable for risk evaluations (Harris and Harper, 1997; Toth and Brown, 1997; Burger and Gochfeld, 2001, 2006a, 2007; Holloman and Newman, 2006).

Additional factors to consider in assessing mercury exposure and toxicity are foods eaten at the same time and co-occurring chemicals that can modify the effects of mercury. For example, green and black tea extracts can reduce the bio-accessibility of mercury (Shim et al. 2009). There has been considerable interest in the ability of selenium to reduce the effects of mercury through a variety of mechanisms. Selenium is thought to be protective for mercury exposure (Satoh et al., 1985); lower levels of non-fatal heart attacks have been associated with higher levels of selenium (Mozaffarian, 2009) and studies with animal models have suggested that some of the adverse impacts of high methylmercury exposure are a result of pathologic effects from impaired selenium-dependent enzyme activities (Watanabe et al., 1999; Ralston, 2008, 2009; Ralston et al., 2008).

Finally, it is customary to examine human exposure to mercury from the viewpoints of both the general public and workers, both in factories and in home operations such as gold mining (Maramba et al., 2006). Gold-mining operations provide a good example of the possible routes of exposure. Miners are exposed to gaseous elemental mercury and gold dust, infants and children ingest mercury through hand-to-mouth activity, and finally, mercury can seep into rivers, and with methylation, move up the food chain to species that are consumed by people.

Noncancer End Points and Reference Doses

Risk for noncancer effects of mercury on people focus on neurobehavioral effects in adults or neurodevelopmental effects on the fetus (ATSDR, 1999; NRC, 2000a; Institute of Medicine [IOM], 2006). These approaches use the RfD (EPA), MRL (ATSDR), or ADI (FDA) to arrive at levels of mercury that are not expected to cause harm (Table 12.4). Although for most risk assessments, one usually makes assumptions about exposure that involve a 70-kg adult over a 50- to 70-year lifespan, for mercury, risk assessments for women and children are usually made because of the sensitivity of the developing fetus and young children (ATSDR, 1999; USEPA, 2006). The RfD, the EPA's approach to an ADI, is computed by dividing a NOAEL (if available), by a denominator combining all applicable uncertainty factors. The choice of NOAEL is critical. The uncertainty factors include: (1) extrapolating from animal data to humans (using a default UF of 10), (2) intraspecific variability to protect the most sensitive individuals (such as pregnant women or children [default UF of 10]), (3) calculating a lifetime risk from a study that used only an acute or subacute (short-term) exposure (default UF of 10), and (4) when the RfD is based on a LOAEL rather than a NOAEL (UF of 10). Other safety factors might account

for multigenerational effects. If all of these uncertainty factors apply, they would be multiplied to serve as the denominator.

However, for mercury, the NOAELs are based on human data; this greatly reduces uncertainty. The RfD for mercury was first based on retrospective studies of an incident of poisoning in Iraq in which grain, contaminated with a methylmerury fungicide, was used in the baking of bread. Although the exposure lasted only a few months, it was quite high, and resulted in neurologic effects in both adults and infants (Shipp et al., 2000). When data from several child development studies became available, the USEPA revised its chronic oral RfD for methylmercury to 0.1 µg/kg/day (USEPA, 2001c). In this and in the following discussions, refer to table 12.4 for concentrations and risk levels set by various agencies.

EPA's Reference Dose for Methylmercury

The RfD is based on the assumption that thresholds exist for certain toxic effects such as cellular necrosis. It is expressed in milligrams per kilogram per day and is defined as follows: "In general, the RfD is an estimate (with uncertainty spanning perhaps an order of magnitude) of a daily exposure to the human population (including sensitive subgroups) that is likely to be without an appreciable risk of deleterious effects during a lifetime" (USEPA, 2006). In, 1985 EPA set the RfD for methylmercury at 0.0003 mg/kg/day (0.3 µg/kg/day) (Rice et al., 2000; Schierow, 2004), based on neurodevelopmental effects observed in the 1970s Iraq poisoning epidemic (this was subsequently lowered to 0.0001 mg/kg/day, see next paragraph). The Iraq epidemic resulted from direct human consumption of fungicide-treated grain intended for planting. Subsequent to the EPA's comprehensive mercury report (USEPA, 1997), new epidemiologic data based mainly on exposure through fish consumption, became available. The EPA's reassessment relied mainly on results from studies in New Zealand and the Faroe Islands that detected neurobehavioral deficits related to prenatal mercury levels. At the same time the USFDA and the ATSDR arrived at comparable estimates of about 0.4 µg/kg/day and 0.3 µg/kg/day, respectively. The FDA has set an action level of 1 ppm methylmercury in commercial fish, above which level fish could be seized. From that level FDA arrived at an ADI of 0.4 µg/kg/day using average consumption levels (Schierow, 2004). The ATSDR arrived at an MRL of 0.3 µg/kg/day based on the "negative" Seychelles Island study. In 2004, the Joint FAO/WHO Expert Committee on Food Additives (JECFA) established a methylmercury guideline (PTWI) of 3.3 µg/kg body weight per week for methylmercury based on adult data from the Iraq epidemic (Schierow, 2004). It continued this level at its 1999 meeting (JECFA, 1999), based on reassuring preliminary results from the Seychelles study (Davidson et al., 1998). At its 2003 meeting, it revised the PTWI to 1.6 µg/kg/day, based on an evaluation of both

TABLE 12.4

Guidance and Risk Levels for Methylmercury Determined by Different Agencies

Agency and measure	Year	Value	Basis
USEPA, long-term oral RfD	1985	0.3 µg/kg/day	Effects on adults in Iraq
	1995 IRIS	0.1 µg/kg/day	Developmental effects in Iraq
	2001 IRIS	0.1 µg/kg/day[a]	Studies in New Zealand and Faroe Islands
ATSDR MRL (oral)	1994 Toxicological profile	0.1 µg/kg/day	Seychelles study
	1997 Draft profile	0.5 µg/kg/day	Seychelles study
	1999 Toxicological profile	0.3 µg/kg/day	Seychelles study
USFDA ADI	1984	0.4 µg/kg/day	Corresponds to 1 ppm action level
UN FAO/WHO	1993	3.3 µg/kg/wk	Based on studies in Iraq with no fetal consideration
JECFA	Reaffirmed 1999	1.6 µg/kg/wk[b]	JECFA (1999)
Guidance value	Revised 2003	0.23 µg/kg/day	JECFA (2003)
PTWI			Seychelles and Faroes

NOTE: Some agencies do not distinguish between total mercury and methylmercury or assume that all mercury is methylmercury (the typical conversion is 90%).

a. Method recommended by NRC (2000a). There is no separate provision for adults.

b. Accepted and used by the European Food Safety Authority (2004). JECFA (2006) notes that the 1.6 value is to protect the fetus and probably children and that adults may tolerate twice the PTWI.

ADI = acceptable daily intake; MRL = minimal risk level; PTWI = provisional tolerable weekly intake; RfD = reference dose.

Faroes and Seychelles data (JECFA, 2003), but subsequently acknowledged that adults could tolerate twice that level, while data for children under 17 was uncertain (JECFA, 2004, 2006) (see Table 12.4).

The Seychelles are tropical islands in the Indian Ocean. The study has been conducted mainly by the University of Rochester. The islands' residents, largely Muslim, consume fish daily and the Seychelles Child Development Study, which began at the same time as the Faroes study, has not found evidence of harm from prenatal exposure to methylmercury at the levels encountered in that population. Fish from the surrounding reefs and ocean are a major source of protein. This study is generally considered "negative," although there has been evidence of a late effect on children whose mothers had high mercury levels in hair (Davidson et al., 2006), although in many studies, the causal relationships are unclear (Myers et al., 2009).

The Faroe Islands in the North Atlantic are inhabited mainly by people of Scandinavian background. Oceanic fish are a major source of protein, and some families also capture Pilot Whales periodically, which are a major source of both methylmercury and polychlorinated biphenyls. A prospective study of mother–child pairs was initiated in 1990; there was evidence of impaired neurobehavioral functions in children at the age of 7 years, who had higher in utero exposure to mercury, particularly during the third trimester (Grandjean et al., 1998). The EPA's reassessment lowered the RfD to 0.1 µg/kg/day based on the positive Faroes study, although its reasoning has been criticized (e.g. Davidson et al., 2004). The literature review,

risk-estimation procedures, and rationale are detailed in the USEPA's IRIS database (USEPA, 2001c).

Both the Faroe and Seychelles studies involved populations with very high fish consumption, and extensive efforts have been devoted to contrasting the studies and reconciling the apparent differences. Probable confounders include ethnic differences, the high levels of polychlorinated biphenyls ingested intermittently in the Faroe Islands after Pilot Whale hunts, the higher levels of fresh fruit consumption in the Seychelles, and differences in measurement techniques.

An Example of a Formal Human Risk Assessment

In response to the need for coordinated risk communication by the Department of Energy and the States of South Carolina and Georgia, we undertook a risk assessment for people consuming fish from the Savannah River. We assumed that the people who actually fished the river were most likely to consume large amounts of fish, and we took a dual approach. We captured fish from the river, including species sought and favored by sportsmen, and analyzed their edible tissues, and we interviewed fishers to determine how much fish they ate. Our risk assessment included radionuclides as well as mercury, but only the latter is reported here (Table 12.5). We have conducted similar risk assessments in New Jersey, around the Oak Ridge nuclear facility, and in the Aleutians near Amchitka Island, where there were three underground nuclear tests in the 1965–1971 period (Campbell et al., 2002; Burger and Campbell, 2004; Burger et al., 2005, 2007b; Burger and Gochfeld, 2007).

TABLE 12.5a

Mercury Concentration in Five Commonly Eaten Fish from the Savannah
River and Percentage of Fish Exceeding 0.5 ppm and 1.0 ppm

Species	No.	Mean Hg (±SE) in ppm wet weight	% exceeding 0.5 ppm	% exceeding 1.0 ppm	μg of mercury in 8 oz (227 g)
Bowfin (Amia calva)	58	0.94 ± 0.05	81%	45%	214
Largemouth Bass (Micropterus salmoides)	48	0.46 ± 0.04	38%	4%	105
Yellow Perch (Perca flavescens)	39	0.28 ± 0.02	10%	0%	64
Black Crappie (Pomoxis nigromaculatus)	53	0.24 ± 0.02	9%	0%	55
Channel Catfish (Ictalurus punctatus)	45	0.20 ± 0.02	1%	0%	46

NOTE: These values are for total mercury (about 90% of which is methylmercury). (Additional data are provided in Burger et al., 2001a).

TABLE 12.5b

Distribution of Fish Intake (g/day) for Fishermen and Women Interviewed along the Savannah River (from Burger et al., 1999)

Fish eaters	Median	Mean	95th percentile
Black males	51.8	70.1	187.9
White females	12.8	26.1	90

NOTE: Of the four groups tested (black males and females and white males and females), black males reported the highest and white females the lowest fish consumption.

Data on the distribution of mercury levels in fish commonly caught and eaten by local anglers along the Savannah River is provided in Table 12.5a, b. We interviewed the anglers for many features, including the amount of fish that they and their family members consumed. To stabilize the estimate of meal size we showed them a model equivalent to about 8 oz (227 g) of fish. Table 12.6 combines mercury concentration data with fish consumption data to estimate the hazard quotient (daily mercury intake divided by both the ATSDR MRL (0.3 µg/kg/day) and the EPA's RfD (0.1 µg/kg/day).

Table 12.5 shows the sample size and average total mercury concentration (micrograms per gram, or parts per million [ppm], of muscle on a wet weight basis) in five of the fish species we sampled from the Savannah River, as well as the number (and percent) exceeding a conservative action level of 0.5 ppm and the current USFDA action level of 1.0 ppm. The final column is the amount of mercury (micrograms of total mercury) in an 8 oz (227 g) serving. On average, about 90% of this mercury would be methylmercury. We provide more details on the data and methods in Burger et al. (2001c).

We calculated mercury intake using the median, mean, and 95th percentile of the fish consumption estimates from our interview studies (see Table 12.6). It should be noted that some risk evaluations are based on much lower default assumptions derived from the general population, whereas fish consumption risks fall mainly on the large number of people who are population outliers (high fish consumers). We illustrate the risk evaluation using Bowfin (see Table 12.6), the fish with the highest mercury content (mean 0.94 µg/g [ppm]). Of the four populations—white male and female and black male and female—the black males had the highest average consumption and white females the lowest. Using their median, mean and 95th percentile consumption in grams per day, the table shows the mercury intake in micrograms per day. This is then converted to methylmercury using a conversion value of 90% (from many published studies). We then divided the daily intake by 70 kg for males and 60 kg for females to arrive at a daily intake in micrograms per kilogram of body weight. These are the units that both the ATSDR and the

TABLE 12.6

Risk Assessment for Bowfin and Channel Catfish from the Savannah River using the Data from Table 12.5a & b for Fishermen and their Families. Data are Given for a Hypothetical Black Male (70 kg) and Hypothetical White Female (60 kg)
The last two lines for Channel Catfish (mean mercury 0.20 µg/g) show the corresponding hazard quotients (HQ) if that species only were consumed.

	Black males intake (70 kg)			White females intake (60 kg)		
	Median[a]	Mean	95th %	Median	Mean	95th %
Daily intake of fish (g/day)	51.8 g	70.1 g	187.9 g	12.8 g	26.1 g	90 g
Bowfin						
Total mean Hg concentration in fish	0.94	0.94	0.94	0.94	0.94	0.94
[Hg] µg/day mean intake	48.7	65.9	176.6	12.0	25.5	84.6
Methylmercury intake/day	43.8	59.3	159	10.8	22.1	76.1
MeHg/kg	0.63	0.85	2.27	0.18	0.37	1.27
HQ (MRL)	**2.09**	**2.82**	**7.57**	0.60	**1.23**	**4.23**
HQ (RFD)	**6.26**	**8.47**	**22.7**	**1.8**	**3.68**	**12.7**
Channel Catfish						
Total mean Hg concentration in fish	0.2	0.2	0.2	0.2	0.2	0.2
HQ(MRL)	.44	.60	**1.6**	0.13	0.26	0.90
HQ(RfD)	**1.33**	**1.80**	**4.84**	0.38	0.78	**2.70**

a. Median, mean and 95th percentile intake in grams per day.

b. The mean concentration of total Hg in each fish.

c. Mean mercury intake (µg/day).

d. This row converts total to methylmercury assuming that about 90% of total mercury is methylmercury.

e. These rows calculate the Hazard Quotient (dividing the daily intake by some guidance value; an HQ > 1 indicates excessive exposure. The daily intake of MeHg (µg/kg-day) is divided by the Minimal Risk Level (MRL) of 0.3 µg/kg-day to yield a hazard quotient (intake divided by daily allowance or HQ[MRL]).

f. calculation of HQ(RfD) obtained by dividing daily intake by 0.1 µg/kg-day which is the EPA's Reference Dose (RfD).

EPA used for the MRL (0.3 µg/kg/day) and RfD (0.1 µg/kg/day), respectively. We divide the daily intake by the MRL to arrive at an HQ, which we designate as HQ(MRL), and also divide intake by the RfD to arrive at a different HQ, which we designate at HQ(RfD) (see Table 12.6). If an HQ is >1, then the intake is clearly excessive, and these are denoted by bold type.

We also show the resultant HQs for Channel Catfish (average total Hg, 0.20 µg/g). This illustrates the value of also choosing low-mercury fish, even from the same body of water, so that people know which species of fish they can eat safely. However, even if the black fishers in our sample confined their diet to Channel Catfish, more than half of them would exceed the HQ(RfD), since at their median consumption rate, the HQ is 1.33.

It is also possible to translate the daily intake data into advisories regarding the frequency with which such fish could be consumed. The FDA and states often use this approach. We reported that one should eat an 8-oz meal of Bowfin less than once a month (to avoid adverse effects), but could eat an 8-oz meal of Channel Catfish about once a week (Burger et al., 2001c).

Human Health Safety Guidelines

Another shorthand method of determining potential risk from mercury is to develop "safe" human health standards, such as consumption advisories based on levels of mercury in foods (usually fish and shellfish, or marine mammals for Native hunters). Such advisories can reduce levels of intake, particularly of canned fish (Shimshack et al., 2007). These health standards are based on risk assessments, but do not require a separate risk assessment; they rely merely on a comparison to a standard or guideline.

Mercury effects can also be assessed using neurobehavioral end points for screening. For example, effects from exposure to mercury vapor in miners and smelters may be assessed by comparing urine analysis with data on hand tremors. Neurobehavioral test results can then be compared both to patient mercury levels and to known effects levels (Fiedler et al., 2007: Iwata et al., 2007).

Action levels are another type of guidance value that may or may not be based on risk. The USFDA develops action levels for specific contaminants, which are the levels above which an agency takes some action to control exposure, restrict access, conduct research, or in the case of fish, seize shipments in interstate commerce. The USFDA action level for methylmercury in fish is 1.0 ppm (micrograms per gram, wet weight), but this is a regulatory action level, rather than a risk level (USFDA, 2001, 2003, 2005, 2006). In contrast, the risk level that would trigger an advisory by the USEPA of one meal per week for human consumption is 0.2 ppm (Rothschild and Duffy, 2002). The 0.2 ppm exposure tolerance limit established by the USEPA was intended to protect adult human health and likely does not protect the fetal or neonatal brain (Landrigan et al., 2006). Using these action levels in conjunction with levels of mercury in fish, agencies develop consumption advisories. The issuing of consumption advisories for mercury is generally the responsibility of states, although the USFDA has issued some advisories, and such advisories often target sensitive populations (Scherer et al., 2008).

In 1982, the European Commission set an Environmental Quality Standard for mercury; the mean concentration of mercury in a representative sample of fish shall not exceed 0.3 ppm (wet weight). Many countries have set the maximum permitted level of mercury in fish at 0.5 ppm, including Australia, Sweden, and Canada (IOM, 1991; Denton and Burdon-Jones, 1996). The established criteria for mercury in fish muscle in the United Kingdom and the European Union is now 0.5 ppm in edible fish (with up to 1 ppm allowed for certain "exempt" predatory fish species) (EC, 2008). China has set standards for methylmercury in canned fish (parts per million wet weight) of 0.5 ppm (except 1 ppm is allowed in shark, sailfish, tuna, pike, and other high-mercury fish). Similarly, many U.S. states have set 0.5 ppm or lower limits on mercury in fish (Burger and Gochfeld, 2004b). The World Health Organization standard is also 0.5 ppm for fish consumption, although large predators may be excepted.

Some examples of levels of mercury in fish that people in the general population of the United States eat are presented in Table 12.7. Using these tables, it is possible to determine whether people are eating fish that exceed the action levels of the United States (1.0 ppm), as well as more conservative countries, such as those in the European Union (0.5 ppm) and the level used by the European Commission (0.3 ppm) (Burger and Gochfeld, 2001). We present mercury data in fish from supermarkets in New Jersey and Illinois, for recreational and subsistence fish in South Carolina and Tennessee, and for Native American subsistence fish from the Aleutians. As is clear, some of the fish people eat exceed the action levels. Armed with this type of information, people can make informed risk decisions on whether and when to eat fish and how much of it to eat, although people also consider other factors (e.g. cost, availability) in making their decisions (Burger et al., 2005).

One problem with determining risk from per capita mercury intake estimates is the variability in mercury concentration data in fish or shellfish consumed. That is, spatially refined mercury concentration data for a range of fish species is required to determine risk from consuming such fish (Sunderland, 2007). As Tables 12.7 indicates, there is variation both within a region and between regions. Cod (*Gadus morhua*), for example, had mean mercury levels of 0.1 ppm in New Jersey and the closely related *G. macrocephalus* averaged 0.2 ppm from the Aleutians. More interesting, perhaps, is the maximum value obtained from different regions: mercury levels of 0.1 ppm from New Jersey and 0.9 ppm from the Aleutians. Thus, there was little variation in the mercury concentrations in cod obtained in New Jersey supermarkets, but a great deal of variation in cod caught by subsistence fishers in the Aleutians. This is of particular interest because it has been suggested that even one meal of a high-mercury fish may pose a problem to developing fetuses (Ginsberg and Toal, 2000). If this is the case, then consumers should be provided with information not only on the mean levels of mercury in fish, shellfish, and other wild-caught foods, but with some estimate of variance and the maximum values from their region. These differences suggest that site-specific data on mercury levels are required both for states to make decisions about issuing advisories, and for individuals to decide what species (and amounts) of fish to consume.

Setting water quality standards by using mercury concentrations in fish is another way of reducing the risk from mercury. In, 1982 the European Commission set an Environmental Quality Standard for mercury: the mean concentration of mercury in a representative sample of fish shall not exceed 0.3 ppm (wet weight). Further, the USEPA (2001b) promulgated 0.3 ppm as an ambient freshwater quality criterion in, 2001, but this value was developed using a mercury consumption level (7 μg/day for a 70-kg person) that is far less than the exposure of many recreational or subsistence fishers. While by Treaty, Tribal Nations have the right to set their own water quality standards, they generally do not do so.

Ecological Risk Assessment for Mercury

The interest in the risks to humans and the environment from mercury derive directly from the general public, managers, conservationists and other scientists, regulators, and policy makers. Formal ERA for mercury involves similar steps as used in HRA. Cancer is not an end point of concern for mercury for either ERA or HRA. There are numerous

Mean (± standard error) Concentrations of Total Mercury in Fish from Various Samples and the Percent Exceeding Various
Guideline and Action Levels
0.3 ppm is EPA's freshwater fish criterion concentration. 0.5 ppm is the allowable level for mercury in fish in the European Union.
1.0 ppm is the U.S. FDA action level for methylmercury in fish.

Species	No.	Mean (±SE)	% >0.3 ppm	% >0.5 ppm	% >1 ppm
Commercial fish					
Illinois[a]					
Salmon	18	0.031 ± 0.009	0	0	0
Canned tuna (gourmet)	18	0.060 ± 0.013	0	0	0
Canned tuna (light)	20	0.097 ± 0.019	10	0	0
Grouper	18	0.258 ± 0.056	44	17	0
Canned tuna (white)	22	0.310 ± 0.033	64	9	0
Tuna steak	18	0.345 ± 0.058	56	22	0
Walleye	18	0.508 ± 0.129	44	22	22
Orange Roughy	19	0.570 ± 0.059	95	58	5
Swordfish	18	1.310 ± 0.185	94	89	67
New Jersey[b]					
Shrimp (large)	12	0.010 ± 0.001	0	0	0
Scallops	12	0.013 ± 0.001	0	0	0
Shrimp (small)	12	0.015 ± 0.001	0	0	0
Whiting	16	0.035 ± 0.004	0	0	0
Flounder	54	0.047 ± 0.005	0	0	0
Porgy	16	0.095 ± 0.013	0	0	0
Cod	7	0.108 ± 0.006	0	0	0
Croaker	14	0.144 ± 0.019	0	0	0
Red Snapper	4	0.240 ± 0.008	0	0	0
Bluefish	50	0.263 ± 0.017	32	2	0
Chilean Sea Bass	7	0.375 ± 0.055	71	29	0
Tuna (Yellowfin)	49	0.648 ± 0.089	65	43	22
Recreational fish					
New Jersey[c]					
Peanut Bunker (Menhaden)	5	0.011 ± 0.001	0	0	0
Bonito	3	0.045 ± 0.004	0	0	0
Ling	11	0.066 ± 0.017	0	0	0
Weakfish	22	0.079 ± 0.020	5	0	0
Porgy	22	0.084 ± 0.017	0	0	0
Dolphin	14	0.124 ± 0.044	14	7	0
Tuna (Yellowfin)	36	0.128 ± 0.017	3	3	0
Atlantic Croaker	14	0.132 ± 0.012	0	0	0
Fluke	195	0.133 ± 0.006	4	0	0
Northern Kingfish	12	0.139 ± 0.020	0	0	0
Black Sea Bass	7	0.166 ± 0.014	0	0	0
Tautog	41	0.181 ± 0.014	12	0	0
Thresher Shark	1	0.406	100	0	0

(continued)

TABLE 12.7 *(continued)*

Species	No.	Mean (±SE)	% >0.3 ppm	% >0.5 ppm	% >1 ppm
Tuna (Bluefin)	8	0.427 ± 0.062	75	50	0
Bluefish	115	0.463 ± 0.032	56	35	7
Striped Bass	118	0.472 ± 0.026	68	42	4
Mako Shark	25	2.170 ± 0.253	100	100	92
Oak Ridge, Tennessee[d]					
Black Crappie	14	0.049 ± 0.014	0	0	0
White Bass	29	0.117 ± 0.015	3	0	0
Striped Bass	15	0.296 ± 0.043	27	13	0
Savannah River, South Carolina[e]					
Red-breasted Sunfish	35	0.127 ± 0.023	9	6	0
Bluegill Sunfish	30	0.140 ± 0.022	7	3	0
American eel	24	0.147 ± 0.031	8	8	0
Catfish	47	0.205 ± 0.020	21	6	0
Shellcracker	36	0.234 ± 0.031	28	14	0
Crappie	53	0.245 ± 0.018	28	9	0
Spotted Sucker	35	0.271 ± 0.039	31	14	3
Perch	39	0.285 ± 0.022	44	10	0
Pickerel	19	0.357 ± 0.033	68	21	0
Largemouth Bass	48	0.465 ± 0.045	65	38	4
Bowfin	58	0.938 ± 0.054	98	81	45
Subsistence fish					
Aleutian Islands, Alaska[f]					
Sockeye Salmon	15	0.042 ± 0.005	0	0	0
Atka Mackerel	19	0.046 ± 0.004	0	0	0
Pacific Ocean Perch	17	0.048 ± 0.009	0	0	0
Northern Rock Sole	15	0.068 ± 0.007	0	0	0
Walleye Pollock	12	0.074 ± 0.018	0	0	0
Rock Sole	27	0.092 ± 0.011	0	0	0
Rock Greenling	83	0.100 ± 0.010	2	0	0
Dolly Varden	75	0.114 ± 0.013	9	1	0
Red Irish Lord	57	0.130 ± 0.010	2	0	0
Pacific Halibut	24	0.158 ± 0.044	13	8	0
Black Rockfish	68	0.167 ± 0.015	18	1	0
Pacific Cod	142	0.173 ± 0.011	13	4	0
Flathead Sole	39	0.276 ± 0.013	33	3	0
Yellow Irish Lord	68	0.281 ± 0.024	35	12	0
Great Sculpin	27	0.366 ± 0.058	48	30	4

NOTE: The amount of mercury in fish varies greatly, making it essential to perform risk assessments using site-specific data for each fish species.

a. Data are from Burger and Gochfeld (2006b).

b. Data are from Burger et al. (2005) and Burger and Gochfeld (2005).

c. Data are from Burger and Gochfeld (unpublished).

d. Data are from Burger and Campbell (2004).

e. Data are from Burger et al. (2001c).

f. Data are from Burger and Gochfeld (2007) and Burger et al. (2007b).

books and over a hundred guidance documents for performing ecological risk assessment, indicating the complexity of such assessments (Bartell et al., 1992; Newman, 1998; Fisher and Burton, 2004; Sorensen et al., 2004; Suter et al., 2005; Barnthouse et al. 2007). This proliferation is due in part to the inherent complexity of ecosystems, to the wide range of species present, and to the diversity of forms (e.g. aquatic, terrestrial), stages (e.g. egg, larvae, young, adult), phases (e.g. moving from aquatic to terrestrial), and life spans (e.g. hours to decades).

Because of ecologic complexity, ERA must be conducted with a particular objective in mind. Merely examining the risk from mercury in the environment is too broad, and requires considerable refinement (the problem- formulation phase). Particular care should be devoted to the inclusion of a wide range of stakeholders at this point to ensure that the final assessment addresses the concerns of interested and affected parties, the general public, and the management and regulatory needs of state, federal and tribal governments. While risk assessment is basically scientific and technical, determining the ecologic end point of concern is mainly social and political (a case in point is that of Pacific Salmon in the Northwest [Lackey, 1996; NRC, 1996]).

Formal risk assessment for mercury in ecosystems follows the general methods described above, including problem formulation, characterization of exposure and pathways, characterization of effects, and risk characterization (refer to Figure 12.2). For an ecologic evaluation of mercury, the question to be addressed must be carefully defined. Further, the difference between assessment end points and measurement end points must be clarified. Uncertainties exist for ERA, particularly for gaps in available data on effects for different species, and in the magnitude of chemical exposures (Washburn et al., 1998). Some of the uncertainty is reduced by using probabilistic rather than deterministic risk assessment for the effects of methylmercury, particularly for consumption exposures in humans (Johnston and Snow, 2007).

As an example, probabilistic risk assessments for the effects of mercury on different species in the Everglades of South Florida relied on literature-derived life history parameters, combined with site-specific concentrations of mercury in species (Duvall and Barron, 2000; Rumbold, 2005). This assessment indicated that alligators had 100% exceedances of long-term risk thresholds, and Great Egrets (*Egretta alba*) had 99% exceedances. Mercury is one of the issues of concern for the restoration of the Everglades (SFWMD, 2007, 2010). Aquatic ecosystems, such as the Everglades, are particularly vulnerable to mercury and other contaminants because of the potential for bio-accumulation and rapid transport through aquatic systems (Burger, 1997b).

Similarly, probabilistic risk models have been used to examine mercury contamination in the East Fork Poplar Creek at the Department of Energy's Oak Ridge Site (Moore et al., 1999). Over 50 years of operation at the site has resulted in contamination of water, sediment, biota, and floodplain soils. Monte Carlo simulations of total daily intake of mercury

by species was integrated with species-specific dose–response curves to estimate risk. Methylmercury posed a risk to mink (24% probability of at least 15% mortality) and to kingfishers (50% probability of at least a 12–28% decline in fecundity (Moore et al., 1999). These estimates allow for a comparison of the relative risk between the two species, although it would be more useful if the same end points had been used for both species (e.g. either mortality or fecundity).

Exposure Assessment

Exposure evaluations for mercury follow directly from the problem-formulation phase. In most cases, exposure assessment involves determining the levels of mercury in whole bodies (usually used for invertebrates and plants) or in tissues, such as liver, kidney, muscle, or blood. Noninvasive techniques for mercury evaluation include examining the feathers for birds, hair for mammals (including humans), and tail tips for reptiles. Levels of mercury in tissues are usually called "biomarkers" of exposure, and optimally they also indicate something about the possible effects of mercury exposure. For example, levels of mercury in blood are usually significantly correlated with fish consumption (Harnly et al., 1997). Once the concentration has been determined, the opportunity for contact and the amount of contaminated prey consumed must be estimated.

Benchmarks

As with human health risk evaluations, an important first step in evaluating a site is to screen for priority chemicals. For aquatic systems, if the levels of a chemical are below background concentrations, they can be ignored, and if the chemical analysis yielded nondetectable levels and the methods were deemed appropriate, the chemical may be ignored. If the chemical concentrations are below concentrations that have been determined to constitute an ecotoxicologic hazard, they may be ignored. Other chemicals also need to be evaluated. The challenge is that there are very few chemicals for which the ecotoxicologic adverse effect level has been adequately demonstrated in any organism.

There are screening level benchmarks, especially for chemicals in aquatic systems that are generally accepted. In the United States, the U.S National Ambient Water Quality Criteria for Protection of Aquatic Life (NAWQC) are used to screen aqueous chemicals. However, there are few such criteria involving very few species, making it useful to develop other benchmarks with the use of the LOELs (lowest observed adverse effect level) and NOELs; there is no NAWQC for mercury. However, the lowest long-term effect values for methylmercury have been determined to be 0.52 µg/L for fish, <0.04 µg/L for Daphnids, and 0.8–4.0 µg/L for plants (Suter, 1996). Values are also given for inorganic mercury, which are lower for fish, and higher for Daphnids. In general, benchmarks are more highly developed for aquatic systems, mainly because of the rapid transport of contaminants in aquatic systems. While other benchmarks can and have been developed, their usefulness depends on the appropriate regulators accepting them for the risk assessment for mercury.

Hazard Quotients

HQs have been used to evaluate the ecologic risk from exposure to mercury (see Table 12.3). One problem, however, is that data on toxicity levels for mercury are available for only a very small percentage of the species, even for birds and mammals in which much of the work has been done. Thus, assessors are forced to extrapolate not only from laboratory studies, but from one species to another, not to mention adjusting for potential differences due to subspecies differences. Very rarely are such toxicity data for mercury validated in the field.

HQs are a type of analysis used for risk characterization in screening assessments. The HQ is derived by dividing the ambient exposure concentration by a toxicologically effective concentration. For wildlife, doses are used in place of concentrations. If the HQ is greater than 1, then the chemical is worthy of concern and further risk evaluations. Large quotient values suggest large effects or greater uncertainty concerning the end point. When more chemicals than just mercury are involved, the sum of the toxic units are added together to produce an index of toxicity (Suter et al., 2000), sometimes referred to as a hazard index. However, there is little empirical evidence to support the additivity of HQs. HQ's less than 1 do not allow a substance to be ignored completely.

Toxicity Reference Value

Another risk assessment approach is the use of the toxicity reference value (TRV), which is based on terrestrial mammal data. Since the TRV for mammals does not incorporate all the uncertainty values of the RfD, it is less conservative (Hung et al., 2007). As with HRA, ERA uncertainty factors include interspecific to intraspecific comparisons, short to long term, lowest (LOAEL) to NOAEL, and laboratory to field extrapolation. There is little standardization in how these uncertainty factors are dealt with in ecological risk assessment (Chapman et al., 1998).

Adverse Effects Levels and Screening Levels

In a practical sense, health professionals interested in risk often use established human health guidelines to determine whether, for example, people should eat fish. Similarly ecotoxicologists use a combination of NOAEL and LOAEL to determine what levels of mercury in animals result in adverse effects. From controlled laboratory experiments, ecotoxicologists and risk assessors can determine screening levels, which are effects threshold values based on toxicity databases (Naito et al., 2006). There is a wide range of benchmarks that can be used in the screening of mercury and other chemicals (Suter, 1996).

Ecosystem Responses to Mercury

Whereas HRA concentrates on only one species (humans), ERA focuses not only on individuals and their populations, but also on ecosystems, since effects at the species level can have cascading effects on the structure and function of the system. Ecosystem approaches to evaluating the risk of mercury involve assessing mercury deposition in airsheds and watersheds (both terrestrial and aquatic components), monitoring and evaluating trends in sediment and water indicators, monitoring and evaluating trends in aquatic biota, and examining wildlife indicators (Harris et al., 2006). All these require evaluating the fate and effects of mercury within components of the ecosystem.

Additional Issues for Risk Evaluations for Mercury

Monitoring, Biomonitoring, and Surveillance

Environmental monitoring examines the status and trends in indicators to determine whether the environment is improving or degrading, and as such, have been used extensively by managers (Suter, 2001). Both human and ecological risk assessment for mercury depend on biologic monitoring of species or tissues. To assess the impact of elevated levels of mercury in media (usually inorganic mercury) or biota (such as methylmercury in fish), biologic monitoring is conducted, usually with regular frequency. For humans, the tissue of choice varies with the type of exposure. Elemental and inorganic mercury exposure is usually monitored with urine analysis for total mercury. Since methylmercury is excreted mainly in the feces, urine monitoring does not provide consistent results, and hair or blood levels are used. The EPA considers hair levels below 10 ppm and blood levels below 5 µg/L to be unlikely to be associated with adverse effects (USEPA, 2006). Such monitoring for mercury is recommended for people who have high levels of consumption of fish or shellfish (Hightower and Moore, 2002), in communities of Native Americans who eat high levels of subsistence foods (Harris and Harper, 1997; Harnly et al., 1997; Wheatley and Wheatley, 2000; Burger and Gochfeld, 2007), for anyone consuming large quantities of fish (e.g. recreationists, high-end commercial fish consumers), and for people living near gold-mining operations (Rojas et al., 2006) and chlor-alkali plants (Ullrich et al., 2007).

Optimally, monitoring plans should be developed to show spatial and temporal trends in mercury levels in media (e.g. soil, sediment, water), biota and the food chain, and humans (and their tissues). Increasingly organizations and governments are designing monitoring plans to assess mercury in the food chain, including humans (Muir et al., 2005). Monitoring data can be used for ecological risk assessment models at the local, regional, and global levels (Barnthouse, 1992), as well as for constructing food-web and population-based models. Burger et al. (2001b) used food-web models at the Department of Energy's Savannah River Site to predict levels of mercury in organisms at different trophic levels at different points of time in the future. The models indicated that methylmercury levels will peak earlier in some organisms than others. Such models can provide useful information for both HRA and ERA in predicting future risks.

There are a number of mercury monitoring systems that provide information about mercury levels in air and water. In turn, these can be used to predict future potential risk through methylation to the food chain. Examples of monitoring systems include individual species (Burger and Gochfeld, 2004c), larger regional areas (SFWMD, 2007), and continent-wide programs such as Mussel-Watch, which began in the mid-1980s and now covers more than 250 sites (CCMA, 2007). Under the Clean Air Mercury Rule issued by the EPA in 2005, most power plants are required to monitor their mercury emissions using such systems beginning in January 1, 2009. In 1994, the National Atmospheric Deposition Program Mercury Deposition Network was established to provide a database of weekly concentrations of total mercury in rainfall (wet deposition) as well as dry deposition in the United States (Driscoll et al., 2006). This is a nationwide scheme, but has not been adequately funded.

Bioindicators

Biomonitoring plans depend on the wise selection of bioindicators (see Table 12.3). Bioindicators can be selected to measure mercury levels (fate of mercury) or the effects of mercury exposure (Wolfe et al., 2006). While biomonitoring usually requires the selection of indicator species, both ERA and HRA require selection of tissues such as urine, blood, and hair for humans and feathers, fur, or internal tissues for biota (Peakall, 1992; NRC, 2000b). Tissue indicators are usually called biomarkers for both ERA and HRA.

For both HRA and ERA, indicators should be biologically, methodologically, and societally relevant (Burger, 2006; Harris et al., 2006). In the case of mercury, indicators should provide early warning, exhibit changes in response to stress, and exhibit changes that result in important effects that can be attributable to a cause and that indicate something to both the organisms themselves and others higher or lower on the food chain. For example, levels of mercury in bass indicate potential uptake from their food (e.g. smaller fish or insects) and potential exposure to their predators (e.g. alligators, larger fish, or people). Methodological relevance means that the samples necessary to measure mercury levels can be easily obtained, that effects caused by mercury can be assessed in the field, that the data are easy to analyze, that the data relate directly to the assessment end points, and that the methods are not too costly. For an indicator to be useful for a long period of time, it must be of interest to the public, regulators, and public policy makers, and must be transparent and easy to understand and relate to other indicators.

Whereas internal tissues can be used as biomarkers of mercury exposure for many animals, these are less useful for people and many species of wildlife. It is often difficult to persuade people to give samples of blood, hair, or urine, and it is unwise to kill endangered species for tissue samples. Noninvasive tissues are usually more useful for long-term biomonitoring programs, such as urine and hair for mammals and feathers and eggs for birds. The bigger question for ERA is what species to select as bioindicators that reflect the ecosystem.

Risk assessors seeking the most sensitive species as bioindicators to predict deleterious effects for all species in an ecosystem are chasing an elusive goal. No one species can represent all other species. Instead, risk evaluators, managers, and regulators must select a suite of species that provide the most information for their particular goal, bringing us back to the importance of the problem-formulation phase for both HRA and ERA.

Since mercury generally accumulates in biota and bio-amplifies up the food chain, the task of selecting bioindicators for mercury includes determining which organisms in the system accumulate the highest levels and which species prey on those organisms. Both accumulation and bio-accumulation vary by species. For fish species that are low on the food chain, mercury normally accumulates more rapidly in bottom-feeding species that are exposed to mercury that has already accumulated in sediments, than those feeding in the water column. For example, in the Savannah River, spotted sucker (*Minytrema melanops*) and catfish (*Ictalurus punctatus*) feeding on the bottom had higher levels (means of 0.27 ppm and 0.20 ppm, respectively) of mercury than sunfish (*Lepomis* species) feeding in the water column (mean, 0.13 ppm) (Burger et al., 2001c). Top-level predatory fish within the system had the highest levels of mercury—Bowfin (*Amia calva*), with mean of 0.94 ppm, and Largemouth Bass with a mean of 0.47 ppm— than other fish lower on the food chain. Similarly, in the New York/New Jersey Harbor Estuary, mean mercury concentrations in Blue Crabs (*Callinectes sapidus*) and Mummichogs (*Fundulus heteroclitus*) were below 0.05 ppm, concentrations in Bluefish and young Striped Bass were about 0.1 ppm, those in White Perch (*Morone Americana*) and adult Bluefish (*Pomatomus saltatrix*) averaged about 0.2 ppm, and concentrations in eel (*Anguilla rostrata*) averaged 2.8 ppm (Iannuzzi et al., 2004). This is a useful suite of bioindicators because there are species low (i.e. crabs and mummichogs), intermediate (i.e. White Perch), and higher (i.e. adult Bluefish) on the food chain. Eel are interesting because they are not high on the food chain, but they feed on the sediment layer.

Bioindicators are most useful when they are of interest for evaluating both human and ecologic health (such as some edible, top-level fish) and when they provide information about the species itself, its population, and those of its prey or predators. For management purposes, mercury levels in indicator species should be measured with some periodicity to provide not only status of mercury concentrations in the system, but also of trends over time. For example, levels of mercury in bass and the feathers of Great Egrets have been monitored for many years in the Everglades, showing overall declines, with some regional hot spots requiring management and restoration (SFWMD, 2007).

Risk Balancing

Health professionals, ecologists, managers and the public must recognize that management of risks involves balancing both the risks and benefits. That is, a person worried about the risk of mercury from fish consumption, will balance that risk against the health benefits of consuming fish, as well as against the risks and benefits of eating replacement foods (such as red meat or other protein sources; Gochfeld and Burger, 2005). Willett (2005) suggested that the recent decline in fish consumption was "probably influenced" by fears about mercury in fish, and concluded that both risks and benefits of fish consumption should always be provided in risk communications.

Another aspect of risk balancing that is important to consider is the possible effect of other elements on mercury toxicity, or of other foods on mercury toxicity. Both aspects could be considered in both risk assessment and risk management. For example, Ralston (2008, 2009) and others (Cabanero et al., 2007, 2008; Pinheiro et al., 2009, Ralston and Raymond, 2010), have suggested that selenium reduces the toxicity of mercury, and thus some reasonable molar ratio should be used or considered as protective of mercury toxicity in risk assessment decisions. Selenium-mercury interaction may reduce the bioavailability or toxicity of methylmercury, and conversely some mercury toxicity may be due to impaired selenium-dependent enzyme synthesis or activity (Ralston et al., 2008). Recent work has included great variation in the selenium: mercury molar ratios within a species for both freshwater (Burger, 2011) and marine fish (Burger and Gochfeld, 2011, in press). Such variability makes it difficult to predict how much selenium may be available to reduce mercury toxicity. While the practical implications of the modification of mercury toxicity by selenium for risk assessment and management are unclear at this time, future work may include such considerations.

A third aspect that bears examination is the rational regulation of environmental hazards, such as mercury, should enhance the average quality of life for individuals, with some degree of equity in the distribution of risks and benefits (Gilbert, 1984; Bullard, 1990; Holloman and Newman, 2006). This leads to considerations of balancing the risks among people such that no one group bears the risks, while another group reaps the benefits. This is more likely to be the case with the siting of plants that expose people to mercury (e.g. chlor-alkali plants; Ullrich et al., 2007) or downwind of coal fired plants (Bradley and Suter, 2002). The question of environmental equity has moved to the fore, and should be considered when siting plants or considering the risk from mercury in fish.

For ecosystems, managers often must choose between prior study and adaptive management, choosing the proper level of biological organization (individual, populations, communities, ecosystem), and selecting among short-term versus long-term goals (Elms, 1997; Wilson and Lantz, 2000). Is the goal overall individual health and well-being, population health and well-being, or community health and well-being. Risk balancing often involves issues with mitigation and remediation because of mercury. A balanced risk design is one where the risks of adverse effects are balanced against one another such that the total risk is minimized, within a framework that is transparent to all parties. For example, is it "better" to remove soil that is contaminated with mercury, or leave it *in situ* because to remove the soil disrupts the total ecosystem for little gain in reduction of health effects due to mercury? Soil characteristics and mercury speciation influencing bioavailability are also important (Gochfeld, 2003). Inorganic mercury sequestered as sulphide requires less interference than more mobile or available species.

Environmental managers often must balance the risks and benefits of actions based on considerations of the exposure of people and other receptors to mercury through the food chain. For example, mercury in fish in the Savannah River, coming from the Department of Energy's Savannah River Site, posed a potential risk to people consuming fish from the river (Burger et al., 1999, 2001a, 2001c). Several risk-management strategies were considered: (1) Soil and sediment from Steel Creek could be removed to reduce the source of the mercury. (2) Other remediation strategies upstream could be considered, and (3) Consumption advisories could be promulgated to reach the at-risk populations. The resolution of the issue required obtaining site-specific data on mercury levels and consumption patterns and determining risk. Then it became a risk-balancing issue: What was the relationship between remediation (soil removal) and risk to people versus the ecosystem? Soil removal would clearly degrade or destroy the existing ecosystem (which had remained relatively unchanged for over 50 years). This had to be balanced against the risk to fish consumers. After considerable involvement of a range of stakeholders, including state officials, regulators, fishers, and the public, it was decided that developing a Fish Fact Sheet aimed at the target audience of fishers (and consumers) from the Savannah River would reduce risk to these consumers, while not increasing the risk to valuable aquatic and riparian ecosystems.

Finally, few studies have attempted to evaluate or rank the risks to ecosystems from different stressors, chemical as well as physical disruptions. The EPA has provided a framework for cumulative risk assessment that involves three phases: (1) planning, scoping, and problem formulation, (2) analysis, and (3) interpretation and risk characterization (Callahan and Sexton, 2007; Zartarian and Schultz, 2009). This is a necessary first step in evaluating multiple stressors (or multiple chemicals). Evaluating different risks can also involve a relative risk model to rank and sum individual risks numerically (Wiegers et al., 1998). Stressor sources and effects must be measured for each measurement end point. These can then be compared and ranked.

The task of integrating the risk from mercury with other stressors provides a great and continuing challenge. This is an area requiring considerable development of methods.

Future Research Needs

Mercury risk evaluations change frequently with respect to methods, information available, technologic advances, and the questions the public, health professionals, ecologists, and governments ask. It is increasingly clear, however, that the risks from mercury can be controlled only by determining sources of mercury in the environment, the pathways of exposure, and the concentrations of mercury in its different forms, in environmental media and the food chain. The concentrations in biota then must be calibrated to effects, ranging from sublethal effects to mortality; dose–response curves need to be developed not only for mortality (the percent of organisms that die at each exposure), but to several levels of sublethal effects. Compiling dose–response curves for a range of effects from mercury in different species (including humans) will provide information on interspecific (among species) variability. A major shortcoming of modern risk evaluation is the assumption that doses are distributed equally day by day, while recurrent exposures and intermittent or pulsed doses are simply averaged. This is no more logical than a person taking seven pills once a week rather than one pill a day and assuming that efficacy and toxicity would be the same. The interaction among toxicants, particularly mercury and PCBs (polychlorinated biphenyls), requires continued attention, as does the interaction of mercury and selenium. Far more studies of mercury levels and effects in a wide range of biota are required to illuminate a pattern in which interspecific extrapolation is reasonable. Intraspecific (within a species) variability is also critical, especially as a function of life stage (i.e. fetus, young, and adult) and other vulnerabilities. The body of data on fate and effects of mercury is increasing daily, and will continue to do so, providing insights into interindividual, intraspecific, and interspecific differences that can help manage the risks from mercury. The evaluation of the risks from mercury involves multiple media, species, exposure routes, and effects.

Armed with information on fate and effects of mercury in humans and other receptors, society still faces a number of issues that require scientific and social inputs and that require political and public policy decisions. These include determining the risk to populations, communities, and ecosystems; how to balance human and ecologic risk from mercury; how to balance the risks from mercury against the benefits of exposure (through fish consumption, industrial production, mining); how to evaluate intermittent high exposures; how to incorporate multiple stressors into risk assessment; and what is acceptable risk for humans, other receptors, and ecosystems.

Acknowledgments

We have had stimulating discussions about both human and ecological risk assessment, and on mercury, with many colleagues, and we thank them now: C. Chess, K. Cooper, M. Gallo, B.D. Goldstein, D. Kosson, M. Peterson, C. W. Powers, M. Lemire, D. Mergler, N. Ralston, E. Silbergeld, A. Stern, and D. Wartenberg. We thank C. Jeitner and T. Pittfield for help with the graphics. Over the years our research has been funded by the NIMH, EPA, NIEHS (P30ES005022), the Department of the Interior, the Department of Energy (through the Consortium for Risk Evaluation with Stakeholder Participation, AI # DE-FG 26-00NT 40938 and DE-FC01-06EW07053), the New Jersey Department of Environmental Protection (Office of Science, and Endangered and Nongame Species Program), Trust for Public Lands, New Jersey Audubon, the Jersey Coast Angler's Association, and EOHSI. The conclusions and interpretations reported herein are the sole responsibility of the author, and should not be interpreted as representing the views of the funding agencies.

References

ATSDR (Agency for Toxic Substances and Disease Registry). 1999. *Toxicological profile for mercury.* Atlanta, GA: Centers for Disease Control Prevention.

Bachman, R., A.L. Barton, J.R. Clark, P.L. deFur, S.J. Ells, S. J. Ells, C.A. Pittinger, M.W. Slimak, R.G. Stahl, and R.S. Wentsel. 1998. *A multi-stakeholder framework for ecological risk management: summary from a SETAC technical workshop.* Pensacola, FL: SETAC.

Barnthouse, L.W. 1992. The role of models in ecological risk assessment: a 1990s perspective. *Environmental Toxicology and Chemistry* 11:1751–1760.

Barnthouse, L.W. 1994. Issues in ecological risk assessment: the CRAM perspective. *Risk Analysis* 14:251–256.

Barnthouse, L.W., W.R. Munns, Jr., M.T. Sorensen. 2007. *Population-level ecological risk assessment.* Pensacola, FL: Society for Environmental Toxicology and Chemistry.

Barron, M.G., S.E. Duvall, and K.J. Barron. 2004. Retrospective and current risks of mercury to panthers in the Florida Everglades. *Ecotoxicology* 13:223–229.

Bartell, S.M., R.H. Gardner, and R.V. O'Neill. 1992. *Ecological risk estimation.* Boca Raton, FL: Lewis.

Bascietto, J., D. Hinckley, J. Plafkin, and M. Slimak. 1990. Ecotoxicity and ecological risk assessment: regulatory applications at EPA. *Environmental Science and Technology* 24:10–14.

Beate, L., B. Stephan, and D. Gustav. 2010. Proposal for a revised reference   243concentration (RfC0 for mercury vapour in adults. *Science of the Total Environment* 408:3530–3535.

Bloom, N.S. 1991. On the chemical form of mercury in edible fish and marine invertebrate tissue. *Canadian Journal of Fisheries and Aquatic Sciences* 49:1010–1017.

Boischio, A.A.P., and D.S. Henshel. 1996. Risk assessment of mercury exposure through fish consumption by the riverside people in the Madeira Basin, Amazon, 1991. *Neurotoxicology* 17:169–175.

Bradley, E.S., and G.W. Suter III. 2002. Screening evaluation of the ecological risks to terrestrial wildlife associated with a coal ash disposal site. *Human and Ecological Risk Assessment* 8:637–656.

Brain, R.A., H. Sanderson, P.K. Sibley, and K.R. Solomon. 2006. Probabilistic ecological hazard assessment: evaluating pharmaceutical effects on aquatic higher plants as an example. *Ecotoxicology and Environmental Safety* 64:128–135.

Bullard, R.D. 1990. *Dumping in Dixie: race, class, and environmental quality.* Boulder, CO: Westview Press.

Burger, J. 1997a. The historical basis for ecological risk assessment: preventive strategies for living in a chemical world. *Annals of the New York Academy of Sciences* 837:360–371.

Burger, J. 1997b. Methods for and approaches to evaluating susceptibility of ecological systems to hazardous chemicals. *Environmental Health Perspectives* 105:843–848.

Burger, J. 1999. Ecological risk assessment at the Department of Energy: an evolving process. *International Journal of Toxicology* 18:149–155.

Burger, J. 2006. Bioindicators: types, development, and use in ecological risk assessment and research. *Environmental Bioindicators* 1:22–39.

Burger, J. 2007. The effect of ecological systems of remediation to protect human health. *American Journal of Public Health* 97:1572–1578.

Burger, J. 2009. Risk to consumers from mercury in bluefish (*Pomatomus saltatrix*) from New Jersey: size, season and geographical effects. *Environmental Research* 109:803–811.

Burger, J. 2011. Selenium: mercury molar ratios in fish from the Savannah River: implications for risk management. *Journal of Risk Research.* 201:1–18.

Burger, J., and K.R. Campbell. 2004. Species differences in contaminants in fish on and adjacent to the Oak Ridge Reservation, Tennessee. *Environmental Research* 96:145–155.

Burger, J., K.F. Gaines, and M. Gochfeld. 2001c. Ethnic differences in risk from mercury among Savannah River fishermen. *Risk Analysis* 21:533–544.

Burger, J., and M. Gochfeld. 1997a. Paradigms for ecological risk assessment. *Annals of the New York Academy of Sciences* 837:372–386.

Burger, J., and M. Gochfeld. 1997b. Risk, mercury levels, and birds: relating adverse laboratory effects to field biomonitoring. *Environmental Research* 75:160–172.

Burger, J., and M. Gochfeld. 2001. On developing bioindicators for human and ecological health. *Environmental Monitoring and Assessment* 66:23–46.

Burger, J., and M. Gochfeld. 2004a. Bioindicators for assessing human and ecological health. In: *Environmental monitoring* Wiersma G.B. (ed.). Boca Raton, FL: CRC Press, pp. 541–566.

Burger, J., and M. Gochfeld. 2004b. Mercury in canned tuna: white versus light and temporal variation. *Environmental Research* 96:239–249.

Burger, J., and M. Gochfeld. 2004c. Metal levels in eggs of common terns (*Sterna hirundo*) in New Jersey: temporal trends from 1971 to 2002. *Environmental Research* 94: 336–343.

Burger, J., and M. Gochfeld, M. 2005. Heavy metals in commercial fish in New Jersey. *Environmental Research* 99:403–412.

Burger, J., and M. Gochfeld. 2006a. A framework and information needs for the management of the risks from consumption of self-caught fish. *Environmental Research* 101:275–285.

Burger, J., and M. Gochfeld. 2006b. Mercury in fish available in supermarkets in Illinois: are there regional differences. *Science of the Total Environment* 367:1010–1016.

Burger, J., and M. Gochfeld. 2007. Risk to consumers from mercury in Pacific cod (*Gadus macrocephalus*) from the Aleutians: fish age and size effects. *Environmental Research* 105:276–284.

Burger, J., and M. Gochfeld. 2011. Environmental justice: conceptual model for evaluating exposure pathways in low income, minority, Native American, and other unique exposure populations. *American Journal of Public Health.* 101: Suppl. 1:553–563.

Burger, J., and M. Gochfeld. 2011. Potential moderating effects of selenium on mercury uptake and selenium/mercury ratios in fish from Oak Ridge. Waste Management 2011.

Burger, J., and M. Gochfeld. (in press). Selenium and mercury ratios in saltwater fish from New Jersey: individual and species variations complicate possible use in human health consumption advisories. *Environmental Research.*

Burger, J., M. Gochfeld, C. Jeitner, S. Burke, T. Stamm, R. Snigaroff, D. Snigaroff, R. Patrick, and J. Weston. 2007a. Mercury levels and potential risk from subsistence foods from the Aleutians. *Science of the Total Environment* 384:93–105.

Burger, J., M. Gochfeld, C.W. Powers, D.S. Kosson, J. Halverson, G. Siekaniec, A. Morill, R. Patrick, L.D. Duffy, and D. Barnes. 2007b. Scientific research, stakeholders, and policy: continuing dialogue during research on radionuclides on Amchitka Island, Alaska. *Journal of Environmental Management* 85:232–244.

Burger, J., M. Gochfeld, C.W. Powers, L. Waishwell, C. Warren, and B.D. Goldstein. 2001a. Science, policy, stakeholders, and fish consumption advisories: developing a fish fact sheet for the Savannah River. *Journal of Environmental Management* 27:501–514.

Burger, J., S. Harris, B. Harper, and M. Gochfeld. 2010. Ecological information needs for environmental justice. *Risk Analysis* 30:893–905.

Burger, J., J. Hunter, and K. Cooper. 2001b. Using integrated food-web and population-based models for environmental monitoring, remediation decisions, and long-term planning. *Remediation,* 2001:87–102.

Burger, J., C.S. Stephens, S.C. Boring, M. Kuklinski, J.W. Gibbons, and M. Gochfeld. 1999. Factors in exposure assessment: ethnic and socioeconomic differences in fishing and consumption of fish caught along the Savannah River. *Risk Analysis,* 19:217–229.

Burger, J., A.H. Stern, and M. Gochfeld. 2005. Mercury in commercial fish: optimizing individual choices to reduce risk. *Environmental Health Perspectives* 113:266–271

Cabanero, A.I., C. Carvalho, Y. Madrid, C. Batoreu, and C. Camara. 2005. Quantification and speciation of mercury and selenium in fish samples of high consumption in Spain and Portugal. *Biological Trace Elements Research* 103:17–35.

Cabanero, A.I., Y. Madrid, and C. Camara. 2007. Mercury-selenium species ratio in representative fish samples and their bioaccessibility by an in vitro digestion method. *Biological Trace Element Research* 119:195–211.

Callahan, M.A., and K. Sexton. 2007. If cumulative risk assessment is the answer, what is the question? *Environmental Health Perspectives* 115:799–806.

Campbell, K.R., R.J. Dickey, R. Sexton, and J. Burger. 2002. Fishing along the Clinch River arm of Watts Bar Reservoir adjacent to the Oak Ridge Reservation, Tennessee: behavior, knowledge and risk perception. *Science of the Total Environment* 299:145–161.

Castilhos, Z.C., S. Rodrigues-Filho, A.P.C. Rodrigues, R.C. Villas-Boas, S. Siegel, M.M. Veiga, and C. Beinhoff. 2006. Mercury contamination in fish from gold mining areas in Indonesia and human health risk assessment. *Science of the Total Environment* 368:320–325.

CCMA. 2007. National Status and Trends Program: Mussel Watch. Center for Coastal Monitoring and Assessment. National Oceanic and Atmospheric Administration, Washington DC. http://ccma.nos.noaa.gov/stressors/pollution/nsandt (accessed December 31, 2007).

Chapman, P.M., A. Fairbrother, and D. Brown. 1998. A critical evaluation of safety (uncertainty) factors for ecological risk assessment. *Environmental Toxicology and Chemistry* 17:99–108.

Clark, J.R., K.H. Reinert, and P.B. Dorn. 1999. Development and application of benchmarks in ecological risk assessment. *Environmental Toxicology and Chemistry* 18:1869–1870.

Constantinou, E., M. Gerath, D. Mitchell, C. Seigneur, and L. Levin. 1995. Mercury from power plants: a probabilistic approach to the evaluation of potential health risks. *Water, Air and Soil Pollution* 80:1129–1138.

Corburn, J. 2002. Environmental justice, local knowledge, and risk: the discourse of a community-based cumulative exposure assessment. *Environmental Management* 29:451–466.

Davidson, P.W., G.J. Myers, C. Cox, C. Axtell, C. Shamlaye, J. Sloane-Reeves, E. Cernichiari, L. Needham, A. Choi, Y. Wang, M. Berlin, and T.W. Clarkson. 1998. Effects of prenatal and postnatal methylmercury exposure from fish consumption on neurodevelopment: outcomes at 66 months of age in the Seychelles Child Development Study. *Journal of the American Medical Association* 26:701–707.

Davidson, P.W., G.J. Myers, C. Shamlaye, C. Cox, and G.E. Wilding. 2004. Prenatal exposure to methylmercury and child development: influence of social factors. *Neurotoxicology and Teratology* 26:553–559.

Davidson, P.W., G.J. Myers, B. Weiss, C.F. Shamlaye, and C. Cox. 2006. Prenatal methylmercury exposure from fish consumption and child development: a review of evidence and perspectives from the Seychelles Child Development Study. *Neurotoxicology* 27:1106–1109.

Davis, S., and J.C. Ogden. 1994. *Everglades: the ecosystem and its restoration*. Boca Raton, FL: CRC Press.

DeForest, D.K., K.V. Brix, and W.J. Adams. 2007. Assessing metal bioaccumulation in aquatic environments: the inverse relationship between bioaccumulation factors, trophic transfer factors and exposure concentration. *Aquatic Toxicology* 84:236–246.

Denton, G.R.W., and C. Burdon-Jones. 1996. Trace metals in fish from the Great Barrier Reef. *Marine Pollution Bulletin* 17:201–209.

DiGuillio, R.T., and E. Monosson (eds.). 1996. *Interconnections between human and ecosystem health*. London: Chapman & Hall.

Donatuto, J., and B.L. Harper. 2008. Issues in evaluating fish consumption rates for Native American tribes. *Risk Analysis* 28:1497–1506.

Dorea, J.G. 2009. Studies of fish consumption as a source of methylmercury should consider fish-meal-fed farmed fish and other animal foods. *Environmental Research* 109:131–132.

Dorea, J.G. 2010. Research into mercury exposure and health education in subsistence fish-eating communities of the Amazon Basin: potential effects on public health policy. *International Journal of Environmental Research and Public Health* 7:367–3477.

Driscoll, C.T., M. Abbot, R. Bullock, J. Jansen, D. Leonard, S. Lindberg, J. Munthe, N. Pirrone, and M. Niles. 2006. Airsheds and watersheds. In: *Ecosystem responses to mercury contamination*. Harris, R. Krabbenhoft, D.P. Mason, R. Murray, M.W. Reash, R. and Saltman, T. (eds.). Boca Raton, FL: CRC Press, pp. 12–46.

Duvall, S.E., and M.G. Barron. 2000. A screening level probabilistic risk assessment of mercury in Florida Everglades food webs. *Ecotoxicology and Environmental Safety* 47:298–305.

European Commission. 2008. Commission Regulations: setting maximum levels for certain contaminants in food stuffs. EC-No-629/2008. Geneva, Switzerland.

Ehrlich, R. 2001. The impact of pollution from a mercury processing plant in KwaZulu-Antal, South Africa, on the health of fish-eating communities in the area: an environmental health risk assessment. *International Journal of Environmental Health Research* 11:41–50.

Eisler, E. 2003. Health risks of gold miners: a synoptic review. *Environmental Geochemistry and Health* 25:325–345.

Elms, D.G. 1997. Risk balancing in structural problems. *Structural Safety*, 19:67–77.

European Food Safety Authority. 2004. Opinion of the Scientific Panel on Contaminants in the Food Chain [CONTAM] related to mercury and methylmercury in food. EFSA-Q-2003-030 Adopted: 24 February, 2004. *EFSA Journal* 34:1–14. http://www.efsa.europa.eu/en/scdocs/scdoc/34.htm (accessed 9 Dec 2011).

FAO/WHO. 2003. Joint FAO/WHO Expert Committee on Food Additives, Sixty-first meeting Rome, 10–19 June, 2003. Geneva Switzerland: Food and Agriculture Organization of the United Nations and World Health Organization. JECFA/63SC.

Fiedler, N., J. Burger, and M. Gochfeld. 2007. Neurobehavioral toxicity. In: *Public health and preventive medicine*. Wallace, R.B. (ed.). New York: McGraw Hill, pp. 523–543.

Fisher, D.J., and D.T. Burton. 2004. Comparison of two U.S. environmental protection agency species sensitivity distribution methods for calculating ecological risk criteria. *Human and Ecological Risk Assessment* 9:675–690.

Fitzgerald, W.F., and R.P. Mason. 1996. The global mercury cycle: oceanic and atmospheric aspects. In: *Global and regional mercury cycles: sources, fluxes and mass balances*. Baeyens, W. Ebinghaus, R. Vasiliev, O. (eds.). Dordrecht, the Netherlands: Kluwer Academic, pp. 85–108.

Fung, Y., and M.P. Molvar. 1992. Toxicity of mercury from dental environment and from amalgam restorations. *Journal of Toxicology* 30:49–61.

Gilbert, T.L. 1984. Problems of risk balancing for regulating environmental hazards. U.S. Department of Energy Technical Report. Washington DC: National Technical Information Service. NTIS, PC A02/MF A01.

Ginsberg, G.I., and B.F. Toal. 2000. Development of a single-meal fish consumption advisory for methylmercury. *Risk Analysis* 20:41–47.

Gochfeld, M. 2003. Cases of mercury exposure, bioavailability, and absorption. *Ecotoxicology Environmental Safety* 56:174–179.

Gochfeld, M., and J. Burger. 2005. Good fish/bad fish: a composite benefit-risk by dose curve. *Neurotoxicology* 26:511–520.

Gochfeld, M., and J. Burger. 2007. Environmental and ecological risk assessment. In: *Public health and preventive medicine*. Wallace, R.B. (ed.). New York: McGraw–Hill, pp. 545–562.

Goldblum, D.K., A. Rak, M.D. Ponnapalli, and C.J. Clayton. 2006. The Fort Totten mercury pollution risk assessment: a case history. *Journal of Hazardous Materials* 136:406–417.

Grandjean, P., P. Weihe, R.F. White and F. Debes. 1998. Cognitive performance of children prenatally exposed to "safe" levels of methylmercury. *Environmental Research* 77:165–172.

Greenberg, M., J. Burger, M. Gochfeld, D. Kosson, K. Lowrie, H. Mayer, C.W. Powers, C.D. Volz, and V. Vyas. 2005. End-state land uses, sustainability protective systems, and risk management: a challenge for remediation and multigenerational stewardship. *Remediation* Winter:91–105.

Groth, E. III. 2010. Ranking the contribution of commercial fish and shellfish varieties to mercury exposure in the United States: implications for risk communication. *Environmental Research*. doi:10.1016/j.envres.2009.12.006.

Harnly, M., S. Seidel, P. Rojas, R. Fornes, P. Flessel, D. Smith, R. Dreutzer, and L. Goldman. 1997. Biological monitoring for mercury within a community with soil and fish contamination. *Environmental Health Perspectives* 105:424–429.

Harris, S.G., and B.L. Harper. 1997. A Native American exposure scenario, and a tribal risk model. *Risk Analysis* 17:789–795.

Harris, R., D.P. Krabbenhoft, R. Mason, M.W. Murray, R. Reash, and T. Saltman (eds.). 2006. *Ecosystem responses to mercury contamination*. Boca Raton, FL: CRC Press.

Hays, S.M., R.A. Becker, H.W. Leung, L.L. Aylward, and D.W. Pyatt. 2007. Biomonitoring equivalents: a screening approach for interpreting biomonitoring results from a public health perspective. *Regulatory Toxicology and Pharmacology* 47:96–109.

He, Q.L., Z.F. Yan, Q.H. Wang, and F.S. Li. 2006. The application of earthworm avoidance test in ecological risk assessment of naphthalene-contaminated soils. *Journal of Agro-Environmental Science* 26:538–543.

Hightower, J., and D. Moore. 2002. Mercury levels in high-end consumers of fish. *Environmental Health Perspectives* 111:604–608.

Holloman, E.L., and M.C. Newman. 2006. A probabilistic assessment of mercury exposure to African Americans consuming local fish and shellfish. *Transactions of the American Geophysical Union* 87:suppl 36.

Hughner, R.S., J.K. Maher, and N.M. Childs. 2008. Review of food policy and consumer issues of mercury in fish. *Journal of the American College of Nutrition* 27:185–194.

Hung, C.L.H., R.K.F. Lau, J.C.W. Lam, T.A. Jerrerson, S.K. Hung, M.H.W. Lam, and P.K.S. Lam. 2007. Risk assessment of trace elements in the stomach contents of Indo-Pacific humpback dolphins and finless porpoises in Hong Kong waters. *Chemosphere* 66:1175–1182.

Hunsaker, C.T., R.L. Graham, G.W. Suter II, R.V. O'Neill, L.W. Barnthouse, and R.H. Gardner. 1990. Assessing ecological risk on a regional scale. *Journal of Environmental Management* 14:325–332.

Hylander, L.D., E.C. Silva, L.J. Oliveira, S.A. Silva, E.K. Kuntze, and D.X. Silva. 1994. Mercury levels in Alto Pantanal: a screening study. *Ambio* 33:478–484.

Iannuzzi, T.J., T.N. Armstrong, J.B. Thelen, D.F. Ludwig, and C.D. Firstenberg. 2004. Chemical contamination of aquatic organisms from an urbanized river in the New York/New Jersey harbor estuary. *Human and Ecological Risk Assessment* 10:389–413.

IOM (Institute of Medicine). 1991. Seafood Safety. National Academy Press, Wasington, DC.

IOM, 2006. Seafood choices: balancing benefits and risks. Washington, DC: National Academies Press.

Iwata, T., M. Sakamoto, X. Feng, M. Yoshida, X.J. Liu, M. Dakeishi, P. Li, G. Qiu, H. Jiang, M. Nakamura, and M. Kaysuyuki. 2007. Effects of mercury vapor exposure on neuromotor function in Chinese miners and smelters. *International Archives of Occupational and Environmental Health* 80: 381–387.

Jewett, S., C.X. Zhang, A.S. Naidu, J.J. Kelley, D. Dasher, and L.K. Duffy. 2003. Comparison of mercury and methylmercury in northern pike and Arctic grayling from western Alaska rivers. *Chemosphere* 50:381–392.

JECFA (Joint FAO/WHO Expert Committee on Food Additives). 1999. Evaluation of certain food additives and contaminants. Fifty-third report of the Joint FAO/WHO Expert Committee on Food Additives. *WHO Technical Report Series* 896. Geneva: World Health Organization, pp 87–93.

JECFA (Joint FAO/WHO Expert Committee on Food Additives). 2003. Summary and conclusions of the sixty-first meeting of the Joint FAO/WHO Expert Committee on Food Additives (JECFA), pp. 18–22. http://www.who.int/pcs/jecfa/Summary61.pdf (accessed 18 Jan 2011).

JECFA. 2004. Methylmercury. In: *Safety evaluation of certain food additives and contaminants*. Report of the 61st Joint FAO/WHO Expert Committee on Food Additives. Geneva: World Health Organization, International Programme on Chemical Safety. WHO Technical Report Series 922, pp 132–139. http://whqlibdoc.who.int/trs/WHO_TRS_922.pdf (accessed 1 Jan 2011).

JECFA. 2006. Methylmercury. Summary and conclusions of the 67th Joint FAO/WHO Expert Committee on Food Additives. Geneva, World Health Organization, International Programme on Chemical Safety. WHO Technical Report Series 940. www.who.int/ipcs/food/jecfa/summaries/summary67.pdf (accessed February 23, 2012).

Johnston, J.J., and J.L. Snow. 2007. Population-based fish consumption survey and probabilistic methylmercury risk assessment. *Human and Ecological Risk Assessment* 13: 1214–1227.

Lackey, R.T. 1996. Is ecological risk assessment useful for resolving complex ecological problems? In: *Pacific Salmon and their ecosystems: status and future options*. Stouder, D.J. Bisson, P.A. and Naiman, R.J. (eds.). New York: Chapman & Hall, pp. 525–540.

Landrigan, P.J., A.L. Golden, and H.J. Simpson. 2006. Toxic substances and their impacts on human health in the Hudson River watershed. In: *Hudson River Estuary*. Levinton, J. S. and Waldman, J.R. (eds.). New York: Cambridge University Press, pp. 413–427.

Lange, T.R., H.E. Royals, and L.L. Connor. 1994. Mercury accumulation in largemouth bass (*Micropterus salmoides*) in a Florida lake. *Environmental Contamination and Toxicology* 27:466–471.

Lansens, P., M. Leemakers and W. Vaeyens. 1991. Determination of methylmercury in fish by headspace-gas chromatography with microwave-induced-plasma detection. *Water, Air and Soil Pollution* 56:103–115.

Loredo, J., A. Periera, and A. Ordonez. 2003. Untreated abandoned mercury mining works in a scenic area of Asturias (Spain). *Environment International* 29:481–491.

Mahaffey, K.R., R.P. Clickner, and R.A. Jeffries. 2009. Adult women's blood mercury concentrations vary regionally in the United States: association with patterns of fish consumption (NHANES, 1999–2004). *Environmental Health Perspectives* 117:47–53.

Maramba, N.P.C., J.P. Reyes, A.T. Francisco-Rivera, L.C.R. Panganiban, C. Dioquino, N. Dando, R. Timbang, H. Akagi, M.T. Castillo, C. Quitoriano, M. Afuang, A. Matsuyama, T. Eguich, and Y. Fuchigame. 2006. Environmental and human exposure assessment monitoring of communities near an abandoned mercury mine in the Philippines: a toxic legacy. *Journal of Environmental Management* 81:135–145.

Marins, R.V., J.B. DeAndrade, P.A. DeP.Pereira, E.C. Paiva, and H.H.M. Paraquetti. 2000. Sampling techniques for the assessment of anthropogenic vapour and particulate mercury in the Brazilian Amazon atmosphere. *Journal of Environmental Monitoring* 2:325–328.

Moore, D.R.J., B.E. Sample, G.W. Suter, B.R. Parkhurst, and R.S. Teed. 1999. A probabilistic risk assessment of the effects of methylmercury and PCBs on mink and kingfishers along East Fork Poplar Creek, Oak Ridge, Tennessee, USA. *Environmental Toxicology and Chemistry* 18:2941–2953.

Mozaffarian, D. 2009. Fish, mercury, selenium and cardiovascular risk: current evidence and unanswered questions. *International Journal of Environmental Research and Public Health* 6:1894–1916.

Mueezzinoglu, A. 2003. A review of environmental consideration on gold mining and production. *Critical Reviews in Environmental Science and Technology* 33:45–71.

Muir, D.C.G., R.G. Shearer, J. van Oosdam, S.G. Donaldson, and C. Furgal. 2005. Contaminants in Canadian arctic biota and implications for human health. *Science of the Total Environment* 351–352:539–546.

Myers, G.J., S.W. Thurston, A.T. Pearson, P.W. Davidson, C. Cox, C.F. Shanmlaye, E. Cernichiari, and T.W. Clarkson. 2009. Potential exposure to methylmercury from fish consumption: a review and new data from the Seychelles Child Development Study. *Neurotoxicology* 30:338–349.

Naito, W., Y. Gamo, and K. Yoshida. 2006. Screening-level risk assessment of Di(2-ethylhexyl)phthalate for aquatic organisms using monitoring data in Japan. *Environmental Monitoring and Assessment* 115:451–471.

Newman, M.C. 1998. *Fundamentals of ecotoxicology*. Boca Raton, FL: Lewis.

Nichols, J.W. 2001. Use of indicators in ecological risk assessment for persistent, bioaccumulative toxicants. *Human and Ecological Risk Assessment* 7:1043–1057.

NJDEP (New Jersey Department of Environmental Protection). 2001. Final Report: NJ Mercury task force. Trenton, NJ.

Norton, S.B., D.J. Rodier, J.H. Gentile, W.H. van der Schalie, W.P. Wood and M.W. Slimak. 1992. A framework for ecological risk assessment for EPA. *Environmental Toxicology and Chemistry* 11:1663–1672.

NRC, 1983. *Risk assessment in the federal government*. Washington DC: National Academies Press.

NRC, 1986. *Ecological knowledge and environmental problem-solving*. Washington DC: National Academies Press.

NRC, 1993. *Issues in risk assessment*. Washington DC: National Academies Press.

NRC, 1994. *Building consensus through risk assessment and management of the Department of Energy's Environmental Remediation Program*. Washington DC: National Academies Press.

NRC, 1996. *Upstream: salmon and society in the Pacific Northwest*. Washington DC: National Academies Press.

NRC, 2000a. *Toxicological effects of methylmercury*. Washington DC: National Academies Press.

NRC, 2000b. *Ecological indicators for the nation*. Washington, DC: National Academies Press.

NRC, 2009. *Science and decisions: advancing risk assessment*. Washington, DC: National Academies Press.

Odum, E.T., 1957. *Fundamentals of ecology*. Philadelphia: Saunders.

Pacyna, E.G., J.M. Pacyna, F. Steenhuisen, and S. Wilson. 2006. Global anthropogenic mercury emissions inventory for, 2000. *Atmospheric Environment* 40:4048–4063.

Paruchuri, Y., A. Siuniak, N. Johnson, E. Levin, K. Mitchell, J.M. Goodrich, E.P. Renne, and N. Basu. 2010. Occupational and environmental mercury exposure among small-scale gold miners in the Talensi-Nabdam District of Ghana's Upper East region. *Science of the Total Environment* 408: 6079–6085.

Payne, R.T. 1966. Food web complexity and species diversity. *American Naturalist* 100:65–75.

Peakall, D. 1992. *Animal biomarkers as pollution indicators*. London: Chapman & Hall.

Pinheiro, M.C.N., J.L.M. de Nascimento, L.C.L. Silveira, J.B.T. daRocha, and M. Aschner. 2009. Mercury and selenium – a review on aspects related to the health of human populations in the Amazon. *Environmental Bioindicators* 4:222–245.

Power, M., and L.S. McCarty. 1997. Fallacies in ecological risk assessment practices. *Environmental Sciences and Technology* 31:370A–375A.

PCCRARM, 1997. *Framework for environmental health risk assessment*. Washington DC: US Congress.

Ralston, N.V.C. 2008. Selenium health benefit values as seafood safety criteria. *Eco-Health* 5: 442–455.

Ralston, N.V.C. 2009. Introduction to 2nd issue on special topic: selenium and mercury as interactive environmental indicators. *Environmental Bioindicators* 4:286–290.

Ralston, N.V., and L.J. Raymond. 2010. Dietary selenium's protective effects against methylmercury toxicity. *Toxicology* 278:112–123.

Ralston, N.V.C., C.R. Ralston, J. L. Blackwell III, and L.J. Raymond. 2008. Dietary and tissue selenium in relation to methylmercury toxicity. *Neurotoxicology* 29:802–811.

Rasmussen, N.C. 1981. The application of probabilistic risk assessment techniques to energy technologies. *Annual Review of Energy* 6:123–138.

Rice, G., J. Swartout, K. Mahaffey, and R. Schoeny. 2000. Deviation of U.S. EPA's oral Reference Dose (RfD) for methylmercury. *Drug Chemistry and Toxicology* 23:41–54.

Riley, D.M., C.A. Newby, T.O. Leal-Almeraz, and V.M. Thomas. 2001. Assessing elemental mercury vapor exposure from cultural and religious practices. *Environmental Health Perspectives* 109:779–784.

Rojas, M., D. Siejas, O. Agreda, and M. Rodriguez. 2006. Biological monitoring of mercury exposure in individuals referred to a toxicological center in Venezuela. *Science of the Total Environment* 354:278–285.

Rothschild, R.F.N., and L.K. Duffy. 2002. Preliminary study on total mercury in the common prepared subsistence foods of a rural Alaskan village. *Alaska Medicine 2002*; 44:89–103.

Rowe, G., and L.H. Frewer. 2000. Public participation methods: a framework for evaluation. *Science, Technology and Human Values* 25:3–29.

Ruckelshaus, W.D. 1985. Risk, science and democracy. *Issues in Science and Technology* 1:19–38.

Rumbold, D. 2005. A probabilistic risk assessment of the effects of methylmercury on great egrets and bald eagles foraging at a constructed wetland in South Florida relative to the Everglades. *Human and Ecological Risk Assessment* 2:365–388.

Satoh, H., N. Yasuda, and S. Shimai. 1985. Development of reflexes in neonatal mice prenatally exposed to methylmercury and selenite. *Toxicological Letters* 25:199–203.

Scherer, A.C., A. Tsuchiya, L.R. Younglove, T.M. Burbacher, and E. M. Faustman. 2008. Comparative analysis of state fish consumption advisories targeting sensitive populations. *Environmental Health Perspectives* 116:1598–1606.

Schierow, L.-J. 2004. *Mercury in the environment: sources and health risks.* CRS Report for Congress. http://ncseonline.org/NLE/CRSreports/04Jun/RL32420.pdf (accessed 6 Oct 2011).

Schoeny, R. 1996. Use of genetic toxicology data in U.S. EPA risk assessment: mercury study report as an example. *Environmental Health Perspectives* 104:Suppl 3:663–674.

Seigneur, C., P. Pai, M. Gerath, D. Mitchell, G. Hamby, G. Gong, C. Whipple, and L. Levin. 2006. Probabilistic assessment of regional mercury exposure. *Water, Air and Soil Pollution* 97:159–168.

Selin, N.E., E.M. Sunderland, C.D. Knightes, and R.P. Mason. 2010. Sources of mercury exposure for U.S. seafood consumers: implications for policy. *Environmental Health Perspectives* 118:137–143.

SFWMD (South Florida Water Management District). 2007. *South Florida Environmental Report: 2007.* G. Redfield (ed.). West Palm Beach, FL: SFWMD.

SFWMD (South Florida Water Management District). 2010. *South Florida Environmental Report: 2010.* G. Redfield (ed.). West Palm Beach, FL. SFWMD.

Sheehan, P.J. 1984. Effects on community and ecosystem structure and dynamics. In: *Effects of pollutants at the ecosystem level.* P.J. Sheehan, D.R. Miller, G.C. Butler and P. Bourdeau (eds.). Chichester, England: Wiley, 22: 51–100.

Sheridan, S.K., T.G. Townsend, J.L. Price, and J.T. Connell. 2000. Policy options for hazardous-building-component removal before demolition. *Practice Periodical of Hazardous, Toxic, and Radioactive Waste Management* 4:111–117.

Shimshack, J.P., M.B. Ward, and T.K.M. Beatty. 2007. Mercury advisories: information, education, and fish consumption. *Journal of Environmental Economics and Management* 53:158–179.

Shim, S.M., M. Ferruzzi, Y.C. Kim, E.M. Janie, and C.R. Santerre. 2009. Impact of phytochemical-rich foods on bioaccessibility of mercury from fish. *Food Chemistry* 112:46–50.

Shipp, A.M., P.R. Gentry, P.R. Gentry, G. Lawrence, C. Van Landingham, T. Covington, H.J. Clewell, K. Gribben, and K. Crump. 2000. Determination of a site-specific reference dose for methylmercury for fish-eating populations. *Toxicology and Industrial Health* 16:335–438.

Sorensen, M.T., W.R. Gala, and J.A. Margolin. 2004. Approaches to ecological risk characterization and management: selecting the right tools for the job. *Human and Ecological Risk Assessment* 10:245–269.

Steevens, J.A., M.R. Reiss, and A.V. Pawlisz. 2005. A methodology for deriving tissue residue benchmarks for aquatic biota: a case study for fish exposed to 2,3,7,8-tetrachlorodibenzo-p-dioxin and equivalents. *Integrated Environmental Assessment and Management* 1:142–151.

Stern, A.H. 2005. A revised probabilistic estimate of the maternal methylmercury intake dose corresponding to a measured cord blood mercury concentration. *Environmental Health Perspectives* 113:155–163.

Sunderland, E.M. 2007. Mercury exposure from domestic and imported estuarine and marine fish in the U.S. seafood market. *Environmental Health Perspectives* 115:235–242.

Sunderland, E.M., M. Cohen, N.E. Selin, and G.L. Chmura. 2008. Reconciling models and measurements to assess trends in atmospheric mercury deposition. *Environmental Pollution* 156:526–535.

Suter, G.W. II. 1996. Toxicological benchmarks for screening contaminants of potential concern for effects on freshwater biota. *Environmental Toxicology and Chemistry* 7:1232–1241.

Suter, G.W. II. 2001. Applicability of indicator monitoring to ecological risk assessment. *Ecological Indicators* 1:101–112.

Suter, G.W. II, R.A. Efroymson, B.E. Sample, and D.S. Jones. 2000. *Ecological risk assessment for contaminated sites.* Boca Raton, FL: Lewis.

Suter, G.W. II, T. Vermeire, W.R. Munns, Jr., and J. Sekizawa. 2003. Framework for an integration of health and ecological risk assessment. *Human and Ecological Risk Assessment* 9:281–301.

Suter, G W. II, T. Vermeire, W.R. Munns, Jr., and J. Sekizawa. 2005. An integrated framework for health and ecological risk assessment. *Toxicology and Applied Pharmacology* 207:611–616.

Swain, E.B., P.M. Jakus, G. Rice, F. Lupi, P.A. Maxson, J.M. Pacyna, A. Penn, S.J. Spiegel, and M.M. Veiga. 2007. Socioeconomic consequences of mercury use and pollution. *Ambio* 36:45–61.

Tannenbaum, I., M. Johnson, and M. Bazar. 2003. Application of the hazard quotient in remedial decisions: a comparison of human and ecological risk assessments. *Human and Ecological Risk Assessment* 9:387–401.

Tardiff, R.G., and B.D. Goldstein. 1992. *Methods for assessing exposure of human and non-human biota.* Chichester, UK: Wiley.

Toth, J.F. Jr., and R.B. Brown. 1997. Racial and gender meanings of why people participate in recreational fishing. *Leisure Science* 19:129–146.

Tran, N.L., L. Barraj, K. Smith, A. Javier, and T.A. Burke. 2004. Combining food frequency and survey data to quantify long-term dietary exposure: a methylmercury case study. *Risk Analysis* 24:19–30.

Ullrich, S.M., M.A. Ilyushchenko, T.W. Tanton, and G.A. Uskov. 2007. Mercury contamination in the vicinity of a derelict chlor-alkali plant. Part II: contamination of the aquatic and terrestrial food chain and potential risks to the local population. In Mercury contaminated sites: characterization, risk assessment and remediation. *Science of the Total Environment* 381:1–26.

USACOE, 1996. *Risk assessment handbook*. Volume II: Environmental evaluations. EM200-14. Washington DC: USACOE.

USDOE, 2009. *Environmental justice at the U.S. Department of Energy*. www.lm.doe.gov/env_justice/ (accessed 8 Sept 2011).

USDOI, 1986. *Natural resource damage assessments: final: final rule. Federal Register* 51:27646–27753.

USEPA, 1986. Risk assessment guidelines for carcinogenicity, mutagenicity, complex mixtures, suspect developmental toxicants, and estimating exposures. *Federal Register* 51:33992–34054.

USEPA. 1995. *Integrated Risk Information System—Mercury, elemental*. http://www.epa.gov/iris/subst/0370.htm

USEPA, 1997. *Ecological risk assessment guidance for superfund process for designing and conducting ecological risk assessments*. Washington, DC: USEPA.

USEPA, 2001. *Ecological risk assessment bulletins—supplement to RAGS, region 4*. Washington, DC: USEPA.

USEPA, 2001a. *Freshwater criterion for fish*. http://www.epa.gov/fedgstr/EPA-WATER/2001/January/Day-08/w217.htm (accessed 7 Jan 2011).

USEPA, 2001b. *Integrated risk information system: methylmercury MeHg*. http://www.epa.gov/ncea/iris/subst/0073.htm (accessed 14 Feb 2011).

USEPA, 2006. *Integrated risk information system data base for methylmercury*. www.epa.gov/iris (accessed 20 Nov 2011).

USEPA, 2009a. *Environmental justice: compliance and enforcement*. http://www.epa.gov/environmentaljustice (accessed 30 July 2011).

USEPA, 2009b. *Integrated risk information system: site help and tools—glossary*. http://www.epa.gov/iris/help_gloss.htm (accessed 1 Jan 2011).

USEPA, 2010. *Superfund risk assessment: human health: exposure assessment*. http://www.epa.gov/answer/riskassessment/index.htm (accessed 1 Aug 2011).

USFDA, 2001. *FDA consumer advisory*. Washington, DC: U.S. Food and Drug Administration. http//www.fda.gov/bbs/topics/ANSWERS/2000/advisory.html (accessed December 1, 2001).

USFDA, 2003. *FDA consumer advisory*. Washington, DC: U.S. Food and Drug Administration. http//www.fda.gov/bbs/topics/ANSWERS/2000/advisory.html (1 January 1, 2004);2003.

USFDA, 2005. *Mercury levels in commercial fish and shellfish*. Washington, DC: Food and Drug Administration. http//www.fda.gov/bbs/topics/ANSWERS/2000/advisory.html (accessed 1 January 1, 2005).

USFDA, 2006 (updated). *Mercury concentrations in fish: FDA monitoring program, 1990–2004*. Washington, DC: U.S. Food and Drug Administration. Available http//www.fda.gov/~dms/admehg3.html. (accessed 2 December 2, 2007).

Van der Schalie, W.H., H.S. Gardner, J.A. Bantle, C.T. DeRose, R.A. Finch, J.S. Reif, R. H. Reuter, L.C. Backer, J. Burger, L.C. Folmar, and W.S. Stokes. 1999. Animals as sentinels of human health hazards of environmental chemicals. *Environmental Health Perspectives* 107:309–315.

Washburn, S.T., C.F. Kleiman, and D.E. Arsnow. 1998. Applying USEPA risk assessment guidance in the 90s. *Human and Ecological Risk Assessment* 4:763–774.

Watanabe, C., K. Yin, Y. Kasanuma, and H. Satoh. 1999. In utero exposure to methylmercury and Se deficiency converge on the neurobehavioral outcome in mice. *Neurotoxicology and Teratology* 21: 83–88.

Wendroff, A.P. 1995. Magico-religious mercury use and cultural sensitivity. *American Journal of Public Health* 85:409–410.

Wheatley, B., and M.A. Wheatley. 2000. Methylmercury and the health of indigenous peoples: a risk management challenge for physical and social sciences, and for public health policy. *Science of the Total Environment* 259:23–29.

WHO, 2005. *Policy paper: mercury in health care*. Geneva: World Health Organization (WHO/SDE/WSH/05.08). http://www.who.int/water_sanitation_health (accessed 7 Feb 2011).

WHO, 2007. *Preventing disease through healthy environments: exposure to mercury: a major public health concern*. World Health Organization Mercury Flyer. http://www.who.int/phe/news/Mercury-flyer.pdf (accessed 18 Jan 2011).

Wiegers, J.K., H.M. Feder, L.S. Mortensen, D.G. Shaw, V.J. Wilson, and W.G. Landis. 1998. A regional multi-stressor rank-based ecological risk assessment for the Fjord of Port Valdez, Alaska. *Human and Ecological Risk Assessment* 4:1125–1173.

Willett, W.C. 2005. Balancing health risks and benefits. *American Journal of Preventive Medicine* 29:321–321.

Williams, B.L., and M.S. Magsumbol. 2007. Emergency preparedness among people living near U.S. Army chemical weapons sites after September 11, 2001. *American Journal of Public Health* 97:1601–1607.

Wilson, E.O. 1986. *Biodiversity*. Washington, DC: National Academies Press.

Wilson, M.V., and L.E. Lantz. 2000. Issues and framework for building successful science-management teams for natural areas management. *Natural Areas Journal* 20:381–385.

Wolfe, M.F., T. Atkeson, W. Bowerman, J. Burger, D.C. Evers, M. Murray, and E. Zillioux. 2006. Wildlife indicators. In: *Ecosystem responses to mercury contamination*. Harris, R. Krabbenhoft, D.P. Mason, R. Murray, M.W. Reash, R. and Saltman, T. (eds.). Boca Raton, FL, CRC Press, pp. 123–190.

Zartarian, V.G., and B.D. Schultz. 2009. The EPA's human exposure research program for assessing cumulative risk in communities. *Journal of Exposure Science and Environmental Epidemiology*, 2009:1–8.

Zeeman, M., and J. Gilford. 1993. Ecological hazard evaluation and risk assessment under EPA's Toxic Substances Control Act (TSCA): an introduction. In: *Toxicology and risk assessment*. Landis, W.G. J.S. Hughes, and M.A. Lewis (eds.). Philadelphia: American Society of Testing and Materials, Vol. 1, pp. 7–21.

Zhang, H., X. Feng, T. Larrsen, T. Qiu, and R. Vogt. 2010. In inland China, rice, rather than fish, is the major pathway for methylmercury exposure. *Environmental Health Perspectives* 118:1183–1188.

Mercury and Public Health

An Assessment of Human Exposure

WENDY McKELVEY and EMILY OKEN

EXPOSURE SOURCES AND HEALTH EFFECTS

Methylmercury in Fish

Ethylmercury in Vaccines

Elemental Mercury in Dental Amalgams

Mercury in Teething Powders, Laxatives, and "Traditional Medicine Products"

Mercury in Skin Care Products and Antiseptics

Ritualistic or Cultural Use of Elemental Mercury

Occupational Exposures and Elemental Mercury Spills

Organomercurials as Fungicides on Seed Grain and in Latex Paint

DERIVATION OF EXPOSURE GUIDELINES FOR METHYLMERCURY

CLINICAL ASSESSMENT OF EXPOSURE TO MERCURY

BIOMONITORING FOR MERCURY EXPOSURE IN HUMAN POPULATIONS

Mercury Levels in Blood and Hair

Mercury Levels in Urine

FUTURE BIOMONITORING EFFORTS

REGULATIONS AND RECOMMENDATIONS FOR REDUCING EXPOSURE TO MERCURY

Fish Consumption Advisories

CONCLUSION

Historically, humans have suffered toxic effects of mercury as a result of purposeful as well as accidental exposures. Mercury has been used in medical remedies for centuries. Some scientists believe it was used during the Middle Ages to treat diseases that manifested with skin lesions, such as syphilis and leprosy (Goldwater, 1972; Rasmussen et al., 2008). Earlier medicinal uses have been documented in China, India, and the Middle East (Goldwater, 1972). Mercury is still used medicinally in some parts of the world (Liu et al., 2008; Saper et al., 2008).

The toxicity of mercury and mercury-containing remedies has also long been recognized. In the 16th century, Paracelsus, the Swiss physician and alchemist, noted harmful effects resulting from high or prolonged doses. The concomitant toxic and presumed curative properties of mercury prompted him to write: "What is there that is not poison? All things are poison and nothing (is) without poison. Solely the dose determines that a thing is not a poison" (Deichmann et al., 1986). This statement is commonly paraphrased as, "The dose makes the poison."

Mercury has many useful properties that have perhaps contributed toward a tendency to overlook its toxicity. Its ability to control the growth of microorganisms led to its use as a fungicide on seed grain and in interior and exterior latex paint, as a topical antiseptic, and as a preservative in cosmetics, eye drops, and vaccination vials. Elemental mercury responds quickly and evenly to changes in temperature and pressure, making it a prime candidate for use in thermometers, barometers, manometers (such as blood pressure gauges) and other measuring devices. Its electrical and chemical properties have led to its use in thermostats, switches, fluorescent lights, batteries, and industrial processes. It has a high reflective index and can be found in antique mirrors, painted behind sheets of glass as an amalgam with tin (Goldwater, 1972). It easily forms alloys with other metals, and the process of amalgamation followed by burning is still used to recover gold from ore. Amalgams of mercury with silver and other metals have been used to fill dental caries for over a century. The interesting appearance of this metal in its liquid state has also led to its use in children's toys and necklaces (Washington State Department of Health, 2008).

Humans may be exposed to mercury in three chemical forms:

• Inorganic compounds, which refer to mercury combined with chlorine, sulfur, oxygen and other noncarbon groups.

- Elemental (or metallic) mercury—also an inorganic form, which is mercury *un*combined with other elements.
- Organic compounds, which refer to mercury combined with methyl, ethyl, or other carbon groups.

Elemental mercury in its silvery, liquid state is perhaps most familiar, although its vapor has a far greater impact on health. The toxicity of mercury varies according to the form and route of exposure, the dose, and the age at which a person is exposed (ATSDR, 1999).

Exposure Sources and Health Effects

Human exposure to mercury today may occur from a number of sources, including dietary fish and seafood, dental amalgams, some vaccines, cosmetics and skin care products, traditional/herbal medicine products, ritualistic practices involving elemental mercury, some occupational settings, and spills or breaks of mercury-containing articles or devices. Methylmercury is arguably the most important form for exposure to mercury worldwide because of its pervasiveness in fish and its neurotoxicity (IPCS, 1990; US EPA, 1997).

Methylmercury in Fish

Methylmercury makes its way into fish tissue through a series of steps that begins with emission of elemental mercury into the atmosphere, in part from natural processes (e.g., volcanic activity, forest fires, weathering of rocks, and degassing from soil and surface water), and also as a result of human activities (e.g., combustion of coal and other fossil fuels, waste incineration, and recycling of previously deposited anthropogenic mercury) (Lindberg et al., 2007).

Atmospheric mercury may travel short or long distances and deposit in the sediment beds of bodies of water, where it can be methylated by microorganisms. Methylmercury then travels up the food chain through a bio-accumulative process when large fish eat smaller fish. The result is that fish species highest on the food chain (e.g., shark and swordfish) and those that have lived the longest have the highest levels. Fish-eating birds and sea mammals can also accumulate high levels of mercury (ATSDR, 1999; US EPA, 1997). Most fish contain at least some mercury in their tissues, most of which is methylated (US EPA, 1997; IPCS, 1976).

Upon ingestion, an estimated 95% of the methylmercury in fish tissue is absorbed into the bloodstream and distributed throughout the body (National Research Council [NRC], 2000; IPCS, 1990). Methylmercury crosses both the blood–brain barrier and the placenta. In humans, it has a whole-body half-life of about 70 days (50 days in blood) (Clarkson et al., 2003; Clarkson and Magos, 2006). Exposure in the general population is believed to occur almost entirely through consumption of fish or seafood.

High doses of methylmercury can cause severe, potentially lethal damage to the nervous system, and the developing nervous system is most sensitive (NRC, 2000). This was tragically demonstrated by the poisonings that occurred during the 1950s and 1960s, in and around Minamata and Niigata, Japan, where several chemical plants that produced acetaldehyde for the manufacture of plastics were discharging methylmercury-containing waste into the local waters (Ekino et al., 2007). The fish from these waters—a dietary staple for residents of the area—accumulated mercury at concentrations in the range of 6 to 36 parts per million (ppm) (Harada, 1995). For comparison, most commercial fish species sold in the United States (US) contain less than 1 ppm (US FDA, 2006).

In Minamata, children exposed prenatally to high doses of methylmercury through maternal fish consumption were born with varying degrees of neurologic damage, including cerebral palsy, mental retardation, seizures, and sensory and reflex disturbances, sometimes resulting in death (Harada, 1995; NRC, 2000). Symptoms in their mothers tended to be less severe, and included numbness and tingling in the arms and legs; lack of coordination or steadiness; disturbances in speech, vision, and hearing; and tremor (Harada, 1995; NRC, 2000). In some cases, symptoms in children and adults improved upon cessation of exposure, while in others they did not show up for months or years, or they worsened over time (Kinjo et al. 1993; Harada, 1995; US EPA, 2008a). Average hair mercury concentration in mothers of affected children was estimated to be 41 ppm (ranging from ~3.8 to ~133 ppm) (Akagi et al., 1998). In the US, hair concentrations are typically under 1 ppm (McDowell et al., 2004).

There is no question that exposure to methylmercury at high doses is neurotoxic (International Program on Chemical Safety [IPCS], 1990; NRC, 2000; US EPA, 2008a); however, there is less agreement on the potential effects of long-term exposure to lower levels (Myers et al., 2003; Stern et al., 2004). In the past, attention has focused on comparing two apparently conflicting studies of the association between lower-level prenatal exposure and neurodevelopmental outcomes in children from populations that consume fish or seafood on a regular basis. One of the studies included 917 children from the Faroe Islands, where prenatal exposure occurred primarily through maternal consumption of the meat from pilot whales (Grandjean et al., 1992). At ages 7 and 14 years, higher prenatal exposure was associated with subtle deficits in attention, language, memory, and possibly visuospatial and motor functions (Grandjean et al., 1997; Debes et al., 2006). The geometric mean total mercury concentration in umbilical-cord blood collected from this cohort of children was ~23 μg/L (interquartile range, 13 to 41), and it was 4.3 ppm in maternal hair at delivery (interquartile range, 2.6 to 7.7). In contrast, a study conducted in the Republic of the Seychelles on

643 children followed up to 17 years of age did not identify neurodevelopmental deficits associated with prenatal exposure (Davidson et al., 1998, 2010; Myers et al., 2003). In the Seychelles, exposure occurred primarily through maternal consumption of ocean fish. The arithmetic mean total mercury concentration in maternal hair at delivery was 6.9 ppm (standard deviation, 4.5). Proposed explanations for the discrepancies between the two studies include hazardous levels of co-occurring compounds, such as polychlorinated biphenyls (PCBs), in pilot whale; co-occurring protective substances in ocean fish; different exposure patterns (intermittent, high doses from pilot whales, as compared with steadier and lower doses from ocean fish); population-specific toxicokinetic differences in response to exposure; choice of biomarker (mercury in hair or cord blood); and the sensitivity of the different neurodevelopmental tests used in each study (NRC, 2000).

One of the difficulties of studying the effect of exposure to methylmercury through fish consumption is that fish also contain nutrients that are beneficial to neurodevelopment and overall health. An observed mercury effect may be offset, or confounded, by co-occurring, beneficial nutrients such as long-chain omega-3 fatty acids. More recently, studies of prenatal exposure have attempted to separate mercury risks from nutrient benefits by estimating a mercury effect while controlling for the nutrients in fish—or frequency of fish meals (Oken et al., 2005, 2008b; Budtz-Jorgensen et al., 2007; Lederman et al., 2008; Strain et al., 2008). A second cohort study of prenatally exposed children from the Seychelles was designed specifically to separate risks from benefits (Davidson et al., 2008). Results from these studies support the hypothesis that nutrients in fish can confound observed associations between prenatal exposure to methylmercury and child development. Both beneficial and adverse effects appear to be strengthened when the effect of each exposure is assessed while simultaneously controlling for the other.

The concern that an observed association between exposure to methylmercury and adverse neurodevelopmental outcomes in fish-eating populations may be attributed to co-occurring PCBs in fish has also been raised. However, results from analyses that have considered both sets of compounds simultaneously lend support to the hypothesis that methylmercury has an independent effect (Budtz-Jorgensen et al., 1999; Suzuki et al., 2010).

Mercury has been measured in breast milk, and maternal fish or seafood consumption can raise levels in a breast-feeding child (Grandjean et al., 1994). However, infants from the Faroe Island cohort who were breast-fed—and therefore had higher hair mercury concentrations (geometric mean, 1.8 ppm)—achieved developmental milestones earlier than children who were not breast-fed (Grandjean et al., 1995). Methylmercury passes into breast milk less readily than inorganic forms of mercury (Skerfving, 1988; Bjornberg et al., 2005). Furthermore, breast milk confers many health benefits to a child, including improved

neurodevelopmental outcomes (Kramer et al., 2008; Oken et al., 2008a). Most, but not all (Davidson et al., 2010), analyses from the Faroe Islands and the Seychelles cohorts that have looked at effects of postnatal mercury exposure—independent of prenatal exposure—have not reported poorer developmental outcomes, underscoring the relative importance of earlier exposure (Debes et al., 2006; Myers et al., 2009).

Several studies in the Amazon and other regions of Brazil have examined effects of methylmercury exposure in adults consuming contaminated fish. Mercury has been used in these areas for mining gold, which has contributed to its accumulation in local fish. Deforestation practices have also contributed to the release of mercury into the environment in this region (Passos and Mergler, 2008). Results from one study of 91 adults reported subtle deficits in visual and motor function associated with an average hair mercury concentration of about 13 ppm (Lebel et al., 1998). Another study of 129 adults with average hair concentrations of about 4 ppm reported subtle decreases in fine motor function and verbal memory (Yokoo et al., 2003). Both studies were cross sectional and could not rule out confounding by exposure at an earlier age. In a case series of high-end fish consumers in the United States, adults and children with total blood mercury levels ranging from 2.0 to 89.5 µg/L reported a variety of nonspecific symptoms including fatigue, headache, decreased memory, decreased concentration, and muscle or joint pain (Hightower and Moore, 2003). However, the extent to which the mercury was causally associated with these symptoms remains uncertain, since there was no control group for comparison. In an urban US population of older adults, total blood mercury was not associated with worse neurobehavioral performance, but average levels were substantially lower than those measured in the studies from Brazil (Weil et al., 2005).

There is some evidence that exposure to methylmercury through fish consumption increases the risk of cardiovascular disease in adults. One of the most methodologically sound studies followed 1871 Finnish men with an average hair mercury concentration of 1.9 ppm, and reported increased incidence and mortality for cardiovascular end points (Virtanen et al., 2007). These associations have been controversial (Mozaffarian and Rimm, 2006; Stern, 2007), since the long-chain omega-3 fatty acids in fish are widely accepted to offer protection from cardiovascular disease. Even more provocative are the relatively low exposure levels at which associations were observed. In another large European study, toenail mercury was positively associated with incident myocardial infarction, whereas docosahexaenoic acid (a cardioprotective omega-3 fatty acid) in adipose tissue was negatively associated with the end point when the two exposures were modeled simultaneously (Guallar et al., 2002). This pattern is consistent with the notion that there may be negative confounding between mercury risks and nutrient benefits associated with fish consumption, similar to what we observe for neurodevelopmental outcomes.

In addition to beneficial nutrients in fish, observational studies of the effects of methylmercury exposure through fish consumption may also be confounded by sociodemographic differences between individuals who choose to eat fish and those who do not. These differences may predict neurodevelopmental *or* cardiovascular outcomes for reasons that are independent of either the nutrient or the contaminant exposures that occur from eating fish.

It is interesting to note that in some heavily polluted areas, such as those near mercury mines in inland China, where fish is rarely eaten, other foods may be more important sources of methylmercury exposure than fish. For example, rice grown in contaminated waters was found to accumulate very high levels of methylmercury (Zhang et al., 2010). Since rice does not contain the beneficial nutrients to offset the harmful effects of methylmercury, toxicity may be even greater from this food source.

Ethylmercury in Vaccines

The US Food and Drug administration (FDA) regulations require that preservatives be present in multidose vaccine vials to prevent bacterial and fungal contamination (Ball et al., 2001). Multidose vials are commonly used because they are less expensive and require less storage space than single-use vials. Since the, 1930s, ethylmercury in the form of thimerosal (sodium ethylmercury thiosalicylate) has been used as a vaccine preservative (Committee on Infectious Diseases and Committee on Environmental Health, 1999).

The FDA Modernization Act of 1997 mandated a reassessment of the risks of mercury-containing food and drugs. In its analysis, it determined that the ethylmercury dose associated with the recommended immunization schedule for the first 6 months of life could exceed the US EPA reference dose for methylmercury—a similar organomercurial compound (Ball et al., 2001). As a result, in July 1999, the American Academy of Pediatrics and the US Public Health Service recommended removing thimerosal from childhood vaccines (US Centers for Disease Control and Prevention [CDC], 1999). They reasoned that although there is no evidence that thimerosal poses more than a minute risk (primarily due to local hypersensitivity reactions), mercury is a known neurotoxicant that should be avoided if at all possible. A primary consideration was the desire to preserve the public's trust in vaccine safety. By 2001, vaccine manufacturers in the United States and Europe had eliminated most multidose infant vaccines containing thimerosal (specifically, the diphtheria–pertussis tetanus and hepatitis B vaccines) (US FDA, 2008b). However, thimerosal is still used widely in infant vaccines in countries that do not have the resources to provide their populations with single-dose preparations. In many of these places, the potentially deadly threats from childhood diseases such as diphtheria, pertussis, tetanus, and hepatitis far outweigh any threats from exposure to thimerosal (Clements and McIntyre, 2006).

At high doses, the toxicity of ethylmercury appears similar to that of methylmercury (Magos et al. 1985; Risher et al., 2002; Clarkson and Magos, 2006). However, the reference dose derived by the US Environmental Protection Agency (EPA) for methylmercury may not be generalizable to ethylmercury. One reason is that ethylmercury clears more quickly from blood, with a half-life of about 20 days in adults, as compared with 50 days for methylmercury (IPCS, 1990; Clarkson and Magos, 2006). A study of infants exposed to ethylmercury through vaccination suggested an even shorter half-life of 3.7 days (Pichichero et al., 2008). The faster clearance, combined with the episodic nature of vaccine-related exposure, is unlikely to result in accumulation of mercury comparable to what might occur from steady exposure to methylmercury from fish consumption.

At the time when the FDA was conducting its review and risk assessment, there was growing public concern that mercury in vaccines was causing an epidemic of autism in children (Baker, 2008). A review of studies on this topic published from 1966 to 2004 was conducted by Parker et al. (2006). The four studies that found evidence for a harmful association were published by the same authors (e.g., Geier and Geier, 2003), used overlapping data sets, and contained critical methodologic flaws. Studies of higher quality did not support the hypothetical association. More recent studies of neuropsychological outcomes in children corroborate the absence of evidence for effects of early exposure to thimerosal on the central nervous system (Thompson et al., 2007; Price et al., 2010). Furthermore, autism rates have not decreased since the removal of thimerosal (Stehr-Green et al., 2003; Fombonne et al., 2006; Schechter and Grether, 2008; Hertz-Picciotto and Delwiche, 2009). Despite the reassuring scientific evidence surrounding thimerosal, large segments of the population remain wary of vaccination (Baker, 2008).

Elemental Mercury in Dental Amalgams

Debate surrounding the use of mercury amalgams for dental restoration dates back to the 19th century, when the first national association of dentists—the American Association of Dental Surgeons—came out strongly against it because of mercury's known toxicity (Goldwater, 1972). A larger group of dentists, who eventually became the American Dental Association, argued in favor of the value of this low-cost material, largely dismissing the notion of health risks.

Amalgam tooth fillings contain about 50% elemental mercury and are a source of persistent, low-level exposure to mercury vapor (IPCS, 1991). Exposure is thought to occur primarily through inhalation (ATSDR, 1999; Berglund, 1992). About 80% of inhaled mercury vapor is retained by the body, predominantly in the kidneys and to a lesser degree in the central nervous system; however, most human studies have focused on neurologic health effects (IPCS, 1991). The whole body half-life of inhaled mercury vapor is about 60 days (Clarkson and Magos, 2006). Once mercury vapor enters the bloodstream, it can also cross the placenta. The presence of amalgam restorations is positively associated with inorganic mercury levels in maternal and umbilical-cord blood (Palkovicova et al., 2008). Brain, blood, and urine mercury levels have also been correlated with the number of amalgam restorations in a person's mouth (Nylander et al., 1987; Akesson et al. 1991; Vahter et al., 2000; Guzzi et al., 2006). Urine mercury concentration increases approximately 1 to 1.8 µg/L for every 10 covered surfaces (Kingman et al., 1998; Dye et al., 2005), but people who chew gum regularly or grind their teeth tend to have higher levels (Barregard et al., 1995; Sallsten et al., 1996). Removing amalgam fillings may also result in transiently higher levels (Molin et al., 1990).

It has been hypothesized that exposure to mercury from dental amalgams may play an etiologic role in neurologic disorders such as Alzheimer's disease, chronic fatigue syndrome, and multiple sclerosis (IPCS, 1991; Siblerud et al., 1994; Mutter et al., 2004; Brownawell et al., 2005; Bates, 2006; Aminzadeh and Etminan, 2007). However, the estimated average daily dose of mercury vapor inhaled from amalgam restorations is low (urine levels typically under 2.0 µg/g creatinine) as compared with levels of occupational exposure, which have been associated with kidney damage and neurologic symptoms (urine levels typically over 50 µg/g creatinine) (IPCS, 1991; Kingman et al., 1998; Clarkson and Magos, 2006). Rigorous scientific studies have failed to provide evidence for neurologic or neurodevelopmental risks associated with the mercury exposure from dental amalgams (Clarkson et al., 2003; Karol et al., 2004; Kingman et al., 2005; SCENIHR, 2008). They have also failed to identify reproductive risks associated with the placement of amalgams during pregnancy (Daniels et al., 2007; Hujoel et al., 2005). One explanation for previous reports of associations is confounding by sociodemographic factors that are related to both the presence of amalgams and poorer neurocognitive outcomes (Lygre et al., 2010). There continues to be interest in this topic.

Research to address the question of whether there are adverse effects from exposure to mercury amalgams has focused on children because of their heightened sensitivity to mercury toxicity. The New England Children's Amalgam Trial has been following 534 children 6 to 11 years of age at enrollment for renal and neuropsychological end points (Bellinger et al., 2006). Children were randomly assigned to receive either amalgam fillings or composite resin. After 5 years of follow-up, no adverse effects of mercury amalgams on neuropsychological measures have been detected (Bellinger et al., 2006). Similarly, another trial conducted in Portugal on 507 children found no evidence for adverse neurobehavioral effects after 7 years of follow-up (DeRouen et al., 2006; Lauterbach et al., 2008; Mackert, 2010). The New England Children's Amalgam Trial reported an

association between amalgam placement and an increased prevalence of microalbuminuria, which is one marker of renal function, but the finding was not corroborated in the Portuguese study (Barregard et al., 2008; Woods et al., 2008). Other markers of renal dysfunction were not associated with the placement of amalgams.

Mercury in Teething Powders, Laxatives, and "Traditional Medicine Products"

Mercury has been used in home remedies and traditional medicine products for centuries. India and China still use inorganic mercury compounds (in addition to other metals) as part of medical systems that date back thousands of years (Saper et al., 2004, 2008; Liu et al., 2008). A 2004 survey of 193 medicines from the Indian Ayurvedic tradition, purchased over the Internet and manufactured in either India or the United States, found that 4% contained mercury (median concentration, 104 ppm) (Saper et al., 2008), and 6 of 70 Ayurvedic medicines produced in South Asia and purchased from stores in Boston in 2003 contained a median mercury concentration of 20,000 ppm (Saper et al., 2004). Until the mid-20th century, calomel (mercurous chloride) was an ingredient of teething powders and deworming products sold in the United States, Europe, and other parts of the world. In some areas, these products were used by as much as 40–50% of the population (Warkany and Hubbard, 1953). Calomel has also been used in laxative preparations, as has elemental mercury (Goldwater, 1972).

Gastrointestinal absorption of inorganic mercury compounds varies from less than 0.2% for mercury sulfide (cinnabar) to 7–15% for mercuric chloride [corrosive sublimate] (Liu et al., 2008). Absorption in young children may be higher (Clarkson and Magos, 2006). Only a fraction of exposure to inorganic compounds crosses the blood–brain barrier. The kidney is most sensitive to the toxic effects of inorganic compounds, but the central nervous system may also be affected by long-term exposure. Central nervous system damage, and death due to renal failure, occurred in several instances of long-term ingestion of a calomel laxative (Clarkson and Magos, 2006). In contrast, elemental mercury is not absorbed by the gastrointestinal tract in any significant amount (IPCS, 1991).

By the 1950s, it became known that mercury compounds used in teething powders and other products could cause acrodynia—or Pink disease—in children (Warkany, 1966). It took years to establish mercury as the cause, because the disease occurred in only one of several hundred exposed children. Acrodynia manifests with a variety of cardiovascular, dermal, and neurologic symptoms. Sensitive individuals may suffer from elevated blood pressure, tachycardia, pink palms and soles—sometimes with peeling skin, gingivitis and loosening of the teeth, profuse sweating and salivation, irritability, insomnia. and photophobia (Warkany and Hubbard, 1953). Despite efforts to completely eliminate mercury-containing teething and other products, sporadic reports of their use persist. In 2003, several poisonings occurred in toddlers living in Canada because of the use of a teething powder containing calomel that had been purchased in India (Weinstein and Bernstein, 2003).

Mercury in Skin Care Products and Antiseptics

Mercury compounds have also long been used in skin care products and antiseptics (Goldwater, 1972; IPCS, 1991). Mercuric chloride was used to disinfect diapers and as a treatment for diaper rash until the 1950s, when it became known that such use could also cause acrodynia in sensitive children (Clarkson, 2002). Mercurochrome is an organomercurial that was used for treating minor cuts and scrapes in the United States until 1998, when the FDA declared that it was "not generally recognized as safe and effective." Mercury compounds are used as preservatives in some eyedrops, nasal sprays, and contact lens solutions. Skin-lightening creams that contain inorganic mercury compounds are used in many parts of the Middle East and Asia, the Caribbean and Latin America, and Africa (IPCS, 1991).

In the United States, it is illegal to sell any skin care product that contains more than 1 ppm mercury, with the exception of cosmetics or drops for the eye area, which may contain up to 65 ppm. However mercury-containing creams and soaps remain unregulated and available in other countries (IPCS, 1991). These products have been identified on the shelves of stores on the U.S.–Mexican border and in New York City (McKelvey et al., 2010; Weldon et al., 2000). Several poisoning incidents have been traced to the use of skin-lightening creams (6–10% mercury by weight) that were brought into the United States from the Dominican Republic and Mexico (NYC Department of Health and Mental Hygiene, 2005; CDC, 1996). In a 1997 survey of Hispanic communities on the Texas–Mexico border, 5% of households reported that at least one person had used a mercury-containing skin-lightening cream in the past year (Weldon et al., 2000).

Inorganic and organic mercury compounds used in skin care products and antiseptics are easily absorbed through the skin. Low concentrations of inorganic compounds do not readily cross the blood–brain barrier or the placenta, and prolonged cutaneous exposure—similar to oral routes of exposure—most typically results in kidney damage. However, there have been instances when long-term dermal exposure accompanied by high urine levels has been associated with nervous system dysfunction as well (Weldon et al., 2000; Kern et al., 1991).

Ritualistic or Cultural Use of Elemental Mercury

Elemental mercury may be used in certain Afro-Caribbean and Latin American traditions, including santeria, espiritismo, palo mayombe, and voodoo (US EPA, 2002; Newby et al., 2006). It is sometimes referred to in Spanish as azogue and in Haitian Creole as vidajan. Rituals involve sprinkling it around a home, wearing it in an ampule or amulet, burning it in a candle, or mixing it with perfume (Riley et al., 2001). These practices are believed to ward off evil, provide protection, and bring good luck (US EPA, 2002). Surveys conducted in New York, Chicago, and other cities in the United States and Puerto Rico in the 1990s found that elemental mercury was widely available for sale in botanicas—stores that specialize in selling herbal remedies and religious items in Latino and Afro-Caribbean neighborhoods (Zayas and Ozuah, 1996; US EPA, 2002). A 2001 survey documented mercury for sale in 14 of 15 botanicas visited in New Jersey, Pennsylvania, and New York, although store personnel denied that they were selling it when approached by cultural "outsiders" (Riley et al., 2001).

There has been disagreement over how extensively elemental mercury is used by the general Latin American and Afro-Caribbean populations (Wendroff, 1997). In a study of 100 children from a New York City neighborhood where botanicas are common, 3 had urine mercury levels over 10 µg/L (Ozuah et al., 2003). However, the 95th percentile for the sample (2.8 µg/L) was lower than the 95th percentile measured in a population-based study of German children from 1990–1992 (3.9 µg/L), which was conducted prior to Germany's elimination of mercury amalgams for dental restoration in children (Schulz et al., 2007b). Nonetheless, it is plausible that mercury vapor is present in homes where the metal has been used for ritualistic purposes, especially when large amounts, high temperatures, and frequent activities are involved (Riley et al., 2001). In contrast, infrequent practices with small amounts are not likely to result in mercury vapor concentrations above the US EPA reference level (0.3 µg/m³) (Riley et al., 2001). Results from two studies of children living in areas of New York and Chicago where botanicas are common did not support the notion that use of elemental mercury is widespread (Rogers et al., 2007, 2008).

Elemental mercury can vaporize, particularly when agitated or heated, and inhalational exposures can result in high urine and blood concentrations (Forman et al., 2000). Vaporized mercury crosses blood–brain and placental barriers. It has a whole-body half-life of about 60 days (Clarkson and Magos, 2006). The central nervous system and kidney are the primary targets of toxicity (Solis et al., 2000; Clarkson and Magos, 2006).

Occupational Exposures and Elemental Mercury Spills

A famous example of occupational exposure to mercury dates back to the 17th century, when mercuric nitrate was used to turn fur into felt in the manufacture of fur felt hats (Goldwater, 1972). The psychological symptoms that sometimes developed as a result of exposure have been referred to as "Mad Hatter's Disease." Recognition of this occupational hazard in the hat manufacturing industry led the US Public

Health Service to ban the use of mercury in fur felting in 1941 (Goldwater, 1972).

Occupational exposure to mercury today can occur in a number of industries. Mercury vapor can be present during the manufacture of chlor-alkali compounds (i.e., caustic soda and chlorine), fluorescent lighting, and mercury-containing devices. It is released when elemental mercury is added to finely ground gold-containing ore and then burned off to obtain pure gold. In low-income communities that rely on gold mining for their livelihood, children as young as 8 years old participate in this rudimentary extraction method (Bose-O'Reilly et al., 2008). Mining or smelting of mercury-containing ore can pose exposure hazards as well (Feng and Qiu, 2008). Dentists and their staff may be exposed when working with mercury amalgams. Handling of mercury-contaminated waste and demolition of buildings that have used fluorescent or high-intensity discharge lamps represent additional potential for exposure.

Mercury spills generally involve the release of elemental mercury (Zeitz et al., 2002). They can occur when a mercury-containing object or device breaks. Breakages of household thermometers have been relatively common, typically involving release of approximately 1 g of mercury. Larger releases have been associated with breakage of meters and gauges, such as those used to measure blood pressure, and removal of mercury-containing gas-pressure regulators, which were used with older gas meters in homes (Hryhorczuk et al., 2006). In several instances, elemental mercury spills have been discovered in residential buildings (as well as a day care center) that were converted from industrial buildings in which mercury was used (e.g., thermometer and mercury vapor lamp manufacturing) (Lee et al., 2009). Mercury spills may also occur when children—attracted to the unusual appearance of the metal—discover an unsecured store and share it with friends, unknowingly contaminating their home or school environment (Lee et al., 2009). When spilled, elemental mercury can persist in a school, work, or home environment for many years if it is not removed properly (Carpi and Chen, 2001).

Elemental mercury is not readily absorbed across the skin or gastrointestinal tract, so ingestion or dermal exposure rarely results in poisoning. However, because elemental mercury can volatilize, and the vapor is readily absorbed, there have been instances of acrodynia and neurologic disturbances resulting from handling or playing with it (CDC, 1991; Risher et al., 2003; Abbaslou and Zaman, 2006). Attempts to vacuum a spill have resulted in high exposures due to enhanced volatilization (Baughman, 2006). Cleaning up releases of elemental mercury can be straightforward in the case of small items such as a household thermometer (US EPA, 2008b), but large spills can be very expensive to clean up (Zeitz et al., 2002). The way the spill is handled is an important determinant of ensuing exposure in a community.

Organomercurials as Fungicides on Seed Grain and in Latex Paint

Organomercurials were used to preserve seed grain beginning in the early 20th century, after these compounds were determined to have antimicrobial properties (Goldwater, 1972). Such use was banned as a result of several incidents of widespread poisoning that occurred when treated grain was inadvertently ingested directly. The 1971–1972 Iraqi epidemic involving exposure to methylmercury was catastrophic, with thousands admitted to the hospital and hundreds dying (Bakir et al., 1973). Treated seed grain had been imported from Mexico and distributed to farmers and their families in the fall of 1971. The seed sacks were labeled, but the warnings were in Spanish, and they used an unfamiliar skull and crossbones symbol. The grain was colored with a red dye, but this could be removed by washing, which gave the false impression that the poison could also be removed. Because the grain arrived at the end of the planting season, families used it to prepare bread directly, thereby ingesting poisonous amounts of methylmercury.

The Iraqi epidemic differed from Minamata in that extremely high levels of exposure occurred over a shorter period (several months). Maternal hair mercury concentration reached almost 700 ppm (infant blood levels were over 4000 μg/L within 2 months after delivery) (Marsh et al. 1987). Similar to the Minamata incident, children exposed prenatally suffered more severe and permanent neurologic damage than mothers (Amin-Zaki et al. 1979). Other incidents involving accidental ingestion of treated grain on a smaller scale had occurred previously in Iraq and also in Pakistan, Guatemala, and several other countries (Bakir et al. 1973).

Organomercurials were also used for their antimicrobial properties in the latex paint manufacturing industry. Since the early 20th century, manufacturers sometimes added phenylmercuric acetate to latex paint to prevent the growth of mildew and bacteria (Goldwater, 1972). It has been shown that mercury levels are higher in homes where mercury-containing paint has recently been applied (Agocs et al. 1990; Beusterien et al., 1991), and on several occasions, children have been poisoned by the mercury vapor (Hirschman et al., 1963; CDC, 1990). In 1989, acrodynia and neurologic symptoms developed in a 4-year-old within a month of exposure in an unventilated, newly painted home (CDC, 1990). His urine mercury level was 65 μg/L. The indoor paint contained over 900 ppm mercury, which was substantially over the 300 ppm limit recommended by the EPA at the time. The EPA subsequently banned use of mercury in interior paint, and its use in exterior paint has been discontinued in the United States as well.

Derivation of Exposure Guidelines for Methylmercury

The severity of neurologic damage that can result from ingesting methylmercury—demonstrated by the poisonings that occurred in Japan and Iraq—has led governmental and public health organizations to devote a great deal of time and attention to determining an acceptable level of exposure (NRC, 2000). Guidelines have varied across agencies, countries, and time as a function of the key studies and uncertainty factors used in risk assessments (Table 13.1). The US Agency for Toxic Substances and Disease Registry (ATSDR) has derived a minimal risk level (MRL) of 0.3 µg/kg of body weight per day (µg/kg-bw/day), based on neurodevelopmental risks assessed in the Seychelles study (ATSDR, 1999). In 2003, the WHO Joint Expert Committee on Food Additives (JECFA, 2003) reduced its provisional tolerable weekly intake (PTWI) from 3.3 to 1.6 µg/kg-bw/wk (0.23 µg/kg-bw/day), based on results from both the Faroe Island and Seychelles studies, after considering neurodevelopment to be the most sensitive health outcome. Health Canada (2007) uses the same PTWI for women of childbearing age and young children, but allows a higher ingestion rate (0.47 µg/kg-bw/day) for members of the general population. The European Union used the Faroe Islands and Seychelles studies to arrive at a "no observed adverse effect level" (NOAEL) of 0.1 µg/kg-bw/day (Mahaffey et al., 2009). It is not always clear whether exposure guidelines are meant to apply specifically to sensitive subgroups (e.g., the developing child) or the general population.

The EPA recommends using a reference dose (RfD) of 0.1 µg/kg-bw/day, based on data from the Faroe Islands, the Seychelles and a study of prenatal exposure in children from New Zealand (Rice et al., 2003; Rice, 2004). The RfD is defined as "an estimate (with uncertainty spanning perhaps an order of magnitude) of a daily exposure to the human population (including sensitive subgroups) that is likely to be without an appreciable risk of deleterious effects during a lifetime" (Rice et al., 2003). It allows a 60-kg woman a weekly consumption of about 4 oz (120 g) of albacore tuna (assumed to contain an average of 0.35 µg of methylmercury per gram) (US FDA, 2008a). Blood levels below 5.8 µg/L are considered to be within the RfD (NRC, 2000). Some have argued that because the RfD is based on cord blood, which concentrates methylmercury from maternal blood by a factor of about 1.7, an even lower screening value for mercury in blood (e.g., 3.5 µg/L) is warranted (Stern and Smith, 2003; Rice, 2004; Mahaffey et al., 2009).

Clinical Assessment of Exposure to Mercury

The form and timing of suspected mercury exposure determines the appropriate laboratory test. Conversely, results from various laboratory tests—and different biologic matrices—can help to identify an exposure source. Mercury is typically measured in blood, urine, or hair. It has also been measured in organ tissue (i.e., autopsy studies), cord blood, breast milk, and other matrices for research purposes.

Total mercury concentration in whole blood is usually indicative of exposure to methylmercury unless there is concurrent exposure to a significant source of inorganic mercury or mercury vapor (NRC, 2000; Mahaffey et al., 2004). Blood methylmercury is present almost entirely in the red cells (Kershaw et al., 1980). Blood concentrations of 5.8 µg/L and above (other screening values are sometimes used) are reportable in some US states as a means of monitoring exposure in the general population. Germany uses a similar screening value of 5.0 µg/L (Schulz et al., 2007b).

Scalp hair is a useful matrix for measuring methylmercury exposure, particularly when the purpose is to determine cumulative or long-term exposure or to determine exposure that occurred at sequential points of time in the past (e.g., during specific trimesters of pregnancy) (Cernichiari et al., 1995; NRC, 2000). Methylmercury makes up more than 80% of the mercury in hair, and the remainder is likely to have been methylmercury that has been converted to the inorganic form in the follicle (Cernichiari et al., 1995; Phelps et al. 1980). Concentrations of methylmercury in hair correlate well with concentrations in blood (Grandjean et al., 1992). The ratio of maternal hair to maternal blood concentration is approximately 250:1, but it varies (IPCS, 1990; Gill et al., 2002; McDowell et al., 2004). Maternal hair mercury has been shown to be a good predictor of levels in the fetal brain (Cernichiari et al., 1995). Total mercury concentration in hair is not an appropriate proxy for exposure to methylmercury in a person who works or lives in an area with high ambient mercury concentration—for example, in or around mercury mines, gold-mining operations, or chlor-alkali plants, because it may not be possible to remove external contamination under these circumstances (Li et al., 2008). Hair mercury concentrations of 1 ppm and above have been equated with exposure exceeding the EPA's RfD for methylmercury (NRC, 2000).

Urine testing is preferred when measuring exposure to inorganic mercury compounds or mercury vapor because almost all urine mercury is of the inorganic form (IPCS, 1990; ATSDR, 1999). If spot urine samples are collected, mercury concentrations are sometimes expressed per gram of creatinine to account for differences in urine dilution. In the United States, some states require physicians and laboratories to report urine mercury levels that exceed 20 µg/L. Germany has proposed a human biomonitoring value of 7 µg/L or 5 µg/g creatinine (Schulz et al., 2007a). Urine concentrations decline with a mean half-time of about 90 days (Roels et al., 1991).

The best approach to treating elevated blood or urine mercury is to remove the exposure source, since levels drop quickly in response to removal. In cases of acute and extremely high exposure, chelation therapies have been used, although their effectiveness depends on selecting the appropriate agent for the form of exposure (Flomenbaum

TABLE 13.1
Summary of Risk Assessments for Methylmercury

Agency, year	Key studies	Biomarker and exposure level	Critical dose	Uncertainty factor	Acceptable level
US EPA, 2001	Seychelles (Davidson et al., 1998); Faroe Islands (Grandjean et al., 1997); New Zealand (Crump et al., 1998). Final value based on all three studies.	Cord blood, 58 µg/L	Benchmark dose, 1.0 µg/kg-bw/day	10	RfD, 0.1 µg/kg-bw/day
European Union, 2002	Seychelles study (Davidson et al., 1998); Faroe Islands (Grandjean et al., 1997). Final value based on Faroes.	Cord blood, 58 µg/L	Benchmark dose, 1.0 µg/kg-bw/day	10	NOAEL, 0.1 µg/kg-bw/day
Health Canada, 2007	Seychelles study (Davidson et al., 1998); Faroe Islands (Grandjean et al., 1997); New Zealand (Crump et al., 1998). Final value based on Faroes.	Maternal hair, 10 ppm	Benchmark dose, 1.0 µg/kg-bw/day	5	PTDI, 0.2 µg/kg-bw/day (for women of childbearing age and young children)
WHO JECFA, 2003	Seychelles (Davidson et al., 1998); Faroe Islands (Grandjean et al., 1997); New Zealand (Crump et al., 1998). Final value based on Faroes and Seychelles.	Maternal hair, 14 ppm	10.2 µg/kg-bw/wk (1.5 µg/kg-bw/day)	6.4	PTWI, 1.6 µg/kg-bw/wk (equivalent to 0.23 µg/kg-bw/day)
US ATSDR, 1999	Seychelles (Davidson et al., 1998)	Maternal hair, 15.3 ppm	NOAEL, 1.3 µg/kg-bw/day	4.5	MRL, 0.3 µg/kg-bw/day

SOURCE: NRC, 2000, Mahaffey et al. 2009.

NOTES: MRL = minimal risk level; NOAEL = no observed adverse effect level; PTDI = provisional tolerable daily intake; PTWI = provisional tolerable weekly intake; RfD = reference dose.

et al., 2006). The time between exposure and treatment may also impact the effectiveness of chelation (NRC, 2000; Clarkson et al., 2003). Chelation therapy is unlikely to reverse damage to the central nervous system, particularly after exposure to methylmercury, but it may prevent further deterioration (Clarkson et al., 2003).

Biomonitoring for Mercury Exposure in Human Populations

The mission of public health institutions is to protect and improve the health of people and communities by educating, promoting healthy lifestyles and environments, and conducting research on causes and prevention of disease and injury. We can measure public health achievements by tracking exposures and related health outcomes. The dramatic success in lowering childhood and adult blood lead levels that occurred by eliminating lead from automobile gas and house paint has been well documented by sequential, population-based studies (Pirkle et al., 1994). Mercury is currently a component of biomonitoring efforts in North America, Europe, and Asia (CDC, 2012; Schulz et al., 2007b; Wong and Lye, 2008; Son et al., 2009).

Mercury Levels in Blood and Hair

Mercury exposure in the general population can vary enormously, and it does so primarily as a function of type and frequency of fish consumption (NRC, 2000). Blood concentrations range from well under 1.0 μg/L in those who eat fish infrequently to more than 8 μg/L in frequent consumers (Brune et al., 1991).

Germany began conducting population-based biomonitoring for mercury as part of its German Environmental Surveys (GerES) in the western part of the country in 1985–1986, and upon reunification, in the eastern part in 1990–1992. In 1998, the estimated geometric mean total blood mercury concentration (based on measurements in 3973 adults aged 25–69 years from both parts of the country) was 0.61 μg/L (Schulz et al., 2007b). The 2003–2006 estimate in children aged 6–14 years (based on 1240 measurements) was 0.24 μg/L. The 95th percentiles for adults and children, respectively, were 2.4 μg/L and 1.0 μg/L.

In the United States, the National Health and Nutrition Examination Survey (NHANES) began population-based mercury biomonitoring in 1999–2000 (CDC, 2012). During 1999–2002, the survey measured mercury levels in women of reproductive age (16–49 years) and children (ages 1–5 years); more recent data include men and older ages. In 2003–2006, the geometric mean total blood mercury concentration in males and females 1 year of age or older was 0.83 μg/L (based on 16,780 measurements); the median concentration in the subset of 1879 children 1 to 5 years of age was 0.30 μg/L (Caldwell et al., 2009). The 95th percentiles were 4.76 and 1.60 μg/L, respectively. An assessment of changes over time suggests that geometric mean mercury levels have been stable since 1999–2000, however, the upper end of the distribution (95th percentile) may be decreasing (Caldwell et al., 2009; Mahaffey et al., 2009). The 95th percentile from data collected on women in 1999–2000 was 7.2 μg/L (95% confidence interval, 5.30–11.30), as compared with 4.48 μg/L (95% confidence interval, 3.88–5.60) in 2005–2006.

Other Western countries have reported average mercury levels similar to those in Germany and the United States. The Canadian Health Measures Survey measured total blood mercury concentration in Canadians 6 to 79 years of age. The 2007–2009 estimated geometric mean was 0.76 μg/L (based on 2678 measurements) (Wong and Lye,

2008). An estimate of geometric mean total blood mercury among adults in the Czech Republic was 0.82 (based on measurements from 1188 blood donors during 2001–2003) (Batariova et al., 2006). These estimates represent relatively low average exposure.

Mercury concentrations in hair specimens collected from women and children were measured in the 1999–2000 NHANES (McDowell et al., 2004). Women had a geometric mean hair mercury concentration of 0.20 ppm; the geometric mean in children was 0.12 ppm. Similar to results for blood mercury, average levels were low, but the 95th percentiles for women and children who consumed fish most frequently (at least three times in the past 30 days) were higher (2.75 and 2.00 ppm, respectively), probably reflecting the presence of small groups with high fish consumption.

Estimates of mean values can obscure heterogeneity of exposures within a population, especially in countries that are culturally diverse. Regional differences in blood mercury levels have been noted in both the United States and Germany (Schulz et al., 2007b ; Mahaffey et al., 2009). A local HANES conducted in New York City in 2004 reported higher total blood mercury levels than the national HANES (McKelvey et al., 2007). About 25% of adult New Yorkers had levels that equaled or exceeded the New York State reportable level (5 μg/L), as compared with about 10% of adults nationally in 1999–2000 (Mahaffey et al., 2004). Data from NHANES suggest that the northeast United States and coastal regions, in general, may have similarly elevated levels (Mahaffey et al., 2009). In New York City, Asian and foreign-born Chinese New Yorkers had an even higher prevalence of elevated blood mercury levels. An estimated 72% of foreign-born Chinese residents had levels of 5.0 μg/L and above (McKelvey et al., 2007). A 2003–2004 study conducted among children 1.5 to 5 years of age living in Vancouver, Canada, also reported the highest blood mercury concentrations in the Chinese, as compared with the other racial/ethnic groups sampled (Innis et al., 2006). These differences were all attributed to more frequent fish consumption.

In general, studies conducted in communities where fish constitute an important part of the diet have reported higher blood and hair mercury levels. A 2000–2001 study of 1057 consecutive births in Hong Kong found that 78% of the neonates had cord-blood mercury concentrations greater than or equal to 5.8 μg/L (Fok et al., 2007), as compared with 10% of US women from the combined 1999–2004 NHANES, who had levels greater than or equal to 3.5 μg/L (assuming a ratio of about 1.7 for cord:maternal blood concentration) (Mahaffey et al., 2009). Mean fish consumption in Hong Kong was 67 g/day based on a food-frequency questionnaire, whereas dietary recall studies of adults in the United States estimate an average consumption rate of approximately 15 g/day (weight after cooking) (US EPA, 2002). In a 2000–2002 survey of 3686 participants from five districts in Japan, the geometric mean hair mercury concentrations were 2.55 ppm in men and 1.43 ppm in women; 92% of men and 72% of women had levels greater than 1.0 ppm (Yasutake et al., 2003). Average hair mercury in Japanese and Korean communities in the state of Washington measured six and three times, respectively, the national level (geometric means, 1.23, 0.61, and 0.2 ppm, respectively), and fish consumption was similarly elevated relative to national levels (Tsuchiya et al., 2008). Fish is an important component of the diet in some Native American cultures as well, and average hair mercury concentrations over 5 ppm have been measured among Cree Indians living in Northern Quebec (McKeown-Eyssen and Ruedy, 1983). The relatively high mercury levels in the fish-eating populations living in the Faroe Islands, the Republic of the Seychelles, and the Amazon region of Brazil were described previously (Grandjean et al., 1992; Myers et al., 2003), and many more examples exist, particularly from island populations (Mahaffey et al., 2009).

Thus far, Korea is the only Asian country that has begun ongoing population-based biomonitoring for mercury exposure (Son et al., 2009). Preliminary results for 2007–2008—available for a subset of 2342 adult study participants—are consistent with other studies that have measured blood mercury concentration in Asians. The geometric mean was 3.8 µg/L and the 95th percentile was 14.94 µg/L. There was also a pattern of increasing mercury exposure with increasing socioeconomic status that was attributed to greater fish consumption.

In the United States, people with higher education and socioeconomic status may also have higher blood and hair mercury levels due to consumption of more expensive, predatory fish (e.g., swordfish and sushi-grade tuna), which tend to be higher in mercury (Hightower and Moore, 2003; Knobeloch et al., 2005; McKelvey et al., 2007). Approximately one in six patients visiting a middle- to high-income internal medicine clinic in San Francisco was deemed likely to be ingesting methylmercury above the EPA's RfD. Indeed, among those selected for their high fish consumption, 89% had total blood mercury concentrations greater than or equal to 5.0 µg/L; 16% had levels of at least 20 µg/L (Hightower and Moore, 2003). Swordfish consumption was most strongly correlated with elevated mercury levels. The seven children included in this study had blood mercury levels from 11 to 26 µg/L and hair levels ranging from 3 to 15 ppm.

Mercury Levels in Urine

Urine mercury concentration in the general population is most consistently associated with the presence of mercury amalgams used for dental restoration. Other exposure sources, including mercury-containing skin-lightening creams, traditional medical remedies, and ritualistic practices, may also be present in some subgroups of the population. Perhaps because of demethylation of methylmercury in vivo, or the concurrent presence of inorganic mercury in fish tissue, frequent fish consumption has also been associated with higher urine mercury levels (Apostoli et al., 2002; Levy et al., 2004; McKelvey et al., 2010).

The GerES first collected population-based biomonitoring data on mercury in urine as part of its 1985 survey. In 1998, the geometric mean urine mercury concentration, measured in 4730 adults 18–69 years old from both parts of the country was 0.34 µg/g creatinine (95th percentile of 2.0 µg/g) (Becker et al., 2003). The geometric mean was highest (0.89 µg/g) among those who had mercury amalgams on more than eight teeth. The geometric mean urine mercury concentration measured in 1354 children 6–14 years of age was only 0.10 µg/L (95th percentile of 0.52 µg/L) in 2003–2006, which was statistically significantly lower than the 1990–1992 estimate of 0.54 µg/L (95th percentile of 3.9 µg/L) (p value for the difference between geometric means, <0.01), most likely because Germany eliminated the use of mercury amalgams for dental restoration in children during this period (Schulz et al., 2007b). Levels measured in 619 Czech children in 2001–2003 were similar to earlier German levels (geometric mean, 0.45 µg/g; 95th percentile, 4.18 µg/g) (Batariova et al., 2006).

The most recent data on urine mercury concentrations in the US population come from, 2001–2002 NHANES data. The geometric mean was 0.62 µg/g creatinine (95th percentile, 3.0 µg/g) based on data from 1960 women 16 to 49 years of age (CDC, 2005). Estimates were higher than in the German population, but lower than levels measured among 160 adult female blood donors in the Czech Republic in 2001–2003 (95th percentile, 11.8 µg/g) (Batariova et al., 2006). In the Czech study, women had significantly higher urine mercury levels than men. The NYC HANES identified elevated urine mercury levels in a subgroup of Dominican women, some of whom were later found to have been using mercury-containing skin-lightening creams (Mckelvey, 2011).

Future Biomonitoring Efforts

Biomonitoring for a chemical is most appropriate when there are suspected health effects and uncertain exposure patterns in the population, when an adequately accurate and economically feasible laboratory test exists, and when there are known interventions for reducing population risks. Mercury meets these criteria and therefore is considered a high priority on many governmental agendas. The European Union has included biomonitoring for mercury in its Environment and Health Action Plan 2004–2020 (Smolders et al., 2008), and Canada has included it in its Canadian Health Measures Survey (Wong and Lye, 2008). The US NHANES continues to conduct mercury biomonitoring in blood and urine from children and adults, both male and female (CDC, 2012). At a state level, California and Minnesota have passed legislation to develop biomonitoring programs, and mercury is a priority chemical (California Office of Environmental Health Hazard Assessment, 2009; Minnesota Department of Health, 2009). Korea is the only Asian country that has begun a national biomonitoring effort.

Regulations and Recommendations for Reducing Exposure to Mercury

A number of laws have been enacted in the United States to prevent or reduce the release of mercury into the environment. The Clean Water Act requires states to adopt water-quality standards for their rivers, streams, lakes, and wetlands. These standards identify maximum levels for mercury and other pollutants to protect the health of humans, as well as fish and wildlife. The Clean Air Act is another key environmental law that regulates 188 hazardous air pollutants, including mercury. In the United States, the EPA is responsible for developing and enforcing many of the regulations that implement federal environmental laws (US EPA, 2008a). EPA regulations include rules for reducing mercury emissions from coal-fired power plants, chlor-alkali and other industrial plants, boilers, solid-waste combustion, and other sources.

Individual states share responsibility for developing and enforcing related regulations. In 1999, states in the Northeast and other parts of the country began to enact legislation to reduce mercury in products and waste. In 2001, the Northeast Waste Management Officials' Association (NEWMOA) launched the Interstate Mercury Education and Reduction Clearinghouse (IMERC) to provide technical and programmatic assistance to states that have enacted mercury education and reduction legislation (NEWMOA, 2007). The IMERC also provides information on mercury-added products and member states' mercury education and reduction programs to industry and the public. State legislation has included bans on the sale of mercury-containing thermometers, toys, and other products and regulations for their disposal; prohibition of elemental mercury sale for anything other than research, medical, or manufacturing purposes; as well as bans on the use of elemental mercury in classrooms.

More controversial legislation involves limiting the use of mercury amalgams for dental restorations. In several US states, dentists must now obtain informed consent from patients receiving mercury amalgam restorations (Edlich et al., 2008), and the FDA is considering a recommendation to limit use during pregnancy. Legislators in Denmark, Sweden, and Norway have banned the use of mercury amalgams (Edlich et al., 2008), while Germany limits their use to adults and nonpregnant women (Schulz et al., 2007b). Some claim that the absence of evidence for harmful effects of amalgams combined with their affordability and durability argues against limiting their use (Beazoglou et al., 2007).

Fish is probably the most important source of exposure to mercury in the general population, because the methylmercury in fish tissue can be severely neurotoxic. However, regulating exposure directly from fish consumption is difficult. It is prohibitively expensive and time-consuming to screen all fish and seafood products that come into the market. Even fish species known to contain the highest concentrations of mercury will have varying levels, depending on the source and size of the specimen (Sunderland, 2007).

The FDA has set an informal "action level" of 1 ppm for mercury in fish. Agencies in the European Union, United Kingdom, and Canada have used 0.5 ppm as a criterion, with exceptions for certain predatory species, which are allowed to contain up to 1 ppm. The potential difficulties of enforcing government regulations have led some seafood restaurants and retailers in the United States to start their own screening and labeling programs (Burros, 2008).

Fish Consumption Advisories

As an alternative to regulation, advisories can help guide individuals in reducing exposure to methylmercury from fish consumption on their own. In January 2001, the FDA disseminated a consumer advisory on mercury in fish directed at groups considered to be at the highest risk: women who might become pregnant, women who are pregnant, nursing mothers, and young children. The advisory recommended avoiding the four most contaminated fish species (shark, swordfish, king mackerel, and tilefish) and limiting overall consumption of fish and shellfish to 12 oz/week or less. In 2004, the FDA reissued the advisory jointly with the EPA, emphasizing the nutritional benefits of fish, adding a suggested restriction in consumption of canned white (albacore) tuna, and including examples of species that are low in methylmercury (FDA/EPA, 2004).

Individual states have primary responsibility for collecting data and issuing advisories on mercury in recreationally caught fish from local bodies of water. Some states and localities provide advice for commercial fish consumption as well (US EPA, 2008c). Their recommendations may include information on a greater number of species that are of potential relevance to the local population (New York City Department of Health and Mental Hygiene, 2007; Washington State Department of Health, 2008). Advisories differ from state to state based on the choice of guidelines for determining allowable methylmercury intake, fish species listed, and definitions of average body weight and portion size.

In addition to advice issued by federal and state governments, not-for-profit groups also provide information on mercury in fish directly to consumers. For example, the Natural Resources Defense Council and the Turtle Island Restoration Network provide online mercury calculators (www.nrdc.org and www.gotmercury.org), which allow consumers to calculate whether their mercury intake exceeds the EPA's RfD, based on their body weight and combinations of fish species consumed. Other groups, such as Physicians for Social Responsibility and the Environmental Working Group, provide web-based lists of fish species with higher and lower mercury concentrations, along with consumption guidelines.

Several studies have attempted to assess the level of influence that the FDA/EPA advisories have had on fish consumption in the United States. Knowledge of methylmercury in fish was measured in the nationally representative Food Safety Surveys, 2001 and 2006 (Lando and Zhang, 2011). Awareness of mercury as a problem in fish rose from

69% to 80% during that time. A cohort of well-educated pregnant women in Massachusetts reported consuming less dark meat fish, canned tuna, and white meat fish after publication of the FDA 2001 advisory (Oken et al., 2003). Total fish consumption declined 1.4 servings per month (about 17%) between December 2000 and April 2001, with a further decline as of February 2002. An analysis using data from the US Consumer Expenditure Survey found that education and newspaper readership were associated with reduced fish consumption after release of the national advisory (Shimshack et al., 2005). A simulation study found that reducing the total amount of fish consumed (e.g., to no more than 12 oz/wk) was more effective at eliminating the high end of the exposure distribution than changing the types of fish consumed (Carrington et al., 2004).

Awareness of recreational fish consumption advisories in the United States is generally low, ranging from 8% to 32% (Anderson et al., 2004; Knobeloch et al., 2005; Gliori et al., 2006). Furthermore, results from several surveys suggest that awareness of recreational fish advisories is not more common among higher-risk subgroups, such as pregnant women, nor does awareness necessarily predict lower mercury levels or less frequent consumption of higher-mercury fish (Knobeloch et al., 2005; Silver et al., 2007; Karouna-Renier et al., 2008; Burger and Gochfeld, 2009).

There have been several studies examining the influence of national advisories in other countries. In 1998, authorities in the Faroe Islands issued guidelines recommending that pregnant and nursing women abstain from eating pilot whale meat and blubber (Weihe et al., 2005). Of 1180 eligible women, 415 responded to an initial survey and 270 to a follow-up survey 1 year later. Mean hair mercury concentrations declined over the year in this responsive subset of the population. In France, exposure to a fish advisory that simultaneously addressed methylmercury risk and omega-3 fatty acid benefits led to a significant decrease in total fish consumption and exposure to mercury that was greatest in children less than 6 years old (Verger et al., 2007). There was no change in consumption of the most contaminated fish listed in the advisory, which were rarely consumed.

It appears that messages that are simple, or targeted at well-known fish species, are more likely to be effective. In focus groups, participants preferred simple messages (Nesheim and Yaktine, 2007). However, they did not always respond appropriately to the messages. For example, almost all participants reported that they would avoid species designated "Do not eat" regardless of whether or not they were in the targeted audience. Presentation also matters; in a survey of sport fishermen, responses varied whether "risks" or "benefits" were listed first (Knuth et al., 2003).

There is concern that an unintended consequence of promoting fish consumption advisories could be a reduction of intake in groups that are likely to benefit from eating fish (Cohen et al., 2005; Mozaffarian and Rimm, 2006), potentially having an overall detrimental impact on public health. In addition to harmful contaminants, fish contains a number of beneficial nutrients, including protein, iodine, and vitamin D, and it is the primary dietary source for long-chain omega-3 fatty acids, including docosahexaenoic acid (DHA) (Nesheim and Yaktine, 2007). DHA is a necessary structural component of the brain and eye, and its developmental benefits have been shown in some randomized trials of supplementation during pregnancy and early infancy (Hadders-Algra et al., 2007; Helland et al., 2003). Higher DHA intake is also believed to be protective against cardiovascular outcomes such as stroke and sudden cardiac death, so if groups at high risk for heart disease were to reduce their intake of fish to avoid exposure to methylmercury, they would also lose this potential benefit (Cohen et al., 2005; Mozaffarian and Rimm, 2006). Some jurisdictions, such as New York City, have opted to promote more frequent consumption of the fish lowest in mercury to counter the potential for reduction in fish consumption overall (New York City Department of Health and Mental Hygiene, 2011).

Developing effective and beneficial fish consumption guidelines is a challenge (Hughner et al., 2008). Part of the difficulty lies in communicating the message with an easy-to-understand conceptualization of the trade-offs between benefits and risks (Nesheim and Yaktine, 2007). There is also the challenge of synthesizing information on co-occurring contaminants in fish (e.g., PCBs and contaminants associated with aquaculture) for which limited data are available. Disagreement across federal agencies in the United States, and among agencies within and outside the United States, over what constitutes "safe" methylmercury intake can confuse rankings of fish species into categories of recommended consumption frequency. The best outcome would be expected if pregnant women and other higher-risk populations substituted more-contaminated with less-contaminated fish, while maintaining overall fish intake at a level sufficient to provide an adequate supply of omega-3 fatty acids. For frequent fish consumers, this may be difficult. However, there are a number of fish species that are both high in beneficial nutrients and low in methylmercury (Figure 13.1) (Nesheim and Yaktine, 2007; Mahaffey et al., 2008). It is encouraging that data for the US population are now suggesting a shift toward consumption of lower-mercury fish without a concurrent drop in overall fish consumption (Mahaffey et al., 2009).

Conclusion

Mercury is an established toxicant with diverse exposure sources. Methylmercury in fish is probably the most important source of exposure worldwide because of its pervasiveness and neurotoxicity. However, the effects of low-level, long-term exposure—and how these effects vary across sensitive subgroups of the population—are still not well understood. Ultimately, reducing health risks requires a thorough understanding of the human contribution to the release of mercury into the environment and a societal commitment to control these releases.

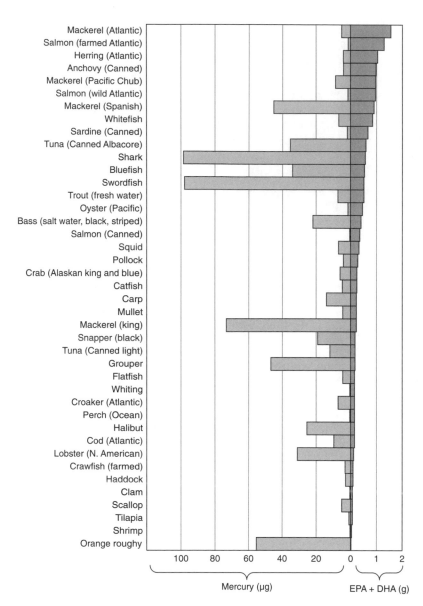

FIGURE 13.1   Comparison of estimated mercury and omega-3 fatty acid levels in 100 g of fish.
NOTES: The scales used in this figure are arbitrary. Estimates are for raw specimens, except for canned items.
SOURCES: Nesheim and Yaktine, 2007; US FDA 2008a.

References

Abbaslou, P., and T. Zaman. 2006. A child with elemental mercury poisoning and unusual brain MRI findings. *Clinical Toxicology (Philadelphia, Pa.)* 44 (1):85–8.

Agocs, M. M., R. A. Etzel, R. G. Parrish, D. C. Paschal, P. R. Campagna, D. S. Cohen, E. M. Kilbourne, and J. L. Hesse. 1990. Mercury exposure from interior latex paint. *New England Journal of Medicine* 323(16):1096–101.

Akagi, H., P. Grandjean, Y. Takizawa, and P. Weihe. 1998. Methylmercury dose estimation from umbilical cord concentrations in patients with Minamata disease. *Environmental Research* 77(2):98–103.

Akesson, I., A. Schutz, R. Attewell, S. Skerfving, and P. O. Glantz. 1991. Status of mercury and selenium in dental personnel: impact of amalgam work and own fillings. *Archives of Environmental Health* 46(2):102–9.

Amin-Zaki, L., M. A. Majeed, S. B. Elhassani, T. W. Clarkson, M. R. Greenwood, and R. A. Doherty. 1979. Prenatal methylmercury poisoning: clinical observations over five years. *American Journal of Diseases of Children* 133 (2):172–7.

Aminzadeh, K. K., and M. Etminan. 2007. Dental amalgam and multiple sclerosis: a systematic review and meta-analysis. *Journal of Public Health Dentistry* 67 (1):64–6.

Anderson, H. A., L. P. Hanrahan, A. Smith, L. Draheim, M. Kanarek, and J. Olsen. 2004. The role of sport-fish consumption advisories in mercury risk communication: a 1998-1999 12-state survey of women age 18-45. *Environmental Research* 95 (3):315–24.

Apostoli, P., I. Cortesi, A. Mangili, G. Elia, I. Drago, T. Gagliardi, L. Soleo, T. Valente, G. F. Sciarra, C. Aprea, A. Ronchi, and C. Minoia. 2002. Assessment of reference values for mercury in urine: the results of an Italian polycentric study. *Science of the Total Environment* 289 (1–3):13–24.

Agency for Toxic Substances and Disease Registry (ATSDR). 1999. Toxicological profile for mercury. Atlanta, GA: Agency for Toxic Substances and Disease Registry.

Baker, J. P. 2008. Mercury, vaccines, and autism: one controversy, three histories. *American Journal of Public Health* 98 (2):244–53.

Bakir, F., S. F. Damluji, L. Amin-Zaki, M. Murtadha, A. Khalidi, N. Y. al-Rawi, S. Tikriti, H. I. Dahahir, T. W. Clarkson, J. C. Smith, and R. A. Doherty. 1973. Methylmercury poisoning in Iraq. *Science* 181 (96):230–41.

Ball, L., K. R. Ball, and R. D. Pratt. 2001. An assessment of thimerosal use in childhood vaccines. *Pediatrics* 107 (5):1147–54.

Barregard, L., G. Sallsten, and B. Jarvholm. 1995. People with high mercury uptake from their own dental amalgam fillings. *Occupational and Environmental Medicine* 52 (2):124–8.

Barregard, L., F. Trachtenberg, and S. McKinlay. 2008. Renal effects of dental amalgam in children: the New England children's amalgam trial. *Environmental Health Perspectives* 116 (3):394–9.

Batariova, A., V. Spevackova, B. Benes, M. Cejchanova, J. Smid, and M. Cerna. 2006. Blood and urine levels of Pb, Cd and Hg in the general population of the Czech Republic and proposed reference values. *International Journal of Hygiene and Environmental Health*, 209 (4):359–66.

Bates, M. N. 2006. Mercury amalgam dental fillings: an epidemiologic assessment. *International Journal of Hygiene and Environmental Health*, 209 (4):309–16.

Baughman, T. A. 2006. Elemental mercury spills. *Environmental Health Perspectives* 114 (2):147–52.

Beazoglou, T., S. Eklund, D. Heffley, J. Meiers, L. J. Brown, and H. Bailit. 2007. Economic impact of regulating the use of amalgam restorations. *Public Health Report* 122 (5):657–63.

Becker, K., C. Schulz, S. Kaus, M. Seiwert, and B. Seifert. 2003. German Environmental Survey, 1998 (GerES III): environmental pollutants in the urine of the German population. *International Journal of Hygiene and Environmental Health*, 206 (1):15–24.

Bellinger, D., C. F. Trachtenberg, L. Barregard, M. Tavares, E. Cernichiari, D. Daniel, and S. McKinlay. 2006. Neuropsychological and renal effects of dental amalgam in children: a randomized clinical trial. *Journal of the American Medical Association* 295 (15):1775–83.

Berglund, A. 1992. Release of mercury vapor from dental amalgam. *Swedish Dental Journal Supplement* 85:1–52.

Beusterien, K. M., R. A. Etzel, M. M. Agocs, G. M. Egeland, E. M. Socie, M. A. Rouse, and B. K. Mortensen. 1991. Indoor air mercury concentrations following application of interior latex paint. *Archives of Environmental Contamination and Toxicology* 21 (1):62–4.

Bjornberg, K., A. M. Vahter, B. Berglund, B. Niklasson, M. Blennow, and G. Sandborgh-Englund. 2005. Transport of methylmercury and inorganic mercury to the fetus and breast-fed infant. *Environmental Health Perspectives* 113 (10):1381–5.

Bose-O'Reilly, S., B. Lettmeier, R. M. Gothe, C. Beinhoff, U. Siebert, and G. Drasch. 2008. Mercury as a serious health hazard for children in gold mining areas. *Environmental Research* 107 (1):89–97.

Brownawell, A., M. S. Berent, R. L. Brent, J. V. Bruckner, J. Doull, E. M. Gershwin, R. D. Hood, G. M. Matanoski, R. Rubin, B. Weiss, and M. H. Karol. 2005. The potential adverse health effects of dental amalgam. *Toxicology Review* 24 (1):1–10.

Brune, D., G. F. Nordberg, O. Vesterberg, L. Gerhardsson, and P. O. Wester. 1991. A review of normal concentrations of mercury in human blood. *Science of the Total Environment* 100 (Spec No):235–82.

Budtz-Jorgensen, E., P. Grandjean, and P. Weihe. 2007. Separation of risks and benefits of seafood intake. *Environmental Health Perspectives* 115 (3):323–7.

Budtz-Jorgensen, E., N. Keiding, P. Grandjean, and R. F. White. 1999. Methylmercury neurotoxicity independent of PCB exposure. *Environmental Health Perspectives* 107 (5):A236–7.

Burger, J., and M. Gochfeld. 2009. Perceptions of the risks and benefits of fish consumption: individual choices to reduce risk and increase health benefits. *Environmental Research* 109 (3):343–9.

Burros, M. 2008. More testing of seafood to address mercury concerns. *New York Times*, January 30. http://www.nytimes.com/2008/01/30/dining/30mercury.html (accessed Feb. 1, 2012).

Caldwell, K. L., M. E. Mortensen, R. L. Jones, S. P. Caudill, and J. D. Osterloh. 2009. Total blood mercury concentrations in the US population:, 1999-2006. *International Journal of Hygiene and Environmental Health* 212 (6):588–598.

California Office of Environmental Health Hazard Assessment. 2009. *California Environmental Contaminant Biomonitoring Program*. http://www.oehha.ca.gov/multimedia/biomon/index.html (accessed September 16, 2009).

Carpi, A., and Y. F. Chen. 2001. Gaseous elemental mercury as an indoor air pollutant. *Environmental Science and Technology* 35 (21):4170–3.

Carrington, C., D. B. Montwill, and P. M. Bolger. 2004. An intervention analysis for the reduction of exposure to methylmercury from the consumption of seafood by women of child-bearing age. *Regulatory Toxicology and Pharmacology* 40 (3):272–80.

Cernichiari, E., R. Brewer, G. J. Myers, D. O. Marsh, L. W. Lapham, C. Cox, C. F. Shamlaye, M. Berlin, P. W. Davidson, and T. W. Clarkson. 1995. Monitoring methylmercury during pregnancy: maternal hair predicts fetal brain exposure. *Neurotoxicology* 16 (4):705–10.

Clarkson, T. W. 2002. The three modern faces of mercury. *Environmental Health Perspectives* 110 (Suppl 1):11–23.

Clarkson, T. W., and L. Magos. 2006. The toxicology of mercury and its chemical compounds. *Critical Reviews in Toxicology* 36 (8):609–62.

Clarkson, T. W., L. Magos, and G. J. Myers. 2003. The toxicology of mercury—current exposures and clinical manifestations. *New England Journal of Medicine* 349 (18):1731–7.

Clements, C. J., and P. B. McIntyre. 2006. When science is not enough—a risk/benefit profile of thimerosal-containing vaccines. *Expert Opinion on Drug Safety* 5 (1):17–29.

Cohen, J. T., D. C. Bellinger, W. E. Connor, P. M. Kris-Etherton, R. S. Lawrence, D. A. Savitz, B. A. Shaywitz, S. M. Teutsch, and G. M. Gray. 2005. A quantitative risk-benefit analysis of changes in population fish consumption. *American Journal of Preventive Medicine* 29 (4):325–34.

Committee on Infectious Diseases and Committee on Environmental Health. 1999. Thimerosal in vaccines—An interim report to clinicians. American Academy of Pediatrics. Committee on Infectious Diseases and Committee on Environmental Health. *Pediatrics* 104 (3 Pt 1):570–4.

Crump, K. S., T. Kjellstrom, A. M. Shipp, A. Silvers, and A. Stewart. 1998. Influence of prenatal mercury exposure upon scholastic and psychological test performance: benchmark analysis of a New Zealand cohort. *Risk Analysis* 18 (6):701–713.

Daniels, J. L., A. S. Rowland, M. P. Longnecker, P. Crawford, and J. Golding. 2007. Maternal dental history, child's birth outcome and early cognitive development. *Paediatric and Perinatal Epidemiology* 21 (5):448–57.

Davidson, P. W., A. Leste, E. Benstrong, C. M. Burns, J. Valentin, J. Sloane-Reeves, L. S. Huang, W. A. Miller, D. Gunzler, E. van Wijngaarden, G. E. Watson, G. Zareba, C. F. Shamlaye, and G. J. Myers. 2010. Fish consumption, mercury exposure, and their associations with scholastic achievement in the Seychelles Child Development Study. *Neurotoxicology* 31 (5):439–47.

Davidson, P. W., G. J. Myers, C. Cox, C. Axtell, C. Shamlaye, J. Sloane-Reeves, E. Cernichiari, L. Needham, A. Choi, Y. Wang, M. Berlin, and T. W. Clarkson. 1998. Effects of prenatal and postnatal methylmercury exposure from fish consumption on neurodevelopment: outcomes at 66 months of age in the Seychelles Child Development Study. *Journal of the American Medical Association* 280 (8):701–7.

Davidson, P. W., J. J. Strain, G. J. Myers, S. W. Thurston, M. P. Bonham, C. F. Shamlaye, A. Stokes-Riner, J. M. W. Wallace, P. J. Robson, E. M. Duffy, L. A. Georger, J. Sloane-Reeves, E. Cernichiari, R. L. Canfield, C. Cox, L. S. Huang, J. Janciuras, and T. W. Clarkson. 2008. Neurodevelopmental effects of maternal nutritional status and exposure to methylmercury from eating fish during pregnancy. *Neurotoxicology* 29 (5):767–775.

Debes, F., E. Budtz-Jorgensen, P. Weihe, R. F. White, and P. Grandjean. 2006. Impact of prenatal methylmercury exposure on neurobehavioral function at age 14 years. *Neurotoxicology and Teratology* 28 (5):536–47.

Deichmann, W., B. D. Henschler, B. Holmsted, and G. Keil. 1986. What is there that is not poison? A study of the Third Defense by Paracelsus. *Archives of Toxicology* 58 (4):207–13.

DeRouen, T. A., M. D. Martin, B. G. Leroux, B. D. Townes, J. S. Woods, J. Leitao, A. Castro-Caldas, H. Luis, M. Bernardo, G. Rosenbaum, and I. P. Martins. 2006. Neurobehavioral effects of dental amalgam in children: a randomized clinical trial. *Journal of the American Medical Association* 295 (15):1784–92.

Dye, B. A., S. E. Schober, C. F. Dillon, R. L. Jones, C. Fryar, M. McDowell, and T. H. Sinks. 2005. Urinary mercury concentrations associated with dental restorations in adult women aged 16-49 years: United States, 1999-2000. *Occupational and Environmental Medicine* 62 (6):368–75.

Edlich, R. F., C. L. Cross, J. J. Dahlstrom, W. B. Long, 3rd, and A. T. Newkirk. 2008. Implementation of revolutionary legislation for informed consent for dental patients receiving amalgam restorations. *Journal of Environmental Pathology, Toxicology and Oncology* 27 (1):1–3.

Ekino, S., M. Susa, T. Ninomiya, K. Imamura, and T. Kitamura. 2007. Minamata disease revisited: an update on the acute and chronic manifestations of methyl mercury poisoning. *Journal of the Neurological Sciences* 262 (1–2):131–44.

Feng, X., and G. Qiu. 2008. Mercury pollution in Guizhou, Southwestern China—an overview. *Science of the Total Environment* 400 (1–3):227–37.

Flomenbaum, N. E., L. R. Goldfrank, R. S. Hoffman, M. A. Howland, N. A. Lewin, and L. S. Nelson. 2006. *Goldfrank's toxicologic emergencies.* 8th ed. New York: McGraw-Hill.

Fok, T. F., H. S. Lam, P. C. Ng, A. S. Yip, N. C. Sin, I. H. Chan, G. J. Gu, H. K. So, E. M. Wong, and C. W. Lam. 2007. Fetal methylmercury exposure as measured by cord blood mercury concentrations in a mother-infant cohort in Hong Kong. *Environment International* 33 (1):84–92.

Fombonne, E., R. Zakarian, A. Bennett, L. Meng, and D. McLean-Heywood. 2006. Pervasive developmental disorders in Montreal, Quebec, Canada: prevalence and links with immunizations. *Pediatrics* 118 (1):e139–50.

Forman, J., J. Moline, E. Cernichiari, S. Sayegh, J. C. Torres, M. M. Landrigan, J. Hudson, H. N. Adel, and P. J. Landrigan. 2000. A cluster of pediatric metallic mercury exposure cases treated with meso-2,3-dimercaptosuccinic acid (DMSA). *Environmental Health Perspectives* 108 (6):575–7.

Geier, D. A., and M. R. Geier. 2003. An assessment of the impact of thimerosal on childhood neurodevelopmental disorders. *Pediatric Rehabilitation* 6 (2):97–102.

Gill, U. S., H. M. Schwartz, and L. Bigras. 2002. Results of multiyear international interlaboratory comparison program for mercury in human hair. *Archives of Environmental Contamination and Toxicology* 43 (4):466–72.

Gliori, G., P. Imm, H. A. Anderson, and L. Knobeloch. 2006. Fish consumption and advisory awareness among expectant women. *Wisconsin Medical Journal* 105 (2):41–4.

Goldwater, L. 1972. *Mercury: A history of quicksilver.* Baltimore, MD: York Press.

Grandjean, P., P. J. Jorgensen, and P. Weihe. 1994. Human milk as a source of methylmercury exposure in infants. *Environmental Health Perspectives* 102 (1):74–7.

Grandjean, P., P. Weihe, P. J. Jorgensen, T. Clarkson, E. Cernichiari, and T. Videro. 1992. Impact of maternal seafood diet on fetal exposure to mercury, selenium, and lead. *Archives of Environmental Health* 47 (3):185–95.

Grandjean, P., P. Weihe, and R. F. White. 1995. Milestone development in infants exposed to methylmercury from human milk. *Neurotoxicology* 16 (1):27–33.

Grandjean, P., P. Weihe, R. F. White, F. Debes, S. Araki, K. Yokoyama, K. Murata, N. Sorensen, R. Dahl, and P. J. Jorgensen. 1997. Cognitive deficit in 7-year-old children with prenatal exposure to methylmercury. *Neurotoxicology and Teratology*, 19 (6):417–28.

Guallar, E., M. I. Sanz-Gallardo, P. van't Veer, P. Bode, A. Aro, J. Gomez-Aracena, J. D. Kark, R. A. Riemersma, J. M. Martin-Moreno, and F. J. Kok. 2002. Mercury, fish oils, and the risk of myocardial infarction. *New England Journal of Medicine* 347 (22):1747–54.

Guzzi, G., M. Grandi, C. Cattaneo, S. Calza, C. Minoia, A. Ronchi, A. Gatti, and G. Severi. 2006. Dental amalgam and mercury levels in autopsy tissues: food for thought. *American Journal of Forensic Medicine and Pathology* 27 (1):42–5.

Hadders-Algra, M., H. Bouwstra, S. A. van Goor, D. A. Dijck-Brouwer, and F. A. Muskiet. 2007. Prenatal and early postnatal fatty acid status and neurodevelopmental outcome. *Journal of Perinatal Medicine* 35 (Suppl 1): S28–34.

Harada, M. 1995. Minamata disease: methylmercury poisoning in Japan caused by environmental pollution. *Critical Reviews in Toxicology* 25 (1):1–24.

Health Canada. 2007. *Human health risk assessment of mercury in fish and health benefits of fish consumption.* http://www. hc-sc.gc.ca/fn-an/pubs/mercur/merc_fish_poisson-eng.php (Last accessed January 16, 2012).

Helland, I., B. L. Smith, K. Saarem, O. D. Saugstad, and C. A. Drevon. 2003. Maternal supplementation with very-long-chain n-3 fatty acids during pregnancy and lactation augments children's IQ at 4 years of age. *Pediatrics* 111 (1):e39–44.

Hertz-Picciotto, I., and L. Delwiche. 2009. The rise in autism and the role of age at diagnosis. *Epidemiology,* 20 (1):84–90.

Hightower, J. M., and D. Moore. 2003. Mercury levels in high-end consumers of fish. *Environmental Health Perspectives* 111 (4):604–608.

Hirschman, S., Z. M. Feingold, and G. Boylen. 1963. Mercury in house paint as a cause of acrodynia. effect of therapy with *N*-acetyl-D,l-penicillamine. *New England Journal of Medicine* 269:889–93.

Hryhorczuk, D., V. Persky, J. Piorkowski, J. Davis, C. M. Moomey, A. Krantz, K. D. Runkle, T. Saxer, T. Baughman, and K. McCann. 2006. Residential mercury spills from gas regulators. *Environmental Health Perspectives* 114 (6):848–52.

Hughner, R. S., J. K. Maher, and N. M. Childs. 2008. Review of food policy and consumer issues of mercury in fish. *Journal of the American College of Nutrition* 27 (2):185–94.

Hujoel, P., P. M. Lydon-Rochelle, A. M. Bollen, J. S. Woods, W. Geurtsen, and M. A. del Aguila. 2005. Mercury exposure from dental filling placement during pregnancy and low birth weight risk. *American Journal of Epidemiology* 161 (8):734–40.

Innis, S., M. J. Palaty, Z. Vaghri, and G. Lockitch. 2006. Increased levels of mercury associated with high fish intakes among children from Vancouver, Canada. *Journal of Pediatrics* 148 (6):759–63.

International Program on Chemical Safety (IPCS). 1976. *Environmental health criteria 1: mercury.* Geneva: World Health Organization.

International Program on Chemical Safety. 1990. *Environmental health criteria 101: methylmercury.* Geneva: World Health Organization.

International Program on Chemical Safety. 1991. *Environmental health criteria 118: inorganic mercury.* Geneva: World Health Organization.

Joint FAO/WHO Expert Committee on Food Additives (JECFA). 2003. *Joint FAO/WHO Expert Committee on Food Additives sixty-first meeting: summary and conclusions.* ftp://ftp.fao.org/es/esn/jecfa/jecfa61sc.pdf (accessed November 15, 2008).

Karol, M. H., S. Berent, J. V. Bruckner, J. Doull, M. E. Gershwin, R. D. Hood, G. Matanoski, R. Rubin, and B. Weiss. 2004. *Review and analysis of the literature on the potential adverse health effects of dental amalgam.* Bethesda, MD: Life Sciences Research Office.

Karouna-Renier, N. K., K. Ranga Rao, J. J. Lanza, S. D. Rivers, P. A. Wilson, D. K. Hodges, K. E. Levine, and G. T. Ross. 2008. Mercury levels and fish consumption practices in women of child-bearing age in the Florida Panhandle. *Environmental Research* 2008 Nov; 108(3):320–6.

Kern, F., N. Roberts, L. Ostlere, J. Langtry, and R. C. Staughton. 1991. Ammoniated mercury ointment as a cause of peripheral neuropathy. *Dermatologica* 183 (4):280–2.

Kershaw, T. G., T. W. Clarkson, and P. H. Dhahir. 1980. The relationship between blood levels and dose of methylmercury in man. *Archives of Environmental Health* 35 (1):28–36.

Kingman, A., J. W. Albers, J. C. Arezzo, D. H. Garabrant, and J. E. Michalek. 2005. Amalgam exposure and neurological function. *Neurotoxicology* 26 (2):241–55.

Kingman, A., T. Albertini, and L. J. Brown. 1998. Mercury concentrations in urine and whole blood associated with amalgam exposure in a US military population. *Journal of Dental Research* 77 (3):461–71.

Kinjo, Y., H. Higashi, A. Nakano, M. Sakamoto, and R. Sakai. 1993. Profile of subjective complaints and activities of daily living among current patients with Minamata disease after 3 decades. *Environmental Research* 63 (2):241–51.

Knobeloch, L., H. A. Anderson, P. Imm, D. Peters, and A. Smith. 2005. Fish consumption, advisory awareness, and hair mercury levels among women of childbearing age. *Environmental Research* 97 (2):220–7.

Knuth, B., A. A. Connelly N, J. Sheeshka, and J. Patterson. 2003. Weighing health benefit and health risk information when consuming sport-caught fish. *Risk Analysis* 23 (6):1185–97.

Kramer, M., S. F. Aboud, E. Mironova, I. Vanilovich, R. W. Platt, L. Matush, S. Igumnov, E. Fombonne, N. Bogdanovich, T. Ducruet, J. P. Collet, B. Chalmers, E. Hodnett, S. Davidovsky, O. Skugarevsky, O. Trofimovich, L. Kozlova, and S. Shapiro. 2008. Breastfeeding and child cognitive development: new evidence from a large randomized trial. *Archives of General Psychiatry* 65 (5):578–84.

Lando, A.M. and Y. Zhang. 2011. Awareness and knowledge of methylmercury in fish in the United States. *Environmental Research* 111: 442–450.

Lauterbach, M., I. P. Martins, A. Castro-Caldas, M. Bernardo, H. Luis, H. Amaral, J. Leitao, M. D. Martin, B. Townes, G. Rosenbaum, J. S. Woods, and T. Derouen. 2008. Neurological outcomes in children with and without amalgam-related mercury exposure: seven years of longitudinal observations in a randomized trial. *Journal of the American Dental Association* 139 (2): 138–45.

Lebel, J. D., Mergler, F. Branches, M. Lucotte, M. Amorim, F. Larribe, and J. Dolbec. 1998. Neurotoxic effects of low-level methylmercury contamination in the Amazonian Basin. *Environmental Research* 79 (1):20–32.

Lederman, S. A., R. L. Jones, K. L. Caldwell, V. Rauh, S. E. Sheets, D. Tang, S. Viswanathan, M. Becker, J. L. Stein, R. Y. Wang, and F. P. Perera. 2008. Relation between cord blood mercury levels and early child development in a World Trade Center cohort. *Environmental Health Perspectives* 116 (8):1085–91.

Lee, R., D. Middleton, K. Caldwell, S. Dearwent, S. Jones, B. Lewis, C. Monteilh, M. E. Mortensen, R. Nickle, K. Orloff,

M. Reger, J. Risher, H. S. Rogers, and M. Watters. 2009. A review of events that expose children to elemental mercury in the United States. *Environmental Health Perspectives* 117 (6):871–8.

Levy, M., S. Schwartz, M. Dijak, J. P. Weber, R. Tardif, and F. Rouah. 2004. Childhood urine mercury excretion: dental amalgam and fish consumption as exposure factors. *Environmental Research* 94 (3):283–90.

Li, Y. F., C. Chen, B. Li, J. Wang, Y. Gao, Y. Zhao, and Z. Chai. 2008. Scalp hair as a biomarker in environmental and occupational mercury exposed populations: suitable or not? *Environmental Research* 107 (1):39–44.

Lindberg, S. ,R. Bullock, R. Ebinghaus, D. Engstrom, X. Feng, W. Fitzgerald, N. Pirrone, E. Prestbo, and C. Seigneur. 2007. A synthesis of progress and uncertainties in attributing the sources of mercury in deposition. *Ambio* 36 (1):19–32.

Liu, J., J. Z. Shi, L. M. Yu, R. A. Goyer, and M. P. Waalkes. 2008. Mercury in traditional medicines: is cinnabar toxicologically similar to common mercurials? *Experimental Biology and Medicine (Maywood, N.J.)* 233 (7):810–7.

Lygre, G., B. L. Bjorkman, K. Haug, R. Skjaerven, and V. Helland. 2010. Exposure to dental amalgam restorations in pregnant women. *Community Dentistry and Oral Epidemiology* 38 (5):460–9.

Mackert, J. R. Jr. 2010. Randomized controlled trial demonstrates that exposure to mercury from dental amalgam does not adversely affect neurological development in children. *Journal of Evidence-Based Dental Practice* 10 (1):25–9.

Magos, L., A. W. Brown, S. Sparrow, E. Bailey, R. T. Snowden, and W. R. Skipp. 1985. The comparative toxicology of ethyl- and methylmercury. *Archives of Toxicology* 57 (4): 260–7.

Mahaffey, K.R., R.P. Clickner, and C. C. Bodurow. 2004. Blood organic mercury and dietary mercury intake: National Health and Nutrition Examination Survey, 1999 and, 2000. *Environmental Health Perspectives* 112 (5):562–570.

Mahaffey, K. R., R. P. Clickner, and R. A. Jeffries. 2008a. Adult women's blood mercury concentrations vary regionally in USA: association with patterns of fish consumption (NHANES, 1999-2004) (Supplemental Material). http://www.ehponline.org/docs/2008/11674/suppl.pdf (accessed January 16, 2012).

Mahaffey, K. R., R. P. Clickner, and R. A. Jeffries. 2008b. Methylmercury and omega-3 fatty acids: co-occurrence of dietary sources with emphasis on fish and shellfish. *Environmental Research* 107 (1):20–9.

Mahaffey, K. R., R. P. Clickner, and R. A. Jeffries., 2009. Adult women's blood mercury concentrations vary regionally in the United States: association with patterns of fish consumption (NHANES, 1999-2004). *Environmental Health Perspectives* 117 (1):47–53.

Marsh, D. O., T. W. Clarkson, C. Cox, G. J. Myers, L. Amin-Zaki, and S. Al-Tikriti. 1987. Fetal methylmercury poisoning. Relationship between concentration in single strands of maternal hair and child effects. *Archives of Neurology* 44 (10):1017–22.

McDowell, M. A., C. F. Dillon, J. Osterloh, P. M. Bolger, E. Pellizzari, R. Fernando, R. Montes de Oca, S. E. Schober, T. Sinks, R. L. Jones, and K. R. Mahaffey. 2004. Hair mercury levels in US children and women of childbearing age: reference range data from NHANES, 1999-2000. *Environmental Health Perspectives* 112 (11):1165–71.

McKelvey, W., R. C. Gwynn, N. Jeffery, D. Kass, L. E. Thorpe, R. K. Garg, C. D. Palmer, and P. J. Parsons. 2007. A biomonitoring study of lead, cadmium, and mercury in the blood of New York city adults. *Environmental Health Perspectives* 115 (10):1435–41.

McKelvey, W., N. Jeffery, N. Clark, D. Kass, and P. J. Parsons. 2011. Population-based inorganic mercury biomonitoring and the identification of skin care products as a source of exposure in New York City. *Environmental Health Perspectives* 119 (2): 203–9.

McKeown-Eyssen, G. E., and J. Ruedy. 1983. Methyl mercury exposure in northern Quebec. I. Neurologic findings in adults. *American Journal of Epidemiology* 118 (4):461–9.

Minnesota Department of Health. 2009. *Environmental public health tracking and biomonitoring.* http://www.health.state.mn.us/divs/eh/tracking (accessed September 16, 2009).

Molin, M., B. Bergman, S. L. Marklund, A. Schutz, and S. Skerfving. 1990. Mercury, selenium, and glutathione peroxidase before and after amalgam removal in man. *Acta Odontologica Scandinavica* 48 (3):189–202.

Mozaffarian, D., and E. B. Rimm. 2006. Fish intake, contaminants, and human health: evaluating the risks and the benefits. *Journal of the American Medical Association* 296 (15):1885–99.

Mutter, J., J. Naumann, C. Sadaghiani, R. Schneider, and H. Walach. 2004. Alzheimer disease: mercury as pathogenetic factor and apolipoprotein E as a moderator. *Neuroendocrinology Letters* 25 (5):331–9.

Myers, G. J., P. W. Davidson, C. Cox, C. F. Shamlaye, D. Palumbo, E. Cernichiari, J. Sloane-Reeves, G. E. Wilding, J. Kost, L. S. Huang, and T. W. Clarkson. 2003. Prenatal methylmercury exposure from ocean fish consumption in the Seychelles child development study. *Lancet* 361 (9370):1686–92.

Myers, G. J., S. W. Thurston, A. T. Pearson, P. W. Davidson, C. Cox, C. F. Shamlaye, E. Cernichiari, and T. W. Clarkson. 2009. Postnatal exposure to methyl mercury from fish consumption: a review and new data from the Seychelles Child Development Study. *Neurotoxicology* 30 (3):338–49.

National Research Council (NRC). 2000. *Toxicological effects of methylmercury.* Washington, DC: National Academies Press.

Nesheim, M.C., and A.L. Yaktine, eds. 2007. *Seafood choices: balancing benefits and risks.* Washington, DC: National Academies Press.

New York City Department of Health and Mental Hygiene. 2007. *Eat fish, choose wisely.* http://www.nyc.gov/html/doh/downloads/pdf/edp/mercury_brochure.pdf (accessed September 16, 2009).

Newby, C., D. M. Riley, and T. O. Leal-Almeraz. 2006. Mercury use and exposure among Santeria practitioners: religious versus folk practice in Northern New Jersey, USA. *Ethnicity and Health* 11 (3):287–306.

Northeast Waste Management Officials' Association (NEWMOA). 2007. *About the Interstate Mercury Education & Reduction Clearinghouse* (IMERC). http://www.newmoa.org/prevention/mercury/imerc/about.cfm (accessed November 24, 2008).

Nylander, M., L. Friberg, and B. Lind. 1987. Mercury concentrations in the human brain and kidneys in relation to exposure from dental amalgam fillings. *Swedish Dental Journal* 11 (5):179–87.

Oken, E., K. P. Kleinman, W. E. Berland, S. R. Simon, J. W. Rich-Edwards, and M. W. Gillman. 2003. Decline in fish consumption among pregnant women after a national mercury advisory. *Obstetrics and Gynecology* 102 (2):346–51.

Oken, E., R.O. Wright, K.P. Kleinman, D. Bellinger, C.J. Amarasiriwardena, H. Hu, J.W. Rich-Edwards, and M.W. Gillman. 2005. Maternal fish consumption, hair mercury, and infant cognition in a US Cohort. *Environmental Health Perspectives* 113 (10):1376–1380.

Oken, E., M. L. Osterdal, M. W. Gillman, V. K. Knudsen, T. I. Halldorsson, M. Strom, D. C. Bellinger, M. Hadders-Algra, K. F. Michaelsen, and S. F. Olsen. 2008a. Associations of maternal fish intake during pregnancy and breastfeeding duration with attainment of developmental milestones in early childhood: a study from the Danish National Birth Cohort. *American Journal of Clinical Nutrition* 88 (3):789–96.

Oken, E., J. S. Radesky, R. O. Wright, D. C. Bellinger, C. J. Amarasiriwardena, K. P. Kleinman, H. Hu, and M. W. Gillman. 2008b. Maternal fish intake during pregnancy, blood mercury levels, and child cognition at age 3 years in a US cohort. *American Journal of Epidemiology* 167 (10):1171–81.

Ozuah, P. O., M. S. Lesser, J. S. Woods, H. Choi, and M. Markowitz. 2003. Mercury exposure in an urban pediatric population. *Ambulatory Pediatrics* 3 (1):24–6.

Palkovicova, L. M., V. Ursinyova, V. Masanova, Z. Yu, and I. Hertz-Picciotto. 2008. Maternal amalgam dental fillings as the source of mercury exposure in developing fetus and newborn. *Journal of Exposure Science and Environmental Epidemiology* 18 (3):326–31.

Parker, A., A. W. Staggs, G. H. Dayan, I. R. Ortega-Sanchez, P. A. Rota, L. Lowe, P. Boardman, R. Teclaw, C. Graves, and C. W. LeBaron. 2006. Implications of a 2005 measles outbreak in Indiana for sustained elimination of measles in the United States. *New England Journal of Medicine* 355 (5):447–55.

Passos, C. J., and D. Mergler. 2008. Human mercury exposure and adverse health effects in the Amazon: a review. *Cadernos de Saúde Pública* 24 Suppl 4:s503–20.

Phelps, R. W., T. W. Clarkson, T. G. Kershaw, and B. Wheatley. 1980. Interrelationships of blood and hair mercury concentrations in a North American population exposed to methylmercury. *Archives of Environmental Health* 35 (3):161–8.

Pichichero, M., E. A. Gentile, N. Giglio, V. Umido, T. Clarkson, E. Cernichiari, G. Zareba, C. Gotelli, M. Gotelli, L. Yan, and J. Treanor. 2008. Mercury levels in newborns and infants after receipt of thimerosal-containing vaccines. *Pediatrics* 121 (2):e208–14.

Pirkle, J. L., D. J. Brody, E. W. Gunter, R. A. Kramer, D. C. Paschal, K. M. Flegal, and T. D. Matte. 1994. The decline in blood lead levels in the United States. The National Health and Nutrition Examination Surveys (NHANES). *Journal of the American Medical Association* 272 (4):284–91.

Price, C. S., W. W. Thompson, B. Goodson, E. S. Weintraub, L. A. Croen, V. L. Hinrichsen, M. Marcy, A. Robertson, E. Eriksen, E. Lewis, P. Bernal, D. Shay, R. L. Davis, and F. DeStefano. 2010. Prenatal and infant exposure to thimerosal from vaccines and immunoglobulins and risk of autism. *Pediatrics* 126 (4):656–64.

Rasmussen, K. L., J. L. Boldsen, H. K. Kristensen, L. Skytte, K. L. Hansen, L. Mølholm, P. M. Grootes, M.-J. Nadeau, and K. M. F. Eriksen. 2008. Mercury levels in Danish Medieval human bones. *Journal of Archaeological Science* 35 (8):2295–2306.

Rice, D. C. 2004. The US EPA reference dose for methylmercury: sources of uncertainty. *Environmental Research* 95 (3):406–13.

Rice, D. C., R. Schoeny, and K. Mahaffey. 2003. Methods and rationale for derivation of a reference dose for methylmercury by the US EPA. *Risk Analysis* 23 (1):107–15.

Riley, D. M., C. A. Newby, T. O. Leal-Almeraz, and V. M. Thomas. 2001. Assessing elemental mercury vapor exposure from cultural and religious practices. *Environmental Health Perspectives* 109 (8):779–84.

Risher, J. F., H. E. Murray, and G. R. Prince. 2002. Organic mercury compounds: human exposure and its relevance to public health. *Toxicology and Industrial Health* 18 (3):109–60.

Risher, J. F., R. A. Nickle, and S. N. Amler. 2003. Elemental mercury poisoning in occupational and residential settings. *International Journal of Hygiene and Environmental Health*, 206 (4–5):371–9.

Roels, H., A. M. Boeckx, E. Ceulemans, and R. R. Lauwerys. 1991. Urinary excretion of mercury after occupational exposure to mercury vapour and influence of the chelating agent meso-2,3-dimercaptosuccinic acid (DMSA). *British Journal of Industrial Medicine* 48 (4):247–53.

Rogers, H. S., J. McCullough, S. Kieszak, K. L. Caldwell, R. L. Jones, and C. Rubin. 2007. Exposure assessment of young children living in Chicago communities with historic reports of ritualistic use of mercury. *Clinical Toxicology (Philadelphia, Pa.)* 45 (3):240–7.

Rogers, H. S., N. Jeffery, S. Kieszak, P. Fritz, H. Spliethoff, C. D. Palmer, P. J. Parsons, D. E. Kass, K. Caldwell, G. Eadon, and C. Rubin. 2008. Mercury exposure in young children living in New York City. *Journal of Urban Health* 85 (1):39–51.

Sallsten, G., J. Thoren, L. Barregard, A. Schutz, and G. Skarping. 1996. Long-term use of nicotine chewing gum and mercury exposure from dental amalgam fillings. *Journal of Dental Research* 75 (1):594–8.

Saper, R. B., R. S. Phillips, A. Sehgal, N. Khouri, R. B. Davis, J. Paquin, V. Thuppil, and S. N. Kales. 2008. Lead, mercury, and arsenic in US- and Indian-manufactured Ayurvedic medicines sold via the Internet. *Journal of the American Medical Association* 300 (8):915–23.

Saper, R. B., S. N. Kales, J. Paquin, M. J. Burns, D.M. Eisenberg, R. B. Davis, and R. S. Phillips. 2004. Heavy metal content of ayurvedic herbal medicine products. *Journal of the American Medical Association* 292 (23):2868–2873.

Scientific Committee on Emerging and Newly-Identified Health Risks (SCENIHR). 2008. *Scientific opinion on the safety of dental amalgam and alternative dental restoration materials for patients and users.* Brussels, Belgium: SCENIHR.

Schechter, R., and J. K. Grether. 2008. Continuing increases in autism reported to California's developmental services system: mercury in retrograde. *Archives of General Psychiatry* 65 (1):19–24.

Schulz, C. J., Angerer, U. Ewers, and M. Kolossa-Gehring. 2007a. The German Human Biomonitoring Commission. *International Journal of Hygiene and Environmental Health* 210 (3–4):373–82.

Schulz, C. A., Conrad, K. Becker, M. Kolossa-Gehring, M. Seiwert, and B. Seifert. 2007b. Twenty years of the German Environmental Survey (GerES): human biomonitoring—temporal and spatial (West Germany/East Germany) differences in population exposure. *International Journal of Hygiene and Environmental Health* 210 (3–4):271–97.

Shimshack, J. P., M. P. Ward, and T. K. M. Beatty. 2005. Are mercury advisories effective? Information, education, and fish consumption. Tufts University Working Paper, 2004-23. Medford, MA: Tufts University Department of Economics.

Siblerud, R., L. J. Motl, and E. Kienholz. 1994. Psychometric evidence that mercury from silver dental fillings may be an etiological factor in depression, excessive anger, and anxiety. *Psychological Reports* 74 (1):67–80.

Silver, E., J. Kaslow, D. Lee, S. Lee, M. Lynn Tan, E. Weis, and A. Ujihara. 2007. Fish consumption and advisory awareness among low-income women in California's Sacramento-San Joaquin Delta. *Environmental Research* 104 (3):410–9.

Skerfving, S. 1988. Mercury in women exposed to methylmercury through fish consumption, and in their newborn babies and breast milk. *Bulletin of Environmental Contamination and Toxicology* 41 (4):475–82.

Smolders, R., G. Koppen, and G. Schoeters. 2008. Translating biomonitoring data into risk management and policy implementation options for a European Network on Human Biomonitoring. *Environmental Health* 7 (Suppl 1):S2.

Solis, M., T. E. Yuen, P. S. Cortez, and P. J. Goebel. 2000. Family poisoned by mercury vapor inhalation. *American Journal of Emergency Medicine* 18 (5):599–602.

Son, J. Y., J. Lee, D. Paek, and J. T. Lee. 2009. Blood levels of lead, cadmium, and mercury in the Korean population: results from the Second Korean National Human Exposure and Bio-monitoring Examination. *Environmental Research* 109 (6):738–44.

Stehr-Green, P., P. Tull, M. Stellfeld, P. B. Mortenson, and D. Simpson. 2003. Autism and thimerosal-containing vaccines: lack of consistent evidence for an association. *American Journal of Preventive Medicine* 25 (2):101–6.

Stern, A. H. 2007. Public health guidance on cardiovascular benefits and risks related to fish consumption. *Environmental Health* 6:31.

Stern, A. H., and A. E. Smith. 2003. An assessment of the cord blood:maternal blood methylmercury ratio: implications for risk assessment. *Environmental Health Perspectives* 111 (12):1465–70.

Stern, A. H., J. L. Jacobson, L. Ryan, and T. A. Burke. 2004. Do recent data from the Seychelles Islands alter the conclusions of the NRC Report on the toxicological effects of methylmercury? *Environmental Health* 3 (1):2.

Strain, J. J., P. W. Davidson, M. P. Bonham, E. M. Duffy, A. Stokes-Riner, S. W. Thurston, J. M. Wallace, P. J. Robson, C. F. Shamlaye, L. A. Georger, J. Sloane-Reeves, E. Cernichiari, R. L. Canfield, C. Cox, L. S. Huang, J. Janciuras, G. J. Myers, and T. W. Clarkson. 2008. Associations of maternal long-chain polyunsaturated fatty acids, methyl mercury, and infant development in the Seychelles Child Development Nutrition Study. *Neurotoxicology* 29 (5):776–82.

Sunderland, E. M. 2007. Mercury exposure from domestic and imported estuarine and marine fish in the US seafood market. *Environmental Health Perspectives* 115 (2):235–42.

Suzuki, K., K. Nakai, T. Sugawara, T. Nakamura, T. Ohba, M. Shimada, T. Hosokawa, K. Okamura, T. Sakai, N. Kurokawa, K. Murata, C. Satoh, and H. Satoh. 2010. Neurobehavioral effects of prenatal exposure to methylmercury and PCBs, and seafood intake: neonatal behavioral assessment scale results of Tohoku study of child development. *Environmental Research* 110 (7):699–704.

Thompson, W., W. C. Price, B. Goodson, D. K. Shay, P. Benson, V. L. Hinrichsen, E. Lewis, E. Eriksen, P. Ray, S. M. Marcy, J. Dunn, L. A. Jackson, T. A. Lieu, S. Black, G. Stewart, E. S. Weintraub, R. L. Davis, and F. DeStefano. 2007. Early thimerosal exposure and neuropsychological outcomes at 7 to 10 years. *New England Journal of Medicine* 357 (13):1281–92.

Tsuchiya, A., T. A. Hinners, T. M. Burbacher, E. M. Faustman, and K. Marien. 2008. Mercury exposure from fish consumption within the Japanese and Korean communities. *Journal of Toxicology and Environmental Health A* 71 (15):1019–31.

United States Department of Agriculture (USDA). 2011. National Nutrient Database for Standard Reference. http://ndb.nal.usda.gov/ (accessed June 1, 2011).

US Centers for Disease Control and Prevention (US CDC). 1990. Mercury exposure from interior latex paint—Michigan. *Morbidity and Mortality Weekly Report* 39 (8):125–6.

US Centers for Disease Control and Prevention. 1991. Acute and chronic poisoning from residential exposures to elemental mercury—Michigan, 1989-1990. *Morbidity and Mortality Weekly Report* 40 (23):393–5.

US Centers for Disease Control and Prevention. 1996. Mercury poisoning associated with beauty cream—Texas, New Mexico, and California, 1995-1996. Morbidity and *Mortality Weekly Report* 45 (19):400–3.

US Centers for Disease Control and Prevention. 1999. Thimerosal in vaccines: a joint statement of the American Academy of Pediatrics and the Public Health Service. *Morbidity and Mortality Weekly Report* 48 (26):563–5.

US Centers for Disease Control and Prevention. 2005. *Third national report on human exposure to environmental chemicals*. Atlanta, GA: Centers for Disease Control and Prevention.

US Centers for Disease Control and Prevention. 2012. *National Center for Health Statistics (NCHS). National Health and Nutrition Examination Survey*. http://www.cdc.gov/nchs/nhanes.htm (accessed January 25, 2012).

US Environmental Protection Agency (US EPA). 2002. *Estimated per capita fish consumption in the United States, 2002.* http://www.epa.gov/waterscience/fish/files/consumption_report.pdf (accessed September 17, 2009).

US Environmental Protection Agency. 1997. *Mercury report to Congress.* Washington, DC: US EPA.

US Environmental Protection Agency. 2002. *Task Force on Ritualistic Uses of Mercury report.* http://www.epa.gov/superfund/community/pdfs/mercury.pdf (accessed November 13, 2008).

US Environmental Protection Agency. 2008a. *Integrated risk information system: methylmercury (MeHg)* (CASRN 22967-92-6). http://www.epa.gov/iris/subst/0073.htm (accessed November 15, 2008).

US Environmental Protection Agency. 2008b. Mercury: spills, disposal and site cleanup. http://www.epa.gov/mercury/spills/index.htm (accessed November 13, 2008).

US Environmental Protection Agency. 2008c. Advisories where you live. http://www.epa.gov/waterscience/fish/states.htm. (Last accessed January 16, 2012).

US Environmental Protection Agency. 2008d. Laws and Regulations. http://www.epa.gov/mercury/regs.htm (accessed October 24, 2008).

US Food and Drug Administration/Environmental Protection Agency [FDA/EPA]. 2004. Consumer advisory: An important message for pregnant women and women of childbearing age who may become pregnant about the risks of mercury in fish. http://www.fda.gov/Food/ResourcesForYou/Consumers/ucm110591.htm (accessed January 16, 2012).

US Food and Drug Administration (US FDA). 2008a. *Mercury levels in commercial fish and shellfish*. http://www.cfsan.fda.gov/~frf/sea-mehg.html (accessed November 15, 2008.

US Food and Drug Administration. 2008b. *Thimerosal in vaccines*. http://www.fda.gov/CBER/vaccine/thimerosal.htm (accessed November 15, 2008).

Vahter, M. A. Akesson, B. Lind, U. Bjors, A. Schutz, and M. Berglund. 2000. Longitudinal study of methylmercury and inorganic mercury in blood and urine of pregnant and lactating women, as well as in umbilical cord blood. *Environmental Research* 84 (2):186–194.

Verger, P., S. Houdart, S. Marette, J. Roosen, and S. Blanchemanche. 2007. Impact of a risk-benefit advisory on fish consumption and dietary exposure to methylmercury in France. *Regulatory Toxicology and Pharmacology* 48 (3):259–69.

Virtanen, J. K., T. H. Rissanen, S. Voutilainen, and T. P. Tuomainen. 2007. Mercury as a risk factor for cardiovascular diseases. *Journal of Nutritional Biochemistry* 18 (2):75–85.

Warkany, J., and D. M. Hubbard. 1953. Acrodynia and mercury. *Journal of Pediatrics* 42 (3):365–86.

Warkany, J. 1966. Acrodynia—postmortem of a disease. *American Journal of Diseases of Children* 112 (2):147–56.

Washington State Department of Health. 2008. *Health concerns about mercury in necklaces* http://www.doh.wa.gov/ehp/ts/IAQ/MercuryNecklaces.html (accessed November 12, 2008).

Weihe, P., P. Grandjean, and P. J. Jorgensen. 2005. Application of hair-mercury analysis to determine the impact of a seafood advisory. *Environmental Research* 97 (2):200–7.

Weil, M., J. Bressler, P. Parsons, K. Bolla, T. Glass, and B. Schwartz. 2005. Blood mercury levels and neurobehavioral function. *Journal of the American Medical Association* 293 (15):1875–82.

Weinstein, M., and S. Bernstein. 2003. Pink ladies: mercury poisoning in twin girls. *Canadian Medical Association Journal* 168 (2):201.

Weldon, M. M., M. S. Smolinski, A. Maroufi, B. W. Hasty, D. L. Gilliss, L. L. Boulanger, L. S. Balluz, and R. J. Dutton. 2000. Mercury poisoning associated with a Mexican beauty cream. *Western Journal of Medicine* 173 (1):15–9.

Wendroff, A. P. 1997. Magico-religious mercury exposure. *Environmental Health Perspectives* 105 (3):266.

Wong, S. L., and E. J. Lye. 2008. Lead, mercury and cadmium levels in Canadians. *Health Reports*, 19 (4):31–6.

Woods, J. S., M. D. Martin, B. G. Leroux, T. A. DeRouen, M. F. Bernardo, H. S. Luis, J. G. Leitao, J. V. Kushleika, T. C. Rue, and A. M. Korpak. 2008. Biomarkers of kidney integrity in children and adolescents with dental amalgam mercury exposure: findings from the Casa Pia children's amalgam trial. *Environmental Research* 108 (3):393–9.

Yasutake, A., M. Matsumoto, M. Yamaguchi, and N. Hachiya. 2003. Current hair mercury levels in Japanese: survey in five districts. *Tohoku Journal of Experimental Medicine*, 199 (3):161–9.

Yokoo, E. M., J. G. Valente, L. Grattan, S. L. Schmidt, I. Platt, and E. K. Silbergeld. 2003. Low level methylmercury exposure affects neuropsychological function in adults. *Environmental Health* 2:1–8.

Zayas, L. H., and P. O. Ozuah. 1996. Mercury use in espiritismo: a survey of botanicas. *American Journal of Public Health* 86 (1):111–2.

Zeitz, P., M. F. Orr, and W. E. Kaye. 2002. Public health consequences of mercury spills: Hazardous Substances Emergency Events Surveillance system, 1993–1998. *Environmental Health Perspectives* 110 (2):129–32.

Zhang, H., X. Feng, T. Larssen, L. Shang, and P. Li. 2010. Bioaccumulation of methylmercury versus inorganic mercury in rice (Oryza sativa L.) grain. *Environmental Science and Technology* 44 (12):4499–504.

CHAPTER 14

Mercury Exposure in Vulnerable Populations

Guidelines for Fish Consumption

JOHN DELLINGER, MATTHEW DELLINGER,
and JENNIFER S. YAUCK

In the 1950s, a mysterious epidemic hit the Japanese fishing village of Minamata. An unusual number of residents began to exhibit odd behaviors, such as slurring their speech, stumbling, or trembling uncontrollably. Hearing and vision impairments developed in some, and paralysis in others. The malady even affected newborn babies, some of whom were born with physical deformities, cerebral palsy, or mental retardation.

An investigation eventually linked the village's strange outbreak of health problems to a pollutant in Minamata Bay: mercury. For years, a local chemical plant had discharged organic mercury into the bay's waters, where the pollutant moved up the food chain and eventually accumulated in fish. The villagers, whose diet consisted largely of seafood, were exposed to excessive amounts of mercury

through the contaminated fish. In all, several thousand people were reportedly affected by what came to be known as Minamata disease (Ministry of the Environment, 2002).

More than 60 years later, mercury-contaminated fish still pose a threat to human health. According to the U.S. Environmental Protection Agency (USEPA) and the U.S. Food and Drug Administration (USFDA), nearly all fish contain trace amounts of mercury (USEPA and USFDA, 2004). Fish consumption, in fact, is the main route by which humans are exposed to the metal, typically in a highly absorbable form known as methylmercury (Agency for Toxic Substances and Disease Registry [ATSDR], 1999). However, outright poisonings from exposure to excessive levels of mercury in fish—like the poisonings that occurred in Minamata—are rare. More commonly, human exposure to mercury in fish is long term in nature and occurs at relatively low levels.

In an effort to safeguard human health, international, national, state, local, and tribal agencies establish guidelines for fish consumption. However, developing such guidelines can be a challenging task. This is because fish, although it contains mercury, is also a highly nutritious food. Fish consumption, therefore, has both risks and benefits. Moreover, in populations like Minamata's, where fish is a dietary staple, restricting or removing fish from the diet can introduce health risks by diminishing the intake of critical nutrients. Ideal fish-consumption guidelines, therefore, attempt to balance the health risks of mercury exposure against the health risks of absent or diminished dietary benefits.

Risks of Mercury in Fish

Prior to the Minamata disaster, little was known about the human health effects of mercury. Today, it is well established that high-dose mercury poisonings in adults can cause severe neurologic damage or death (USEPA, 1997; Mozaffarian and Rimm, 2006). The estimated lethal dose of methylmercury is 10 to 60 mg/kg of body weight (ATSDR, 1999). High-dose exposures in utero can result in delayed cognitive and neuromuscular development in children (USEPA, 1997; Mozaffarian and Rimm, 2006).

The health effects of long-term exposure to mercury at lower doses are less well defined. Studies of adults with low-dose mercury exposures have shown both positive and negative associations between mercury levels and various neurologic outcomes (Mozaffarian and Rimm, 2006; Mergler et al., 2007). Although some evidence has suggested an association between low-dose mercury exposure in adults and an increased risk of cardiovascular disease, the overall body of research on adult cardiovascular outcomes is inconclusive (Mozaffarian and Rimm, 2006; Mergler et al., 2007). Mercury's carcinogenicity is also questionable. The USEPA and the World Health Organization's International Agency for Research on Cancer both classify methylmercury as a "possible carcinogen," based on inadequate data in humans and limited evidence of carcinogenicity in animals (National Research Council [NRC], 2000; USEPA, 2008). Studies of nonadults with low-dose, prenatal, or postnatal mercury exposures—including a well-known study in the Faroe Islands—have shown an association between mercury and adverse outcomes (NRC, 2000), including neurobehavioral deficits (Grandjean et al., 1997) and decreased heart rate variability (Grandjean et al., 2004). However, another major study in the Seychelles found no adverse effects on IQ or neurodevelopment in young children from prenatal or postnatal mercury exposure (Davidson et al., 1998).

Benefits of Nutrients in Fish

Although fish as a food source may harbor mercury, it also offers many dietary benefits. Fish contains important nutrients, including protein, vitamins, omega-3 polyunsaturated fatty acids (omega-3 PUFAs), and selenium.

Like the protein in other animal food sources, the protein in fish is complete, meaning it contains all of the essential amino acids required by the human body (Medline Plus, 2008a). However, fish is lower in saturated fats than many other animal foods.

Oily fish in particular are a good source of the fat-soluble vitamins A, D, and E. Vitamin A is an antioxidant that is needed for vision, promotes cell growth, and is important for embryo development. Vitamin D promotes the uptake of calcium and phosphorous by the body and may help prevent bone fractures. Vitamin E is an antioxidant and helps repair body tissues. Almost all fish are a source of some B vitamins, which aid metabolism (Medline Plus, 2008b).

Omega-3 PUFAs are essential nutrients, meaning they cannot be manufactured by the body, and therefore must be obtained through food. Highly oily fish such as salmon and sardines are especially high in omega-3 PUFAs, most notably eicosapentaenoic acid (EPA) and docosahexaenoic acid (DHA). Omega-3 PUFAs reduce triglycerides and the formation of plaque in blood vessels and have repeatedly demonstrated cardiovascular health benefits. Numerous studies have linked omega-3 PUFA intake with a decreased risk of death from coronary heart disease (Mozaffarian and Rimm, 2006). In addition, some evidence suggests that DHA, which accumulates in the developing brain, is beneficial for cognitive and neurologic development (Daniels et al., 2004; Mozaffarian and Rimm, 2006; Mergler, et al., 2007).

Like omega-3 PUFAs, selenium is an essential nutrient. It also is a trace mineral, required by humans in only small amounts, that plays a role in protecting tissues from oxidative damage (ATSDR, 2003).

Potential Complicating Factors

The challenge of developing guidelines that account for both the risks of mercury in fish and the benefits of nutrients in fish can be complicated further by dietary and other factors. Such factors introduce complexity by attenuating, enhancing, or confounding the effects of mercury (NRC, 2000).

For example, mercury and selenium, both found in fish, have a high affinity for each other and are known to bind together to form mercury selenides. In doing so, selenium makes mercury less bio-available, and thus may protect against mercury toxicity, an effect that has been observed in various animal studies (USEPA, 1997; Raymond and Ralston, 2004). However, as Raymond and Ralston (2004) note, the binding of these two elements may also make the converse true: mercury may make selenium less bioavailable. This may lead to a disruption in the formation and activity of selenoproteins, which are essential for normal neurologic development, an effect hinted at by some animal studies (Raymond and Ralston, 2004). The health effect ultimately experienced from consuming both mercury and selenium, then, may depend on which element is more abundant. If this indeed is the case, it may in part explain the conflicting results in health outcomes noted previously between the people of the Faroe Island population (who consume whale, which may contain more mercury than selenium) and the Seychelles population (who consume fish, which may contain more selenium than mercury) (Raymond and Ralston, 2004). It would also underscore the importance of understanding the specific consumption behaviors and nutrient intake of a particular population when developing fish-consumption guidelines.

Likewise, the health effects associated with mercury and omega-3 PUFAs may compete with each other, although not through a direct chemical interaction like that of mercury and selenium. As noted earlier, substantial evidence suggests that omega-3 PUFAs decrease the risk of death from coronary heart disease. Meanwhile, limited evidence suggests that mercury may increase the risk of cardiovascular disease and even death from coronary heart disease, possibly by promoting lipid peroxidation and therefore

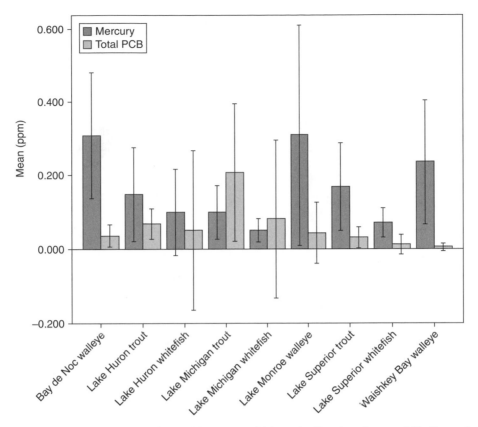

FIGURE 14.1   Mercury and PCB levels in Great Lakes fish, by lake source and fish species. Error bars denote ±2 SD. (*Sources:* Inter-Tribal Fisheries and Assessment Program (ITFAP), 2003, 2004, 2005.)

hardening of the arteries (Salonen et al., 1995). Several authors point out that the risk of cardiovascular disease as it relates to fish consumption, therefore, may ultimately be determined by the balance between omega-3 PUFAs and mercury in the fish consumed (Salonen et al., 1995; Guallar et al., 2002). Should this prove true, the risk of cardiovascular disease could range from relatively low in populations that eat fish that are very oily and have minimal mercury content to relatively high in populations that eat fish that are less oily and have high mercury content. As in the case of mercury and selenium, this demonstrates the potential importance of recognizing the specific consumption behaviors and nutrient intake of a particular population when developing fish-consumption guidelines.

Another complicating factor is the possible co-contamination of fish with other chemical pollutants that can contribute to cancer and other adverse health outcomes. Polychlorinated biphenyls (PCBs) and dioxins, for example, are industrial contaminants that can persist in the environment and are likely carcinogenic. Although levels of these two contaminants are on an overall decline in the environment because of a ban on PCBs and the reduction of dioxin emissions, numerous studies document their presence in fish (Flint and Vena, 1991; Gerstenberger and Dellinger, 2002; Mozaffarian and Rimm, 2006; Stahl et al., 2009) as well as in fish consumers and their offspring (Falk, et al.,

1999; Hanrahan et al., 1999; Stewart et al., 1999; Schaeffer et al., 2006). Meanwhile, various emerging contaminants appear to be on the rise in fish, including polybrominated diphenyl ethers (PBDEs), polychlorinated diphenyl ethers (PCDEs), and polychlorinated naphthalenes (PCNs). Knowledge of the health effects of these contaminants is currently limited (Domingo et al., 2007). Co-contaminants like those mentioned here can confound the adverse effects of mercury in fish.

A separate but related issue is the fact that the levels of mercury and co-contaminants in fish do not necessarily vary together (Figure 14.1). In other words, a fish that is relatively low in mercury can be relatively high in another type of contaminant. This leads to an important point: to truly protect human health, fish-consumption guidelines cannot be created in isolation, only with mercury (and its interaction with factors like selenium) considered. Instead, effective guidelines must consider the comprehensive risks of mercury *and* other contaminants in fish.

Guidelines for Fish Consumption

Fish Advisories in the United States

The fish that people consume generally fall into one of two categories: (1) noncommercial fish caught for sport or subsistence from local sources, and (2) commercial fish, bought in stores and restaurants, that may be domestic or imported. In the United States, the USEPA is responsible for addressing issues of mercury in noncommercial fish, while the USFDA is responsible for addressing issues of mercury in commercial fish. Although most of the fish consumed in the United States comes from commercial sources (Sunderland, 2007), most guidance on safe fish consumption focuses on noncommercial fish (USEPA, 2007).

In the United States, guidelines for consumption of noncommercial fish are issued in the form of fish advisories, which are nonregulatory, voluntary recommendations. The first such fish advisories were issued in the early 1970s (USEPA, 2000). The objective of an advisory is to enable people to make informed decisions about their fish-eating behaviors. A typical advisory includes information about contaminants of concern and the benefits of eating fish, and provides guidance on how to minimize contaminant exposure. Included in this guidance may be information on how to choose fish based on their source, size, and species; advice on how to prepare fish; and recommendations on how frequently certain types of fish may be consumed, if at all. Advisories may be issued for the general population or for specific populations.

Developing Fish Advisories

State, local, and tribal agencies hold primary responsibility for developing and issuing advisories for noncommercial, locally caught fish in the United States. Each agency makes its own determinations about the scope and extent of its contaminant monitoring, about the decision-making process used to issue an advisory, and about the specific advice that is issued (USEPA, 2007). However, the USEPA encourages agencies to follow the standardized methods contained in its *Guidance for Assessing Chemical Contaminant Data for Use in Fish Advisories* manual (USEPA, 2000). These methods are summarized here in order to illustrate the basic process of the development of fish advisories.

The USEPA manual outlines four main steps for developing and issuing advisories: (1) fish sampling and analysis, (2) risk assessment, (3) risk management, and (4) risk communication. The first step involves screening local waters to identify areas where targeted fish species have concentrations of targeted contaminants above predetermined screening values. A screening value represents the concentration of a contaminant in fish that is of potential public health concern, and it is used as a threshold value against which to compare monitoring data. Screening is followed by more intensive sampling and analysis of tissues from fish in potentially problematic areas. Through the follow-up sampling and analysis, size-specific levels of contamination in targeted fish species are determined, and the magnitude and geographic extent of contamination are assessed.

The second step involves using risk-assessment procedures to evaluate the nature and extent of risk to the population that consumes local fish. The general steps in a risk

assessment are hazard identification, dose–response assessment, exposure assessment, and risk characterization. A risk assessment considers technical information such as the dose at which a particular contaminant is likely to result in adverse health effects in humans, as well as additional factors that influence risk, such as any hardships that may result from fishing restrictions or any characteristics of a particular population that may make it more or less sensitive to a contaminant. Through risk assessment, risk-based fish-consumption limits are developed that are the basis of fish advisories. For noncarcinogenic contaminants such as mercury, basic consumption limits for a particular location are calculated from five variables:

- a dose–response variable known as the reference dose,
- the average body weight for the human population of interest,
- the measured concentration of a contaminant (from the fish sampling and analysis step) in a given species of fish,
- the average fish meal size of the population of interest, and
- a specified time period.

The USEPA provides dose–response variable values for multiple contaminants. As of 2011, the reference dose for mercury was 0.1 µg/kg of body weight per day, but some questions have been raised about the validity of this value (Stern and Smith, 2003; Mahaffey et al., 2009). The USEPA also provides default values for the acceptable risk level, body weight, and meal size variables, but recommends that agencies adjust these values according to their specific situations to arrive at appropriate consumption limits. Consumption limits may be refined further based on additional factors that influence risk, as mentioned previously. Typically, consumption limits are expressed as the amount of fish that can safely be consumed per day, or the number of meals of fish that can safely be consumed over a given period.

The third step of the USEPA's approach, risk management, involves combining the scientific information obtained in the risk-assessment step with various policy considerations to arrive at a design for a fish advisory program. A program can be designed to use any of a number of options for managing fish consumption, ranging from taking no action, to issuing specific advisories, to issuing fishing bans. The design of an advisory program is determined in part by factors such as the goals the program is intended to achieve, the availability of staff and financial resources, and local issues—such as the potential impacts of an advisory on traditional practices, tourism, or community relations—that should be considered.

The fourth and final step of the USEPA's approach, risk communication, involves determining the best way to successfully deliver fish-consumption advice to the population

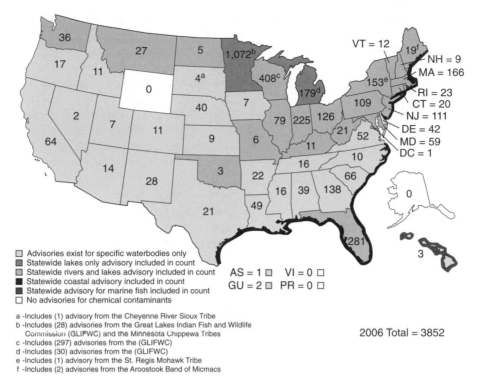

FIGURE 14.2 Total number of fish-consumption advisories per state in 2006. Note that state advisory totals are influenced by the scope of each state's contaminant testing program. Some states perform more testing than others. (*Source:* USEPA 2007.)

for which it is intended. This requires identifying a target audience and determining a communication strategy that is appropriate for them. Ideally, evaluations are carried out throughout this step to ensure that the advisory information is being communicated correctly and effectively and to ensure that it is having its intended impact on the fish-consumption behaviors of the target audience.

Mercury Advisories

According to the USEPA (2007), 3852 total fish advisories were in effect throughout the nation in 2006 (Figure 14.2). This represented 38% of the nation's total lake acreage (not including the Great Lakes or their connecting waters) and 26% of the nation's total river miles (Table 14.1). Although advisories were issued for 44 different contaminants in the United States that year, 3080 of them (nearly 80%) were due at least in part to mercury. This represents about 35% of the nation's lake acres and about 25% of the nation's river miles under advisory due to mercury.

In addition to the advisories issued by state, local, and tribal agencies, the USEPA and USFDA in 2004 issued a joint mercury advisory for consumption of noncommercial *and* commercial fish by women of reproductive age, nursing mothers, and young children (USEPA and USFDA 2004). Typically, the USEPA issues advisories for noncommercial fish only, while the USFDA issues advisories for commercial fish only; this joint advisory marked the first time the two agencies combined their advice into a single advisory. Nonetheless, because

mercury concentrations in fish vary by region and water body, the USEPA recommends that consumers of noncommercial fish always consider local advisories first.

Vulnerable Populations

Recognizing Variations in Risks and Benefits

As noted throughout this chapter, fish-consumption guidelines are ideally based on both the risks and the benefits of eating fish. The consideration of risks and benefits is usually accomplished during the risk-assessment and risk-management steps of the fish advisory development process. A critically important point to recognize during this stage of the process is that the risks and benefits of fish consumption can differ among populations. Risks and benefits, therefore, are best weighed in the context of the population for which the advisory is being developed. Vulnerable populations, in particular, need to be evaluated differently from the general fish-eating population.

Defining Vulnerable Populations

In the case of mercury, vulnerable populations generally fall into one of two categories: (1) populations that are unusually susceptible or sensitive to mercury, and (2) populations that have potentially high mercury exposures.

Populations that are unusually susceptible or sensitive to mercury typically experience poorer health outcomes

TABLE 14.1
Percentage of Lake Acres and
River Miles Under Advisory for One or More
Contaminants by State in 2006

State	% Lake acres under advisory[a]	% River miles under advisory[a]
Alabama	0.1	0.7
Arizona	1.2	0.1
Arkansas	0.7	0.3
California	19.7	0.1
Colorado	16.5	0.0
Delaware	8.9	24.3
Georgia	11.2	4.2
Hawaii	0.0	16.2
Idaho	29.8	0.0
Iowa	0.2	0.2
Kansas	0.0	0.1
Louisiana	3.5	1.2
Michigan	100.0	3.5
Minnesota	100.0	3.5
Mississippi	7.2	0.3
Nebraska	3.9	0.9
Nevada	0.0	0.4
New Mexico	19.5	0.1
North Carolina	0.1	0.2
Oregon	2.6	0.5
South Carolina	16.7	5.2
South Dakota	1.4	0.0
Tennessee	9.2	0.6
Texas	12.5	0.1
Utah	0.0	0.1
Virginia	9.3	4.7
United States	38.0	26.0

SOURCE: Adapted from USEPA (2007).

NOTE: Alaska and Wyoming had no advisories in 2006. The remaining 22 states and the District of Columbia had 100% of their lake acres and river miles under advisory in 2006.

[a] Does not include the Great Lakes or their connecting waters; 100% of the Great Lakes and their connecting waters were under advisory in 2006.

at a particular level of mercury exposure than the general population does. Included in this category are developing fetuses (and, therefore, women who are pregnant or of reproductive age) and young children. In Minamata, infants exposed to mercury in utero experienced marked

developmental delays even though their mothers showed little or no signs of toxicity, as noted in a USEPA report (1997). The difference in susceptibility between adults and developing fetuses may be a result of mercury's direct disruption of developmental processes. In addition, children may experience continued susceptibility due to the lack of a complete blood–brain barrier, decreased mercury excretion, or increased absorption of mercury from milk during the developmental stage (USEPA, 1997).

Other populations are vulnerable because of potentially high mercury exposures resulting from consumption behaviors. While PCBs and other contaminants that accumulate in the fat of fish can largely be removed by trimming or cooking, mercury accumulates in muscle tissues, from which it cannot be removed. When people eat contaminated fish, therefore, they are exposed to mercury. However, the extent of exposure is influenced by the source, size, and species of fish consumed, as well as by the frequency and size of fish meals eaten. A report by the ATSDR (1999) notes that sport fishers and subsistence fishers—including some Native American tribes (Dellinger, 2004)—who consume fish from local, contaminated waters can experience greater exposure to mercury than people who eat commercial fish from a variety of sources. Similarly, people who eat fish that likely have relatively high accumulations of mercury in their tissues—like larger (and therefore presumably older) fish, and piscivorous (fish-eating) fish species—have a higher risk of exposure. Finally, individuals who routinely consume large amounts of fish are more likely to be exposed to mercury than those who eat little or no fish (ATSDR, 1999).

Although vulnerable populations may be at a higher risk of adverse health effects from mercury than the general population, some of these populations also obtain greater benefits from consuming fish than does the general population. As a result, restricting or removing fish from the diets of these vulnerable populations can introduce risks that might not occur when fish consumption is restricted or avoided in the general population. For this reason, when developing fish-consumption advisories targeted toward vulnerable populations, special care must be taken to understand the unique benefits obtained by the population from fish—and the unique risks that can result from removing those benefits. The remainder of this section illustrates some of the unique risk–benefit issues of vulnerable populations.

Unusually Susceptible or Sensitive Populations

NUTRITIONAL RISKS OF LIMITING FISH IN DIETS

Given fish's high nutritional content, the restriction or removal of fish from the diet can itself introduce health risks. One of the populations for which this can be a special concern is developing fetuses. A study by Hibbeln et al., (2007), for example, found that, despite mercury's potential ability to affect the developing brain, children whose mothers ate larger amounts of seafood (defined in this study as >340 g/wk) during pregnancy experienced better neurodevelopmental outcomes. Children whose mothers ate smaller amounts of seafood, however, were not protected from certain adverse neurodevelopmental outcomes, such as suboptimal IQ and social development scores. The authors concluded that limiting seafood consumption during pregnancy could actually be detrimental and that the risk of harm from a loss of nutrients can be greater than the risk of harm from exposure to presumably trace amounts of contaminants in seafood.

EFFORTS TO BALANCE RISKS AND BENEFITS

Recognizing that the developing fetus is sensitive to mercury but may also derive cognitive developmental or other benefits from fish, the 2004 joint mercury advisory issued by the USEPA and USFDA (USEPA and USFDA, 2004) encourages women of reproductive age to eat fish, but to choose fish that are lower in mercury. Not only does the advisory list fish that should be avoided, but it also lists examples of fish that are lower in mercury and emphasizes the nutritional benefits that can be obtained from fish. Assuming reproductive-age women follow the advice as intended—that is, by avoiding or reducing their intake of fish with high mercury content, rather than avoiding or reducing fish intake altogether—they would be likely to minimize the risks and maximize the benefits of eating fish. The joint advisory was one of the earliest to include information about the benefits of fish for reproductive-age women.

Populations with Potentially High Mercury Exposures

NUTRITIONAL RISKS OF LIMITING FISH IN DIETS

The restriction or removal of fish from the diet may also lessen benefits or introduce risks in traditional or subsistence populations for which fish is a dietary staple, and therefore a major source of nutrients. For instance, in a study of the James Bay Cree of Canada, Dewailly et al. (2002) determined that omega-3 PUFAs may favorably influence some risk factors for cardiovascular disease, and concluded that the Cree should therefore be encouraged to maintain their traditional fish-based diet. Similarly, Dellinger (2004) reported that in some Great Lakes tribes with diets rich in locally caught fish, the body burden of mercury is low, while obesity, diabetes, and heart disease are major health concerns. The author suggested that, for these tribes, replacing the traditional fish diet with a highly processed, market-based diet that is potentially higher in saturated fats and lower in omega-3 PUFAs may in fact do more harm than good. Indeed, because traditional populations are often remotely located, it may be too difficult or too expensive for them to obtain a healthy variety of commercial

foods to replace missing traditional foods (Kuhnlein and Receveur, 1996; Egeland and Middaugh, 1997). A number of studies have, in fact, shown a decrease in the nutritional and health statuses of traditional populations following advice to limit fish consumption, as noted by Egeland and Middaugh (1997) and the Institute of Medicine (2007).

In addition, diets can vary significantly among individual traditional populations, and therefore may confer different risks and benefits. For instance, as mentioned earlier, the net impact of fish on a population's neurodevelopmental or cardiovascular health may be influenced by the ratio of mercury to selenium or omega-3 PUFAs contained in the fish. Because of this, fish-consumption advisories that do not consider the specific dietary intakes of specific groups, and instead are based on the idea that "one size fits all traditional populations," could actually unnecessarily eliminate certain dietary benefits.

SOCIOCULTURAL RISKS OF LIMITING FISH IN DIETS

In addition to having nutritional impacts, limiting fish in the diets of traditional populations may also have social and cultural impacts. Fishing is of great social and cultural significance to many traditional populations. A report from the Columbia River Inter-Tribal Fish Commission (CRITFC, 1994) captures this idea, stating: "Fish is not just a major food source for tribal members, it is the essence of the tribes' cultural, economic, and spiritual well-being." Restricting or removing fishing may lead to a decrease in culture-specific food activities and knowledge (Kuhnlein and Receveur, 1996) and undermine some of the social stability that contributes to good health.

Also notable is the fact that some traditional populations view fish-consumption advisories as a sign of disrespect to their cultures. The advisories are seen as excusing polluters from the responsibility of cleaning contaminated waters and passing the negative impacts of contamination on to socioeconomically disadvantaged communities (USEPA, 2000).

TRADITIONAL ECOLOGIC KNOWLEDGE AND FISH CONSUMPTION

Another important consideration to take into account when weighing the risks and benefits of fish consumption in traditional populations is the role that traditional ecologic knowledge can play in influencing health. *Traditional ecologic knowledge* refers to knowledge about the natural world acquired over generations by indigenous and other peoples through direct interaction with their local environment. Traditional ecologic knowledge often leads to the adoption of behaviors that are sustainable for both the environment and the community that depends on that environment. Dellinger et al. (2005) hypothesized that some traditional ecologic knowledge–based cultural practices may be among the first mercury "guidelines" ever developed for fish consumption.

As an example, Polynesian culture has depended heavily on fish for over 2000 years. It is conceivable that during this period, Polynesians would have been impacted by natural emissions of volcanic mercury and developed practices that steered people away from the fish most contaminated by such emissions. Dellinger et al. (2005) reported a Tahitian taboo that bans women from eating "outside fish"—fish from outside the lagoon—during pregnancy and while nursing. Similarly, a Hawaiian practice bans women from eating two specific types of pelagic, piscivorous fish during pregnancy. In limiting Polynesian women to the smaller and often nonpiscivorous fish of lagoons, these practices in effect reduce the health risks from mercury while maintaining the nutritional benefits of eating fish.

As another example, among Native American Ojibwe tribes, walleye is a traditional food that is often consumed with wild rice. Although walleye is a piscivorous fish that is potentially high in mercury, wild rice provides a supplementary source of selenium (Dellinger, 2004) and may mitigate some of mercury's adverse effects, as noted earlier. Dellinger further noted that selenium content varies considerably among different stands of rice (unpublished data) and that according to anecdotal reports, the Ojibwe favor certain rice stands, possibly those that are higher in selenium. Thus, this traditional diet may be allowing Ojibwe fish consumers to obtain dietary health benefits while reducing mercury-related health risks, and may be another instance of traditional ecologic knowledge at work.

The possibility that these practices may be functioning as informal "guidelines" that both maintain benefits and mitigate risks provides reason to be cautious about encouraging changes to long-established harvesting traditions that are not yet fully understood.

EFFORTS TO BALANCE RISKS AND BENEFITS

Health agencies and experts around the world have recognized the important role of locally caught fish in the diets and cultures of traditional populations for several decades (Department of Health and Welfare, Canada, 1979; WHO, 1999; USEPA, 2000; International Joint Commission [IJC], 2004). For example, a 1999 report from a World Health Organization (WHO) committee on food additives stated:

> The Committee noted that fish makes an important contribution to nutrition, especially in certain regional and ethnic diets, and recommended that its nutritional benefits be weighed against the possibility of harm when limits on methylmercury concentrations in fish or fish consumption are being considered. (WHO, 1999)

But despite this long-standing recognition of the unique benefits of fish for traditional populations, in practice, historical efforts to alter the fish-consumption patterns of such populations have often focused on these groups' higher risks from mercury while failing to adequately consider the risks introduced by limiting fish consumption.

Dellinger (2004) cites an instance of one tribal nutritionist who, when asked what advice she gives to expectant mothers, replied that she tells them, "Don't smoke, don't drink, and don't eat fish." In other cases, advisories have not been developed for traditional populations at all, leaving only general-population advisories to inappropriately advise them.

However, this trend began changing in about the mid-1990s, and now some traditional populations take a more active role in developing their own advisories and their own strategies for communicating the risks and benefits of fish consumption to community members.

Communicating Risks and Benefits

The Importance of Communication

When done properly, risk assessment and risk management can lead to useful and well-designed fish advisories. However, before a fish advisory can have an impact on consumption behaviors, it must be communicated to its target audience successfully. Research indicates that the impacts of advisories for both noncommercial and commercial fish can vary widely (Jardine, 2003), and illustrates some of the potential challenges faced by communicators of advisory information.

A study by Oken et al. (2003), for example, suggested that after the USFDA issued a mercury advisory in 2001 recommending that pregnant women avoid eating certain long-lived predatory fish and limit their consumption of all other fish, pregnant women acted in accordance, reducing their total fish consumption by 1.4 servings per month. The authors pointed out that this advisory was well publicized through the mainstream media and health care providers. (An aside: these authors questioned the public health implications of the advisory's apparent success in altering consumption behavior, given the potential nutritional benefits of fish for the developing fetus.)

Meanwhile, other studies suggest that the advisory message does not always get across to consumers. A telephone survey by Imm et al. (2005) showed that only about half of the adults who ate fish caught from the Great Lakes were aware of applicable fish advisories. This rate was the same as that found in a similar, initial survey conducted almost a decade earlier. Moreover, despite a campaign to raise awareness of fish advisories among women, awareness in this group dropped from 38 to 30% between the two surveys. Similarly, in a study of two Canadian populations (Jardine, 2003), only about half to one third of people were aware of applicable fish advisories, and only about half of those who were aware knew which species of fish were included in the advisory.

In other cases, studies show that, even if successfully delivered, advisory messages can be misconstrued. Many participants in Jardine's study (2003) indicated they had ceased eating *all* fish from a local area covered under an advisory, despite the advisory applying only to specific fish species. Cohen et al. (2005) argue that such unintended changes in consumption behavior could have negative net impacts on public health. For instance, under the 2004 joint USEPA/USFDA mercury advisory, reproductive-age women are advised to avoid eating high-mercury fish and to instead eat low-mercury fish. Assuming certain benefits from eating fish and certain risks from ingesting mercury, Cohen et al. calculated that women who modify their fish intake in accordance with the advisory would likely benefit the development of their offspring while experiencing few negative impacts. However, if they instead decrease their total fish consumption, the risks would substantially reduce the net benefits. Furthermore, Cohen et al. determined that if adults other than reproductive-age women reduce their fish consumption—that is, even though the advisory does not apply to them—the net public health impact would be negative.

Still other studies show that people obtain advisory information through a variety of sources and that they instinctively trust some sources more than others. The mainstream media, the Internet, health care providers, health fairs, and fishing guide publications are some of the avenues through which advisory information is delivered. A Canadian study found that about one third of fish consumers surveyed turned to conventional sources of information, such as the media, when deciding whether to eat their catch; another third depended on unconventional sources of information, such as bait shop owners and other interpersonal contacts (IJC, 2004). In Jardine's Canadian study (2003), many study participants indicated a lack of trust in their government, which was responsible for issuing advisories.

Jardine (2003) suggests that if a fish-consumption advisory is to be effective, fish consumers must be aware of the advisory, understand the advisory, and trust the agency that issued the advisory. Furthermore, Jardine also suggests that to achieve this, public participation and communication during the advisory development process are necessary.

Community-Based Participatory Research

A relatively new health research approach known as *community-based participatory research,* or CBPR (Agency for Healthcare Research and Quality [AHRQ], 2003). incorporates both public participation and communication. CBPR aims to impact the health of a particular community directly, quickly, and effectively by actively involving members of the studied community in all aspects of the research process. In contrast to the traditional approach to health research, under a CBPR approach, community members are partners with researchers rather than just research subjects, and the community is involved in the project from beginning to end (AHRQ, 2003).

Under this arrangement, the community's knowledge and input guide the research, thereby helping researchers identify and better understand the community's unique health issues and concerns and enabling them to design interventions that are effective and relevant for that specific community (AHRQ, 2003; Israel et al. 2005). Because they are directly involved in CBPR, community members are more likely to trust both the researchers and the research itself, which in turn increases the likelihood that the community will accept and comply with a particular intervention (Jardine, 2003). In addition, under the CBPR approach, the benefits of research are often experienced immediately by the community. This is usually not the case under the traditional health research approach (AHRQ, 2003).

CBPR is a type of *translational research,* which the National Institute of Environmental Health Sciences (NIEHS) defines as the conversion of environmental health research into information, resources, or tools that can be used by public health and medical professionals and by the public to improve overall health and well-being, especially in vulnerable populations (NIEHS, 2008). Indeed, because of its community-specific focus and ability to build trust, the CBPR approach can be a particularly effective way to tackle health problems in communities that are marginalized, disadvantaged, or otherwise overlooked.

The CBPR approach thus lends itself well to the process of developing and communicating effective fish advisories, especially for vulnerable populations. In particular, Jardine (2003) points out that public participation in the fish-advisory process ensures that community information is being incorporated into the process, that the information requirements of the community are being met, and that this information is being communicated to the affected people.

The following examples from the work of two of this chapter's authors and/or their collaborators in the Great Lakes region illustrate how CBPR can be applied to the development and communication of fish-consumption guidelines for vulnerable populations.

EXAMPLE 1: THE HMONG

Milwaukee, Wisconsin, is home to a relatively large number of Hmong, an Asian ethnic group that aided the United States in fighting the North Vietnamese during the Vietnam War and then sought political refuge in the United States after the country withdrew from Vietnam in 1975. As avid and traditional anglers, Hmong people frequently fish in local and regional waters. However, many Hmong have a limited understanding of the contaminants present in Wisconsin's waterways and fish.

To address this problem, the NIEHS Children's Environmental Health Sciences Core Center (NIEHS CEHSC), formerly the NIEHS Marine and Freshwater Biomedical Sciences Center, at the University of Wisconsin–Milwaukee partnered with the Sixteenth Street Community Health Center and the Hmong/American Friendship Association to develop an outreach program (Thigpen and Petering, 2004). The goal of the program was to communicate the risks of eating contaminated fish to inner-city Hmong in a way that would result in their active consideration of the issues within the context of their fishing practices.

The program's main outreach product was a video. To ensure that the video would be culturally relevant, authentic, and appealing, project partners enlisted the input of a community focus group of 12 Hmong men and women. The group took on the role of cultural critic and advisor and was involved in every step of the video-production process. Shaped by the group's efforts, the video is titled, "Nyob Paug Hauv Qab Thu" ("Below the Surface") and is presented in both Hmong and English. It includes interviews with community leaders and presents scientifically sound information about fish consumption. It also acknowledges the Hmong tradition of fishing, while showing which fish are safest to eat and demonstrating ways to prepare fish to make them safer to eat.

To help people remember the video's message while catching or cooking fish, each video is packaged with a laminated tackle box card and a kitchen magnet. Both items contain summary information about how to safely catch and prepare fish. The video cover, magnet, and card all contain Hmong-oriented designs or artwork.

After producing the materials, the next step was to distribute them to the target community. Project partners did this through local stores, doctors' offices, and at Hmong festivals, where the video was showcased. Finally, they assessed the video's impact on consumption behaviors through pre–video-viewing and post–video-viewing evaluations. According to the evaluation, after viewing the video, 71% of respondents said they would change the type of fish they catch, 76% said they understood which parts of fish are safer to eat, and 84% said they would alter how they prepare their fish (David Petering, personal communication).

EXAMPLE 2: THE ANISHNAABE

The Anishnaabe (or Ojibwe or Chippewa) comprise several Native American tribes that reside in the upper Great Lakes. The Anishnaabe people have a rich tradition of subsistence fishing that dates back hundreds of years. Since European contact, they also have been highly involved in commercial fishing, and many tribal members make a living from fishing in the Great Lakes.

In order to assess the Anishnaabe's awareness of safe fish-consumption practices, the Inter-Tribal Council of Michigan conducted several focus groups with men and women from the community (Dellinger, 2007). Focus-group participants completed surveys about fish consumption and fish advisories, and then discussed these topics in a traditional Native American "talking circle" format. They also participated in a traditional fish dinner. Information gathered from the focus groups was combined with risk-assessment data and used to guide the creation of various outreach products.

One of the products that resulted from the project was a video, titled "Nindamwaa Giigoon: An Anishnaabe Guide to Eating Fish," which was produced in collaboration with the NIEHS CEHSC and the Chippewa–Ottawa Resource Authority. The first part of the title means, "We are eating fish." The video features community experts who give scientifically sound advice on fish consumption and contains cultural images and music. It is narrated by Ada Deer, who, as the first Native American woman to lead the Bureau of Indian Affairs and the director of Native American Studies at the University of Wisconsin–Madison, is widely recognized by the target population.

Feedback from focus groups was also used to guide the development of an informational brochure and poster (Dellinger, 2007). Both the brochure and the poster incorporate culturally relevant illustrations and/or designs, elements that focus-group participants suggested would make the materials more appealing to tribal members. The brochure and poster simplify fish-consumption advice by outlining the three major "S" factors that affect the level of risk associated with eating fish: the source, size, and species of fish. They also provide guidelines for preparing fish in a way that reduces the intake of contaminants.

Following production, the video, brochure, and poster were distributed to the target community through tribal health clinics and other community outlets, and evaluated for their impact on consumption behaviors through pre–video-viewing and post–video-viewing surveys (Dellinger, 2007). According to the evaluation, after viewing the video, most respondents said they would not change the amount of fish they eat, but about half said they would probably or definitely eat different fish species. In addition, 88% of respondents said the video helped them to "learn which pollutants cause problems for people who eat fish," and 83% said it helped them "learn which fish parts should not be eaten" (Dellinger et al., 2008).

Conclusion

Fish consumption can both expose consumers to mercury-related health risks and provide them with nutritional health benefits. The objective of fish-consumption guidelines is to help consumers make informed, healthy choices about the fish they eat so that they can minimize the risks and maximize the benefits of eating fish.

As such, ideal fish-consumption advisories should be developed through a process that recognizes and carefully weighs both the risks and benefits of eating fish. The process should also recognize that specific risks and benefits vary among populations, and account for this accordingly. This is especially important in the case of vulnerable populations—such as developing fetuses or traditional peoples—for whom fish provide unique benefits, and for whom fish restrictions or avoidance have potential to introduce risks.

Fish advisories should be carefully and thoughtfully developed and communicated. To impact consumption behavior as intended, fish advisory information must be received, understood, and trusted by the targeted population. Community-based participatory research, which involves community members as partners in the research process, is well suited for use in developing and communicating effective fish advisories, especially for vulnerable populations.

Under current policies, worldwide anthropogenic emissions of mercury and other pollutants are expected to increase in the future. As concentrations of environmental mercury approach concentrations historically observed only following major volcanic emissions, protecting vulnerable populations by both minimizing the risks and promoting the benefits of fish consumption will become even more important. Although a deeper understanding of mercury biotransformation, biomagnification, fate, and transport may be necessary to further research and to guide future policy decisions, simplified messages—such as those emphasizing the source, size, and species of fish consumed—may aid in protecting vulnerable populations.

References

Agency for Healthcare Research and Quality. 2003. *The role of community-based participatory research: Creating partnerships, improving health* (AHRQ publication no. 03-0037). http://www.ahrq.gov/research/cbprrole.htm (accessed February 10, 2008).

Agency for Toxic Substances and Disease Registry. 1999. *Toxicological profile for mercury.* Atlanta: U.S. Department of Health and Human Services, Public Health Service.

Agency for Toxic Substances and Disease Registry. 2003. *Toxicological profile for selenium.* Atlanta: U.S. Department of Health and Human Services, Public Health Service.

Cohen, J.T., Bellinger, D.C., Connor, W.E., Kris-Etherton, P.M., Lawrence, R.S., Savitz, D.A., Shaywitz, B.A., Teutsch, S.M., and Gray, G.M. 2005. A quantitative risk-benefit analysis of changes in population fish consumption. *American Journal of Preventive Medicine* 29(4): 325–334.

Columbia River Inter-Tribal Fish Commission. 1994. *Summary of preliminary results: A fish consumption survey of the Umatilla, Nez Perce, Yakima and Warm Springs Tribes of the Columbia River Basin.* Portland, Oregon.

Daniels, J.L., Longnecker, M.P., Rowland, A.S., Golding, J., and the ALSPAC Study Team—University of Bristol Institute of Child Health. 2004. Fish intake during pregnancy and early cognitive development of offspring. *Epidemiology* 15(4): 394–402.

Davidson, P.W., Myers, G.J., Cox, C., Axtell, C., Shamlaye, C., Sloane-Reeves, J., Cernichiari, E., Needham, L., Choi, A., Wang, Y., Berlin, M., and Clarkson, T.W. 1998. Effects of prenatal and postnatal methylmercury exposure from fish consumption on neurodevelopment: outcomes at 66 months of age in the Seychelles Child Development Study. *Journal of the American Medical Association* 280(8): 701–707.

Dellinger, J.A. 2004. Exposure assessment and initial intervention regarding fish consumption of tribal members of the Upper Great Lakes Region in the United States. *Environmental Research* 95: 325–340.

Dellinger, J.A., Hudson, J., Krabbenhoft, D., and Murphy, H. 2005. Pacific volcanoes, mercury contaminated fish, and Polynesian taboos. *Clinical Toxicology* 43: 595–596.

Dellinger, J.A., Haverkate, R., Hickey, A., Dellinger, M., Pritchard, D., Farmer, A., Vignavong, S., and Petering, D. 2008. "Eat more fish but choose wisely" risk reduction strategy for Michigan Anishnaabe tribes: preliminary evaluation of DVD. Poster presented at Native American Health Research Conference Portland, Oregon, August 25–28, 2008.

Dellinger, M.J. 2007. Using translational research to create culturally relevant fish consumption advisories. Master's thesis, University of Wisconsin–Milwaukee.

Department of Health and Welfare, Canada. 1979. Methylmercury in Canada: Exposure of Indian and Inuit residents to methylmercury in the Canadian environment. Ottawa, ON: Minister of National Health and Welfare.

Dewailly, E., Blanchet, C., Gingras, S., Lemieux, S., and Holub, B.J. 2002. Cardiovascular disease risk factors and n-3 fatty acid status in the adult population of James Bay Cree. *American Journal of Clinical Nutrition* 76: 85–92.

Domingo, J.L., Bocio, A., Falcó, G., and Llobet, J.M. 2007. Benefits and risks of consumption—Part I. A quantitative analysis of the intake of omega-3 fatty acids and chemical contaminants. *Toxicology* 230: 219–226.

Egeland, G.M., and Middaugh, J.P. 1997. Balancing fish consumption benefits with mercury exposure. *Science* 278(5345): 1904–1906.

Falk, C., Hanrahan, L., Anderson, H.A., Kanarek, M.S., Draheim, L., Needham, L., Patterson, D., Jr., and the Great Lakes Consortium. 1999. Body burden levels of dioxin, furans, and PCBs among frequent consumers of Great Lakes sport fish. *Environmental Research* 80(2): S19–S25.

Flint R.W., and J. Vena. 1991. *Human health risks from chemical exposure: The Great Lakes ecosystem.* Chelsea, MI: Lewis.

Gerstenberger, S.L., and Dellinger, J.A. 2002. PCBs, mercury, and organochlorine concentrations in lake trout, walleye, and whitefish from selected tribal fisheries in the Upper Great Lakes region. *Environmental Toxicology* 17: 513–519.

Grandjean, P., Weihe, P., White, R.F., Debes, F., Araki, S., Yokoyama, K., Murata, K., Sorensen, N., Dahl, R., and Jorgensen, P.J. 1997. Cognitive deficit in 7-year-old children with prenatal exposure to methylmercury. *Neurotoxicology and Teratology* 19(6): 417–428.

Grandjean, P., Murata, K., Budtz-Jørgensen, E., and Weihe, P. 2004. Cardiac autonomic activity in methylmercury neurotoxicity: 14-year follow-up of a Faroese birth cohort. *Journal of Pediatrics* 144(2): 169–176.

Guallar, E., Sanz-Gallardo, M.I., van't Veer, P., Bode, P., Aro, A., Gómez-Aracena, J., Kark, J.D., Riemersma, R.A., Martín-Moreno, J.M., and Kok F.J., for the Heavy Metals and Myocardial Infarction Study Group. 2002. Mercury, fish oils, and the risk of myocardial infarction. *New England Journal of Medicine* 347(22): 1747–1754.

Hanrahan, L.P., Falk, C., Anderson, H.A., Draheim, L., Kanarek, M.S., Olson, J., and The Great Lakes Consortium. 1999. Serum PCB and DDE levels of frequent Great Lakes sport fish consumers—a first look. *Environmental Research* 80(2): S26–S37.

Hibbeln, J.R., Davis, J.M., Steer, C., Emmett, P., Rogers, I., Williams, C., and Golding, J. 2007. Maternal seafood consumption in pregnancy and neurodevelopmental outcomes in childhood (ALSPAC study): an observational cohort. *Lancet* 369: 578–585.

Imm, P., Knobeloch, L., Anderson, H.A., and the Great Lakes Sport Fish Consortium. 2005. Fish consumption and advisory awareness in the Great Lakes basin. *Environmental Health Perspectives* 113(10): 1325–1329.

Institute of Medicine. 2007. *Seafood choices: balancing benefits and risks*. Washington, DC: National Academies Press.

International Joint Commission. 2004. *Great Lakes fish consumption advisories: The public health benefits and risks*. Washington, DC: International Joint Commission.

Inter-Tribal Fisheries and Assessment Program. 2003. Fish Contaminant Monitoring Program: Lake Trout and Whitefish from Northern Lake Michigan, 2003. Administrative Report 04-1. Sault Ste. Marie: Inter-Tribal Fisheries and Assessment Program.

Inter-Tribal Fisheries and Assessment Program. 2004. Fish Contaminant Monitoring Program: Lake Trout and Whitefish from Lake Superior and Walleye from St. Mary's River and Bay de Noc, 2004. Administrative Report 05-1. Sault Ste. Marie: Inter-Tribal Fisheries and Assessment Program.

Inter-Tribal Fisheries and Assessment Program. 2005. Fish Contaminant Monitoring Program: Lake Trout and Whitefish from Northern Lake Huron, 2005. Administrative Report 06-1. Sault Ste. Marie: Inter-Tribal Fisheries and Assessment Program.

Israel, B.A., Parker, E.A., Rowe, Z., Salvatore, A., Minkler, M., Lopez, J., Butz, A., Mosley, A., Coates, L., Lambert, G., Potito, P.A., Brenner, B., Rivera, M., Romero, H., Thompson, B., Coronado, G., and Halstead, S. 2005. Community-based participatory research: lessons learned from the Centers for Children's Environmental Health and Disease Prevention Research. *Environmental Health Perspectives* 113(10): 1463–1471.

Jardine, C.G. 2003. Development of a public participation and communication protocol for establishing fish consumption advisories. *Risk Analysis* 23(3): 461–471.

Kuhnlein, H.V., and Receveur, O. 1996. Dietary change and traditional food systems of indigenous peoples. *Annual Review of Nutrition* 16: 417–442.

Mahaffey, K.R., Clickner, R.P., and Jeffries, R.A. 2009. Adult women's blood mercury concentrations vary regionally in the United States: association with patterns of fish consumption (NHANES 1999-2004). *Environmental Health Perspectives* 117(1): 47–53.

Medline Plus. 2008a. *Dietary proteins*. http://www.nlm.nih.gov/medlineplus/dietaryproteins.html (accessed January 14, 2008).

Medline Plus. 2008b. *Vitamins*. http://www.nlm.nih.gov/medlineplus/vitamins.html (accessed January 14, 2008).

Mergler, D., Anderson, H.A., Chan, L.H.M., Mahaffey, K.R., Murray, M., Sakamoto, M., and Stern, A.H. 2007. Methylmercury exposure and health effects in humans: a worldwide concern. *Ambio* 36(1): 3–11.

Ministry of the Environment, Government of Japan. 2002. *Minamata disease: the history and measures*. http://www.env.go.jp/en/chemi/hs/minamata2002/index.html (accessed December 9, 2007).

Mozaffarian, D., and Rimm, E.B. 2006. Fish intake, contaminants, and human health: evaluating the risks and the benefits. *Journal of the American Medical Association* 296(15): 1885–1899.

National Institute of Environmental Health Sciences. Office of Translational Research. 2008. http://www.niehs.nih.gov/about/od/otr/index.cfm (accessed February 10, 2008).

National Resource Council. 2000. *Toxicological effects of methylmercury*. Washington, DC: National Academies Press.

Oken, E., Kleinman, K.P., Berland, W.E., Simon, S.R., Rich-Edwards, J.W., and Gillman, M.W. 2003. Decline in fish consumption among pregnant women after a national mercury advisory. *Obstetrics and Gynecology* 102(2): 346–351.

Raymond, L.J., and Ralston, N.V.C. 2004. Mercury: selenium interactions and health implications. *SMDJ Seychelles Medical and Dental Journal* 7(1): 72–77.

Salonen, J.T., Seppänen, K., Nyyssönen, K., Korpela, H., Kauhanen, J., Kantola, M., Tuomilehto, J., Esterbauer, H., Tatzber, F., and Salonen, R. 1995. Intake of mercury from fish, lipid peroxidation, and the risk of myocardial infarction and coronary, cardiovascular, and any death in Eastern Finnish men. *Circulation* 91: 645–655.

Schaeffer, D.J., Dellinger, J.A., Needham, L.L., and Hansen, L.G. 2006. Serum PCB profiles in Native Americans from Wisconsin based on region, diet, age, and gender: implications for epidemiology studies. *Science of the Total Environment* 357: 74–87.

Stahl, L.L., Snyder, B.D., Olsen, A.R., and Pitt, J.L. 2009. Contaminants in fish tissue from US lakes and reservoirs: a national probabilistic study. *Environmental Monitoring and Assessment* 150: 3–19.

Stern, A.H., and Smith, A.E. 2003. An assessment of the cord blood:maternal blood methylmercury ratio: implications for risk assessment. *Environmental Health Perspectives* 111(12): 1465–1470.

Stewart, P., Darvill, T., Lonky, E., Reihman, J., Pagano, J., and Bush, B. 1999. Assessment of prenatal exposure to PCBs from maternal consumption of Great Lakes fish: an analysis of PCB pattern and concentration. *Environmental Research* 80(2): S87–S96.

Sunderland, E.M. 2007. Mercury exposure from domestic and imported estuarine and marine fish in the U.S. seafood market. *Environmental Health Perspectives* 115(2): 235–242.

Thigpen, K.G., and Petering, D. 2004. Fish tales to ensure health. *Environmental Health Perspectives* 112(13): A738.

US Environmental Protection Agency. 1997. *Mercury study report to Congress*. Washington, DC: U.S. Environmental Protection Agency.

US Environmental Protection Agency. 2000. *Guidance for assessing chemical contaminant data for use in fish advisories*. Washington, DC: Office of Water, Office of Science and Technology.

US Environmental Protection Agency. 2007. *Fact sheet: 2005/2006 national listing of fish advisories*. http://www.epa.gov/waterscience/fish/advisories/2006/tech.pdf (accessed January 27, 2008).

US Environmental Protection Agency. 2008. *Integrated Risk Information System (IRIS) on methylmercury*. http://www.epa.gov/ncea/iris/subst/0073.htm (accessed February 2, 2008).

US Environmental Protection Agency and US Food and Drug Administration. 2004. *What you need to know about mercury in fish and shellfish*. http://www.epa.gov/waterscience/fish/files/MethylmercuryBrochure.pdf (accessed December 9, 2007).

World Health Organization. 1999. Safety evaluation of certain food additives and contaminants. WHO Food Additive Series 44. Geneva, Switzerland: WHO.

Environmental Justice

The Mercury Connection

JEROME NRIAGU, NILADRI BASU, and SIMONE CHARLES

POPULATIONS AT RISK

DISPARITIES IN SITING OF MERCURY SOURCES

Brownfield Development

DISPROPORTIONATE EXPOSURE AROUND HOT SPOTS OF MERCURY

Grassy Narrows, Ontario (Chlor-Alkali)
James Bay Cree of Quebec (Hydroelectric Dam)
Pomo Tribe at Clear Lake (Cinnabar Mine)
Selected Tribes within the Great Lakes Basin

IMMIGRANT POPULATIONS FROM ASIA

NON-HISPANIC BLACK URBAN ANGLERS

CURSE FROM THE WIND: CONTAMINATION OF THE ARCTIC REGION WITH MERCURY

DO FISH-CONSUMPTION ADVISORIES PROMOTE ENVIRONMENTAL INJUSTICE?

Environmental justice and sustainable development are two recent concepts that have provided exciting and normative framework for public debate and environmental planning in many countries. Although both concepts are difficult to define and lack precision as analytic policy tools, each paradigm has a potential to effect long-lasting changes on how we relate to and manage the environment (Agyeman, 2005). What makes the concepts unique is that both promote environmental equity using communitarian-approach to issues at the local, regional, and global scales.

As defined by Bullard (1994), environmental justice "embraces the principle that all people and communities are entitled to equal protection of environmental and public health laws and regulations." The United States Environmental Protection Agency (USEPA) offers a somewhat different definition—"the fair treatment and meaningful involvement of all people regardless of race, color, national origin, or income with respect to the development, implementation, and enforcement of environmental laws, regulations, and policies." Fair treatment means that no group of people, including racial, ethnic, or socioeconomic groups, should bear a disproportionate share of the negative environmental consequences resulting from industrial, municipal, and commercial operations or the execution of federal, state, local, and tribal programs and policies. Meaningful involvement means that: (1) potentially affected community residents have an appropriate opportunity to participate in decisions about a proposed activity that will affect their environment and/or health; (2) the public's contribution can influence the regulatory agency's decision; (3) the concerns of all participants involved will be considered in the decision-making process; and (4) the decision makers seek out and facilitate the involvement of those potentially affected (USEPA, 2008).

Other authors view environmental justice through a broader prism that encompasses ethics, civil rights, public health, and social disparities. Bunyan Bryant (a pioneer in this field) notes that

> Environmental Justice is broader in scope than environmental equity. It refers to those cultural norms and values, rules, regulations, behaviors, policies, and decisions to support sustainable communities, where people can interact with confidence that their environment is safe, nurturing, and productive. Environmental justice is supported by decent paying and safe jobs; quality schools and recreation; decent housing and adequate health care; democratic decision-making and personal empowerment; and communities free of violence, drugs, and poverty. These are communities where both cultural and biological diversity are respected and highly revered and where distributed justice prevails. (Bryant, 2008)

The concept of environmental justice is being increasingly embraced in other countries with regard to communities with perceived disadvantages (for instance, because of their race, ethnicity, socioeconomic status, immigration status, lack of land ownership, geographic isolation, formal education, occupational characteristics, political power, gender, or other characteristics) that put them at disproportionate risk for being exposed to environmental hazards (Claudio, 2007). Internationally, environmental justice has also been extended to scenarios such as exporting of wastes and polluting industries by industrialized countries to the developing nations. Increasingly, environmental justice is being synergized with human rights as a means for: (a) reinforcing the normative claims of international environmental health laws, (b) strengthening advocacy for rights to a clean environment, and (c) bridging the divide between environmental health practitioners and human rights advocates in contemporary public health domains (Nixon and Forman, 2008).

It is clear from the definitions above that the concept of environmental justice is still evolving as different actors and researchers weigh in on the debate (Payne-Sturges and Gee, 2006). The diverging views on environmental justice encompass, to differing degrees, three important elements: economic, environmental, and policy (legal or political). People who view environmental justice through the environmental lens emphasize the balancing of benefits and burdens, better environmental health, and overall improvement in the quality of life, and elimination of health inequalities that characterize environmentally devastated neighborhoods and poor or minority communities (Solitaire and Greenberg, 2002). As an economic discourse, environmental justice has been contextualized in terms of increase in number and type of jobs, an increase in the tax base, or an improvement in infrastructure and education in marginalized communities. From the policy perspective, environmental justice embraces the empowerment of the disenfranchised in ways that include the legitimization of community knowledge and partnerships, community-based planning and participatory research, and an increase of community-driven decision making that is supported by elected leadership, the business community, and middle-class residents (Solitaire and Greenberg, 2002). This chapter views environmental justice primarily through the environmental lens.

Many aspects of mercury pollution, from distribution of sources to differential vulnerabilities and heightened exposures and impacts can be contextualized within the policy framework of environmental justice as contained in the Executive Order 12898 (Federal Action to Address Environmental Justice in Minority Populations and Low-Income Populations) issued on February 11, 1994, by President Bill Clinton. The Presidential Memorandum accompanying the Executive Order provides that existing laws can be used to meet the environmental justice objectives. Specifically, President Clinton noted that. "Environmental and civil rights statutes provide many opportunities to address environmental hazards in minority communities and low-income communities. Application of these existing statutory provisions is an important part of this administration's efforts to prevent those minority communities and low-income communities from being subject to disproportionately high and adverse environmental effects." According to this Executive Order, environmental justice populations can be regarded as communities that are most at risk of being unaware of or unable to participate in environmental decision making or to gain access to federal or state resources. From the perspective of environmental justice communities, mercury is clearly an exemplary case. Any group that relies on fishing for dietary sustenance, cultural identity, spiritual well-being, or economic prosperity is more vulnerable to mercury pollution. It has become ironic that some programs under the Executive Order have the unintended consequence of exacerbating environmental injustice in the at-risk populations.

The risk of exposure of women to methylmercury is of heightened concern because of the potential for damaging the developing brain of the fetus. The disparity in blood mercury levels remains a matter of health and reproductive inequality of global proportion.

Populations at Risk

Consumption of fish represents the primary means by which humans are exposed to mercury. The general population of the United States consumes an average 17.5 g of fish per day but certain groups consume more (Agency for Toxic Substances and Disease Registry [ATSDR], 1999; USEPA, 2000). Recreational anglers consume 30 g of fish per day; subsistence fishers consume 142 g of fish per day. These two groups consume significantly more fish than the average U.S. citizen and are therefore vulnerable to fishborne mercury. Various ethnic populations, such as Asians, Pacific Islanders, and Indigenous peoples of North America, also rely heavily on fish for sustenance (Hightower and Moore, 2003; Hightower et al., 2006). Not surprisingly, the groups that consume the highest amounts of fish are disproportionately exposed to higher levels of mercury (this book, chapters 11 and 12).

Over 20 states and 1 tribe have issued advisories covering every one of their lakes and/or rivers, while 12 states and 1 tribe have advisories that cover their entire coastal waters (O'Neill, 2004). These advisories are symptomatic of extensive contamination of the aquatic resources of this country with mercury and suggest that the number of communities that depend on these waters for subsistence fishing are disproportionately at risk of exposure to high levels of mercury.

The biomonitoring data from the National Health and Nutrition Examination Survey (NHANES) carried out by the Centers for Disease Control and Prevention (CDC) during 1999–2002 showed that 16.6% of adult female participants who self-identified as Asian, Pacific Islander, Native American, or multiracial had blood mercury levels ≥5.8 µg/L, while 27.3% had levels ≥3.5 µg/L. By comparison, 5.1% of the entire survey population (n = 3497)

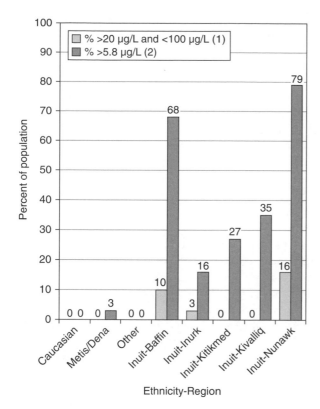

FIGURE 15.1 Maternal blood guideline exceedances for organic mercury in Arctic Canada, by region and ethnicity. (*Source:* Van Oostdam et al., 2005.)

had blood mercury levels ≥ 5.8 µg/L and 10.9% had levels ≥ 3.5 µg/L (Hightower et al., 2006). Another observation from the NHANES database that was of equal concern was that about 8% of all U.S. women of childbearing age were found to have blood mercury levels ≥ 5.8 ppb, a level considered by the USEPA to cause an increased risk of adverse health effects to babies (Woodruff et al., 2003). Native Americans, Asians immigrants, and Pacific Islanders represent a high-risk group for dietary exposure to methylmercury as evidenced by the fact the mean number of fish and shellfish meals consumed by this particular racial/ethnic group was higher than the average for the general population (Figure 15.1). The lowest fish and shellfish consumption rate was by Mexican Americans, and this population also had the lowest blood mercury levels (Figure 15.1).

Biomonitoring of blood mercury concentrations in a representative sample of 1811 New York City (NYC) residents as part of the NYC Health and Nutrition Examination Survey found the geometric mean blood mercury concentration among NYC adults to be 2.73 µg/L (McKelvey et al., 2007). About one quarter (24.8%) or 1.4 million NYC adults, had blood mercury concentrations equal to or exceeding the New York State reportable level of 5 µg/L. The 97.5th percentile for blood mercury concentration for all participants was 15.37 µg/L. Women 20–49 years of age (n = 1049) had a geometric mean blood mercury level of 2.64 µg/L with a 23.8% prevalence of blood mercury ≥ 5 µg/L. Frequent consumption

of fish or shellfish was associated with increasing mercury levels ($p < 0.01$ for trend test for geometric mean and prevalence ≥ 5 µg/L). Almost half of adult Asian New Yorkers (46.2%) had blood mercury levels ≥ 5 g/L. Among the foreign-born Chinese New Yorkers in the survey, 73% had blood mercury concentrations ≥ 5 µg/L, and 20% of these were ≥ 15 µg/L (McKelvey et al., 2007). These epidemiologic studies point to the fact that the body burden of a significant fraction of the population of United States is elevated but the health consequences have not been fully assessed.

Disparities in Siting of Mercury Sources

Industrial sources of mercury in the environment are a major environmental health issue because they tend to be located in predominantly built-up areas, especially in communities of color and socioeconomically depressed neighborhoods. Incinerators and coal-fired power plants are notorious emitters of mercury because the pollution-control devices in these plants are not 100% effective in removing gaseous mercury from waste gas streams. In a detailed assessment of industrial emissions of mercury into the air in the Great Lakes basin during 1999–2000, Murray and Holmes (2004) showed that coal-fired electric utilities accounted for 52.7% of the region's mercury emissions, varying from 20.2% of the total in New York to 67.5% in Ohio. Chang et al. (2000) reported that mercury removal efficiencies of pollution-control devices of two large-scale municipal solid-waste incinerators in Taiwan were less than 50%. Much of the mercury was emitted as oxidized mercury. Similar results were observed by Lee et al. (2004), who measured percentages of elemental mercury in the flue-gas emissions of 9.5–31.4% from coal-fired power plants and 1.3–3.7% from industrial-waste incinerators in Korea. Other important contributors to regional emissions included municipal-waste combustion (5.6%), mercury-cell chlor-alkali plants (4%) and hazardous waste incinerators (4%), stationary internal combustion engines (3.5%), industrial, commercial, and institutional boilers (3.3%), and lime manufacturing (3.0%). Medical-waste incineration accounted for 1–4% of the regional emissions. These types of factories are characteristically found in the old parts of towns, where environmental justice communities tend to aggregate (Atlas, 2001). Indeed, the United States General Accounting Office in 1983 stated that 75% of off-site commercial hazardous waste facilities in EPA Region 4 were located in African-American neighborhoods, the residents of which make up 20% of the region's population. The fact that in the early 20th century, local zoning bodies routinely zoned many residential African-American communities as "industrial" while zoning similar regions in white communities as "residential" is well documented (Bullard, 1994). Such residential segregation via zoning ordinances would inevitably create unequal distribution of ethnic minorities and low-income people around the mercury-emitting factories.

The scientific literature is rich with studies that have reported on disproportionate placing of old, polluting (and mercury-releasing) coal-fired power plants and other industries, including refineries, chemical plants, hazardous-waste dumps and processing sites, and incinerators in economically depressed neighborhoods (Bullard et al., 2007; Mohai and Saha, 2006). The 1994 and 2007 United Church of Christ studies on toxic waste and race in the United States highlighted the following inequalities in the location of environmental hazards:

1. Race was the single most important factor in the location of hazardous-waste treatment facilities after accounting for urbanization and regional differences. Race was a stronger predictor of the location of hazardous-waste facilities than income, education, or socioeconomic status.
2. Penalties were higher for polluters when pollution occurred in predominantly white areas as compared with minority areas. "Vulnerable communities, populations and individuals often fell between the regulatory cracks."
3. Inequalities existed in the chosen option of waste treatment where permanent treatment of hazardous versus containment was available (Bullard et al., 2007).

It is estimated that 68% of all African Americans live within 30 miles of a coal-fired power plant, as compared with 56% of whites (Bullard, 1994). The rates of poverty are 1.5 times higher in communities hosting hazardous-waste facilities as compared with non-host areas (Bullard et al., 2007). There are many studies showing that power plants and incinerators are disproportionately located and concentrated in communities of color and the working class (Bullard, 1994; Mohai and Saha, 2006). Anderton et al. (1994, 1997) and Davidson and Anderton (2000) also conducted studies in low-income areas with disproportionate numbers of hazardous waste or toxic-type facilities; minorities and poor whites tend to dominate the low-income profile in these studies.

Disparities between neighborhoods hosting hazardous waste facilities and those not hosting such facilities were reported throughout the EPA Regions: Region 1 (36% vs. 15%), Region 4 (54% vs. 30%), Region 5 (53% vs. 19%), and Region 6 (63% vs. 42%). On the state level, examples of significant disparities between host and non-host neighborhoods include Michigan (66% vs. 19%), Nevada (79% vs. 33%), and Kentucky (51% vs. 10%). Well-known examples of environmental justice communities where disproportionately large numbers of industries known to release mercury into the local environment are located in relation compared to neighboring Caucasian communities include:

1. "Chicagoland," Illinois, whose minority communities represent 50% or more of the area, are disproportionately cluttered with coal-fired power plants, steel plants, and oil refineries.

2. Waterfront South in Camden County, New Jersey, which contains the largest minority percentage in the county also houses the St. Lawrence Cement Company, which emits significant particulate matter, mercury, lead, manganese, and other air pollutants.
3. Macon, Georgia, where more than 60% of African-American residents live within 30 miles of a coal-fired power plant.

Although not generally realized, natural gas and crude oil also contain mercury in trace amounts, which can readily build up in the local environment when huge quantities are processed (USEPA, 2001). For example, minority children in Texas are being disproportionately endangered given the location of over 100 refineries and chemical plants located within 2 miles of 216 schools located in just eight counties (Bullard et al., 2007). Within these counties, the school population is predominantly minority—over 70% African American and Hispanic, as compared with 47% statewide. Mercury was not considered as one of the air toxins of concern in the study, however.

It is impossible to establish direct causal relationships between mercury emission and health effects in disparate communities. Population groups differ in health outcomes because of greater exposure to environmental risk factors according to where they live, work, or play (Sexton et al., 1993; Bullard, 1994; Mohai and Saha, 2006). For example, people of color are more likely to live in high-poverty neighborhoods and be employed in more hazardous occupations than the general population (Bullard, 1994, 2007; Saha and Mohai, 2006) and disparities in industrial exposure often translate into increased risk for illness. Sexton et al. (1993), Brooks and Sethi (1997), among others, have shown that non-Hispanic blacks were more likely to reside in census tracts with higher total air toxin concentrations. The United Church of Christ used a meta-analysis of 64 studies in the United States to provide an overwhelming body of empirical evidence that people of color and low incomes face disproportionate environmental impacts. This report eloquently noted that "Because people of color and the poor are highly concentration in neighborhoods with multiple facilities, they continue to be particularly vulnerable to the various negative impacts of hazardous waste facilities" (Bullard et al., 2007).

Brownfield Development

Brownfields, an important derivative of the environmental justice program under the USEPA, are hotspots of pollution that often include mercury. Although brownfields can be found in neighborhoods that range from affluent suburban communities to some of the poorest urban ghettos, most are located in blighted neighborhoods. They are located next to abandoned residential and commercial properties, near infrastructure and public facilities in poor or dilapidated condition, and neighborhoods that are experiencing major job losses and high crime rates. In these places, brownfields represent socioeconomic burdens because they can lower property taxes, diminish the natural beauty of the area, and most importantly contaminate the water supply and the air.

Brownfields represent a significant health hazard to the community. An abandoned factory may become an exploratory playground for children who become unknowingly exposed to toxins including mercury, lead, arsenic, and solvents. Depending on the type and level of mercury contamination, brownfields can release significant amounts of this toxin into the air (mercury compounds are notoriously volatile) or drinking water. The practice of building of new schools on brownfields may serve to perpetuate environmental injustice with regard to mercury. Opponents of the practice argue that children remain exposed to the degassing of residual mercury (and other contaminants) in the remediated brownfields and hence represent a liability to the school system (Solitaire and Greenberg, 2002). Proponents, including many developers, claim that brownfields can be cleaned up to acceptable levels for use in building schools and that they pose a greater health risk if left underdeveloped. There are currently no reliable data to support either claim. Regardless, the hazard (mercury) is never completely removed, and affected communities must bear the burden of taking steps to shield themselves from the risk of any residual mercury in the brownfields.

Disproportionate Exposure around Hot Spots of Mercury

Evidence that hot spots of mercury generally coincide with areas that are home to communities of color, low-income and immigrant communities, as well as tribes and indigenous peoples has been discussed above. These hot spots impose a profound burden on subsistence and sport fishers and their families, for whom fish and fishing are important for physiologic, economic, social, political, cultural, and spiritual health. Among the groups at risk, the local tribes and indigenous peoples are the most vulnerable and often the most highly exposed to mercury. Examples of such communities include several indigenous peoples found throughout North America, such as the Cree in Quebec (Dumont et al., 1998; Muckle et al., 2001a), Ojibwe in the Great Lakes basin (Dellinger, 2004) and Ontario (Kinghorn et al., 2007), Rancheria in Northern California (Harnly et al., 1997), and the Mohawk in Quebec (Chan et al., 1999) and New York (Schell et al., 2003).

Using available databases, Roe (2003) identified 655 watersheds across the United States where Native communities exist. By examining the concentrations of mercury in fish within these watersheds, 19 Native communities were classified as having a severe risk for mercury intoxication, 70 as having a high risk, and 59 as having a moderate risk. Such a comparison reveals that the geographic location of tribes puts many Native peoples at a disproportionate risk of mercury exposure (O'Neill, 2004).

This section briefly outlines selected cases from indigenous peoples across North America who are exposed to mercury from various local sources (e.g., cinnabar mines, hydroelectric dams, chlor-alkali plants, pulp and paper mills, coal-fired power plants). In each case, the presence of mercury has been shown to negatively impact the health, culture, spirituality, and identity of these communities. These communities are cases for environmental injustice in the sense that they have derived little or no benefit from the products and services of the industries that release the mercury and are now bearing the burden of the wastes left behind.

Grassy Narrows, Ontario (Chlor-Alkali)

The Grassy Narrows First Nations People live in northwestern Ontario, about 130 km downstream of Dryden. In the mid-1900s a chlor-alkali plant was built in Dryden. Between 1962 and 1970 the plant discharged over 10,000 kg of mercury into the English–Wabigoon river system (Armstrong and Hamilton, 1973). Northern pike and walleye inhabiting these waters had mercury levels as high as 27.8 and 10.4 µg/g, respectively (Fimreite and Reynolds, 1973). Fish levels that warrant regulatory action range between 0.5 and 1 µg/g. Contamination extended as far as 320 km downstream of the Dryden discharge point (Fimreite and Reynolds, 1973). Not surprisingly, many residents of Grassy Narrows had extremely high levels of blood mercury, including one individual with a level of 660 µg/L (Wheatley and Paradis, 1995). Furthermore, reports revealed that fish-eating wildlife, including mink and river otter, were severely intoxicated (Wren, 1985). Owing to this contamination and associated media reports (Wheatley and Paradis, 1995), in May 1970 the Ontario Ministry of Energy and Resource Management halted fishing in the region.

The people of Grassy Narrows were immediately impacted by this fishing ban. Locally caught fish were an important component of their diet, spirituality, and culture. Fishing and fishing-related industries, such as hunting and lodging, represented a primary source of income for many people (Kinghorn et al., 2007). Community members started to change their views towards traditional foods (fish, plants) and lifestyles (hunting, fishing, gathering). Instead of subsistence hunting/fishing, many started to purchase and consume commercially available market foods and adopt a more sedentary, Western lifestyle.

Thirty years have passed since mercury was discharged into the English-Wabigoon river system but pollution continues to plague Grassy Narrows. In 2002, Kinghorn et al. (2007) sampled fish in the region and found that walleye, bass, and northern pike still had levels of mercury that exceeded protective guidelines recommended by Health Canada. A study on 57 residents of Grassy Narrows found that a range of clinical symptoms related to mercury poisoning, including numbness, tremors, pain in the extremities, and several sensory disturbances, still persisted (Harada et al., 2005). It is evident that mercury pollution continues to affect the traditional ways at Grassy Narrows. Two community meetings were held and it was decided that consumption of fish should still be discouraged from certain bodies of water in the area (Kinghorn et al., 2007). For more than 30 years the residents of Grassy Narrows have not had access to fish with safe levels of mercury and very little monitoring work has been carried out in the area.

James Bay Cree of Quebec (Hydroelectric Dam)

For nearly 5000 years the James Bay Cree have resided in the region of northwest Quebec. In recent years, this area has become impacted by mercury from several industrial operations. Between 1961 and 1978, a pulp and paper mill plant using chlor-alkali cells released mercury into the Lac Quevillon area. More importantly, the government of Quebec initiated the development of a massive hydroelectric plant in James Bay in 1971. A series of stations were built along the La Grande watershed. While there was much resistance to this development by the James Bay Cree, their social and environmental concerns were not immediately addressed.

The newly created reservoirs and associated flooding events promoted the methylation of mercury in sediments and subsequent biomagnification through the aquatic food chain. One study reported that concentrations of mercury in fish were five times greater than levels measured before the development (Brouard et al., 1994). Many fish samples had total mercury concentrations that exceeded 0.5 µg/g. The concern of mercury's presence in the James Bay region was quickly realized given the previous experience with the events in Grassy Narrows, Ontario. In fact, when referring to mercury the Cree adopted the term *nemasahkosiwin*, which literally translates to "sick fish."

A surveillance and education program was initiated in the early 1980s by the Cree Board of Health and Social Service (Noël et al., 1998). In one survey from 1988, nearly 15% of Cree (2613 individuals) had levels of mercury in hair exceeding 15 µg/g (Dumont et al., 1998). These levels were high enough to cause tremors in many individuals, but associations with other neurologic outcomes were not as clear (Auger et al., 2005). Owing to education programs, hair levels have decreased since the 1980s (Dumont et al., 1998). Though, as levels of mercury remain elevated in the fish (Belinsky et al., 1996), decreased hair mercury levels are associated with reduced consumption of locally caught fish. These species of fish (e.g.., whitefish, lake trout, pike), which were once regularly harvested and consumed by James Bay Cree, were excellent sources of proteins, minerals, vitamins, and fatty acids.

Pomo Tribe at Clear Lake (Cinnabar Mine)

The Pomo people are found primarily in Northern California, a region rich in cinnabar (HgS). Between 1865 and 1957, this mercury ore was mined in the Sulphur Bank Mercury Mine on Clear Lake. Though mining operations ceased half a century ago, nearly 2 million cubic yards of mine wastes and tailings remain in the area. The site is now listed by the USEPA as a superfund site.

Concentrations of mercury in the soil surrounding Clear Lake are 100 times greater than background levels, and local fish are highly contaminated (Harnly et al., 1997). Nearly 20% of fish sampled from the lake had mercury levels exceeding 1.0 µg/g. Many individual fish samples exceeded 0.5 µg/g. While urinary mercury (reflects exposure to inorganic mercury) levels in tribal members were at background levels, mean levels of blood mercury (reflects fish consumption) were about sevenfold higher as compared with non–fish consumers (15.6 µg/L vs. 2 µg/L; Harnley et al., 1997). Furthermore, 20% of the people had blood mercury levels that exceeded a protective guideline of 20 µg/L. Consumption of locally caught fish (60 g of fish per day) is an important component of this group's culture. Like other indigenous groups, the presence of mercury in fish has caused cultural distress and negatively affected nutritional habits.

Selected Tribes within the Great Lakes Basin

There are several Native communities located along the shores of the Great Lakes basin. For centuries these people have relied on this massive body of water and its abundant natural resources for their livelihood and traditional lifestyles. Over the past 200 years, the Great Lakes ecosystem has undergone major developments, particularly in the areas of agriculture, urbanization, forestry, shipping, and transportation. More recently, numerous industries have flourished in the Great Lakes basin, including coal-fired power plants, which are the single largest source of mercury pollution in the region and are responsible for ensuring that fish-consumption advisories remain constant throughout the basin (Cohen et al., 2004). Given the cultural, economic, spiritual, and/or nutritional importance of fish to Native Peoples, these consumption advisories have impacted traditional lifestyles in several communities. Four examples are provided below with additional details provided by Dellinger et al. (this book, chapter 14).

The Mohawks of Akwesasne (reservation at the border of the State of New York and the provinces of Ontario and Quebec) are a fishing and agriculturally based traditional culture of about 10,000–12,000 people. Their 4000-acre land sits in close proximity to three (two Alcoa and one General Motors) Superfund sites. Traditionally, the Mohawks of Akwesasne have depended on fish as a crucial supplement to their diets. Expectedly, contamination from three local Superfund sites and from other atmospheric pollutants in the area has threatened the safety of those consuming large quantities of fish and has presented the difficult task of getting community members to limit their consumption. Several public health studies involving their people have been conducted from the 1980s to the present, which document undue exposure to mercury because of their heavy reliance on natural resources. A number of risk-management strategies have been implemented, including fish consumption advisories issued by the St. Regis Mohawk Tribe Health Service in 1986, the New York State Department of Health (NYS DOH) in 2005, and Environment Canada. The warnings from 1986 specify that women and children should not consume area fish and men should consume only one fish meal per week. The NYS DOH set specific advisories to avoid consumption of fish from the Grasse River and the bay at General Motors along with other general advisories. The Canadian environmental agency advisories included greater species specificity, a regional breakdown of the St. Lawrence River, and allowance for meals of several species of fish. The Mohawks have conducted their own workshops to teach people how to clean and prepare fish to reduce contaminants. The exact benefits and costs of the various risk-management strategies have yet to be adequately assessed.

Kahnawake is another Mohawk community of 6500 located just south of Montreal, Quebec. Chan et al. (1999) performed a dietary assessment in the community and found that 33 of 42 participants actively fished in the region. On average, they had fished for 27 years. Daily fish consumption (23 g/day) was higher than in the general American population but comparable to other fish-eating Native Peoples throughout the Great Lakes basin. Most of the Mohawks surveyed indicated that they were eating less locally caught fish than they did 5 to 15 years ago. This decrease stemmed from the perception that fish are now unhealthy to eat because of chemical pollutants. Concentrations of mercury were also measured in fish locally caught near the Kahnawake, and in some cases, levels approached or exceeded the Health Canada guideline of 0.5 µg/g. Despite these levels, Chan et al. (1999) concluded that the nutritional and cultural benefits of consuming locally caught fish far outweigh the relatively lower risks associated with consuming polluted fish.

Chippewa Indians practice the traditional art of spearfishing walleye, a species of fish with quite high mercury burdens. Peterson et al. (1994) surveyed 175 adults from five Wisconsin Chippewa tribes to assess their fish-consumption habits and to assess levels of blood mercury. About 50% of participants ate one or fewer fish meals per week, while 21% ate three or more per week. Twenty percent of the participants had levels of blood mercury >5 µg/L but only one exceeded the 20 µg/L threshold. From this work, the authors concluded, presumably prematurely, that levels of mercury are not a health concern for Chippewa adults.

Immigrant Populations from Asia

In most Asian countries, fish is consumed almost daily and represents an important source of protein. Although their rate of fish consumption may decrease when they emigrate to the United States, surveys done in many parts of this country show that many Asian immigrants practice fishing. In particular, the immigrants of Southeast Asia who were closely connected to the natural environment where hunting and fishing were important skills for survival naturally become avid anglers in their adopted new countries. A survey of Hmong immigrants in California showed that 50% still practiced fishing (Ikeda et al., 1991). Hmongs are one of the largest groups of Southeast Asian immigrant groups in the United States. They were recruited by the Central Intelligence Agency and fought for the United States in the Vietnam War in the 1960s. After the war, they fled persecution by the communist regime into refugee camps in Thailand and later into the United States, where they began arriving in 1975. They continue to be admitted as refugees, mainly to California, Minnesota, and Wisconsin. Today, about 100,000 Hmong live in California alone. Other Southeast Asian immigrant groups with strong track records for sport fishing in Canada and the United States include Vietnamese, Cambodian, Thai, Burmese, Mien, and Lahu.

A survey of southeast Asians in Rhode Island found that 91% ate fish and 58% caught their own fish (Getz et al., 2006). Among those who ate fish, 47% were categorized as "infrequent fish consumers" (ate fish less than once a week), 49% were regular eaters (ate fish one to four times per week), and only 5% were frequent eaters (ate fish four or more times per week). Those in the frequent consumption category relied almost exclusively on what they caught and never purchased fish. Only one third of the study participants had ever heard of a ban on fishing or fish consumption (Getz et al., 2006). A study of Vietnamese women in Hamilton, Ontario, found that most of them ate more than 40 meals per year of Great Lakes fish, with some reporting 100–200 fish meals per year (Cavan, 1993). They claimed that the Great Lakes fish were important to them because they tasted good, were not expensive, were fresh and nutritious, and reminded them of their fishing activity in Vietnam (Shatenstein et al., 1999).

In addition to consuming more fish overall, Asian immigrants also demonstrate other risk behaviors that distinguish them from fishermen (and fisherwomen) in the larger sport fishing context. Among these risk behaviors are: (a) predatory species (i.e., those with higher contaminant loads) and bottom dwellers (especially carp) make up a large percentage what is eaten; (b) many anglers consume all and any fish they catch; and (c) in addition to the fillet, almost every fish organ is consumed, often as delicacies. As noted previously, population-based studies of blood mercury levels in Rhode Island, Minnesota, Wisconsin, New York City, and other parts of the United States have identified Southeast Asian immigrants as being among the most at risk with respect to mercury exposure.

Non-Hispanic Black Urban Anglers

The demographics of communities in watersheds where the fish tissue levels of mercury substantially exceed the national health criteria suggest that non-Hispanic black

(NHB) anglers, especially in urban areas are at increased risk for exposure to methylmercury. About 90% of NHB anglers fish in the Midwest, Northeast, and South regions of the United States (Henderson, 2004), where most of the fish advisories for mercury have been issued. It is not a coincidence that the NHB population and the sources of mercury contamination are often co-located within and around urban areas. The persistence of subsistence fishing in polluted waters by non-Hispanic urban blacks is driven by economic deprivation. They often live in so-called food deserts of inner cities, where the supply of fresh seafood is limited. Since many NHBs cannot afford to buy boats, they are more likely to fish from the shore for benthic organisms in the most contaminated waters. Over 1 million NHB anglers fish for catfish, and more black anglers consume catfish than do non-Hispanic white anglers in the United States (Weintraub and Birnbaum, 2008). In fact, catfish consumption has been shown to be a major contributor to elevated PCB levels in an NHB population (Weintraub and Birnbaum, 2008), and this is likely to be true for disparities in mercury exposure.

A cultural angle to the fishing practices of NHBs has been advanced by Weintraub and Birnbaum (2008). During slavery, fishing for nocturnal catfish enabled NHB anglers to supplement diets, develop knowledge of rivers along the Underground Railroad, and, in some cases, earn money (Cecelski, 2001). The Jim Crow legislation limiting economic opportunity and access to arable land further perpetuated subsistence fishing. The historical legacy may explain why the rate of fishing among NHB anglers is similar regardless of income levels (Henderson, 2004; Weintraub and Birnbaum, 2008). The way the fish is prepared is a cultural trait that may result in increased absorption of mercury by NHBs. Frying, for instance, can reduce the water content of the fish, resulting in a final product with a higher methylmercury concentration (Burger et al., 2003). Also, NHB anglers are less likely to trim off the fat (where PCBs and other organic pollutants tend to accumulate), and are more likely to eat whole fish than non-Hispanic white anglers. Because tissue organs accumulate mercury, consumption of the whole fish (versus fillets) results in elevated exposures to mercury (Burger et al., 2001).

Disparities in exposure and body burden of mercury may also stem from racial differences in fish consumption. The percentage of high-end consumers (respondents that consumed fish three times a week or more) was significantly higher for NHBs (15%) as compared with the white sub-population (11.6%) (USEPA, 2000). Various other surveys have reported that NHB anglers generally consume 50–100% more fish than non-Hispanic white anglers (Gibson and McClafferty, 2005). Studies in Pennsylvania and South Carolina found that NHB anglers consume fish at more than four times the rate of that of non-Hispanic white anglers (Burger, 2002).

Curse from the Wind: Contamination of the Arctic Region with Mercury

Mercury is released from many human industrial activities in a gaseous form. As such, it can travel long distances through the atmosphere and be transported to remote ecosystems (Mason and Fitzgerald, 1996; Van Oostdam et al., 1999). A study of streams and rivers throughout the western United States detected mercury in every one of 2707 fish tested, and an atmospheric source was suggested as a key factor responsible for mercury in these fish (Peterson et al., 2007). Because of a variety of factors, the Arctic region has become a major sink for mercury released from industrial sources in Europe and Asia (Arctic Monitoring and Assessment Programme [AMAP], 1998; 2005; Macdonald et al., 2005). As the flux of mercury into the Arctic region increases, the inorganic mercury becomes methylated and biomagnified in the local food chain, making the species feeding at high trophic positions more vulnerable to mercury exposure via their diet (AMAP, 2003).

The environmental and human health implications of mercury pollution in Arctic region have been of public health concern and scientific interest since the early 1970s. The flux of industrial pollutants into the northern polar region via atmospheric and oceanic long-range transport mechanisms and the subsequent impacts on wildlife and human health have been the focus of a number of major initiatives, such as the Arctic Environmental Strategy's Northern Contaminants Program initiated in 1991 by the Canadian government and the Arctic Monitoring and Assessment Programme, a circumpolar multicountry program established to assess the state of multiple compartments in the Arctic ecosystem, including human health (AMAP, 1998). These programs have conducted detailed investigations of the sources and extent of contamination of the Arctic food chain with mercury, assessments of exposure, characterizations of risk, human biomarkers, and risk–benefit analysis pertaining to mercury in the Arctic region (AMAP, 2003, 2005; Braune et al., 2005; Macdonald et al., 2005; van Oostdam et al., 2005). Results of these investigations provide solid evidence that mercury has increased in the Arctic food chain to the point at which it represents a hazard to human health. The studies also show significant differences in exposure and mercury levels among people living in this region and in their vulnerability to the mercury hazard. Mercury pollution in the Arctic is thus an international environmental justice issue, since the communities that are impacted negatively derive no benefit from the factories in North America, Europe, and Asia that emit the mercury, nor do they have the opportunity to participate in decisions on how to mitigate the mercury risk.

The indigenous people of the Arctic region have become vulnerable to the risk of mercury exposure because they rely heavily on natural resources for their livelihood. The traditional foods of indigenous peoples in the circumpolar countries consist of raw, boiled, or dried meat, blubber, and offal from several seal species (Greenland seal, bearded seal, ringed seal), baleen and toothed whale species, walrus and bear, various birds, and a number of saltwater and freshwater fish (fresh or dried). In the summertime, leaves, roots, and flowers become increasingly featured in local diets (Deutch et al., 2007). More than 250 different species of wildlife, plants, and animals have been identified as forming the rich framework of the traditional food systems of Arctic peoples (van Oostdam et al., 2005). Some studies show that traditional (country) food use as a percent of total dietary energy varies from a low of 6% in communities close to urban centers, to over 40% in more remote areas (van Oostdam et al., 2005). Chemical analyses of these traditional food items of animal and plant origins now show elevated levels of mercury, along with other toxic metals, and persistent organic pollutants (Chan and Receveur, 2000; van Oostdam et al., 2005; Deutch et al., 2007). There is strong evidence to suggest a health inequity that is lined to contamination of traditional components of diets with dangerous levels of mercury.

A survey of 79 species of marine mammals, terrestrial mammals, birds, fish, and plants in northern Canada found that the high levels of mercury contamination in many parts of northern Canada exceeded the guideline level of 0.5 μg/g total mercury because of the enhanced methylation of mercury in local aquatic ecosystems (Chan and Receveur, 2000). About 32% of mammal meat samples and 64% of terrestrial mammal samples tested exceeded 0.5 μg/g. Assessment of exposure to mercury in one Inuit community on Baffin Island, 16 Dene/Métis communities in Denendeh, Northwest Territories (NWT), 10 Yukon First Nations communities, and one Mohawk community in Quebec showed that over 50% of residents had dietary exposure levels that exceeded the provisional tolerable daily intake (PTDI) in the Inuit community, with the intake levels for high-end consumers (i.e., 95th percentile) being six times higher than the PTDI (Chan and Receveur, 2000). The increase in exposure with age was associated with the corresponding age-related increased intake of country food (van Oostdam et al., 2005). The point to be emphasized is that the exposures for a large percentage of the native populations exceed the tolerable daily intake value (van Oostdam et al., 2005).

The association of the intake of traditional food items, as determined by dietary surveys, with blood mercury levels has been demonstrated in a number of epidemiologic studies in the Arctic (see Hansen et al., 1990). The awareness of the potential for high exposure to mercury and risk to human health in the early 1970s has led to extensive programs aimed at assessing mercury levels in indigenous people in many areas of the Arctic. As Bjerregaard (1995) noted, the "Inuit have been studied intensively, possibly more so than any other ethnic group. In Greenland, the saying goes that one scientific book has been written for each indigenous Greenlander. In Canada, the average Inuit family is said to consist of a mother, a father, two children and an anthropologist." These studies have produced a rich database that documents the fact that the indigenous populations of the

Arctic region are being disproportionately exposed to mercury as compared with other populations in their countries.

From 1971 to December 1992, the screening program in Canada conducted 71,842 tests in 514 native communities across the country. Out of the 38,571 individuals tested, 1.4% had blood or blood-equivalent mercury levels in the 100–199 μg/L range and 0.2% had levels >200 μg/L (Wheatley and Paradis, 1995). The high-enders were fish eaters except in the NWT, where exposure was largely through consumption of sea mammals. Of the 99 individuals with mercury levels >100 μg/L, 27% were found to have some abnormalities not attributable to methylmercury, 11% had neurologic findings possibly attributable to methylmercury, and 62% had no significant abnormalities (Wheatley and Wheatley, 2000).

Considerably more data (Table 15.1) have become available since the report by Wheatley and Wheatley (2000). Walker et al. (2006) and van Oostdam (2005) report that among the mothers from NWT/Nunavut and Nunavik, only Inuit exceeded the Canadian total mercury level of concern of 20 μg/L and, more importantly, almost no Caucasian or Dene/Métis mothers exceeded the lower guideline of 5.8 μg/L for methylmercury, the benchmark no-effect level (van Oostdam et al., 2005). The differences among ethnic groups were attributed to divergence in dietary habits. Among the five Inuit regions studied by Walker et al. (2006), the percentage that exceeded the Canadian guideline level of concern of 20 μg/L for organic mercury were highest in Nunavik (16%) and Baffin (10%). The percentage that exceeded the 5.8 μg/L blood guideline for methylmercury among Canadian Inuit women ranged from 16% in Inuvik to 79% in Nunavik and 68% in Baffin (van Oostdam et al., 2000).

Other studies in northern Canada consistently show elevated levels of mercury in maternal and cord blood (see Table 15.1). In Nunavik (northern Quebec), for instance, the reported mean concentrations of mercury in maternal and cord blood were 10.4 and 18.5 μg/L, respectively, in a prospective longitudinal study of the effects of methylmercury and PCB exposure on infant development (Muckle et al., 2001b). Similar patterns of exceedances are evident in other circumpolar countries. In two communities of Alaska, maternal blood mercury concentration above the 5.8 μg/L threshold varied from 0% for women in Barrow, where the primary seafood for residents was terrestrial mammals and bowhead whales (plankton feeders), to 48% for women in Bethel, where residents consumed freshwater fish and some marine mammals (AMAP, 2003).

In northern Greenland, where the highest mercury exposure in Greenlanders is documented, more than 80% of the population exceed the benchmark level of concern of 5.8 μg/L and 16% exceed the World Health Organization minimum toxic blood concentration in nonpregnant adults of 20 μg/L mercury in blood (Hylander and Goodsite, 2006). In the Nuuk Region of Greenland, it was reported that 3% of mothers had blood mercury concentrations that exceeded 20 μg/L, while 27% had levels that exceeded the 5.8 μg/L threshold for methylmercury. In two other regions

TABLE 15.1
Concentrations of Total Mercury (μg/L) in Human Blood Samples from Different Countries of the Arctic Region

Location	Ethnic group	Geometric mean	Sample type	Year collected	No. of subjects	Reference
Canada (average)						
	Caucasian	0.87	Maternal	1994–1999	134	Deutch et al. (2007)
		1.22	Cord	1994–1999	134	Deutch et al. (2007)
	Dene/Métis	1.35	Maternal	1994–1999	92	Deutch et al. (2007)
		1.62	Cord	1994–1999	86	Deutch et al. (2007)
	Inuit	3.51	Maternal	1994–1999	146	Deutch et al. (2007)
		6.96	Cord	1994–1999	169	Deutch et al. (2007)
	Baffin Inuit	6.72	Maternal	1994–1999	31	Deutch et al. (2007)
		12.2	Cord	1994–1999	61	Deutch et al. (2007)
	Inuvik Inuit	2.13	Maternal	1994–1999	31	Deutch et al. (2007)
		3.08	Cord	1994–1999	30	Deutch et al. (2007)
	Kivalliq Inuit	3.66	Maternal	1994–1999	17	Deutch et al. (2007)
		8.01	Cord	1994–1999	16	Deutch et al. (2007)
	Kitikmeot Inuit	3.42	Maternal	1994–1999	63	Deutch et al. (2007)
		6.26	Cord	1994–1999	58	Deutch et al. (2007)
Western NWT	Dene	14.4	Cord	1878–1982	5	Wheatley (1994)
	Dene	10.7	Maternal	1982–1983	76	Wheatley (1994)
N. Quebec	Inuit	12.1	Cord	1993–1995	299	Dewailly et al. (2001)
	Inuit	18.5	Maternal	1996–2000	95	Muckle et al. (2001a)
	Inuit	10.4	Cord	1996–2000	130	Muckle et al. (2001b)
S. Quebec	Nonindigenous	0.97	Cord	1993–1995	1109	Rhainds et al. (1999)
Ontario	Fish eaters	2.2	Adults	1992–1993	176	Kearney et al. (1995)
Greenland						
Average: 6 regions	Inuit	34.8	Men	1995–2005	510	Walker et al. (2006)
	Inuit	23.1	Women	1995–2005		Walker et al. (2006)
Ittoqqortoormiit	Inuit	18.5	Men	1995–2005		Walker et al. (2006)
	Inuit	20.8	Women	1995–2005		Walker et al. (2006)
Tasssilaq	Inuit	31.6	Men	1995–2005		Walker et al. (2006)
	Inuit	20.6	Women	1995–2005		Walker et al. (2006)
Nuuk	Inuit	26.7	Men	1995–2005		Walker et al. (2006)
	Inuit	3.31	Women	1995–2005		Walker et al. (2006)
Sisimiut	Inuit	7.72	Men	1995–2005		Walker et al. (2006)
	Inuit	10.1	Women	1995–2005		Walker et al. (2006)
Uummannaq	Inuit	60.5	Men	1995–2005		Walker et al. (2006)
Qaanaaq	Inuit	69.8	Men	1995–2005		Walker et al. (2006)
	Inuit	57.2	Women	1995–2005		Walker et al. (2006)

(continued)

TABLE 15.1 *(continued)*

Location	Ethnic group	Geometric mean	Sample type	Year collected	No. of subjects	Reference
Disko Bay	Inuit	12.8	Maternal	1994–1996		Bjerregaard and Hansen (2000)
Ilullisat	Inuit	25.3	Cord	1994–1996		Bjerre gaard and Hansen (2000)
Finland (average)						
		1.4	Maternal	1996–1998	130	AMAP (2003)
Russia (Siberia)						
Taymir	Indigenous	2.7	Maternal	1995–1996	18	AMAP (2003)
Taymir	Indigenous	2.9	Maternal	1996–1998	12	AMAP (2003)
Norilsk	Nonindigenous	1.4	Maternal	1995–1996	49	AMAP (2003)
United States (Alaska) (average)						
	Inuit	5.5	Maternal	2000	23	
Bethel	Inuit	1.3	Maternal	2000	23	AMAP (2003)
Barrow						AMAP (2003)

SOURCES: 1=Deutch et al., 2007. 2=Wheatley (1994). 3=Dewilly et al. (2001). 4a=Muckle et al. (2001). 4b=Muckle et al. (2001b). 5=Rhainds et al. (1999). 6= Kearney et al. (1995). 7=Walker et al. (2006). 8=Bjerregaard and Hansen (2000). 9=AMAP (2003).

in Greenland that have been studied, maternal exceedances of the 5.8 µg/L threshold were 68% and 80% (AMAP, 2003). An epidemiologic study of 510 men and women in six Greenland districts found that human blood mercury levels were very high (mean values ranged from 3.3 to 69.8 µg/L, especially in the northern communities, where people depended on local foods for their diet (Deutch et al., 2007). Except for women from Nuuk, the mean blood mercury levels were found to be above the 5.8 µg/L guideline, while values above 20 µg/L were recorded in four of the six districts for men and women (see Table 15.1).

Methylmercury crosses the placental barrier and is able to penetrate the blood–brain barrier. The fetus is thus particularly vulnerable to the risk of mercury exposure; therefore, the accumulation of mercury in the Arctic food must be viewed with some concern. A number of studies have determined the mercury level in cord blood to be a bioindicator of fetal exposure. In one of the first such studies, the analysis of 2405 umbilical cord blood samples taken from communities in the Arctic regions of Canada found that 22% of the samples had mercury levels >20 µg/L, with the highest recorded concentration being 224 µg/L (Wheatley and Wheatley, 2000). In a subsequent study, Walker et al. (2006) found the geometric mean total mercury concentration in cord blood from different indigenous communities in Canada to be 2.7 µg/L. The geometric mean concentration of methylmercury in cord blood ranged from 1.14 µg/L in Caucasians to 6.16 µg/L in Inuit participants, with the mean concentration being

significantly higher in Inuit samples than in the rest of the ethnic groups (see Table 15.1). Considerable individual variability was found in cord-blood mercury levels among the Inuit, with values ranging from 0.0 to 70 µg/L, as well as marked regional differences, with the levels of participants from the Baffin Region being significantly higher than those for Inuit participants from the Inuvik Region. The study showed that 56% of Inuit and 5% of Dene/Métis cord-blood samples were greater than the 5.8 µg/L threshold for methylmercury (Walker et al., 2006). There were significant and important regional differences in the exceedance of the 5.8 µg/L threshold, such as the 11–58% rate for maternal samples from Kitikmeot and Baffin participants and the 20–75% for samples from Inuvik, the Baffin, and Kivalliq regions (see Table 15.1). In contrast to Canada, nearly 75% of the children born in Greenland are estimated to have cord-blood mercury levels >5.8 µg/L (Hylander and Goodsite, 2006).

The ratio of total mercury in cord blood to the level in maternal blood for communities in Canada ranged from 0.44 to 4.5, with a geometric mean value of 1.4, while the corresponding methylmercury ratio ranged from 0.15 to 10.3, with a mean value of 1.6 (Walker et al., 2006). Studies of other biomarkers of mercury exposure are consistent with the blood data in showing disproportionate exposure for indigenous people that consume traditional foods. A study of autopsy samples from 102 ethnic Greenlanders found the highest levels of mercury in kidney (1.4 µg/g wet weight) followed by liver (0.53 to 1.4 µg/g wet weight) and the spleen (0.53 to 1.4 μg/g wet weight) (Johansen et al., 2007). Total mercury levels in the liver and kidneys from Greenlanders were elevated by factors of 7–8 as compared with values for similar organs from people in Denmark, Norway, and Sweden, and were higher than the levels found in the general populations of Spain, Poland, Korea, and Japan (Johansen et al., 2007). Significantly elevated mercury concentrations have been reported in the brains of Greenlanders; an autopsy study of 17 Greenlanders and 12 Danes found that the median total mercury concentration was 174 ng/g wet weight in Greenlanders and 4 ng/g in Danes (Pedersen et al., 1999).

Do Fish-Consumption Advisories Promote Environmental Injustice?

For most contaminants, the focus of environmental regulatory efforts has been on risk reduction by targeting the first link in the chain that connects environmental contamination with adverse impacts on human health, namely preventing or limiting emissions and remediating contaminated sites. Fish advisories warn of health risks from the consumption of contaminated fish and are intended to reduce exposure through reduced or eliminated fish consumption. For mercury, the widely accepted risk-management strategy by regulatory bodies has become risk avoidance, in which the focus is on breaking the chain link at the point of human exposure (O'Neill, 2004). As such, the onus is placed on individuals who bear the burdens of mercury exposure to avoid the risk by changing their fish-consumption practices. This strategy places the environmental justice communities in a lose–lose situation: either eat the fish and suffer the health effects from contaminants or do not eat the fish and suffer the health and cultural effects of losing a critical diet food.

Various studies reviewed above converge on the fact that the adverse health impacts of mercury pollution fall primarily on poorly resourced and geographically vulnerable communities of indigenous people, Asia immigrants, and urban poor. For the Native Americans, decreased consumption of traditional food is likely to have negative health consequences by changing the balanced dietary intakes of total fat, saturated fat, and sucrose; lowering the intake of vitamins A, D, and E, riboflavin and B_6; and reducing intakes of the important minerals iron, zinc, copper, magnesium, manganese, phosphorus, potassium, and selenium (Kuhnlein et al., 2004). A shift away from traditional-food diets has also been linked to rises in obesity, diabetes, and cardiovascular disease among Aboriginal peoples in the United States and Canada (Young, 1993; Young et al., 1993). Increased compensatory consumption of saturated fat, sucrose, and alcohol in diets has led to higher incidences of gallbladder disease, tooth decay, alcoholism, and fetal alcohol syndrome. Poor diet (which excludes the traditional fish protein) has also been associated with higher incidences of anemia, otitis media, a variety of infections, and some kinds of cancer (Kuhnlein and Receveur, 1996).

The way of life for Aboriginal peoples in North America is very much defined by the ability to borrow from the natural capital of their ecosystem. Today, traditional foods still remain central to cultural, social, and spiritual well-being in many regions (e.g., Condon et al., 1995; Receveur et al., 1998; Van Oostdam et al., 1999, 2005). Hunting, fishing and gathering of wild resources and the subsequent sharing of those items with individuals throughout the community are social activities that bring individuals, families, and generations together and are often the harbinger for celebrations and festivities (van Oostdam et al., 2005). A number of studies have documented the following cultural, social and economic benefits of collecting and using traditional food among adult Inuit in five regions of the Canadian Arctic: (a) it contributes to physical fitness and good health; (b) it provides people with healthy food; (c) it favors sharing in the community; (d) it is an essential part of the culture; (e) it is an occasion for adults to display responsibility for their children; (f) it provides education about the natural environment; (g) it contributes to children's education; (h) it provides skills in survival; and (i) it provides skills in food preparation at home Kuhnlein et al. (2001). As one indigenous community elder ruefully observed: "Inuit foods give us health, well-being and identity. Inuit foods are our way of life. Total health includes spiritual well-being. For us to be fully healthy, we must have our foods, recognizing the benefits they bring. Contaminants do not affect our souls. Avoiding food from fear does" (Egede, 1995).

Balancing the risks of mercury exposure with the loss of beneficial traditional food raises several concerns (Van Oostdam et al., 1999). When country food is compromised by mercury contamination, more than Aboriginal peoples' health is affected; their economy, culture, spiritual well-being, and way of life are also threatened. The importance of traditional foods is further stressed by the lack of healthy, accessible, and economically viable nutrition alternatives in many communities and for many individuals. Many market foods are expensive and of lower nutritional value and they deprive Aboriginal people of the cultural and social significance and other benefits of hunting and consuming country food. Consequently, current risk-management programs aimed at reducing the impacts of mercury-contaminated traditional food raise problems that go far beyond the usual confines of public health and cannot be resolved simply by risk-based health advisories or food substitutions. It is a form of cultural discrimination.

In a review article, O'Neill (2004) has argued that the regulatory shift in policy from risk reduction to risk avoidance is a promoter of environmental injustice. In the first place, the burden of undertaking risk-avoidance measures falls disproportionately on communities of color, Southeast Asian immigrants, and indigenous peoples, which are likely to be most vulnerable. Nor do risk avoidance measures impose their burdens equally. Communities who are disproportionately exposed are called on to change their behaviors and lifestyles while the general public is not required to make any sacrifices. In addition to distributive inequities, environmental injustice also stems from cultural discrimination because of differences in normative values attached to fish, fishing, and fish consumption. For indigenous populations in particular, fish, fishing, and fish consumption are indispensable to their physical, social, economic, political, spiritual, and cultural health, practices that the general population cannot relate to and tend to ridicule. The implicit cultural discrimination associated with the policy of risk avoidance is well captured in the following commentary by Harper and Harris (2008, p. 66):

> This [not eating fish] is not only a decision paradigm of balancing risks against benefits, but also of adding more risk due to contaminants to a pre-existing cultural and possible health deficit from lost nutrition and the other negative effects of lost fish. Although agency decision makers, drawn largely from the general population, may think that tribal members make poor decisions by eating the fish knowing they contain unsafe levels of contaminants, there are other perspectives. . . . Many traditional people give no further consideration to further reducing their fish consumption, other than to recognize that they now bear an additional burden of chemical contaminants, one that they willingly share with their swimming relatives.

Since fish advisories are not always effective, they may actually perpetuate the health inequalities. The problem becomes magnified when the people affected do not speak English, are culturally different from the general population, and/or are opposed to elements of this particular risk-management strategy on philosophical, moral, or cultural grounds. It has been reported that half of the people consuming fish caught recreationally on the Great Lakes were not aware of the relevant fish-consumption advisories, with people of color, women, and those without a high-school education showing the least awareness (Tilden et al., 1997). For many people in the environmental justice community, it is difficult to understand the complex risk–benefit information to make an informed choice of balancing chemical risk with the health and cultural benefits,

even to the point of incurring more risk than the general public accepts because of the greater cultural importance of fish (Harper and Harris, 2008).

Fish advisories may result in un-intended risk tradeoffs that can exacerbate health inequalities. O'Neill (2004) elaborated on this point rather eloquently:

> If those exposed change their ways in order to avoid risks posed by contamination, they may adopt practices that subject them to a different set of risks. To the extent that those affected "comply" with fish consumption advisories, the potential for countervailing risks is a serious concern, given the celebrated nutritional benefits of frequent fish consumption. Fish are an efficient source of protein, omega-3 fatty acids, selenium, and other nutrients important to human health. By forgoing these benefits, those affected may open themselves to an increased risk of coronary and other diseases. In addition, for those for whom fish forms a part of a traditional diet, including those in the fishing tribes of the upper Great Lakes, regular consumption of fish and other traditional foods may function to promote health and to combat diabetes, a particular concern for tribes given the high rate of diabetes among American Indians and Alaska Natives.

Thus, by promoting a policy that allows significant mercury contamination to remain in place and relying instead on fish-consumption advisories, the regulators are helping to perpetuate a long history of cultural discrimination against American Indian peoples.

By intervening late in the chain linking contamination and human health effects, fish-consumption advisories as a tool fail to address any of the various other adverse effects of mercury that do not directly threaten human health, such as the effects on all nonhuman components of contaminated ecosystems. "Loons cannot read fish consumption advisories" as O'Neill (2004) curtly noted. This calls into question the validity of risk–benefit models used to support the policies on fish-consumption advisories. Any policies or programs that disproportionately burden the natural resources must be considered an injustice to the people that depend on such resources.

References

Agyeman, J. 2005. Where justice and sustainability meet. *Environment* 47: 10–23.

AMAP. 1998. *Assessment report: arctic pollution issues.* Arctic Monitoring and Assessment Programme, Oslo, Norway.

AMAP. 2003. *Assessment 2002: Human health in the Arctic.* Arctic Monitoring and Assessment Programme, Oslo, Norway.

AMAP. 2005. *Assessment 2002: heavy metals in the Arctic.* Arctic Monitoring and Assessment Programme, Oslo, Norway.

Anderton, D., Anderson, A., Oakes, J., and Fraser, M. 1994. Environmental equity: the demographics of dumping. *Demography* 31 (2): 229–248.

Anderton, D., Anderson, A., Rossi, P. Oakes, J., Fraser, M., Weber, E., and Calabrese, E. 1994. Hazardous waste

facilities. "Environmental equity" issues in metropolitan areas. *Evaluation Review* 18 (2): 123–140.

Anderton, D., Oakes, J., and Egan, K. 1997. Environmental equity in Superfund: demographics of discovery and prioritization of abandoned toxic sites. *Evaluation Review* 21 (1): 2–26.

Armstrong, F.A.J., and Hamilton, A.L. 1973. Pathways of mercury in a polluted Northwestern Ontario lake. In: Singer, P.C. (Ed.), *Trace metals and metal-organic interactions in natural waters.* Ann Arbor Science, Ann Arbor, MI, pp. 131–156.

Atlas, M.K. 2001. Safe and sorry: risk, environmental equity, and hazardous waste management facilities. *Risk Analysis* 21 (5): 939–954.

ATSDR. 1999. *Toxicological profile for mercury.* http://www.atsdr.cdc.gov/toxprofiles/tp46.html (accessed September 15, 2008).

Auger, N., Kofman, O., Kosatsky, T., and Armstrong, B. 2005. Low-level methylmercury exposure as a risk factor for neurological abnormalities in adults. *Neurotoxicology* 26(2): 149–157.

Belinsky, D.L., Kuhnlein, H.V., Yeboah, F., Penn, A.F., and Chan, M.H. 1996. Composition of fish consumed by the James Bay Cree. *Journal of Food Composition and Analysis,* 9: 148–162.

Braune, B.M., Outridge, P.M., Fisk, A.T., Muir, D.C.G., Helm, P.A., Hobbs, K., et al. 2005. Persistent organic pollutants and mercury in marine biota of the Canadian Arctic: an overview of spatial and temporal trends. *Science of the Total Environment* 351/352: 4–56.

Bjerregaard, P. 1995. Health and environment in Greenland and other circumpolar areas. *Science of the Total Environment* 160/161: 521–527.

Bjerregaard, P., and Hansen, J.C., 2000. Organochlorines and heavy metals in pregnant women from the Disko Bay area in Greenland. *Science of the Total Environment* 245: 195–202.

Brooks N, and Sethi, R. 1997. The distribution of pollution: community characteristics and exposure to air toxics. *Journal of Environmental Economics and Management* 32: 233–250.

Brouard, D., Doyon, J.-F., and Schetagne, R. 1994. Amplification of mercury concentrations in lake whitefish (*Coregonus clupeaformis*) downstream from the La Grande 2 Reservoir, James Bay, Quebec. In: Watras, C.J., and Huckabee, J.W. (Ed.), *Mercury pollution integration and synthesis.* New York, Taylor & Francis, pp. 369–380.

Bryant, B. 2008. *Environmental justice.* http://wwwpersonal.umich.edu/~bbryant/poems1.html (accessed September 22, 2008).

Bullard, R.D. 1994. Environmental justice for all. In: R. D. Bullard (Ed.), *Unequal protection: environmental justice and communities of color.* Sierra Club Books, San Francisco, pp. 3–22.

Bullard, R.D., Mohai, P., Saha, R., and Wright, B. 2007. *Toxic wastes and race at twenty 1987–2007: grassroots struggles to dismantle environmental racism in the United States.* United Church of Christ Justice and Witness Ministry, Cleveland, OH.

Burger, J. 2002. Daily consumption of wild fish and game: exposures of high end recreationists. *International Journal of Environmental Health Research* 12: 343–354.

Burger, J., Gaines, K.F., and Gochfeld, M. 2001. Ethnic differences in risk from mercury among Savannah River fishermen. *Risk Analysis* 21: 533–544.

Burger, J., Dixon, C., Boring, C.S., Gochfeld, M. 2003. Effect of deepfrying fish on risk from mercury. *Journal of Toxicology and Environmental Health* 66: 817–828.

Cavan, K.R. 1993. Report II for the Hamilton Health Department on the results of the Great Lakes Health Effects Pilot Study. City of Hamilton, Hamilton, ON.

Cecelski, D.S. 2001. *The waterman's song: slavery and freedom in maritime North Carolina.* University of North Carolina Press, Chapel Hill, NC.

Chan, H.M., Trifonopoulos, M., Ing, A., Receveur, O., and Johnson, E. 1999. Consumption of freshwater fish in Kahnawake: risks and benefits. *Environmental Research.* 80(2):S213–S222.

Chan, H.M., and Receveur, O. 2000. Mercury in the traditional diet of indigenous peoples in Canada. *Environmental Pollution* 110(1): 1–2.

Chang, M.B., Wu, H.T., and Huang, C.K. 2000. Evaluation on speciation and removal efficiencies of mercury from municipal solid waste incinerators in Taiwan. *Science of the Total Environment* 246 (2–3): 165–173.

Claudio, L. 2007. Standing on principle: the global push for environmental justice. *Environmental Health Perspectives* 115(10): A499–A503.

Cohen, M., Artz, R., Draxler, R., Miller, P., Poissant, L., Niemi, D., Ratté, D., Deslauriers, M., Duval, R., Laurin, R., Slotnick, J., Nettesheim, T. and McDonald, J. 2004. Modeling the atmospheric transport and deposition of mercury to the Great Lakes. *Environmental Research* 95: 247–265.

Condon, R.G., Collings, P., and Wenzel, G. 1995. The best part of life: subsistence hunting, and economic adaptation among young adult Inuit males. *Arctic* 48(1): 31–46.

Dellinger, J.A. 2004. Exposure assessment and initial intervention regarding fish consumption of tribal members of the Upper Great Lakes Region in the United States. *Environmental Research* 95(3): 325–340.

Davidson, P., and Anderton, D. 2000. Demographics of dumping II: a national environmental equity survey and the distribution of hazardous materials handlers. *Demography* 37 (4): 461–466.

Deutch, B., Pedersen, H.S., Asmund, G., and Hansen, J.C. 2007. Contaminants, diet, plasma fatty acids and smoking in Greenland 1999–2005. *Science of the Total Environment* 372: 486–496.

Dewailly, E.; Ayotte, P.; Bruneau, S.; Lebel, G.; Levallois, P.; Philippe, W. 2001. Exposures of the Inuit population of Nunavik (Arctic Quebec) to Lead and Mercury. *Archives of Environmental Health: An International Journal* 56: 350–357.

Dumont, C., Girard, M., Bellavance, F., and Noel, F. 1998. Mercury levels in the Cree population of James Bay, Quebec, from 1988 to 1993/94. *Canadian Medical Association Journal* 158 (11): 1439–1445.

Egede, I. 1995. Inuit food and Inuit health: contaminants in perspective. Presentation to Inuit Circumpolar Conference, Seventh General Assembly, Nome, Alaska, July, 1995.

Fimreite, N., and Reynolds, L.M. 1973. Mercury contamination of fish in northwestern Ontario. *Journal of Wildlife Management* 37(1): 62–68.

Getz, T., Migliore, B., Ratnapradipa, D., Zarcadoolas, C., Esposito, V., Caron, C., and Peterson, C. 2006. Rhode Island Southeast Asian community fish ingestion project report. RI Department of Environmental Management. http://www.dem.ri.gov/programs/benviron/waste/pdf/finalfis.pdf (accessed September 20, 2008).

Gibson, J.C., and McClafferty, J.A. 2005. Chesapeake Bay angler interviews. Publication no. CMI-HDD-05 01. Virginia Polytechnic Institute Conservation Management Institute, Blacksburg, VA.

Hansen, J.C., Tarp, U., and Bohm, J. 1990. Prenatal exposure to methylmercury among Greenlandic Polar Inuits. *Archives of Environmental Health* 45: 355–358.

Harada, M., Fujino, T., Oorui, T., Nakachi, S., Nou, T., Kizaki, T., Hitomi, Y., Nakano N., and H. Ohno. 2005. Followup study of mercury pollution in indigenous tribe reservations in the province of Ontario, Canada, 1975–2002. *Bulletin of Environmental Contamination and Toxicology* 74(4): 689–697.

Harnly, M., Seidel, S., Rojas, P., Fornes, R., Flessel, P., Smith, D., Kreutzer, R., and Goldman, L. 1997. Biological monitoring for mercury within a community with soil and fish contamination. *Environmental Health Perspectives.* 105(4): 424–429.

Harper, B.L., and Harris, S.G. 2008. A possible approach for setting a mercury risk-based action level based on tribal fish ingestion rates. *Environmental Research* 107: 60–68.

Henderson, E. 2004. Participation and expenditure patterns of African-American, Hispanic, and women hunters and anglers: addendum to the 2001 national survey of fishing, hunting, and wildlife-associated recreation. Report 2001-4. U.S. Fish and Wildlife Service, Arlington VA.

Hightower, J.M., and Moore, D. 2003. Mercury levels in high-end consumers of fish. *Environmental Health Perspectives* 111: 604–608.

Hightower, J.M., O'Hare, A., and Hernandez, G.T. 2006. Blood mercury reporting in NHANES: identifying Asian, Pacific Islander, Native American, and multiracial groups. *Environmental Health Perspectives* 114(2): 173–175.

Hylander, L.D., Goodsite, M.E. 2006. Environmental costs of mercury pollution. *Science of the Total Environment* 368: 352–370.

Ikeda, J.P., Ceja, D.R., Glass, R.S., Hardwood, J.O., Lucke, K.A., and Sutherlin, J. M. 1991. Food habits of the Hmong living in central California. *Journal of Nutrition Education* 23: 168–174.

Johansen, P., Mulvad, G., Pedersen, H.S., Hansen, J.C., and Riget, F. 2007. Human accumulation of mercury in Greenland. *Science of the Total Environment* 377: 173–178.

Kearney, J., Cole, D., and Haines, D. 1995. Report on the Great Lakes Anglers Pilot Exposure Assessment Study. Health Canada, Ottawa, Ontario.

Kinghorn, A., Solomon, P., and Chan, H.M. 2007. Temporal and spatial trends of mercury in fish collected in the English-Wabigoon river system in Ontario, Canada. *Science of the Total Environment* 372(2–3): 615–623.

Kuhnlein, H.V., and Receveur, O. 1996. Dietary change and traditional food systems of indigenous peoples. *Annual Review of Nutrition* 16: 417–442.

Kuhnlein, H.V., Receveur, O., Chan, H.M., and Loring, E. 2000. *Assessment of dietary benefit/risk in Inuit communities.* Center for Indigenous Peoples' Nutrition and Environment (CINE), McGill University, Ste-Anne-de-Bellevue, Quebec.

Kuhnlein, H.V., Receveur, O., Soueida, R., and Egeland, G.M. 2004. Arctic indigenous peoples experience the nutrition transition with changing dietary patterns and obesity. *Journal of Nutrition* 134: 1447–1453.

Lee, J.S., Hong, J., Gyu Lee, T., Park, J., Seo, Y., Jurng, J., and Hyun, J. 2004. Mercury emissions from selected stationary combustion sources in Korea. *Science of the Total Environment* 325 (1–3): 155–161.

Macdonald, R.W., Harner, T.T., and Fyfe, J. 2005. Recent climate change in the Arctic and its impact on contaminant pathways and interpretation of temporal trend data. *Science of the Total Environment* 342: 5–86.

Mahaffey, K.R. 2005. Update on mercury. In: *Proceedings of the 2005 National Forum on Contaminants in Fish.* Publication no. EPA-823-R-05-006. http://epa.gov/waterscience/fish/forum/2005 (accessed September 15, 2008).

Mason, R.P., and Fitzgerald, W.F. 1996. Sources, sinks and biogeochemical cycling of mercury in the ocean. In: Baeyens W (Ed.), *Global and regional mercury cycles: sources,* *fluxes and mass balances.* Kluwer Academic, Dordrecht, the Netherlands. pp. 249–272.

McKelvey, W., Gwynn, C., Jeffery, N., Kass, D., Thorpe, L.E., Renu, K., Garg, R.K., Palmer, C.D., and Parsons, P.J. 2007. A biomonitoring study of lead, cadmium, and mercury in the blood of New York City adults. *Environmental Health Perspectives* 115(10): 1435–1441.

Mohai, P., and Saha, R. 2006. Reassessing racial and socioeconomic disparities in environmental justice research. *Demography* 43(2): 383–399.

Muckle, G., Ayotte, P., Dewailly, E., Jacobson, S., and Jacobson, J. 2001a. Determinants of polychlorinated biphenyls and methylmercury exposure in Inuit women of childbearing age. *Environmental Health Perspectives* 109: 957–963.

Muckle, G., Ayotte, P., Dewailly, E., Jacobson, S.W., and Jacobson, J.L. 2001b. Prenatal exposure of the northern Québec Inuit infants to environmental contaminants. *Environmental Health Perspectives* 109(12): 1291–1299.

Murray, M., and Holmes, S.A. 2004. Assessment of mercury emissions inventories for the Great Lakes states. *Environmental Research* 95: 282–297.

Nixon, S., and Forman, L. 2008. Exploring synergies between human rights and public health ethics: a whole greater than the sum of its parts. BMC International Health and Human Rights. http://www.biomedcentral.com/1472-698X/8/2 (accessed November 23, 2008).

Noel, F., Rondeau, E., and Sbeghen, J. 1998. Communication of risks: organization of a methylmercury campaign in the Cree communities of James Bay, Northern Quebec, Canada. *International Journal of Circumpolar Health* 57 (Suppl 1): 591–595.

O'Neill, C.A. 2004. Mercury, risk, and justice. Environmental Law Institute. http://www.eli.org (accessed September 15, 2008).

Payne-Sturges, D., and Gee, G.C. 2006. National environmental health measures for minority and low-income populations: tracking social disparities in environmental health. *Environmental Research* 102: 154–171.

Pedersen, M.B., Hansen, J.C., Mulvad, G., Pedersen, H.S., Gregersen, M., and Danscher, G. 1999. Mercury accumulations in brains from populations exposed to high and low dietary levels of methyl mercury. *Circumpolar Health* 58: 96–107.

Perlin, S.; Woodrow, R.; Creason, J.; Sexton, K. 1995. Distribution of industrial air emissions by income and race in the United States: An approach using the toxic release inventory. *Environmental Science and Technology*, 29 (1): 69–80.

Peterson, D.E., Kanarek, M.S., Kuykendall, M.A., Diedrich, J.M., Anderson, H.A., Remington, P.L., and Sheffy, T.B. 1994. Fish consumption patterns and blood mercury levels in Wisconsin Chippewa Indians. *Archives of Environmental Health* 49(1): 53–58.

Peterson, S.A., Sickle, J.V., Herlihy, A.T., and Hughes R.M. 2007. Mercury concentrations in fish from streams and rivers throughout the western United States. *Environmental Science and Technology* 41: 58–65.

Receveur, O., Kassi, N., Chan, H.M., Berti, P.R., and Kuhnlein, H.V. 1998. Yukon First Nations assessment of dietary benefit/risk Centre for indigenous peoples' nutrition and environment (CINE). McGill University, Montreal, PQ.

Rhainds, M., Levallois, P., Dewailly, E., and Ayotte, P., 1999. Lead, mercury and organochlorine compound levels in cord blood in Quebec, Canada. *Archives of Environmental Health* 54: 40–47.

Roe, A. 2003. Fishing for identity: mercury contamination and fish consumption among indigenous groups in the United States. *Bulletin of Science, Technology and Society* 23(5): 368–375.

Saha, R., and Mohai, P. 2005. Historical context and hazardous waste facility siting: understanding temporal patterns in Michigan. *Social Problems* 52(4): 618–648.

Schell, L.M., Hubicki, L.A., DeCaprio, A.P., Gallo, M.V., Ravenscroft, J., Tarbell, A., Jacobs, A., David, D., Worswick, P., and Akwesasne Task Force on the Environment. 2003. Organochlorines, lead, and mercury in Akwesasne Mohawk youth. *Environmental Health Perspectives* 111(7): 954–961.

Sexton, K., Gong, H., Jr., Bailar, J.C., 3rd, Ford, J.G., Gold, D.R., Lambert, W.E., and Utell, M.J. 1993. Air pollution health risks: do class and race matter? *Toxicology and Industrial Health* 9(5): 843–878.

Shatenstein, B., Kosatsky, T., Tapia, M., Nadon, S., and Leclerc, B.S. 1999. Exploratory assessment of fish consumption among Asian-origin sportfishers on the St. Lawrence River in the Montreal region. *Environmental Research* Section A 80: S57–S70.

Solitaire, L., and Greenberg, M. 2002. Is the U.S. Environmental Protection Agency Brownfields Assessment Pilot Program environmentally just? *Environmental Health Perspectives* 110(Suppl 2): 249–257.

Tilden, J., Hanrahan, L.P., Anderson, H., Palit, C., Olson, J., and Kenzie, W.M. 1997. Health advisories for consumers of Great Lakes sport fish: is the message being received? *Environmental Health Perspectives* 105: 1360–1365.

USEPA. 2000. *Guidance for assessing chemical contaminant data for use in fish advisories.* Volume 1. *Fish sampling and analysis*, 3rd ed. EPA 823-B-00-0007. Office of Science and Technology, Washington DC.

USEPA. 2001. *Mercury in petroleum and natural gas: estimation of emissions from production, processing, and combustion.* Publication no. EPA-600/R-01-066. US Environmental Protection Agency, Washington, DC.

USEPA. 2007. *The 2005/2006 national listing of fish advisories.* Publication no. EPA 823-F-07-003. Office of Science and Technology, Washington DC.

USEPA. 2008. *Environmental justice.* http://www.epa.gov/Compliance/basics/ejbackground.html (accessed September 15, 2008).

Van Oostdam J., Gilman A., Dewailly, E., Usher, P., Wheatley, B., Kuhnlein, H, et al. 1999. Human health implications of environmental contaminants in Arctic Canada: a review. *Science of the Total Environment* 230: 1–82.

Van Oostdam, J., Donaldson, S.G., Feeley, M., Arnold, D., Ayotte, P., Bondy, G., Chan, L., Dewailly, E., Furgal, C.M., Kuhnlein, H., Loring, E., Muckle, G., Myles, E., Receveur, O., Tracy, B., Gill, U., and Kalhok, S. 2005. Human health implications of environmental contaminants in Arctic Canada: a review. *Science of the Total Environment* 351/352: 165–246.

Van Oostdam, J., Donaldson, S., Feeley, M., and Tremblay, N. (Eds.). 2003. *Toxic substances in the arctic and associated effects—human health.* Canadian Arctic Contaminants and Assessment Report II. Indian and Northern Affairs Canada. Ottawa, ON.

Walker, J.B., Jan Houseman, J., Seddon, L., McMullen, E., Tofflemire, K., Mills, C., Corriveau, A., Weber, J.P., LeBlanc, A., Walker, M., Donaldson, S.G., and Van Oostdam, J. 2006. Maternal and umbilical cord blood levels of mercury, lead, cadmium, and essential trace elements in Arctic Canada. *Environmental Research* 100: 295–318.

Weintraub, M., and Birnbaum, L.S. 2008. Catfish consumption as a contributor to elevated PCB levels in a non-Hispanic black subpopulation. *Environmental Research* 107: 412–417.

Wheatley, B., 1994. Exposure of aboriginal peoples in Canada to methylmercury with an emphasis on the Northwest Territories. In: Mercury—a health concern in the N.W.T? Workshop Proceedings. Unpublished report. Government of the Northwest Territories, Canada.

Wheatley, B., and Paradis, S. 1995. Exposure of Canadian aboriginal peoples to methylmercury. *Water, Air and Soil Pollution* 80: 3–11.

Wheatley, B., and Wheatley, M.A. 2000. Methylmercury and the health of indigenous peoples: a risk management challenge for physical and social sciences and for public health policy. *Science of the Total Environment* 259(1–3): 23–29.

Woodruff, T.J., Axelrad, D.A., Kyle, A.D., Miller, G., and Nweke, O. 2003. America's children and the environment: measures of contaminants, body burdens, and illnesses. U.S. Environmental Protection Agency, Office of Children's Health Protection and Office of Policy, Economics, and Innovation. http://www.epa.gov/envirohealth/children (accessed August 30, 2006).

Wren, C.D. 1985. Probable case of mercury poisoning in a wild otter, Lutra Canadensis, in Northwestern Ontario. *Canadian Field Naturalist* 99(1): 112–114.

Young, T.K. 1993. Diabetes mellitus among native Americans in Canada and United States: an epidemiological review. *American Journal of Human Biology* 5: 399–413.

Young, T.K., Moffat, M.E.K., and O'Neil, J.D. 1993. Cardiovascular diseases in a Canadian Arctic population. *American Journal of Public Health* 83: 881–887.

CHAPTER 16

Integrating Mercury Science and Environmental Policy

A State Perspective

C. MARK SMITH

Persistent, bio-accumulative, and toxic (PBT) pollutants are of particular concern to environmental and public health policy makers because of their potential for adverse multi-generational effects that often range far beyond their site of initial release. PBTs, like mercury, which cause adverse neurodevelopmental effects, raise additional concerns because of their long-term individual and societal impacts as well as ethical considerations relating to the involuntary nature of the exposure. Personal and societal concerns about the well-being of children are also paramount. These attributes underpin the priority status that mercury pollution has been afforded by many states as well as their focus on precautionary approaches to the issue.

Mercury is also a multimedia pollutant that is subject to atmospheric transport, with both long-range and near-field deposition. Atmospheric transport of mercury from upwind emission sources creates important geopolitical policy issues for many states and countries (U.S. Environmental Protection Agency [USEPA], 1997a; Fitzgerald, et al. 1998; Northeast States For Coordinated Air Use Management [NESCAUM], 1998b; United Nations Environment Programme [UNEP]. 2003). This is particularly the case for the Northeast states, where local and regional pollution-reduction efforts have proven insufficient to address the adverse impacts of many air pollutants, including mercury, acidifying pollutants, ozone, and particulates, attributable to upwind emission sources (NESCAUM, 1998a, 2003; Miller, 1999; Smith and Trip, 2005).

In the United States, innovative environmental policies are frequently initiated at the state level (Smith and Trip, 2005). U.S. environmental statutes facilitate state policy and regulatory experimentation by allowing the states, in most instances, to establish regulations more stringent than those adopted federally. Concerned over evidence of widespread mercury contamination of fish and faced with what many perceived as insufficient federal efforts to address mercury pollution through the mid-2000's, the states have taken a leadership role in many mercury pollution reduction efforts. This chapter briefly highlights some of the state mercury initiatives underway and the roles of science and monitoring in helping to inform and guide these efforts.

State Mercury Initiatives: A National Overview

The majority of states have programs addressing one or more issues relating to mercury. These include actions to reduce mercury pollution attributable to air emission point sources, wastewater discharges and sludge reuse; reduce mercury use in products; increase recovery and recycling of end-of-life mercury-added products; monitor mercury levels and trends in the environment; and educate consumers, businesses, and the general public about mercury (e.g., New Hampshire Department of Environmental Services, 1999; Massachusetts Executive Office of Environmental Affairs, 2000). In addition to individual state initiatives, several collaborative multistate efforts at the regional and national level are also underway, including the New England Governors and Eastern Canadian Premiers Mercury Action Plan, the Great Lakes Binational Toxics Strategy, the Great Lakes Mercury in Products Phase Down and Emission Reduction Strategies, and the Quicksilver Caucus, among others (USEPA 1997a; Conference of New England Governors–Eastern Canadian Premiers 1998; Smith and Trip, 2005; Great Lakes Regional Collaboration, 2008, 2010).

To help delineate the scope and diversity of state activities addressing mercury, a national survey of state environmental protection agencies was completed in 2005 by the Environmental Council of States (ECOS, 2005). Additional, more focused surveys of state activities have also been completed by other organizations, including a survey of state mercury-reduction programs targeting coal-fired electricity-generating units by the National Association of Clean Air Agencies (NACAA, 2007) and regional surveys and summaries of state activities addressing mercury-added products by the Northeast Waste Management Officials' Association (NEWMOA, 2008a).

The responses to these surveys highlight the leadership role the states have assumed in many areas to reduce mercury pollution. Of the 45 states that responded to the ECOS 2005 national survey, 22 reported that they either had a mercury action plan or strategy in place to manage and coordinate their mercury activities (16 states) or planned to develop one (6 states). All of the responding states reported that they engaged in outreach or education efforts on mercury, including communications about fish-consumption advisories and consumer products, often in multiple languages. Many states also reported considerable activity in the areas of mercury-added products, emission source control, monitoring and research, and interstate coordination and information sharing.

Mercury-Added Products

More than 40% of state respondents reported taking actions to reduce pollution attributable to the use and disposal of mercury-added products. These efforts include legislative, regulatory, and voluntary programs to phase out the sales of certain mercury-added products, label products containing mercury, and enhance the collection and recycling of end-of-life mercury-added products.

State legislation addressing mercury-added products has far eclipsed federal action. The last national law addressing unnecessary uses of mercury was the federal Mercury-Containing and Rechargeable Battery Management Act of 1996 (P.L. 104-142), which prohibited the sale of certain mercury-added batteries. Even in this case, federal action followed the adoption or introduction of legislation addressing mercury-added batteries in 13 states (Hurd et al., 1993).

Over the past several years, at least a dozen states have adopted more comprehensive mercury products legislation comprised of one or more of the following elements: restrictions on the sale of mercury-added products for which environmentally preferable alternatives exist, labeling requirements for mercury-added products that continue to be sold to inform consumers about their mercury content and the need for proper disposal or recycling at end-of-life, requirements that manufacturers report their mercury-added product sales, and requirements that manufacturers support collection and recycling programs for end-of-life products. Many of these elements have been adopted by all the New England States and many others (NEWMOA, 2008a, 2008b, 2008c, 2008d).

Emission Sources

Many states also reported adopting regulations on mercury emission sources that are more stringent than federal requirements, in particular with respect to municipal solid-waste combustors, medical-waste incinerators, and coal-fired electricity-generating units (EGUs). As the largest national point source category of mercury emissions and a large source of electric generating capacity in the United States, coal-fired EGUs have received considerable attention from the states.

In March 2005, the USEPA adopted the Clean Air Mercury Rule (CAMR) to regulate mercury emissions from EGUs (USEPA 2005a). The rule established a nationwide mercury emissions cap for this sector and an interstate emissions trading program. The initial cap, applicable through 2018, was set at a level high enough to be achievable by pollution-control measures to address other pollutants. Mercury-specific controls were not required. Emissions under the final cap were estimated to be about 70% lower than the baseline.

In the deliberations leading up this rule the EPA initially determined in 2000 that EGUs should be classified as a source of hazardous air pollutants (HAP), in particular because of mercury emissions. The EPA also determined that "regulation of HAP emissions from coal and oil fired electric utility steam generating units under Section 112 of the Clean Air Act (CAA) was appropriate and necessary" (USEPA, 2000). Under the 1990 CAA amendments, this determination would have necessitated that these units meet a strict maximum achievable control technology (MACT) standard to reduce mercury emissions. Subsequently, in 2005, with, according to many observers, considerable evidence of undue reliance on industry information and documents, the EPA reversed its decision to regulate EGU under Section 112 of the CAA and instead determined that regulation under the provisions of Section 111 of the CAA, using a cap-and-trade program instead of MACT controls, was appropriate (USEPA 2005a, 2005b).

Many states and other organizations criticized CAMR on the grounds that the EPA's decisions and the rule itself did not comport with the requirements of the CAA, did not achieve sufficient mercury emission reductions, established compliance deadlines that were overly long, and could perpetuate or contribute to mercury deposition hot spots through the rule's trading provisions (Christen, 2004; NESCAUM, 2004; NACAA, 2005). Because of these concerns, several states joined in a legal challenge to the rule. This challenge was ultimately successful, and CAMR was vacated on February 8, 2008, by the D.C. Circuit Court (U.S. Court of Appeals, 2008). The EPA initially petitioned the Supreme Court to review this decision, but on February 6, 2009, following the election of President Barack Obama, the Agency dismissed this request. On February 23, 2009, the Supreme Court denied the Utility Air Regulatory Group's request to review the U.S. Circuit Court of Appeals decision.

In March 2011, the EPA proposed standards for emissions of mercury and other toxic air pollutants from coal and oil-fired EGUs under Section 112 of the Clean Air Act. These regulations established emission limits based on Maximum Achievable Control Technology and did not include emissions trading provisions. These standards were finalized in December, 2011. Based on EPA estimates these standards will control mercury emissions from this sector by approximately 90% when fully implemented (USEPA, 2011).

Prior to the CAMR vacatur, many states had already decided to adopt more stringent regulations on EGUs. To help the states advance their own programs targeting this sector, NACAA developed a model rule (NACAA, 2005). This model was largely based on provisions in regulations, and/or legislation, that had already been adopted or proposed by a number of states, including Massachusetts and Connecticut (Connecticut General Assembly, 2003; MassDEP, 2004a; NACAA, 2007). Under the NACAA model rule, interstate mercury emission trading was not allowed, addressing state concerns regarding the potential contribution of EGUs to mercury deposition hot spots. The model also included more stringent emission-control requirements and a faster implementation timeframe using a two-phase approach. Under the first phase, the model stipulated that a mercury removal efficiency of 80% or an emission limit of 0.010 lb/GWh be achieved by 2009. The second phase, to be achieved by 2013, required either 90–95% removal efficiency or an emission limit of 0.0060–0.0025 lb/GWh. New EGUs were required to meet the Phase 2 90–95% removal requirement.

By 2007, based on a survey conducted by NACAA, about a dozen states had adopted legislation or regulations on mercury emissions from the coal-fired EGUs that were more stringent than CAMR (NACAA, 2007).

Monitoring and Research

With respect to mercury monitoring and research, states across the country have invested in numerous initiatives addressing mercury. Based on 2005 ECOS survey information, the states estimated allocating well in excess of $50 million on mercury research and monitoring over the previous 15 years. Of the responding states, 62% indicated that they conducted research and/or studies related to mercury. Twenty-nine states, 64% of those responding, reported that they maintained an inventory of in-state mercury sources. These state databases underpin national emission inventories and are often based on source testing that exceeds federal requirements both in scope and frequency.

In addition to maintaining inventories of mercury sources, states are also supporting atmospheric and ecologic monitoring and research, including sediment-core and fish-tissue monitoring for both public health purposes and trend analyses. The states also support air deposition monitoring, and in 2005, twenty-one states participated in the National Mercury Deposition Network, often funding site operation. Michigan, Florida, Massachusetts, Connecticut, Minnesota, Vermont, Wisconsin, Maine, New Jersey, and New York have also supported additional monitoring and modeling efforts in collaboration with academic research groups.

Thirty-nine states reported that they engaged in ongoing fish tissue sampling for mercury (e.g., Massachusetts Department of Environmental Protection (MassDEP), 2004b; Hutcheson et al., 2008). Overall, states have sampled fish from many hundreds of water bodies across the United States. Twenty-eight states reported that they have conducted other scientific research related to mercury. Research projects have included co-sponsored testing of continuous emission monitoring technologies for mercury, as part of the EPA Environmental Technology Verification Program, research on dental amalgam separators, evaluations of in-state mercury pollution sources and impacts, assessments of fugitive mercury releases, mercury transport model development, assessments of emissions from mine fires and oil combustion, and environmental trend analyses. The states have also supported research on mercury levels in and releases from mercury-added products, including a New Jersey assessment of environmental releases from broken linear fluorescent tubes and a Maine analysis of indoor mercury releases attributable to broken compact fluorescent lamps (CFLs) (Aucott et al., 2003; Stahler et al., 2008).

Interstate Coordination

The scope and diversity of state activities to address mercury have led to efforts to improve coordination between the states, enhance information sharing, and build capacity at the state level to both improve efficiency and influence national and international agendas to reduce mercury pollution. Many examples of multistate coordination and planning on mercury initiatives exist, including efforts by the Great Lakes Regional Collaboration Executive Committee, the Great Lakes Regional Pollution Prevention Roundtable, the Southern States Mercury Task Force, the Interstate Mercury Education and Reduction Clearing House, the Quicksilver Caucus (QSC) and its member organizations, and the New England Governors and Eastern Canadian Premiers Mercury Action Plan (NEG-ECP MAP), among others. The QSC, a multistate national group and the NEG-ECP MAP, a regional binational state and provincial mercury pollution reduction plan are discussed in more detail below.

The Quicksilver Caucus

Overview

The QSC was formed in May 2001 by a coalition of state environmental associations to facilitate collaboration on mercury-related issues, share technical and policy information, and encourage multimedia approaches to reducing mercury pollution. The QSC also provides a mechanism for multimedia state input on national and international mercury-reduction programs and strategies. Caucus members include the Environmental Council of the States, the Association of State and Territorial Solid Waste Management Officials, the National Association of Clean Air Agencies, the Association of State and Interstate Water Pollution Control Administrators, the Association of State Drinking Water Administrators, and the National Pollution Prevention Roundtable. Many individual states have also been active participants in the QSC.

The QSC has focused its efforts on several priority areas. These include information sharing and capacity building between the states, the EPA, and UNEP; pollution prevention and stewardship approaches to reduce mercury in the environment; and the safe, long-term storage of excess commodity elemental mercury. These are briefly discussed below.

Information Sharing and Capacity Building between the States, the EPA, and UNEP

To facilitate information sharing and joint planning, the QSC has organized and held state workshops focused on mercury, which were attended by environmental agency leaders and their representatives. These meetings provided opportunities for the states to share information about various mercury reduction initiatives and identify common priorities and potential areas of collaboration. Based on discussions at these meetings the QSC has implemented a number of activities to facilitate state mercury-reduction progress. The members of the QSC also hold regular conference calls and have completed several reports on issues of concern to the states.

Since its inception, the QSC has also provided input to the EPA on national efforts to address mercury, in particular, advocating for the EPA's adoption of a strong national mercury action plan with specific implementation commitments, reduction goals, and timelines.

Because of the significant contribution of global sources to mercury deposition in the states, which makes it difficult to meet mandated clean water goals established under the U.S. Clean Water Act, the states have also provided technical and policy input to the UNEP mercury program. In 2001, the UNEP Governing Council initiated a global evaluation of mercury pollution and impacts. Based on this assessment the UNEP Governing Council concluded "that there is sufficient evidence of significant global adverse impacts from mercury to warrant further international action to reduce the risks to humans and wildlife from the release of mercury to the environment" and called for immediate actions to address the issue (UNEP, 2003). In February 2009, the Governing Council of UNEP agreed to work toward a global legally binding agreement addressing mercury. Although mandatory requirements have yet to be established through the UNEP process, negotiations are now underway (UNEP, 2009).

Within the context of international mercury-reduction efforts, the United States and several other countries initially supported an implementation program relying on voluntary initiatives, arguing that this mechanism would result in faster progress than would be achieved through a negotiated binding agreement. A number of voluntary partnerships were established under this effort, with staff and monetary support from the United States and other countries. Throughout this process, the QSC supported efforts to advance global reductions in mercury pollution and consistently advocated for the initial partnerships to be strengthened by the inclusion of objective mercury-reduction goals, timelines, and detailed work plans, which in many cases were ultimately included. The QSC also advocated for the United States to support development of a binding global agreement. The United States is currently a leading advocate of this approach, and the states, through the QSC, continue to provide technical and policy input to the EPA and the State Department to help inform and support U.S. negotiating positions.

To facilitate the partnership efforts and help expand international capacity to reduce mercury pollution the QSC, with EPA support, formed a resource network in 2007. This network is comprised of state technical, policy and program implementation experts interested in assisting UNEP. As of the fall of 2008, participating states provided staff time and the EPA travel expenses for state experts to participate in three international capacity-building workshops focused on mercury.

Pollution Prevention and Stewardship Approaches to Reduce Mercury in the Environment

Mercury releases attributable to the dental sector and mercury-added consumer products were identified by the QSC as priorities for state action. Mercury amalgam filling material contains about 50% mercury. Mercury is discharged into dental office wastewater when amalgam is placed, shaped, and removed. Numerous mercury-added products exist that can result in mercury releases and exposures if broken in use or upon disposal. The QSC has expended considerable efforts to facilitate and encourage progress on these sources.

Two QSC documents published in 2008 summarize state and local actions to address mercury discharges from the dental sector. At that time, 11 states reported having legislation or regulations in place to reduce mercury pollution from the dental sector. The QSC reports *Dental Mercury Amalgam Waste Management White Paper* and *Case Studies of Five Dental Mercury Amalgam Separator Programs* provided background information about the environmental significance of mercury attributable to the dental sector and specific information about state and local government programs that address dental mercury amalgam discharges (QSC 2008a, 2008b). Information-sharing webinars have also been held to facilitate state actions on this sector. QSC and ECOS also advocated for stepped-up national efforts to reduce mercury pollution from the dental sector. In December 2008, the EPA announced a Memorandum of Understanding with the American Dental Association calling for voluntary efforts to reduce mercury amalgam discharges to wastewater (USEPA, 2008). Although supportive of these efforts, the QSC urged the EPA to take additional steps to ensure timely progress. In 2010, QSC and ECOS further urged the EPA to back up the voluntary effort by including dental facilities for rulemaking in its effluent guidelines program plan and by requiring the use of best management practices, including amalgam separator mercury-pollution controls, at dental facilities (ECOS, 2010; QSC, 2010). Soon thereafter, the EPA announced that it was initiating an effluent guideline rulemaking for dental facilities, with a draft rule expected in 2011 and a final rule in 2012 (USEPA, 2010).

The QSC also issued the *Product Labeling: Information for States* report to stimulate discussion about the value and effectiveness of state mercury-added product labeling requirements, which have been adopted by many states. Labeling helps to ensure that consumers are informed about the mercury content of various products and serves as a mechanism to encourage the use of nonmercury alternatives (QSC, 2006b). The QSC report provides information about labeling activities in nine states. The companion *Mercury-Added Product White Paper* identified five mercury containing product types in which significant reductions in mercury use and releases could be achieved through state and federal pollution prevention initiatives (QSC, 2006a).

The QSC also engaged with car manufacturers, steel makers, the auto recycling industry, environmental organizations and the EPA to help establish and implement the *Memorandum of Understanding to Establish the National Vehicle Mercury Switch Recovery Program* (NVMSRP). This agreement was developed to enhance the recycling of mercury switches from automobiles as a mechanism to reduce mercury emissions from scrap metal furnaces (USEPA, 2006). Prior to 2003, over 200 million mercury switches, containing approximately 0.5 to 1 g of mercury, were installed in vehicle lighting applications (e.g., trunk lights), anti-lock brake sensors, and some airbags. When vehicles are scrapped, the mercury switches may be broken, immediately spilling their contents, or they may enter scrap metal wastes destined for high-temperature reclamation.

By 2010, over 3.3 million mercury switches had been collected from over 9000 participating recyclers. Although an impressive total, the recycling targets established under the NVMSRP have not been achieved and the industry-supported fund established to provide recyclers an incentive payment for each switch diverted from the waste stream has been depleted. Discussions to further fund and improve the program, which is scheduled to run through 2017, are ongoing. QSC has worked to evaluate the program and continues to monitor its implementation (QSC, 2009).

Safe, Long-Term Storage of Excess Commodity Elemental Mercury Nationally and Internationally

Since its inception, the QSC has voiced its opposition to U.S. elemental mercury stockpile sales and advocated for a federal plan to manage the long-term storage of excess commodity elemental mercury. To inform QSC positions on this issue, a series of workgroup assessments were completed in 2003 addressing commodity mercury management, storage, best management practices, markets, and policy option issues (QSC, 2003a, 2003b, 2003c, 2003d, 2003e). These reports were the basis of a set of QSC principles regarding the collection and management of elemental commodity grade mercury and ECOS Resolution 06-1: Mercury Retirement and Stockpiling, which advocated against the market sales and export of elemental commodity grade mercury from the U.S. federal strategic mercury stockpile. Communications from the QSC and its member organizations to federal decision makers also contributed to the Defense National Stockpile Center's environmental impact statement regarding the disposition of the federal stockpile and the ultimate decision to indefinitely suspend sales and consolidate the stockpile for safe long-term storage (Defense National Stockpile Center Defense Logistics Agency, 2004).

The ECOS also testified in support of federal U.S. legislation, the Mercury Export Ban Act of 2008 (S.906), cosponsored by U.S. Senators Barack Obama (D-IL) and Lisa Murkowski (R-AK), and Representative Tom Allen (D-ME), among others (Smith, 2007). This Act prohibits the export of elemental mercury from the United States starting in 2013 as well as commercial sales from the federal mercury stockpiles held by the Department of Energy and the Department of Defense. It also directs the Department of Energy to provide for the permanent safe storage of collected/recycled U.S. mercury in excess of domestic demand. In addition to the ECOS, the Natural Resources Defense Council, American Chemistry Council, National Mining Association, and Chlorine Institute also supported this Act. The Act was overwhelmingly approved in both the Senate and House of Representatives in September 2008 and signed into law by President George W. Bush in October 2008.

TABLE 16.1
Objectives of the New England Governors and Eastern Canadian Premiers Mercury Action Plan

Action area/objectives
Regional mercury task force
Coordinate, prioritize, monitor, and report on progress; revise plan.
Emission reductions
Long-term goal: virtual elimination of anthropogenic mercury releases to the environment.
2003: 50% reduction in regional mercury emissions.
2010: 75% reduction in regional mercury emissions.
Strict emissions limits for major point sources included.
Source reduction and safe waste management
Eliminate or reduce nonessential uses of mercury.
Segregate and recycle mercury from remaining uses to maximum degree possible.
Outreach and education
Potential adverse impacts and ways to reduce exposures.
Alternatives to mercury-added products.
Proper waste management.
Research, analysis and strategic monitoring
Support and expand research and analysis.
Support strategic monitoring to measure and track progress.
Stockpile management
Minimize mercury stockpile sales.

New England Governors and Eastern Canadian Premiers Mercury Action Plan

Overview

The Conference of New England Governors (NEG) and the Secretariat of the Eastern Canadian Premiers (ECP) have collaborated on cross-border economic and environmental issues since 1973. In light of the findings in the Northeast Regional Mercury Study (NESCAUM, 1998b); the Mercury in Massachusetts report (MassDEP, 1996); and the USEPA Mercury Study Report to Congress (USEPA, 1997b) the NEG-ECP directed their environmental agencies to develop a regional binational action plan to reduce mercury pollution in the New England states and Eastern Canadian provinces.

The resulting NEG-ECP Mercury Action Plan (MAP), the first such binational regional pollution-reduction plan to be initiated and implemented at the state and provincial level, was unanimously endorsed by the region's Governors and Premiers in 1998 (Conference of New England Governors-Eastern Canadian Premiers [CNEG-ECP], 1998). Support for the MAP crossed political party lines, with endorsement by Republican, Democrat, and Independent governors in the United States and by Premiers representing three political affiliations in Canada.

The MAP is, by design, multimedia and comprehensive in scope, combining end-of-pipe control strategies and pollution-prevention approaches where best applied. The plan extends across traditional media and programmatic boundaries as well as political borders. It includes 45 specific elements in six action areas (Table 16.1) (CNEG-ECP, 1998). The action areas address emission reductions, source reduction and waste management, outreach and education, research, analysis and monitoring, and mercury stockpile management. A regional Mercury Task Force (MTF) was also established, providing a mechanism to develop and fine-tune implementation work plans, revise and adapt the MAP as needed, coordinate activities across the jurisdictions, and report on progress to the region's environmental agency leaders, as well as the governors and premiers.

The MAP established a long-term regional goal of virtually eliminating anthropogenic mercury releases, with an interim 50% reduction target by 2003 (CNEG-ECP, 1998). A 75% reduction goal was subsequently adopted for 2010 (CNEG-ECP, 2001). To achieve these reductions, the MAP included emission limits for major point sources, which were set at levels much more stringent than the federal U.S. or Canadian requirements in effect at the time. For example, the MAP established a mercury emission value for municipal solid-waste combustors at 0.028 mg mercury/dry standard cubic meter (mg/dscm), about threefold more stringent than the EPA's limit of 0.080 mg/dscm. The MAP emission value for medical-waste incinerators was set 10 times lower than the EPA's value. For other sources, the MAP directed the jurisdictions to achieve maximum feasible reductions. Commitments to reduce unnecessary mercury use in products, increase the recycling of end-of-life mercury-added products, implement outreach and education programs to inform the public about mercury risks, and support environmental monitoring and research efforts were also endorsed. Lastly, the MAP specifically called for the continued safe storage and ultimate retirement of the U.S. strategic stockpile of over 5000 tons of elemental mercury rather than its sale into the international commodities market.

Basis of the Mercury Action Plan

The NEG-ECP MAP was established on the principles that environmental policies addressing mercury should be based on sound science; take a precautionary approach where scientific uncertainties exist; adopt comprehensive, multimedia, lead-by-example policies; include concrete goals with measurable milestones and timelines; provide implementation flexibility to the jurisdictions; and include mechanisms for coordination, oversight, accountability and reporting.

The 1998 Northeast States and Eastern Canadian Provinces Mercury Study: A Framework for Action (NESCAUM, 1998b) summarized the state of the science regarding mercury in the region and was the primary technical basis for the NEG-ECP MAP. This assessment summarized data on regional mercury emissions by category, ranking source estimates by their degree of uncertainty, and on mercury impacts in the region, based on deposition modeling and monitoring data and information on mercury levels in fish and other biota. This assessment and other reports helped to capture the attention of state policy leaders in the northeast and drive action (USEPA 1997a; NESCAUM, 1998b; MassDEP, 1996; UNEP, 2003; Agency for Toxic Substances and Disease Registry, [ATSDR]. 1999).

Although data indicated that wildlife resources in the region were at risk, the substantial body of science indicating that mercury can impair neurologic development in the fetus was the primary risk concern (National Research Council, 2000). The extensive data demonstrating that mercury levels exceeded public health guidelines in freshwater fish from lakes and ponds across the region, even in remote areas with no nearby sources, was also important to policy leaders, as were modeling and monitoring results indicating that the mercury entering the region's water bodies was attributable to atmospheric deposition from sources located both within and outside the area (MassDEP, 1996; NESCAUM, 1998b). The widespread nature of the problem and its sources argued for

TABLE 16.2
Summary of Mercury Emission Reductions in New England and Eastern Canada (metric tons/yr)

Context	New England	Eastern Canadian provinces	Total	Percent reduction
1998 baseline	7.10	2.74	9.82	55%
2003 estimate	2.85	1.55	4.40	

NOTE: Values based on emission estimates reported by the jurisdictions. Emission categories included municipal solid-waste incinerators, medical-waste incinerators, chlor-alkali plants, commercial and industrial boilers, electricity-generating units, residential boilers, wood-burning facilities, and area sources. The 2003 emission estimates focused on sources where regulatory or other actions to reduce mercury emissions were implemented since the 1998 Mercury Action Plan was adopted. Emission estimates for some categories were not updated, including area source emissions due to a lack of new data, and industrial, commercial and residential boilers, as no activity directed at addressing emissions from these sources occurred.

a regional approach. The identification of major sources of mercury releases within the region highlighted opportunities for action that could result in significant local benefits. The contribution from out-of-region sources supported a clean-hands, lead-by-example approach in order to support regional advocacy for stronger national and international efforts.

Progress as of 2008

EMISSION REDUCTIONS

Substantial reductions in emissions from most major point sources in the region were achieved under the MAP. Overall, as compared with baseline emissions in the mid-1990s, the region achieved approximately a 55% reduction in emissions from the source categories included in the baseline inventory by 2003, exceeding the 50% reduction target (Table 16.2) (NESCAUM, 1998b). Overall emission reductions in the New England states are now estimated to exceed 70% (NESCAUM, 2005, 2007). In Massachusetts, overall mercury emissions were recently documented to have been reduced by approximately 91% since the mid 1990's, with the largest reductions being achieved from municipal solid waste combustors, medical waste incinerators and coal-fired power plants (NESCAUM, 2011).

These reductions were achieved by addressing major in-region point emission source categories. Based on stack test data, regional emissions from municipal solid-waste combustors were reduced by 2004 by about 85% through new air-pollution controls and reduced inputs of mercury in solid waste (e.g., MassDEP, 1998). Medical waste incinerator emissions were reduced by more than 95%, in large part because many facilities ceased operation in response to the more stringent mercury emission limit as well as a stringent EPA limit on dioxin emissions. Emissions from chlor-alkali facilities were also reduced by more than 90% though the use of best management practices at a facility in New Brunswick and the closure of a facility in Maine.

Regulations and legislation targeting coal-fired EGUs in New England are now being implemented and will result in further substantial reductions in regional mercury emissions. These state requirements will achieve considerably greater emission reductions under faster implementation timeframes than the vacated CAMR. For example, legislation adopted in Connecticut in June 2003 established an emission control target of 90% by 2008 for coal-fired units in that state (Connecticut General Assembly 2003). In 2004, Massachusetts adopted stringent emission limits for this sector based on an analysis of mercury emission levels and control technology options (MassDEP, 2002, 2003, 2004a). The regulations phase in emission reduction requirements in two steps, culminating in a 95% emission control requirement in 2012. The anticipated emission reductions under these regulations are depicted in Figure 16.1.

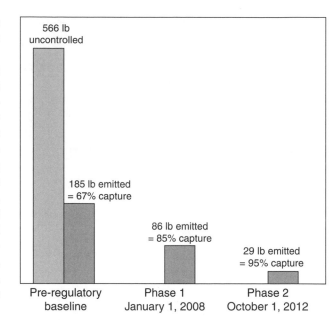

FIGURE 16.1 Massachusetts emissions standards for power plants, 310 CMR 7.29.

POLLUTION PREVENTION

The region has continued to advance effective mercury pollution-prevention initiatives on many fronts. The New England states have taken cutting-edge leadership positions regarding product stewardship for mercury-added prod-ucts. Comprehensive mercury products legislation has been adopted in all the New England states (Table 16.3) (NEW-MOA, 2008). The details of specific requirements for each state can be found on the respective state's websites. To briefly summarize, the laws in effect in 2008 typically required

TABLE 16.3

Status of Mercury Education and Reduction Legislation and Regulation in the New England States: June 2008

Requirement	CT	MA	ME	NH	RI	VT
Mercury-added product notification	√	√	√	√	√	√
Bans on sale of certain mercury-added products	√	√	√	√	√	√
Bans on sale of certain mercury-added novelty items	√			√	√	√
Ban on sales of mercury fever thermometer	√	√	√	√	√	√
Bans on use of mercury-added educational products in K–12 schools		√	√	√	√	√
Phase out of mercury-added product sales, with exemptions	√	√	√		√	√
Product labeling	√	√	√		√	√
Bans on disposal of most mercury-added products		√	√		√	√
Plans for collecting mercury-added products	√	√			√	
Disclosure of mercury content in certain products for hospitals		√	√		√	
Control on sale of elemental mercury	√		√	√	√	√
Public education and outreach	√	√	√	√	√	√
Dental amalgam separators	√	√	√	√	√	√
Mercury auto switch removal	†	√	√	V	√	√

SOURCE: Adapted from the Northeast Waste Management Officials' Association (2008).

√Provisions that have been implemented.

†Authority exists to implement under existing laws or policies.

V = voluntary program in place.

that mercury-added products be labeled; that the sales of many specific mercury products for which alternatives exist be phased out; that manufacturers notify the states about mercury-added products they are selling; and that manufacturers and government institutions enhance the collection and recycling of end-of-life mercury products.

The Interstate Mercury Reduction and Education Clearinghouse (IMERC) was established by the states to collect and manage the data submitted under legislative mercury product notification requirements. IMERC also helps in the implementation of other aspects of state mercury-products laws. IMERC data are currently the only source of information on total mercury use and trends in use in products in the United States. Manufacturer notifications indicate that, concurrent with the implementation of state mercury-products legislation, mercury use in fabricated and formulated products decreased nationally by about 11%, or about 14 tons per year, between 2001 and 2004 (NEWMOA, 2008e).

Many other mercury pollution-prevention initiatives have also been implemented across the region. Details of these efforts can be found at the respective state agency websites. These include legislation requiring manufacturer-funded recycling programs targeting thermostats (Maine and Vermont) and vehicle mercury switches (Maine and Massachusetts). Programs to educate students and teachers about mercury and to conduct school mercury cleanouts have also been implemented across the region and have resulted in the removal of several thousand pounds of mercury from the region's high schools and middle schools. Several states (Massachusetts, Connecticut, and Vermont) have also implemented statewide mercury thermometer exchange programs, which have collected over 150,000 mercury fever thermometers.

The region has also taken the lead in addressing mercury pollution from the dental sector attributable to the installation, shaping, and removal of amalgam fillings, which contain approximately 50% mercury. All jurisdictions under the MAP have implemented initiatives to reduce this source using pollution prevention and control approaches. Regional emission inventory estimates indicated that sewage sludge incinerators (SSI) were responsible for a significant share of the region's mercury emissions (NESCAUM, 2005). To address this sector the Mercury Task Force has focused on efforts to reduce mercury inputs to wastewater. This approach was viewed as preferable to mercury emission control requirements on SSIs because additional release pathways related to the handling and treatment of wastewater and treated sludge would also be addressed. The beneficial reuse of treated biosolids, discharge of untreated wastewater during high-flow storm events, emissions during wastewater and sludge treatment, and discharge of treated wastewater all result in releases of mercury. Reducing mercury inputs to wastewater addresses all these pathways.

Considerable research demonstrates that the dental sector has been a significant contributor to mercury loadings in municipal wastewater (Arenholt-Bindslev and Larsen, 1996; Andersen, 2001; Cain et al., 2004). The Massachusetts Water Resources Authority estimated that dentists accounted for 13–79%, with a midpoint estimate of 46%, of mercury inputs to its system in the 1990s (Massachusetts Water Resources Authority, 1997). Other studies suggest values in the range of 30% to >60%.

Goals for the dental sector were established under the MAP in 2005. These stipulated that 75%, by 2007, and 95%, by 2010, of the region's dentists who generate mercury-containing wastewater from dental amalgam would have amalgam separator pollution controls installed and be using other Best Management Practices (BMPs) to minimize mercury pollution. Amalgam separators are devices that rely on a number of relatively simple technologies to capture mercury amalgam particulates and, in some cases, soluble mercury. Units typically cost from $500 to $2,000 and can reduce mercury discharges from dental practices to wastewater by 95–99% (Agedembo et al., 2002; Strategic Envirotechnology Partnership, 2003). BMPs minimize mercury pollution by stipulating proper waste amalgam handling and disposal practices be followed.

The jurisdictions have pursued a variety of approaches to achieve the MAP goals for this sector. The Canadian provinces are implementing the Canada-wide Standard for Mercury in Dental Amalgams, which was adopted in 2000 (Canadian Council of Ministers of the Environment, 2000). Under this policy, mercury releases from the dental sector were to be reduced by 95% by 2005 through the voluntary use of best management practices and amalgam separators.

Several New England States also initially tried voluntary approaches to encourage the use of amalgam separators, but by 2007, all had adopted legislation and or regulations requiring their use. Overall, these efforts have been very successful. By 2007, >91% of dentists in New England and >53% in the Canadian provinces were estimated to have appropriate amalgam separators installed. For the region as a whole, approximately 9054 dentists (2038 in the Canadian provinces and 7016 in the New England states), or 78% of the total, had installed amalgam separators in their offices, exceeding the 2007 regional goal of 75%. As the overall Canadian result falls short of the reduction target established under the Canada-wide Standards, the provinces are considering next steps, which may include installation requirements.

Although the American Dental Association (ADA) had opposed state and national regulations requiring the use of amalgam separators for many years, instead favoring voluntary approaches, amalgam separators were included in the Association's recommended "Best Management Practices for Amalgam Wastes" (American Dental Association, 2004). To date, purely voluntary efforts by the states to encourage amalgam separator use have not met with great success, and as a result, as of 2009 amalgam separator requirements had been adopted in 11 states.

OUTREACH AND EDUCATION

Most of the pollution-prevention efforts in the region have also included outreach components to educate consumers, teachers, students, and businesses about mercury. A variety of communication channels have been used to reach different target audiences, including brochures about healthful fish consumption distributed at health care clinics and supermarkets, toll-free mercury hotline numbers, mercury educational displays and information for schools and other institutions, and mercury fact sheets made available in hard copy and on the web (e.g., Maine Bureau of Health, 2004). A regional mercury-products clearing house and topic hub was also developed (NEWMOA, 2008c).

The region has taken a number of steps to clarify and improve communications regarding the safe use of compact fluorescent lights (CFLs) and their cleanup if broken. CFLs and other fluorescent lighting offer excellent energy efficiency as compared with regular incandescent lights and can thus reduce emissions of a number of pollutants, including greenhouse gases. CFLs also contain mercury, some of which is released to the air if a bulb is broken, either accidently during use or upon disposal. To address health concerns of consumers, MEDEP scientists completed a research study on mercury releases to indoor air from broken CFLs prior to and following various cleanup procedures (Stahler et al., 2008). They found that under some circumstances, broken CFLs can lead to mercury levels in indoor air high enough to be of potential concern to young children and pregnant women. Because of the increasing use of CFLs, some attributable to energy-conservation efforts supported by the states, the MTF coordinated work to update and harmonize CFL cleanup guidance across the region. This effort was completed in the spring of 2008 and all the New England states now have consistent cleanup protocols for broken CFLs posted on their websites (e.g., MassDEP, 2008). Several states also revised their recommendations for CFL use, encouraging consumers to take steps to minimize breakage, especially in areas frequented by young children. The region is also providing ongoing input on follow-up studies planned by the EPA.

REGIONAL MERCURY TOTAL MAXIMUM DAILY LOAD ASSESSMENT

Under the U.S. Clean Water Act, states are required to develop total maximum daily load (TMDL) estimates for mercury inputs to impaired water bodies. A TMDL is a calculation of the maximum amount of a pollutant that a water body, or group of water bodies, can receive and still meet applicable water-quality standards, in this case fish that are safe to eat. An implementation plan to achieve the TMDL is also required. To comply with this requirement the New England Interstate Water Pollution Control Commission (NEIWPCC), the New England States, and New York completed an innovative regional TMDL for mercury-impaired water bodies primarily impacted by air deposition of mercury (NEIWPCC, 2007). This TMDL built on a statewide TMDL approach completed by Minnesota and was approved by EPA Regions 1 and 2 on December 20, 2007.

The regional assessment documented that, in the northeast states, over 10,000 water bodies and over 46,000 river miles were impaired for fish consumption because of mercury. The TMDL assessment concluded that, on a regional basis, anthropogenic mercury inputs would need to be reduced by 86–98% for fish from the region's freshwaters to meet the EPA fish-tissue consumption criterion for mercury (NEIWPCC, 2007). These TMDL estimates were based on a regional data base of mercury concentrations in fish and assumed a simple linear relationship between mercury water-body inputs and fish-tissue concentrations across the region, an approach used in other TMDL assessments and recommended by the EPA. The document endorsed the MAP as an initial TMDL implementation plan and highlighted the need for emission reductions from upwind sources. The regional TMDL estimates, as well as similar findings by Minnesota and New Jersey, support the aggressive reduction goals of the MAP and emphasize the need for commensurate federal action, including emission reductions from coal-fired utilities greater than the 70% stipulated under the vacated EPA Clean Air Mercury Rule.

State Perspectives on Mercury Policy and Science

Communication and collaboration between research scientists and policy makers has helped inform state initiatives addressing mercury as well as other environmental issues. Although science has played a critical role in state mercury initiatives, it is important to note that policy makers and scientists have different informational needs and operate under different decisional frameworks. In order for science to effectively inform policy, key policy drivers and concerns must be identified and the relevant technical information made accessible and understandable. To ultimately solve many environmental issues, policies and research agendas must be based on an iterative, adaptive process that allows new scientific information and new policy priorities to be taken into account. This can be accomplished only if environmental agencies support key scientific research and monitoring and if scientists take the time to effectively communicate their findings to policy makers.

Toward these ends, the states have funded numerous scientific efforts addressing mercury, as summarized previously, and have supported expanded federal resources in these areas. Better information on mercury sources, exposures, and trends is needed to ensure that state, federal, and international mercury policies are successful and efficient in reducing adverse impacts.

Given that much regulatory activity addressing mercury is occurring at the state rather than the federal level, state agency and organization input should be an integral part of any national or international mercury monitoring and research program. As partners in the process, the states can be strong advocates for appropriate federal support. Expanded programs should also be designed to inform and support key state policy and regulatory concerns. The states are particularly interested in the following areas:

- **Environmental Indicators.** Approaches and data to evaluate the results of state, regional, and global mercury policy initiatives are critical to ensuring accountability and optimizing efforts. Improved data on trends in mercury levels in the environment and exposures are needed, based on consistent, or at least comparable, methods. Resources to allow for more coordinated and robust mercury monitoring are needed nationally and globally.
- **Mercury Sources and Inventories.** Improved data on trends in mercury production, recycling, use, and releases are also needed based on transparent tracking and reporting mechanisms. Of particular interest are improved estimates of emissions attributable to oil combustion and refining, mobile sources, mining, and releases attributable to mercury-added products. Improved global inventories on a country and sector basis will ultimately be needed to effectively develop, implement, and track global reduction initiatives.
- **Elemental Mercury Exposures and Impacts.** The potential for exposures to elemental mercury attributable to various products and resulting risks are uncertain. Results from a research project completed by the State of Maine suggest that elemental mercury from broken CFLs may, if not cleaned up properly, result in inhalation exposures of potential concern to young children and pregnant women. Better information on elemental mercury releases from broken products and effective cleanup procedures and on elemental mercury toxicity under short- and long-term exposures is needed to optimize guidance for safe product use and spill cleanup in homes, businesses, and schools (Centers for Disease Control and Prevention, 1995; Carpi and Chen, 2001; Riley, et al. 2001; ATSDR 2003; MEDEP, 2007).
- **Determinants of Mercury Levels in Fish and Other Biota.** Improved understanding of the factors that influence mercury levels in fish would help target fish testing and consumption outreach as well as allow environmental responses to various interventions to be better assessed.
- **Outreach and Communications.** Information on the effectiveness of outreach and education efforts relating to fish consumption advisories and the benefits of fish consumption, safe mercury product use, and mercury spill cleanups is also needed. Communication is also a key to better coordination and integration of research and monitoring programs across state and federal programs. Yet communications between scientists and policy makers often do not occur in a timely fashion because of funding, workload, and travel limitations. Improved communications would help target research to policy priorities, improve coordination and data sharing between state and academic initiatives, and build support for expanded research and monitoring. Given the significant interest and commitment of resources to mercury research and monitoring already made by the states, opportunities to maximize these efforts and leverage existing initiatives should be pursued. Expanded monitoring and research programs should reflect and build on the state efforts already underway. A collaborative regional data assessment and communication effort in the Northeast provides a successful example, which involved state, federal, and academic researchers and communicated summary data to policy makers in an effective format (Evers, 2005; Evers and Clair, 2005).

Given that many states are actively implementing mercury monitoring and research programs, national mercury monitoring and research initiatives should seek to involve the states as active partners, facilitate participation of state scientists and policy experts and leverage existing programs to the degree possible. Travel budget issues often preclude state participation in scientific meetings, which limits opportunities for project development, coordination, collaboration, and sharing of information about research results, priorities, and available state funding. This is especially the case for international meetings. Increased support for state participation at such meetings would help ensure better coordination and integration.

Conclusions

Until recently efforts to reduce mercury pollution in the United States were, in large part, led by the states. These state initiatives were implemented in response to scientific data as well as public concerns over mercury's health and environmental impacts, especially to children. Key policy drivers underlying these initiatives include the extensive toxicology and epidemiology database demonstrating mercury's developmental neurotoxicity, as well as data documenting that a significant number of people are being exposed to mercury at levels of toxicologic concern. Other findings supporting action include the widespread contamination of freshwater fish from water bodies across the United States; contamination of marine species that are popular seafoods; elevated levels of mercury in "signature" wildlife species; the significant contribution of anthropogenic sources to local, regional, and global mercury loadings; and the identification of many preventable sources.

Over the past decade, the states, individually and in some cases collectively, have implemented mercury policy and regulatory initiatives far more aggressive than those adopted by the EPA. State programs and policies include numerous examples of successful and innovative approaches to address mercury pollution and demonstrate what can be accomplished technologically, economically, and politically. Taking a lead-by-example approach, the New England states, the Great Lake states, New Jersey, and other states have collaborated through regional and national state organizations on the mercury issue. As discussed in this chapter, examples of such efforts include the adoption in 1998 of the NEG-ECP MAP and the formation of the QSC in 2001.

Many states have adopted more aggressive mercury-control regulations on the EGU sector, trash and medical-waste incinerators, and other sources than the EPA initially required. The states have also led efforts to reduce the unnecessary uses of mercury through the adoption of comprehensive mercury products legislation phasing out the sale of many mercury-added products, requiring the labeling of mercury-added products still being sold, and mandating extended producer responsibility regarding mercury product recycling. State regulations and legislation to reduce mercury

pollution attributable to the dental sector have also far outpaced federal programs. Finally, the states have also been advocates for stronger national and international efforts to reduce mercury pollution and have helped to build mercury-reduction capacity by sharing their expertise nationally and globally. Most recently, the EPA, the State Department and other federal agencies under the Obama administration have made renewed efforts to more aggressively address sources of mercury pollution both within the United States and globally, often building on successful state initiatives.

Mercury research and monitoring, often supported by state agencies, has motivated and informed many actions on mercury. Ongoing research and monitoring will be critical to the adaptive management and evaluation of these efforts. Because of increasingly tight state budgets, enhanced federal support for these efforts will be needed to ensure that policy efforts are most effectively targeted and implemented.

References

Agedembo, A., Watson, P., and Lugowski, S. 2002. The weight of wastes generated by removal of dental amalgam restorations and the concentration of mercury in dental wastewater. *Journal of the Canadian Dental Association* 68(9): 553–558.

Agency for Toxic Substances and disease Registry. 1999. *Toxicological profile for mercury.* U.S. Department of Health and Human Services, Agency for Toxic Substances and Disease Registry, Atlanta, GA. http://www.atsdr.cdc.gov/toxprofiles/ tp.asp?id=115&tid=24 (accessed November 15, 2010).

Agency for Toxic Substances and disease Registry. 2003. *National alert: a warning about continuing patterns of metallic mercury exposure.* U.S. Department of Health and Human Services, Agency for Toxic Substances and Disease Registry, Atlanta, GA. http://www.atsdr.cdc.gov/alerts/970626.html (accessed November 15, 2010).

American Dental Association. 2004. *Best management practices for amalgam waste.* American Dental Association, Chicago, IL. http://www.ada.org/sections/publicResources/pdfs/topics_ amalgamwaste.pdf (accessed November 15, 2010).

Anderson, C.T. 2001. Community-wide dental mercury study. *Metropolitan Council Environmental Services (MCES) and the Minnesota Dental Association Report Number 01-507.* Metropolitan Council, St. Paul, MN.

Arenholt-Bindslev, D., and Larsen, A.H. 1996. Mercury levels and discharge in waste water from dental clinics. *Water, Air and Soil Pollution* 86(1–4): 93–96.

Aucott, M., McLinden, M., and Winka, M. 2003. Release of mercury from broken fluorescent bulbs. *Journal of the Air and Waste Management Association* 53: 143–151.

Cain, A., Krauel, R., Diroff, N., and Thomas, A. 2004. *Options for dental mercury reduction programs: information for state/ provincial and local governments a report of the Binational Toxics Strategy Mercury Workgroup co-chairs.* Battelle, Columbus, OH. http://www.epa.gov/region5/air/mercury/ dentaloptions3.pdf (accessed November 15, 2010).

Carpi, A., and Chen, Y.-F. 2001. Gaseous elemental mercury as an indoor air pollutant. *Environmental Science and Technology* 35(21): 4170–4173.

Canadian Council of Ministers of the Environment. 2000. *Canada wide standards for mercury emissions.* http://www .ccme.ca/assets/pdf/mercury_emis_std_e1.pdf (accessed November 15, 2010).

Centers for Disease Control and Prevention. 1995. Mercury exposure in a residential community—Florida, 1994. *Morbidity and Mortality Weekly Report* 44(23): 436–437.

Christen, K. 2004. Mercury trading scheme raises concerns *Environmental Science and Technology Science News.* March 4.

Connecticut General Assembly. 2003. *Public Act 03-72: an act concerning mercury emissions from coal-fired electricity generators.* Adopted June 3, 2003. http://www.cga.ct.gov/asp/cgabillstatus/ cgabillstatus.asp?selBillType=Bill&bill_num=HB06048&which_ year=2003 (accessed November 15, 2010).

Conference of New England Governors–Eastern Canadian Premiers. 1998. *New England Governors and Eastern Canadian Premiers Mercury Action Plan.* New England Governors' Conference, Boston, MA. http://www.mass.gov/dep/toxics/ priorities/negecp.pdf (accessed November 15, 2010).

Conference of New England Governors–Eastern Canadian Premiers. 2001. *Resolution 26-3.* Adopted at the 26th annual conference, Westbrook, CT. New England Governors' Conference, Boston, MA. http://www.negc .org/documents/NEG-ECP_Overview07_03.pdf (accessed November 15, 2010).

Defense National Stockpile Center, Defense Logistics Agency. 2004. *Final mercury management environmental impact statement.* Defense National Stockpile Center, Defense Logistics Agency, Washington, DC.

Environmental Council of States. 2005. *Compendium of states' mercury activities.* The Environmental Council of the States, Washington, DC. http://www.ecos.org/section/2005_ mercury_compendium (accessed November 15, 2010).

Environmental Council of States. 2010. Implementing a national vision for mercury, ECOS Resolution 07-1, Revised March 24, 2010. http://www.ecos.org/section/ committees/cross_media/quick_silver (accessed November 15, 2010).

Evers, D.C. 2005. *Mercury connections: the extent and effects of mercury pollution in northeastern North America*. BioDiversity Research Institute, Gorham, ME.

Evers, D.C., and Clair, T.A. 2005. Mercury in northeastern North America: a synthesis of existing databases. *Ecotoxicology* 14 (1&2): 7–15.

Fitzgerald, W.F., Engstrom, D.R., Mason, R.P., and Nater, E.A. 1998. The case for atmospheric mercury contamination in remote areas. *Environmental Science and Technology* 32(1): 1–7.

Great Lakes Regional Collaboration. 2008. Great Lakes mercury in products phase-down strategy. http://www.glrppr.org/glmst (accessed November 15, 2010).

Great Lakes Regional Collaboration. 2010. Great Lakes mercury emissions reduction strategy. http://www.glrppr.org/glmst (accessed November 15, 2010).

Hurd, D.J., Muchnick, D.M., Schedler, M.F. and Mele, T. 1993. Recycling of consumer dry cell batteries. *Pollution Technology Review No 23*. Noyes Data, Park Ridge, NJ.

Hutcheson, M.S., Smith, C.M., Wallace, G.T., Rose, J., Eddy, B., Sullivan, J., Pancorbo, O., and Rowan-West, C. 2008. Freshwater fish mercury concentrations in a regionally high mercury deposition area. *Water, Air, and Soil Pollution* 191 (1–4): 15–31.

Maine Bureau of Health. 2004. *Freshwater fish safe eating guidelines*. Maine Center for Disease Control and Prevention, Augusta, ME. http://www.maine.gov/dhs/ehu/fish/ (accessed November 15, 2010).

Massachusetts Department of Environmental Protection. 1996. *Mercury in Massachusetts: an evaluation of sources, emissions, impacts and controls*, C.M. Smith and C. Rowan-West, eds., Office of Research and Standards, Boston, MA. http://www.mass.gov/dep/toxics/stypes/hgexsum.htm (accessed November 15, 2010).

Massachusetts Department of Environmental Protection. 1998. *Complete regulation package for municipal waste combustor regulation*. Massachusetts Department of Environmental Protection, Boston, MA. http://www.mass.gov/dep/toxics/stypes/hgres.htm#understand (accessed November 15, 2010).

Massachusetts Department of Environmental Protection. 2002. *Evaluation of the technological and economic feasibility of controlling and eliminating mercury emissions from the combustion of solid fossil fuel, pursuant to 310 CMR 7.29—emissions standards for power plants*. Massachusetts Department of Environmental Protection, Boston, MA. http://www.mass.gov/dep/toxics/stypes/mercfeas.pdf (accessed November 15, 2010).

Massachusetts Department of Environmental Protection. 2003. *Background document and technical support for public hearings on proposed amendments to 310 CMR 7.00 et seq.: 310 CMR 7.29 "Emissions Standards for Power Plants."* Massachusetts Department of Environmental Protection, Boston, MA. http://www.mass.gov/dep/toxics/laws/hgtsdx03.pdf (accessed November 15, 2010).

Massachusetts Department of Environmental Protection. 2004a. *Massachusetts emissions standards for power plants, 310 CMR 7.29*. Massachusetts Department of Environmental Protection, Boston, MA. http://www.mass.gov/dep/toxics/stypes/hgreg.pdf (accessed November 15, 2010).

Massachusetts Department of Environmental Protection. 2004b. *Fish mercury levels in northeastern Massachusetts lakes, December 2003*. Office of Research and Standards, Massachusetts Department of Environmental Protection, Boston, MA. http://www.mass.gov/dep/toxics/stypes/fishmerc.pdf (accessed November 15, 2010).

Massachusetts Department of Environmental Protection. 2008. *Consumer information: compact fluorescent light bulbs (CFLs) and guidance for cleaning up broken compact fluorescent light bulbs (CFLs)*. Massachusetts Department of Environmental Protection, Boston, MA. http://www.mass.gov/dep/toxics/stypes/cflinfo.htm (accessed November 15, 2010).

Massachusetts Executive Office of Environmental Affairs. 2000. *Massachusetts zero mercury strategy*. Massachusetts Executive Office of Environmental Affairs, Boston, MA. http://www.mass.gov/dep/toxics/stypes/hgres.htm#doing (accessed January 21, 2012).

Massachusetts Water Resources Authority. 1997. *Mercury in dental facilities*. Charlestown Navy Yard, Boston, MA. http://www.mwra.com/03sewer/html/dentsum.htm (accessed November 15, 2010).

Miller, P.J. 1999. Lifting the veil of smog: why a regional ozone strategy is needed in the Eastern United States. *EM: Environmental Manager* April: 19–23.

National Association of Clean Air Agencies. 2005. *Regulating mercury from power plants: a model rule for states and localities*. National Association of Clean Air Agencies, Washington, DC. http://www.4cleanair.org/FinalMercuryModelRule-111405.pdf (accessed November 15, 2010).

National Association of Clean Air Agencies. 2007. *State mercury programs for utilities*. National Association of Clean Air Agencies, Washington, DC. http://www.4cleanair.org/Documents/StateTable.pdf (accessed November 15, 2010).

National Research Council. 2000. *Toxicological effects of methyl mercury*. National Academies Press, Washington, DC. http://books.nap.edu/books/0309071402/html/index.html (accessed November 15, 2010).

New Hampshire Department of Environmental Services. 1999. *The New Hampshire mercury reduction strategy*. New Hampshire Department of Environmental Services, Concord, NH. http://des.nh.gov/organization/commissioner/p2au/pps/ms/mrpptp/reduction_strategy.htm (accessed November 15, 2010).

Northeast States For Coordinated Air Use Management. 1998a. *The costs of ozone transport: achieving clean air in the east*. Northeast States for Coordinated Air Use Management, Boston, MA.

Northeast States For Coordinated Air Use Management. 1998b. *1998 Northeast states and eastern Canadian provinces mercury study: a framework for action*. Northeast States for Coordinated Air Use Management, Northeast Waste Management Officials Association, New England Interstate Water Pollution Control Commission and Canadian Ecological Monitoring and Assessment Network, Boston, MA.

Northeast States For Coordinated Air Use Management. 2003. *Mercury emissions from coal-fired power plants, the case for regulatory action*. Northeast States for Coordinated Air Use Management, Boston, MA. http://www.nescaum.org/topics/mercury (accessed November 15, 2010).

Northeast States For Coordinated Air Use Management. 2004. Comments to Docket Number OAR-2002-0056 on:

Proposed National Emission Standards for Hazardous Air Pollutants; and in the Alternative, Proposed Standards of Performance for New and Existing Stationary Sources: Electric Utility Steam Generating Units (69 FR 4652-4752). NESCAUM, Boston, MA. http://www.nescaum.org/documents/proposed-national-emission-standards-for-hazardous-air-pollutants/ (accessed January 21, 2012).

Northeast States For Coordinated Air Use Management. 2005. *Inventory of anthropogenic mercury emissions in the northeast.* NESCAUM, Boston, MA. http://www.nescaum.org/documents/inventory-of-anthropogenic-mercuryemissions-in-the-northeast. http://www.nescaum.org/topics/mercury (accessed November 15, 2010).

Northeast States For Coordinated Air Use Management. 2007, October. *Modeling mercury in the northeast United States.* NESCAUM, Boston, MA. http://www.nescaum.org/topics/mercury (accessed November 15, 2010).

Northeast States For Coordinated Air Use Management. 2011. Massachusetts State Anthropogenic Mercury Emissions Inventory Update. NESCAUM and MassDEP, Boston, MA. http://www.nescaum.org/topics/emissions-inventories (accessed January 23, 2012).

New England Interstate Water Pollution Control Commission (NEIWPCC). 2007. Northeast Regional Mercury Total Maximum Daily Load. NEIWPCC, Lowell, MA. http://www.neiwpcc.org/mercury/mercurytmdl.asp (accessed on January 21, 2012).

Northeast Waste Management officials' Association. 2008a. *Mercury reduction & education legislation in the IMERC— member states: 2008.* Northeast Waste Management Officials' Association, Boston, MA. http://www.newmoa.org/prevention/mercury/modelleg.cfm (accessed November 15, 2010).

Northeast Waste Management officials' Association. 2008b. *Mercury education and reduction model act.* Northeast Waste Management Officials' Association, Boston, MA. http://www.newmoa.org/prevention/mercury/final_model_legislation.htm (accessed November 15, 2010).

Northeast Waste Management officials' Association. 2008c. *Interstate mercury education & reduction clearinghouse (IMERC) mercury-added products database.* Northeast Waste Management Officials' Association, Boston, MA. http://www.newmoa.org/prevention/mercury/imerc.cfm (accessed November 15, 2010).

Northeast Waste Management officials' Association. 2008d. *Mercury Program.* Northeast Waste Management Officials' Association, Boston, MA. http://www.newmoa.org/prevention/mercury/ (accessed November 15, 2010).

Northeast Waste Management officials' Association/Interstate Mercury Reduction and Education Clearinghouse. 2008e, June. *Trends in mercury use: summary of the Interstate Mercury Education & Reduction Clearinghouse (IMERC) mercury-added products database.* NEWMOA, Boston, MA. http://www.newmoa.org/prevention/mercury/imerc/factsheets/mercuryinproducts.pdf (accessed November 15, 2010).

Quicksilver Caucus. 2003a. *Mercury stewardship: best management practices.* The Environmental Council of the States, Washington, DC. http://www.ecos.org/section/committees/cross_media/quick_silver (accessed November 15, 2010).

Quicksilver Caucus. 2003b. *Mercury stewardship: storage of mercury.* The Environmental Council of the States, Washington, DC. http://www.ecos.org/section/committees/cross_media/quick_silver (accessed November 15, 2010).

Quicksilver Caucus. 2003c. *Mercury stewardship: best management practices.* The Environmental Council of the States, Washington, DC. http://www.ecos.org/section/committees/cross_media/quick_silver (accessed November 15, 2010).

Quicksilver Caucus. 2003d. *Mercury stewardship: mercury commodity review.* The Environmental Council of the States, Washington, DC. http://www.ecos.org/section/committees/cross_media/quick_silver (accessed November 15, 2010).

Quicksilver Caucus. 2003e. *Mercury stewardship: market policy options.* The Environmental Council of the States, Washington, DC. http://www.ecos.org/section/committees/cross_media/quick_silver (accessed November 15, 2010).

Quicksilver Caucus. 2006a. *Mercury-added product white paper.* The Environmental Council of the States, Washington, DC. http://www.ecos.org/section/committees/cross_media/quick_silver (accessed November 15, 2010).

Quicksilver Caucus. 2006b. *Product labeling: information for states.* The Environmental Council of the States, Washington, DC. http://www.ecos.org/section/committees/cross_media/quick_silver (accessed November 15, 2010).

Quicksilver Caucus. 2007. *Letter to Deputy Assistant Secretary of State for Environment, Mr. Daniel Reifsnyder.* Communication regarding state concerns about US international positions on mercury pollution. The Environmental Council of the States, Washington, DC. http://www.ecos.org/files/2518_file_QSC_State_Dept_Letter_Jan_09_final.pdf?PHPSESSID=fbbe92769a4d2060929d279f3ad70917 (accessed November 15, 2010).

Quicksilver Caucus. 2008a. *Dental mercury amalgam waste management white paper.* The Environmental Council of the States, Washington, DC. http://www.ecos.org/section/committees/cross_media/quick_silver (accessed November 15, 2010).

Quicksilver Caucus. 2008b. *Case studies of five dental mercury amalgam separator programs.* The Environmental Council of the States, Washington, DC. http://www.ecos.org/section/committees/cross_media/quick_silver (accessed November 15, 2010).

Quicksilver Caucus. 2009. *National Vehicle Mercury Switch Recovery Program status report.* http://www.ecos.org/files/3461_file_NVMSRP_Status_Report_Jan_09_Revised_Final.pdf (accessed November 16, 2010).

Quicksilver Caucus. 2010. Quicksilver Caucus comment letter on US EPA's annual review of effluent guidelines. http://ecos.org/files/4062_file_QSC_Letter_to_EPA_on_Effluent_Guidelines_FINAL_Sent.pdf (accessed November 15, 2010).

Riley, D.M., Newby, A., Leal-Almeraz, T.O., and Thomas, V.M. 2001. Assessing elemental mercury vapor exposures from cultural and religious practices. *Environmental Health Perspectives* 109(8): 779–784.

Smith, C.M. and Trip, L.J. 2005. Mercury policy and science in northeastern North America: the mercury action plan of the New England Governors and Eastern Canadian Premiers. *Ecotoxicology* 14 (1&2): 19–37.

Smith, C.M. 2007. *Collection and management of commodity grade elemental mercury.* Testimony of June 22, 2007 before the House Energy and Environment Committee; Subcommittee on Environment and Hazardous Materials, Washington, DC. The Environmental Council of the States, Washington, DC. http://www.ecos.org/files/2798_file_Arleen_O_Donnell_Testimony_on_Hg_6_22_07F.pdf (accessed November 15, 2010).

Stahler, D., Ladner, S., and Jackson, H. 2008. *Maine compact fluorescent lamp breakage study report.* Maine Department of Environmental Protection, Augusta, ME. http://www.state.me.us/dep/rwm/homeowner/cflreport/cflreportwoapp.pdf (accessed November 15, 2010).

Strategic Envirotechnology Partnership. 2003. *Development, evaluation and implementation of a testing protocol for evaluation of technologies for removal of mercury from dental facilities: part I—field studies and protocol evaluation June 2003.* Strategic Envirotechnology Partnership (STEP), Massachusetts Executive Office of Environmental Affairs, Boston, MA.

United Nations Environment Programme. 2003. *Global mercury assessment report.* The Inter-organization Programme for the Sound Management of Chemicals', United Nations Environment Programme, Geneva, Switzerland. http://www.chem.unep.ch/mercury/default.htm (accessed November 15, 2010).

United Nations Environment Programme. 2009. Mercury—the negotiating process. http://www.unep.org/hazardoussubstances/MercuryNot/MercuryNegotiations/tabid/3320/language/en-US/Default.aspx (accessed November 15, 2010).

United States Court of Appeals for the District of Columbia Circuit. 2008. *No. 05-1097, State Of New Jersey, et al., Petitioners V. Environmental Protection Agency, Respondent Utility Air Regulatory Group, et al., Intervenors.* Argued December 6, 2007 decided February 8, 2008. http://pacer.cadc.uscourts.gov/docs/common/opinions/200802/05-1097a.pdf (accessed November 15, 2010).

US Environmental Protection Agency. 1997a. *Great Lakes binational toxics strategy.* http://www.epa.gov/glnpo/bns (accessed November 15, 2010).

US Environmental Protection Agency. 1997b. *Mercury study report to Congress.* EPA-452/R-97-003, United States Environmental Protection Agency, Washington, DC. http://www.epa.gov/mercury/report.htm (accessed November 15, 2010).

US Environmental Protection Agency. 2000, December 20. Regulatory finding on the emissions of hazardous air pollutants from electric utility steam generating units. *Federal Register* 65(245): 79825–79831.

US Environmental Protection Agency. 2005a, March 29. Revision of December 2000 regulatory finding on the emissions of hazardous air pollutants from electric utility steam generating units and the removal of coal- and oil-fired electric utility steam generating units from the Section 112(c) (40 CFR Part 63 [OAR–2002–0056; FRL–7887–7] RIN 2060–AM96). Federal Register 70(59): 15994.

US Environmental Protection Agency. 2005b, May 18. Standards of performance for new and existing stationary sources: electric utility steam generating units (40 CFR Parts 60, 72, and 75 [OAR–2002–0056; FRL–7888–1] RIN 2060–AJ65). *Federal Register* 70(95): 28606.

US Environmental Protection Agency. 2006, August 11. Memorandum of understanding to establish the national Vehicle Mercury Switch Recovery Program. http://www.epa.gov/mercury/pdfs/switchMOU.pdf (accessed November 15, 2010).

US Environmental Protection Agency. 2008. Memorandum of understanding on reducing dental amalgam discharges. http://water.epa.gov/scitech/wastetech/guide/dental/upload/2008_12_31_guide_dental_mou.pdf (accessed November 15, 2010).

US Environmental Protection Agency. 2010. Dental amalgam effluent guideline. http://water.epa.gov/scitech/wastetech/guide/dental/index.cfm (accessed November 15, 2010).

US Environmental Protection Agency. 2011. Final Mercury and Air Toxics Standards (MATs) for power plants. USEPA, Washington, DC. http://www.epa.gov/airquality/powerplanttoxics/actions.html (accessed 1/22/2012)

INDEX

Tables are indicated by a 't' after a citation, and figures with an 'f.'

Nyanza Superfund site case study, mercury contamination, 158–161

O

occupational exposure to mercury, public health research on, 272–273
ocean
   mercury settling and transport in, 13, 170–176, 171f, 172t–174t, 175f–176f, 199–200
   natural mercury emissions in, 9
omega-3 polyunsaturated fatty acids, fish consumption, mercury-contaminated fish, 290–291
open ocean. *See* marine environment, mercury contamination in; ocean
ores
   isotopic mercury ratios, 63
   soil-based mercury association with, 104–105
organic mercury compounds
   in agricultural products and paints, 273
   in aqueous media, 37
   calibration and quality control procedures for, 46–47
   chemical speciation, 29, 39–40
   derivatization methods, 43
   determination techniques, 36–42, 38f–39f
   differential reduction, 44
   distillation-based determination, 37–38, 38f
   environmental matrices, 42
   hyphenated determination techniques, 39, 39f
   in natural waters, 36, 39–40
   quantification, 44–45
   in saline waters, 168–170, 169f–170f
   separation techniques, 44
   in solid matrices, 42
outreach on mercury contamination prevention, New England Governors and Eastern Canadian Premiers Mercury Action Plan, 325–328
oxic water masses, marine environment mercury concentrations and, 187
oxidation
   atmospheric mercury deposition, 75
   mercury toxicity studies and, in fish, 223–225

P

paints, ancient mercury use in, 19–23
particulate-bound mercury, 5
   chemical speciation, 11, 13–14
   in marine environments, 187–188
   particle scavenging and sediment burial, 189
   terrestrial watersheds, mercury cycling in, 125–126, 126f
particulate organic carbon, terrestrial watersheds, mercury cycling in, 125–126, 126f
per capita mercury intake measurements, mercury risk evaluation using, 253–256, 254t–255t
perturbation effects, terrestrial watersheds, mercury cycling in, 134–135
phase speciation, organic mercury determination, 39–41
   chromatographic conditions, 44
pH effects, soil-based mercury association with, 105

photo-acoustic spectroscopy, total mercury determination, 36
photodecomposition, monomethylmercury, in marine environments, 188
photodemethylation, isotopic mercury, 67
photoreduction, isotopic mercury, 65, 67
phytoplankton, mercury in, 193–195
plants, mercury concentrations in, Arctic region contamination, 308–312
point mercury sources, atmospheric mercury transport and, 13–14
policy requirements, mercury monitoring and assessment procedures, 83
pollution prevention initiatives
   New England Governors and Eastern Canadian Premiers Mercury Action Plan, 324–326
   state policies for, 320–321
polychlorinated biphenyls (PCBs), fish consumption, mercury-contaminated fish and presence of, 291, 291f
Pomo Tribe at Clear Lake case study, mercury exposure, 306
population monitoring, mercury toxicity
   in amphibians, 227
   environmental justice, at-risk populations, 302–303, 303f
   fish consumption guidelines for vulnerable human populations, 293–299
preconcentration analysis
   isotopic mercury measurement, 56–57
   organic mercury compounds, derivatization, 43
   sampling strategies, 58
preindustrial mercury cycle, 5–6
preservation methods, mercury sampling and storage, 31–33, 31f, 32t
Presidential/Congressional Commission on Risk Assessment and Risk Management (PCCRARM), mercury risk assessment protocol, 242–243
probable effect level (PEL) measurements, large lake ecosystem mercury contamination, 156–158, 156t, 291f
problem formulation principles, mercury risk assessment protocols, 244
protein, monomethylmercury binding, 68–69, 69t
public health policies, mercury exposure and, 267–280
   biomonitoring in human populations, 275–277
   clinical assessment protocols, 274–275, 275t
   environmental justice issues surrounding, 312–313
   future biomonitoring efforts, 277
   methymercury guidelines, derivation of, 273–274
   regulations and recommendations for exposure reduction, 278–279, 280f
   sources of exposure and health effects, 268–273
   state perspectives on, 326–328

Q

quality control, organic mercury identification, 46–47
quantification methods, organic mercury compounds, 44–45
Quicksilver Caucus (QSC), state mercury control initiatives and, 320–321

R

racial disparities in mercury toxicity, environmental justice principles, 303–304
radioactive mercury tracers, identification of, 45–46
reactive gaseous mercury (RGM)
   atmospheric deposition, 74–75
   basic properties, 5
   oxidation and reduction, 75
   in soil, 102
reactive oxygen species (ROS), mercury toxicity and, in fish, 223–225
redox cycling, soil-based mercury emissions, 107
reduction processes
   atmospheric mercury deposition, 75
   isotopic mercury, 65–68, 66t, 67f
re-emission, previously deposited mercury, 11
reference doses, mercury risk evaluation
   EPA methylmercury reference dose, 249–250
   methylmercury exposure guidelines, 273–274
   noncancer risk assessment, 249–250
   toxicity reference value, 257
regulation of mercury emissions
   emission sources, 318–319
   information sharing and capacity building, 320
   interstate coordination, 319–320
   mercury-added products, 318
   monitoring and research initiatives, 319
   national overview of, 317–318
   New England Governors and Eastern Canadian Premiers Mercury Action Plan, 322–326, 322t–324t, 324f
   pollution prevention and stewardship initiatives, 320–321
   public health policies and, 278–279, 280f
   Quicksilver caucus, 320–321
   regional mercury total maximum daily load assessment, 326–328
   state mercury initiatives, 318–328
   storage policies for excess elemental mercury, national and international commissions, 321
reproductive function, mercury toxicity and
   in birds, 229–233
   in fish, 225
reptiles, mercury toxicology research on, 227–228
research methodology, state regulations for, 319
reservoirs case study, mercury hotspots, 152–156, 154f
   age of reservoir and fish mercury levels, 155–156
   downstream methylmercury sources, 155
   hydropower *vs.* fossil fuels and, 156
   methylation sites, 153–155, 154f
   organic matter and methylation, 153
   water-level fluctuations, 155
riparian zones, terrestrial watersheds, mercury cycling in, 132, 132f
risk assessment protocols
   fish consumption guidelines based on, 291–293, 293f, 294t
   mercury risk evaluation and, 240–243, 241t, 242f–243f
risk/benefit analysis techniques
   fish consumption guidelines mercury exposure reduction, 293–299